Blondie, From Punk to the Present

Blondie,
From Punk to the Present:
A Pictorial History

Allan Metz, compiler

Prologue by Chris Stein

Musical Legacy Series,

Number 1

Springfield, Missouri: Published by Musical Legacy Publications, an imprint of Barnabas Publishing Services

BLONDIE, FROM PUNK TO THE PRESENT: A PICTORIAL HISTORY

© 2002 by Allan Metz

Editing, graphics, layout and cover design by Robert W. Betts

Technical proofreading by Amy G. Oravec

Typesetting and composition by Maryann D. Betts

Cover photograph by Joe Ryan

Frontis piece photographs by Frances Garrett, Plymouth Pavilions, Plymouth, England, November 29, 1998

Title page photograph by Teresa R. Hale, Dockland Arena, London, November 13, 1999

First Edition, published 2002

by Musical Legacy Publications,

an imprint of Barnabas Publishing Services

Springfield, Missouri 65804 U.S.A.

Library of Congress Control Number: 2001118378

ISBN 1-892477-23-8 (paperback: alk. paper)

Table of Contents

Part I: Then

BACKGROUND

PUNK

BLONDIE AND PUNK

Part II: Between Acts

Part III: Now

INTERVIEWS

PROFILES

ALBUM REVIEWS

CONCERT PREVIEWS AND REVIEWS

ON THEIR CRAFT

Part IV: In Retrospect

OVERVIEWS

COMPREHENSIVE DISCOGRAPHY COMMENTARY

APPRECIATIONS

This book is dedicated to the members of Blondie,
true pioneers in every sense of the word.

Acknowledgments

This book never would have been possible without the cooperation and enthusiasm of numerous people who helped to sustain and encourage me throughout the various stages of compiling and publishing this book.

Special thanks to Victor Bockris for writing the Foreword, an original essay on Blondie and punk, providing photos as well as granting permission to reprint an essay on the 1970s, an unedited version of an interview he conducted with Deborah Harry, plus previously unpublished quotes accompanied by his original commentary.

Special thanks also to the webmasters of the official Blondie web site, Barry L. Kramer and Louis A Bustamante, for assisting in obtaining permission from Chris Stein to adapt and edit his original essay as the Prologue and to, of course, Mr. Stein for granting the permission. Barry and Louis also were indispensable in providing other assistance with this book and my Blondie web sites. Thanks also to Barry L. Kramer for helping to secure Chris Stein's permission to adapt and edit his remembrance of Joey Ramone. I also would like to take this opportunity to publicly thank Chris for the inclusion of his material in this book, which, however, does not constitute and should not be viewed as an endorsement by him, Blondie or its management of this book. The same holds true of the publicity photos provided by Beyond Music. Therefore, this book is unofficial and unauthorized and, as such, is published independently of the band, Blondie, Beyond Music, and its management, Left Bank. A further statement to this effect may be found at the end of the Acknowledgments.

I am most grateful to Robert Betts, Editor; Amy Oravec, Associate Editor; and typesetter Maryann Betts of *The Blondie Review*, who provided those same services for this book and did so with great determination and hard work. Thanks to graphic designer, Sheryl Jenkins, of Jenkins Studio for initial work done. I also very much appreciate the digital imaging done by Michael Chittenden of Colorspace: A Photo Lab, Springfield, Missouri.

Regarding the photography utilized for the book, I would like to thank all the photo contributors and agencies whose credits are found accompanying their respective photos, which reflect the three major stages of Blondie and Deborah Harry's careers: the early Blondie period through to its initial success and fame, an interim period when Harry pursued a solo career after the band disbanded in 1982, and the contemporary Blondie reunion.

And thanks to Edward Fay from the *New York Daily News*, Fred Jordan from Fromm International Publishing Corp., Laurie Hanson and Maria Carpico from the *Pittsburgh Post-Gazette*, and Jeff Johnson and *Fabula* magazine for granting permission to reproduce quotations on the back cover as well as to all those involved in granting permission to utilize previously published articles, unedited versions of published articles, unpublished work, and original work written specifically for this book, including professional photographers who also contributed text, captions, and extended captions to accompany their respective photos. They and those who helped secure permissions for written selections are too numerous to mention individually. Subscribers to the DHBIS (Deborah Harry and Blondie Information Service) listserv and its moderator, Louis A Bustamante, proved to be invaluable on many occasions by providing information and answering inquiries.

I would like to take this opportunity to thank Gary Swadley, director of Computer Services at Drury University, Chris Long, and the rest of the staff for assisting me with computer applications pertaining to the book and its web component as well as webmaster, Victoria Johnson, and computer instructor, Duane Bedell. Similar kudos go out to Edward S. Proctor, Electronic Resources Librarian and Webmaster, Duane G. Meyer Library, Southwest Missouri State University. I thank all the written contributors to this book who granted me permission to reprint and adapt their material. Thanks also to Barry L. Kramer (president of the Debbie Harry Collector's Society—DHCS), Joe Ryan, Liz Vap, Ursula J. Hull, Lisa Diedrich, Kevin Munns, John Sibby, Edward Kary, Theresa Heinz, Cathay Che, Jon Erkider, Bob Neumann, Teresa R. Hale, Ross MacDonald, the late Robert Jacks, Scott Coblio, and Ralph Heibutzski for providing valuable feedback and assistance. The efforts of Reta Spears (Barnabas Publishing Services) regarding the various aspects of registering the book are much appreciated. I also extend appreciation to the following libraries and their respective staffs: F.W. Olin Library, Drury University, especially Katherine Bohnenkamper and her student assistants, Breana Uzzell and Crystal White, for interlibrary loan assistance; the Springfield-Greene County public library system; and the Duane G. Meyer Library of Southwest Missouri State University as well as that university's music library. Preliminary research on the theme of women in rock/pop music was conducted at the music libraries of the University of California at Berkeley and Stanford University.

All these people helped make this book possible. If, somehow, someone who should have been acknowledged was not, it assuredly was unintentional and I apologize in advance.

Blondie, From Punk to the Present: A Pictorial History and its publisher, editor, compiler, and contributors are not connected in any way with the artists, agents, management, promotions or any other business concerns of any of the persons, venues or organizations discussed herein, unless specifically stated. All opinions expressed in *Blondie, From Punk to the Present* are solely those of the specific editor, writer, or contributor and not necessarily those of the publisher or compiler. Every effort has been made to give proper photo credit, when and where applicable.

All of the original and previously published articles and essays in this book are the property of the authors or publishers (where applicable) and are presented here, as close as possible, as submitted.

Allan Metz

Preface

Allan Metz: My question for Leigh would be his assessment of the musical legacy of Blondie. In other words, what impact/influence has the band had on rock/pop music (and what are recent/contemporary examples of this legacy)? And what has been Deborah Harry's influence on female musical artists who followed her (such as Madonna onward)?

Leigh Foxx: When we played at RFK Stadium, we shared the bill with the Cardigans, the Mighty Mighty Bosstones, Beck, etc...and when we were on stage, a lot of the band members were on the side of the stage watching. It was then that I realized the influence that the band has on younger artists not to mention the reception that we got from the 70,000+ fans *(source:* Bustamante*).—Evaluation by Leigh Foxx, bassist for Blondie, of the band's legacy and influence. Reprinted with permission.*

This book is an edited collection of interpretative narrative on Blondie from a variety of sources through text and the visual medium of photography. To understand this phenomenon, it is necessary to trace Blondie's roots by first considering the decade in which it emerged in an analytical essay on the 1970s by Victor Bockris, who collaborated with Deborah Harry and Chris Stein on the book entitled *Making Tracks: The Rise of Blondie*, and is generally acknowledged as the de facto Blondie biographer as a result of this book and his subsequent work. Attention next turns to the nature of punk, punk music in the United States (primarily New York City) and how it differed from its British counterpart, the punk scene in New York City where the band originated, and then proceeds to a discussion of Blondie within this context through to the present time.

The book opens with a Prologue by Blondie co-founder and guitarist Chris Stein, adapted from a piece he originally wrote for *Blondie, The Official Web Site*, www.blondie.net. The Foreword is by Victor Bockris, who provides a new overview of Debbie and Blondie together with the observations and insights that only he could provide. The Introduction is based on, and is an elaboration of, the introduction to a published annotated bibliography I compiled, which has been since adapted and supplemented since its submission* and is followed by a heartfelt note from editor, Robert Betts.

All ten selections in the "Punk" section of Part I are adapted from Jessamin Swearingen's typescript of her Division III examination from Hampshire College and her web site, which adapted the thesis to a web format.** Both direct and so insightful, her compelling writing eloquently captures the punk ethos. Appended to the chapter on the Ramones are an Associated Press obituary on Joey Ramone and quotes from his contemporaries, the Go-Go's and Chris Stein. The section "Blondie and Punk" consists of selections by Robert Betts, Russell White, former Blondie bassist Gary Valentine, another essay from Jessamin Swearingen, a film review by Jon Erkider, and an original essay by Victor Bockris commissioned specifically for this book. All provide retrospective looks at the band and its roots and round out the section.

Part II addresses the period between Blondie's breakup in 1982 and its reunion efforts beginning in the mid-1990s. The first selection in this section is written by Lisa Diedrich, a very knowledgeable and articulate Blondie observer. The next selection is an addendum to the previous selection, consisting of my reflections and elaborations on the points made by Lisa plus incorporating her additional observations on this period. Daniel Porter's selection on Deborah Harry's solo career offers a British perspective, serving as a complement to the previous two selections. Next, is an insightful 1989 Deborah Harry performance review by Scott Coblio followed by a reprint of a 1991 interview with Richard Harry (Deborah Harry's father) conducted by Brian La Fountain. Jazz is the subject of the next two selections in Part II—reviews of Jazz Passengers' concerts featuring Deborah Harry. In addition to writing the Foreword, the original essay "Blondie's Punk Roots" plus the adapted essay on the 1970s, Victor Bockris further enhances this book with a previously unpublished original uncensored version of a 1996 *High Times* magazine interview with Deborah Harry. Part II concludes by returning to the subject of jazz with an insightful article by Robert L. Doerschuk on Deborah Harry as a jazz vocalist and the distinction between singing jazz versus rock and roll.

Part III consists of reprinted magazine and newspaper articles plus a number of unedited versions of previously published articles, which makes them unique. Many contain both a recent account of contemporary

Blondie as well as an historical perspective on the band. The relative newness of these writings has the twofold advantage of providing a perspective by placing the band in this historical musical context in relation to its reunion and focusing on the present and future without overly dwelling on the past because this reunion is not about nostalgia, but what exciting and groundbreaking territory Blondie has yet to explore. This section is arranged as follows: Interviews, Profiles, Album Reviews, Concert Previews and Reviews, and On Their Craft. All these sections are arranged in either exact or at least approximate chronological order to attain a better flow of the text, with the exception of On Their Craft, which worked better with a nonchronological sequence of selections as Clem Burke, Chris Stein, and Deborah Harry discuss the finer technical points of their musicianship. Of course, while some of these selections could have been placed in one or more other categories, achieving a balance among the selections was an important consideration.

Part IV concludes the main text of the book and consists of three sections: the first contains overviews of the band—the first two selections are both historical and contemporary, while the remaining selections in this section are in the form of an essay on Blondie's visual image, a poem, and commentary by Victor Bockris on previously unpublished quotes he compiled from Deborah Harry on a wide variety of subjects. The next section offers comprehensive critical analyses of Blondie's discography from an American and then British perspective. Part IV ends on a personal note with a series of Appreciations, both adapted and original remembrances which articulately sum up Blondie and Deborah Harry's appeal to a number of the book's contributors and other writers.

A section of appendices follows Part IV consisting of a genealogy/chronology, a selective album discography listing with album tracks, an interview with a major mover among Blondie fandom, two photo exhibit reviews, a unique and interesting physiological analysis of Clem Burke during concert performances, a listing of libraries that own the *Making Tracks* book, and a selective listing of major web site links. An Afterword by John Sibby closes the text with his unique poetic style. The Afterword is followed by an extensive References/ Bibliography section, which includes material either directly about Blondie or related to the band. Four detailed indexes (Album/Song/Video, Band/Group, Name, and Subject) complete the book.

In addition to the text, photography is the book's other focal point. The photos capture Blondie then, now, and in between and are arranged in three separate photo sections corresponding to the text. The first photo section contains photos by professional photographers as they portray the electricity and intensity of Blondie at their height of fame on both sides of the Atlantic—the U.S. and Great Britain. The second photo section, focusing on Deborah Harry's solo career, contains numerous photos provided by fans and professional photographers, including many outstanding ones of Deborah Harry with the Jazz Passengers both in the U.S. and Europe. Blondie's tours in 1998 and 1999 afforded professional and fan photographers alike ample opportunity to capture the band on film once again. You will see and enjoy the fruits of their labor in the third photo section.

Allan Metz

*Allan Metz, "The Musical Legacy of Blondie: An Annotated Bibliography." *Bulletin of Bibliography* 56, 4 (December 1999): 189-217.

**Jessamin Swearingen, "We Created It: Let's Take It Over!: The Emergence of Punk in America." Typescript of a Division III examination in the School of Social Science, Hampshire College, May 1993. A corresponding web site, *We Created It, Let's Take It Over,* may be accessed at www.inch.com/~jessamin

Prologue: "Insomnia...Sleepless in Scotland"

by Chris Stein
(adapted and edited by Allan Metz)

Originally published on Blondie—The Official Web Site, www.blondie.net—Ed.

All in all, although the last year and a half or so has found us away from home for all but 10 weeks (I just got this information last week and, correct or not, on hearing it, I developed insomnia), the whole of this touring has been mostly positive...of course, things being the mass of contradictions they usually are, now that we're at the end with everyone fried, the band is of course at a well-oiled high point and I'm confident that these last shows we're doing represent an all time high for Blondie performances...

One, of course, might argue that the "old days" found us younger and more insane, perhaps more energetic, but I have tapes of lots of that stuff and I can assure you it often bears little resemblance to the music on the records, frequently sounding like some kind of psychedelic punk-funk mix, not necessarily bad, but the musicianship pales by comparison to what's going on now. And now that I think about it, I'm becoming ageist in my discussion here. Yeah, that's bullshit. We're AS energetic as ever, more sober, but there are still threads of madness throughout. Fear not. The problem is that there is so much down-time involved with touring and I've now come to a place where I've got to decide how to use my time...when I started this thing over three years ago, I was still recovering from years of drug use. Now that I've got a much better feeling of forward motion, I find sitting in hotel rooms watching T.V. to be more unbearable than ever...in a way, I feel at the height of my powers now and I'd rather spend time doing more modern things than dragging around in airports and hotel lobbies...I can speak for the whole crew in saying that we all love doing the shows and I know that people are always going to want to see Debbie and the band in the flesh, but...it's a difficult split...

No matter what anyone says, it's impossible to write on the road, and I've got to make new music, not just endlessly play old songs...so really I'm making more of a deal out of this than it is. We just have to go into another mode of operation for a while...I guess in a way I am a bit sad about not being out doing shows (more contradiction) since I feel really close to all the people that come to see us. I get really emotional on stage now; hearing everyone sing along never fails to make me completely sentimental. Playing the song [*"Under the Gun"*—Ed.] about Jeff Pierce always just makes me tearful even though it's not a familiar one. I can't forget about his death depriving us of who knows what...so...after New Year's Eve in Miami, Blondie will be off the road for a time...I don't know if we'll ever do another year and a half straight again, but we'll for sure do more live events...

Chris—Glasgow Scotland—Nov. 26 '99

Foreword

by Victor Bockris

I have known Debbie Harry since 1977. I first met her at the photographer Christopher Makos' apartment on the night of the great New York Blackout. We were sitting in a pitch black room. So I couldn't see her. But her partner in all things at that time, Chris Stein, and Debbie radiated an intense, focused energy. Their minds were so totally appropriate to their times that I had one of those "immediate" experiences. We became friends.

In 1979 they asked me if I would work with them on a book of Chris Stein's photographs. At the time I was working on Andy Warhol's book of photographs *Exposures* and my book on William Burroughs *A Report from the Bunker*. Their project fit perfectly between them. In fact, I attempted to begin work on their book in the style of my Burroughs book by arranging a dinner party with Andy Warhol and taping the conversation. But that was completely the wrong approach. It took us a while to figure out what was the right approach, but once we hit upon our target I had with them one of the very best collaborative experiences of my life.

I worked with Debbie on writing the text of what was to become *Making Tracks: The Rise of Blondie*. We toiled on it at their apartment, at my apartment, and out in L.A. when they were recording *Autoamerican*. When we had finished the text Debbie had to go to Toronto to film "Videodrome," leaving Chris and I in New York to complete the selection of the photographs and design of the book. I had gotten to know Debbie well. Now I got to know Chris well. I have always been fascinated by collaboration. Their collaboration is an extraordinary model matched in rock 'n' roll perhaps only by John and Yoko's, although with a completely different dynamic, and it continues in one form or another to this day. It is certainly no coincidence that they are still among the most successful survivors of the punk era.

When *Making Tracks* was published in the U.S. in 1982, Chris had a great show of his photographs at the prestigious Daniel Wolf Gallery on 57th Street in Manhattan. Then they went on the American leg of "The Hunter" tour and I saw them perform before 50,000 people at an open air concert in Philadelphia. But by then Chris was seriously ill. Standing backstage dressed from head to foot in black and holding a balloon, he looked like a ghost in a Fellini movie.

The Hunter turned out to be a dreadful failure and much of their U.S. tour and their entire European and Far East tours were cancelled. The album's failure had nothing to do with the music. It was just as good as the previous Blondie albums and contains to my mind at least three No. 1 singles. "English Boys" is one of my favorite Blondie songs. (I also like "Victor" on *Eat to the Beat*). In between *Autoamerican* and *The Hunter*, Debbie had recorded a solo album, *Koo Koo*, with Bernard Edwards and Nile Rodgers of Chic producing. There were some lovely Harry/Stein songs on *Koo Koo*, but the production didn't do them justice. It was too sparse, there were too many gaps in the music. And the cover by H.R. Giger (designer of the Alien movies), on which three large needles pass through Debbie's face from left to right, confused a lot of the Blondie fans who had always pinned her as a comic book heroine, and not the serious beatnik-based and souled artist which she essentially is. Furthermore, rock is the fastest business and in the interim between *Autoamerican* and *The Hunter* much had changed.

In 1980, Debbie and Chris had moved to an enormous mansion on East 72nd Street on the Upper East Side. Now they pretty much retired to the bedroom as they experienced one of the most precipitous falls in rock history, followed by Chris being hospitalized on the critical list with a rare skin disease which took his doctors several months to diagnose. This was one of the toughest passages in Debbie's tough life, and perhaps more than anything indicates what a strong, resilient and loyal person she is.

I think in many ways that Debbie is probably happier today than she was during Blondie's greatest period of success. The strain of that kind of success, the number of people tugging on your time, the number of things you have to keep in mind, confuse and disturb the artistic vision and leave little time for true creativity. Today she lives in a comfortable apartment in one of the best buildings in New York. Her solo records will soon become classics, her film work is steadily developing, she's singing jazz, increasing her vocal range, and right now she's in a successful play.

I adore her and admire her. She is truly one of the most extraordinary, beautiful on the outside and inside, and talented people I know. She is also well balanced, centered and capable. I don't know what she could add to her life to make it better, more perfect than it is at the moment. (Perhaps a man). It is hard to think of a person in New York who has weathered more and come through so well. She once told me that she realized early on in her career that she could take the negative route and be a tragic singer like Billie Holiday or Janis Joplin, but that she wanted to make music that would make people happy and live for a long time. I think that has something to do with it. When she writes her autobiography, it will undoubtedly be an international No. 1 blockbuster. Meanwhile, this book will stand as another worthwhile contribution to the literature of Blondie/Debbie Harry, and I hope you enjoy it. Above all, I hope it sends you back to the music, to the Best of Blondie.

Victor Bockris, New York, 2001.

Editor's Note

Assembling a Blondie Book

by Robert Betts

Putting this book together was a monumental task—it drew heavily upon our collective energy reserves, consumed thousands of (collective) personal hours and tested our deepest tenacity—it really was a lot of work. It was not because we are amateurs in this business or unskilled in researching, editing, proofing, typesetting, or publishing. And it was not because we didn't have the required talent available. It was because of the great vicissitude of the subject matter and the overwhelming amount of historical and rhetorical material available. Were this book concerned with another topic, this volume may not have happened. But, it did happen—it happened quite smoothly and methodically despite the intensity of our involvement. The single greatest factor in achieving our goal was that it has been a labor of love. This was the glue that bound us to the effort. That was the drive that pushed us forward. Truly, the fuel that fired our determination to achieve our goal was Deborah Harry and Blondie—plain and simple. We wanted this book...and we were going to have it!

Allan Metz had been collecting Blondie material for many years. His efforts in gathering articles, essays, photographs, and historical data would rival the most thorough researcher. With the Blondie reunion tour, albums, and appearances having peaked, it became apparent that it was time to publish this book. Allan had already known me as a Blondie archivist and publisher of *The Blondie Review*, a quarterly fan journal, which is what prompted him to call on me to assist him in assembling this tome. Our meeting, early this year, lasted only a few minutes before I asked him when I should begin. The decision was a foregone conclusion; for me, this was a given, I knew it had to happen. I am curiously suspicious as to whether Allan had any question or doubt concerning my dedication and passion of the subject matter. I firmly believe he knew my answer long before our meeting.

It was the end of May 2000 when I scheduled a meeting with my good friend and dedicated Blondie fan, Amy Oravec, in the Chelsea district of New York City. This was just a few hours before the well-known Deborah Harry book release party given by Cathay Che at Mother's night club. With other friends and band members showing up, it quickly turned from a meeting into a party (quite by accident, one of the best I've ever given). During brief moments of business-like seriousness, Amy and I decided to produce what's now known as *The Blondie Review* magazine. By the time Amy finished with my draft of the first issue, I was very aware of her proofreading and composition talents. Those drafts then went to my wife, Maryann whose typesetting and formatting expertise led to the premiere issue of the magazine—in less than three months time! After discussing the plans Allan had for his book, I knew that I must have their assistance. What a team we were assembling! The rest, as they say, is history.

Actually, this whole project has been a synergy of souls. I must thank Amy for her unquestioning dedication, drive and ability. Her guidance and expertise have been invaluable. Without Amy, we'd still be sorting out our prepositions and conjunctions. Additionally, I am morally bound to express my appreciation for the understanding and tolerance of my wife, Maryann, and daughter, Stacy. They have seen the tightest and loosest of family relationships. They have worked closely with me, but also lived without me as I dedicated much of our family time to *The Blondie Review* and then, as though that weren't enough, tackled the duties of this book at the same time. Thanks. Additionally, I offer my most sincere thanks and gratitude to the legion of fans who have shared their knowledge and materials and helped us so much along the way. Many are new acquaintances and some are old and dear friends. They run the spectrum from the casually interested to the sincerely and passionately dedicated. Without the fans, collectors, writers, and photographers, this book would not exist. Finally, I wish to thank Allan Metz for enlisting me as his editor in this most ambitious and rewarding effort. It otherwise would have been a missed opportunity for me that I would have regretted...forever. Having the chance to help collect and assemble so much material, all in one place, for all the dedicated fans and interested readers alike is a most flattering compliment and satisfying achievement. I appreciate Allan's trust in my advice, decisions, and ability.

I truly hope you enjoy this product of our passion.

Robert Betts
Shelton, Connecticut, USA
August 2002

"Squeezebox at Don Hill's"

New York City, May 18, 2001

(adapted and edited by Robert Betts)
web site, www.rocketcityrecords.com

Deborah with Cherie Currie. Cherie rocketed to international super-stardom as the teenage lead vocalist for the legendary all-female rock band, The Runaways, alongside bandmates Joan Jett, Lita Ford, Sandy West & Jackie Fox.

Sandy West is one of the hardest hitting drummers in the world. This sweet-faced blonde was the source of the thundering rhythm that powered The Runaways. As headliners, their shows were opened by the likes of Tom Petty & The Heartbreakers and Cheap Trick.

Plasmatics' Guitarist Richie Stotts made a rare appearance in his nurses uniform to play alongside Debbie and the amazing Toilet Boys.

Debbie with Runaways Cherie and Sandy.

Introduction

by Allan Metz

"...You are a True Original who has inspired millions through your Music, Style, Integrity, and Attitude **NO ONE DOES IT BETTER** THANK YOU!!!" (Bartolini, 2 July 2000)—*Posted message to the imusic.com Blondie Bulletin Board. Reprinted with the permission of the author.—Ed.*

"Okay...Let's remind everyone one more time...Are you ready? Listen up...Before Madonna, Cyndi Lauper, Courtney Love, Gwen Stefani, and Shirley Manson...There was the ORIGINAL GODDESS ICON—DEBORAH HARRY." (Bartolini, 2 July 2000)—*Posted message to the imusic.com Blondie Bulletin Board. Reprinted with the permission of the author.—Ed.*

"I am [a] No Doubt fanatic stopping by. Today I have to bow down to the Queen who started it all. Without Deborah Harry, Gwen Stefani (and others) would not be here today! Thanks DEBBIE [for] influencing [the] artists of today." (HairColor80, 3 July 2000).—*Posted message to the imusic.com Blondie Bulletin Board. Reprinted with the permission of the author.—Ed.*

Blondie is (current lineup in alphabetical order):

Clem Burke (drums)
Jimmy Destri (keyboards)
Deborah Harry (vocals)
Chris Stein (guitar)
With:
Paul Carbonara (guitar)
Leigh Foxx (bass)

This book offers both a contemporary and retrospective look at the pop/new wave rock band, Blondie, and its lead singer, Deborah Harry, through text and the medium of photography. Although the band's height of international fame was in the late 1970s to the early 1980s when the group broke up acrimoniously, its influence continues to this day. "But though Blondie had split, there was already an influx of new wave/post-punk bands capitalizing on the group's power pop sound, carrying the band's influence into the next decade" (Gaar, 261). Prior to that: "Among the bands of the 'punk' or 'new wave' genre trying to put the primal energy back into rock'n'roll in the 1970s and the early 1980s, the one that first crossed over to a mass audience and maintained hegemony there was Blondie..." ("Harry, Debbie," *Current Biography Yearbook*, 191). While punk in its origins largely had been perceived as a British phenomenon, the other side of the Atlantic witnessed "subversive bubblegum. Blondie set the trend Stateside for cute harmonic pop songs with a blistering edge, a sound that echoed later through muscular pop outfits like The Go-Go's...with a power pop barbed by punk mores" (O'Brien, Lucy, 137). And "the woman who was probably most identified with [the] rise of punk and new wave in America was undoubtedly Debbie Harry,...who simultaneously updated and poked fun at the conventions of '60s pop and the girl group persona" (Gaar, 258).

A new chapter in Blondie's distinguished history is now being written in the form of a reunion, planned since the mid-1990s. This reunion serves as an opportune time to explore the Blondie legend. There have been many descriptions of the band and its captivating lead singer, Deborah Harry, the "self-mocking pin-up of punk...Harry's pretty come-hither-and-drop-dead face, accented by its painted pout, became the most photographed in the rock music world..." ("Harry, Debbie," *Current Biography Yearbook*, 191). This look, both in appearance and attitude, can be at least partially attributed to "punk's do-it-yourself philosophy [which allowed] women in the '70s...to express their sexual identities and preferences without outside interference. Long before

Madonna or Courtney Love, New Wave trash-glam diva Debbie Harry was pushing the irony button on the myth of the dumb blonde. With her torn fishnets and black eye make-up juxtaposed against her classically beautiful features, the singer of Blondie warped familiar images with humor and subtlety" (Gaines, 94). Harry has since served as a role model and inspiration for many other women in the rock music industry from Madonna to contemporaries like Shirley Manson of the band, Garbage, Gwen Stefani of No Doubt, and Nina Persson of the Cardigans.[1] This legacy is reflected in much of the photography contained in this book because when you see Deborah Harry fronting Blondie, you also can visualize these and many other subsequent bands. Blondie helped to establish the template for a band with a female lead singer fronting its remaining male members at a time when such an arrangement was not the norm.

Blondie and Deborah Harry also have influenced numerous other bands and singers. "It's possibly more difficult to name a band fronted by a woman that is not influenced by Blondie than it is to name one who could not have existed without them. And although elements of Deborah Harry (then Debbie)—her look, her attitude, her delivery—appear everywhere in music and fashion today, as they have throughout most of the 80s and 90s, Blondie's sound has been just as influential as their style" (Johnson, 27). And, by the same token, Blondie is a reflection of the pop culture it later influenced. "Of all the CBGB[2] bands, none was more influenced by [Andy] Warhol than Blondie, with its cartoon name, plastic themes, pop visuals...[Harry]...was the first rock & roller to exploit blond sex object as shtick. She would not be the last" (O'Dair, 281-282). Before proceeding further, some background on the band is in order.

Background

New York City-based Blondie was formed in 1974, honing its musical skills at the famous club, CBGBs, and eventually emerging on top of the new wave scene and then crossing over to the pop music mainstream. After a number of band name and personnel changes, Blondie had its greatest success with the following lineup: Deborah Harry, vocals; Chris Stein, guitar; Jimmy Destri, keyboards; Clem Burke, drums; Frank Infante, guitar; and Nigel Harrison, bass. The self-titled first album, *Blondie*, on the Private Stock record label, reflected a punk ethos and 1960s girl group sensibilities ("Blondie," *Encyclopedia of Popular Music*, vol. I, p. 598)—or, "The Ramones meets the Ronettes," as one music critic opined (Boyd, 63). Blondie made six albums from 1976 to 1982, the most successful was *Parallel Lines*, considered by many music critics to be one of the best rock albums of all time. Within this time span, from the late '70s to the early '80s, Blondie constituted a major force on the rock/pop scene, producing a string of hit singles internationally. The most well-known of these singles are the reggae-inspired "The Tide Is High," the rap song, "Rapture," and the disco-flavored "Heart of Glass" and "Call Me." A number of factors led to Blondie's demise—dissension among band members over the focus on photogenic lead singer Harry, tensions and disputes with management and their record company (Chrysalis), a disappointing showing of the band's sixth album, *The Hunter*, and a tour curtailed by a rare disease, pemphigus, which afflicted guitarist Chris Stein (*Encyclopedia of Popular Music*, vol. I, p. 598). Regarding Chrysalis, however, Harry recently has observed that: "It wasn't all bad with Chrysalis, they did a good job on promoting Blondie and introducing it in such a way that our reputation has remained. We still exist today because of the way they marketed us" (Malins, 14). Following a long-term recovery by Stein, Harry and Stein remained active in the music industry with Deborah embarking on a solo career. The other band members pursued careers in and out of the music business. Harry released one solo album while Blondie still was together in 1981 (*Koo Koo*) and three subsequent albums (*Rockbird*, 1986; *Def, Dumb and Blonde*, 1989; and *Debravation*, 1993), the latter two with the musical collaboration of Chris Stein. These albums and the singles (for example, "French Kissin in the USA" and "I Want That Man") they spawned, however, did not approach the commercial attainment of the more successful Blondie material, although they generally fared better in the United Kingdom. Following the breakup of Blondie, Harry also branched out into film, theater, television, and modeling. Musically, in addition to her solo work, she also began singing in the 1990s with the avant-garde jazz group, the Jazz Passengers, performing the vocals on the critically acclaimed album, *Individually Twisted* as well as on other Passengers' albums ("Harry, Deborah," *Encyclopedia of Popular Music*, vol. III, pp. 2418-2419).

Considering the musical experimentation of Blondie, it is not surprising that either Harry plunged into other fields or successfully challenged her vocal talents with jazz. Chris Stein provided the major impetus to reunite Blondie both for artistic and commercial reasons, not wanting the later regret of not having made this attempt. In the mid-1990s, Stein broached the reunion idea with Harry, who was reluctant at first. Stein's persistence, however, paid off as Harry agreed along with two other original band members, Clem Burke and Jimmy Destri. (Two former band members, Frank Infante and Nigel Harrison, are not part of the Blondie reunion and sued over the use of the Blondie name. Infante and Harrison later lost the lawsuit. They are replaced by bassist, Leigh Foxx and guitarist, Paul Carbonara. Gary Valentine, who was the band's bassist from 1975 to 1977, currently is not a member of the band).[3] Legal matters aside, the band went ahead with its plans, rehearsing and doing occasional live performances to fine-tune its sound. By 1998, the group was ready and this process included a European tour in the fall of 1998.

The big year of the Blondie reunion so far has been 1999. Album-wise, the original plan had been to record two new songs as part of yet another compilation album of earlier songs. Rather than following the route of other '70s and '80s band reunions, the group decided to release a CD with all new original material and signed on with an independent label, California-based Beyond Music. The album, entitled *No Exit*, was released in the United States on February 23, 1999, and the first single ("Maria") from the new album the following month. The winter of 1999 witnessed a media blitz for Blondie in support of the new album—television and radio appearances, some concert dates, and much exposure in the print media. From mid-May through the end of the year, Blondie toured both Europe and the United States. The reunion effort has been promising. The single, "Maria," debuted at No. 1 in England, making this song the sixth No. 1 single for the group in that country. With this hit single, Blondie reached yet another milestone—the first band to have had a No. 1 single in each of the last three decades in the United Kingdom. Following past trends, "Maria" did not fare as well in the United States, debuting and remaining in the lower reaches of the top 100 singles. The album, however, fared better, debuting at number 18 in the *Billboard* album charts and remaining in the top 100 for nine weeks. International album sales exceeded one million in the first month following *No Exit*'s release ("Blondie Announces"). A *Blondie Live* album was released on November 23, 1999 in the U.S. and a British counterpart, *Livid*, in April 2000. Having already attained this level of commercial and artistic success, a new album is scheduled for 2003. Blondie is among "the Class of 2002 potential first-time nominees"[4] for the Rock and Roll Hall of Fame (Cohen and Grossweiner).[5] Induction into the Hall would be a fitting tribute to this innovative band. In the meantime, we all await with anticipation as to what Blondie holds in store for us in the future.

As detailed in the Preface, the book begins with a narrative of the punk music scene in New York City along with the placement of Blondie within this context and is followed by a consideration of Deborah Harry's solo career and Blondie's reunion. The latter has certainly served as a catalyst for a consideration anew of Blondie both then and now. Deborah Harry and Blondie's influence is undeniable back when the band had its initial success, through their period of inactivity when their music continued to be played and heard, and, finally, when the four original band members reunited. And the fact is that Blondie has never been better. This book will document the fact that the group has made a significant contribution to, and has had a substantial impact on, pop and rock music as reflected in both the text and photography of this book.

To close this introduction, I will leave you with (as best I can reconstruct), a brief conversation I had with Deborah Harry (DH) at a "meet and greet" event I had the fortune of attending following a Blondie concert at the Concord Pavilion (since renamed the Chronicle Pavilion) in Concord, California on August 20, 1999:

AM: I've been doing extensive research for a book on Blondie's legacy and influence. You must be tired of all the discussion of the band's legacy by now.

DH: Oh, no. I really appreciate all your efforts. I think it's wonderful. Good luck (with it).

AM: Thanks, I'll need it!

DH: Don't we all...

Notes

1. For Deborah Harry's brief observations on women in rock, see Deborah Harry, "Foreword," in Amy Raphael, *Never Mind the Bollocks: Women Rewrite Rock* (London: Virago, 1995). A year later, it was published in the United States as Amy Raphael, *Grrrls: Viva Rock Divas*, 1st St. Martin's Griffin ed. (New York: St. Martin's Griffin, 1996).

2. Full name CBGB OMFUG, standing for "Country, Blue Grass and Blues, and Other Music For Uplifting Gormandizers" or CBGBs, or CBs, for short.

3. For Valentine's remembrances of "early" Blondie and his stint with the band, see: Gary Valentine, "'Must Be Into the Shangri-Las...,'" *Mojo: The Music Magazine* (United Kingdom) 63(February 1999): 76-83, which is reprinted in this book. For observations by Deborah Harry on Blondie and herself, see Debbie Harry, Chris Stein, and Victor Bockris, *Making Tracks: The Rise of Blondie*, 1st Da Capo Press ed. (New York: Da Capo Press, 1998) and the original: *Making Tracks: The Rise of Blondie* (New York: Dell Publishing Company, 1982). For observations on Blondie and Deborah Harry by three distinguished music critics in book form, see Lester Bangs, *Blondie* (New York: Simon and Schuster, 1980) as well as in these two critics' edited volumes: "The Story of Blondie (1986)" in Kurt Loder, *Bat Chain Puller: Rock and Roll in the Age of Celebrity* (New York: St. Martin's Press, 1990), 180-198 and "Ripped to Shreds" in Greil Marcus, *Ranters & Crowd Pleasers: Punk in Pop Music, 1977-92*, 1st ed. (New York: Doubleday, 1993), 105-108. See also Fred Schruers, *Headliners: Blondie* (New York: Tempo Books, 1980).

4. The others are Boston, the Ramones, and Peter Tosh, according to the source cited in the next footnote. The inductees for 2002 in the Performer category are Isaac Hayes, Brenda Lee, Tom Petty and the Heartbreakers, Gene Pitney, the Ramones, and the Talking Heads, as announced December 13, 2001 on the Rock 'n' Roll Hall of Fame web site (www.rockhall.com).

5. Jane Cohen and Bob Grossweiner, "A Rock And Roll Hall Of Fame Analysis," *CD-NOW* web site, 22 September 1999, Accessed 7 April 2000 <www.cdnow.com>.

Part I: Then

Chris Stein and Deborah Harry, May 21, 1982
credit: © Mirror Syndication International

Background

"Visions of the Seventies: The Rise and Fall of a Cultural Challenge"

By Victor Bockris

"The 1970s were America's low tide. Not since the Depression had the country been so wracked with woe. *Never*—not even during the Depression—had America's pride and self-confidence plunged deeper. But the decade was also, paradoxically, in some ways America's finest hour...

"For a short time...[Americans] behaved foolishly, and on one or two occasions, even disgracefully. Then they recouped. They rethought. They reinvented. They rediscovered in their own past the governing principles of their future. Out of the failure and trauma of the 1970s they emerged stronger, richer, and—if it is not overdramatic to say so—greater than ever."—*David Frum,* How We Got Here: The 70's: The Decade That Brought You Modern Life (For Better or Worse) *(New York: Basic Books, 2000, p. 289).*

Nobody would argue that America, in the second half of the 20th Century, went through a social revolution equal to the industrial revolution in its effect on how people lived. There is, however, mounting disagreement as to when this transformation took place. The majority says it was the 1960s; a pushy new minority is arguing it was the 1970s. Of course, they are both wrong because history doesn't happen in decades. I would say that 1965-82 was the period in which we saw the unified playing out of a set of cultural ideas. Focusing in on them, one might say that 1975-80 was the period in which we really let it rip! Whatever one believes, the '70s is a much maligned and grossly ignored decade. And until we cut it out, identify it and give it a chance to speak for itself, the argument has no base.

As far as I'm concerned, the only history worth reading is about people. What I look for is how the images of men and women changed, along with the way they relate to one another. The following is an introduction to the '70s, in terms of how the artists who played the strongest roles in shaping those changes played out their hands, linking themselves to each other in the unique collaboration that was the '70s signature.

The '70s are widely and mistakenly seen as an embarrassment; portrayed in films, magazines, books and television shows as an empty-minded, tasteless decade characterized by bellbottoms, barbiturates, disco music and bad hair. Yet the figures who defined the period, such as John Lennon, Lou Reed, Andy Warhol, Debbie Harry, Patti Smith and Jean Michel Basquiat, are more widely respected now than then. Despite the conservative view of what President Nixon called "The Silent Majority," the political upheaval that had forced President Johnson out of office in 1968 became in the '70s a social upheaval in habits, beliefs and morals, affecting not just the avant-garde but the entire country. Many of the most radical ideas of the '60s took root and became facts in the '70s and continue to influence the way we view and live life today. If we don't see this, we are walking around in a world we cannot understand.

The thrust of the '70s was an attempt to, in Muhammad Ali's poignant words, "make America be America," a land of freedom of expression with room for experiments in different ways of living not tied to the nuclear family or the jobs and economics of big business.

The early '70s (1970-72) was a period of pause. Having expended an enormous amount of energy in the '60s with questionable results, we didn't want to blunder on blindly. As John Lennon pointed out in a 1971 interview, the same bastards were still running the show. We had to re-examine everything. The '70s began to find a voice they could call their own in 1974—with the ousting of the corrupt and reactionary Nixon administration as a result of the Watergate scandal; with Muhammad Ali's return to his throne as the heavyweight champion of the world, a title that had been stripped from him when he refused to be inducted into the Army to fight in Vietnam in 1967; with Andy Warhol's move out of the Factory at 33 Union Square where he had been shot and almost killed in 1968 into a grander space that heralded a new period of growth and success; with William Burroughs' return from 25 years of self-imposed exile from the United States to live in New York, where he too would experience a period of great success; with the recognition that Lou Reed was, in the words of David

Bowie, "the most important person in rock'n'roll"; with Patti Smith's first single, "Piss Factory"; and with Television, the Ramones, the Talking Heads and Blondie performing in a tiny Bowery bar called CBGB. These people were all outsiders who would, in the short, magic interlude between 1975-80, suddenly all find themselves in the right places at the right times.

The 1976-80 period, in which the Southern Democrat Jimmy Carter occupied the White House, was the most permissive period in the history of the United States. Never before had so many people taken so many drugs; never before had so many people had so much sex with so many different kinds of people in so many ways. Never before had so many great works from so many different fields found themselves fueled by a unique artistic cross pollination. And nowhere were these experiments more extensively practiced than in the New York Underground.

New values and new tastes in art and entertainment historically emerge from the Bohemian Underground of the major cities. As I see it, NYC played the key role in shaping the social changes of the '70s. Its thriving downtown salons, lofts, art galleries and clubs became the seedbed of much that would turn out to be the best and much that would turn out to be the worst in American culture.

The remnants of the '60s counterculture gathered there and were joined by aspirant avant-garde dissidents from all over the country and abroad. These were attractive, dynamic people who led vibrant, exciting lives. They interacted ferociously, delving into each other's minds and bodies. There was an intensity to all their connections, which made them impossible to ignore. They weren't just tired and going through the motions. They were living real life to its breaking points.

Some of them were established figures making a comeback, such as Ali, Burroughs, Warhol and Reed. Others achieved fame for the first time as part of the '70s culture, such as Debbie Harry, David Byrne, Robert Mapplethorpe, Jim Carroll, Richard Hell, Keith Haring, Stephen Sprouse, Jean Michel Basquiat and many others. These artists shared the goal of subverting the mores of the society they were living in, and in the mid-to late '70s they came tantalizingly close to succeeding in making America be America.

In the end, however, the forces of creativity fell because they were susceptible to emotions, to unrealistic romanticism. The forces of darkness returned, epitomized by the materialistic Reagan administration, which came to power at the beginning of the 1980s and had no such illusions.

Sex, drugs and money were three of the major catalysts, although in my opinion there was something more to the revolt of the '70s. Something happened all over New York during these years, which was the product of a collective dream that opened people's minds to other, perhaps greater ways of being. At the very least, we tried, as Burroughs put it, to "blow a hole in time." At the very least, we asked the right questions.

LENNON, THE STONES AND WARHOL:
STEPPING INTO THE BREACH, 1970-74

The stage was set at the end of the '60s. By 1969, the FBI's infiltration and smear campaigns against the leading figures of left-wing cultural and political movements—from the Beats to the Black Panthers—had decimated the upper echelons of the counterculture. Without leaders, the "movement" of the '60s, which had gone underground in the form of the Weathermen or soldiered on in the form of the Yippies, floundered. The New Left, which was more of a humanitarian issue-specific protest against the Vietnam War than a genuine left-wing movement, shifted toward the issue-specific radicalism of the women's liberation, gay liberation and ecology movements. The image of the heterosexual male was reeling from the Manson murders and the violence at the Rolling Stones' free concert at Altamont. No one knew what to think or how to behave.

In my opinion, three artists—John Lennon, the Rolling Stones and Andy Warhol—stepped into the breach. With their bold work and equally bold personalities, they gave people some sense of shape and definition they would not have been able to find anywhere else. Above all, they offered new images of men and women in the first period of the decade, 1970-72, when we were most unsure of ourselves.

In 1970, Lennon left the Beatles and began issuing records more as bulletins than as songs: his blistering singles "Cold Turkey," "Instant Karma" and "Give Peace a Chance" and his first solo album, *John Lennon/ Plastic Ono Band.* In this first, and best of his five solo albums, he informed his audience that the dream of the '60s was over and introduced himself as an individual painfully seeking his way in uncharted territory. He began spending time in New York ("I could see that the '70s were going to be all America's," he said).

In 1971, Lennon's myth-destroying interview, "Lennon Remembers," was published in *Rolling Stone* and was later issued as a mass paperback. That same year, he made his life-changing move to New York and in 1972 released a double album (the first with wife Yoko Ono), *Sometime in New York City*. It dealt with the political questions of the new decade in songs celebrating, among others, the jailed black revolutionary Angela Davis and the rock'n'roll White Panther John Sinclair, who had been sentenced to ten years in jail for the possession of two joints. And "Attica State" chronicled the 1971 prison rebellion, which resulted in the killing of 38 inmates.

In 1970, the Rolling Stones released their 1969 concert film, "Gimme Shelter." Filmed for the Stones by the Maysles brothers, it was a superbly shot and beautifully edited work. As the band moved across the country from the East to the West, the film cut back and forth between the building of the scaffold-like stage at Altamont to the deserted raceway in the desert outside San Francisco where the band would give a free concert at the end of the tour. Some of the Stones' best performances were captured on the film, which closed with the brutal murder of a black man 20 feet from the front of the stage. The band played on, forcing us to question our deification of rock stars as role models. Nicolas Roeg's "Performance," starring Mick Jagger, came out two weeks later, after a two-year censorship delay.

These films had a strong impact on men's styles of the early '70s. In 1971, the band left England, relocated in France and released the drug-drenched *Sticky Fingers,* with a cover by Andy Warhol. An interview with the Stones' Keith Richards—of the same scope and length as Lennon's—appeared in *Rolling Stone*. In it, Richards emerged as the leader of the band and a major trendsetter of the decade.

In 1972, the Stones reached their apotheosis with the double album *Exile on Main Street,* with a sleeve by Beat photographer Robert Frank. They toured the States that summer, ending up in New York. The film of this tour, shot by Robert Frank and titled "Cocksucker Blues," was never released. Like Lennon's work, the Stones' songs of the early '70s were short stories full of torn and frayed characters personifying the wrecked, but still standing, population of the underground. Rock songs, pictures of the times as they happened, became a strong unifying force in a time of political and social confusion.

The period was equally defined by Andy Warhol's films "Trash" (1970) and "Heat" (1972), as well as by his gossipy *Interview* magazine. The characters in Warhol's films and magazine, which was much more radical in the early '70s than it later became, were similar to the characters in the Stones' music—desperate but still insisting on their rights to live in the world of Nixon's "Silent Majority." Warhol made one of his sharpest, most overt political statements with his return to painting in the majestic portraits of Chairman Mao. Warhol painted a companion portrait of Nixon, who had just returned from his historic visit to Mao in China. When the Democrats asked Warhol for a contribution to George McGovern's 1972 campaign against Nixon for the Presidency, Warhol simply scrawled "VOTE MCGOVERN" across the bottom of the Nixon portrait, in which the green-faced figure looked like the personification of evil, and gave them permission to use it as their campaign poster. It was a typical Warhol gesture—hard, deft and far more powerful than the standard poster. It also earned him a prominent place on Nixon's hit list.

The above works would make a good retrospective of the period. It was the combination of each work and its creator's life, however, which became in the early '70s equal to and part of the work and that played the strongest role in reshaping the counterculture's lifestyles, habits and attitudes at the crucial beginning of the decade.

THE OUTING OF THE GAY COUNTERCULTURE:
A NEW WAY OF BEING, 1974-78

The American male went through a radical transformation in the mid-70s. Previously, he had worn the same suit that all men wore. Conversation was not a word in his vocabulary. If you had put him at a European dinner table, he would've had no idea what was going on. But in the '70s, he would turn into a clotheshorse who wore designer suits. He had his hair cut in a salon, used lotions on his skin and dined in French restaurants, ordering wine from a list he understood. He even wore cologne.

This about-face was almost completely engineered by gay men. The Beat Generation's leading figures were gay, and the leading figures in the Warhol world were gay. Lou Reed was gay. Halston was gay. The attitude toward gay men in the heterosexual community went through a 180-degree turn. In 1973, I could not invite a gay man to dinner with heterosexual friends without them being embarrassed into making fun of him. By 1975, I couldn't have a dinner without my gay friends; they had become so popular.

As far as heterosexual men were concerned, Norman Mailer was everywhere in the '70s, debating against the women's liberation movement and writing about graffiti art, Vietnam, Marilyn Monroe and crime. John Lennon pointed the way for men who were trying to live on an equal footing with women in "Woman is the Nigger of the World" and made it the subject of many interviews.

But the strongest hetero statements and images, albeit not often in favor of the women's movement, came from punk rock, the most sexual art movement of the '70s. The way I—and a number of my friends—saw it, sexually the '70s was the healthiest of times. We were getting rid of many blocks and taboos. We were meeting girls who were as strong as we were. In fact, many of them took more risks than their boyfriends, often leading the way. As the singer Deerfrance put it, "If you had one room with no heat, you would not be alone at night. The juices were flowing, and it made the bands and everyone want to go out and meet each other. It was real life."

The '70s was the first decade in which American men were encouraged to have emotions. "Trust your feelings, Luke," says Obi-Wan Kenobi at the peak of "Star Wars" (1977). There was also a desire for collaboration on all fronts, as witnessed by the proliferation of group psychology movements and cults. People wanted to be told what to do; they desperately needed leaders. From where I sat, the culture heroes around whom people gathered in New York were the best because, rather than constantly answering people's questions with a lot of mumbo jumbo, they focused on pointing the way to asking the right questions. When they did give advice, it was carefully thought out, such as: "People need to be aware of having to learn how to live," Andy Warhol said. "Because life happens so fast, and sometimes it goes away too quickly."

There were two climaxes in the '70s. The first one came in 1975, the year America finally withdrew all its forces from Vietnam. Several major figures had landmark successes in April of that year, when the Beat Generation made a significant comeback at a Columbia University group reading by Allen Ginsberg, Peter Orlovsky, Gregory Corso and William Burroughs. From 1975 onward, Burroughs and Ginsberg grew steadily more famous among the young, as they constantly toured colleges and clubs, reading their works and giving interviews to the underground and local press.

In July and August, the Rolling Stones toured the United States, capturing the imaginations primarily of young men who copied the way they walked, spoke and looked—utterly stoned. Keith Richards was arrested in Arkansas but eluded a court appearance due to the influence of ex-FBI agents working as his personal security. This above-the-law status the Stones flaunted was very much a part of the times. It allowed all of us to feel beyond the old controls, despite reality.

In the spring, Bob Dylan returned to the streets of Greenwich Village, which he had haunted ten years earlier as a folk singer. He gathered together performers from the Beat Generation and the folk rock, glam rock and punk rock generations and wove them into the Rolling Thunder Review, which became the most inventive and inspirational rock tours of the decade. Rolling Thunder reached its first climax in December at Madison Square Garden in New York. The concert was a benefit for the wrongfully jailed boxer Rubin "Hurricane" Carter, the subject of Dylan's hot new single, "Hurricane." Muhammad Ali made an appearance, phoning Carter in prison from the stage. For a moment, the counterculture felt united and proud again.

In September, *The Philosophy of Andy Warhol* was published. It was well received and widely reviewed, with *The New York Times* calling Warhol "the bellwether of America." Although it sold poorly at the time, it has stayed in print for the last 25 years.

I would argue that it is a key text of the decade. Read today, it captures the tone and attitude that made Warhol so attractive to young people across the country in the '70s. Serious in intent, it delivers its points on love, sex, money, friendship, work, success and death with humor. Besides, who else could have published a book called "The Philosophy Of" before his name? Around the time of its publication, Warhol managed to infiltrate the Ford White House and turn his visit into an extraordinarily successful international publicity campaign for the book. And with the success of this work, Warhol began to reach a level of intensity and influence in the mainstream that he had never before known.

The most successful TV comedy show of the decade, "Saturday Night Live!," commenced its long, highly successful run from New York City. In the ominous times of the Ford administration, the show built a bridge between "underground" and mainstream humor. Two of its stars, John Belushi and Dan Aykroyd, opened a bar in downtown Manhattan where they celebrated every Saturday night. The show, and particularly Belushi, became a rallying point. "SNL" flourished in the New York Underground, where it became the seminal show for a second generation of TV viewers.

From July 16–August 3, 1975, CBGB mounted a rock festival in which more than 40 bands performed. This summer festival was a turning point in the history of New York Underground rock. Not only was it the first rock festival to cater to unrecorded punk bands, it also inspired new bands, attracted wider audiences and subsequently the national press. Punk was getting into a position to become a force in the second half of the decade.

Watergate had given the counterculture an enormous shot in the arm that—along with Ali's surprise 1974 victory over George Foreman and his even greater defeat of Joe Frazier in the 1975 Thrilla in Manila, combined with the above works and events—created the illusion that "we" could win, that something was happening here that only we understood. In short, there still was a counterculture, something that had definitely been in doubt in the painful days of the early '70s. This feeling was strengthened in the Underground by the assault of punk rock, which began in earnest that November when Patti Smith released her first breakout album, *Horses*. *The New York Times Sunday Magazine*'s December profile of her was the first sign, as far as the public was concerned, that a new Beat generation, named Punk, was upon us. Blondie closed out the year, playing a New Year's Eve concert in Central Park that made the midnight news.

Suddenly a new social network that cross-pollinated the art, beat, punk, Warhol factory and New York School poetry worlds was transforming New York from a broken-down city full of potholes into a gay, sparkling city full of exhilarating people and astonishing new places, out of which a new way of being would grow.

THE GODFATHERS RECOGNIZE THEIR CHILDREN:
A POCKET OF LIGHT, 1975-80

In the mid-70s, gay men became an important economic force. They ran the best clubs, restaurants, bookshops, clothes shops, gyms, limousine services and private airlines. And they gave the best parties. Gay people were the wittiest, the most up-to-date and the most image-conscious. They also had the best drugs, and they were generous with them. The success of disco was largely due to the gay influence, creating the impression that gay men lived more pleasurable lives and—so it seemed at the time—had the most pleasurable future ahead of them. Two male salaries combined, with none of the financial responsibilities of bringing up children, made them the envy of many heterosexuals who were putting off getting married and settling down well into their 30s, sometimes their 40s.

This was a heady period. For the first time, gay choices were considered the wave of the future. They were on the cutting edge. At the same time, everybody in that world knew they were careening toward an abyss, which made it even more exciting in and of itself. According to one writer, "There was a mystic wildness about the partying, the music, the drugs, the clothes, the free sexuality—the interchange of partners, the constant fucking of boys, girls—it was so shocking and exhilarating." Homosexuality had been an unspeakable vice in the '60s. In the '70s, their assertion of the right to lead an entirely new way of life brought the gay rights movement to a level with the civil rights and women's movements in the minds of liberal Americans.

When *Punk* magazine's premiere issue hit the stands in January 1976 with Lou Reed on its cover, one sensed that something else unique was shaking itself into existence. There were several useful publications of the period (*N.Y. Rocker, The Soho Weekly News*), but *Punk* was the most creative and intelligent. It made the scene by treating the musicians, who were unknown outside the Lower East Side, like stars, but with an irreverent sense of humor. It also defined the punk community in embracing not only Reed, but also mentors from an even earlier generation such as Warhol and Burroughs, something unique to the era.

As I see it, in the 1975-80 pocket of light, we experienced a three-generational artistic collaboration that has never been, and probably never will be, equaled. Ali and Burroughs were as important to Patti Smith as her colleagues in the punk band Television were. To Debbie Harry, Andy Warhol and Lou Reed were as relevant as her friends in the Ramones. For the first time, the new generation did not have to kill its fathers. We just promoted them to Godfathers! And the Godfathers recognized their children and welcomed the fresh energy they brought with them.

In 1976, the Ramones, Television, Talking Heads, Richard Hell and the Voidoids, the Dead Boys and Blondie all made their first albums and began attracting international attention. Although punk continued the tradition of the boys club, it was also open to gay people. There were a number of strong creative women in the punk scene, including Debbie Harry and Patti Smith. As managers of groups, record executives, fashion designers, poets, playwrights, actresses, magazine editors, film directors, photographers like Marcia Resnick, performance artists like Laurie Anderson, writers like Susan Sontag and underground painters like Susan Williams and Sarah Charlesworth, they all made an impact. The groundbreaking punk girls such as Anya Phillips, Marcia Resnick and Tina l'Hotsky, who were important muse figures at the clubs and among the many bands, also had a beneficial influence.

Sex was exceptionally free of consequences in the '70s. Pornography became much more widespread in magazines, and this was the first time sexually-explicit films could be shown, such as "Deep Throat" (1973), "Behind the Green Door" (1973) and "The Devil and Miss Jones" (1974). Their stars, Marilyn Chambers and Linda Lovelace, became household names. Not only was this a time before AIDS, but in Manhattan the nuclear family was set aside in exchange for sex and success. Children did not feature (except in horror films like "The Exorcist" (1974) and "The Omen" (1975) and Andy Warhol's "Bad" (1977), in which a baby was tossed out the window of a high-rise apartment building).

The disco scene reached its zenith with the opening of Studio 54 in April 1977. Studio 54 revolutionized the concept of the club by introducing the velvet rope across its door. Nobody could enter unless chosen by the doorman. Although 54 was associated prominently with disco, ironically in the end it did more to kill rather than support it by taking what was essentially a lower-class urban music and turning it into a "limited to only the best people" style.

At first, however, the competition between punk and disco created a healthy tension that gave both scenes shape and definition. It was a time in which the demarcation between the street philosophy of the Beats and the chic philosophy of the Warhol Factory met. Warhol's paintings that year would have been perfect covers for Burroughs' books. It was the first time that Warhol, who had been betrayed by Reed in 1966, finally praised Reed's work in public and Reed spoke openly of his debt to Warhol.

Burroughs interviewed Patti Smith for *High Times*. Warhol painted Debbie Harry's portrait. It was a moment in which the forces linked. It was the climax in which the underground surfaced and the mainstream applauded. In the mid- to late-70s, the rest of the country took several big steps toward catching up with New York. This was due in part to the relentless traveling and proselytizing of our subjects.

Although disco was always far more popular than punk on the radio, in clubs and record sales, the punk bands built a national constituency by touring constantly, bringing their style to impressionable teenagers and young adults across the land. Ginsberg and Burroughs gave readings throughout the country, mostly at universities and punk rock clubs. Andy Warhol traveled as relentlessly as any rock star, publicizing his work. In the spring of 1976, the opening of his "Hammer and Sickle" paintings was mobbed by ecstatic punks. And what could have been more punk than the "Piss" paintings and the "Sex Parts" series he started turning out in 1977. His film "Bad," about a gang of girl punks who will do anything, including murder, for hire, was something of a financial disaster, but today it is a cult classic.

The fact that 1976 was the USA's Bicentennial and 1977 saw the Silver Jubilee of Queen Elizabeth II in the UK made this the perfect time for twin attacks on authority and tradition. The artistic relationship between London and New York had always been strong, starting with the British Invasion of 1964-69, but during punk it became more of a two-way street. The success of Blondie and the Ramones in London was equaled by the impact of the Clash and the Sex Pistols in New York, even though the Pistols were temporarily unable to get USA visas. On hearing their savage rendition of "God Save the Queen," William Burroughs wrote them a letter of support.

THE SECOND CLIMAX:
THE ANNUS MIRABILIS, 1978-79

1978 was the second climax of the decade and its annus mirabilis—the climax of everything that had packed itself into this powerful post-war period. Everybody had a good year. Everyone rose to the challenge, as one brilliant work followed hard on the heels of another. It started with the Sex Pistols' January/February American tour. Although they pointedly ignored the big cities and toured the South and West, the tour was intensively covered by *Punk* magazine, and a *High Times* magazine film crew made a documentary film of the tour, "Dead On Arrival." After the band broke up at the end of the tour in San Francisco, Johnny Rotten and Sid Vicious stopped in New York on their way back to England. Vicious moved to New York later in the year and became the most famous punk rock star when he killed his girlfriend, Nancy Spungen, in the Chelsea Hotel.

The Rolling Stones, who had sunk into a torpor from which session musicians could not rescue them during the 1973-76 seasons, snapped back into focus with *Some Girls,* their best album since *Exile on Main Street,* as Keith Richards finally kicked heroin in the teeth. *Some Girls* was a series of love songs recorded in Paris and presented to America via "Saturday Night Live."

Lou Reed, who had stepped back from the front lines in '76 and '77, returned to the front in top form with *Street Hassle,* in which he once again relied upon a Warhol superstar for his shoreline (Eric Emerson, who had appeared in a number of Warhol's films). Reed also came out with the magnificent double live album *Take No Prisoners,* in which he emerged as the Lenny Bruce of rock'n'roll with his monologues and asides to the audience. He had finally become himself; he had finally learned how to live.

Warhol himself exploded onto the canvas with a series of beautiful, if sometimes brutal, works in the "Skull" and awesome "Shadows" series. Blondie released *Parallel Lines,* which contained their first American #1 single "Heart of Glass," cracking the carapace of punk to appear as a disco band. Studio 54 became the most important club in the world, mesmerizing and astonishing roomfuls of people. A giant neon Man in the Moon loomed over the dance floor, lifting his glittering coke spoon to his nose. Beneath his benevolent gaze, the most beautiful girls and boys in the world danced with abandon. Hedonistic, elitist, often racist, it was the most decadent place in the world. Andy Warhol dropped by every night, often just standing like a slab of stone-silent oracle, the essence of emptiness. Celebrities appeared like shimmering apparitions. But then Studio 54 was raided by the police, its owners were arrested and thrown in jail and everyone went downtown to the Mudd Club.

The Mudd Club, which opened in October 1978, was the polar opposite of Studio 54. Representing punk, it consisted of two bare rectangular rooms and two very active bathrooms, in which the gender line had finally been completely erased. It shared with Studio 54 a sense of spectacle, putting on events such as the Dead Rock Stars party, which consisted of a series of shrines to Janis Joplin, Jimi Hendrix, Brian Jones and Jim Morrison. We were very aware of our dead that year.

The Mudd instantly became the greatest club in the world, branching out into the nightclub as a performance space and having art exhibitions and literary readings, as well as rock'n'roll shows. Mickey Ruskin, whose Max's Kansas City had been the gathering place of the downtown crowd from 1966 to 1973, opened two additional bars and restaurants, The Ocean Club, 1976-77 and Chinese Chance, 1978-83. Both became key meeting places for the downtown rock art fashion avant-garde scene.

William Burroughs now inherited the throne of this new society as King of the Underground. His new book about collaboration, *The Third Mind* (1978, with Brion Gysin), was another key text of the decade. The Nova Convention at the Entermedia Theatre on the Lower East Side that December was a celebration of his life and work by beat, punk, pop, art and rock figures. (Jean Michel Basquiat, hardly known outside the graffiti art world, was in the audience, and another young unknown painter, Keith Haring, wrote in his journal of the complete awakening the Nova Convention brought him.)

"One has the feeling of being in the middle of something here," Burroughs wrote Paul Bowles in Tangier. He was at the center of the climax of the most creative cultural period in the history of New York. Never before had so many different artists and their audiences been connected by a landscape. Furthermore, the highly successful movies of Woody Allen ("Annie Hall" and "Manhattan") and Martin Scorsese ("Mean Streets" and "Taxi Driver") and other films like "Saturday Night Fever" and "Dog Day Afternoon" painted the city in beautiful, if sometimes violent, imagery.

Television went through many revolutions in the '70s, mirroring the social changes, particularly in women's roles. Two of the best programs, "Mary Hartman, Mary Hartman" (starring Allen's first wife, Louise Lasser), about a housewife whose obsessions are the waxy yellow buildup on her kitchen floor and her husband's impotence and "Saturday Night Live" (on which Burroughs read to an audience of 100,000,000 in 1981), were proud of being from New York. The shows and their actors became as much a part of the fabric as the artists, writers and musicians.

By the end of 1978, the mass consumption of these films and TV shows, the popularity of the new music and the national press stories about the activities in the clubs had familiarized the rest of the country with present-day New York, creating a two-way street of communication that made people like Ali, Burroughs and Warhol, who had previously been impossibly distanced by their heavy metal images, less frightening, even intriguing.

It did not hurt, of course, that both Warhol and Ali infiltrated the White House several times during the '70s, that Burroughs was accepted into the Academy of Arts and Letters before he left New York or that Allen Ginsberg won the Gold Medal in Literature from the National Arts Club in 1979. Also to coincide with the publication of his book of photographs of the '70s, *Exposures* (1979), and the simultaneous opening of his "Portraits of the Seventies" at the Whitney Museum in New York, a major TV station profiled Andy Warhol on the popular "20/20" show, which had an audience of 80 million.

As the lifestyles of the New York Underground figures rose from the surface of their work to become accepted by a significant part of the mainstream, New York—which had seemed like a forbidden city in the first two-thirds of the decade—ended it by becoming more a part of the tapestry of America than before.

HEROIN: THE SUCKER PUNCH, 1979-83

In 1979, a terrific new creative energy exploded all over New York in the form of graffiti art on the walls and subways and in break-dancing, hip-hop and rap music in the streets. This was also the year when the initially all-white MTV was launched. The predominantly black artists in graffiti and rap were so numerous, so talented and so confident and young that, regardless how many were shot by the police, some got through.

The top three graffiti men were the extraordinary Jean Michel Basquiat, known as the Radiant Child, and the two white boys, Keith Haring and Kenny Scharf. In 1980-81, Glenn O'Brien shot a movie, "Downtown 81," about Basquiat and the downtown music scene starring James Chance and Kid Creole and the Coconuts. This new energy took the style of the late '70s into the early '80s. Everything was moving so fast that whole movements began and ended in a year.

By late 1981, Basquiat had a one-man show in a Soho gallery, and his work on canvas was called Neo-Expressionist. His next move would be collaboration with Andy Warhol. Haring also got a lot of publicity, and they both became stars and started to make a lot of money.

The New York/No Wave bands Teenage Jesus and the Jerks, Lydia Lunch, the Contortions and James White and the Blacks were like graffiti musicians. S&M became the latest sexual fashion. The world of Christopher Isherwood's *Berlin Stories* continued to find a home in this setting. Lou Reed's mojo was still working. Blondie reached number one repeatedly from 1979 to '81, particularly with the reggae crossover "The Tide is High" and the rap crossover, "Rapture." In 1979, Warhol painted Blondie lead-singer Debbie Harry's portrait in one of the perfect pop marriages of artist subject and form.

However, in the spring of 1979, a dark and horribly destructive element entered the picture. As a result of the Mafia losing control of its distribution after the French Connection bust in 1971 and the Ayatollah Khomeini kicking the CIA-backed Shah out of Iran, the Persian heroin trade the Shah had been sitting on was opened up. A tsunami of strong heroin hit downtown New York, bringing the decade to a tragic end in a chemical blizzard.

Heroin had never been sold in a white neighborhood to white middle-class people before; you would have had to go up to Harlem to purchase it. Now, heroin supermarkets proliferated on the Lower East Side. Ironically, one of the most famous was right across the street from where William Burroughs lived in his famous "Bunker" at 222 Bowery. For a while, its hottest bag was Dr. Nova, named after Burroughs' novel *Nova Express*. No group seemed immune to its influence. It permeated the rock world, the art world and the literary world with a devastating effect upon this very special time and its cast of characters.

For me, the shock troops of the '70s were heroes because of the risks they took. They carried the brunt of the revolution to the streets via their work and entertained very real danger, as the casualty reports testify. In 1979, William Burroughs, half of Blondie, Dee Dee Ramone and Jean Michel Basquiat, among many others at all levels of the counterculture, became junkies. After stabbing Nancy Spungen to death in the Chelsea Hotel, Sid Vicious, the bass player in the Sex Pistols, became the poster child of the junkies. In October 1979, he overdosed and died. This gave the media the opportunity to cut punk rock down to a stupid movement propagated by madmen and killers.

New York had always been looked upon by the rest of America as a mad, bad, dangerous place to live; here was further confirmation. In late 1978, the publisher and editor-in-chief of *High Times,* Tom Forcade, committed suicide. In 1979, the drug smuggler who starred in a movie Forcade had been producing, "Cocaine Cowboys," also killed himself. The casualty reports would increase year by year.

Another exodus now began. In February 1980, Lou Reed got married, turned his back on the scene, went into Alcoholics Anonymous and bought a house in the country. In March, Patti Smith broke up her band, got married and moved to Detroit. In October, Muhammad Ali, who had fought valiantly but at great cost throughout 1976-78, shuffled off-stage after a dismal loss to deal with what would soon become severe physical problems.

But nothing sounded the death knell of the decade as much as the murder of John Lennon outside his apartment building, the Dakota, in December 1980. It was the negation of just about everything that we could hold onto in the counterculture; it deflated an entire culture. In 1981, by which time people were dropping like flies, John Belushi, the most popular star of "Saturday Night Live," which had been a strong proponent of the '70s lifestyle, died of a heroin overdose.

In February 1981, the first novel in Burroughs' new trilogy, *Cities of the Red Night,* was published to international acclaim. Burroughs, now on the methadone program, left the Bunker in 1981 and moved to Kansas, where he would spend the rest of his life. Two months later, Allen Ginsberg, who had lived on the Lower East Side since the 1940s, also left New York, relocating in Boulder, Colorado.

Blondie had pretty much disappeared from the scene, spending all their time on the road or in the studio. In 1982, after a Debbie Harry solo album, *Koo Koo,* and a Blondie album, *The Hunter,* that were disastrous failures, the band broke up. Its songwriter and co-leader, Chris Stein, almost died of a rare skin disease.

The inauguration of Ronald Reagan as President in January 1981 confirmed the end of the permissive '70s. And that December, Andy Warhol put Nancy Reagan on the cover of his magazine. Warhol reached the nadir of his career in 1982 with his "Dollar Bill" paintings. For the first time in his career, he failed to sell a single canvas when the show opened at the Castelli Gallery in New York.

In 1983, the heterosexual community in New York woke up to the threat of AIDS. The gays circled their wagons. As a heterosexual who had spent a lot of time deep inside the gay community, I felt a definite chill. Simultaneously, when I signed a contract to write Andy Warhol's biography, I was expelled from the Factory. That year, Andy moved to a new Factory, slamming the door on those still trapped in the mindset of the old one.

The owner of the Mudd Club, Steve Mass, was arrested on tax evasion charges. In May 1983, seminal club owner Mickey Ruskin died. His packed funeral on the Lower East Side was the surest sign that the counterculture and its underground no longer existed. Now all the rooms in which the stars of the '70s scenes had worked, made love, glittered and danced were empty and silent.

The courage to move forward comes from the courage to look back. "1975-1980 was a time in which people insisted on doing what they weren't supposed to do," wrote Debbie Harry in her memoir, *Making Tracks: The Rise of Blondie.* In the magic of civil disobedience comes obedience. What do we look for in the past? Through a glass darkly, I can see the faces of the allies who befriended us, the heroes who painted, wrote, played, the hands that extended hope, asked not what we could do for ourselves but for each other. So I saw the '70s rise and fall. Great were the men and women at the wall.

Punk

"The Emergence of Punk in America"

by Jessamin Swearingen
(adapted and edited by Allan Metz)

"We Created It: Let's Take It Over"!
web site, 1999-2001

Discussion of American punk and how it differed from its British counterpart.—Ed.

In 1976, Patti Smith ended her rendition of The Who's "My Generation" with the declaration, "We created it; let's take it over!" She knew what she was talking about. Punk rock by birthright was an American creation, originated by New York City musicians during the mid-1960s, but the British version of punk was more famous. Punk was born with the Velvet Underground in New York City. Although the Velvets achieved cult status and eventually critical acclaim, British bands such as the Sex Pistols were better known. As a result, twenty-five years later, punk is falsely considered a British creation.

New York's punk rock is difficult to explain. It eludes blanket generalizations of content and philosophy and never became popular enough during its original inception to be incorporated into mass culture. New York punk's philosophy evolved out of necessity. Jon Savage captured the idea in his book, *England's Dreaming: Anarchy, Sex Pistols, and Beyond.* For his book, Savage interviewed Richard Hell of the New York band Television, and established that Hell considered rock music to be "secret teenage news" (Savage, 88). Punk was about youth; it borrowed the street and rebellion element from rock's origins, and promised individuality. The best way to describe punk is to say what it was not. In the imagination of rock music audiences, the pop charts of the late 1960s and early 1970s are saturated with rebellion and sexual revolution. In reality, the charts reflected a homogenized landscape of bland pop. Punk rock certainly did not crack the veneer of pop, but it expanded pop's boundaries.

Billboard's Top Ten of 1973 is a perfect example of punk's lack of influence on popular music. The number-one song of 1973 was "Tie A Yellow Ribbon Round The Ole Oak Tree" by Tony Orlando and Dawn. To be fair, *Billboard* is a representation of the popular music charts, rather than exclusively of rock music. However, if "Tie A Yellow Ribbon" was the number-one selling record of the year, popular music was completely alienated from rock music. Punk, on the other hand, kept the essence of rock rebellion and innocence alive. The mid-1970s, at least in the *Billboard* charts, have some parallels to the mid-1950s. Rock's first chart success happened in the mid-1950s, in the midst of Tin Pan Alley. Arnold Shaw's book, *The Rockin' Fifties: The Decade That Transformed the Pop Music Scene*, cites Tin Pan Alley as an era of lush ballads designed to soothe a nation immediately after World War II (Shaw, xv). The rock music that emerged in the 1950s was not calm balladry. Punk rock follows this pattern in that the mid-1970s, as reflected by the *Billboard* charts, was about maintaining calm. Punk, like the original rock in the 1950s, disrupted this order. Compare Barbra Streisand's melodramatic number-one record of 1974, the soundtrack for the film, "The Way We Were," to the New York Dolls' "Personality Crisis" from 1973; Streisand's "misty water-colored memories" to the Doll's "prima ballerina on a spring afternoon." Where Streisand tried to remain cool and reserved, the Dolls were pointed and deliberate. Punk revitalized rock music.

The difference between New York City punk and British punk was in its range of perspective and influence. Jon Savage described New York punk bands during the early 1970s as a mixture of styles incorporating the teen bubble gum pop of the girl groups with the harder aggression of the Rolling Stones (Savage, 60). Savage's description of New York punk begins to define its sound and attitude. New York punk was aggressive 1970s rock music that recreated the power of rock's roots in the 1950s but did not lose the power of introspection or a sense of humor. A large division emerged between the alternate forms of punk rock image and the music. Some New York bands like the Ramones acted the part of violent, drug-addicted street thugs; others such as the New York Dolls' leader David Johansen, fashioned themselves after French Symbolist poets like Rimbaud, and

31

wrote songs about urban decay (Savage, 58). Some punks, such as Television, played the part of the introspective artists; others like the Velvet Underground exhibited strains of a self-destructive and hedonistic nature toward the band's end. In a press release from Mercury, the Dolls' record company, Johansen said:

> "Rimbaud would write about the monstrous city and the effects it would have on the species. And here it is 1973 and everything is very fast moving and I try to understand how people feel about it, how they relate to the environment. That's what my songs are about" (Savage, 58).

Punk music followed this path as well. Some bands played at assaultively high voltage and volume. The Ramones exploited the three-chord simplicity of 1950s rock music but took it one step beyond with ear-splitting volume and street-hoodlum apparel. Their songs averaged two minutes in duration and sounded like a subway train roaring out of the station. While Television's Tom Verlaine, who named himself after nineteenth century French Symbolist poet Paul Verlaine (Lazell, 503), favored drawn-out guitar solos and cryptic poetic lyrics; others, such as Blondie, focused on tight pop formations, avoiding the abrasive theatrics. All of these styles meshed together to become "punk" rock—a startling rebirth of old form rock'n'roll music with the new. The seeds of the punk rock sound were planted in the 1950s with the early strains of American rock'n'roll. A direct imitation of the rebellious "race" music of the mid-1950s, rock enticed young listeners and offered alternatives to the drab music on the radio. In doing so, rock revitalized American music and established a pattern for rebellion. White rock stars such as Elvis Presley captured the intensity of this early music and packaged it for other white listeners. The process of copying and reforming, long a tradition in rock format, was the essence of punk rock. In a sense, New York City punk was a game of finding the influence.

New York City punk rock, unlike its British imitation, did not claim to be the end of established rock music. While British punk claimed to be completely new and without previous influence, the New Yorkers paid close attention to their influences. British punk bands such as the Sex Pistols and their manager, Malcolm McLaren, promised that their punk rock was the be-all-end-all of rock. The British borrowed from the influences across the water and exaggerated them until the fashion and sound fit the anger and hopelessness of their own socio-political environment. For this reason, New York City punk was inherently different from British punk. But the most obvious of the differences stemmed from their respective economies.

British punks were mostly unemployed and facing a lagging economy. Their anger was exemplified by songs such as the Sex Pistols' "No Future" and the Clash's "London's Burning." The bitterness expressed in British songs was blatant. The New Yorkers expressed anger and frustration as well, but their themes were more concerned with the arts and literature. While the Sex Pistols named themselves Johnny Rotten and Sid Vicious, Tom Verlaine paid homage to his literary influences. The British were more apocalyptic, attempting to be ahistorical with such declarations as the Sex Pistols' "No Future." New York punks researched history and borrowed from the fertile building ground American rock'n'roll had left behind. On her first album in 1975, Patti Smith recorded a version of Van Morrison's late 1960s hit, "Gloria," thus perpetuating rock's legacy into punk. Unlike its New York influence, British punk not only claimed that there was no future, but in the words of British rock critics Julie Burchill and Tony Parsons, in the title of their book on the subject, punk was the "obituary of rock'n'roll." *The Boy Looked At Johnny": The Obituary of Rock'n'Roll*, though overly British in focus, took its title from a Patti Smith song. Even in criticism, punk was an American creation.

Before British punks even breathed the words "no future," punk rock was carving out its history in Manhattan. Enter the players of the New York City scene in the mid-1960s. They were not interested in writing rock'n'roll's obituary; they were in love with rock music and paid homage to their influences while creating new sounds. Their sounds were varied, but the themes about teenagers and rock'n'roll and the streets were generally the same. By the early 1970s, the rock'n'roll world was populated by distant pop stars in limousines. Rock radio was reflective of such established bands as the Rolling Stones, who in their success had lost the street element and awareness that had once made them vital. Their image, which had once been youthful and demanding, like 1965's "Satisfaction," had been transformed into the chic jet-setting disco of 1978's "Miss You." In contrast, New York City punkers were a part of the street element. Punk music in both countries was about relevance. The simplicity of the Ramones' "Beat On The Brat" made light of the Ramones' street-thug image by poking fun at violence. And Blondie's "Love At The Pier" described hanging out and teen romance and spoke directly of rock's sensibilities.

Punk, particularly in the United States, brought rock music back to its roots. To understand New York City punk and its significance, it is important to note the influences on the musicians who participated in the original punk movement. The punk movement's cultural influences spanned generations, from the American literary expatriates who left the country for Paris during the 1930s to bands formed during the late 1960s in New York City and Detroit. The original punks considered themselves as lost as the 1930s' "lost generation," but they found an emerging voice in their own generation. New York punk was rock music, which became a highly stylized adaptation of literature for the post-World War I "lost" American expatriates and the beatniks of the late-1940s and mid-1950s (Savage, 90). The music unified an entire group of people, giving them an identifying code.

What was to become New York punk evolved from various backgrounds. New York's seminal punk band, the Velvet Underground, was made up of three classically trained musicians who created the most assaulting and unique rock music to date. Bands on the opposite end of the musical spectrum were equally influential. The Shangri-Las and their girl group peers combined teen-angst theatrics with tight harmonies and a smart pop sense. The group's "Leader of the Pack," released in 1964, capitalized on a generation of parental scare tactics. The song told the tale of teen romance without parental consent, starting in the candy store and ending in a fatal motorcycle accident. Although completely different visual- and audio-wise from the Velvet Underground, the girl group style had its own unique place in punk style.

The rumblings of this new American music were heard in different areas of the country as well. The Detroit sound, although often thought of exclusively as Motown's combined perfection of pop and soul, began to show more underground leanings. Among the Detroit punk groups to stake their claim to individual rock music were the Stooges, led by the 1960's version of the lovable idiot, Iggy Stooge (later Iggy Pop), and a garage band turned social activist choir named MC5.

The Stooges created rock music sprinkled with the inner dialogue of a juvenile delinquent's diary. A song on their first album, entitled "I Wanna Be Your Dog," created a sound and an aesthetic that was to be emulated for years to come. By 1969, the release of the Velvet Underground's third album and the Stooges' and MC5's first albums had a direct influence on a new generation of music fans and potential performers. The seeds of punk rock had been planted on American soil. For the next ten years, new music emerged from urban America that would create punk rock.

On "Rapture," Hip Hop, and Punk

"If white listeners heard any rap at all..., it was via Blondie's tribute to the form..."

"An exhilarating fusion of rawk guitar, new wave keyboards, hip hopping bass, and charmingly droll rap shout-outs to Flash, Fab 5 Freddy, and punk rock, 'Rapture' influenced countless pop recordings (Cake's '96 hit 'Going the Distance,' for one)."

"...one of the first white bands to turn rap music into a hit was new wavers Blondie, whose 1980 'Rapture'...turned a Sugarhill Gang refrain into 'Don't stop, do punk rock.'"

Source of quotes: Alan Light, ed. *The Vibe History of Hip Hop* (New York: Three Rivers Press, 1999), pp. 27, 48, and 244, respectively.

"I Belong to the _____ Generation"

by Jessamin Swearingen
(adapted and edited by Allan Metz)

"We Created It: Let's Take It Over"!
web site, 1999-2001

The Beat Generation as a precursor to punk rock.—Ed.

The Beat Generation, which emerged in the late-1940s, followed in the tradition of Western culture's youth-obsessed artistic and literary idealists. Beatniks claimed to be outside the ranks of cultural norms, but they were actually products of a middle class heritage that in turn influenced their work. In late nineteenth century France, a group of young artists and writers known as bohemians disavowed the restrictions and norms of their cultural heritage. The Beats copied these French bohemians and their romantic ideals of artistic productivity.

The Beats saw themselves as a modern version of the "lost" generation of post-World War I and as outcasts in a society recovering from a war in which they were too young to fight. The "lost" generation established a new pattern of migration—instead of flocking to Paris as expatriates, the Beats fled to such urban environments as New York City and San Francisco.

The Beats also influenced later generations of youth subcultures. The early punk movement during the mid-1970s emulated beat poetry and lifestyle to forge a new genre of rock'n'roll music. These musicians borrowed heavily from both the beats and the French romantic poets to emerge as distinct from the rock musicians of the time.

The self-styled French bohemians of the late 1800s idealized youth as freedom and believed they could live their lives to the fullest by attempting to separate from the confines of the French middle class. Jerrold Siegel, author of *Bohemian Paris*, acknowledges the true essence of the bohemian lifestyle. "Bohemia was not a realm outside bourgeois life but the expression of a conflict that arose at its very heart" (p. 10).

The term "bohemian" stems from a region in Czechoslovakia—Bohemia where the Gypsies lived. The French bohemians found themselves mirroring Gypsy life. Siegel comments, "The bohemians located themselves in a twilight zone between ingenuity and criminality" (p. 4). This was only one way in which their lifestyle did not fit into the cultural mainstream. The Bohemians received a fair amount of criticism from the established middle class. Because most participants in the Bohemian culture during the late 1800s were artists and writers, the conflict surrounding their lifestyle arose out of the need of artistic output versus the need for societal support. Siegel argues that the conflict of French Bohemian identity emerged out of this conflict. He asked, "At what point did personal cultivation cease to be beneficial or acceptable to the society that sponsored it?" (p. 11). This aspect of Bohemian culture and practice is repeated throughout history.

Like members of other movements who saw themselves as outside the cultural norm, the beats thought they were boldly new and different. Like the "lost" generation of writers and artists who fled the United States for Paris in the early twentieth century, the Beats wanted to remove themselves from their decidedly American backgrounds, but unlike the "lost" generation of the past, the beats did not need to leave the States to feel exiled.

John Clellon Holmes' novel *Go!* is a narrative of the author's experience as a beat during the late 1940s. The novel is crammed with factual stories of the prime thinkers and their life stories. At one point in *Go!*, the characters are celebrating a July fourth weekend in New York City that illustrates this feeling of expatriation: "Everyone's enthusiasm rose continually during the two days, as if all cherished in the heart's privacy some extraordinary memory of the holiday, long since considered infantile but still capable of evoking for each the hot, lost forenoons in all their American home towns" (p. 131). This passage suggests the author and characters' attempts to misplace their suburban American heritage and create a new identity in New York City. The Beats, much like the "lost" generation, found solace in urban environments far from home.

The members of the self-proclaimed "lost" generation were in exile from the aftermath of World War I. Those who thought themselves to be "lost" were expatriates of a postwar culture that was obsessed with rebuilding its American identity. Many artists fled to Paris, breaking ties with American tradition and adopting new identities as free spirits within their literary or artistic circles.

Fifty years later, similar notions of alienation were brewing within the literary and musical circles of New York City. Much like the beats and the preceding generations who influenced them, the early punk rock songwriters and musicians thought themselves to be forging new artistic territory within the confines of established society. The musicians who formed the nucleus of the New York City punk scene were mostly transplanted suburbanites hoping to start a new life in the city. Punk rock itself emerged much like the literary work of the early Beats—it was different from the mainstream, but definitely middle class in origin.

Those involved in what would later be called punk rock were members of an elitist grouping of musicians and poets who were acting out youthful impulses under the guise of artistic rebellion. Musically, the early punks were creating a distinct division between what was heard on the radio and what they were writing and performing in New York City. The early punk aesthetics combined simplistic, often abrasive music and daring, sometimes offensive fashion, with nihilistic and uncompromising lyrics. While established pop music during the early and mid-1970s was often soothing and musically intricate in performance and production, punk rock stood apart. The early strains of New York City punk music received no airplay and never reached the charts. The punks saw themselves as heirs to the Bohemian throne.

Songwriter/poet Richard Hell changed his name from Richard Meyers and left his hometown in the early 1970s. He migrated to New York City and a few years later wrote the song "Blank Generation," a punk rock equivalent to a generation calling itself lost. Jonathan Savage, author of *England's Dreaming*, an account of British punk, cites Hell's efforts: "Early in 1975, Hell wrote a protean song of escape. The idea was borrowed from an early sixties beat cash-in, Rod McKuen's Beat Generation, but Hell was ambitious, attempting to turn fake culture—suspect?—into real culture" (p. 90).

Savage notes the same dilemma that Siegel acknowledges in his portrayal of the bohemians in *Bohemian Paris*. The artist claims to be outside of society but in turn needs support (and has a background) in the culture he tries to deny. Richard Hell saw the fissure and chose to exploit it. Punk, like any other cultural grouping thinking itself to be outside society, had market value and Hell hoped to profit from it. Hell wasn't economically successful, but he achieved cult status equivalent to that of the Beats and the expatriates of the "lost" generation.

The original beats relived aspects of the French bohemians and the post-World War I lost generation experiences. They moved away from their suburban hometowns to cities and with that migration forced themselves to reevaluate what it meant to be an American citizen and artist. The Beats' cultural and literary output forced the American mainstream to acknowledge their presence and, in turn, support their efforts.

The beatnik movement had an enormous influence on the creative output of the United States after World War II. The boundaries of art and expression with which the beats concerned themselves were tested again ten years later with the hippies and again ten years after that with punk rock. Jerrold Siegel summed it up best when he noted: "Artistic, youthful, unattached, inventive or suspect, Bohemian styles are reoccurring features of modern life" (p. 5).

"The New York City Punk Scene"

by Jessamin Swearingen

(adapted and edited by Allan Metz)

"We Created It: Let's Take It Over"!
web site, 1999-2001

The New York City punk scene in the 1970s and its music venues similar to Max's Kansas City and the famed CBGBs.—Ed.

"From this apartment which Gloria has gotten for the summer, only a few doors over from Park Avenue South on 22nd street, it's become a nightly routine to walk down to Max's [Kansas City] to meet Gloria, hear the Velvet Underground (who are playing upstairs twice a night, six nights a week), or just hang out in the back room. On my way there tonight I realized just how clever this unknown conceptual artist is— the one who designed the laser beam that runs seven blocks in every odd direction, winding up finally, on the wall in the back room of Max's itself" (Carroll, 41).

In order to grow and establish themselves within the music industry, bands must play live shows. Playing live is not only invaluable practice, but it is also a way to form a kinship with the audience and community. By playing live shows, the Velvet Underground influenced the next generation of New York punks. Through their live shows, the New York Dolls confirmed the potential of glam, short for glamor, or glitter rock and proved to be the scenemakers of the lower Manhattan grouping of glitter bands.

For the generation of rock acts that reigned during the early- to mid-1970s, the New York club scene provided necessary live experience. New York City rock critic, Richard Nusser, wrote for the *Village Voice* during the early punk movement and noted that the New York scene's new crop of bands was the last to be directly affected by the 1960s, meaning that these kids watched rock music become an economic product and were directly affected by the possibilities of punk's newness and potential. Whereas rock was becoming another adult-oriented product, as the *Billboard* charts of the early 1970s reflect, punk meant youth and youth culture. Barbra Streisand's 1974 "The Way We Were" was the movie theme song for an adult love story. Patti Smith's "Piss Factory" single of the same year was completely youth-oriented. It narrated Smith's adolescent dreams of getting out of her small hometown and how she wanted to "be so big, I'm gonna be a big star," how she would "go on that train/ I'm going to New York City/ I'm gonna be somebody." Critic Dave Marsh rated "Piss Factory" number 718 in his book, *The Heart of Rock & Soul: The 1001 Greatest Singles Ever Made*. Marsh put his finger right on what made Smith and her contemporaries so exciting and so different from accepted popular music. He wrote: "Smith unites herself perfectly with the material, a blast of rage and revenge, a shaggy dog story posing as a dirty joke that winds up as an anthem to show biz ambition..." (Marsh, 462).

Punk, being a post-1960s commodity, was about the rebirth and cleansing of rock to regain its freshness and youth. If 1960s rock was music's most influential product, then by the 1970s, the product was getting old. When the 1960s' most successful acts could no longer speak to the next generation, punk filled this gap. Punk was also a part of a link in the long chain of New York City's influence on America's mainstream music, ultimately overshadowed by more accessible versions of the same or similar music. Like early folk, punk rock started in the city, later becoming more popular in a different location. In folk's case, it was a migration from New York's Greenwich Village to the west coast or upstate New York near a town called Woodstock, whereas punk started in New York City and moved to the streets of Britain.

New York, because of its immensely dense and diverse population, is a difficult environment in which to maintain a strong musical following. In New York City, the audience is so large and diverse that it is difficult to promote a band. Because of this, many bands slipped back into the woodwork. In the case of most New York punk bands, their output and image was so brutally urban that marketing them to middle America seemed almost blasphemous. The Velvet Underground and the Dolls fell into New York's black hole of obscurity in the early 1970s. Neither band was heard on the radio nor marketed nationally. The Velvet Underground broke up in 1970 and although they were influential among other musicians, the band never achieved the national or chart success such as their contemporaries, the Jefferson Airplane. New York bands were isolated from the rest of the country in that promoters thought New York City to be either too weird or risque for the rest of America. Many New York bands achieved more fame in London than in the States. In her book *Break All Rules! Punk Rock And The Making of a Style*, Tricia Henry explores, via Lou Reed and his Velvets, how the rest of America ignored New York's music but England paid close attention. In London, David Bowie primed the cultural and musical market for Reed's imagery and subject matter with more success than Reed and his fellow American musicians.

The New York City clubs that booked punk bands from the late 1960s to mid-1970s were indispensable to punk rock's future. More than rock's previous turnouts, punk literally grew up on stage. The bands thrived off their audiences. Jon Savage notes that the New York Dolls' leader David Johansen claimed his band was merely a reflection of its audience. New York City punk was a musical "show and tell," and the bands needed to do so on stage. The Dolls did not survive into the mid-1970s to play at a small emerging club in New York City's Bowery called CBGBs. However the Doll's progeny, such as Television and Blondie, put the small club on the market by 1974. According to Roman Kozak's account of CBGBs in its early years, *This Ain't No Disco: The Story of CBGB*, it was the best place for underground bands to play if they were starting out (Kozak, 17).

Eventually CBGBs became the club most pivotal to the early New York punk scene. Preceded by Max's Kansas City and the Mercer Arts Center, CBGBs was the next generation of punk performers' home away from home. It was, during its heyday, the main club that catered to "underground" rock. Max's Kansas City and the Mercer Arts Center were influential, but not as abundantly stocked with different bands. Whereas Max's Kansas City and the Mercer Arts Center were fueled by their seedy clientele and glam rock dress code, CBGBs broke away from the glam and became, for lack of a better term, punk.

Max's Kansas City was the frontrunner for New York City's concert-hall-meets-social-hangout association. The club established itself as the New York underbelly's meeting ground in the late 1960s. Owner Mickey Ruskin started a cabaret in his unused upstairs dining room, and it soon became a lounge for those who hung out in the club. After that, bands like the Velvet Underground established a residency in the club. The Velvets recorded an LP there, *Live At Max's Kansas City*, which was produced during their six-month stint at the club.

In the early 1970s everything in the New York scene seemed to center around Max's. These emerging rock clubs established the cornerstones and influences for what would become punk. The Velvet Underground and Warhol's crowd frequented the club. Blondie's Deborah Harry waited tables there during the early 1970s. The New York Dolls became heirs to the Velvet's throne and played at Max's regularly. It was the place to be and be seen, and every band wanted a piece of the action.

Other clubs that featured alternative rock acts were obscure and equally seedy, but the most notable was the Mercer Arts Center. The Mercer Arts Center was a tangle of boutiques and performance spaces located a few blocks east of the outskirts of Greenwich Village. Located within the wreckage of old New York's most prominent downtown hotel, the Broadway Central, it had a series of back rooms and one large ballroom, where the bands played. The Kitchen, which later moved locations to become its own club, was located in the hotel's actual kitchen. The Oscar Wilde Room was the most frequented section of the club (Kozak, 8).

By 1972 the New York Dolls secured a Tuesday night gig in the Oscar Wilde Room, and the scene started to expand. In a *Rolling Stone* article from October 1972, author Ed McCormack quoted Dolls' guitarist Johnny Thunders: "'They didn't even want us at the Mercer Arts Center until they counted the bar receipts'" (McCormack). If the New York Dolls were a reflection of their audience, which was composed of burned-out New York socialites (i.e., the Warhol crowd), then the Mercer Arts Center was a reflection of New York's music scene. In Roman Kozak's insightful account of the CBGBs era, *This Ain't No Disco*, Elda Gentile, an original member of the Stilletoes, a precursor to Blondie, recounts how the Mercer Arts Center fell apart, literally. A band called the Magic Tramps, which featured Blondie's Chris Stein on guitar, was practicing when the walls fell down. Gentile says that the band left practice and their equipment and ran. "They could see across Broadway. They ran for their lives" (Kozak, 9).

With the Mercer Arts Center in rubble and every up-and-coming band in New York City vying to play Max's Kansas City, CBGBs was a necessary addition to the scenery. Originally a country bar, CBGBs and its owner Hilly Kristal changed the course of punk rock. On the top of the Bowery, a slummy equivalent to Times Square, CBGBs was originally a bar that catered to the upstairs hotel's crusty customers. The Palace Hotel was a flophouse for the neighborhood's many indigents. CBGBs, named for Kristal's musical loves—country, blues, and bluegrass—was a derelict country honky-tonk bar. Kristal was forced out of the West Village for conflicting with noise regulations, and by 1974 moved his bar to the Bowery in hopes of bringing a breakfast-oriented club to life with country music (Kozak, 1-2).

Early in 1974, Tom Verlaine and Richard Hell of Television found CBGBs owner Hilly Kristal on top of a stepladder in front of his club. Verlaine learned that Kristal was looking for bands and convinced him that Television would play country music. Obviously Verlaine and company did not play country, but they were the first punk rock band to play the club (Kozak, 13). Television's manager, Terry Ork, was a patron of the arts to New York's influential downtown scene. He did freelance work for Andy Warhol and had a loft where Television practiced six nights a week. The band's first single, "Little Johnny Jewel," was on his Ork label, and he also managed the Ramones and Stilletoes. Ork was influential regarding who would play at CBGBs, and he helped form the nucleus of what would become the mid-1970s punk scene.

What set CBGBs apart from other New York clubs was its sound system. Unlike other downtown clubs whose live acts were more in the style of a makeshift hootenanny than a planned-out concert, CBGBs evolved into something quite different. For one, the bands helped decide who played, and before record companies began to show interest there was a sense of community among the bands. New York punk bands all knew each other and borrowed the others' equipment. The blanket label of "punk rock" came out of the band's community and possibly from the magazine called *Punk* which published its first issue in January 1975. On the issue's cover was a illustration of Lou Reed drawn with electronic pieces coming from his head. Much like the New York Dolls' 1973 ode to New York glam rock, "Frankenstein," the magazine named the next generation of rock fans.

The punk label became a stance of doing it yourself. Nearly twenty years later, Rhino Records released a weakly executed compilation of American punk entitled, *D.I.Y.* as in, Do It Yourself. The bands who played CBGBs chose their opening acts and, because of this, friends played with friends. And like any social grouping where people begin to mirror each other socially, eventually the mid-1970s downtown Manhattan bands were called punk. New York punk eluded the obvious visual representation of Britain's punk youth—the dyed hair and self-mutilation were absent. New York punk lacked England's fashion entrepreneur, Malcolm McLaren, and even people in Manhattan failed to notice the city's private musical explosion. But it was the club, CBGBs, in the mid-1970s that gave New York's small group of bands a chance to try out their style. The club had an impressive sound system. Kristal acted out the role of proud scout leader, and the bands were his troops. As CBGBs put New York City punk on the map by giving the mid-1970s punk bands and fans a place to play, Kristal invested in a proper, live sound system to accommodate the growing talent of his acts.

Until late 1974 when Arista records signed Patti Smith for a recording contract, CBGBs was a hospitable community of bands and their friends. However, as soon as record companies began to show interest, the community feeling was lost. Bands being assessed for recording potential became jealous and no longer willing to help others out with equipment or shows. Ironically, the club that weaned punk rock initiated the mainstream interest that helped kill it.

In April 2002, *Q* magazine's "Punk Special" publication features a Foreword by Deborah Harry and contains other items on Blondie, including reviews of *Blondie, Plastic Letters,* and *Parallel Lines*.

"Lou Reed and the Velvet Underground"

by Jessamin Swearingen
(adapted and edited by Allan Metz)

"We Created It: Let's Take It Over!"
web site, 1999-2001

The influence of Lou Reed and the Velvet Underground on punk rock.—Ed.

Lou Reed's influence on punk rock in New York and Britain was unequaled. So important was Reed's worth that in Roman Kozak's documentary of the club, CBGBs, *This Ain't No Disco*, the author asks if, "had there been no Velvet Underground a couple years earlier, would there have been a CBGB?" (Kozak, xiv). With his band the Velvet Underground, Reed gained the status of punk's forefather. Although Reed left the Velvet Underground by 1970, Reed's songwriting and collaboration with the Velvets left its mark on the New York live music scene.

The Velvets began performing in New York City in 1966 and became the earliest example of the nihilism punk would later act out. The Velvets far surpassed the artistic pout of Dylan and the Stones and clarified the political ravings of the 1960s protest genre. According to Fred Bronson's book, *Billboard's Hottest Hot 100 Hits*, popular music in the late 1960s was fattened with songs like "I'm A Believer" by the Monkees in 1966 and Lulu's theme to the 1967 movie "To Sir With Love." As in the later years of punk, the music in New York City was in no way reflected on the pop charts. In New York, Lou Reed's songwriting portrayed the horrors of alienation and drugs in the Big City. The 1967 release of the Velvet Underground's first album, *The Velvet Underground & Nico*, contained songs like "Heroin," which changed rock music forever. The song was an ode to a killer narcotic, and it basked in a subtle moral decay that had never before been heard in a rock song. Other Reed songs had undercurrents of sadomasochism, for example, the first album's "Venus in Furs," a song that hinted at the aggressive fashion to come in British punk fashion scene. Reed's lyrics made references to leather boots and whiplashes. Years later, British punk would offer its equivalent. Malcolm McLaren's clothing shops sold "strict fetish clothing in rubber, leather, and vinyl" (Savage, 68), which seemed the obvious evolution from Reed's lyrics.

Lou Reed wrote graphic songs about drug abuse and sexuality that disturbed rock critics but inspired fans. His depiction of drag queen Candy Darling in "Candy Says," although beautiful and insightful, deviated completely from the blanket Puritanism enforced by most white pop. In his book, *The Rockin' Fifties: The Decade That Transformed the Pop Music Scene*, Arnold Shaw describes the groundwork for white pop music. With roots in Tin Pan Alley, white pop evolved out of the post-World War II timeframe and was meant to soothe (Shaw, xv). Tin Pan Alley specifically "...lived on three other types: ballads, i.e., romantic songs; rhythm tunes, considered lightweight, like "I'm Looking Over A Four-Leaf Clover" or "Cruising Down the River," and novelty songs like "I Taut I Taw a Puddy Cat" or "Papa Loves Mambo"—these were either overnight smashes or bombs" (Shaw, 14). Tin Pan Alley's effect on white pop was noticeable. Shaw also noted that: "Direct references to physical contact or sex were taboo. But lyric writers had a drawerful of Victorian euphemisms that conveyed the idea" (Shaw, 15). This pattern continued into the next decades of pop. Pop music shunned mentioning practices that deviated from the norm, and the 1960s did little to bring pop music out of its Victorian age. The bubble gum shyness of 1969's Tommy James & the Shondells' hit "Crimson and Clover" was much more typical than 1969's sexually suggestive Rolling Stones' hit "Honky Tonk Women." James' song sweetly declared that while he hardly knew a girl, he thought he loved her. Songs like this were much more plentiful than the Stones' sexual frankness in "Honky Tonk Women." This frankness was a rarity, but the Stones were popular enough to get away with it. "Honky Tonk Women" was one of 1969's most successful songs, but most pop songs failed to crack the veneer of sexual innocence that record producers and radio broadcasters tried to maintain. Reed's subject matter broke open the myth of the pop chart's sterile sexuality, enabling future pop stars to wear clothes or sing songs that were outside of the cultural norm. His daring lyrics influenced English pop star David Bowie's glam (glamour) rock pose and set the stage for New York's glam/punk band the New York Dolls. Although marginal in cultural acceptance and isolated within New York punk, glam rock's outrageous costumes and sexual suggestiveness provided the perfect foil for the punk aesthetic. Glam's theatrics, in turn, made punk look harder and more dangerous.

Throughout his career, Reed wrote and performed songs of questionable subject matter and often musically brutal content. This made its impression on the generation coming of age during the late 1960s. Reed and the Velvet's effect on 1970s punk bands was obvious. The Velvets were the house band at Max's Kansas City for a month during 1970, their last year together. Max's was a club in lower Manhattan that reflected its audience with such room names as the "Oscar Wilde Room." The Velvet's reign as house band at Max's laid the floor plan for the New York Dolls' explosion onto the Manhattan scene. But in order to understand the New York Dolls and the significance of glam rock, one must trace glam's roots back to Reed's songs.

On the Velvet's third album, the self-titled *The Velvet Underground*, released in 1969, Reed wrote the monumental ballad, "Candy Says"—a narration of Candy Darling, a drag queen in the Warhol scene. Reed's adoption of Darling's drag queen perception, and unflinching portrayal of Darling's sexual identity were completely different from the ultra-manly heterosexual rock'n'roll culture of the era. Reed anticipated the early 1970's trend of sexual openness and promiscuity, predating Marc Bolan, the flamboyant centerpiece for the English rockers, T. Rex. Reed also set the stage for Detroit's most self-indulgent and violent act, the Stooges. Iggy Stooge toyed with Reed's aggressive vocal sneer, and was cutting himself up onstage five years before Sid Vicious sliced the name "Nancy" into his chest. In turn, Reed's indirect influence on the likes of Bolan and Stooge was adopted by a brilliant performer named David Bowie.

With a prepackaged rock star that would make the Monkees look like the cartoon characters they were, David Bowie turned glam rock into a household name—"Ziggy Stardust." Bowie's creation of the Ziggy Stardust character was a brilliant career move that manipulated an image to its maximum (Henry, 33), a tactic only to be achieved again by the likes of the Sex Pistols and later Madonna. Ziggy was the quintessential glam rocker. While the Dolls, T. Rex, and even Iggy Stooge fell flat, Ziggy soared. He was the bisexual martian who had fled a world doomed with only "Five Years" to survive. The mammoth album told a story of young Ziggy (note Iggy tribute), who through a series of Reed-inspired character sketches tries to find "Soul Love" and "falls asleep at night" dreaming of being a "Rock'n'Roll star." Adding to the twisted maze of allusions and homage, Bowie produced Reed's second solo album, which contained the single "Walk on the Wild Side" (Henry, 37). Reed's commercially successful single became the calling card of his generation. "Wild Side" was like a Warhol film chock-full of cameos from larger-than-life characters, an impressive name-dropping of the who's who of the late 1960s/early 1970s New York City scene. Poet Jim Carroll kept a diary of that period. In his second book of published diary excerpts, *Forced Entries: The Downtown Diaries 1971-1973*, Carroll notes that during the Velvet's Max's Kansas City month-long residency, the band played twice a night, six nights a week. Often within his diary entries, Carroll describes his habitual journey to Max's to see the band play. He describes it as if it were Andy Warhol's fun house: many of Warhol's associates are mentioned as part of Max's scenery. Reed and his band provided New York's downtown scene with musical entertainment and a cultural meeting ground that would influence the coming generation.

According to Ed McCormack's article, "New York City's Ultra-Living Dolls," in *Rolling Stone* (#119, 10/26/72, p. 14), the Dolls were the talk of the town by 1972. In the same issue, Reed's effect on the New York scene was described in an article about his upcoming album, *Transformer*. The biggest hit of Reed's career, "Walk on The Wild Side," was on this album. The song anticipated the Dolls' glam rock pose, and set the mold for the era's sexual personae. Tricia Henry noted that: "By placing the lyrics of 'Walk on the Wild Side' within a popular musical structure, Reed laid the groundwork for tolerance of gender blurring and other previously unacceptable subject matter by mainstream audiences" (Henry, 34).

In Mick Rock's article, "Velvet Memories: Lou Reed Sees the Future, Darkly," the author catches Reed discussing his legacy on the New York City scene. Rock notes: "And there's a band now causing a few ripples called the Dolls. 'Something might happen with them, y'know. I seem to inspire transvestite bands'." (*RS* #119, 10/26/72, p. 12)

Reed's single, "Walk On The Wild Side," was bathed in references to Reed's observations of the Warhol era—a scene filled with two-bit performers with stardom in their eyes and a willingness to exploit themselves for the sake of stardom. Reed made note of these characters, occasionally referring to them in earlier Velvet Underground works. But in "Walk On the Wild Side," the effect was more obvious. Each verse contained an image that completely deviated from accepted sexual norms, including the transvestite "Holly."

Although Reed's decendents, the New York Dolls, were practicing heterosexuals, their obsession with clothes and sometimes with female attire could not have been permissible without the go-ahead from a scene already accustomed to sexual ambivalence in their music. For the Dolls, their love of dressing up evolved into a game of rock'n'roll charades. For most of the rock community, glam rock, though making the notion of homo- or bisexuality less taboo, just meant that straight guys could get off on dressing up in girls' clothes—and so did the girls (Savage, 60). While the idea does not seem so groundbreaking today, the climate of sexual permissiveness within the pop industry, as Arnold Shaw described it, was quite unnerved by the Dolls. Their image and drag were not popular within the industry, and they were shunned (Savage 61). If not for the Velvet Underground and Lou Reed's daring subject matter, the glam era would have had no impact.

Reed's influence on the punk scene went beyond sexual politics. Reed's punk progeny took cues from his poetic credentials as well. While in college at Syracuse University in the mid-1960s, Reed studied with mentor Delmore Schwartz, an alcoholic poet who threatened to haunt Reed if he sold out. Reed dedicated the song "European Son" to Schwartz on the first Velvet Underground album. The importance of poetics within rock music was restricted to the likes of sophomoric love poems in the teen pop genre and the protest arena of Bob Dylan's music. Dylan, though a lyricist of poetic merit, conveyed his chilling cynicism in a more global direction. Interested in politics and wars, he obsessed over forcing his alienation onto his listeners. Whereas Dylan refused to acknowledge the origin of a song's subject matter directly, Reed flaunted his. Reed's cynicism was devastating. He wrote locally, named the parties concerned, and talked about his paths taken on the city streets. His narratives of the day-to-day occurrences of Union Square in the first album's "Run Run Run," and his list of so-and-so says songs—"Candy Says," "Stephanie Says," and "Lisa Says"—were based on personal experience. Where Dylan alludes to a conversation in his songs, Reed would relay the words spoken verbatim.

Reed's poetic viciousness affected punk rock to come and resurfaced in his desire to return to poetry in rock lyrics during the New York punk movement. Reed's influence combined French Symbolist poetry and song lyrics and titles modeled after the beat writers. Those involved with the punk scene made it seem as if the connection were obvious. New York Doll David Johansen likened his songwriting to that of Rimbaud (Savage, 58), and the June/July 1976 issue of *Trouser Press* stated that Patti Smith played her first gigs with guitarist Lenny Kaye as "Rock'n'Roll Rimbaud readings" (Rose, 28). One-time Television band member, Richard Hell, borrowed Beat poet Rod McKuen's "Beat Generation," to write the punk staple, "Blank Generation" in 1977 (Savage, 90). Patti Smith achieved the same accusatory viciousness of Reed's lyrical honesty in 1978's "Rock'n'Roll Nigger" on her album *Easter*.

The next generation's musical output was inspired by Reed's attempt to describe his literary ambitions through rock music. Reed, like many others of his generation, felt compelled to write the all-American novel. In a 1987 interview with *Rolling Stone*, Reed says he saw the possibilities of capturing everything a novel would, but in the shape of rock songs (RS #512, 12/10/87, p. 292). Even more than the literary tone of Reed's subject matter, the Velvet Underground as a band set the musical tone for punk rock to come. The abrasive guitars and unrelenting rhythms, along with the distorted wail of John Cale's electric viola in the early Velvet's material, set the standard for a sound that would flirt with punk aggression. The Ramones used Velvet Underground-inspired rhythms in almost all of their songs, a driving 4/4 beat propelling itself like a locomotive. The band Television used the Velvet's two-guitar dynamics to fill pockets of sound answering itself melodically and brilliantly. The Velvet Underground added guitar distortion and feedback to rock's vocabulary. Drummer Maureen Tucker's unusually spastic drumming added an impulsive chaotic rush to the music, and her style was so different that it is impossible to imitate.

In fashion as well, the Velvets created the image before there were words to describe it. The early Velvet Underground promotional pictures set the standard for the nihilistic antisocial atmosphere that later flavored most punk wardrobes. The Velvets dressed in black, an obvious departure from the flowery garb of the hippie era. Reed and company wore wraparound sunglasses, creating an obstacle between performer and audience. While stardom created this obstacle for most 1960s performers—the limousines and arena concerts of the Beatles and Rolling Stones being a perfect example—the Velvets were merely acting out their separation from the mainstream. Later punk exemplified even more dramatically this self-imposed alienation through fashion.

Richard Hell is said to have created the punk look. Hell looked perpetually fresh out of bed-tousled cropped hair, torn t-shirt, and straight-off-the-street jeans and sneakers (Kozak, 15). This simplistic or unkempt look was in contrast to the calculated (or at least more obviously thought out) wardrobe of the established arena rock stars. Ironically, Sex Pistols promoter Malcolm McLaren was so enamored with the potential of Hell's fresh-out-of-bed appeal that he tried to convince the unimpressed Hell that he could be a star in England if he would join McLaren's ranks. Hell stayed in the States, but McLaren took note of Hell's image and formulated the blueprint for what would become the emblem of punk fashion, the Sex Pistols (Savage, 92). Another Malcolm McLaren side project that took note of the Velvet's image and fashion was the New York Dolls. The Dolls saw how fashion, even if subtle (as in the case of the Velvets), could make an impact. What better way to comment on the ridiculous name-dropping flamboyance of their era than by dressing the part? The New York Dolls realized that wearing certain clothes could personify and highlight certain aspects of music and image. They learned this lesson from the Velvets. Establishing themselves and recording ten years earlier than most of the bands on the punk scene, the Velvets were the quintessential punk band. Their influence on rock music, be it punk, glam, American, or British was enormous. No other band, save for the Beatles, has had so much influence on the rock music that would succeed it (Kozak, xiv). The band's four albums and five years on the New York City scene created a style that is still present decades later.

"Straight White Punks In Drag"

by Jessamin Swearingen
(adapted and edited by Allan Metz)

"We Created It: Let's Take It Over!"
web site, 1999-2001

What the New York Dolls meant to punk.—Ed.

Watching the aggressively macho strains of heavy metal rock videos today, it is difficult to fight the urge to dismiss most of the bands as cheap clones of the New York Dolls. The forces urging male rock stars in the early 1970s to wear women's clothing onstage returned full force with the arrival of MTV-ready heavy metal. What was once called "glam rock" reemerged in the early 1980s to affirm that whatever provoked male rock stars in the early 1970s to dress in female attire still meant "bad boy" in the rock industry. By adopting a female persona by wearing makeup and women's clothing, the heavy metal musicians asserted an even more daring male identity than that of the typical male rocker. Dressing in drag for these bands held no connotation of homosexuality; it was merely a means of getting attention.

Glam rock stemmed directly from the Velvet Underground's portrayal of so-called deviant sexuality. The cross-dressers and name-droppers clinging to Andy Warhol's Factory studio space in the late 1960s provided ample material for Lou Reed's impressive narrative lyrical skills. Author Tricia Henry notes that in 1971, after the ending of his career with the seminal Velvet Underground, Reed was visited by English pop star David Bowie. Bowie recognized Reed's talent and saw the potential of his subject matter. During the sexually permissive atmosphere of the late 1960s, it was in vogue for pop stars to experiment with drugs and sexual partners. Bowie wrote "Queen Bitch" on his 1971 LP, *Hunky Dory*, in homage to the Velvet Underground. The song patterned Lou Reed's chanting drawl and straight-from-the-street narration. Reed's influence on Bowie is also evident in Bowie's song "Andy Warhol." Bowie understood Warhol's powers of media manipulation, whereby Warhol and the "silver screen" were indistinguishable.

What Warhol did for images in film, Reed emulated in his songwriting and the Velvet Underground carried out in performance. In the mid-1960s, Warhol's films were excessive and obvious pieces of voyeurism with titles such as "Sleep" and "Vinyl." Tricia Henry insightfully captured the Warhol and Reed connection: "Warhol's films of this period, diametrically opposed to the cinematic sensibilities of Hollywood, paralleled the Velvet Underground's departure from mainstream tastes in popular music. The films contained both a technically unpolished style and subject matter offensive to the general public" (Henry, 22).

Reed created characters who were blatantly themselves and made no attempt to conform to social norms. Factory regular and Warhol superstar, Candy Darling, was the perfect subject matter for Reed's daring songwriting. Reed's stories of drag queens were magnified into a full-blown fantasy by David Bowie. By 1972, as previously noted, Bowie was performing as his "Ziggy Stardust" character. Although enormously successful and entertaining as a recipe full of rock's best ingredients, Bowie's Ziggy was still too far removed from the street element on which rock'n'roll thrived. Bowie's experimental and less than conventionally masculine appearance was threatening to mainstream male rock. The street element of original rock music, its iconography of fast cars and women, had no relevancy for an extraterrestrial bisexual martian.

The New York Dolls filled the void between pedestrian and performer left by Bowie and were on the forefront of the glam phenomenon. Donning makeup and girlish wardrobe, but maintaining the character of a street thug rather than of a space-age cartoon, the Dolls were New York's answer to glam rock and wondered aloud whether their version of rock'n'roll could make it in the industry. The song "Frankenstein" on their 1973 first album, *New York Dolls*, retells the story of the man-made monster, but this time he's in more makeup. In typical Dolls tongue-in-rouged-cheek humor, David Johansen painted the picture of the ultimate drag monster, Frankenstein.

Many critics wondered during the Dolls' rise to infamy about the motivation behind their wardrobe. The Dolls had a killer transvestite image, which made the recording industry hesitant to sign, much less support, the new act. "Frankenstein" anticipated the record industry's intolerance of the Dolls. Certainly the Dolls' provocative image kept the mainstream radio and the rest of America at a safe distance. And as Johansen predicted, the Dolls were getting a "feeling of" their "own ordeal."

Punk photographer Bob Gruen noted that many thought the Dolls' campy clothing and act meant that the band was gay, but in actuality the band just knew a good gimmick when it saw one, not to mention the girl groupies who thought it was cute. Through this daring manipulation of image, the Dolls became a symbol out of rock rebellion and gained an entrance into the fashionable underground of the New York City scene. When Gruen describes the sexual tone of the era, he notes lead Doll, David Johansen, saying the flavor of the era was not necessarily bisexuality, but "trysexuality," as in "try anything" (Savage, 60).

Musically, the Dolls merely rehashed 1960s standards of girl-group schtick and Rolling Stones swagger. Building on the aggressive pout of the Stones' guitar-charged rock and accented with the likes of the Shangri-Las' theatrics, the Dolls stood apart from most early 1970s rockers. Much of the music of that time was community-oriented and less abrasive in tone. Such songs as "Teach Your Children Well" by Crosby, Stills and Nash acknowledged rock music as a commodity both aged and established enough to be concerned with parenting. The New York Dolls and their other punk counterparts rejuvenated rock'n'roll by retaining the childlike charm of dress up and street-thug, cops-and-robbers games.

By playing dress up, the Dolls showcased their belief in the youth-oriented essence of rock music. Fashion has been an integral part of rock'n'roll's marketing since the industry's inception. Acts found their marketing angle and audience in the unifying dress codes of specific rock genres. Fashion is also the way for rock bands and managers to convey a certain image. The Beatles' manager, Brian Epstein, used fashion in the group's early career to present an image of a cultured and pleasant rock band. The Beatles' tasteful gray suits were a means of identifying the band as a unit as well as sanitizing their rock background.

The New York Dolls used fashion to express a kinship to the seedy New York City underworld. No doubt having been influenced by the Velvet Underground's sexually deviant ambiance, the Dolls took fashion one step further. They used their girlish clothing and makeup to accentuate bad boy rock. In a sense, by wearing this clothing they were accentuating their male-based rock ambitions. The origins of their sexually ambivalent image seemingly stemmed from Lou Reed's accounts of the Warhol menagerie that influenced his subject matter. Much like Reed, lead Doll David Johansen wrote songs about sexual flamboyance from a calloused, street-thug perspective.

Critics and neighboring bands wanted to discredit the New York Dolls as flaky transvestites, but the Dolls were an integral element of the savage guitar-based rock that was emerging out of the mainstream arena rock. The Dolls' short-lived career spanned roughly from 1972 to 1975. During that time, the best-selling rock acts included the worst elements of pop music. The New York Dolls were the complete opposite of the chart toppers of that era. Foreign to the soothing schmaltz of 1974's *Billboard*'s top-selling singles, such as the adult-oriented tranquilizers Barbra Streisand and Sammy Davis Jr., the New York Dolls were hardened criminals (Bronson, 266). Their music sounded like the Rolling Stones on a bad day, but looked even worse. Whereas the Stones only flirted with makeup and girlish frocks, the Dolls wore their outrageous near-drag clothing on the street. Fashion's impact on the New York Dolls' career in rock was longstanding. The Dolls' image was that of bored teenagers and high school delinquents rather than that of the calm and controlled fashion of more established rock or pop acts. The street element in the Dolls' fashion eventually led the band to Malcolm McLaren, the P.T. Barnum of the rock'n'roll age.

McLaren, who is best known as the manager of the British punk band the Sex Pistols, had been following the fashion trends since the early 1970s. McLaren and partner Vivian Westwood opened Let It Rock, a clothing store dedicated to the changing fashion of London teenagers. Through McLaren's participation with the youth/fashion subculture, he gained an essential understanding of the power of clothing to say the unmentionable and shock the unshockable.

The Dolls and McLaren originally met in New York City in 1973 while attending an international boutique show at the McAlpin Hotel. Representing Let It Rock, McLaren presented clothing that would lay the groundwork for the English punk aestheticism, featuring blouses with cigarette burns. New York Doll Syl Sylvain was also making clothes and met McLaren at the boutique show. Later, when the Dolls were on their first tour of London, McLaren met the rest of the band.

During his time with Let It Rock, McLaren resurrected the Teddy Boy style made fashionable in the late 1950s. Teddy Boys were elegant street hoodlums, impeccably dressed in tailored clothing and bright colors and were walking personifications of 1950s rock hero Eddie Cochran's ode to "Pink Peg Slacks." According to rock critic Dave Marsh in the 1983 edition of the *New Rolling Stone Record Guide*: "Another great Fifties rock & roller more honored abroad than at home, Eddie Cochran was virtually the prototype of the angelic punk...Cochran created a series of teenage fictions..." (Marsh, 104). Eddie Cochran died in 1960, but his flair for clothes and the youth-oriented strains of rock music kept him alive for the next generations of rock fans.

The Dolls were impressed with McLaren's love and knowledge of clothing, and a friendship ensued between McLaren and the band. At that point, the Dolls were combining a street-boy-tough look with a camped-out-city-granny-on-acid look. McLaren made a note of the Dolls' visual impact, in particular the way in which it shocked people into taking notice. Later when the Dolls were near the end of their career, McLaren stepped in once again. By late 1973, the Dolls were falling apart because of their label's lack of financial support, not to mention the toll of severe alcohol and drug abuse. McLaren went back to New York City and tried to revive the Dolls. Somehow he could sense the potential of a band of their caliber. But the Dolls were close to their end, and nothing short of a miracle would rekindle their recording career.

To keep the Dolls in the public eye, McLaren devised a scheme that would pave the way for the shocking fashion and statements that would come from later punk acts. McLaren toyed with some of the slogans from the French students' Revolution of 1968. In 1974, he borrowed their question, "What are the politics of boredom?" (Savage, 87) and dressed the band in red patent leather. The red, combined with the boredom banner boasting a sickle and hammer, had many asking if the Dolls had gone too far. From drag to communism, the Dolls had once again overextended themselves, and this time failed miserably. McLaren tried to resurrect the Dolls' career by sending the band on a tour of the South. The tour ended when the band broke up in Florida in 1974. Guitarist Johnny Thunders and drummer Jerry Nolan left the Dolls in the middle of a tour because they could not find heroin in Florida (Savage, 88).

Consequently, both Thunders and Nolan are now dead, but the Dolls' tragic drug dependency only heightened the States' intolerance of punk. Punk as a philosophy, in the case of the New York Dolls, lived up to the term "punk," as in hoodlum slang. The Dolls were living parodies of their own self-destruction, and although they were animated fixtures of rock'n'roll mythology, they burned themselves out. Punk rock was a product of this quick-burning flame; it was short-lived and all-consuming, but once it was over, it was quickly forgotten and replaced. The Dolls were punk because they were central to the themes that punk reasserted in rock'n'roll. Youth and fashion were the keys to self expression, and playing original, or at least individual, music regardless of the popular music charts was what the New York Dolls did. Because of their dedication to preserving rock's individuality, the Dolls were the link between late-1960s and mid-1970s punk rock.

Hammersmith Odeon, London, September 9, 1978
credit: © copyright Mick Mercer, web site: www.mickmercer.com, e-mail: mercerm@supanet.com

"I Feel Just Like Some Misplaced Joan of Arc"

by Jessamin Swearingen
(adapted and edited by Allan Metz)

"We Created It: Let's Take It Over!"
web site, 1999-2001

What Patti Smith meant to punk.—Ed.

In 1974, Patti Smith was the first to be signed from the initial wave of bands that played CBGBs. For that alone she has earned the title "Godmother of punk" (Kozak, 38). Smith's influence on the punk scene, however, is not confined to her CBGBs association. Smith was one of the genre's most prolific artists regardless of medium. Her accomplishments, both independent and in terms of the punk movement, are significant. Smith became a rock star on her own terms. Starting as rock's biggest fan, she published her poetry and rock criticism. She also tried playwriting with Sam Shepard on "Cowboy Mouth" before becoming a rock musician herself. Smith was also one of the few (if not first) women to succeed in rock music without becoming a sex symbol. She showed off her rock'n'roll hero worship and created powerful rock pieces out of her collection of rock influences. As in her playwriting, she created narrative and texture with her songs.

Smith released her first single independently in 1974. One-time roommate and friend, Robert Mapplethorpe, put up the money for his label "Mer" to press some copies of "Piss Factory." On the record were Smith and what was the beginning of the Patti Smith Group. "Piss Factory" describes Smith's job in a factory during high school, weaving the tale of being "sixteen and time to pay off." As the record spins, Smith's poetry, backed by Lenny Kaye on guitar and Richard Sohl on piano, takes the listener on a ride through Smith's past. Her verse is crammed with references to a rock'n'roll upbringing. She cites the dizzying soul of the "Wicked" Wilson Pickett's "Mustang Sally" in one verse, then the name brand of the cough syrup on which rock critic extraordinaire, Lester Bangs, overdosed in the next. Her list of influences also includes James Brown, "Twist & Shout," and Philadelphia DJ, George Woods. "Piss Factory" is significant because never before had an artist been so vocal about the impact of rock music and its influences. "Piss Factory" launched itself from where Chuck Berry's autobiographical rock anthem "Johnny B. Goode" left off. Berry's classic is autobiographical, but Smith's sensationalizes her own life story to the point of mythology.

Her monumental first record, *Horses*, released in 1975, broke new ground in rock music. Produced by ex-Velvet Underground member, John Cale, *Horses* forced rock music to be sanctioned as an art form. Smith's rock was more focused than that of the Beatles and less self-absorbed than Jim Morrison's drunken verse. She gained the listener's attention with street-smart on-target fiction.

The album's first song set the standard for the punk attitude, and because *Horses* was the first album released out of the CBGB era of New York punk, Smith in a sense set the tone with references to Jesus and sin. Smith's three lines of self-indulgent religious iconography was the essence of punk. The mixture of educated but disrespectful rebellion maintained the youthful swagger and literary appeal of typical New York punk. The song "Gloria" was a cover of Van Morrison's 1960s rocker. Smith performed the song from a male narrative, thereby at least for the duration of one song, freed women in rock music by doing so. By performing a typically male-based song and retaining the male narrative as a female performer, Smith enabled people to get beyond their assumptions about rock music. Women in rock's past, while powerful in performance, were not strong as women. Aside from Grace Slick of Jefferson Airplane and Stax/Voltrecording label's soul women such as Mable John and Carla Thomas, women of that era remained objects in rock'n'roll. Janis Joplin was a slave to her bottle and sexual dependency. Tina Turner's career was made as the T&A ("tits and ass") visual of Ike Turner's sideshow. Smith changed this by enabling women to be rock fans and, more importantly, participants, without compromising themselves. In addition, she virtually reinvented the narrative voice in rock music. With the overwhelming extent of subject matter conquered on her debut LP, it is no wonder Smith is called "Godmother of punk rock."

Smith moves from the hedonistic perspective of a male rock musician in "Gloria" to the scene of locker room violence with a backdrop of 1960s soul classics in "Land." "Land," an anthem to the underdog, weaves the tale of the hero, Johnny, getting beat up in the locker room. In the background are taunts. Smith narrates the life of the American teenager coming of age via the backbeat of rock'n'roll. Her obsessive love for the art form breathed new life into it, and she stayed true to her roots. From the loving allusions to her rock-obsessed adolescence in "Piss Factory" in 1974, Smith determined to revive rock'n'roll. And now, almost twenty years later, her vision and impact remain equally significant. In today's recording industry, any strong female songwriter or performer who surfaces is compared to Patti Smith. Smith was the first female rock performer to make gender irrelevant in her songwriting and performances. Combining the headstrong brashness of punk with her aggressive pose, Smith allowed women to imagine themselves in rock music as a participant, not just as an observer. If Smith's efforts freed male and female rock fans from their assumptions of women in rock, punk offered the same lesson to rock fans. While Smith's music showed women that they could create and consume rock music on their own terms, punk did the same for rock fans regardless of gender. Punk chronicler, Legs McNeil, best summed up Smith's accomplishment in a July 1989 issue of *Spin* magazine.

> "Patti Smith kicked ass so hard she knocked down the whole fucking wall. She was the first woman in rock'n'roll that guys aspired to be like. She was the first woman to get it down so good that it didn't matter what planet she was from. Patti kicked gender in the balls and made great rock'n'roll by following her own agenda, without falling into the role of the victim. And in the process, Patti opened the doors for every woman who looked up on the stage and didn't imagine herself down on her knees blowing the rock god, but becoming one" (*Spin,* 7/89, p. 6).

I was personally present at Blondie's performance back then. I was 19 at the time. Blondie's appearance was on a Saturday, the last day of the rock concerts. Sunday was always the jazz day and the last day of the festival. Man, Debbie was wild on stage and performing exceptionally well. She had the crowd entirely in her power. Being in the press space right in front of the stage, I was standing perhaps five to six meters from her. I can even tell you what she wore that night, a white dress. It was an experience I won't ever forget.
—*Rudi Keunen, web designer of Jazz Bilzen web site—www.jazzbilzen.be*

Jazz Bilzen Rock/Jazz Festival, Bilzen, Belgium, August 12, 1978. Other acts at this four-day festival included James Brown, Fairport Convention, Larry Coryell, One Truth Band and John McLauglin, Gruppo Sportivo, the Jam, the Boomtown Rats, and Lou Reed.
credit: © Philippe Carly—http://users.skynet.be/phicarly

Reprinted with permission of Rudi Keunen

"Live Cultural Criticism Starring Amiki Baraka and Patti Smith"

by Jessamin Swearingen
(adapted and edited by Allan Metz)

"We Created It: Let's Take It Over!"
web site, 1999-2001

Reflections on the Beats, women in rock, jazz, punk, parallels between black poet and writer Amiri Baraka and Patti Smith, and more.—Ed.

Expressing alienation through poetry is a strong vehicle for social criticism. Amiri Baraka (full name, Imanu Amiri Baraka) and Patti Smith approached their critiques through tales of personal alienation during live poetry readings with musical backdrop. Baraka used jazz in the late 1980s to articulate his anger toward a racist culture that was trying to deny the influence of black people on society. Smith used a rock band to describe how artists—especially women—were thought of as dangerous once they had a cultural voice.

Although different in ethnicity and medium but similar within the context of their respective genres, Baraka and Smith spoke to society with the same message. In Baraka's "In The Tradition" and Smith's "Babelogue/Rock'n'Roll Nigger," the artists related living and creating within a society that wants to quiet opinions because of skin color, gender, or perceived threat to society. Both Baraka, as a black male writer and poet, and Smith as a female rock musician, approached the mainstream from an outside perspective. In live poetry and music, their articulated social criticism is veiled in a more easily digestible model. Baraka and Smith are creators within a world unaccustomed to standards other than those established by white male ideas of art and cultural identity. Both poets make their work's message aggressive and pointed with their words, but accessible to their audiences because of the musical backdrop.

Baraka began his writing career with the name Leroi Jones but in time renamed himself Amiri Baraka to reclaim his African American identity. At twenty-three, he moved from his home in New Jersey to New York City, and by the late 1950s he had become part of the Beat movement. His cultural alienation as one of the few blacks participating in the Beat movement created an interesting dichotomy within the liberal-identified beatnik culture. Most beats thought it hip to go to jazz shows and associate with the musicians, yet few white beatniks acknowledged black culture until it became fashionable within the medium of jazz.

In a chapter entitled "The Village" from his autobiography, *The Autobiography of Leroy Jones* (1984), Jones discusses the racism he experienced during the late 1950s in the Village with the sharp perception of hindsight. He reminisces about meeting other young black men who wanted to write, socializing with the Beat crowd, and discovering a pattern of black exile: "But it is significant that most of those blacks I met...who were "artists left this country never to return" (Jones, 125). Much of the beatnik movement borrowed from a sense of hip that, according to Norman Mailer's essay "The White Negro" [*contained in a collection of his writings entitled* Advertisements for Myself—Ed.], evolved out of black culture and lifestyle. Specifically, jazz music and style became increasingly fashionable to white society, which unconsciously tokenized these aspects of black culture as a white commodity.

Later as Amiri Baraka, Jones performed a series of poetry readings. One poem in particular, "In The Tradition," confronts the white culture's racist notion that American art derives purely from European influences. The poetry reading on the album is accompanied by jazz musicians. Baraka's use of jazz behind his poetry helps answer his own question: "Where's your American music, man?" Jazz is an American music form that had to gain acceptance in Europe before being accepted in mainstream American culture. Baraka states in his poems "We are the composers" and "We are the artists," knowing his "we" is not represented in American history.

Baraka's performance of "In The Tradition" is strong criticism of the cultural negation of black arts in white culture. The argument is strengthened by his choice of a jazz background in the performance of the poetry. Jazz music as a musical genre was disregarded by white mainstream America until the mainstream could find a way to make it a commodity. Baraka's performance uses black music and speaks from a black perspective, but it is still accessible to white audiences.

Baraka's live poetry was copyrighted in 1979 and 1981, but poet musician Patti Smith was covering the same ground in 1978 on her album *Easter* with a song titled "Babelogue/Rock'n'Roll Nigger." Smith created in a climate similar to Baraka/Jones. The oldest child of working class New Jersey parents, Smith moved to New York City in the late 1960s to pursue her artistic ambitions. She began her rock career as a poet, giving readings around lower Manhattan. Accompanied by Lenny Kaye on guitar, her poems took shape as rock songs.

Smith's participation in the rock world has patterns comparable to Baraka's experience within the Beat movement. Both were creators in a medium that catered to artists of different makeups. Baraka was a black artist in a white culture that had little interest in preserving black culture's influence on whites, often denying the influence at all. Smith's case was similar within the rock'n'roll system. Rock had been a male-based industry since the birth of the blues at the beginning of the nineteenth century. Rock'n'roll, slang for sexual activity, excluded women unless they were being used for sexual outlet. Within the context of rock'n'roll, Smith used punk rock as a means to create within rock in the same way Baraka used the beat movement within the white mainstream. Through Smith's punk association, she was able to create and not sugarcoat her message to survive in the male-based rock world. Artists are easier to accept if they can be classified in the mainstream's terms. In the same vein that white culture felt more comfortable with black authors if they associated with the beats, unclassified rock performers were easier to market and describe if called "punk." Smith never disassociated herself from the punk movement the way Baraka/Jones did with the beats. Smith's battle for identity emerged from her association with the rock industry as a female performer. The rock industry realized Smith's power as a performer but did not know how to market her as a woman within the industry. The marketing label of punk made Smith seem more classifiable, and thus more acceptable within the rock mainstream.

In a sense, the new division of punk rock allowed Smith to retain her impact and even aided her refusal to become a pawn to the male-dominated music industry. Smith as a female rock musician tested cultural norms in a society that expected women to be docile folk singers or pretty sex symbols. Smith succumbed to neither. She performed and wrote as a rock-based performer, but never as an object. On her third album, *Easter*, Smith recorded a song that made rock critics cringe. "Rock'n'Roll Nigger," with a spoken word introduction, "Babelogue," placed Smith in the position of cultural critic.

"Babelogue," which also appeared in her book of poetry, *Babel*, focuses on images of male power in rock music. Her account of male sexuality on the stage is insightful as an outsider, but Smith never approached rock as a boys-only sport. Smith was also a rock'n'roll performer and discusses her experience as a woman performer. She describes most men's shock when they saw that she was determined to succeed within rock regardless of gender. In an industry that was prepared to view womanhood as a handicap to rock performers and writers, Smith refused to participate in their mind-set.

The spoken word piece, "Babelogue," ends with Smith claiming her rights to art and then leads into "Rock'n'Roll Nigger." Although abrasive in title, the song rings true in content. "Rock'n'Roll Nigger" sets the pace for strong social commentary to the tune of a hard rock song. The title's significance mirrors Baraka's question: Where was the American music?, and Smith knew. Rock'n'roll was a recipe of black influences modified to suit white tastes, and in the tradition of mainstream culture, a money-making product. Smith also was making note of the position of women within the world of the rock product. Before Smith, John Lennon's ambitious 1972 single, "Woman Is the Nigger of the World," made clear his observation of women within the mainstream.

The first verse in "Rock'n'Roll Nigger" describes an unruly girl, "a black sheep" and "a whore," the good girl gone bad. What better way to describe the depiction of women in rock music? Smith alludes to the woman character who needs "something...more," and taking the role of the "Rock'n'Roll Nigger" in the song's refrain, Smith realizes that she longs to be outside society. It is not hard to imagine that a woman within the world of rock music would feel herself in a state of exile, not unlike Leroi Jones' early artist friends expressing their alienation by leaving the US for good. Smith's position as a woman in rock gave her insight into other artists who had been excluded from the cultural mainstream such as Jimi Hendrix and Jackson Pollock as well as Jesus and "Grandma." Patti as a female participant in rock culture was experiencing much of the fear and criticism black authors did in attempting to retain self-identity in the Beat movement.

Whether battling sexism or racism, both poets confronted their cultural misgivings in a manner that was more accessible to their audiences through live performance and musical backdrop. By using rock or jazz as a medium, the artists empowered cultures whose claims of influence and legacies were denied. Through their performances, both artists presented their material in an active, rather than passive, manner proving that, at least for the duration of a song or poem, their influence would no longer be negated because of race or gender.

"Broadway Looks So Medieval"

by Jessamin Swearingen
(adapted and edited by Allan Metz)

"We Created It: Let's Take It Over!"
web site, 1999-2001

On the band, Television—Ed.

Patti Smith was the Godmother of punk rock, but her Bowery neighbors, the highly intellectual band Television, were the high priests. Formed from a nucleus of Tom Verlaine and Richard Hell, Television was the quintessential musical backdrop for self-obsessed poetry. Television's music gave form to the early New York punk's poetic wanderings and created the look for what later was termed *punk*. Bandmates Verlaine and Hell met at a reform/boarding school in Delaware and ran away from school together in the early 1970s (Savage, 88). In the liner notes to Richard Hell & the Voidoid's *Blank Generation* CD, author John Piccarella writes:

"Sometime in the mid-1960's, Richard Meyers and Tom Miller, two teenagers who had been missing from a prep/reform school in Delaware, were arrested in Alabama for setting a field on fire. One said he wanted to keep warm (He later changed his name to Verlaine). The other said he just wanted to watch it burn (He changed his name to Hell)" (Sire/Warner Bros.).

Piccarella's account of Verlaine and Hell's juvenile exploits, while comical, sets the tone for Television's career. The constant rivalry between Verlaine and Hell caused Hell to leave and form the Voidoids after a short stint with the Heartbreakers, with one-time New York Doll Johnny Thunders. When Hell was with Television, there was a constant tension in the band. Hell states, "Tom and I kind of hated each other from the beginning but there was some mutual ground which we didn't share with anyone else." Hell cites his and Verlaine's shared interest in "the self-conscious twisted estheticism of the French 19th century," which fostered a working bond between competitors, if not friends.

Their competition and working relationship is apparent in Piccarella's account of their arrest in Alabama. A pattern of rivalry is immediately obvious. The young Miller, who later took the surname of the nineteenth century French Symbolist poet Paul Verlaine, masked his intentions by claiming he was cold. Hell, on the other hand, flat out declared that he "wanted to watch it burn." Where Verlaine was tricky, Hell was blatantly rebellious, and this pattern is reflected throughout their music. After the Alabama arrest, they migrated to New York City to form the poetry-rock combination, the Neon Boys (Lazell, 503). By 1973 the band, with the addition of Billy Ficca on drums and the New Jersey guitarist Richard Lloyd, was renamed Television.

Television was significant to the formation of a New York City punk identity. Although their live debut was pretty much ignored by the press, Television eventually played CBGBs and was the first rock band to do so. CBGBs, which stands for "country, blues, and bluegrass" (Kozak, 1) was a bar in the Bowery of lower Manhattan. According to Roman Kozak, who wrote the definitive account of the CBGBs scene, *This Ain't No Disco*, Verlaine and Hell stumbled upon bar owner Hilly Kristal outside of his country and western bar in 1974. The band needed a place to play, and were practicing six nights a week in Terry Ork's lower Manhattan loft. Kristal permitted them to play the following Sunday, and CBGBs connection with punk was formed. CBGBs launched a whole new generation of bands, and if not for Verlaine's sly conniving, CBGBs could have remained a country bar. When Kristal asked if they played country music, Verlaine said, yes, but the lie got them a place to play.

Television's christening of CBGBs was the catalyst for its generation of punk rock bands. Within six months, CBGBs was the place to play in lower Manhattan, and Television had recorded its first single on its manager's label. Because of Terry Ork's business maneuvers, punk established itself, at least for Hilly Kristal's Bowery bar, as a justifiable rock trade. Ork advised Kristal about who should play and, in doing so, brought in bands like Blondie and the Ramones. Ork not only invited other bands to open for Television, but also advertised the shows. CBGBs' Sunday night concerts became the place for bands to play and develop their styles, and it was Television and Ork's involvement that started the tradition (Kozak, 14).

During the year 1974, Television developed a reputation as being overly cynical and cryptic. What began as their fashion of blunt immediacy was turning into disorder. While Verlaine and Hell's appreciation of words and rebellion drew from teenage revolt, it emerged into evasive pretension. Critics either loved Television's overly wordy delivery, or called them too smart for their own good—no one understood them. Verlaine wrote the most cryptic and musically intricate songs, while Hell wrote the more basic rock'n'roll homages. Hell described his rock'n'roll yearnings in the book *England's Dreaming*.

"When you're a kid you think you know everything. I felt I was seeing the reality of human existence that everybody else was deluded about. The best way to reach these people, I thought was with a Rock'n'Roll band. When I was a teenager, there was a feeling of radio as a secret network. Songs were the secret teenage news and you'd get the news by listening to the radio" (Savage, 88).

Hell knew rock music could transform people and wanted to see how far he could push rock music to suit his needs. If Television was visually different from most of its punk neighbors, it was because it did not have a specific image. The Dolls had glitter rock and Blondie had Debbie Harry. The Ramones all looked like hoodlums and Patti Smith did not need any props. Television looked like it had "rolled out of bed" and gone immediately to the show (Kozak, 15). Television's image gave punk more substance, but Hell stole the show. Television's image, between the dueling Verlaine and Hell, gave punk a two-sided example. Hell, one-upped the Ramones by making street tough a little smarter, and Verlaine outshined both Hell and the Ramones with his obsessive poetic stance. In Kozak's book, a picture of Hell playing at CBGBs in 1977 shows him in a ripped t-shirt with a picture of Bugs Bunny wearing a leather jacket. Handwritten on the shirt are the words, "Bugs Bunny has too much money." Hell wore his punk fashion statements on his back; combined with the Ramones' hoodlum image, punk fashion was born.

Hell's torn t-shirt and slogan package led Tom Verlaine to kick the more pronounced "punk" personality, Richard Hell, out of the group. Band tensions had mounted. Verlaine wanted Television signed to a record company, but he also wanted Hell out of the show. Hell's torn t-shirt and ragamuffin hair distracted attention from Verlaine's more austere poetics and aloofness toward the audience. Richard Hell went on to form the Voidoids and slipped to the ranks of cult hero, but his wiped-out look inspired Malcolm McLaren and his future band, the Sex Pistols. Once Hell was out of the picture, Verlaine went about turning Television into his machine. After Blondie's first show at CBGBs, he recruited Blondie's Fred Smith for bass.

Although Verlaine wanted to establish the band, within the New York scene Television stuck out. According to Debbie Harry in *Making Tracks: The Rise of Blondie*: "These guys dressed like Bowery bums while everybody else was semi-glitter wearing tight pants or panty hose" (Harry, Stein, Bockris, 12). The band was different musically as well. Television was actually musically and lyrically eloquent. Verlaine and second guitarist Richard Lloyd grew into impressive and original guitarists, creating a sound that could not be confined to the narrow boundaries of punk stereotype: three chords and unchanging time structure. In contrast to the length of one Ramones song (approximately two minutes), Television would just be completing its introduction. Most punk bands of the time were reliving the simplicity of traditional three-chord rock. Television was a band that could actually play its instruments. Verlaine and Lloyd created musical spirals of sound that circled around each other. Television's music was an intricate pattern of call-and-response melody and tricky unintelligible lyrics. For example, in "Prove It," Verlaine shows off his love of odd rhymes. According to *Boston Phoenix* writer, Howard Litwak, Television stuck out because it was, "shamelessly, gloriously, a guitar band that reveled in soiling excess." This set Television apart from its contemporaries, who acted out their version of punk rock with a minimalist approach.

Television and its New York peers performed and recorded music that spoke of or evoked New York City imagery. Television, like the Velvet Underground, could not have come from any other place on earth. Tom Verlaine's dry wit and sly narratives, though not as obvious as Lou Reed's dialogues, were completely urban-inspired. On the first Television album, *Marquee Moon*, the City's ambiance is inescapable. A marquee moon could only happen in the City, an area where man-made objects overpower nature's own beauty and in time actually become the natural object. "Venus De Milo," also on the band's debut LP, describes this phenomena. The Venus De Milo is a sculpture with no arms, and Verlaine could not resist the pun of falling into Venus De Milo's arms. *Marquee Moon* is full of this tricky word play. Later on in "Venus," Verlaine pays homage to the urban teenage pranks he and ex-bandmate Hell enjoyed. The interchange is also a prime example of their interactions where Richie suggests that they imitate cops. Verlaine decides that they had better not, protecting himself much like he did when they were arrested in Alabama. Verlaine masks his illicit intentions while Hell tries to provoke the worst.

After kicking Hell out of the band, Verlaine continued with Television, contributing an intellectual edge to the emerging punk rock. Hell went on to the Heartbreakers then the Voidoids, but his image, along with the Ramones, typified punk's teenage bad-boy pose. Though as a band Television never achieved the international world fame and notoriety of the other punks, it exemplified the punk dichotomy. While highly intelligent and talented, the band never achieved the fame or notoriety of the neighboring bands. In 1978, Television released a second LP, *Adventure*, but the band split and fell into obscurity soon afterward. Verlaine and Lloyd continued recording, and Hell continued to write. Then in 1992, Television reunited for a mildly successful self-titled album and concert tour.

Television was a departure from conventional punk, and standard rock. It indulged in lengthy guitar solos and cryptic lyrics, but was not typical radio-ready album-oriented rock. As a unit, Television seemed much more album-ready than its contemporaries, but once the band recorded, it fell flat. Their live dynamic and image could not be captured on vinyl, nor was their sound typical aggressive three-chord punk. Nor was Television pop—the band was too alienating to be pop music. Television was in a class by itself, and irreplaceable in the history of New York City punk.

"I'm a Teenage Lobotomy"

by Jessamin Swearingen
(adapted and edited by Allan Metz)

"We Created It: Let's Take It Over"!
web site, 1999-2001

On the Ramones and New York City punk. An obituary of Joey Ramone (who died on April 15, 2001) plus reflections on Joey by his west coast contemporaries, the Go-Go's, and by Chris Stein are appended at the end of this selection.—Ed.

The Ramones were the New York personification of punk rock. In fact, when CBGBs owner Hilly Kristal picked American bands to tour in England, he chose the Ramones. So in a sense, the Ramones were the first American punk band ever seen by the future generation of English punks. The Ramones turned the rebellion of 1950s roots rock into a high decibel and speed assault on the senses. The Ramones put punk rock on the map with such seemingly effortless classics as "I Wanna Be Sedated," "Beat On The Brat," and "Rock'n'Roll High School." The Ramones put the youth back into rock music, and it permanently stunted the band's growth. It seemed that they never made it out of high school.

While bands such as Blondie and the Dolls slipped into camp and Television and Patti Smith were too poetic and wordy, the Ramones were so punk as to be a parody of themselves. The four young men from Queens, in leather motorcycle jackets and sharing the Ramone surname, gave punk a name much in the same way the Beatles and their contemporaries put the "British Invasion" on the pop map. The Ramones and Beatles connection is applicable on other levels. The Ramones were merely reciting the lessons that rock culture and the Beatles had taught them. Early in the Beatles' career, they were the fab four, and were focussed on as members of a band; four young men with similar haircuts and a modest collective image, an image which made them accessible as a commodity. The Ramones used the same tactic, employing the same last names and leather jackets.

"Ramon" was Paul McCartney's alias when booking reservations in hotels during the early waves of Beatlemania (RS, #507, p. 135). Ramon became Ramone, and in 1974 they assumed the last name and an image that would typify punk rock for years to come. Their wardrobe of ripped jeans, sneakers, and leather personified punk. Dressing in their day-to-day street clothes made glam obsolete, and brought rock back to the on-the-streets teenage element.

The Ramones were the fab four of punk; they made punk accessible as a visual commodity. Visualizing punk was important. Creating an image is usually the catalyst from idea to product. The Beatles, with their matching haircuts and suits, sang their way into the hearts of millions. The Ramones, with their teenage casualness and simplistic edge, wormed punk into the brains of the next generation of rock fans. The Ramones' music was simplistic three-chord rock. No other music of their era, aside from the Dolls and Blondie's homage to the girl groups, recalled rock's innocence.

Their teenage subject matter became rock iconography—the band's loving documents of the rock age, such as "Do You Remember Rock'n'Roll Radio?" and the immortal cult favorite, "Rock'n'Roll High School," which was adapted into a movie in 1979. The Ramones' "anyone-can-do-this" image and approach inspired an era of burgeoning rock fans and critics. Never before had rock looked and sounded so simple. In some ways, this was one of the Ramones' problems. Because of their casual delinquent approach, few took the Ramones seriously. Were they a novelty or a complete resurrection of rock music? In essence, to stay true to their intentions, the Ramones remained simplistic, but the irony often failed to come through. While it looked and sounded as though the Ramones' music and aesthetic were completely easy—a farce; their sound was so raw and yet so tight that few could duplicate its power.

The Ramones were a rock'n'roll melting pot. Their original lineup had Joey, the lead vocalist, on drums and original drummer Tommy as producer. Soon Tommy replaced Joey on drums, and their naive stab at the rock industry turned into industrious luck. The Ramones got their first gig at CBGBs in 1974, and they became fixtures by 1975. By 1976, they were signed to Sire Records and primed the nation for punk rock. Their first album, *The Ramones,* failed to make it into the US top 100, but the band's impact was seeping into the rock world's sensibilities.

On the back cover of a 1976 June/July issue of *Trouser Press,* an ad for the first Ramones album is almost a parody of itself. "Their music's swept the Bowery...Now it's gonna sweep the country!" It is almost humorous to imagine the Ramones fitting into today's standards of beauty and glamour. The ad shows four skinny guys in leathers and Keds sneakers. Tommy's belly is showing, and Joey looks like a broken marionette. But there is something in their stares—none of them show respect for the camera. The picture looks like a police lineup in juvenile detention hall.

The ad promises that "The Ramones are so punky you're gonna have to react!" On the bottom of the ad is an excerpt from the British rock critic Charles Shaar Murray's *New Musical Express* article: "They're simultaneously so funny, such a cartoon vision of rock and roll, and so genuinely tight and powerful that they're just bound to enchant anyone who fell in love with rock and roll for the right reasons." Murray's description was right on the money. The Ramones were a perfect rock band. They wrote and performed seemingly simple rock songs about nothing, but in the absence of extravagant chord changes and rock star poses, the Ramones mastered rock's fundamentals.

Typically, rock personified the teenage lifestyle—fast enough for short attention spans, yet not heavy enough to distract the listener from having a good time. Like the Beach Boys, the Ramones' music appeared to be lighthearted descriptions of cars and girls—a perpetual teenage outlook and subject matter—but in the Ramones' simplicity lounged the quintessential essence of rock'n'roll. Their music was layered with flawless fast-rock music and subject matter. In "Rockaway Beach," a song about the New York City waterfront, rock was returned to the basics—including the simple enjoyment of chewing bubble gum on a sunny day.

The Ramones realized that rock music was not about being pretentious; it was about doing what you could as well as you could. Unfortunately, the Ramones never excelled past their original goals, and a dilemma arose regarding their image as pop stars. In their simplistic image, the Ramones seemed barbaric and a parody of the freshness they embodied. The band wreaked of calculated havoc—the assumed Ramone surname and punk wardrobe made it too easy to chalk the Ramones off as a novelty act. Now, even after their "break up," the Ramones still surprisingly sound the same, as if they themselves believed the silent but deadly rock image that the media created for them.

Unlike their peers who transcended the confines of punk rock marketing loopholes and radio intolerance, the Ramones eventually became a parody of the punk brashness they once exuded. In a sense, the punk aggression the band once controlled soon became passe, but the Ramones could not transcend the image they had created for themselves. As a band, the Ramones had created the perpetually teenage image, and they could not get out beyond it even when they grew up.

Like the punk icons, the Sex Pistols, the Ramones immediately stagnated. Both bands' impact was so severe and brash that to evolve would mean softening and nullifying punk's aggressiveness. Growing up, in a sense, would be selling out. The Ramones got trapped by that which made them punk. Their youthful ideals and simplistic naivete held them captive. This trap kept punk from staking its claim on the media. The Sex Pistols had Malcolm McLaren's mastermind publicity techniques, not to mention the sensationalism of the band's tabloid life. The Ramones merely failed to grow up and got lost in the shuffle. They became instant relics of a musical era that would influence the rock world, but fail to make much money in the United States.

"Punk Rocker Joey Ramone Dead at 49"

Associated Press, *Monday, April 16, 2001*

NEW YORK (AP)—Singer Joey Ramone, the punk rock icon whose signature yelp melded with the Ramones' three-chord thrash to launch an explosion of bands like the Clash and the Sex Pistols, died Sunday. He was 49.

Ramone, the gangly lead singer with the leather jacket, tinted glasses and permanently-torn jeans, was hospitalized last month with lymphoma. His death was confirmed Sunday by Arturo Vega, the Ramones' longtime artistic director.

The Ramones—its four members adopted the common last name after forming the band in 1974—came out of Queens, a motley collection of local losers with limited musical skills. Joey became the lead singer only after his drumming proved too rudimentary to keep up with his bandmates' thunderous riffs.

While British bands such as the Sex Pistols and Clash received the media attention once punk rock exploded, both were schooled by the Ramones' tour of England that began on the U.S. Bicentennial—July 4, 1976.

"They changed the world of music. They rescued rock and roll from pretentiousness and unnecessary adornments," said Vega.

Their "do-it-yourself," garage-rock influence still echoes today in bands like Green Day and the Offspring. The low-tech Ramones spent just two days and $6,000 recording their 1976 debut album.

"They're the daddy punk group of all time," said Joe Strummer, lead singer of the Clash, in a recent *Spin* magazine interview.

Despite their influence and critical acclaim, the Ramones never cracked the Top 40.

Bruce Springsteen, after seeing the Ramones in an Asbury Park, N.J., club, wrote "Hungry Heart" for the band—but his manager convinced The Boss to keep the eventual hit single.

The Ramones' best-known songs reflected their twisted teen years in Queens: "Beat on the Brat," "I Wanna Be Sedated," "Now I Wanna Sniff Some Glue," "Teenage Lobotomy," "Sheena Is a Punk Rocker."

Joey Ramone was born Jeffrey Hyman on May 19, 1951. His career started during the early 1970s glam-rock era, when he played in several New York bands—occasionally under the name Jeff Starship.

But his collaboration with Dee Dee, Johnny and Tommy Ramone was something special. They became fixtures in downtown clubs like CBGBs and Max's Kansas City, joining fellow punkers like Patti Smith and Richard Hell.

The scene eventually produced commercially successful bands like Blondie and the Talking Heads.

The Ramones recorded their first album of two-minute, three-chord blasts in February 1976. The band then earned a loyal cult following with a seemingly endless string of tours where they would crank out 30 songs in 90 minutes.

In 1979, Joey and the band appeared in the Roger Corman movie "Rock'n'Roll High School," contributing the title song to the soundtrack. They also did the title track for the film "Pet Sematary," based on the book by Ramones fan Stephen King.

Their last real stab at commercial success came in a bizarre 1980 collaboration with producer Phil Spector—a session that bassist Dee Dee Ramone recalled most for Spector's pulling a gun on the band inside his Beverly Hills mansion.

Joey eventually wound up singing a syrupy version of Spector's classic "Baby, I Love You"—the strangest recording of the band's 22-year career. The Spector-produced "End of the Century" did become the Ramones' best-selling record, hitting No. 44 on the charts.

Five years later, the band released "Bonzo Goes to Bitburg"—Joey Ramone's angry rant about President Reagan's visit to a German military cemetery.

The Ramones disbanded in 1996 after a tour that followed their final studio album, *Adios Amigos*. A live farewell tour album, *We're Outta Here!,* was released in 1997.

Since the band's demise, Joey Ramone kept a fairly low profile—occasionally popping up to perform or host shows at Manhattan clubs, making occasional radio show appearances, and working on a solo album that was never released.

"Go-Go's Personal Statement on the Passing of Joey Ramone"

www.gogos.com *web site, April 17, 2001*

The Go-Go's are very saddened by the news that Joey Ramone passed away on Easter Sunday...heartfelt condolences to his family and loved ones. The Ramones were one of the single most important bands ever and their music influenced all of us. We were fortunate to have met Joey on several occasions and one of the highlights of our career was a telegram from the Ramones congratulating us when our album *Beauty and the Beat* went to number 1.

Belinda [Carlisle]: The concert that changed my life was the Ramones at the Roxy in 1977.

Charlotte [Caffey]: The concert that changed my life was the Ramones with Blondie in 1977. I am very, very sad. But I know that every time I hear the Ramones, I will be transported to an altered state.

Kathy [Valentine]: I probably saw the Ramones dozens of times—more than I saw any other band...every chance I got, because they never ever failed to make me happy. I wanted so bad for the Go-Go's and the Ramones to tour together one summer!! Besides being the singer of one of my favorite bands, Joey was sweet, shy, and easy to talk to.

Gina [Schock]: The first time I saw the Ramones was at CBGBs in 1978. They blew me away. I was instantly a fan. I went out and bought four of their albums: *Ramones, Rocket to Russia, Leave Home,* and *Road to Ruin*. I listened to those records over and over, and still can without growing tired of them. They're classics. The band left a huge impression on me which made me want to be part of the whole punk scene. I must have seen the Ramones play a million times, and every time was as incredible as the first. God Bless Joey Ramone!

Jane [Wiedlin]: The Ramones were the first band that made me realize great music could be made with a minimum of parts: a handful of chords, a simple beat, minimalist lyrics and a streamlined melody. They opened up the world of songwriting to me. I can't believe Joey is gone, he will be missed.

"Remembering Joey Ramone"

by Chris Stein
(edited and adapted by Allan Metz)

Message from Chris Stein originally posted to the DHBIS (Deborah Harry and Blondie Information Service) e-mail discussion group on May 7, 2001.—Ed.

dear troops

thanx for all the mail about joey. he called both debbie and me from the hospital about three weeks before he died. at that time we'd all thought he was getting out soon and he said that the doctors told him he couldn't leave yet...i think he knew by then and the brief conversation we had was the most emotional one i'd ever had with him. i told him i'd do anything i could for him and even though he said he'd call me later on, there was a certain finality that i couldn't ignore; for sure he was calling his friends for the last time...

a lot of you might have had personal encounters with joey over the years so you have an idea of what he was like...even though we didn't hang out regularly, i'd see him fairly often. we talked on the phone a lot and i'd go over to his apartment...any way, he was the absolutely nicest guy i've ever encountered in this insane ego-ridden business, and that's not just a remark. joey was such a real person. maybe if he'd been an aggressive maniac like so many others, the ramones would have gotten their just rewards while he was still with us...

so his passing for me is sad and bitter cause i know in my heart that the ramones were a million times better than so many bands that have had much greater success, bands that all drew ideas from the ramones...

i can only say some cliches. we'll miss him a lot...

"On the Nature of Punk"

by Jessamin Swearingen
(adapted and edited by Allan Metz)

"We Created It: Let's Take It Over"!
web site, 1999-2001

Summing up of the distinction between British and American punk, more specifically rooted in New York City, from where Blondie emerged.—Ed.

Punk, or what became punk rock in Britain, was a product of American sources, with roots varying from Bill Haley and his Comets' first chords of rock music to the self-centered poetry of the Beat Generation's best authors. These cultural artifacts influenced American punk, which in turn influenced Britain's. Punk's impact on America was isolated, but its impact on Britain exemplified rock music's pattern of cultural mimicry. British punk was a recreation of America's best offerings modified to suit British tastes. Punk business man, Malcolm McLaren sensed America's influence on British punk. After the New York Dolls broke up in 1975, McLaren gave Sex Pistols' guitarist, Steve Jones, one of the Dolls' old guitars (Savage, 97-99). McLaren studied rock and its history and knew that rock music thrived on cultural thievery.

Today, nearly twenty-five years after punk's reign on the New York scene, punk is still considered a British creation. It is no surprise that a conflict arises concerning punk's origins. Cultural creations are always being modified, and fickle pop audiences are more likely to grant authenticity to the latest output, rarely seeking out its origin. To add to the confusion, Britain's Sex Pistols and the Clash looked more punk than America's Patti Smith or Television. During Britain's adoption of punk, New York audiences and music critics saw record companies losing interest in American bands. This caused the critics to wonder what was so special about the British. American writer Alan Betrock criticized the rock media's attention for being prone to "malcolmization" (a take-off on Malcolm McLaren's first name), and noted that "New York has been historically maligned." Betrock documented New York's origination of such musical styles as the 1960s girl sound to the City's Greenwich Village folk scene, and pointedly asked why New York did not get credit for the discovery (Betrock, 43, 46). He added that British punk became more popular because the only American group that truly looked punk were the Ramones.

The two versions of punk, the antecedent American and its British descendent, were very different. British punk was aggressive and violent. It demanded immediate change and had no interest in working for the solution. The Sex Pistols typified British punk with songs such as "Anarchy in the UK," which did not give a thought to anarchy's effect. American punk seemed lazy by comparison. It was sarcastic while the English was violent and poetic while the former was illiterate. The American originator offered lessons for the British to copy, and the British pushed one step further, thus gaining more recognition.

Britain's economic climate inspired youth fashion in extremes of image-conscious violence and self-abuse. In her book, *Break All Rules: Punk Rock and the Making of a Style,* Tricia Henry cites Britain's stagnant economy as the reason for punk's success. "Great Britain in 1975 had one of its highest unemployment rates since World War II" (Henry, 68). Punk in Britain was more accurate as a description of the national youth sentiment than it was Stateside. If British punk was confrontational, New York punk seemed almost noncommittal in comparison. British punk overshadowed its New York influences in popularity because bands such as the Sex Pistols and its punk-manifesto approach and subject matter in songs like "God Save The Queen" or "Anarchy in the UK" complimented British aggression.

The hostility stemmed from Britain's social and economic climate and offered little incentive for British youths to peacefully coexist and be optimistic. The war cry of "No future/No future for you" in the song "God Save The Queen" was an apt one, and it seemed, at least momentarily, to apply. The generation of British youths coming of age during punk graduated from high school into a climate of harsh unemployment statistics and little options for upward mobility. This bleak scenario offered little alternative, and punk for the British youth was a way to act out on their feelings of inadequacy. As British teenagers struggled with the demoralizing effects of welfare and unemployment, American youth involved with punk chose the bohemian lifestyle. Economic conditions were not as difficult

55

for the young Americans who formed punk bands. Most of those involved moved to New York City by choice, fashioning themselves as urban expatriates.

Much like the mid-1960s British Invasion, British punk bands borrowed American musical styles and turned their interpretations into cash. Britain reclaimed punk rock much like early British rock bands exported American blues back to American audiences. Recalling the Rolling Stones' effect on her impressionable teenage mind, Patti Smith wrote an article for *Creem* magazine in 1976. In it, she wrote that the Rolling Stones were "five white boys as sexy as any spade." Smith was saying that the Stones made rock music that was as authentic as its original blues inspiration. The bands cited as part of the British Invasion mimicked their early rock influences—black blues musicians—and tried to recreate their rock'n'roll.

Undoubtedly the rock'n'roll era was unstoppable when the British Invasion reached American soil; but if not for American influences, the British Invasion would have been meaningless. With a careful recipe of imitation and freshness, British musicians managed to make American R&B (rhythm and blues) and blues seem like uncharted territory to young American audiences. The same happened with punk. America's influence on British punk was renamed "new wave." As Betrock's article notes, American punk was lost in Britain's shadow. In the rock industry, super stars of lesser stature than Elvis and the Beatles have a quick turnover. Unless their initial popularity is enormous, bands generally fade into the oblivion from which they emerged. Rock audiences are flippant, a buying crowd reluctant to pay attention to anything that does not suit its needs. Pop stars play into the audience's needs in order to survive. Within the rock industry of the mid-1950s, Elvis survived in the industry as a white artist who recorded black-styled rock music. His white skin kept him from alarming the industry, which at the time was catering to white artists.

Arnold Shaw's insightful look into rock's roots is an invaluable account of the musical climate of the 1950s. His book, *The Rockin' 50s: The Decade That Transformed the Pop Music Scene,* shows how rock was manipulated to serve the buyer's or the producer's market. Shaw discusses Elvis's success in terms of practicality. Until 1954, the *Billboard* charts kept black and white musicians separated by two different charts—R&B and pop charts. It was not until 1954 that a black artist had chart success on the pop charts (Shaw, 73-74). Still, by 1955 the established white songwriters who reigned before rock's emergence wanted to keep their whiter "pop" alive (Shaw, 3). Elvis' manipulation of racism, much like Deborah Harry's manipulation of sexism, enabled him to succeed within the industry. Rock, since its birth in the mid-1950s, had set a pattern of borrowing to see how much the borrower could get away with. In this vein, British punk was successful because it was playing on something the British-buying audience needed, while in the case of American punk, American-buying audiences did not understand the new bands or their music. The United States' economy was not at the bottom like England's, which made punk less relevant in the states.

After a pleasant decade of the late-1960s love and happiness, the baby boom generation, the largest record-buying population since rock's inception, was complacent. The consumer audience was getting older and settling into young adulthood. American punk was peaking in 1972, but American pop charts certainly did not reflect the occurrence. According to *Billboard's* Hot 100 Hits, the chart toppers during the early years were not reflections of punk, but reflections of pop, from the 1973 hit "Tie a Yellow Ribbon Round The Ole Oak Tree" by Tony Orlando and Dawn to Barbra Streisand's 1974 movie theme, "The Way We Were." Punk was nowhere to be found on American pop charts, but it was busy repackaging itself for British consumption. Punk's peak occurred during the late Nixon and early Carter years, and the nation seemed to want glossed-over niceness, not aggressive or hard-to-understand music. The 1960s were still alive in the consumer's imagination, and punk was not yet part of the picture. In *Rock Eras: Interpretations of Music & Society, 1954-1984,* Jim Curtis defines a generation that came of age during the Nixon era—kids who grew up with Nixon as their "father figure." If the 1960s was this generation's childhood, then punk was its late adolescence, and a new generation of music fans was coming of age. Curtis explains that, "Only when Nixon resigned were the sixties finally over" (Curtis, 296). Nixon resigned on August 9, 1974, five months before Patti Smith became the first American punk act to get signed. By the time record companies were signing bands, the main surge of punk was over in America. And if one were to believe Curtis' time line, punk was lost in a shuffle between one decade and the next.

Punk may have been lost in time, but it created a music and style that was a new aesthetic, and it meant that one did not have to be a hippie or a genius musician to be in a rock band. The extended guitar solos of 1960s rock staples became passe; punk was about simplicity. Anyone could be in a punk band; it was a do-it-yourself, all-invited occasion, and the results were inspiring. Bands came out of the woodwork to stake their claim on the new music. The idea took off and eventually moved to England but failed to sell records stateside. The American version of punk rock was forgotten while the British turned theirs into a household name.

Because of its style, punk fit more comfortably in British music and fashion than in New York's. A punk used to be a hoodlum, and New York punk was too weird to be purely street-tough-enough to be "punk." The New Yorkers were either flamboyant and campy or too overtly intellectualized and dreamy. American bands like the Velvet Underground and the New York Dolls maintained a street edge, but their versions of the rock and street aesthetic never became as popular as British punk. No matter how hard-hitting the New York message was, the British made it even more obvious. If Lou Reed's poetic slurs brought the ideas of desperate nihilism to the surface, British bands such as the Sex Pistols brought the message home. With his band the Velvet Underground, Reed wove tales of modern depravity. His songs were full of people trapped by the temptations of the city's streets or their own desires. Speaking to and from the perspective of drug addicts and transsexuals, his subject matter confronted alienation but wrapped it in the modern cloth of rock music. British punk took it one step further. Instead of New York Doll David Johansen's tight narratives about having a "Personality Crisis," such British punks as the Sex Pistols screamed about there being "No Future." The New York Dolls' "Personality Crisis" is deliberately tongue-in-cheek, whereas the Sex Pistol's lyrics are abrasive.

Back in the States, the pop charts were a reflection of America's disenchantment with punk. The examples of number-one hits during punk's early years show a country wanting to be comforted. The late 1960s put the buying market in the mindset of the Beatles' "All You Need Is Love." Why create tension with lyrics about "Heroin" or a "Personality Crisis" when you could avoid reality with "Tie A Yellow Ribbon Round The Ole Oak Tree?" Britain's success with punk, as opposed to America's comparative failure, acted itself out like sibling rivalry; the younger one trying to outdo the older one, capitalizing on the elder's accomplishments for the younger's success. British punk took the most obvious aspects of New York City punk—fashion, simplicity, and rebellion—to build its own monster. The younger British punk gained more media attention because its message was the most blatant. British bands flaunted their aggression with names such as the Sex Pistols and the Clash. They borrowed the rumpled-hoodlum look from Television's Richard Hell, and they didn't give the New Yorkers credit. During New York punk's peak, Malcolm McLaren recognized America's punk potential and tried to convince members of collapsed New York punk bands to migrate to England. McLaren knew he could turn punk rock into a viable commodity that would speak to British youth. He admired the urban fallout-shelter atmosphere of the New York Dolls and Richard Hell, and knew he could package their aesthetic into a more obvious and accessible product. Because of his keen observations, British punk and its fashion played into British emotional and economic exile, eventually emerging out of McLaren's clothing shops. He and partner Vivien Westwood created visually confrontational wardrobes to suit the modern nihilist. Because of McLaren and Westwood's fashion instincts, when people think of punk, their images are inspired by McLaren's clothing and shops. His and Westwood's talent for accessorizing fetishes made punk style more memorable. While New Yorkers favored a toned down, bohemian-jeans-and-ripped t-shirt look, the British went all out. Meticulously ripped clothing held together with safety pins and dotted with intentional cigarette burns were topped with cropped and dyed vertical hair. British punk fashion embodied the extreme, not the casual or poetic, like the wanderings of their New York influences.

New York punk was an era of music that for lack of a better term is now called *punk*. In Alan Betrock's 1977 *New York Rocker* article, most of the American bands were calling themselves "new wave," and leaving punk to the British. New wave was a less severe and more artistic version of the same idea, and stylistically it could more easily encompass the differences between the New York bands. Britain's success with popularizing punk came from the consistency of its musical and visual output; years of redundant offerings eventually hit home. Names like the Clash, the Damned, and the Sex Pistols finally registered with their audience, and British bands developed a uniform fashion code of belligerence. New York's punk was not as easy to categorize; its scene revolved around an eclectic melting pot of influences. Whereas British punk meant aggression and immediacy, its New York antecedents combined aspects of aggression and immediacy with everything from bubblegum pop records to French bohemian poets (Savage, 86). New Yorkers were not dressing to shock; their aesthetic was strictly come-as-you-are, which for Manhattan's glamor and intrigue was statement enough.

New York City punk set the standard for punk fashion and musical style. Although expanded and manipulated to suit Britain's cultural fads, it still remains relatively unique within the boundaries of pop's homogeneous leanings. Punk music, whether British or American, was not as safe as pop, but it exemplified rock's pattern of borrowing and reclaiming. Rock music originally was about youth and creation and began as a separation from the status quo. Punk, either the American original or its British offspring, continued the trend.

Blondie and Punk

"Blondie, Punk and All the Other Stuff"

or

(If I Had Been a Better Drummer, Clem Would Be Unemployed)

by Robert Betts

This original article was extracted and adapted from The Blondie Review, *Volume 2, Issue 1, December, 2001.*—Ed.

Punk (pungk) slang, n. 2. A young hoodlum or tough. A young thug. Youth, usually associated with wild or careless behavior. Displaying a seemingly bitter personality toward the establishment. Antagonistic toward social or cultural standards. Sincere or staged antiestablishment attitude, actions, or demeanor. Of, or relating to, being or acting purposely bizarre.—*Webster's Collegiate Dictionary, Yale-Literary Edition, (Yale/Buckley, New Haven, Connecticut) 1963.*

I went to the "vault" purposely (just) to retrieve a pre-punk rock dictionary. I wanted to see what the definition was prior to the existence and subsequent influence of lower Manhattan's new music. My suspicions were confirmed; the definition applies.—Ed.

I was one. Or, at least, that's what I wanted everyone who saw me to think. But, at the time, I was never quite clear on the whole punk thing. Was I supposed to really live it? Or was it just an attitude—a social expression describing contemporary feelings in a traditional culture? And why just music...and clothing? Why not speeches in the park? If they (we) were so serious about it there would be some kind of social movement—upheaval. But there really wasn't. It was just music and clothes...and, of course, attitude. That really seemed to be the prime ingredient—attitude. Anyhow, here's my story, to the best of my recollection...

IN THE BEGINNING

From Beat to Grease

I was a teenager when the beatniks settled into Greenwich Village coffeehouses and recited what we thought was deep and probing poetry describing all form and manner of the failing, futile social and governmental systems. That peaked, ran its course, and declined almost as quickly as the caffeine buzz that originally sustained it. William S. Burroughs, Gregory Corso, Allen Ginsberg and all the contemptible contemporaries remained as significant notables, but for the most part, had faded from the underground prominence as the baby boomers began to realize that our (world's) socioeconomic system was way off kilter. Now it was the early 70s and the war children were starting to figure things out—this now, was all different. The punk movement was how they handled the situation. It was a reaction, plain and simple—they were reactionaries. This punk thing had substance. It was very real. The kids believed in it and it was going somewhere. It had direction...well, sort of; we just were not too sure which direction. In those days, I would dutifully report to the Bowery, Lower East Side, and East Village, anywhere in lower Manhattan, in full uniform. I say uniform because, by definition, that is exactly what it was. Many of us 20-somethings wore the costume de facto of the neo-greaser—the quasi-biker look: black leather motorcycle jacket over a white t-shirt, jeans and engineer boots. In retrospect, we were almost cookie-cutter punks—except for our hairdos, the only real vestige of individuality, we were clones. Strangely, there seemed to be this kind of late-50s retro feeling in the air. It was, if nothing else, an airing out for our souls. The irony of it all was that in our efforts to display our rebellious attitudes we were, in fact, conforming, at least within and amongst our own circle.

Dress Up and Dance

At the other end of town, I should say, uptown, the guys were dressing up in flashy polyester leisure suits and the girls in ballroom dance dresses and patent leather shoes. With the wisdom that can only come from prejudiced idealism, we noted the lemming-like attraction this electro-techno predictable, formula music had upon the scrubbed, shaved and pressed unthinking masses. They called it disco and it was catching on—big time. This disco stuff combined Latin rhythms with funk, a soulful earthy down-home blues, and produced a strong, driving, steady, unnatural techno beat that was a natural for the dance floor—the discotheques. Disco returned dancing to the people along with the spirit, fun, excitement and sexuality of popular music.

Our punk music was, in part, a backlash against the glitz and glam of the sequins, light shows and superficial polish of the preformulated electronic drumbeat, say nothing, do nothing, so-called music. There was no statement, we thought. In retrospect, I must admit that I was enamored with all the gorgeous "chickies." In some kind of grand, delusional, but magnificent accident, this social twist managed to effect a complete social turnaround...overnight. No longer were the kids of the hippie generation wandering about the parks and streets of New York in army fatigues and combat boots. The men shaved, got haircuts and donned stylish, albeit often garish, clean, pressed suits. With their impeccable dressings and adornments, they resembled escorts at a fashionable Hollywood awards show. In contrast to their earlier olive drab canvas coverings, the girls became women, in the Victorian sense, gorgeous, cosmopolitan fashion creatures. True eye candy. When we scanned the field of polyester and flesh, it was always the next one being more desirable than the last. Soft flowing hair and outfits that tightly fit all the right contours and revealed enough skin to be daring, but not slutty...just a little naughty.

You Angry Punks!

The punk movement was a reaction to all of this predictable, mindless nonsense. This was not the place for black artists to get recognized just because they dressed well and looked good like Earth, Wind and Fire, Chic, Donna Summer and Gloria Gaynor. This was not the place for the gay community to gain social acceptance just because they presented a harmless, fun, and at times, cute persona a la The Village People. That's what we told everyone who'd ask. We were thinkers. We had comments to share on politics and society. We wanted to express our feelings, emotions and desires. We were going to do all that through our music.

And we did do that through our music. The "we" being all the like-minded punks and punkettes. Our punk rock reaction of the mid-1970s was a strategy, or at least a tactic, to launch a rock revolution. Even British bands such as the Sex Pistols and the Clash brought a new raw energy to rock. It was not unlike the drive of acid rock and other "head music" from a decade before. The punks were fueled by an anger of the materialism in our society and the lack of inspiration in early 1970s "la-la" pop music. Punk wasn't a big commercial success, but it had a great impact on rock music. It demonstrated that new styles could still develop outside of the established rock industry. It showed that young musicians, with new and creative ideas, could express themselves without formal music schooling, expensive equipment and years of practice. The acceptance and success of punk convinced many established non-punk musicians to make their music more direct, more energetic, beatier, faster, and more distinct.

A New Wave Rolls In

New York City bands such as Blondie, the Talking Heads and the Patti Smith Group took a more methodical and artistically deeper approach to punk rock. Their music was more lyrical, poetic and original in concept than the existing punk rock. These stylized groups became punk's new wave of rock. We called it *new wave,* but it was still punk—just a little more Republican. The music of punk and new wave bands represented a live, driven and aggressive alternative to the established musicians who dominated the rock industry, its economy, and in general, the record industry's almighty dollars. It may be argued that new wave legitimized punk, if in name only. As a more middle of the road presentation, that's understandable. Naturally, anyone who first heard the name of this new music, *punk,* knew right away that it had to be bad. The term *new wave* sounds kind of cute, at least less threatening, more benign. According to record sales of the period, there was no argument: new wave outsold punk many times over. It didn't carry the baggage of bad boys and girls rebelling against the norms of the day. In fact, not many civilians, particularly the moms and dads of the mid-1970s, had a clue as to just what this new wave stuff was all about. It is suspicious that parental cognizance even acknowledged it at all. Once again, youth outmaneuvered the old folks. Ha!

From the Bowery to Studio 54

We all agreed that disco and punk were social and artistic opposites. But, in music, the unlikely often happens—and it did. They came together in the late 1970s. Blondie enjoyed hits that combined disco rhythms with the spirit of new wave rock. Was it a stretch? Well, one is given pause to ponder that amalgamation. It would seem that Blondie purposely softened punk into new wave so that it would become the ambassador between the warring factions of punk and disco. Personally, and with all due respect to discoers everywhere, I see it as an easy "step-down" transition for Blondie. The anatomy of disco is basically "high-melody, la-la" vocals with fair to nothingness meaning and predictable, clocklike syncopation. But, what's wrong with that? It served its purpose—it was "fun dance music"...no more, no less. Regardless of the merits, Blondie jumped in with both feet and took it to the top. The downtown to uptown transition was complete. "Heart of Glass" is just one, albeit the biggest, of the Blondie contributions to fluffy hair and big shiny belt buckles.

Harlem Meets the Lower East Side

Another diametrically opposed entertainment style crept in with the stealth and cunning of a drunken hippo. This wasn't like the 1960s acapella doo-wop, a marriage of rhythm and blues and race music sung by Italian Romeo-types and Negro harmonizers, performed on the stoops of Brooklyn brownstones. Nor was it the intricate, tangled melodies and rhythms of the ad hoc progressive jazz ensembles found in every uptown park on every sunny Sunday. No. This was a more raw, straight from the ghetto, street manifestation. This was new, bold and in-your-face expressionism. This one in particular was an especially, culturally significant, down-in-the-street, art form that plundered its way to the top with the grace and elegance of a train wreck. It was the raw, inner-city sounds of rap music. The black kids of the ghetto slammed and breakdanced their way into notoriety. So did Blondie. Once again Debbie and the boys threw caution to the wind and just did it! They cross-cultured themselves into a world of racial specificity. Unified ethnic acceptance seemed unlikely. But then, we under-estimated Blondie! The short story is that "Rapture" enjoyed the ultimate crossover status, the sharing of the black and white pop experience—highly unlikely, but very, very successfully. "Rapture" opened the door to the guarded, but seething, underground ghetto music and made it legitimate for airplay on top 40 radio stations. Like it or not, now the masses were going to hear this new "word-rhyme music" expressing the anger and discontent of the inner city. Blondie and "Rapture" were putting rap music right in the public's face—it was turned loose on the world! Although somewhat commercialized, "Rapture" demonstrated Blondie's apathy toward social angst amongst young black and white musicians in a time when all of America was painfully aware of the tensions in the racial divide. It was perfectly shown that when mellow, but poignant ghetto rhythms of Harlem from the likes of Fab Five Freddie can combine with the hot and cold intensity of the angry, white youth of the Bowery, then all is right in mainstream eyes. It sometimes takes a war, but human nature always finds a way. Knowing the black street music ethic as well as the white punk revolution, it was nothing short of an epiphany when I first heard "Rapture" and saw the video! This was highly unlikely—nay, impossible. But it did happen. Debbie and the boys pulled it off.

Dreadlocks and Rhythms

We had all heard the so-called "island music." I don't have to go into the details of its foreign feeling to our "must be invented here" American music ethic and its alien standing in the modern, popular music of the early 1980's. We all knew that no one in America listened to this music, "...hey, what is that? Calypso? Where is that stuff from, Jamaica?" "Bermuda?" Well, Blondie did. And for the third time they jumped off the deep end without fear—without looking. Born was "Island Of Lost Souls." I have no idea what inspired them to do it except for their ever present experimental attitudes. After seeing the video, I couldn't be sure if it was a genuine foray into that genre or a spoof of the requisite "happiness" that accompanies the land of splief stereotypes. Whatever it was, it worked. Blondie pulled it off smooth and easy. And why not? After all, "Island" is a fun song.

All Bases Covered

Songs like "Rapture," "Heart Of Glass," "One Way Or Another," "Sunday Girl," "Island Of Lost Souls" and several others somehow managed to weave the styles of rap, disco, pop, island, and rock in general, into the socially acceptable top 40. This was nothing short of genius! "HOG" became a standard at discotheques. "OWOA" was played ad nauseam on middle-of-the-road FM radio stations. "IOLS" brought all of America closer to tropical musical influence and its easy-listening, fun melodies. And "Rapture" told white America that a musical subculture was sprouting up all over the cities like weeds from those very same sidewalk cracks.

TODAY'S REALITY

Death, Diversion and Division

I won't go into the issues of the socioeccentric, sociopathic behavior of the holier-than-thou ego-gods who landlorded disco. And I won't comment on the blatant stupidity of such self-involved habits as tax evasion and self-effacing drug use and trafficking practiced daily by disco's paternal faction. Those stories have all been told. Suffice to say, disco died a slow and unceremonious death, plain and simple. Like any majestic beast, it ruled supreme throughout its prime years—the *Tyrannosaurus rex* of socialized music. After it peaked, it immediately became ill—seriously, terminally ill. It then lingered in a long, slow, deep, dark vortex while its flesh rotted on the very skeleton that once supported its mighty presence. Studio 54, leisure suits and lighted glass dance floors drifted out to sea toward the horizon. The vision remained in sight, but its image was shrinking, fading. It was all so self-agonizing. Sad, really. The empires of high fashion, pride in appearance, along with precise, fluid dance execution, designer drugs, overpriced alcohol and obsessive narcissism were rapidly turning to a grungy, pathetic existence of depravity, debauchery and decadence. The expensive overcut cocaine was quickly replaced by street-level heroin, special K, Ecstasy, barbiturates and methamphetamine. The top-shelf scotch and bourbon from the elegant, mirrored bars became cheap wine and vodka from the corner discount store. It took a long time, but by the early 1990s disco as a lifestyle had decomposed to dust. All that was left to do was to shovel the fallen dirty remains from the gutters in front of the once elegant and fashionable fantasy lands back onto, what is now, the graves of the self-shattered.

Islands in the Skyscrapers

Island music is stronger today in mainstream music than it was when the fifth generation of Blondie laid down those happy, "la-la" rhythms of "Island Of Lost Souls." It has many descendants, stylizations and names. It laterally transposed to reggae and ska. It has even managed to imbed itself into Latin and soul music. It has seldom peaked on the commercial top 40 charts, but it never especially waned in record sales either—it just seems to always "be" there. Blondie demonstrated to the world, with "Island" that a handful of punks from the island of Manhattan can make successful island music.

Out In The Streets

Rap is going to be here for a while. Since the early 1980s it has done nothing but grow taller and expand sideways. Here too, stylizations have branched out to cover the whole spectrum from the crude and raw to the (quasi-) melodic and sensitive. It can be brutally angry or sweetly romantic, but always finds its target audience. Rap is pretty much devoid of melody. Some may question the validity of calling this stuff legitimate music if it has no tune, no melody. It can't be hummed or whistled. You can't play it on a lead guitar or keyboard. Can pseudo-harmony and raw driving rhythm be music? It would seem that is the case. Rap's demographics are primarily young and middle-aged black and Latino of both sexes with a fairly healthy percentage of young white males thrown in for balance, albeit, I believe, mostly for their own vicarious reasons. Regardless, it's going to be with us for a while...and our first commercially successful taste of it came in the form of "Rapture."

No Debbie At CBGB

　　We hit all the "in" punk places of SOHO, NOHO, and the East Village back in the days of sociocultural confusion and our population's lobotomy-like political, social and economic disorientation. That's when we self-medicated to become mindless and happy—that's when disco reined supreme...one of the medications. I was mostly a "weekender," having maintained enough cognitive brain power to appreciate the capital advantages of my day job. I always felt bad about missing something on the weeknights. But, there was still plenty to do and see and talk about on those occasional weeknights. Certainly, we made up for lost time every weekend. There were always the likes of Max's Kansas City, the Mudd Club, Mercer Arts Center and every little dive over on First Avenue, Avenue A, the Bowery, up at St. Marks Place, all around Tompkins Square Park and everywhere else on the lower East Side. But we always gravitated back to CBGB's—this year-old club seemed like home to us. There was always some kind of crowd outside those doors. Sometimes sparse, sometimes large, but always someone to "hang" with. That's what made the place so warm, comfortable and friendly. We felt safe and secure there among our own kind. I'm willing to bet that I bumped into some pretty famous people back then, a quarter of a century ago. But then again, I bumped into a lot of people back then. None were famous at that time—a good excuse to not remember most of them. Most were young. All were punks, with the exception of the occasional tourist. Chances are very good that I shared a beer or cigarette, or certainly some casual philosophical words with the likes of Iggy Pop, Johnny Thunders, Richard Hell, Tish and/or Snooky Bellomo, Elda Gentile, Amanda Jones, Rosie Ross, Billy O'Conner, Fred Smith, Jackie, Julie or possibly someone from Television, Dictators, Agnostic Front, Shirts, Dead Boys, Patti Smith Group, New York Dolls, Heartbreakers, Talking Heads, Ramones and, yes, Blondie...maybe—just maybe. I don't know that for sure, but chances are very good that happened—likely, many times. Usually, the names and faces lasted only as long as the beers and the cigarettes. There were just so many—a bunch of kids hanging out, much too many to remember. There were few events monumental enough to create a significant synapse memory. It was just night after night, month after month of the same thing: lots of talking, commiserating, and very loud music. Lots of beer, lots of cigarettes. It was all so social; we would hang out front in the afternoon then attend the shows all night—so much fun...just fun, fun, fun. I do remember the names of the Ramones, Television, Patti Smith, I think, and some others. But there were lots of bands, lots of people, lots and lots of party fun. So much going on that much of it is just a blur now. But...the one thing I'm clear on is that I really missed the boat—big time. I never saw Debbie. It was in the late summer of 1974 and beginning to sink into my naïve, idealistic brain that maybe I really didn't belong here anymore—maybe it wasn't meant to be. I had an established career on the other side of the microphone, designing all the same kind of audio equipment that cluttered the stage of CBGBs. Engineering was a good, solid and respected career. The job paid well and now I had a house in the woods of neighboring Connecticut to attend to. The responsibilities of domestication were nipping at my heals. The clock was beating against my heart's desires—my dreams. It was almost the middle of the decade and time for me to make some serious decisions...about my career—my life. I had to be practical and think with my head—it was time to move on. It was a great ride. I'd do it all again—exactly the same...but, now it was over. I left there. Oh, sure, there were casual return trips where I felt more like a tourist than part of the crowd, but for the most part, the ride was over for me. So, I can honestly say, I never saw Debbie. I'd know if I did, but I'm sure I never did. I may have heard of the band "Blondie," but don't remember the name Debbie Harry. She would not have been one of the monofaced ships that passed in the Manhattan night like all the others. I would have felt then, as I do now, about that face. I would have remembered that. I can categorically state that I never saw Debbie there. So I guess that means I never saw "Blondie" or the "Stilettos" or "Angel and the Snake" or "The Banzai Babies" either. Even in the crowd hanging outside 315 Bowery, I never saw her. Chris, Clem, Jimmy, Frank, Nigel, Gary, maybe...who would have known who they were back then, but Debbie, no. I just know I never saw Debbie...that's a shame. I just dropped out too early—probably, only a month or two too early...but, I digress.

　　Anyhow, my point is that the whole place, if not just CBGBs, certainly the neighborhood, was an interesting focal point. I might call it, "an island of lost (punk) souls." It seemed like an endless stream of leather jackets, chrome epaulette chains and cute miniskirted chickie-punkettes that paraded through the door of that club. Most of the guys seemed to be straight from the wardrobe room of a motorcycle B movie. Few others appeared as early British Invasion leftovers from a decade before with tight tapered pants and pointy toed, high heeled, half boots all in the requisite "everything-all-black" style. The "babes" always looked squeezable. Half of them appeared in heavy eye and face makeup and go-go boots. The other half in t-shirts and tight jeans as nitty-gritty street smart hoodlumettes. Regardless of their coverings, they all looked gorgeous and desirable. Simply stated, the dress code, if there really was one, would be those basic themes. My casual attire was leather and denim—beaten, raggedy, weathered and chrome adorned—formal dress was pegged pants, sport jacket, skinny tie—all black. Pictures of early Blondie, with the "guys" in their black suits, bring back memories to me that transcend any form of description—kind of a retro deja vu. It's a bittersweet memory, the kind that pulls your heart deeper into your chest. I see pictures of the boys during the *Parallel Lines, Plastic Letters, Autoamerican* and self-titled period...and I see a mirror.

CONCLUDING PERSONAL THOUGHTS

There are hundreds of potential memories from back then, but really nothing monumentally memorable. Just a few names, a few faces and a few recollections to cherish as the years go by. It really was the definitive bittersweet time. There was a lot of good conversation, but little wisdom gained, no money, but good friends; no jobs, but lots of talent; no activity, but lots of time; no firm prospects, but faith and hope; nothing to celebrate, but good times had by good companions.

If I paint a dark picture, forgive me. That's not my intention. We had fun...lots of it. It's just that the specter of being in "the underground" and its associated stigma to the general populace is, most often, depressing to me. That term, *underground,* seems to define a lack of talent or a reason to not be taken seriously. But, that is not true! Many famous entertainers around today came from some sort of underground. Here I am, 25 years later and it's obvious that it's truer now than ever before. I recently attended a benefit party in New York City designed to dispel that very thing. Romy Ashby, a songwriter and collaborator on Blondie's *No Exit* album along with coauthor and publisher Foxy Kidd held the affair. Several, so-called underground artists were being honored at the party just as they were in Romy and Foxy's publication, *Goodie Magazine*. I can report that there is talent that, for whatever reason, hasn't gotten the breaks and recognition it takes to "make it." If you aren't already aware of it, I must tell you that, "The economics of capitalism does influence our artistic opportunities and can certainly suppress those very same freedoms." What a waste. And therein lies the reality of the entire situation. That's how it was on the Bowery back then—it's really no different today.

Having said all that, I often wonder what the percentages are...what the odds were for success. How many other Blondie-type bands could there have been? Not necessarily just like Blondie per se, but the break-through, girl-lead, modern rock band. And how about the Ramones, the pioneer-types that literally broke ground for those that followed? How many upstart musicians gave up just scant days before the first big break was about to come? I wonder. Back then, I walked the streets of lower Manhattan with a pair of Gene Krupa model drumsticks in my back pocket, sat in on many jams, did relief sets and talked nicely to any of the older people who didn't seem to fit in, in hopes of their being a talent scout for some big record label or maybe a magazine writer with some credibility or even a hungry agent or manager. Oh well, like I said, "I wonder what the odds were."

THERE REALLY IS NO EXIT

Blondes Have More Fun

But Blondie persevered. Man, did they ever! Their struggle must have been tremendously torturous at times. Gratifying at other times, I'm sure. The other bands either died on the vine or went on to some level of success from barely passing to moderately significant accomplishment. Many of the groups split up and the fallout produced still other bands that either made it or didn't. A few groups produced the underlyings of things to come. The Ramones is such a group. Never achieving the fame and fortune due their insight and talent, they smoothed the path to the future for countless others.

Throughout its six generations, Blondie has collectively been a mixed-fusion presentation of the best of the best. The individual talents are just the tip of the whole. Arrangements, stage presence, musical direction and harmonious musical unity have dictated this band's survival and success in four decades of trials, tests and tribulations. They have never been afraid to be different. They've always taken chances—most uncalculated. They have risen where others have fallen. Most importantly, they represent the maternal and paternal roots of a musical faction that they wouldn't let fade away. They raised and nurtured a piece of musical history that is now so broad and diverse as the ancestral house it was born in—rock and roll. That very important little slice of rock's heritage is now a quarter-century old, has performed and entertained since the 70s, and is still going strong in a new millennium. How presumptuous are these punks to claim such credentials!

The Boys in the Band

There have been many. A complete genealogy and chronology appeared in an early issue of *The Blondie Review*, [*and also in this book*—Ed.] but the "core-four," have a certain collective air about them. It's almost as though one feeds the other, in a most vital way. Individually, they are talents in the superlative. Together, they define a synergy of a greater magnitude. Chris Stein, Jimmy Destri and Clem Burke *are* "the boys in the band." Yes, there have been others, all talents in their own right—the current reunion lineup with Leigh Foxx and Paul Carbonara added, probably, being the best musical collection ever. But the core-four, three guys and a girl, are the quarter-century Blondie that I know...and love.

THE QUEEN OF PUNK

Peroxide for Breakfast

Deborah Harry opened the doors for female front persons. No longer did the "girl in the band" have to be relegated to back-up harmonies or used as a miniskirted, go-go showpiece. Gone was the stereotypical, sweetheart, good, wholesome, girl-next-door, Annette Funicello, Leslie Gore and Shelley Fabares stigma. No longer did they have to look sweet like apple pie and behave as Catholic schoolgirls. Now they could front the band, express their feelings and project the emotions of the material they performed. Deborah Harry did that in a way no female ever did it before—ever! Her trailblazing thereafter left a path for others to follow. From the soft, sultry, alluring and beckoning sweetheart who breathed "Sound Asleep" to the vicious, ferocious and nasty street corner punk who stylized "Rip Her To Shreds" and "Victor" and to everything else in between, she delivered the feeling and emotion of the song. Her chameleon capabilities are beyond belief. Every three minutes, after each song's end, she's somebody different—someone else in a different place. She puts all of her resources together in such a synergistic fashion that the product never fails to amaze and delight her audience.

It's All in the Rinse

Yes, she's a part of the band, but like a batter is part of a baseball team, she's pretty much on her own out there at home plate in the heat of the spotlight and the audience's unforgiving eyes. Yes, she's a part of the team, but the term, *front person,* carries a heavy burden. Her tools are her clothes, expressive movements, makeup, overacted facial expressions, self-styled footwork, critically timed hair waving, stylized arm and hand gestures and, of course, her face—that face! She choreographs all those assets into an unmistakable, single, harmonious vision. Her voice can be ethereal, melodic, sweet, angry, guttural, romantic or demanding. She can be sweetly melodic, get-up-and-dance rhythmic, sing-along lyrical or depressingly...pathetically blue. That voice could lullaby a rabid dog into the arms of Morpheus or force a thug to find religion. Her stylizations satisfy and complement rock, punk, ballad, rap, reggae, disco, torch, pop, bubblegum, jazz, doo-wop, blues and just about any other musical genre she's tackled. She's sung all over this globe—solo, guest and with several other groups. She's acted from Broadway to Hollywood and in between on stage, screen and television. Her sensitivities run the spectrum from reading poetry to wrestling. She is brave, bold and courageous. No new project is beyond her ambition or daring. There is no genteel trepidation—she rushes in with blind leaps of confidence and assurance. She is sociable. She is "street people" and always has time for her subjects. She handles the throngs of fans, whether polite and devoted or rude and unruly, with the grace and dignity of royalty. She's been the pioneer, from her rough and raw "Bowery punkette" beginnings to a polished and refined cosmopolitan debutante, and throughout it all she has remained the reining queen. She is a breed apart—timeless, omnitalented, divinely beautiful and a one-in-forever—*she is our Deborah Harry...*

...supremo bella femmina cantante!

"Ripped To Shreds"

by Russell White

Original unedited version of published article entitled "Going Blonde at CBGBs," Total Guitar, April 1999.—Ed.

With Blondie's return to live performance and the forthcoming release of "No Exit", their first new material since 1982's "The Hunter", Russell White assesses the recording career of the most successful band of the American new wave.

In today's pop marketplace, where nostalgic reunions are increasingly commonplace, the return of Blondie is as welcome as any. Although prime movers on the new wave scene of the mid to late seventies and early eighties, Blondie's music is extraordinarily diverse, and defies attempts at rigid classification. Over the course of an eight year career, the group's "power pop" sound combined punk, surf music, disco, reggae and rap. Yet in America at least, Blondie were stigmatised by the punk tag, and were largely rejected by the mainstream music industry. As Jon Savage notes in *England's Dreaming*, although Blondie "were playing what they thought was pop, it was a long way from the industry expectation". Blondie's punk pedigree had been established by their links to New York venues such as Max's Kansas City, the Mercer Arts Center and most famously the CBGB OMFUG club (the acronym stands for Country, Blue Grass and Blues, and Other Music For Urban Gourmets). CBGB's formed a focal point for the new wave scene.

In Britain, the combination of tuneful pop songs and Debbie Harry's glamorous image proved a potent commercial combination. The group's five U.K. number ones ("Heart of Glass", "Sunday Girl", "Atomic", "Call Me" and "The Tide is High"), together with a string of top twenty hits, represents a level of success which was unmatched by Blondie's new wave contemporaries: The Ramones, Talking Heads, The Patti Smith Group and Television. The group formed in 1974 when former Playboy bunny Debbie Harry met art student and guitarist Chris Stein after Stein had seen Harry perform in the Stilettoes, a theatrical girl group whose Supremes meet the Shangri-Las sound reflected their sixties girl group influences. Stein joined the Stilettoes as part of the backing band, but by August 1974 internal disagreements caused the group to split. Harry and Stein left with the Stilettoes' rhythm section of Fred Smith (bass) and Billy O'Connor (drums) to form Angel and the Snake, supplementing their sound with two backing singers.

After several months playing the New York club circuit, the group changed their name first to Blondie and the Banzai Babies and then to Blondie. By May 1975 O'Connor had left to pursue a career in medicine, and had been replaced by Clem Burke, while Smith had left to replace Richard Hell in Television. Smith's departure had a profound effect on both Harry and Stein who felt that this was part of a wider conspiracy against Blondie on the CBGB's scene. As Harry noted: "we were struck dumb by the whole thing, by the whole movement against us. I may be paranoid but I think that whole clique wanted to destroy us". Avoiding the overt intellectual and artistic pretensions of Television and the Patti Smith Group, many in the CBGB scene shunned them. Yet as Burke told the *Guardian*'s Paul Burston in a recent interview [*see pp. 208-212—Ed.*], Blondie had consciously based their aesthetic on the combination of art and commerce. Drawing an analogy between Blondie's music and Warhol's art, Burke says: "We wanted to reach as many people as possible. That's why Warhol made paintings of brillo boxes and Campbell's soup cans, because everyone could relate to that".

Galvanised by Burke's faith in the band's abilities, Blondie regrouped after a period of introspection, recruiting bass player Gary Valentine in July 1975 and keyboard player Jimmy Destri in February 1976. This line up, Harry (vocals), Stein (guitar), Burke (drums), Destri (keyboards) and Valentine (bass) would record the group's eponymously titled debut album with Private Stock Records. Produced by Richard Gottehrer, "Blondie" was recorded at the Plaza Sound Studio and Radio City Music Hall during August and September of 1976.

Blondie's first album highlighted the band's ongoing obsession with popular culture and a kitsch aesthetic that Mary Harron saw as central to the scene. For Harron, "[Punk] was about saying yes to the modern world.

[...] Like Warhol, [punk] embraced everything that cultured people, and hippies, detested: plastic, junk-food, B-movies, advertising, making money—although no one ever did. You got so sick of people being so nice, mouthing an enforced attitude of goodness and health. Punk was liberating and new: the idea of smoking sixty cigarettes a day and staying up all night on speed". Blondie embraced kitsch trashiness on such tracks as "Kung Fu Girls", "A Shark in Jet's Clothing" and "The Attack of the Giant Ants", all of which sound like the titles of sensationalist B-movies.

By October 1977, Blondie had moved to Chrysalis records with whom they recorded their follow up album, "Plastic Letters", again with Gottehrer producing. The band's relationship with Valentine had deteriorated to the extent that he left the band before recording began. However, his legacy to the band, "(I'm Always Touched By Your) Presence Dear", was the album's best track. A much darker affair than their debut, "Plastic Letters", retained elements of the sugary girl group sound of the band's past, most obviously in "Denis", a cover of a fifteen year old hit by Randy and the Rainbows.

In 1978 Blondie began work on their third and most successful album "Parallel Lines". Produced by Mike Chapman, an Australian who had worked with, among others, Suzi Quatro and Mud, the album featured Valentine's replacement Nigel Harrison and rhythm guitarist Frank Infante who had been playing with the band since July of 1977 but had not played on "Plastic Letters". Sharing the songwriting duties amongst all six band members, "Parallel Lines" hinted at the diversity that would be cemented on later albums. The album yielded four hits, "Picture This", "Hanging on the Telephone" originally recorded by Californian band The Nerves, "Heart of Glass" and "Sunday Girl". Although "Sunday Girl" provided the band with their first U.K. number one, it is the disco inflected "Heart of Glass" which is most memorable, finally breaking the band into the American market.

Their fourth album "Eat to the Beat" was recorded in 1979 with Mike Chapman again producing. Although not as consistent as "Parallel Lines", "Eat to the Beat" nonetheless yielded another three hit singles, "Dreaming", "Union City Blue" and "Atomic". In between "Eat to the Beat" and the band's next album "Autoamerican", Blondie recorded the Giorgio Moroder penned "Call Me", a track written for the film "American Gigolo". The single would provide their fourth U.K. number one. After contemplating asking Moroder to produce their next album, the band again hired Mike Chapman. Recorded in 1980, "Autoamerican" is arguably their most ambitious project. In an era in which the mixing and matching of genres is an entrenched formula, Blondie's flirtation with [Ennio] Morricone inspired Spaghetti Western soundtracks on "Europa", reggae on "The Tide is High", originally recorded by The Paragons and rap on "Rapture" was a daring move. Unfortunately, the same cannot be said of the band's final album, "The Hunter". Critically derided at the time, the song "Island of Lost Souls" would be Blondie's final hit single.

Internal strife had by now afflicted the band. Chris Stein had fallen ill with a rare skin disease Pemphigus Vulgaris, while Frank Infante sued the band on the grounds that he had been excluded from group activities and, specifically, the decision to dissolve the group. The group finally went their separate ways in 1982. Harry pursued a moderately successful solo career and continued to collaborate with Stein, whilst the rest of the members found employment with other groups. Ultimately Blondie will be remembered as the most successful American export of the 1970s. A great singles band, Blondie were never punk rock; they were the perfect epitome of punk as pop.

"'Must Be Into the Shangri-Las...'"

by Gary Valentine

Mojo magazine, February 1999

Gary Valentine, former Blondie bassist from 1975 to 1977, recalls the band's early days.—Ed.

Fashion victim. Barely house-trained. Partial to jailbait. No bass-playing experience whatsoever. Gary Valentine was just the plunker Blondie were looking for and an ideal flatmate too...

I first met Chris Stein and Debbie Harry in 1975. I was 19, had left home the year before, and was living in a storefront on East 10th Street, between First Avenue and Avenue A, in New York's East Village. The neighbourhood, on the fringe of Alphabet City, sported junkies, prostitutes, East European immigrants and gangs of Hispanic kids. Back then it was a sort of no man's land, but nowadays yuppie moms wheel their prams through the reclaimed streets without a second thought. If you throw a rock in any direction, you're bound to hit a Starbuck's Coffee Shop, or a Gap. Maybe a Tower Records.

Not too long ago I walked through the old neighbourhood, remembering what it was like. A lot of places remained, like the Russian baths on 10th Street that William Burroughs mentions in one of his books, and the B&H Dairy Restaurant on Second Avenue, where you can get hot borscht and challah bread like nowhere else. But some places had changed. The store-front I lived in, for example: 23 years ago the windows were so filthy it was an even bet whether the shades were drawn or not. Today a Thi Chi studio is there, and a big Yin and Yang symbol advertises the place. The shop windows, filled with holistic health notices, are very clean. Apparently it's true: you can't go home again.

I moved to New York from my parents' house in New Jersey; just across the Hudson River, more or less behind the Statue of Liberty. A series of misadventures, culminating in my underaged girl friend becoming pregnant and my being arrested for it (the 'autobiographical material' behind my song X-Offender, Blondie's first single), led my parents to giving me an ultimatum. Change my ways, get a job, think about returning to university and forget about rock'n'roll. I packed a bag and left. A friend had sublet the store-front from a friend of his, who had converted it into a studio. 'Converted' is too extravagant a word for its condition. There were mounds of unwashed laundry, a couch that was more holes than couch, a dilapidated stereo, ashtrays overflowing with cigarette butts and roaches, and stacks of greasy dishes. It was dark, dirty and stale. Perfect, I thought. My hero at the time was Henry Miller and my plan was simple: I was going to become a poet.

My friend was eccentric. He divided his time between working for the Manhattan Transit Department, studying the Bible for hints about the end of the world and wanting to be a rock'n'roll star. He also squeezed in a considerable number of drugs. He wore eye-liner too, a leftover from the glitter days of The New York Dolls and Club 82, an old drag club on East Fourth Street, between Second and Third Avenues, which for a brief time a year before was the centre of the New York 'underground' scene. We had a vague plan to start a band, and one item in the store-front helped: an old, shattered piano. Practically every other key on it was broken, but this didn't matter. I taught myself how to play and started writing lyrics instead of poetry.

Most of the time I was hungry. I had barely enough money to cover my rent, and occasionally I shoplifted food. It was the kind of life you're supposed to lead if you want to write or paint or be any kind of artist. At least that's what I told myself those days I hadn't eaten, when I tried to quell the pains in my stomach by drinking warm water, a trick I picked up from the French writer, Rene Daumal. It didn't help Daumal much: he died of tuberculosis at 36. Luckily for me, something happened in the summer of 1975 that gave me something more substantial to sink my teeth into.

Clem Burke, who I knew from high school and who had been drumming in bands since he was a kid, had started playing with a band in New York. I had seen Clem play for years, and we had become friends. He was always on top of what was cool. He had some sixth sense about what was going to be the Next Big Thing, and more times than not he was right. He knew about David Bowie before anyone else, and in '73 was already walking around with lipstick or his eyelids painted red, a dangerous thing in New Jersey. I admired Clem for his commitment to the rock life.

It was something of a coup to have a place in the city, and he was always dropping in, bringing some grass or a bottle of wine and a handful of new records. Most of the time we had *Ziggy Stardust,* All The Young Dudes, *Fun House, White Light/White Heat* or *Highway 61* blaring, and we'd sit and talk about how we were going to be bigger than The Beatles. Clem was still in college and occasionally he'd ask me to write a paper for him, or a poem for a creative writing class. His band was playing somewhere in the Wall Street district. Did I want to come?

Yeah, sure. What're they like?

"Oh, sorta campy. The guitarist's a real nut. But the singer's sexy. We do some weird songs."

Yeah. What're you called?

"Blondie. You saw them once at Club 82. They were The Stilettoes then."

I vaguely remembered: Club 82, to me, was a melange of the Dolls, Rock The Boat, glitter shoes, drag queens, transvestites, earrings, lipstick, a brief encounter with Lou Reed and David Bowie, too many Tequila Sunrises and an unfortunate whiff of amyl nitrate. But I think I saw them on the same bill as Wayne County.

Yeah. Sure. I remember.

He told me the name of the place. White's Pub, a dive somewhere in the financial district. If I wanted to go I should be there when he got there.

I had already been to CBGBs Country, Blue Grass and Blues—on the Bowery—to see Patti Smith and Television, and I had observed Richard Hell prowling the streets of the East Village with what seemed like a perpetual sneer cut into his face. Like him, I had taken to wearing shades just about all the time. I had picked up the habit from peering at Ian Hunter albums and old Dylan photos, and what I gained in imperturbable cool I lost in eyesight.

In those days there really weren't many places for unsigned bands to play, especially bands like the early Television, who were working, more or less, on a 'learn as you go' basis. Max's Kansas City hadn't re-opened yet, Club 82 had lost its cachet when glitter dried up and 'real' venues like The Bottom Line wouldn't look twice at the likes of the bands who would start to bring crowds to what used to be a biker bar in what still is a pretty ratty part of the city. Walking around Second Avenue and St. Mark's Place, I'd see little flyers for Television or Patti Smith posted to street lamps, or spread across abandoned storefronts. But they were just a small part of the samizdat self-advertising that goes on in any big city, competing with notices for avant-garde theatre productions and political rallies. In that early summer of 1975, things were still pretty quiet on the rock'n'roll front. Hence Blondie husking in the depths of downtown Manhattan.

I don't remember a great deal about the show. A friend, Ronnie Toast, a maniac poet who later wrote a couple songs for Blondie, went with me, and I remember sitting in the back, huddled in a dark corner, nursing the one beer we could afford. My hair was long and I don't think I said much. The place was practically empty. White's wasn't exactly on the clubbing circuit, and what I remember of the audience is a handful of barflies occasionally letting out a frank appraisal of the singer. If they didn't always appreciate the material, at least they liked her looks. It was only later I found out they got the gig because Debbie worked there as a waitress.

My memories of Debbie from that night are vague. But I was impressed by Chris's voodoo attire. He was always covered in skulls, pentagrams, crossbones and swastikas, this last item a bit odd for a Jew. (Recently, when I met him again after 20 years, I saw his tastes hadn't changed. His loft in New York is somewhere between The London Dungeon and a Damien Hirst installation.) He wore dark eye-liner, his nails were long and black (he never used a plectrum, and played his guitar as if it were a banjo), and his hair fell around his rouged face in gypsy ringlets. Later, when I joined the band, and Blondie had its first incarnation in '60s retro gear, I always thought Chris felt out of place in Mod suit, skinny tie and Beatle boots.

Also there that night was Fred Smith. When he left Blondie to join Television—after Tom Verlaine had given Richard Hell his walking papers—it probably seemed a chance he couldn't pass up. After all, Blondie then—and for a long while after—were really little more than a joke. Television were getting press. Verlaine's surreal lyrics and switchblade guitar were grabbing critics' attention. Blondie had little more going for them than Debbie's looks. It was a good move for me, because soon after Clem asked me if I wanted to play bass with the band.

Before the proper ingredients congealed into the distinct bands, Clem was, like Fred, on the look-out to better his situation. He saw an ad for a drummer in the Village Voice. He called. It was Patti Smith. Did I want to go to the audition?

We went to a rehearsal space that night somewhere in uptown Manhattan, above 14th Street, which, for East Villagers, may as well have been the Catskills. He had yet to crop his hair to the moptop he sported on the first Blondie LP and, like Chris, was still hanging on to the remnants of glitter. A weird Rod Stewart shag, like a flaccid octopus, hung around his head, and he chain-smoked Marlboros with a quick, jerky motion. I guess I was there for moral support. I wasn't really a musician, and my clothes were definitely uncool. When I thought about it, all I had going for me were my dark glasses.

Inside the room were some amplifiers, a set of drums and two people: Lenny Kaye and Patti Smith. Not one to mince words, Patti came to the point.

"Which one's the drummer?"

Clem twirled his sticks.

Then she looked at me.

"And what about you?"

Silence.

Again the look.

"Well? Whadda you play? Hmmm?"

Nothing.

She looked at Lenny.

"Maybe sunglasses?"

She laughed. Lenny picked up his guitar and started strumming. In a thin, sarcastic voice he sang, "You'll look sharp/Wearing sunglasses after dark." Clem didn't pass the audition.

My own audition for Blondie went somewhat better. After hanging around at a couple of gigs they knew who I was. Clem had told them I was a poet and that I wrote songs—my repertoire on the clapped-out piano was growing—and I guess I looked the part. I was thin. The fact that I couldn't really play the bass was a minor detail. If your standards for rock musicianship were Yes and Emerson, Lake & Palmer then, yeah, practically none of us could 'really play'. But that was unimportant. The whole idea behind the early New York scene was that you didn't have to depend on established rock performers to provide your musical sustenance. If you had the nerve to get up on-stage and bang away, you could do it yourself.

One day Clem came to the store-front, told me Fred had quit and asked if I wanted to audition. I said yes. I could play a little, having picked up a few chords from guitarist friends in Jersey—while they were figuring out Allman Brother licks, I was slugging away at Johnny B. Goode. He said they'd have a bass at the rehearsal space—I didn't have one—and gave me the address.

The place was uptown, in an office building on West 37th Street, near the Port Authority Bus Station, not far from Hell's Kitchen. A year or so before I spent a day panhandling at the bus depot, trying to get enough money for a decent meal (I think Abbie Hoffman in Steal This Book suggested it as a good place to ask for spare change), and at one time my friend and I thought it was great fun to photograph each other talking with the hookers who worked the neighbourhood.

What I remember most from that first jam was realising how attractive Debbie was. Not that I hadn't noticed this before. But sitting across from her, talking, in a small, brightly lit room, was different from seeing her in a dive like White's, where she mumbled a quick "Hi" before and after a set. Like every male who's seen her in the flesh, I knew I was looking at a very sexy woman.

Chris was there, done up as usual in his Bela Lugosi best. Clem was very supportive and somewhat avuncular, jollying me out of my natural shyness, telling them about my poetry and songs. Chris lit a joint, and after it went around, handed me the bass.

"Whaddya know?" Er... "Can you play A and D?"

"Yeah."

"OK. You know the Stones' Live With Me?"

I nodded.

"Awright."

70

We went to it. Chris had a scratchy, plucky way of playing, as if his fingers hit two different chords simultaneously, one hanging into the other. Clem hit a steady beat. I ploughed into the bass, figuring it out with a kind of join-up-the-dots approach. Debbie let the chords churn around for a while before coming in. Casually, in thin T-shirt, ripped jeans and tennis shoes, she sang.

"I got nasty habits..."

I bet she does, I thought.

"C'mon now honey, donchu wanta live with meee..."

An hour later we stopped. Finally Chris said, "OK, you can play." Clem got off the drums and moved over to the piano.

"C'mere," he said. "Play one of your songs." I put down the bass and sat at the upright. The tuning wasn't great, but compared to the one at the store-front, this was a Steinway. I hit a C, got my pitch, and sang something I had just come up with. They nodded.

"OK. Sounds good."

"So?" Clem asked.

"So he can play. So he's in."

"Debbie?"

"Yeah. Sure. He sounds great."

Cool, I said. I had made it. I was officially in a New York rock'n'roll hand.

A lot happened after that audition. For one thing, my friend at the store-front announced he was moving to a kibbutz in Israel (the spot, apparently, would be safe when Armageddon arrived). I had to find a new crib. Rehearsals with the hand were going well, and I was getting better on the bass. There was no way around it. I took a deep breath and knocked on my parents' door.

That lasted a few weeks. The fact that I was playing in a band didn't go down well, and that it was in New York made it even worse—they didn't care for me crawling into bed at 4am after a gig or a night out. I received another ultimatum, packed another knapsack, and left.

For a few nights I crashed at the rehearsal space. Technically *verboten,* I had nowhere else to go. I crashed on another friend's couch in Jersey City, but after a couple of nights his mother didn't care for this and so I was back on the street. Eventually my plight came up at a rehearsal.

"Debbie," Chris said. "Gary doesn't have a place to live."

"Shit."

Then a thoughtful moment.

"Well, I guess he can live with us."

Chris and Debbie lived in a tiny one-bedroom flat above a grocery store on Thompson Street, in the interzone between SoHo and Little Italy, the kind of neighbourhood you'd expect to see in an Al Pacino film. There was hardly enough room in the place for the two of them. Every vertical level surface was covered in photographs. A bulletin board on one wall had flyers for The Stilettoes, an Elvis record cover, a photo of Debbie in her Chevy Camaro, a picture of Billy Doll, the drummer from The New York Dolls, who had OD'ed and been replaced by Jerry Nolan, the inevitable skull and crossbones, a Rolling Stones button with Brian Jones. The refrigerator had pictures of Richard Hell, Johnny Thunders, Eric Emerson from The Magic Tramps, another rock martyr who had met an early end. Crucifixes, magical talismans, voodoo dolls, images of Warhol, The Velvet Underground and junk art Chris picked up from the trash: the bric-a-brac of the streets found its walk-in display case in that small flat.

My other vivid memory is of shivering myself awake most of the first night I spent there, crashing on a small couch and amplifiers, speaker cases and guitars, because I was too shy to ask for a blanket after Chris and Debbie had gone to bed.

Memories: Debbie making coffee in the morning—Café Bustella, a real New York item, like the bottles of Manhattan Special, an absurdly sweet coffee soda we'd get from the deli below. Bleary-eyed, rats'-nest hair, she'd fall out of their bedroom wrapped in a housecoat, then pull out a frying pan, yawn and make scrambled eggs for Chris and I. Most times I had been up already for a few hours, reading, or quietly plucking one of the guitars. I tried to keep out of the way.

She'd kick us out every now and then, just to have the place to herself. Chris would roll a joint and we'd hit the streets, usually heading across Houston to the East Village. I wore his hand me downs—black peg-leg pants, a Canadian Film Festival T-Shirt, a white leather jacket. I even got a new pair of shades—a little less dark—using his Medicare card.

By then we had done a few gigs, recorded the Alan Betrock demo, and I had had my trial by fire. My first performance was at a dive called Monty Python's, on Third Avenue and 12th Street. It was the only time I ever suffered stagefright and played with my back to the audience—mostly another batch of barflies and a few other musicians. In the early days different bands would support one other, turning up to what might otherwise be empty gigs, like people on a desert island taking in one other's washing. (After the A&R people started coming, competitiveness eroded the early camaraderie.)

Chris had sublet a flat on First Avenue to Tommy Ramone of The Ramones (who else?) and brought me around to meet him. Then there were The Miamis. We did a lot of shows with them; they wrote great songs and were a fun band, but were lost in the shuffle when the record companies started signing people. It was at their place that I first met Dee Dee Ramone. The Ramones had just been signed to Sire Records and Dee Dee was feeling rather pleased. We sat at the kitchen table, the inevitable joint had gone around, and Dee Dee was holding court, telling us what it was like dealing with record company people. The usual questions were asked: How much money did they get? When was the album due? Were they going on tour?

Somebody asked if the Ramones would still play CBGBs. "Well, y'know, probably. But not that often. We'd rather do bigger places, y'know, being signed and all that."

He lounged back in his chair, satisfied with his assessment of things. Then suddenly he leaned forward, put his hands on the table and earnestly assured us, "But I'll come to see you guys play. I don't want to lose touch." I hadn't said much. I sighed and shook my head. "Gee, Dee Dee," I said. "It must be lonely at the top."

The others laughed. Dee Dee seemed a little put out. I don't think I made a good impression.

We played a lot of small gigs in those early days—bachelor parties, weddings, forgettable dives with names like Brandy's and Broadway Charlie's. The idea was to get money to eat. Most people think a musician's life is about sex and drugs and rock'n'roll, but most of the time it's about food. After a show we'd hop into Debbie's Camaro and go to Dave's Pot Belly, an all-night coffee shop on Christopher Street, west of Bleecker, in Greenwich Village, and stuff ourselves on cheeseburgers, fries and milkshakes. If the take wasn't good there was Smiler's Deli, on Seventh Avenue and Sheridan Square, for less sumptuous fare, like chicken salad sand-wiches and chocolate milk. For special treats Debbie went to Chinatown and brought a sack of bao back to the flat, steamed buns filled with pork and sweet sauce.

At one party, for the Equestrian Club, somewhere on the upper East Side, we did our originals but filled out the set with covers of the Stones, The Supremes, The Doors, Captain Beefheart, The Velvet Underground—we even did a version of Television's Venus De Milo. We played for three hours but, for lack of material, repeated the same songs over and over. Nobody seemed to mind. The food was good, and so were the drinks. We made about $300, the most money we had seen, and thought, Yeah, this is what it's all about.

In July we debuted at CBGBs Festival of Unrecorded Rock Talent, playing with The Ramones and Talking Heads, and in August, supporting The Heartbreakers, we shared a bill with the Talking Heads. We were known as the band who would open for anyone, and to a degree this was true. We simply weren't that impres-sive. Debbie would forget lyrics. Chris would look at his guitar as if it had just materialised out of thin air. The only one of us who could keep things together was Clem. We rehearsed at a loft on Third Street, just around the corner from CBGBs, owned by Arturo Vega, who later became an art director for The Ramones. But after a few weeks he lost interest in us and we had to find a new place. Meanwhile, the Thompson Street flat was getting too small. Obviously it was time to move on.

We landed in an illegal loft space above a liquor store on the Bowery, two blocks from CBGBs. A friend of Chris's had got a lease on the place, and he rented us a floor. The friend, Benton, was the most peculiar individual I had met to date. Thin as a rail, with a long mane of blond hair, he was an artist of sorts, but spent most of his time wearing biker gear and fantasising about the Hell's Angels. (During the end of our stay there, on a PCP binge, Benton asked an Angel to beat him; he obliged.) Sometimes he wouldn't leave his room for days, and his floor was dotted with Coke bottles filled with his urine.

The loft was unheated; I spent one Christmas Eve (my birthday) burning a stack of Jimi Hendrix posters to stay warm. Any furniture we had was dragged in from the streets. Naturally it was filthy. Outside the sidewalk was covered with winos and down-and-outs; often we had to push the door open in the morning, because a bum had camped out there the night before. One winter morning we discovered one had frozen to death; someone suggested hauling the body inside, but luckily an ambulance arrived. (Benton had got his hands on a series of Tibetan paintings, one of which was a cheery scene of a group of monks eating one of their fellows).

An eerie statue of a nun stood in front of a fireplace. A cross was painted on her forehead, and rosary beads hung from her hand. The fireplace itself was covered in occult formulae. Benton was fond of Aleister Crowley, meditated on the Tarot, and in inspired moments read aloud from Diary Of A Drug Fiend. Between this and Chris's voodoo fascination, the place had the air of a bad satanist film. Chris said the loft was haunted, and that he could feel poltergeists (Chris always had an active imagination). Debbie had brought her cats, and their nonchalant defecation combined with Benton's piss to create a particularly aromatic atmosphere. (Brecht said that the world of culture is built on a mountain of shit: if nowhere else, this observation fitted the New York scene. CBGBs was notoriously known as 'the toilet', and I remember being told that Richard Hell had thrown his girlfriend out because she had flushed the loo.)

The wiring, like everything else in the loft, was faulty, and once when I reached out to move a lamp I suddenly had 110 volts running through me. I couldn't move and I couldn't let go of the lamp. A black mass like a storm cloud rose from the back of my skull and headed toward my forehead; I knew that when it got there I'd be gone. I tried to call out, but my muscles were paralysed. Chris miraculously emerged from the back room and, calmly smoking the ubiquitous joint, stepped over to the socket and unplugged the lamp. I collapsed. For several days after my arm was numb, and I often fell asleep, sitting up, with my eyes open.

Another time I got arrested by an off-duty policeman. A friend of ours was acting in The Tempest, and Clem, Benton and I had gone to a matinee at the theatre in Chelsea. Walking back we shared a joint. From out of nowhere a madman grabbed me, shouting, "No! No! This can't happen. Not in my neigbourhood!" I had no idea what he was talking about. In those days people more or less smoked openly, figuring that the police had better things to do. He never said he was a policeman, showed no badge or ID, just flashed a set of bracelets and tried to cuff me. I fought him off, but he chased me into the street. A crowd gathered, and Benton and Clem looked on, uncertain what to do. Finally, he grabbed my shirt and threw me to the asphalt, my head hitting the deck, stars and tweety-birds whizzing before my eyes. "Is he all right?" I heard. "Do you think he's epileptic?" Someone suggested sticking a wallet in my mouth. I'm in a scientology commercial, I thought, before conking out. The next thing I'm in a police car heading to jail.

We spent the next three nights in three different jails. It was Friday; the courts didn't open until Monday; there was nothing for it but for the three of us to spend the weekend enjoying the hospitality of New York's finest. My head pounded from its recent meeting with West 18th Street. I couldn't see. The police had taken my glasses and had refused to give me pain-killers, suspecting that I might slit my wrists with the broken lenses or overdose on two Excedrin. And I was hungry: Life in the Big Apple. Worse still, we had a show at Max's Kansas City that Monday night and there was no guarantee we'd be released on time. Throughout Clem kept up a mantra of "Shit man, this sucks" and minor variations thereof, which Benton would counter with his single maxim for a philosophy of life: "Learn to love it." The cops didn't know what to make of us, and I was concerned that Benton might taunt one of them into living out one of his masochistic fantasies. Clem asked a black guy for a cigarette. The guy eyeballed him. "Hey; man. You look like Mick Jagger. You want a cigarette? You gotta sing for it, man."

Clem took a deep breath, and let rip.

"I can't get no satisfaction. I can't get no..." He got the smoke.

It's strange, the people you see in a cell. Crumpled up in the back and obviously getting over a bad bout of smack, I saw a guy I knew from the third grade who'd made a habit of beating me up. There was some justice after all.

Monday rolled around and we spent the day in a holding pen, waiting for our case to be heard. Chris and Debbie got a public defender. He told us not to worry. We weren't. We just wanted to get out of there. Finally we were brought before the judge, five minutes before he left for the day. The arresting officer admitted he hadn't identified himself as a policeman, and that was it. Case thrown out. We made it to the soundcheck at Max's. The best thing about it was that I was interviewed by New York Rocker.

Around this time Jimmy Destri joined the band. He had come to our gigs at Mothers, a gay bar on 23rd Street across from the Chelsea Hotel. Every now and then they let rock bands play there, and we had done a few shows with an assortment of sidemen, including a flautist and conga player. Jimmy had played with a group called Milk And Cookies but was axed just as they went to England to record an album. He was a friend of The Fast, another unsung band from the mid-'70s, two of whose members, Miki [Zone] and Mandy, succumbed to Aids. He brought his Farfisa organ to the loft and it sounded right.

One of the first things we did together was the music for a production of Vain Victory; a play by Jackie Curtis, one of the Warhol crowd. Chris and Debbie always aspired to that set and thought it was a coup when Debbie got the part of Juicy Lucy. I remember little of the play but for the lines, "I'm so hungry I could eat you." "You'll do no such thing. Have another saltine." But the party after closing night was a smash. Lisa Persky, an actress, who also wrote for New York Rocker, had been invited by Benton, and in the taxi uptown she sat on my lap and we made out. At the party I got progressively loaded, and went from room to room asking for the redhead I'd arrived with. Eventually I found her. We decided to go to her studio on Christopher Street. The elevator down was a bit abrupt, and when I hit the street I heaved. She huddled me into a taxi, and when we finally got to her place we ran into her father, who had dropped by for a visit. I later wrote (I'm Always Touched By Your) Presence Dear, Blondie's second hit, for Lisa.

Clem went to London for a six week adventure; we took the opportunity to write songs and work Jimmy into the band. The first album grew out of this time. We worked every day. My relationship with Lisa developed. She was acting in an off-Broadway production called Women Behind Bars where twice-nightly she was raped on stage by Divine of Pink Flamingos fame.

When Clem returned from England he brought back the first Dr Feelgood album. We threw a party at the loft and invited everyone. They all came. We had more people there than at any of our gigs. Johnny Thunders, Jerry Nolan, Hell, The Ramones, The Miamis, The Marbles, Lance Loud And The Mumps, The Dictators, Talking Heads, Suicide. Conspicuous by their absence were Verlaine and Patti Smith. They didn't mix much with us or the other bands, and inhabited an exclusive atmosphere of art and self-regard. Chris and Debbie were convinced Patti had a vendetta against them. The paranoia drove them to succeed.

Clem played the Dr Feelgood album over and over. Strange the give and take between New York and London. The stripped-down, straightforward R&B of Dr Feelgood inspired everyone there that night to go on, and not too long after the torn shirts of early Television would turn up in the whole Sex Pistols aesthetic, shipped back to us via Malcolm McLaren.

Blondie's rise to fame and success began with our first shows at CBGBs with Jimmy Destri, in February 1976. The work we put into writing and rehearsing paid off. For the first time, Blondie sounded like a real band. The joke was over. We started building up a following, and were becoming a force. At the time it was a struggle, but looking back the rest seemed to follow as a matter of course. At 20 it's immensely gratifying to see people in different cities across the country wearing peg-leg pants and skinny ties, just because you do. That's what happened in Los Angeles, where we played with The Ramones and Tom Petty, in San Francisco, and later across the States after *Blondie* was released and we opened for Iggy Pop on a nationwide tour.

The same thing happened when we toured the UK with Television in spring 1977. That was my favourite time with the band. I was always an Anglophile, and to find myself playing London, Manchester and Glasgow was a dream, even if I did fall off the stage in Bristol (oddly enough, that was one show I didn't wear my dark glasses). But in July that particular dream ended. I left the band, moved to the West Coast and pursued other goals, one of which was fronting my own group, The Know.

But my life with Blondie wasn't over yet. Almost 20 years later, after I had moved to London and was working as a freelance writer, I got a call from Chris Stein. He had tracked me down through a friend. It was an odd sensation hearing his voice on the telephone after two decades, but what he asked was less expected still. He wanted, he said, to put the original band back together. Was I interested? I had just returned from a tour of Eastern Europe, where I had played guitar in a gypsy band in Istanbul and Macedonia, and had covered an arts festival in Tuzla, Bosnia, for The Guardian. Heading to New York to play pop music again wasn't the first thing on my mind, but I was intrigued, and Chris seemed very eager. I decided to give it a try.

In November 1996 I landed in New York. Jimmy Destri met me at JFK and we drove to Chris's loft in Tribeca. After the initial shock of comparing grey hairs and paunches, things settled into familiar, old routines, the way it is around family. Later that day Debbie showed up and we talked and remembered a few old times. Maybe you can't go home again, but it sure is interesting seeing your old room-mates 20 years on.

"Blondie and the Politics of Power Pop"

by Jessamin Swearingen
(adapted and edited by Allan Metz)

"We Created It: Let's Take It Over!"
web site, 1999-2001

Women and sexism in the music industry and Deborah Harry within this context; punk and "new wave" and the placement of Blondie within this scene.—Ed.

Throughout the annals of music, sexism has pawed its way through rock's history. Women were either marketed as childish nymphets or the sultry accessories to the male rock show. These women focused their careers around these categories and with rare exception (including Patti Smith), those who did not, usually fell into obscurity.

Possibly the most graphic example of sexism and its impact on women in rock was Janis Joplin. Her independence as a performer could not be maintained offstage—if onstage her strengths emerged, offstage her fears raged. Joplin remained painfully aware that she was not "pretty enough" for the rock world until her death. She acted on this insecurity with bouts of drug and alcohol abuse, and her life ended tragically in a heroin overdose.

The rock industry's powerful grip on women musicians and their self-image has dictated how women's musical contributions register in the mainstream. Joplin may have been a powerhouse performer, but in rock's collective memory, she is a tragic heroine. Only beginning in the 1990s, with women-identified rock scenes like "Riot Grrrl," had the perception of female rockers started to change. Still, within the more conventional boundaries of mainstream radio and advertising, the industry has problems publicizing women if they are not attractive and seductive.

Deborah Harry of Blondie was a performer who both profited and lost from the industry's sexism. Blondie, the band which Harry fronted, was one of the late 1970s most consistent hit machines. By the release of their second album, *Plastic Letters*, the band had achieved only moderate success. But with 1978's *Parallel Lines*, Blondie became one of the most eclectic and successful pop bands on the charts.

Regardless of musical achievements, the band's success was overshadowed by Harry's fame as a sexual persona. Her face and dyed blonde hair became the symbol of the band. Because of Harry's image, Blondie lost the status of a band and was perceived as merely her backup group. To this day, people refer to Deborah Harry as "Blondie" as if it were her name.

The media acted as though it were more acceptable for Harry to be an image than a rock performer. An early promotional release for the band showed a picture of Harry in a revealing top, asking, "Wouldn't you like to rip her to shreds?" This infuriated the band. Aside from Harry being alone in the picture, and thus discounting the band, it perpetuated her image as a sexual object. If she had been a male fronting the same band, the marketing strategies might have been different. For example, Mick Jagger, the Rolling Stones' front man, is marketed with the same amount of sex appeal. However, he also is seen as a talented and important songwriter.

Blondie as a band would be remembered as one of the top talents of the late 1970s. Songwriters Deborah Harry, partner/guitarist Chris Stein, and keyboardist James Destri maintained a consistent niche in the late 1970s rock market. The band released a chain of hit singles during a period of time when the industry faced a recession and sales were low. To add to the recording industry's confusion during the sales slump, along came punk rock, a genre of music for which record companies had no way of anticipating. The same companies were putting all their money into established acts like ABBA, Barbra Streisand, and a new dance fad called disco. Punk was too hard to package for mainstream consumption. However, the industry saw punk's potential (if not merely the dollar signs) and signed a few bands, but no one sold records like Blondie.

In the context of punk rock, Blondie was an anomaly, part of the surge of new acts sharing the moniker, "punk." Blondie strived for radio airplay and hit singles. The band adopted the title "power pop" for itself, but faced opposition from an industry refusing to accept it as pop when the band was punk by association. By separating the musical genres, a new category was born. "New wave" filled the void between punk and pop, and it represented a moderated, less vicious form of this new rock aesthetic. It was a less severe and more colorful version of the same punk idea. Stylistically, it could more readily encompass the difference between the New York City punk bands. New wave was a compromise to the severity of punk's separation from the music industry. It, however, was not mainstream, and it appealed to alternative audiences. Blondie did not call itself "new wave," but for the music industry the band was easier to market with that title.

In 1977, punk was becoming a viable business in both the United States and England. Yet the recording industry found few examples of the genre that they knew how to market—punk was just too aggressive. A&R and management teams tripped over themselves trying not to offend record buyers accustomed to the whole-some charm of ABBA's hooked-on-phonics pop or the Bee Gees' blue-eyed (i.e., white) soul. With the girlish charm of Deborah Harry, coupled with the aggressive pop hooks of the band, Blondie became the punk era's best-selling American band.

By 1979 Blondie was a household name. And, ironically, the song that propelled them to their fame was a crossover (meaning that it merged genres) song called "Heart Of Glass." The single was from the band's third and most successful album, *Parallel Lines*, and another example of the band's cross-genre musical attack. Stylistically, the band covered more genres than the average band. Blondie's diversity set it apart from its punk peers and gave it more selling power.

With "Heart Of Glass" Blondie tinkered with disco, but early in their recording career they recreated the 1960s bubblegum and Girl Group sound, alluded to the garage pre-punk sounds of 1960s radio, and emerged as a perfect hybrid of the era's musical fabric. Early Blondie records were a virtual sampling of 1960s radio program-ming. In perfect sync with her influences, Deborah Harry invited Ellie Greenwich, composer of the Shangri-Las' classic, "Leader of the Pack," to sing backup on a track of Blondie's first album. Greenwich agreed, and her voice is heard, but it was Harry who did the arrangement for the vocals.

The band had done its homework—Harry could see the selling power and charm of the girl groups, but molded it into a more powerful image. Excelling from the ranks of Diana Ross and the Supremes, Harry was a female performer in control of the music she recorded. Unlike most girl groups, Harry had artistic control of her music and was never told what to wear. Diana Ross, undoubtedly the best known individual among the girl group performers, did not have control over her music nor the clothes she wore. Harry, although not free from the media's manipulation, was certainly more autonomous than her girl-group influences.

In the history of female pop stars, Harry is often cited as a precursor to Madonna's rise to queen of the industry. Madonna, like Harry, knows the power of image and uses the selling power of an attractive female. Harry, however, was much more rock'n'roll-based than her dance-music progeny, and it was Harry who whetted the media's appetite for a female superstar.

Pop icons come and go, but from the very beginning of Blondie's self-titled 1976 debut, it was obvious that Blondie was the perfect pop band. The first track on side one, "X Offender" starts off with Harry coolly confiding over a Ronettes, "Be My Baby" drum beat. Harry's deadpan delivery was coated in perfect girl group obviousness. It is hard to tell if she is serious as the drums boom, boom, boom back to such a perfectly cliche era of rock. It is even unclear if it is 1977 or 1965. The album was such a carbon copy of the bubblegum teen anthems of the 1960s that it is almost too easy. As a matter of fact, Blondie was such a perfect copy of the bubblegum sound that its first LP is almost boring. Save for the street-smart snarl of "Rip Her To Shreds," Harry hammed her way through the entire album. She knew the material too well, and as a result it sounded too calculated. The band had to move on. And it was the group's strength as a band, not Harry's good looks and sex symbol image, that enabled its survival.

Guitarist and collaborator, Chris Stein, was equally important in Blondie's rise to fame. He co-wrote many of the band's hit singles and added his eclectic musical styles to Blondie's sound. Blondie was too strong as a band to be merely Harry's backup, and Harry's talent as a performer was much more than that of a mere sex symbol. Rarely do women without talent who have the looks to compensate succeed as pop stars past the proverbial sophomore slump. The emphasis on their personalities might be enhanced, as in the case of sometime actress and pop star, Cher. Yet fortunately, as tolerant as the industry is, it does not excuse Cher's self-indulgent wanderings in the music industry as musical talent. Cher is a celebrity, not a musician; Deborah Harry is a musician.

Blondie's first two albums show the band's obsession with pop culture. Song titles ranging from the B-movie suggestiveness of "Kung Fu Girls" to the double-feature goofiness of "The Attack of the Giant Ants" gave the debut an air of calculated innocence. Their songs reveal the band members as icons to their own pop cultural upbringing. Although Harry's looks were both an asset and a drawback to her image as a musician, what better vehicle to guide the band to success than Deborah's movie star features? Through the band's matinee-to-prime-time evolution, Blondie demonstrated its ability to execute several different genres of pop music. Within rock music, a band's evolution is considered respectable and a sign of maturation. Yet in punk, an evolution of sound was either impossible because of the short life expectancy of most punk bands, or a sell out. If a band's sound changed, it might be perceived as compromising to satisfy the mainstream.

Blondie's next album, *Plastic Letters*, on the other hand, seemed weary and damaged. Songs like "Fan Mail" and "Cautious Lip" showed a different side to the band. *Plastic Letters* demonstrated a harder edge, attacking traditional pop with more bite. The creepy spy soundtrack guitar on "Youth Nabbed As A Sniper" and the world-weary teen-angst of "Fan Mail" showed the band's evolution. "Fan Mail" sets the scene for our teenage heroes—the misunderstood teenager meets the rebellious rocker—taking the melodrama of the 1950s movie classic "Rebel Without A Cause" into a higher plane—one of rock'n'roll.

Harry saw the importance of marketing herself as a commodity within the pop world. Her role as a pop performer was that of a character, and the songs were the scripts for her performances. She became the living replica of the Blondie image. Harry wanted Blondie's character to combine the best elements of rock mythology: street smarts, attraction, and a perpetually teenage outlook. The Blondie character would have to be smart, fun, and attractive. By Harry's turning herself into the Blondie character, it became harder for the fans and industry to tell the two apart. Was Harry Blondie, the Marilyn Monroe for the modern rock era, or the brilliant manipulator behind the band?

In more recent times, with a more educated, not to mention jaded, audience, Madonna can maintain this balance with ease. She can be a pop personality, changing her images with more fluidity than David Bowie's chameleon business maneuvers in the early 1970s. Deborah Harry was never given the benefit of the doubt. She was enslaved to the Blondie image and was given no credit for her intelligence or business prowess.

The band's name was ironic—a stab at the sexist imagery Harry was surrounded by. Many fans believe the band's name was adopted from the comic strip, but "Blondie" was a cat call—what men called Harry. Within the dogmatic notions of feminism, naming the band "Blondie" could be interpreted as Harry empowering herself. In a world of leering truck drivers, Harry was usurping their assumptions of her and using her sexuality as power.

Musically, Harry honed the band into the perfect pop machine. Blondie packaged the strong vocals and story telling aspect of the girl groups and combined them with the musical sharpness of soul and R&B bands to become one of the era's most impressive bands. The band thus eventually outshone its influences; like changing clothing fashions, particular genres of music fade from popularity after a while. But a band, like Blondie, able to encompass all genres can evolve rather than stagnate.

In terms of sales and survival rates, Blondie was the most successful band of its peers. Harry manipulated the industry's sexism to become the most notable performer of the era. She used rock's sexist climate to help promote her band, thereby selling records and gaining success within an industry that had little time for the other punk or new wave bands emerging from the same scene.

Blondie, although not as revolutionary or aggressive in fashion or lyrical subject matter as its punk contemporaries, was the most popular of the lot. Harry's looks contributed to the band's fame, but it was the band and its unstoppable pop-music mentality that enabled its rise to fame. Blondie was among the most diverse and talented bands of the late 1970s and early 1980s. If not for the industry's fear of the band's punk association or the tendency to market Blondie in Harry's image, rather than promote the band's talent, Blondie would have the respect that is due them.

"'Downtown 81' in 2001"

by Jon Erkider

A "mini-review" of the film "Downtown 81" by a very knowledgeable chronicler of the New York City scene.—Ed.

"Downtown 81" is amazing! Anyone interested in the art and music scene of the East Village in the aftermath of punk and the true beginnings of raw new wave music and art should go and see it.

Don't pay any attention to reviews written by people who just don't understand what kind of effect punk and pop (as an art form) has had on the masses (where would Beck be without James Chance?). Jean Michel Basquiat is cool and handsome and a perfectly good actor playing the "SAMO" character of himself (remember the walls in "The Hardest Part" video told us that "SAMO IS A MYTH!")?

The film is filled with Blondie, Blondie and more Blondie. Everybody is in it, including all the significant no-wave/art crowd from the 3rd Street set.

"Downtown 81" begins with Debbie cooing the lines: "...Fairy tales can come true, it can happen to you, especially if you're young and live in New York..." And Jean Michel was young, a mere 19 years old and an originator of a new art form that started out with spray cans, abandoned refrigerators and cars, and decaying storefronts.

The story is a day in the life of the artist struggling to find a place to sleep, to locate a beautiful model he'd recently met, and to sell a painting to get money to live.

Throughout his day and night he encounters the most colorful of people, the coolest clubs and the coolest bands (including DNA with Arto Lindsay kicking ass with his crunching and gyrating guitar licks!).

Nowhere else will you ever see interior shots and performances of the Mudd Club, the Rock Lounge and the Peppermint Lounge. This is a fantastic time warp for anyone with a predilection for this new and rare seminal music period.

Jimmy Destri plays a cab driver, Chris Stein plays the lead singer of a punk band (the Felons) and a bearded Clem plays the drummer. A DJ spins and scratches *Autoamerican* in an underground dive while very early MCs rap and freestyle to it (this is historical!).

Chris Stein's "15 Minutes" is played in the film, which was later recycled as the theme song for Andy Warhol's "15 Minutes" show on MTV in 86-87.

Other notables who star or make cameos are a loony and comedic Walter Steding (the violinist on "The Tide Is High" and one-time Animal Records recording artist); Fab Five Freddy and Lee Quinones painting East Village walls; Cookie Mueller (from the John Waters films) as a stripper; Steve Mass (Mudd Club owner) as a drunkard; musicians Tav Falco and John Lurie; artist David McDermott (speed-freaking and ranting while standing on a desolate Astor Place devoid of Starbucks and K-Mart); painter Diego Cortez (one-time video director for Blondie); Glenn O'Brien (who co-hosted "TV Party" with Chris) as a reporter from the *Christian Science Monitor* and Maripol (showing off her new wave fashions) as well as Tish & Snooky [Bellomo] (of Manic Panic and one-time Banzai Babies to an early Blondie); "Blank Generation" filmmaker Amos Poe; and *Making Tracks* co-author Victor Bockris as Mudd Club patrons.

Debbie plays a bag lady who turns into a princess with a kiss from Jean Michel. Debbie is unrecognizable as a dirty vagabond lying in the gutter with rotten teeth and a dirty face. (Only those lips give her away!) Her voice is hilariously disguised when she calls Jean over: "Sonny?...Come here, Sonny..." As a princess, this Debbie is the Debbie from the "Rapture" video—the lithe utterly beautiful rock star doll who was right at the height of her super-fame. Her hair is just an inch longer and she looks fucking amazing. It's exciting to see this rare, unearthed Debbie treasure—even though she's only on screen for about six minutes.

The Village is unrecognizable as well—the buildings are decrepit and collapsed—winos asleep on stoops with trash and debris everywhere.

This little art piece is testimony to the rarely written about period when all the CB's bands were already signed and all these burgeoning artists and musicians rose up from its influence. Blondie was back home in NY and going to the Bronx to see the Funk 4 Plus One More and frequenting all the new clubs where Debbie even played drums and trumpet!

Originally titled "New York Beat," "Downtown 81" is a look into the past; a past in which Debbie and Chris and Blondie were once again breaking ground. New York was theirs and it still is. Even in 2001.

"Blondie's Punk Roots"

by Victor Bockris

Original essay written specifically for this book.—Ed.

When I was young, they had what were called "little fuck books"—which featured characters taken from the comics. Most of them were absurd and grotesque, but there were one or two of genuine erotic interest; *Blondie* comes to mind.—*Terry Southern, interview with Lee Server, 1986*—Puritan *magazine*

The history of punk is appropriately ugly. Punk rock is a music of passion born out of contradiction. Consequently it would be mad to look in its roots for kindness and understanding. It was in fact an ugly competitive uptight movement, full of hostility and hatred. It was also the most exciting glamorous organic movement of real art in its particular moment of creativity, in say 1974-1976, and to be involved in it, to walk around New York knowing about it, was thrilling, sexy and beautiful because it was to live in the present. And anybody who has ever lived in the present will know that it is an experience that you would give up almost anything to have, both because it's rare and grand. Goethe wrote that being an artist is the best way to both avoid life and engage in life, and that's very true of punk. Goethe was a punk.

Punks have existed since the beginning of time, they just tend to erupt at certain moments when cultures need to be cleaned out and taken back to their roots. Thus it takes a certain type of person to, I think, be a punk and in particular a punk rocker, because you would need to have a very educated head as well as an empty, blunt head. You would need to have a great deal of passion and sexuality, as well as being able to deny that passion and sexuality. You would have to be a great lover who could learn to hate. And yet despite how true all of this is I think that Debbie Harry is, as her friend the great Anya Phillips pointed out in Lester Bangs' *Blondie*, one of the nicest people any of us had ever met, and despite all the shit she had to live through to make it, and then incredibly make it again, she never lost that basic niceness, a basic good-heartedness I suppose comparable to say Allen Ginsberg's good heartedness. She never became a jerk or an asshole but she was certainly a punk, pure, magic, alive and filled with the passion to make music. That's why I find it almost impossible to comprehend, sitting here in 2002, that there was a time when a bunch of people in the punk scene were so jealous of Blondie's early success with their first album, they tried to kick the band out of the CBGB nest and deny them their punk roots. They tried to set up the idea that while Patti Smith, Television and the Ramones were artists, for example, Blondie was just some lightweight pop band whose name should not be breathed in the same holy arena as the others. That people came to see them primarily to catch a glimpse of Debbie's panties.

The truth is that along with the Ramones, with whom they shared the most in common, Blondie was not just another punk band, they are the roots of punk. They created punk. They were the second band to play CBGB. They got the Ramones their first gig at CBGB. Debbie and Chris spent all of 1974 through 1976 in the gutter basically playing in sewer bands, knocking it out night after night in rehearsal halls and tiny clubs with audiences of five people trying to find their sound, like a writer trying to find his voice or a boxer trying to find his punch, or a painter trying to find his hand. That they made it came from persistence, intelligence and above all I think the spirit of collaboration, which Debbie Harry and Chris Stein are champions of and/or great examples of. The ability to work together, to be creative together over a long period of time, considering the circumstances of creating rock music and the context, is a remarkable achievement. These are punk roots.

As anyone who reads this book will know, Blondie went through several incarnations before becoming the successful Blondie, the original five piece line up of Debbie Harry, Chris Stein, Clem Burke, Gary Valentine and Jimmy Destri. During these incarnations as the Stilettos, Angel and the Snakes and Blondie and the Banzai Babies they had to eat a lot of shit. They had to play bad gigs that made them feel ill. They had to take criticism from the press, their peers, even their friends. Other bands would steal their musicians, their musicians would leave them because they were so bad. They would feel at times that there was no point in going on. That there was no chance of making it or even making a living out of it, and shit goddamit they just couldn't stand it another moment. Their roots are the fact that, like a great basketball team even when they're fifteen points down in the last five minutes, they wouldn't give up. They just kept coming back and coming back until they did make it, until they did get that sound right, until they did turn themselves on, and turn the audience on, and turn music on and emerge alive in the moment again and again. It's like very few things on earth. I don't believe anything is better than sex, since sex is the ultimate collaboration, the ultimate being with another person, but it's obviously like sex; it's just connecting with a very large number of people and with the other members of the band on different levels. Can you imagine then what it must be like to write songs, create a sound with the person you love, then be able to stand on stage next to them all over the world singing those same songs and turning on a million people and making at the same time a million dollars. Those are punk roots. Those are creative roots. To be able to do that and not crack up, not just disintegrate under the insane 24/7 pressures of the rock business and touring and human beings unbelievable, strange, twisted monsters, assholes, immature, nasty, self destructive passive aggressives, liars, thieves, stupid jerks, hostile pricks, suicidal idiots.

Then there was New York City.

Debbie had, as we know, grown up an adoptee, dreaming that her mother was Marilyn Monroe, and at one time so desperate to sing that until she could she could hardly open her mouth without bursting into tears for fear that she might not be able to. Those are punk roots. In the 1960s she came to New York, like all the other migrant workers who flood into the city every September to make it, and found herself waiting tables at Max's on the Jefferson Airplane the night before they played Woodstock, then as a Playboy Bunny, getting offers left and right that could have driven anyone out of their minds. Those are punk roots. She got addicted to junk, which under the circumstances you can read about in my *High Times* interview, and had to leave to recuperate, reassess and start all over again. When she returned in 1972, via hooking up with Elda Gentile in the Stilettos and meeting Chris Stein, she could not have known it but she had arrived back at the perfect time. Over the next three years America would go through an abstract revolution of the kind much further fetched than what happened in the 1960s. With the fall of Nixon and emergence of the democratic humanist President Carter, with the end of the Vietnam war and the return of the heroin addicted American army, and with the great beat revival, kicked off by William Burroughs' return to New York in 1974, and the great Warhol revival, kicked off by his return to painting with his haunting portraits of Mao in 1972-1974, New York would suddenly emerge like a demon out of the dashboard as the head of America. Rock Central. A place where three generations of artists from the 50s, 60s and 70s would merge together in a cross cultural pollination of fields and generations that had never happened anywhere in the world before, and will probably never happen again, to recreate one of the richest most productive artistic, creative, sexual climates in the history of western civilisation. as we knew it. Those are punk roots.

Walking through the Lower East Side in the summer of 1975, while CBGB was having its punk rock summer festival, through the summer of 77, when everybody essentially took off and went on the road forever, was an historic experience. I remember so many moments in which one felt one was in a movie, not in the sense that it was a good idea that would make money, but in the sense that everybody was playing their part perfectly. It was as if the Warholian idea of putting on a costume and makeup before going out everyday, and acting as if you were the star of your own movie, had suddenly spread to these few hundred people. It was like the pop art revolution ten years earlier, small, intelligent, sexy, fast, clean, sharp, very American, very addictive, very sexy. It was like fucking the American culture, like making love to it. It was a complete acceptance across the boards of the purest American art forms, like TV, basketball and jazz, like eating and drinking and taking drugs, like consuming the wind. Punk roots.

What is art after all? Isn't it living in a place and picking up on the vibrations of the place as if they're in the air and you are an antenna in whatever form you're working in, and then once you get attuned to this, working your ass off at not losing it. Working your ass off at knowing people, at getting out there and taking part in the big game, like walking around in a dream. It was the sort of experience in America that put you in touch with all time. With Edgar Allan Poe and Memory River, with the Shangri-Las and the essence of adolescence, with Lolita and baseball.

I always thought what tied it all together most of all was romance. That the punks were all great romantics, just as Warhol was, just as Burroughs, Corso and Ginsberg were, just as Charlie Parker and Ornette Coleman were. It was one of those give it your all times in which nobody thought about their health or, as Debbie put it so succinctly, people insisted on doing what they weren't supposed to do, but in the healthiest way possible. I fell in love with a punk girl in 1977 and I've been in love with her ever since. Partially it was being in love with those roots, that time when there was still so much good stuff to come but we didn't know it, although we felt it and we were walking up and down in it and being amazed every day. Partially it was about being in love with something that would last always. Remember how Diaghelev told Cocteau to go away and don't come back until you can astonish me and Cocteau came back with Stravinsky and the Rites of Spring and kicked off punk rock in 1914?

I also think punk rock's roots were really in the Second World War. Just as the British Invasion of 1964 was lead by a group of boys who had been born during the war, punk was led by a group of boys and girls who had grown up in the immediate aftermath of the war, whose first comic book images were of insane Nazis grinning like sharks in cold black leather, of horror and concentration. Of the McCarthy hearings and the disgraceful cold war, in which thousands of American boys froze to death in Korea, although nobody knew where it was, just like Vietnam ten years later. We were the children of Hitler and Lolita, myths of madness and sex. People who wanted to turn each other inside out to experience their depths and lick the nacreous grapes of their organs, their vaginas, their assholes, their hearts. Those are all punk roots, deep, deep roots in the darkness of Mingus and Monk. In the hell of Parker and the subway bebop of Dizzy Gillespie, in the magic founderings of the Lounge Lizards and the Contortions. In the Nova ovens, in the feeling that we were the heat and we were closing in. And that we owned New York.

And I think that Debbie Harry reigned over this scene like a war queen, like an abstraction of Cleopatra and Boadicea, in the contretemps of addiction and music, in the hell of memory and her lost childhood, in the catharsis of undressing on the stages of small clubs, without realising it at all at the time of course, but then suddenly getting it like a frigid person who discovers orgasms. Because she turned out to not be Marilyn Monroe's daughter, but rather a healthier version of Marilyn, one who would not die, who would refuse to let the system of jealousy, stupidity and hatred, of those heterosexual dollars, kill her. The spiteful eyes and bent mouths of the creeps and dictated who spewed up in their failures weird shrieks on the Bowery years later, alone, frustrated and denied. Yet Debbie still offers life. I saw her play Joey Ramone's memorial service May 21st 2001. She commanded the stage and threw her voice up and right back into the last row of the three thousand hardcore fans who packed the Hammerstein Ballroom that night in an orgy of nostalgia for being alive in those punk roots, ending with "I Wanna Be Your Boyfriend" and making us cry for the haunting beauty of punk.

Debbie is still alive because she stayed true to her roots, came to know them, sang through them and for them and with them, came to embrace, as Corso would say, the whole shot. In the burned capitol of crime, in the punk city of New York, where heroes walked the streets after hours, through the night till the dawn holding onto the flames of their own fires, totally combusting in the spontaneity of hard won success, in the arrival and deployment of their armies, and in the glitter of their ears. Those ears that are punk roots, those eyes that saw it all, embraced it all. When Gregory Corso was lying on his deathbed his final good time came when he cried out, "I WANT MY DEBBIE HARRY!!!!" And somebody went and found her for him and brought her round and then Gregory knew it would be alright and he went out gentle in the good night, calmed by her spirit, her presence, her song, in the beauty of those punk roots.

Above all Debbie Harry is international. Like all the best American artists she broke out of the hieroglyphic nightmare of the road and took to the air, travelling across oceans and continents, taking her thrilling voice, her thrilling act, her thrilling band around the globe, bound for glory as her entourage touched down in Moscow. The strange thing is that unlike Warhol, whose passion for La Gloire drove him more than anything, Ginsberg, who lusted after fame like Whitman's, who got the moves down before he conquered the language, Debbie was not burned up by ambition so much as just wanting to be true to the moment, alive in the moment. It was her insistence on being alive in the moment that made her, and her constant looking for the way in, so that for example she discovered Stephen Sprouse, who dressed her, Chris Stein, who not only undressed her but photographed her naked with a guitar, creating some of the great lasting punk images of the world.

On July 4th, 1980 Debbie and Chris took Andy Warhol, his boyfriend Jed Johnson and myself to dinner in Harlem. Andy and Jed were breaking up and it was, I think, the last time they went out together, putting a certain strain on the evening, but I remember sitting in the back of the car as Debbie bombed up the West Side Highway straining to hear what she and Andy were saying together, because they were talking about how to make a successful movie, an area Debbie was just getting involved in with Union City and Videodrome. "It's all magic," Andy was saying in his parsimonious way. Something I think he really believed. And I know Debbie believes in magic, and in particular in ritual, in their powers to release creativity, but I don't think for a moment that she thinks any of her success had to do with magic. It had to do with damned hard work, digging deep down into herself and into others to find it, to bring it out. "Let's get it! Let's get it! Get it!" Keith Richards cried out at the beginning of the Stones' Madison Square Garden concert at the end of the 1972 Exile tour, when the whole band was so exhausted they could hardly stand up. Only Keith, bouncing up and down like a mad dragon let out of his cage, pulled them together and pushed it out into the night. Debbie and Chris "got it."

And I know you want to know, because I write books about people who make it, everybody wants to know how they got it. Well, there are elements of magic in it, but in the case of punk it was more an example of the magic of history, of the coming together of all those different influences that were both exploded by and imploded by the Second World War, a five year moment in which fifty million people got their hearts blown out for no apparent reason. By the entering into and staying in the area of that moment and chasing the dragons down the sheets of flames—in the mailed fist, the drive out of the Ardennes in the magic reality of German warfare, the kind of insane discipline that holds an entire army in place at Stalingrad while it is annihilated man by man—and then to remember and not remember, to exist in contradictions, to cowboy the white whale, to cool the mark inside...

Bob Dylan talks of that high mercury sound. That was the sound I heard the first time I walked into CBGB, and heard every time I went there in those magic years when tramps turned into stars while many died in the attempt. Debbie never spoke of fear. She heaped too much garbage to be afraid. Those are punk roots.

For me Debbie will always be the poet of punk. "You say you want to take me down to Puerto Rico, you say you want to take me up to the mountains, the boring mountains. I've been there, I've done it, I'm doing it still..."

"Marilyn and Jean, Jayne, Mae and Marlene...they really had fun..." Lillian Hellman lying on her death-bed the night before she expired whispered to her last friend, "I was fun, wasn't I?" In America, where all we do is work, you better be. Humor is the way in and the way out, so long as you don't get trapped in the pigsty quicksand of the authorities and cop a Lenny Bruce. I'll never know how Debbie survived the years after Blondie, the year when Chris almost died, the long brutal years of the eighties, but I do know that she was walking on the tightrope of her roots, living in her roots, and finding her way back into the heart of the fun that was and is at the roots of Blondie. In the cool underground forests and hidden cities of her memory, her instincts and her role as the great sexual icon of punk, a jazz singer, an actress, a movie star, a songwriter, a punk/pop/rock singer and a beatnik, who is now one of the great citizens of New York. And those are her punk roots.

Tiffanys, Coventry, UK, November 14, 1977, with "special guest," XTC
credit: © Philippe Carly—*http://users.skynet.be/phicarly*

Early Photo Section

Deborah Harry of the pop group Blondie holding Apollo Theatre Glasgow trophy.
credit: copyright © Mirror Syndication International

Deborah Harry, New York City, 1976
credit: copyright © Bob Gruen / Star File

Deborah Harry, New York City, 1977
Also cover photo (or one very similar) for
British music magazine *Rock On!,* October 1978
credit: copyright © Bob Gruen / Star File

Deborah Harry, Paris, 1978
credit: copyright © Bob Gruen / Star File

Deborah Harry—Blondie, The Paradise, Boston, MA,
May 1978
credit: copyright © Ron Pownall / Star File

American Bandstand, Los Angeles, circa 1979
credit: copyright © Michael Ochs Archives.Com, Brian McLaughlin

Flyer promoting the first Blondie Australian tour and the beginning of the first Blondie world tour, 1977
credit: Victor Bockris Archive

Barbarella's, Birmingham, England, February 28, 1978
credit: Alan Perry copyright © The Concert Photo Co.

Newcastle City Hall, Newcastle, England, January 4, 1980
credit: Alan Perry copyright © The Concert Photo Co.

Newcastle City Hall, Newcastle, England, January 5, 1980
credit: Alan Perry copyright © The Concert Photo Co.

Hammersmith Odeon, London, January 11, 1980
credit: Pete Still copyright © The Concert Photo Co.

Hammersmith Odeon, London, January 13, 1980
credit: Pete Still copyright © The Concert Photo Co.

Whiskey A Go Go, Los Angeles, February 9, 1977
credit: copyright © Michael Ochs Archives.Com, Richard Creamer

Debbie performing in 1979 at the Mudd Club for a Red Star Records night, in Walter Steding's all-star band, which included Chris Stein, Richard Lloyd of Television, and filmmaker Amos Poe. Seen here with trumpet, Debbie also played drums.—*Stephanie Chernikowski*
credit: copyright © Stephanie Chernikowski

Blondie performing during the May 4-7, 1978 Blitz Benefit at CBGB, held to pay medical expenses when drummer Johnny Blitz of the Dead Boys was stabbed. It was a three-night event and everyone showed. Debbie, here with master guitarist Robert Fripp who joined the band for a few numbers, reads lyrics from a cheat sheet.—*Stephanie Chernikowski*
credit: copyright © Stephanie Chernikowski

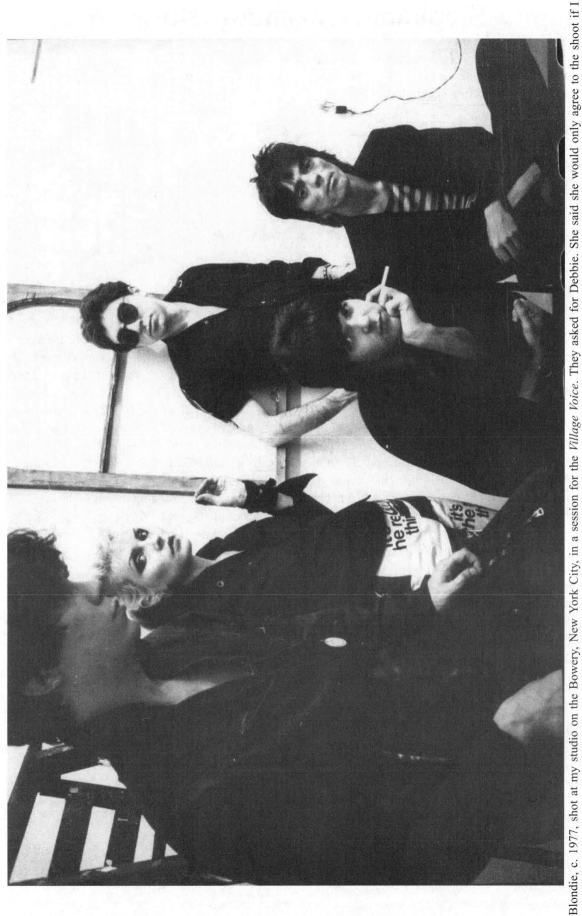

Blondie, c. 1977, shot at my studio on the Bowery, New York City, in a session for the *Village Voice*. They asked for Debbie. She said she would only agree to the shoot if I included the band, so I agreed. When the photo ran, they cropped it down to Debbie.

This session was before stardom when things were still DIY. Some of the band used electrical tape to bind the legs of their pants tighter (bondage pants weren't widely available at the time), while Debbie—a true child of Warhol—wore high Pop Coca-Cola promo pants proclaiming 'It's the real thing.' Her roots always showed.—*Stephanie Chernikowski*

credit: copyright © Stephanie Chernikowski

91

Stephanie Chernikowski

decisive moments
born and reared in east texas bayou country
kissed by elvis as a teen
my rock & roll fate was sealed
first used a 35 mm camera the day of the first moonwalk
i always liked to look
moved to macdougal street nyc 10.75
saw nureyev dance and patti and lenny do piss factory
first assignment for the village voice: alex chilton 2.22.77
walked in cold off the street, didn't know a soul and never showed a "book"
call me lucky
east village streets ragged and still at dawn
last night's guitar roar humming in my ears

SC from *Blank Generation Revisited*

Stephanie Chernikowski moved to New York City from her native Texas on Columbus Day of 1975. She began working as a photojournalist shortly before her move and to the present has continued to view life through a lens. Her concentration has been on 35mm black & white portraiture and documentation of the downtown music and arts scene, with occasional digressions.

In 1996, 2.13.61 Publications released *Dream Baby Dream: Images from the Blank Generation*, "a documentary film in stills," her record of the punk years in New York City. Critically acclaimed it was nominated for a Firecracker Award (the ABA's Independent Press category) for the outstanding art/photography book of the year. The following year she was project coordinator of and a contributor to *Blank Generation Revisited: the Early Years of Punk Rock*, published by Schirmer Books/Simon & Schuster in which six of the era's leading photographers presented photo essays on the period drawn from their contributions to a long-running traveling show.

Chernikowski's images have been commissioned by such diverse artists as R.E.M., Henry Rollins, Stevie Ray Vaughan, Willie Nelson, D Generation, Jon Spencer's Blues Explosion, Daniel Lanois, Alex Chilton, the dBs, Alan Vega, Panasonic, The Cramps, Richard Hell, Richard Lloyd, Eric Ambel, Coyote Shivers, Laura Cantrell, Will Rigby, and Amy Rigby.

Her photojournalism has appeared in numerous publications and books around the world, some of which include *The Village Voice, The New York Times, Rolling Stone, Texas Monthly, Austin Chronicle, Austin American-Statesman, New York Daily News; New Music Express, Melody Maker, Mojo* (UK). It is included in videos aired by BBC, A&E, VH1, and PBS.

As the work has acquired historical significance, demand has increasingly moved to galleries. Chernikowski's solo shows have included "Rough Magic: Punks NYC 1970s," at Great Modern Pictures, NYC, and "Late Night Reruns and Coming Attractions," Congo Bill/Danceteria, NYC. Some of the group shows in which her work has appeared are "Blank Generation Revisited," Earl McGrath Gallery and CBs 313 Gallery, NYC, Stichting Melkweg, Amsterdam, Lubbock or Leave It, Austin TX; Janet Wallace FAC, St. Paul, MN; "The Cool & the Crazy," Earl McGrath Gallery, NYC, Candace Perich Gallery, Ridgefield CT, Govinda Gallery, Washington DC; "Ascent of Western Civilization", Threadwaxing Space, NYC; "The Last Party: a history of nightlife," Serge Sorrokko Gallery, New York & San Francisco; "Angels: from Cherubim & Seraphim & Lucifer's Children," Melkweg Gallery, Amsterdam; "Man and Peace, Third International Photo Exhibition," traveling USSR; The Village Voice group show, Overseas Press Club, NYC; "Traveling Across America" and "The Cat Show," Multi-Media Arts Gallery, NYC.

Chernikowski is also a published writer on lifestyle and popular culture for books and periodicals, most notably for *The Village Voice*, where her work was accompanied by her photographs. She calls those visual/verbal pieces semi(o)fictions.—*Reprinted with permission from web site,* Stephanie Chernikowski Photography, *www.angelfire.com/pop/artpix*

All photos this page: Roundhouse, London, March 5, 1978
credit: copyright © Mick Mercer

All photos this page:
Roundhouse, London, March 5, 1978
credit: copyright © Mick Mercer
web site: www.mickmercer.com
e-mail: mercerm@supanet.com

Mick Mercer

"Photographing Blondie" by Mick Mercer

It's actually a bit weird these days, the way people ask you things, harking back to the days of punk. I'm only 43 years old, but I keep expecting people to think I'm about to hand them a treasure map! Last year a journalist asked me what I thought of Blondie way back when, as they were writing about the reunited version. I said they were punk's ABBA, because of the effortless way their tunes seemed to spew out. Some bands hit a rich vein that last for several years, and Blondie were one of this rare breed.

I've chosen these photos [*on pp. 93-94*—Ed.] because I think they best reflect what happened at the gigs. I went along to try and get photos illicitly, for my fanzine, *Panache*. I'd already been to see Blondie a couple of times in 1977, once at the Hammersmith Odeon supporting the deathly still Television, who were so dull I actually fell asleep, whereas Blondie were a charismatic bundle of spitting fun. Suitably impressed, I squeezed into the rabid Rainbow later that year, and they were even better, if a little smoother.

The best gig was the Roundhouse in early 78. They were magnificent, and the reasons are clear. At a time when punk was glorious but one-dimensional (concentrating on anger), Blondie represented a reflective, cool form of emotional music allied to bristling pop, but also with those gentler, weirder elements. And a sense of mischief.

What was even better was that you knew they were a true punk outfit, because there were something endear-ingly amateurish about them. When Debbie danced, you wondered whether she'd actually seen herself do this on film. She was a chaotic, heaving mess! That sort of summed up the way they came over, so daft in certain ways that they became totally cool...and regardless of their personal problems later, the way they presented themselves was wonderful.

The quality of their music was obvious. Unlike certain bands where people would defensively become dismissive, you never heard anyone slag Blondie off, and consider how many female fans they had. Because Debbie never actually played on her looks, but just threw herself into the songs, everyone rated her. Despite being huge internationally, there was no smugness, no arrogance. They didn't change in the way they came over from start to finish. No band to get as big, or bigger, has even managed that strange sense of dignity again.

The Hammersmith Odeon gigs probably happened at their height in England, where they were even doing mati-nee shows for younger fans. Unlike the Roundhouse, where nobody minded if you took a camera in, the Odeon was patrolled by overzealous mercenaries, so getting an old-fashioned 35 mm camera (no zoom lens possible) wasn't easy. I had to stick it down my trousers. I foolishly chose to do so before going down the steps to the underpass leading the gig, and by the time I got up the stairs at the other side, I was a tearful baby. Considering the results, I think the pain was well worth it.

Blondie were a fabulous band, but with the mystery that is music, the impetus dribbled away. By the time *Eat To The Beat* came out, there were just too many exciting bands around, and Blondie's golden time stopped glowing.

Having said that, it is of course, great to see them back. Most bands should never try reforming because the ideas have shrivelled in their heads by the time they hit thirty-five. Blondie are different. They deserve whatever good things come their way, because they never did anything shite in the first place.

Deborah Harry, October 1, 1981
credit: copyright © Mirror Syndication International

Deborah Harry, May 21, 1982
credit: copyright © Mirror Syndication International

Newcastle City Hall, Newcastle, England, September 12, 1978
credit: Pete Still © The Concert Photo Co.

98

Deborah Harry (with Blondie) at the Palladium, New York City, May 4, 1978
credit: copyright © 1978, 2002 Ebet Roberts

Deborah Harry (with Blondie) at the Palladium, New York City, May 4, 1978
credit: copyright © 1978, 2002 Ebet Roberts

Blondie at Max's Kansas City, March 11, 1977. Pictured are Deborah Harry and Gary Valentine
credit: copyright © 1977, 2002 Ebet Roberts

101

Chris Stein photo book opening, May 4, 1982. Attended by Iggy Pop, Sylvia and Lou Reed, and Andy Warhol. Pictured are Chris Stein and Deborah Harry. credit: copyright © 1982, 2002 Ebet Roberts

Ebet Roberts

Ebet Roberts moved from her native Memphis to New York to paint but switched to photography in 1977, when she began documenting the evolving CGBG scene. Inside the music business she is recognized as the consummate professional who has photographed everyone. Roberts' photography has been reproduced as album and book covers, press shots, and posters for such rock, classical, and jazz musicians as Bob Marley, Neil Young, Ravi Shankar, Philip Glass, Bob Dylan, R.E.M., The Cure, Natalie Merchant, Robert Plant, Bruce Springsteen, Miles Davis, Talking Heads, Bon Jovi, and Michael Jackson, and in over 100 books including *Blank Generation Revisited* and 1988's *This Ain't No Disco, The Story of CGBG.*

Publications include the *Rolling Stone, New York Times, Newsweek, People, Time, USA Today, New York, Vanity Fair,* and *The Village Voice.* Books include *Rock Stars* by Timothy White, *Frozen Fire: The Story of the Cars* by Toby Goldstein, *Written in My Soul* by Bill Flanagan, *The Rolling Stone Illustrated History of Rock & Roll* by Anthony DeCurtis and James Henke, and *Empty Places* by Laurie Anderson.

"Night Wind Sent" by Andrea Farina
Washington, DC USA
The Blondie Review, Art Issue, Fall 2001, copyright © 2001, Andrea Farina.

Deborah Harry, September 10, 1981
credit: copyright © Mirror Syndication International

Deborah Harry, October 1, 1981
credit: copyright © Mirror Syndication International

All photos on this page: Blondie lead singer Deborah Harry seen here dressed as a school girl.
credit: copyright © Mirror Syndication International

Deborah Harry, October 9, 1979
credit: copyright © Mirror Syndication International

Los Angeles?, 1977
credit: copyright © Michael Ochs Archives.Com, Suzan Carson

Deborah Harry with Swiss artist H.R. Giger, August 7, 1981
credit: copyright © Mirror Syndication International

Deborah Harry, the lead singer of the New York punk band Blondie, is shown in this March 1980 photo.
credit: copyright © AP/Wide World Photos

NEW YORK, April 18, 1981—AT "42ND STREET"—Debbie Harry, lead singer of the rock group Blondie, arrives at New York's Majestic Theater Saturday night to attend "42nd Street." With her is the group's lead guitarist, Chris Stein.
credit: copyright © AP/Wide World Photos

Deborah Harry of the punk rock group Blondie, circa 1977
credit: copyright © AP/Wide World Photos

Blondie in Neon Tunnel,
New York City, September 1976
credit: Bob Gruen / Star File

Blondie, New York City, 1978
credit: COPYRIGHT © MICK ROCK 1978, 2002

Mick Rock

London in the late sixties and early seventies was a hotbed of creative interchange. The prevalent hippie philosophy united all manner of artists, musicians, filmmakers, models, designers, actors, writers and photographers. This was the atmosphere in which Mick began his collaborations with the artists of the new decade. The first band Rock photographed was the Pretty Things, in 1969; soon he was photographing the likes of Syd Barrett, David Bowie, and Iggy Pop; emerging artists who would rapidly become international stars.

"They were all very special people to me. They weren't stars when I first met them. To me, they were free-spirited visionaries."—Mick Rock

Rock began travelling back and forth between New York and London, covering tours and capturing the music scene in all its decadent glory. In 1977, Rock moved permanently to New York, and quickly immersed himself in the burgeoning underground new wave scene, capturing the nihilistic spirit of the music of The Ramones, Blondie, and the Talking Heads. As rock and roll has evolved, Rock has continued to capture the essence of the fresh and new. Mick Rock has been instrumental in creating the key visual images of the last three decades. His photographs have been called as "significant as Andy Warhol's paintings in constructing the images we hold in our minds of the larger-than-life figures of our popular culture." Rock's accomplishments extend beyond photography, and include art direction, music video production and three Grammy nominations. Source—*"Bio" on Mick Rock's web site, www.mickrock.com. Reprinted with permission.*

Deborah Harry, New York City, Autumn 1977
credit: COPYRIGHT © MICK ROCK 1977, 2002

Debbie Harry was indeed the Marilyn Monroe of punk (as the press liked to dub her). But as 'punk' as she was, she was also 'glam' as a girl could be. And she always had a great sense of humour about all the attention. She never let it inhibit her ability to get down with the boys. She was (and is) a face for ages. And a pretty good singer and songwriter as a bonus.—*Mick Rock, 1984*

Left: 1980-photo shows Debbie Harry, lead singer with the pop/New Wave group Blondie, in a studio portrait. She is wearing a beige shirt and dress and beige thigh boots.

credit: © Lynn Goldsmith/CORBIS

Right: Deborah Harry posing in front of magazine.
Some things to celebrate. New York: Deborah Harry, lead singer for the band Blondie, has lots to shout about at a party at Studio 54 June 7 that was held to celebrate the 10th anniversary of Andy Warhol's *Interview* magazine. That's a blowup of the magazine's 100th cover and...that's right...it's Deborah who is featured on the cover. Blondie's song "Heart of Glass" has been a big hit recently. And Deborah is starring in a new movie, *Union City,* that should be in theaters soon. (Original caption). Photographed in Manhattan on June 12, 1979.

credit: © Bettmann/CORBIS

Debbie Harry of Blondie lying on stage
c. 1976-1982
credit: © Denis O'Regan/CORBIS

Debbie Harry of Blondie in the dressing room of the Mabuhay
Gardens, San Francisco, 1977 (later Debbie would brag that Blondie
put the first graffiti on the dressing room walls). The photographer
(Jonathan Postal) was also a founding member of the Avengers.
credit: © Jonathan Postal / Retna Ltd

Deborah Harry
credit: © Govert de Roos / Sunshine / Retna Ltd

Deborah Harry
credit: © Govert de Roos / Sunshine / Retna Ltd

Debbie Harry of Blondie, New York City, May 1977
credit: © Chris Walter / Retna Ltd

113

Chrissie Hynde (Pretenders), Debbie Harry (Blondie), Viv Albertine (Slits) 1980
credit: © Michael Putland / Retnauk / Retna Ltd

Blondie performing at the Starwood Theater,
Los Angeles, May 1978
credit: © Armando Gallo / Retna Ltd

This Starwood photo corresponds with the period when Debbie and Chris were living at the Gramercy Park Hotel in NYC and writing *Parallel Lines*. Blondie went back to LA (after Debbie's "solo" press tours to radio stations...) and at the Palladium met Robert Fripp (with whom Debbie was to star in a re-make of Jean-Luc Godard's "Alphaville"). Fripp ended up playing on "Fade Away and Radiate" on *Parallel Lines* and played on the live version of "Heroes" (released on the B-side of the "Atomic" single in the UK).—*Jon Erkider*

Deb in black was shot at TV show taping, possibly "Midnight Special." If so, that was taped at NBC Studios in Burbank, CA. Just down the hall from where Johnny Carson taped "The Tonight Show." The entire band received either a gold or platinum album backstage. Rodney Bingenheimer was in another photo with them. It was either 1979 or 1980.—*Jeffrey Mayer*
credit: copyright © Jeffrey Mayer

Deborah, in green shirt and camo shorts, was hosting a TV show called "Solid Gold" filmed in a studio (I don't know which one) in L.A., January 19, 1981. I have shots of her from this show with George Burns, backstage and on stage. She received a gold or platinum album and single from the president of Chrysalis Records at the time [*possibly, Terry Ellis*—Ed.].—*Jeffrey Mayer*
credit: copyright © Jeffrey Mayer

Deborah Harry, 1980
credit: copyright © Visages 1980 Todd Eberle

The whole band posing in the corridor of their hotel immediately after their Tower Theater gig, Philadelphia, July 13, 1979, during the *Eat to the Beat* tour.

credit: copyright © Marcia Resnick

Deborah Harry backstage having health food after the Tower Theater concert, mugging for the camera.
credit: copyright © Marcia Resnick

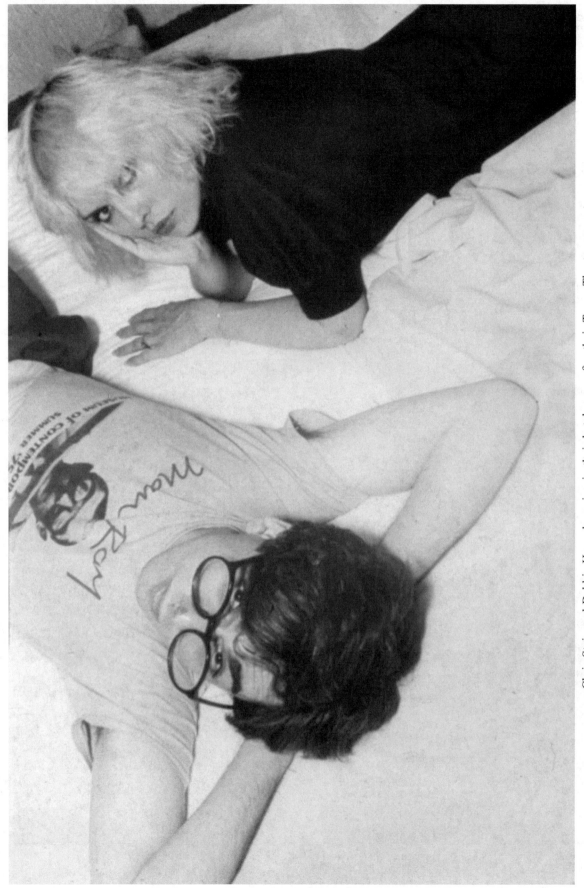

Chris Stein and Debbie Harry lounging in their hotel room after their Tower Theater concert.
credit: copyright © Marcia Resnick

"The Philadelphia Story: Blondie in 1979"

by Marcia Resnick
(adapted and edited by Allan Metz)

Philadelphia was a natural background for the raucous dances and frenetic Motown grooves that accompanied teenage life. According to Phil Spector, it "was just the most insane and the most dynamic city in the history of Rock and Roll" (DeCurtis and Henke, 108). How appropriate, then, to experience Blondie at the Tower Theater in Philly in July 1979.

I, Marcia Resnick, a fine arts educator and freelance photographer (*Soho News*, *New York Rocker*, *Rolling Stone*) was working on a project entitled "Bad Boys, A Compendium of Punks, Poets and Politicians." I was exploring both the nature of power, aggression, fame and sexuality among controversial men and women, and also the ironic gamut of meanings for the word "bad"—from "evil" to "naughty" to "really cool" to "good." It was this very quality of "badness" which rendered my subjects more formidable to their opponents and more endearing to their audience.

In 1979, Blondie was a cool and crazy band with an inherently mod aesthetic. Their unique aura was generated from the time when the 50's met the 60's, when the Lords of Flatbush and other ducktailed types hung out with their "hitter" girlfriends in the backseats of cars or on neighborhood street corners before malls existed. The boys of Blondie, in their pegged pants, narrow lapels and pointy shoes, surrounded the one girl, Debbie, a dazzling blond reminiscent of Ann-Margret in "Kitten With a Whip" or Tuesday Weld in "Lord Love a Duck," wearing shades, a miniskirt, tights and thigh high boots, the kind that were "made for walking." The group "digs" everything and is shocked by nothing. These "enfant terribles" of the Lower East Side music scene stood for the metamorphosis of the Beat Generation into the Blank Generation. Inspired by their cultural heroes, William Burroughs, James Dean, etc., they exuded a sense of villainy co-existing with vulnerability. This time in the life of the band was to become the time when friends, like myself, became fans, and when they were to "find themselves" and finally find their audience because they had found their "sound."

Concert tickets and passes from Blondie's 1977 and 1978 European tours
Courtesy of Philippe Carly—http://users.skynet.be/phicarly

Deborah Harry / The Bottom Line / 1977
credit: copyright © SLPStock / Bobby Grossman

Deborah Harry / backstage at CBGBs after show / Summer 1977
credit: copyright © SLPStock / Bobby Grossman

Rehearsal/sound check at CBGBs, 1977 / l to r: Garry Valentine, Deborah Harry, Clem Burke, Chris Stein
credit: copyright © SLPStock / Roberta Bayley

Blondie performing in an old theater in New Orleans, 1979 / Chris Stein and Deborah Harry
credit: copyright © SLPStock / Roberta Bayley

123

Heart of Glass video, Deborah Harry wearing Stephen Sprouse dress, 1978
credit: copyright © SLPStock / Roberta Bayley

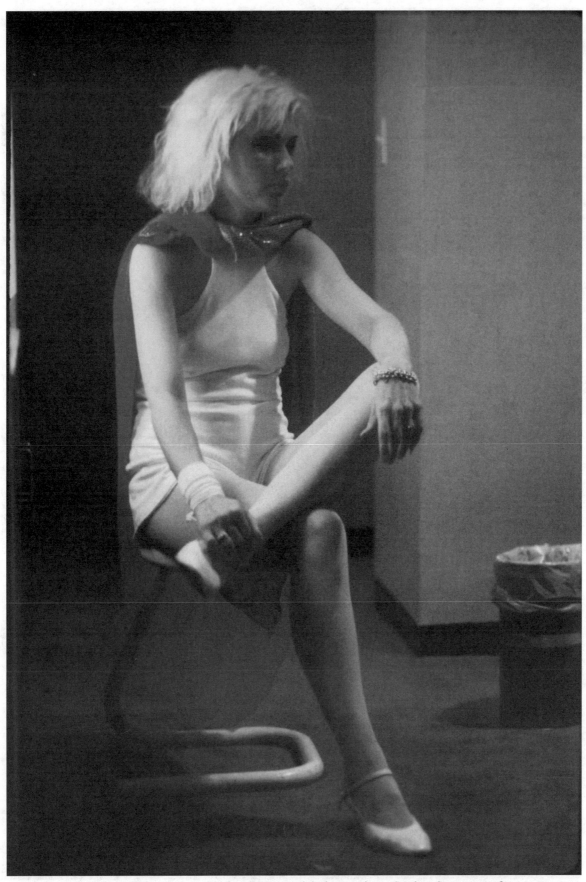

Backstage before a show / Deborah Harry might be wearing a Stephen Sprouse scarf.
The Aladdin Hotel, Las Vegas / the band Badfinger opened the concert, 1979
credit: copyright © SLPStock / Roberta Bayley

Philadelphia Spectrum / Blondie opening for Alice Cooper where they met Alice's snake, 1977
Deborah Harry with roadie
credit: copyright © SLPStock / Roberta Bayley

126

Deborah Harry, Manchester, England / TV dance show / waiting for rehearsal / 1977.
This photo may have been previously published in *Punk Magazine*
credit: copyright © SLPStock / Roberta Bayley

Set of New Jersey television program ("The Soap Factory"), dance party show, 1979
credit: copyright © SLPStock / Roberta Bayley

"She Just Takes Pictures: Interview with Roberta Bayley"

by Charlotte Robinson, Music Critic

PopMatters.com *web site, August 30, 2000*

Slightly edited version of original interview.—Ed.

As the door person at CBGB and photographer for *Punk* magazine, Roberta Bayley was one of the first to document the '70s punk scene in pictures. Her legendary photos have appeared in several significant books about the era, including the photography collection *Blank Generation Revisited: The Early Days of Punk Rock* (1997). Besides photographing and making mischief with some of the most important musicians of the '70s, Bayley is the co-author of an unauthorized biography of Patti Smith and a true renaissance woman. Bayley recently spoke to *PopMatters* from her home in New York, which she shares with her bird Preston, who occasionally tried joining the conversation.

PopMatters: You were originally from California, so what led you to London and then ultimately to New York City in the early '70s?

Roberta Bayley: I grew up in the San Francisco Bay area, about twenty miles north of San Francisco, and I went to school at San Francisco State University until I dropped out in 1971. Then I went to live in London. I basically had some personal things to work out and I wanted to get very far away and that was the farthest I could go where they still spoke English. I ended up in London. I had a friend who was staying at another friend's house and I stayed there. I lived there for a couple of years, working different odd jobs, some waitressing. I was working at a restaurant in Chelsea called the Chelsea Nuthouse on Langdon Street and Malcolm McLaren and Vivienne [Westwood] used to come in and eat there. They always were very fond of Americans and I had a casual relationship with them. I became involved with a friend of theirs named Gerry Goldstein, who was a good friend of Malcolm's. Malcolm had offered Gerry a job in the store [Let It Rock] but Gerry couldn't start right away, so I had offered to fill in for him. I ended up working there just for a few weekends, I think. So I had made that connection when I was in London.

I actually went back to San Francisco and tried to go back to school, but I couldn't bear that so I went back to London again. I was living with Ian Dury—Kilburn and the High Roads was his band then. That didn't work out and I just wanted to get the hell out of London, but I didn't have any money. My friend Andrew got me a one-way ticket to New York and I took it because I just wanted to get out of London. I didn't know anybody at all in New York. I had a list of names of people to look up and everybody I looked up was great. I ended up staying in Brooklyn for awhile and I started working.

How I got involved with the music scene is that one of the people I looked up was this guy David Nofsinger, who was a rock 'n' roll sound guy, a roadie guy. He said, "Let me show you around New York. What do you want to do?" I said, "I want to go see the New York Dolls," because I'd never seen them when I was in London. When they played in London, I was in San Francisco. When they played San Francisco, I was in London. So I was always curious about them. They seemed to be one of the more interesting things happening, even though the mainstream press seemed very down on them. They thought that they were these transvestites or something.

So he said, "Oh great, I was their soundman in Europe." They were playing a tour where they were playing a lot of different clubs in one week. He took me to see them at the Club 82, which was an old drag club in New York. The Dolls actually performed in drag at that show, but because I'd never seen them I thought that was their normal act, wearing dresses and stuff. David [Johansen] had on a strapless dress and high heels. I didn't realize this was a goof for them because they didn't really dress in women's clothes. It was an interesting introduction.

Nofsinger happened to live in the loft directly above the Club 82 and he had a party there afterwards. I met David Johansen that night and I met the Miamis, which was the opening band. Little by little I got introduced to the scene that was happening. I went to see Patti Smith and Television at Max's with Jimmy [Wynbrandt] from the Miamis. That was pretty interesting and I'd certainly never seen anything quite like that before. I stayed in New York from April until September, then I think I was going to try to go back to school again. I went back to San Francisco, but by that time I'd met Richard Hell and we had a correspondence going on and I again couldn't bear school, so I dropped out and got a job. By December I came back to New York, which was about New Year's Eve of 1974, into '75. And I stayed.

PM: How did you get the job working the door at CBGB?

RB: I was going out with Richard Hell and Television was the house band at CBGB. [Television manager] Terry Ork just said, "Will you take the money?" They split all the money at that point, which at the time was about fifty dollars. It might have been less. It was two dollars to get in and the money all went to the band. So they wanted to have somebody that worked for them rather than have somebody who worked at the club, or maybe the club didn't even have anybody to work at the door. It wasn't a happening place at that point. I just worked on the door and Terry gave me ten bucks or something. When CBGB, about a year or so later, did this festival where they had all the different bands playing every night, then [CBGB owner] Hilly [Kristal] asked me if I would come back and do the door, so I did and it became my regular job for a couple of years.

PM: Do you remember a particular strange or interesting thing that happened when you were working there?

RB: Everything was interesting. I don't know if anything was strange. It was just kind of a little scene. People would check out a band and a couple of weeks later they'd start a band. It was a very fun and creative time. Nobody was taking it real seriously, but Patti Smith had started to make some real in-roads and there were people who thought she was going to be successful. There were definitely people that thought that Television was going to be successful. Television with Richard Hell—there was some big excitement about them, that they were really different and maybe they were going to be the new Rolling Stones or something. Looking back, it wasn't a very long-lived thing. Richard left the band and then they became quite a different band. I was never such a great fan of the second version of Television. But there was an excitement and it was interesting.

PM: You started taking photographs of the bands in November 1975?

RB: I probably got a camera right around that time, October or September, and started taking pictures. My friend Guillmette Barbet, who was the photographer for *New York Rocker*, kind of showed me. My friend Jamie gave me a darkroom, which was really nice. He just had one that somebody had left in his house and he wanted to get rid of it. So I acquired a darkroom, which really made a big difference because I could print all my own stuff. Guillmette showed me how to develop film.

I'd had aspirations earlier to be a photographer but I never really pursued it. At one point I had a camera but then I sold that. I didn't really have a clear idea of subject matter, but when I came to CBGB all these bands wanted their pictures taken and it turned out I was pretty good. It was going to work for *Punk* magazine that really opened things up a lot because they really had an interesting take on things. It wasn't just the same old boring, posed pictures. We did all these really creative things, like the fumettis. We did these things that were like comic strips and photos. Two of our issues were just complete stories, a whole story told in photographs of different people. Debbie Harry starred in one, and Joey Ramone, and Richard Hell starred in another one. All the different bands played a part. That was really fun to do.

PM: How did you get the job at *Punk* with John Holmstrom and Legs McNeil?

RB: I remember clearly meeting Legs. He came to the door at CBGB and he said, "I'm Legs McNeil. I get in for free." I said, "Two dollars." I said, "Give me a copy of the magazine and I'll let you in." He said, "It's fifty cents. You can buy one at the bar." I thought he had a good attitude, so I let him in for free. Then I went and bought a copy of the magazine at the bar. I went home that night and read it, and it was the funniest thing I'd ever read. That was the one with the Lou Reed interview. I was like, "I've got to work for these guys!" We actually did a fumetti that never came out about Legs on the town, and Legs going to all these different places and getting thrown out, which we never used but we had a lot of fun shooting it. They liked me and liked my pictures and that's how we started working together.

PM: Did you use color much, or did you usually shoot in black and white?

RB: Pretty early on I would shoot both. I did shoot a lot of color, actually—it's just that there weren't as many places for color to be printed. I always had the idea that when magazines called you, if you had color, it was a good thing. I didn't have any artistic pretensions about the purity of black and white or anything like that. I just took pictures. Money was a consideration because color was expensive. I never really made any color prints. I just sent the slides and a lot of them were published. *Punk* had really excellent color reproduction a little bit later, not in the beginning, but when they went on to much better paper. They did one of my Iggy Pop pictures, a great Ramones picture that was just recently reused on the Ramones anthology, and I did the New York Dolls reunion in color as well.

You have to remember that back then these bands were not really big or anything. Blondie was the only one that people really even wanted color pictures of and that wasn't because they were big—it was just because Debbie [Harry] was very beautiful. If I had color pictures of the Ramones, *Creem* might run a little picture of them or something, but most magazines weren't going to have any interest in color pictures of Richard Hell and Television. There just wasn't really an outlet for it. It didn't really get seen.

PM: Did you go into a shoot with an idea in mind of what you wanted to do?

RB: My first real photo session with a band was the Heartbreakers blood picture, which was on the cover of *Please Kill Me*, and that was Richard [Hell]'s whole concept. He just considered me an adjunct to his genius. [laughs] Literally, I'd had a camera for about a month. I had no idea what I was doing. It's just taken in my apartment up against the wall with flash, I think. There probably wasn't enough natural light the day we did it. Usually I just did very simple pictures with no concept. That was an exception. The *Punk* magazine pictures, of course, were directed by John [Holmstrom] and Legs [McNeil] and some of them have stories and ideas behind them.

I think one of my skills as a photographer is that I work really quickly and I don't tell people what to do. Most of the people I shot knew me and weren't feeling like there was big pressure or anything. Most of these bands, with some exceptions, don't like having their picture taken. It's boring to them and they're just happy to get it over with. If you can work quickly, that's the key to being popular. With Richard

Hell, who was probably one of my main subjects—I probably photographed him more than anybody and I did pretty much all of his records and singles—he felt very comfortable with me. He hates the whole photo process, but with me it was less like that. When I was going out with him, I wasn't a photographer. I didn't have a camera. It was after our relationship, so that really didn't have anything to do with it. It wasn't like I was his girlfriend photographing him. It was long after I was his girlfriend. We'd been friends all this time and it was just less of a deal if someone said, "You need a picture for such and such," to just call me to do it.

PM: Who was your favorite person to photograph?

RB: Iggy [Pop] I liked photographing a lot and I wish I'd photographed him more. My main stuff of him is live and I only did one session with him off-stage. Debbie [Harry]'s great, very easy to photograph, obviously. She "gives" you the picture. I wouldn't take many pictures of her, but she'd look right at you and look amazing, as she does.

I don't know if I think about it that way. I can definitely think of people that I hated photographing, but I wouldn't want to talk about it. [laughs] Part of the reason I stopped was because some people are so annoying and I just don't need it at all. I did it as long as it was really fun. Towards the end, people would ask me to do pictures or I'd think I wanted to get back into it, and then I'd have these really negative experiences. It was a big turn-off.

PM: Did documenting the Sex Pistols' American tour with John Holmstrom, which is discussed in the book *Twelve Days on the Road*, taint your image of punk at all?

RB: It was a really interesting experience. You have to remember that the guy who wrote that book was accusing John and I of being CIA agents. He was a stupid fucking Warner Bros. roadie, Noel Monk—and I'm not talking about Jimmy Guterman, the collaborator with him. But this Noel Monk guy was an old hippie roadie. When I heard he was writing a book, it was hilarious to me. He was screaming, trying to have John and I thrown out of shows saying we were CIA agents. It was so stupid.

The Pistols thing was a drag, but I think they were really just one band. In a way they have kind of a perfect history. I think lingering is not always the best thing to do. As much as I'm happy they could get together and do a reunion tour and make some money and that they were actually pretty good, at least the second night they played here, that was to me was the only mistake they made. But quite frankly most people don't remember that, so who cares? If you see *The Filth and the Fury*, it looks more like a splendid time was had by all.

Yeah, that tour was really quite bleak but John and I were on an expense account. We were hoping we were on an expense account, but really we were on my credit card. It did get paid back eventually. Someone was paying us to stay in hotels with the Sex Pistols and hang out with them. That was interesting. I don't think we looked on it as the end of the punk movement. We could see the band was not very happy. We didn't spend much time with John [Lydon] or Sid [Vicious]. They were traveling on the bus and John and I were flying with Steve [Jones] and Paul [Cook] and Malcolm [McLaren]. We didn't interact that much with John and only minimally with Sid.

PM: Did you think there was a link between the British and New York punk movements?

RB: Yeah, there was. I went over to London. How I got linked personally to that scene was that Dr. Feelgood came over here. They were pub rock but they'd had a number one record in England and they were trying to break them in America. They weren't punk but their tour manager was Jake Riviera, who later started Stiff Records. Jake was into the whole New York thing, the Ramones. Maybe they got the Ramones to open for Dr. Feelgood—I think that's what happened. There was something happening and everybody figured it out, whatever it was. Jake was also the guy who managed Elvis Costello. Things started to get linked together also because of Malcolm. Malcolm had been the Dolls' sort-of manager for awhile and I knew Malcolm, then Malcolm was in New York. All these things were all linking together anyway.

I think the Ramones had a huge influence on what happened in London, which is kind of left out. Say, when you see the film *The Filth and the Fury*, they don't really talk about that. It doesn't take away, to me, from [the British bands'] originality. The kernel for the New York people was the Dolls. Although the Dolls were never successful or anything, they inspired everyone from Richard Hell to whoever because it was like they were acting like stars and they were huge in their own world and they were having a lot of fun and they weren't virtuosos. But there they were, getting more girls in Max's than the Rolling Stones could get in that one particular moment. They were bigger than anybody just within that world, which—that's the only world you're in, is the world you're in. If Max's back room is your world, and you're the biggest person there, then you're the biggest person in the world.

People want to put some noble thing on it, but part of it is about getting chicks and getting adulation. It's not all about "I have to create the new art." There's self-expression, but people have all kinds of motives for doing things in popular art. And that's a good thing. I think the Dolls made people see you could do this. You could start a band, you could be pretty big, you could have a traveling party, you get fans, you hopefully might get money, and get a record deal. It can be done. It's not some far off thing.

Malcolm saw that with the Dolls and he tried to put bands together with Chrissie Hynde, Richard Hell, Syl Sylvain, and all kinds of different people. Then he realized, "Why don't I just get a band from these younger kids?" Then the Ramones came in and influenced the idea of the short song, then came the Sex Pistols and the Damned, who were also managed by Jake Riviera, and they were the first punk band to come over here. It was a very big intermixing.

The scenes were very different in terms of the look. That whole punk look in England didn't really come here until later. There wasn't really a look to the New York scene particularly, which to me was what was nice about it. There was individualism within the bands. That was probably true among the British bands as well, except there was a second wave of copy bands, like the Cortinas and stuff. Remember that? [sings] "You're a fascist dictator." [laughs] All these weird bands that were just really dopey, but that's OK—they were kind of dopey in a fun way. They just threw the politics on top of fast beats. That's always how it goes. There's always one thing and then ten other imitators and some of the imitators are amusing and some aren't.

The Ramones and Blondie and everybody were touring in England by '77. I was over there at that time. I was very good friends with Jake Riviera and that's when the Stiff tour happened, and the Anarchy Tour with the Sex Pistols and the Heartbreakers. It was all very intertwined. I don't think one thing was better than the other. I'd always been quite a bit of an Anglophile and I'd lived in England and knew people there, and I liked that. I never thought about it as two separate things. I just thought we were all having a party.

PM: In *Blank Generation Revisited* you said you dropped out of sight because you were in danger of losing your amateur status. What did you do in the '80s?

RB: Oh, God, everything. What I really like, and it took me a long time to realize what I was doing, but I like to do all kinds of different things. I worked a lot of different jobs. I worked at the Peppermint Lounge for awhile and I worked in sales. I like to take what comes along. It's like an adventure to not be tied into one thing. To me, the most boring thing I could have done was to become a professional photographer. [laughs] If I'd gotten professional and I'd gotten a studio, I'm sure I could have made a lot of money. To me, that's just as boring as being an executive at IBM or something.

My camera was a tool to explore things and have fun and I luckily coincided with something. I never made a living from photography—I always had another job pretty much. Now I'm making almost a living from my photography because of what I did then because I wasn't doing what I did then for money, if that makes sense. I'm making the money now, luckily, because what I had interest in has sustained itself. I do think that there was some artistry in what I was doing even though I don't come from a background where I articulate the great theories that I'm trying to put forth in my work. That's for other people to say about what I do, rather than me. I just take pictures.

PM: You were the only one of the *Blank Generation Revisited* photographers who didn't seem to do it in a careerist way.

RB: Well, they're all still photographers. That's what they do. I'm not sure how much Stephanie [Chernikowski] still shoots, but does she still do sessions [sic]. [David] Godlis is a street photographer. He photographs authors and things like that for jobs, but basically he's just doing his own work out in the street. But Ebet Roberts is working professionally every day, goes to every concert and all that stuff and I'm sure she likes it. For me, I would have killed myself years ago if I still had to go out and photograph bands. Some people like it, so that's good, whatever. [Bob] Gruen is obviously still a working photographer and he's doing a lot of different things.

When people say "What do you do?" I still say "Photographer," but I think the excitement of life is to not define yourself as being one thing. You have to do that if you want to make a lot of money, but luckily making a lot of money was never my motivation. In theory it is, but I know in reality it isn't, because the people who really want to make a lot of money do make a lot of money, I think. So, I must not want to make a lot of money because I never did. That's OK because it gives me a lot of freedom, which is what I really like about life—just seeing what rolls down the path. Luckily, I have Barry Neuman taking care of the gallery, photo, art side of my career, and I have a really good photo agent, Kevin Kushel, who's taking care of the commercial side so I don't have to bother with that stuff, because it interferes with goofing off, which I like doing a lot.

PM: How did you end up working on the Patti Smith biography [*Patti Smith*] with Victor Bockris?

RB: Victor was stuck in a place where he'd done the basic research, but he just couldn't get started on the book. He hired me to come in and help him write the book. I've been a writer when I've been asked to write or forced to write or paid to write. If someone asks, "What do you do?" I don't say, "I'm a writer." I don't wake up every day and write. I don't have a novel that I'm working on. I should be writing my own book, but I'm too lazy and I haven't gotten around to doing that. But I'm working on it because I'm living my life and that will be part of the book. So I'm still doing the research.

PM: Would you ever consider doing another biography?

RB: No. I think some people have a real talent for biography. I had dinner last night with Nick Tosches, who's probably one of the best biographers. The kind of thing he does I could never aspire to. I'm not a writer in that sense. The only way I would do a biography is if some subject matter gripped me so much that I wanted to write about it. I'd really rather read books than write them.

I have my story that I have and nobody else can have. I mean, God forbid—I suppose my payback from Patti is going to be if someone writes my biography. [laughs] I've had an entertaining life, but I certainly wouldn't want it all in print. If I write my book, it's mainly going to be from '74 or '72 to the '80s. I certainly don't have an interest in telling people my whole life story, even though it's mildly amusing. I began as a Beatles fanatic, then there was the whole San Francisco psychedelic scene. All these different things came together, so I think I covered a lot of water.

PM: I was wondering if you were into the San Francisco scene, since you grew up there.

I was going to the Fillmore from the time I was about 17 or 16. We were pretty young, but you still saw all the psychedelia and everything. We went to all the be-ins and love-ins, and this and that. Basically, we were going to see the bands. We weren't going to take LSD—not quite yet. I went to the Monterey Pop Festival, was involved in that whole scene. But the early British Invasion stuff was what I was really into—the Beatles, the Stones, and all that stuff.

PM: You still live and work in New York. Do you feel like the city has retained its cultural importance?

RB: I don't think New York's cultural importance ever is going to change. There isn't any other place like this. Since I've been here all this time—26 or 27 years—maybe I can't even see. I don't know what's happening in the rest of the world and maybe there's a whole big thing out there, but still I don't think there's any place like New York. I don't think I'm that involved in the cultural life or anything except by osmosis. I go to museums or galleries rarely. I just walk around and to me, that's the cultural influence of New York, just walking down the street. I don't think there's any streets like these, but I could be wrong. If I could find another place to live, I'm sure I'd like to live there, but I think I'd really miss New York. I'm from San Francisco, but when I go back there, it's a very nice place but it doesn't even seem like a city to me. It seems like some kind of a weird, clean village. [laughs] Not a lot of grit.

PM: Do you feel like the grit is still in New York in spite of Mayor Giuliani?

RB: The parts of New York that Giuliani has cleaned up, like Times Square—I liked the old Times Square better, but I don't go there. Why would I go there? I'm in my crummy neighborhood. To me, it's improvements. People are saying "Gentrification, gentrification." Hey, if gentrification means I have fifty movie screens within a three-block walking radius of my home, I'm happy about that. I used to have to go uptown for the movies. I don't have to go uptown for anything anymore. Literally, there's five or six theaters within five minutes of where I am. That, to me, is the culture that I like, even though I never go to the movies anymore. But if I want to I can. The same thing about restaurants—I have six good, cheap restaurants within a two-block walking radius. I like that. They can't clean up New York too much. They can do it somewhat, but there will always be some kind of an underbelly here.

In the farther East Village, like Avenue A, B, C, and D, that used to really be very rough, poor, dangerous, drug-dealing, all that. Some of those blocks now are just beautiful. They're not modern or anything. They're just nice. I think that's a good thing. It's unfortunate that everything becomes expensive, but you can't just let things run down and become the South Bronx so they'll stay cheap.

If you want to find bad neighborhoods, there's plenty of them if that turns you on. They're always there. I have a rent stabilized apartment so my rent has only gone up minimally since I've been here. If I lost this apartment and I had to go out and look, I couldn't live in New York. I don't want to work hard enough to pay fifteen hundred a month rent. That's of no interest to me. When would be my time to enjoy my life? So then I would just leave. If gentrification has made the rents go up, I don't know what you can do about these things. I don't have an answer about that stuff.

PM: As a last word, what do you think is the greatest gift punk gave the world?

RB: It's a hard question, because I live on St. Mark's Place between 2nd and 3rd. Anyone who's been in New York knows this block—the "punk rock block." There's still all these kids who are dressed like 1977 in the bondage pants, the mohawk, this and that. What we thought it would have given was the idea of originality and you can be any way you want, you can be different. The idea of punk that I liked was that you don't have to be an expert. An amateur is a good thing. An amateur is somebody who does something because they like doing it. You don't have to be an expert. You can try different things. You could try going on-stage before you were a virtuoso. You could pick up a camera if you hadn't gone to photography school. You can do these creative things.

I guess there are some people who picked up on that idea, but instead they seem to pick up on the bad fashion. I guess that's just the visuals. I'm sure plenty of people were inspired by the punk thing, from R.E.M. to Green Day. Outside of the music thing, though, I find a lot of young people are whiny. They're saying, "We don't have anything. Everything is harder today. You had this. You had the good bands. You were around when..." It's like, "What?!" No, we were around when nothing was happening, so that's why we did it. There were no good magazines around to inspire *Punk* magazine. *Punk* magazine came out of itself. I find so many of the young people are whining about how life's so boring now. No, life was boring then! That's why we did this.

People always say, "Why do you think there's still so much interest in the punk thing?" The reason is because nothing else has happened since then. I'm happy about that because I'm making money. I'm selling my pictures because there's still this continuing, unending interest in the '70s. But why not something new? Wouldn't that be interesting? I always think maybe it's happening out there and I don't know about it because I don't pay attention to these things, but I don't think it is. That's what's scary. I don't think there's anything interesting happening. I wish that wasn't true.

"'You Know When to Take the Picture': Roberta Bayley In Conversation"

by Robert Betts

The Blondie Review (TBR), *December 2000*

An exclusive interview with the noted photographer originally published in TBR.—Ed.

I recently met Roberta for the first time. She is a wonderful person to have on the opposite side of a conversation. I really can't nail it down, exactly, but she exudes that kind of relaxed, friendly openness that makes you feel like you've known each other for a long time. Roberta and I have spoken five times in the past month and I must go on record and tell you that those were some of the most pleasant chats I've had with anyone in recent history (spousal exchanges notwithstanding). Some of the human flavor may be lost in this interview for the lack of Roberta's presence, but at least when I'm done, you'll know something about her talents, accomplishments, who she is, and what she is about.

Roberta Bayley, originally from San Francisco, came to New York City in 1974. It was a time when the music scene was about to undergo a major and important change. Her work appears in *Blank Generation Revisited* and she coauthored *Patti Smith: An Unauthorized Biography* along with Victor Bockris. She worked at CBGB's as a door person in the very early days and as the chief photographer for *Punk* magazine. Roberta's photos ended up on Richard Hell's album [*Blank Generation*/Richard Hell and the Voidoids, 1977], Johnny Thunders' Heartbreakers [*Live at Mothers*, 1994 and *L.A.M.F.: The Lost '77 Mixes*, 1995], David Johansen's [*From Pumps to Pompadour: The David Johansen Story*, 1995], Dave Edmund's *Anthology [(1968-1990), 1993]*, [the Iggy Pop tribute album, *We Will Fall*, 1997], and the Ramones' first album [*Ramones*, 1976] which was chosen by *Rolling Stone* magazine as one of 100 best in rock. She toured with the Sex Pistols and traveled across the United States with Richard Hell in an old 1959 Cadillac. She shot the fumettis for *Punk* magazine. Roberta also worked for Blondie for a year in guerrilla warfare and ran the Blondie Fan Club in the US prior to 1980. Blondie's *Platinum Collection* CD cover is her work. Her solo exhibitions are international and numerous; far too many to list here. When her talent's natural evolution approaches serious and restrictive professionalism, Roberta puts her camera aside for a while. She discusses these and other topics in our little chat.

TBR: Roberta, your work has been viewed by thousands of fans of the punk/new wave generation in the past twenty-something years. It has remained a part of rock history for more than two decades in books such as *The Blank Generation Revisited, Punk* magazine and others. Now, with the revival of *Punk* magazine, it seems that we are going to have so much more of the same to look forward to in 2001.

RB: Thanks for your many kind words. I think it's going to be fun—I think it'll be great. We're excited about it.

TBR: One question I just have to ask is: What was it like working with John Holmstrom and Legs McNeil at *Punk* magazine back then and what are your plans for the future? I mean, is it going to be the same kind of thing?

RB: Well, you know, the great thing about *Punk* was that there was always a lot of enthusiasm and a lot of great ideas flying around. It may, or may not have been so professional, whatever that means, but we did create some great things. And I'm hoping it will be the same thing with flexibility and ideas. We never really had a situation at *Punk* until the very end where there was an actual office and people worked there on a regular basis. At the very beginning *of Punk,* John and Legs, the original publishers, were running things from where they lived which was a horrible place on 10th Avenue and then we had an office on Lafayette Street. But it was a very loose thing. I didn't go to the office very much. I just showed up when there was an assignment...something for me to do.

TBR: It sounds like it was exciting...a lot of freedom, creativity. Is that what you're looking at again?

RB: Well, yah. I've come up with a lot of great ideas for the magazine and John has come up with a lot of great ideas. There are some great new writers, he (John) has found some great new young people. It's gonna be quarterly to begin with and we'll see how it goes.

TBR: I'm sure looking forward to seeing it again. I guess there has been a lot of work already done. What is the prognosis for it?

RB: Oh, we're coming out with it at the launch party—the benefit at CBGBs on January 10th. It's a benefit for charity with photographs shown at the gallery show downstairs. It's going to be a worthwhile event. If you haven't, you should go to the web site.

TBR: You mean *Punk*'s and CBGB's web sites? (www.punkmagazine.com and www.cbgb.com)

RB: Yes, it should all be there. I guess they are fixing up the *Punk* web site now.

TBR: By the way, last time, we talked about the Tom Tom Club, some of the former Talking Heads. I know you are friends with them. I did manage to go and see them in New Haven a few days ago, they were at Toad's Place. I've got to tell you Roberta, they are so alive and fresh...I mean, it was just such a great show. Tina (Weymouth) and Chris (Frantz) and the new group were just fantastic. What a great show they gave us.

RB: Yah, I think they are happy with what they are doing. I think the new record is going good for them. I just spoke to Tina the other day. She said she would come to the *Punk* thing (benefit) but I don't think they are going to play or anything.

TBR: Just off the top of my head (as Bob reads from a cheat sheet) I can remember photographs you've taken of the Heartbreakers, Television, Voidoids, Ramones, Dead Boys, Richard Hell, Andy Warhol, N.Y. Dolls, Billy Idol, Sid Vicious, Sex Pistols, Talking Heads, the Damned, Iggy Pop, Chrissie Hynde, Lou Reed, Patti Smith, David Johansen, Elvis Costello and of course, Debbie Harry and Chris Stein. Do you want to talk about any of them?

RB: I didn't photograph Chrissie Hynde and barely photographed Patti...live only. Same with Lou Reed—his wedding and a little bit live.

TBR: All right. So...I've mentioned about two dozen of the "who's who" of that time. Every time I look at some of those pictures I can feel the mood—the spirit of the moment. How did you manage to do that in almost everything you did? Did you take thousands of pictures and pick out the one that, by chance, happened to be right or did you somehow know when to "capture" the essence of that special moment? I mean, those moments are so fleeting...did you just *wait* for *the* moment, you know, you get Debbie with that special look and...ummm...

RB: Wait? Oh, no, no, no (laughs). I didn't take a lot of pictures. You know, it's just an instinctive thing when to press the shutter—you know when [to] take the picture. Debbie, of all people, is very excellent at giving you the picture. I have two rolls of film...clicking this and that, you [just] know, the picture's perfect.

TBR: I'm looking at the one with Debbie and Joey Ramone on a bed with a newspaper...

RB: Yah, those were posed for *Punk*. No, I have a very casual style. I know that people I have photographed felt relaxed and I also didn't put them under any kind of pressure or make them do things.

TBR: Like Debbie and Chris in the limo?

RB: Yah. That's literally the only picture on the roll. We're going down to New Jersey, I turned and, "click." I take the picture.

TBR: So, that's the answer? Instinctive, intuitive photography? Just like that?

RB: [laughs] I guess so. You know, no pressure...just wait for the moment and take the picture.

TBR: I recorded much of the Vietnam war with an old Pentax. I still have it. Do you still have your Pentax?

RB: No, actually, I sold my Pentax to Lee Brilleaux of Dr. Feelgood.

TBR: Back to the ole days—back to the old neighborhood, who'd you like to hang with...who was fun?

RB: I think David Johansen was the person I most liked hanging out with. He was always very entertaining and had a broad range of knowledge and he also liked to be photographed. It's funny because I'm now friends with his first wife who I barely knew when they were married. She was more in the Warhol crowd than the rock crowd. But I rarely see any of those people now unless they live or work in my neighborhood. I'm a bit of a recluse and homebody. But I'm looking forward to *Punk* magazine and having a forum for my ideas.

TBR: Okay; amateur photographer gets recognized and the stage is set for a professional career and lots of money, but what does she do—she puts her camera away.

RB: It would have been boring. I didn't want that. No, never. I mean, I could have done well and made a lot of money [chuckle]. But, ya know, it's all about fun and artistry and exploring things. If I did that, I'd own a studio and it would've been work [pensive pause]. You know, I just like the adventure.

TBR: Roberta, we're both on tight schedules today. Can we do this again, soon? Maybe at CBGB's in January? I'm sure the readers will want to know more.

RB: Sure. It's going to be fun.

Chris Stein and Deborah Harry, London, May 1982
credit: © Janette Beckman / Retna Ltd

I'm fond of these photos because they were taken during Blondie's last stages. The band was pretty much falling apart by then. Only Debbie and Chris were doing press for *The Hunter,* the Tracks Across America Tour, and the *Making Tracks* book. This period was so significant because it was the last time Blondie would see mainstream success as a band until "Maria" and *No Exit* in Great Britain in early 1999.

It also was an awkward stage because all through the recording of *Koo Koo,* a number of new wave bands—many female-fronted and borrowing from the Blondie character—formed and began having hits; some even taking attention away from Debbie. *Koo Koo* proved not to be the record everyone had been expecting—punk and pop or rock—and Debbie was criticized for being too "R&B" and "urban." Radio stations never played it.

The ironic thing, in the grand scheme of things, is the fact that Debbie and Chris were true innovators and precursors of the future of rock'n'roll itself. At that time music was still segregated. White and black hadn't come together at all (except by maybe the Specials). But look around you now: the charts, the prominent music genre, consist of nothing but that mesh. Debbie and Chris always knew where rock originated. They were the first ones to put the dent in crossover.—*Jon Erkider*

Part II: Between Acts

Deborah Harry, Brixton Academy, London, June 3, 1990
credit: Pete Still © The Concert Photo Co.

"From Breakup to Reunion: The Odyssey of Deborah Harry and Blondie"

by Lisa Diedrich
(adapted and edited by Allan Metz)

An invited original essay written specifically for this book. Covers the period following Blondie's breakup in 1982 through to its reunion, including Deborah Harry's solo career.—Ed.

Koo Koo, The Hunter and "Videodrome"

After Blondie's breakup in 1982, Deborah Harry's career in music continued, but not as a member of a band. Deborah Harry's solo work never achieved the level of success that she had found with the band; that special mix of talent and trouble that seemed to work magic. Deborah's image that is associated with her first solo effort, *Koo Koo,* was an attempt to break away from the Blondie persona that had been associated with Harry since the success of Blondie. The *Koo Koo* album cover was a grotesque H.R. Giger creation that showed a severe, dark-haired Deborah whose visage was impaled with long needles. The videos for the two singles from *Koo Koo* were directed by Giger and in them, Deborah is represented as she never had been in Blondie, with long black hair and an ethereal "witchiness" that seemed suited for a horror film. It is not surprising then that during 1981 Deborah did in fact make a horror movie, "Videodrome," with cult director David Cronenberg. In the film Deborah has dark red hair. It was obvious from "Videodrome" and the image put across with *Koo Koo* that Deborah Harry was trying to make a metamorphosis into a new creation and rid herself of the punk Monroe character of Blondie. Debbie was expressing herself artistically in new pathways, somewhat more disturbing than Blondie's path had been. In the 1979 film, "Union City," Debbie's character finally expresses her true self to her husband when she bleaches her mousy brown hair (a blond epiphany!). However, Nicki Brand in "Videodrome" is different, her blood red hair symbolizes her masochistic obsessions. Nicki exists in a dark netherworld that the character of Blondie would never dare venture.

Blondie reunited for their final album, *The Hunter,* in 1982. *The Hunter* album cover has a blond Debbie on it but it is obviously not a bleached Debbie; this time out Debbie Harry is wearing, quite obviously, a wig. Some of Debbie's TV appearances to support the album also had her sporting a long, white-blond wig. Why not make a TV appearance to sing a Blondie song with blood red "Videodrome" hair? It seems preposterous that Debbie would feel it necessary to don a blond wig in order to promote a Blondie album, but it shows how deeply ingrained the public perception of Debbie as Blondie had become and how Debbie felt obliged to live up to their expectations. Deborah would feel that it was out of character to appear on the British "Top of the Pops" program as a redhead or a brunette to sing a Blondie song. On a David Letterman appearance in 1982, Debbie did appear with her red hair and a man in the audience yells "I thought she was a blond!" Debbie slyly replies, "Oh, do you feel ripped off?" Again here, the character of Blondie is starting to become baggage. It is something that Debbie cannot seem to throw off, at least not as a member of a band whose name was based upon that particular character. This identity problem, although on the surface it may be only one of hair color, had to do specifically with the character of Blondie as Deborah had created her. David Bowie created Ziggy Stardust and Deborah Harry gave us Blondie. Now the problem that Deborah would have to face as Blondie's breakup approached was how to continue the career without the character.

Moroder, Jellybean, and *Rockbird*

Debbie's first solo single after Blondie's breakup was the song "Rush Rush," which appeared on the *Scarface* soundtrack in 1982. The cover of the single shows a very blond Deborah. In fact, the photo seems to have been taken around 1980, with Debbie wearing a revealing pink dress that she had appeared in on the *Plastic Letters* album cover. The song was co-written with Giorgio Moroder, in an attempt to follow up the success of "Call Me." Although the song is good, it is nothing to write home about. It is standard dance music that could be performed by anyone. In fact, it is quite similar to Berlin or Irene Cara songs from that same time period in which Moroder also produced. That special sound that had set Blondie apart from other bands was missing. Debbie is now a vocalist over a dance track and it is a disappointment musically.

What happened next was a career setback for Deborah Harry, no doubt about it. What happened was the rise of New York-based dance music up-and-comer, Madonna to pop music superstardom. Starting in 1983, Madonna's star began to rise and she did not look back. Madonna's sound, new wave meets club dance music, soon took over the airwaves and MTV. Pop music had a new reigning queen and it was not Deborah Harry. Deborah has mentioned that being on the same label as Madonna was not good for her career. Nobody was paying much attention to Harry's career in the mid-80s because all the focus was on Madonna. Debbie even tried the "if you can't beat 'em, join 'em" approach and had her single "Feel the Spin" produced by Jellybean Benitez, Madonna's producer, in 1985, for the *Krush Groove* soundtrack. It is a catchy track, but harks back too closely to Madonna territory to do Harry's career any good.

By 1986, Deborah was co-writing with Chris Stein again and on her *Rockbird* album she goes back to the rock sound that made her famous—producing was Seth Justman who had been in the J. Geils Band. The sound is very mid-80s pop, almost overproduced, and the *Rolling Stone* review described Deborah as sounding like "grandma Madonna." *Rockbird* is a pleasant pop album but not remarkable in the way that Blondie's albums had been. Fortunately, Deborah's acting during the late 1980s continued to blossom; her camp appearance in John Waters' "Hairspray" is wonderful. Deborah also appeared on the cult TV show "Wiseguy" in an almost too close to home role of a singer who had once been top of the charts, but was now struggling with personal fears in order to stage a comeback. In "Wiseguy," Deborah sings the song "Brite Side," a moody ballad that made it on to her next album, *Def, Dumb and Blonde,* probably the best of Deborah's solo projects. First though, an album of remixes was released in 1988, comprising Deborah's few solo hits and remixes of Blondie songs to appeal to the current dance music sound. The album title once again makes reference to that character that just will not go away—it was called *Once More Into The Bleach.* Making reference to that fun, funny, Blondie character was still Deborah's claim to fame whether she liked it or not. It must have been hard for Debbie to believe that a decade had already passed since Blondie became an international sensation.

Def, Dumb and Blonde, Debravation, and The Jazz Passengers

1989 was a good year for Deborah's career. *Def, Dumb, and Blonde* was produced by Mike Chapman. This album included songs written by the Thompson Twins, guest singing by The Cult's Ian Astbury, and even Gary Valentine made an appearance on backing vocals. It was as close to Blondie as Deborah had come since 1982. Although she had no big hits in the US, several songs were successful on the charts in England and Europe. Deborah seemed to have a new confidence, something that was missing from her few appearances to support *Rockbird* in 1986. The songs on the 1989 album are emotion-driven, very different from Blondie's detached music. "Brite Side" is moody, "Bike Boy" is very hard-driving rock, and some tracks are downright depressing, especially "The End of the Run," which is a funeral dirge mourning the passing of Blondie's early years. Deborah appeared on many talk shows and television programs to support her new album and she looked and sounded fantastic. She seemed to be enjoying life at the age of 44.

Unfortunately, for whatever personal or professional reasons, Deborah was unable to follow up the success of *Def, Dumb and Blonde.* It took another four years before her next album, *Debravation,* came out. *Debravation* had some strong songs on it, but the eclecticism, with hard rock and disco, rap and ballads, did not gel as it should. It was not like the magic of Blondie. Deborah went back to red hair. Maybe she was finally tired of not being able to live up to her past; no more was she going to go back to the bleach.

For several years, Deborah quit doing rock music altogether and spent time with the Jazz Passengers, a nonconventional jazz band out of New York City. Deborah was able to expand on her vocal style through this period, but it was the kind of vacation that she could not stay on forever. There was something a little sad about Deborah hanging up her rock'n'roll boots, to this fan anyway. Debbie seemed content to stay out of the limelight in the safety of a relatively obscure jazz band, not unlike the character she played on "Wiseguy," whose insecurities keep her from attempting a comeback.

No Exit

It was Chris Stein's idea to reform Blondie. Through the years, Deborah and Chris have been each other's muses, inspiring themselves to amazing artistic heights. But it is their creativity when combined with the amazing talents of Jimmy Destri and Clem Burke that is Blondie. What a happy ending and an amazing success story that they came back to work with Debbie and Chris to produce such confident, new sounds that are pure Blondie! No other combination of people could create that special blend of music. There can be no doubt that certain bands are together because there is a special chemistry that comes out and creates the music. Clem Burke's drumming was as important to Blondie's sound as Charlie Watts is to the Rolling Stones or John Bonham was to Led Zeppelin. Burke's pounding beats were the anchor for Blondie's songs. Jimmy Destri's return also was a great spark of creativity for the band. Destri had always been the most talented songwriter in Blondie. His songs were the trademark Blondie song structure, and, of course, his trash keyboard playing added something special to Blondie's sound that set them apart from other bands.

I am sure Deborah Harry has moments when she wonders how far the Blondie character can travel considering the inherent ageism of the music business. But when I saw Deborah Harry in 1999 playing with the boys in the band it was obvious that the character of Blondie had jumped back into the bleach and was having more fun than ever before; at that time as interpreted by a 54-year-old Deborah Harry. The defining Blondie sass, swagger and irony are all still there. The songs on *No Exit* are a mix of sounds, the Destri numbers are vintage Blondie, several tracks sound like post-*Hunter* songs, which is amazing, as it took 16 years after *The Hunter* for Blondie to record together again. Blondie even tackles hip-hop (1999 style), country, and a remake of one of their own early covers, "Out in the Streets." Their sound is still new wave, or what was thought of as cutting edge in 1978, but there is nothing wrong with that. A Blondie song is a Blondie song, just like a Stones song is a Stones song. They are staying true to themselves while experimenting with new ground. Blondie toured the world in 1999 and were the comeback story of the year. Blondie's reunion has definitely been productive, and was the right choice for Deborah, Chris, Jimmy, and Clem. A creative team like that one is precious and will continue to enthrall their fans around the world. Their next album will likely be even better than *No Exit*.

"Dreaming": Blondie's Legacy

The character of Blondie was one that Deborah finally could not escape. Debbie created such a fantastic rock'n'roll icon and it became so associated with her personally that eventually there literally was "No Exit"—Deborah had to reclaim her own legacy. Ultimately, the reason that Deborah has been amazingly successful at slipping back into the high-heeled shoes of Blondie is because the character was her alter ego and so much fun to embody on stage. Blondie is a smart, funny, brave character who lives every song as a great adventure. She is either getting tossed into jail in "X Offender," snarling about a groupie supreme in "Rip Her to Shreds," telling a man she does not care about any more to "Just Go Away," mocking the live-now-die-tomorrow culture of America in "Die Young Stay Pretty," or making her way through the war-torn tropical landscape of "War Child" and "Orchid Club." Now she is continuing on, telling a story of a sorry vampire in "No Exit," much the same way she told us about the men from Mars in "Rapture." Blondie's greatest accomplishment was its impeccable combination of humor, irony, glamor, and detachment. Deborah Harry's lyrics broke new ground because they were not concerned with broken hearts. Debbie had more fun talking about men from Mars, cruising the rifle range, and commenting about the absurdities of modern life. Each Blondie song is a mini-movie/music video. Blondie's music was once described as giving the listener the feeling of rotating under glass, and it is an aural pleasure to listen to the singular perfection of Blondie's albums. And Blondie energetically lived up to all that pop stars should be—their presentation of their art was complete, ranging from the attitude of Deborah Harry and the male band members on stage to their album covers.

Blondie did everything that bands were expected to do after the advent of MTV, but they did it years before MTV even happened. Blondie was the first band to release an album in video format with *Eat to the*

Beat in 1979. It is interesting to consider what kind of success Blondie might have had if they had stayed together and flourished during MTV's heyday in the mid-80s. What is certain is that the pop bands that made it big during the 80s owed much to what they learned from Blondie. Blondie paved the way for Pat Benatar and Joan Jett and also opened the doors for the women who would become the leading pop stars of the 1980s with their visual flair, colorful look, and humorous irony—the video music stars like Cyndi Lauper and Madonna.

Blondie's complex mesh of image and sound was misinterpreted by many at the time (the press said Blondie used sex to sell records) and they will probably never be given the due credit they deserve for their groundbreaking music. Deborah was the first rock'n'roll cover girl. When Deborah was featured in fashion magazines circa 1980 that was a first. Today women in rock are constantly on the covers of fashion magazines. Debbie's sense of humor was one of her finest qualities; she was an ironic sex symbol. Today's young pop music singers like Britney Spears and Christina Aguilera, are teenagers with very adult, sexy images. When Debbie became a sex symbol she was over 30. Harry was imitating the public's idea of a sexy blond and making fun of the idea at the same time she was embodying that conception. That sort of irony is missing from today's pop singers who work out their synchronized dancing with deadly earnest looks on their faces or very manufactured smiles. Much of today's music is based solely upon image, with music taking a backseat to generic sounds that provide merely a backbeat to the faces and bodies of the performer on the TV screen. This may be an unfortunate outcome of people misinterpreting Blondie's legacy. Blondie always put the music first; it was their incredibly unique style of music—a music that fused the many diverse elements of surfer sounds, 60s girl groups, Doors' style keyboard, rap, reggae, and punk rock into a completely new musical form that celebrated the utter wackiness and fever of pop music better than any other band of their time. Blondie's success was not a result of Deborah's beauty but because of her talent, and this, hopefully, will be the legacy of Blondie that inspires people in the future.

Deborah Harry with the Jazz Passengers, The Knitting Factory, New York City, May 8, 2002
credit: copyright © 2002 Sylvie Ball

Deborah sang "Imitation of a Kiss" and paused during instrumental sections. Her timing was excellent and her voice was clear and strong and didn't get lost in all that brass.—*Sylvie Ball*

"Addendum"

by Allan Metz and Lisa Diedrich

An elaboration of the previous selection and Blondie's musical legacy.—Ed.

"Maybe I'm Lost"/"I Can See Clearly": Deborah Harry Goes Solo

These two seemingly contradictory song titles reflect the ups and downs of Deborah Harry's solo musical efforts. Following the demise of Blondie and a few years out of the limelight, Deborah Harry launched a solo career, which at least partially represented her attempt to escape from the character she created—so much like David Bowie's Ziggy Stardust problem, except that Bowie, like Madonna, was able to discard the character and continually reinvent himself. Try as she might, however, Harry never achieved the notice and success as when she was the lead singer of Blondie and the same is true of the other band members. This relative lack of success is by no means Harry's fault. Rather, it reflects the attitudes of the male-dominated record industry which collectively believed that there was little, if any, room for more than one female artist at a time, which reflected a sexist attitude. Talk about a glass ceiling! "Pat Benatar is hot, so there is not any room for another female artist like Harry," so the reasoning seemed to be. Then, of course, Madonna, who essentially appropriated Harry's act and took it to dizzyingly new heights, overshadowed Harry—made even more apparent since both Madonna and Harry were on the same record label (Sire/Warner), which slighted Harry attention-wise due to the focus on promoting Madonna. And, speaking of promotion, a painful lesson of Harry's was that an artist needs to be constantly in the limelight and to be promoted and promoting herself. Harry's hiatus (largely due to her helping Chris Stein in his long recovery from a rare disease), while saying a lot about her strength of character and personal loyalty, hurt her career. It is hard to come back "cold" into the music industry. Another factor in explaining Harry's solo career is that, first and foremost, she wanted to be an artist above all and to maintain her artistic control and integrity. She did not have that burning desire to be a star as Madonna did. The bottom line is that with Blondie, the whole was greater than the sum of its parts. This is not uncommon. Other great bands like the Rolling Stones (and, perhaps to a lesser extent, the Beatles) have released comparatively mediocre solo material that just cannot compete with the spectacular sounds they create together. This observation remains true of Blondie originally, during its hiatus period, and now during its reunion.

Blondie's Legacy: "Screaming Skin"

"Screaming Skin" is a popular song on the *No Exit* album, which captures the electricity and excitement of being within the Blondie skin—back to the group's roots in a figurative/symbolic sense. And speaking of the current Blondie reunion, it fits right in with Blondie's legacy. All the members of Blondie are acutely aware of their place in music history. As a takeoff on Andy Warhol, they have more than held on for their fifteen minutes of fame. The reunion is an extension of that legacy. The band wants to enhance and sustain that legacy. Their contributions are both musical and cultural. Even while inactive, that legacy gradually grew with the passage of time and thus was particularly evident in the 1990s because their music remained popular with a staying power of its own. This served as motivation to Chris Stein, along with his sense that the time was ripe on the music scene, to reunite the band. To Chris' credit, once he sets his mind on something, he demonstrates a strong will and determination to realize his goal. Chris persuaded an at first reluctant Harry to go along with his plan, and the other original band members agreed. The reunion has generated numerous articles in the music press, particularly in Great Britain where Blondie has always been very popular and which made the band's first single from the *No Exit* album, the melodious and Blondie-esque "Maria," a number one hit. And a common theme in these articles is to reflect on Blondie's past and its accomplishments by placing the reunion in its proper context. Moreover, Blondie produced six albums before its breakup in 1982, came out with its reunion album, *No Exit* in 1999, and is scheduled to release its next album in 2002. Hopefully, there will be more albums to follow. Thus Blondie has created a body of work. In any one concert, there is never enough time to play all of their best-known songs, as there are so many to choose from; sometimes fans are a bit disappointed when they do not hear a favorite of theirs on a particular night. Although the band lacked artistic control, numerous compilation and remix albums have been produced by Blondie's former record company, Chrysalis, and then EMI, thus further adding to this body of work. The culmination of both Blondie's career and legacy would be their eventual induction into the Rock and Roll Hall of Fame in Cleveland, Ohio. A group or recording artist is eligible to be inducted into the Hall twenty-five years after that group or singer's first record. In Blondie's case, this was 1976 so Blondie would be first eligible in the year 2001. As this book seeks to substantiate, if any group is deserving of this honor, then it would be Blondie since the band was by far the most successful to break out of the New York City punk scene and on to the world stage. And Deborah Harry was ranked number 12 in a poll of music experts for VH1's 100 greatest women of rock—more specifically, between Patsy Cline (at number 11) and Ella Fitzgerald (at number 13)—very special musical company. And in a parallel fan poll conducted by VH1, she was ranked even higher at number six, even ahead of Madonna at number seven!

"Nothing Is Real But the Girl"

The reunion opens up a series of questions. Is Deborah's resurrection of the Blondie character something revolutionary? How will her current status as a half-century-plus sex symbol affect the music business and its inherent ageism? Or has the reformation of Blondie been a step back for Deborah in forging a non-Blondie identity? Or is the character of Blondie so close to something in Deborah that she will never be able to break free from it so why not play it up as only she can? On many of these questions, only time will tell, but they can be the subject of speculation, so here goes.

Deborah's resurrection of the Blondie character is something revolutionary and may contribute to the current trend of women in rock who have resurrected or continued their careers. The names that come readily to mind are Tina Turner, Cher, Donna Summer, and add to that list Deborah Harry, so she is a pioneer in yet another sense. Deborah explains this phenomenon in this way: "I think perhaps it's a fin de siecle thing—a fin de millennium thing, even. Towards the end of every decade, people look back and get nostalgic for the music that they need to enjoy" (Jackson).

Regarding the impact of these veteran divas on the music industry, it could be substantial and already has made an impact. Perhaps people are more accepting of established talent since many of their baby boomer fans themselves are aging right along with them. The Rolling Stones seem to have set the tone in this sense and Deborah Harry has noted that rock and roll has accumulated a venerable history, and so why should the artists involved in that medium not continue to prosper since they, after all, are "younger" than it. On this point, Deborah Harry has stated: "'But what am I supposed to do?...Should I suddenly not do music, or rock, because I'm past a certain age? That sounds really absurd. But I guess it's all relative'" (Varga, 27 May 1999, p. 9). Regarding ageism in general, a parallel may be drawn with the sexism Harry experienced in her first go-around with Blondie. Having fought that battle, she is now poised to take on age-bias.

As to whether the reformation of Blondie represents a step back for Deborah in forging a non-Blondie identity, this assertion is questionable. If there is a legacy (and there certainly is one in Blondie's case), why not reap its benefits? The band could have done this before, but did not. The band does not want to have to look back later and regret not having reconstituted itself when the opportunity was ripe. This is a good segue to the next question posed regarding whether the Blondie character is so close to something in Deborah that she will never be able to break free from it, so why not play it up as only she can? One of the meanings that have been attributed to the title of the 1999 album *No Exit* is that there was "no exit" or escaping from the individual members' identification with Blondie and this reality is particularly true of Deborah Harry. Instead of fighting this identification, as Deborah appeared to be trying to do in her solo career, why not succumb, accept reality, and enjoy it while this reunion lasts?

Blondie and Beyond

There also might be a place in the Blondie legacy for commentary about the newest wave of pop females such as Christina Aguilera and Britney Spears. Their music is obviously more Madonna-derived (they are almost a direct descendent of too many hours in front of the TV watching Madonna videos). But, as it brings up the idea of sex selling music (the perfect example being the cover of Mariah Carey's 1998 *#1's* album), such a discussion might be a good way to close the circle concerning Blondie since this point was made early in Blondie's career. Deborah Harry is *different* from these new teen dreams, most evidently by the fact that she was in her 30s when Blondie broke up but was perceived by the media as having a teen appeal. This point may need to be developed more fully in the future and it may be too early at this point to foresee as the careers of these new stars continue to grow and develop. And Deborah Harry seems to agree on this point: "Just don't ask me to predict who among the new girls will still be here in 25 years' time. God forbid I should condemn anyone else to longevity!" (Jackson).

"Deborah Harry: The Solo Years"

by Daniel Porter
(adapted and edited by Allan Metz)

The Blondie Archive *web site, 1999*

This selection is largely written from a British perspective and thus serves as a complement to the two previous selections, which are written from an American viewpoint.—Ed.

Part I

One of the most unique artists so far to date, Deborah Harry has always been an innovative and creative artist. Along with her aloof beauty, those sharp cheekbones, deep blue green eyes and, of course, the mop of bleached hair with dark roots, Debbie became an obvious target for the fame which eventually came her way. Not just content with releasing a pop album every three years, she has stretched her artistic talents to the brink, first by breaking away from the norm and being the first artist to have a number one hit with a disco song ("Heart Of Glass") and a rap/hip hop song ("Rapture") as the lead singer of Blondie. Subsequently, she became the first pop star to successfully begin and continue a reputable acting career and, in more recent years, has continued to pursue innovation with her stint in the eclectic jazz band, the Jazz Passengers. Born Deborah Ann Harry on July 1, 1945 and adopted at the age of three months to Catherine and Richard Harry, Debbie was brought up in the New Jersey suburbs. After moving to New York, and becoming good friends with Andy Warhol, her rise to fame came at a relatively late age following many years of struggle and dead end jobs, including working as a Playboy bunny and a waitress plus a short stint as a beautician and fitness instructor.

Debbie first started her musical career in 1967 with a folk/rock hippy band called Wind in the Willows, which released one single, "Moments Spent" and one album, *Wind in the Willows*. The band eventually broke up due to its lack of commercial success. Debbie later joined an all-female trio singing group called the Stillettoes featuring Elda Gentile (who is frequently interviewed in Blondie documentaries). It was in this group that she met future musical partner Chris Stein. They met after a Stillettoes show he had attended and Chris eventually joined the band as bass player to get closer to Debbie. Originally called Angel and the Snake, it was not until 1974 that Blondie was formed. In 1976, the band was signed to Private Stock records, and were later bought out by Chrysalis (for half a million dollars), which became the major backer behind Debbie's solo career in years to come. Best known for her work in Blondie, to date the band has sold over 40 million records. Most recently, they have reformed and again set the UK charts alight with their two hit singles—"Maria" (number 1) and "Nothing Is Real But The Girl" (number 22) along with the gold-selling album *No Exit* (number 1). Often described as the face of 80s pop, much of what Deborah Harry worked on following the split up of the then-world's most famous band seems to have been overlooked and shrugged off as a means for Deborah "to keep herself busy." This selection is dedicated to rip that statement to shreds! Debbie's solo years are my personal favorites. A lot of her best material has been released in the period from 1981 to 1999, even though some fans seem to have overlooked these albums and put them down as second best to Blondie's back catalog.

Debbie Goes "Koo Koo!" (1981-1982)

Toward the beginning of Blondie's demise, Debbie was feeling trapped and ready for a change. A new non-Blondie project was needed, she felt, to show that she was more than a piece of blonde fluff on stage backed by five men. She had the hits firmly under her belt—the most recent at that time being "Rapture," a sure sign that things were beginning to evolve and change. "Rapture" was a far cry from the screaming pop singles such as "Atomic" and "Call Me" and proved to be a groundbreaker in the world of pop with Debbie introducing rap to "middle America." After the release of *Autoamerican,* Debbie started working on her first solo project with Chris, *Koo Koo,* along with Nile Rodgers and Bernard Edwards of the Chic organization. This album spawned new, artistic, and fundamentally different songs ranging from pop ("Jump Jump" and "The Jam Was Moving") all the way through to rap ("Military Rap"). Along the same lines as the *Autoamerican* album, *Koo Koo* was the darker side of Debbie showing through. Debbie proved to the world that she was more than a cartoon-type pop star—she was and continues to be a musical artist with talents transcending pouting lips and miniskirts. Along with the new album came a whole new look: the blonde hair was ditched and dyed brown (her natural color) along with a variety of multicolored wigs ranging from bright green to luminous pink [*"shades" of Gwen Stefani's pink-dyed hair!*–Ed.] as shown on the cover of "The Jam Was Moving" 7" single. However artistic its aspirations, this album was slammed by the critics. The album cover, featuring a gaunt-looking Debbie with three massive nails through her face and one through her neck, was banned by the London Underground claiming that children would "try it at home!" (much to Debbie's amusement in later years). Faithful Blondie fans helped this album reach number six in the album charts. *Koo Koo* produced two new singles—"Backfired" and "The Jam Was Moving." There also is a 12" promo-only single of "Chrome." Both the fans and other band members, however, became uneasy with this project. Was a split forthcoming?

Her Stage Presence

The answer was yes. The last album, *The Hunter*, was recorded in 1982 and shunned by the critics as a contract filler, though it remains one of Chris Stein's favorite albums. Debbie dumped the wigs and returned to the peroxide for one last time. However, a cancelled world tour and Chris's serious illness led to the inevitable—the band broke up after seven years of fame in 1982. After this period of constantly being in the public eye, Debbie vanished. Much of the first six months following the spilt were spent in hospital where Chris was recovering from his near-fatal illness. After her previous film appearances—"Union City" (1979) and "Roadie" (1980) (with the rest of the band)—1983 saw two new projects for Debbie—opposite James Woods in "Videodrome" as radio talk show host Nicki Brand. Produced by David Cronenberg, this film caused quite a stir. Debbie appeared on "Nationwide" (a popular UK talk show) and was intensely questioned about the film's integrity and suitability. The year 1983 also saw a major turn in Debbie's career; her one and only (to date!) stage performance in "Teaneck Tanzi: The Venus Fly Trap," a play in which she had the role of a female wrestler. Debbie had to learn all the moves and once said that this was the fittest period of her life. Debbie hoped it also would do well in the US since its British counterpart, "Trafford Tanzi" starring Toyah, had a successful run there. The American production opened at the Nederlander Theatre in New York. The critics, however, panned the play on its opening night and it closed following that initial performance.

Feeling the Spin (1984-1986)

Debbie had maintained a low profile until 1984 when the dance single "Rush Rush" was released, to be featured in the film "Scarface" starring Al Pacino. The single saw a return of the familiar Debbie Harry; the hair was bleached, the face pouting, and the song very much Blondie-based. It demonstrated that this blonde was on her way back. In 1985, Debbie resurfaced with the poppy dance single "Feel The Spin" and a soundtrack to the movie "Krush Groove" was released. The single proved to be a smash at dance clubs, although it failed to chart highly.

The Return of the Rockbird (1986-1988)

The year 1986 witnessed the return of Debbie to the public eye. She had been writing a new album for some months and once her record contractual problems had been sorted out, she concentrated on recording and putting a new album together. Chrysalis UK still had Debbie signed, although Chrysalis USA dropped her from their roster due its greater interest in Madonna at that point. Debbie was later signed to Geffen Records, which helped release and publicize the new album.

Rockbird was written and recorded during a quiet period. After its release, though, Debbie was thrust into the spotlight once again with very heavy publicity. The first single from the new album was the UK smash hit "French Kissin in the USA" released in November 1986, and available on 7", 7" poster sleeve, 12" and 12" picture disc with a variety of remixes. This song reached number eight on the UK charts, peaked at number 57 in the US charts, and topped at number five in Australia. The album eventually charted at 31 in the UK charts. The album cover featured a backdrop painting by Andy Warhol and Debbie wearing a Stephen Sprouse-designed "catsuit" photographed by Guzman. Debbie looks fantastic on this cover, a cross between Alice Cooper and Marilyn Monroe! This album cover, along with *Koo Koo,* are still cited today in magazine polls as among the best album covers of all time. The video for "French Kissin" reveals a sensual-looking Debbie in a leather jacket, showing off pouting lips, and the familiar blonde hair, set in a 1950s/60s pop art period. It was well received by the fans, old and new alike, and the critics. The Blonde Rockbird had proved that she was back. The cleverly titled album was produced by Seth Justman (a new producer for Debbie) and featured some of her best songs, including "French Kissin," "In Love With Love," "Free To Fall," "Rockbird," "Secret Life," and "Beyond The Limit."

The second single, "Free To Fall," was a UK-only release and it peaked at number 46 in the UK charts. The third single, "In Love With Love," was a hit particularly in the clubs. The UK version was different from its US counterpart—the latter opting for the SAW [Stock, Aiken & Waterman] remix (which later launched artists such as Kylie Minogue into the pop industry). It did not chart very highly— number 45 in the UK and number 70 in the US. The budget for this album seemed very high. The videos were all very expensive to make—probably due to the MTV video era at the time.

Debbie made a few appearances on TV both in the UK and US. "Saturday Night Live" featured a slightly thinner Debbie singing "French Kissin" and "In Love With Love" with a number of backing singers, who were gospel oriented; their style did not quite match the songs. The press soon focused in on Debbie, realizing that Madonna had taken over the spotlight, and did to some extent praise and criticize her for returning—both professionally and age-wise. (Debbie was a youthful looking 40 when *Rockbird* was released).

Debbie also extended her film credits by appearing in "Forever Lulu," which was a very walk-on part, in which she played a prostitute who was on the run from a group of gangsters. She also played a voodoo witch in the US show "Tales From The Darkside" in 1987. Although Debbie did not tour with *Rockbird,* she did do a lot of publicity for the album, including an appearance at a New Year's charity party and sang "Walk On the Wild Side" with Lou Reed and Grace Jones. She and Chris also made a Christmas morning MTV appearance; Chris was playing with a stuffed bat. Debbie made an appearance at an awards ceremony clad in her *Rockbird* catsuit and presented an award to Paul Simon—ironically for best solo performer of the year. All was quiet from the Marilyn Monroe of punk until late 1988 with a new "best of" Blondie and Debbie album *(Once More Into The Bleach)* featuring remixes of solo and Blondie work. "Call Me '88" and "Denis '88" were released as singles featuring new promotional photos of Debbie. Debbie and Chris contributed to this album a remix of her '81 single "The Jam Was Moving." The album peaked at number 50 in the UK and the single "Call Me '88" peaked at number 61 in the US charts. During this time, Debbie released another single, "Liar Liar," produced by Mike Chapman of *Parallel Lines* fame (Blondie's most successful album). This single was recorded for the film "Married To The Mob" and still today is only available on a promo CD and general 7". (It is featured on the album's soundtrack, but strangely enough does not appear to be on any compilation albums). Debbie filmed a video for the single, which was recorded in a cellar setting with Debbie interrupting a gangster meeting and more or less beating them up, removing their wigs, stubbing out their cigars, generally causing chaos and eventually making them dance on the table, including the bouncers and geriatric men. It gave the world another view of the Debbie, who had slimmed down since *Rockbird* and looked incredible.

Part II

Def Dumb & (Still) Blonde! (1989-1990)

It was not until late 1989 that Debbie's most successful album was released, *Def, Dumb & Blonde.* Her first name had changed from "Debbie" to "Deborah." ("I'm getting too old to be called Debbie!" she once explained in an interview). A favorite among the fans, it is probably most similar to some of the Blondie material for which Debbie was best known. Featuring a variety of music, today it still holds its ground firmly as an exceptional project. The first single was a smash hit. "I Want That Man" reached number eight on the UK charts and has recently been remixed and released in a compilation album.

Def, Dumb & Blonde charted at number 12 on the UK charts. This album also was produced by Mike Chapman and is very Blondie-influenced and includes some of the best songs Debbie has ever recorded ranging from rap ("Get Your Way" and "Forced To Live") to pop ("Bugeye" and "I Want That Man") to pure melodies such as "Brite Side" and "Maybe For Sure." *Def, Dumb & Blonde* also introduced "Minky" into the pop world. Minky is Debbie's mascot monkey which she found in a garbage skip. The song "Bugeye" was inspired by him. Minky made many appearances in a variety of outfits with Deborah throughout this period including MTV, TOTP ("Top of the Pops") and Terry Wogan. Minky was also still around on stage with the band in the 1998 and 1999 gigs along with many TV shows. Four singles were released from this album: "I Want That Man," "Brite Side," "Sweet and Low," and "Maybe For Sure," the last being the only single not to have a promotional video. This was due to the fact that Debbie had embarked on a world tour, the first time since the breakup of Blondie, and indeed the first time on her own. The lineup for the tour included Chris Stein (guitar), Leigh Foxx (bass), Jimmy Clark (drums), Carla Olla (rhythm guitar), and Suzy Davis (keyboards). As part of this highly successful tour, particularly in the UK and Australia, Debbie performed at the Town and Country Club and The Borderline, both of which sold out. The Town and Country Club gig was broadcast live on Radio One and was also filmed. It has, however, never been released. This tour was a fan favorite, featuring a variety of Blondie and Debbie songs. Debbie commented on the fact that she felt all the songs were relevant to that time and the Blondie songs were very much ahead of their time. Songs featured included "Rapture," "Cautious Lip," "I Want That Man," and "Bike Boy." Debbie did many TV and magazine promotions for this album, the most memorable being a half hour long interview on "One To One" with Annie Nightingale in 1989. Deborah also appeared on MTV, Terry Wogan, Des O'Conner in the UK, "Breakfast TV" ("Good Morning America" in the US), "Request Weekend," and a TOTP-type program in Europe where she sang "I Want That Man" and "Brite Side."

During this period, Deborah continued to expand her film catalog by appearing in the link scenes between "Tales From The Darkside—The Movie," which was shown in cinemas all over the UK and was a huge success. Deborah played a witch who was holding a dinner party with a twist—the twist being the dinner was a small boy locked in her pantry. The boy eventually escaped only to throw Debbie into a flaming oven and kill her with her own cooking instruments. Quite a gory end. In a July 12, 1989 press release, the Disney corporation announced Debbie would play the "Old Woman Who Lived In A Shoe" for the Shelley Duvall-produced "Mother Goose Rock 'n' Rhyme." Debbie appeared wearing a figure-hugging swimming costume and sunglasses, which naturally caught a few headlines and helped promote her in the public eye once again. During this time, Debbie also appeared on a popular US TV show called "Wiseguy" playing Diana Price, a struggling artist who was making a comeback. Debbie performed "Brite Side" live on the show.

The Complete Picture (1991)

After Debbie finished her exhausting world tour for *Def, Dumb & Blonde,* she took a rest—but not for long. The end of 1990/beginning of 1991 also took off. Debbie along with Iggy Pop, who she had known for years from the CBGBs days and who Blondie supported on a tour in 1977, sang a duet on the album *Red Hot + Blue: A Tribute to Cole Porter*. This AIDS benefit album also featured other famous artists including Erasure and Neneh Cherry. Debbie and Iggy's song, "Well Did You Evah!," was originally written by Cole Porter. This was released on a CD single and 12" picture disc. Debbie and Iggy were interviewed about the song on a half hour show while filming the promotional video for the song, which features Debbie and Iggy in many different costumes—posh, common, and plain mad. The video features many animals—a snake (around Debbie's neck), mad chickens, and a bull as well as having Iggy and Debbie rob a bank in bizarre masks—thus constituting one of the funniest promos Debbie has ever made.

Following on from the single, March 23, 1991 saw the release of *The Complete Picture—The Very Best of Deborah Harry and Blondie,* a highly successful twenty-track album featuring all the old Blondie smash hits and also Debbie's solo hits from her first three albums, including "French Kissin," "I Want That Man," "Brite Side," "In Love With Love," and "Sweet And Low," as well as "Well Did You Evah!" The album reached number three in the UK. The artwork and design for this album is especially good, featuring promo shots of Debbie taken throughout her solo career and also opting for a classy white and gold sleeve. This album was available on CD, cassette and double vinyl. The CD is still available today and is featured in many "best of" collaborations. Due to the massive success of this album which was heavily advertised, particularly on UK TV, Debbie then launched into another world tour, including (as noted above) an appearance at the INXS Summer Festival on July 13, 1991. When this was filmed, the press went mad taking photos of Debbie wearing a figure-hugging black swimming costume and slaughtered her in the newspapers over the next week, with the usual criticisms about her weight and age. Clips of Debbie performing "Rapture" and "Atomic" were heavily featured on MTV worldwide.

Hanging on the Telephone (1992)

After the disappointing end to her otherwise successful '91 sold out world tour, Debbie returned to New York and 1992 saw the release of "Intimate Stranger," a relatively low-budget film where Debbie was the star. (There is rarely a scene without her). In a cat and mouse chase of events, Debbie plays Corey Wheeler, a singer performing in a seedy nightclub in downtown Baltimore. Debbie actually performs two cover songs in the film—"Piece Of My Heart" and "I Ain't Gonna Eat Out My Heart Anymore." She is a chain-smoking phone sex girl part time with a sad past. One caller becomes obsessed with "Angel" (her phone sex name). While on the phone, he kills an oriental prostitute and then is set with killing Corey, who brings in a cop. Nick Ciccini, ambitious for promotion, tries to help her. The killer tracks her down and kidnaps her sister by mistake. Corey goes after him, and they end up in an abandoned warehouse where Corey is captured by the killer with a blowtorch in hand. After a struggle, Corey gets hold of the blowtorch and eventually with Nick's help, the killer is subdued—quite a dramatic film which demonstrated Debbie's acting skills. "Intimate Stranger" was well received by the critics in contrast to the some of the criticism on "Videodrome" back in 1983.

The Bleach Is Ditched (1992–1993)

The year 1992 saw the release of "A Prelude To A Kiss," which Debbie recorded for the motion picture of the same title and is available on the soundtrack album. This song was the only single from the album and is only available on a promo CD. It reflected a turn in Debbie's musical style, opting for a more classical piano approach—an emotional song which is variously interpreted by fans. Debbie also released another soundtrack single, "Summertime Blues," a cover for the film "That Night." This was released as a single only in the US and Australia and failed to chart. The cover of this single features an old photo from the *Def, Dumb & Blonde* era. Debbie appeared on a few UK TV programs promoting her film "Intimate Stranger" and also *The Complete Picture* album. The sudden and drastic haircut was a shock to the fans; the blonde locks were replaced by a short brown style, which considerably altered her appearance. The beginning of 1993 saw Debbie in court being sued by ex-Blondie manager Peter Leeds, claiming that he deserved a percentage of her solo earnings, but the case was dismissed.

Debravation (1993)

July 1993 saw the release of the *Debravation* album along with a few other songs available on compilation albums, including one called "In Just Spring." Debbie began to write her fourth and last solo album to date, *Debravation,* in 1991. The sudden success of *The Complete Picture* and the film "Intimate Stranger" delayed its writing. The first song to be written was "Standing In My Way" (1991) and was performed at the INXS concert.

In this album, Debbie returned to the rocky pop that fans had so missed. Standout tracks include "Dog Star Girl," an electropop song which has been somewhat overlooked, along with "The Fugitive," "Stability" (pop/rap), "Rain" (pop), "Lip Service," and, of course, the singles "I Can See Clearly" and "Strike Me Pink." "I Can See Clearly" was released in June 1993, followed by the album in July and then the last single, "Strike Me Pink," in September with a new B-side, "On A Breath." "Strike Me Pink" charted and remained at number 46. "I Can See Clearly" did well in the UK charts (debuting at its top position number 23), but was a smash on the *Billboard* charts reaching number one—Debbie's first number one since the Blondie days. The album debuted and remained at number 24.

Debbie also made her first appearance at the New York "Wigstock" bash on September 5, 1993, where she sang "Heart Of Glass" and "Communion," wearing a blonde wig and orange robe. The press featured many photos of her, she was interviewed at the bash, and the event received additional publicity as a result of Harry's participation.

Jazzing It Up! (1994-1998)

The beginning of 1994 was a difficult time for Debbie. Chrysalis UK dropped her, largely due to the lack of success of her UK tour and album. Chrysalis USA had already dropped her from their books, and it was apparent that Geffen was not involved with her at that stage. The record companies, however, still owned the rights to the old Blondie material. Just as Debbie was getting used to the quieter side of the industry, Chrysalis released a new upbeat remixed "Atomic" (remixed by Diddy), which peaked at number 19 on the UK charts. Debbie actually performed this on TOTP.

Except for a rather successful US tour in May, all else seemed rather discouraging from the career point of view, however, until late 1994 when Debbie was approached by the Jazz Passengers to perform on a track for their then-upcoming album. Always being innovative, Debbie accepted and the song "Dog In Sand" was recorded for the album *In Love*. Debbie then appeared with the Jazz Passengers at the Meltdown Festival on July 8, 1995 along with Elvis Costello. After that, Debbie continued with the band and subsequently recorded two albums with them— *Individually Twisted* (1995) and *Live in Spain* (1998). It was at this point that Debbie gained a new management agency, the Left Bank Organization, which still manages her (and Blondie) to this day. In July 1995, a UK documentary filmed earlier in the year, "Rock Family Trees," saw a return of Debbie on TV, featuring her and Chris Stein.

The latter part of 1995 saw a pick up in Debbie's career. In addition to receiving considerable praise for her work with the Jazz Passengers, she acted in two more films—the first was "Heavy," which costarred Shelley Winters and Liv Tyler. Debbie played a middle-aged waitress named Delores, who was fading fast. The introduction of a new young waitress (Callie played by Tyler) unnerved Delores because she was no longer the star of the diner and she showed some resentment over this changed situation. Victor, the overweight son (played by Pruitt Taylor Vince) of Dolly (played by Shelly Winters), was fascinated with Callie. After constant arguments with Dolly, Dolores took the back seat and watched events unfold. Eventually, Dolly died, Callie left, and Delores was left with Victor to continue running the diner. A sad and artistic film (directed by James Mangold, for whom Debbie has much respect) saw a new style for Debbie and proved that she can hold her own as an actress. The film was a hit with the critics, shown in cinemas worldwide, and was later released on video in 1996. The second film was called "Drop Dead Rock" and was released on DVD on August 10, 1999, in which Debbie plays a record executive.

Remixed, Remade, Remodeled

Following the remixed "Atomic," two new albums were released—*Beautiful: The Remix Album* in the UK and *The Remix Project: Remixed, Remade and Remodeled* in the US. This album spawned four singles—the previously released "Atomic," "Heart Of Glass," (UK, US) "Union City Blue" (UK US), and "Rapture" (US only). "Heart Of Glass" was a smash on the dance charts going to number 1 (the UK charts saw it debut at 15), "Union City Blue" peaked at number 31, and the album reached number 25 in the UK. After the release and relative success of those albums, EMI and EMI Gold released and re-released one album over again, *The Essential Collection*.

The year 1996 saw Debbie tour with the Jazz Passengers, appearing on TV all over the world. Debbie also appeared on "The Big Breakfast" in the UK, where she was asked if Blondie were to ever reform. She shrugged off the question, but then immediately announced that she was "open to suggestion." Amid rumors that the band was reuniting, no official announcement was made. Debbie continued her work with the Jazz Passengers and November/December 1997 saw Debbie perform at the "Last Night Of The Proms," a televised event. Debbie sang three songs— "French Kissin," "Call Me," and "The Tide Is High." This again showed that Debbie had not given up on her solo career. The big news came in 1998. July saw the release of compilation album, *Atomic—The Very Best Of Blondie,* which did exceptionally well, and in September, a UK tour was announced featuring Deborah Harry, Jimmy Destri, Chris Stein, and Clem Burke. Blondie had reformed! Deborah dived into the tour, with a new look—slimmer, blonde hair and looking like the fantastic "Blondie" of yesteryear.

The tour was very successful. Blondie performed new and old songs alike, and a new studio album had been written. Blondie performed live on New Years Eve in Australia where Debbie rang in the new year—and what a year it would be! In January, Blondie performed "No Exit" on the AMAs (American Music Awards) with Coolio and the Wu Tang Clan. At the end of January, Blondie returned to the UK heavily publicizing "Maria," their new single, which, upon release, went straight to number one. Debbie was featured in every major tabloid and musical magazine—all in praise of her return. *No Exit,* the album, including live songs from the UK tour, was released and also was very popular. In addition, *Atomic—The Very Best Of Blondie,* found new life and recharted. Blondie continued with their world tour and returned to the UK in June 1999 and November 1999, making for a huge success.

Two more UK singles were released, "Nothing Is Real But The Girl" (charted at number 22) and "No Exit." A film starring Deborah, "Six Ways To Sunday," was released in August 1999. It received good publicity and reviews, with Debbie attending its opening amid the Blondie reunion. A new live album, *Blondie Live,* was released in the US on November 23, 1999 followed by its UK counterpart, *Livid.* Blondie finished up their world tour in the UK in November and played in Miami on New Year's Eve. The year 2000 represents a lull after a very eventful 1999.

This point in Debbie's career is perhaps the best. She is being recognized and praised for all that she has done and is doing for the musical community and was involved in a number of film projects in 2000. The new millennium will see another new studio album along with another tour. And from then on—who knows? Only Deborah Harry has the key to her future!

"Deborah Harry Takes on 'The World'"

by Scott Coblio
(adapted and edited by Allan Metz)

Edited reprint of concert review originally published in DAKA *Magazine
(Rochester, New York), November 1989.*

The concert took place at The World, New York City, Sunday November 12, 1989.—Ed.

Deborah Harry has become a major icon—as the blonde from Blondie who took a vacation, she's been touted as a mover and shaker who helped lay the foundation for pop culture as we know it. She wore a wedding dress onstage a decade before Madonna "shocked" the nation in one, brought Stephen Sprouse's fashion designs to the fore of world consciousness, and was Warhol's favorite face. And then there was the music; singlehandedly her band Blondie made rap and reggae commercially accessible commodities, and Blondie's first four albums are rock and roll classics.

So after ten years with no tours, there's been a lot of speculation about Deborah Harry. Although she percolated through the eighties with soundtrack projects (*Scarface, Krush Groove, Married to the Mob*) and played lead and supporting roles on the silver screen ("Videodrome," "Forever Lulu," "Hairspray"), her career never quite reached full boil. Even her valiant comeback album, 1986's *Rockbird*, failed to make a major dent. The industry had changed, and Harry was testing the waters.

On this year's *Def, Dumb & Blonde*, she took the dive and did the newest strokes with flair. The debut video, directed by Madonna's Mary Lambert, was encouraging. Harry looked fabulous; the voice was there. A mini-tour began.

I caught up with it at the New York City club, The World. The tension was visible and audible as delays caused fans to wait an extra hour outside the door on opening night. This was THE night, the first major home-town show since Blondie played Central Park in the summer of '79.

No one seemed sure exactly what to expect—how the trademark hair would be tressed or what the extent of Harry's notoriously unpredictable quirkiness would be. Would she roll on the stage as of yore, or be a sphinx? Would she be classy or campy? How would she look and how would she sound? The crowd, having withstood the first delay with these and other questions on their mind, were not the most patient during the opening act, and cries of "DEB-BIE" were no doubt an unnerving but not unexpected reception for Maria Excommunikata, who got through their set in a somewhat economical fashion.

Waiting again, and the sight of a film crew had everybody in double the frenzy. Rumor was that footage was being shot for the next video (called "Brite Side") and suddenly Deborah appeared—spotlighted, walking slowly through the crowd. A roar went up that suggested a coronation. It was several minutes before the cheers receded enough for the first chords of "The Hunter Gets Captured By the Game" to be heard with Deborah whimsically singing about change and what's old seeming to be new, as if just having awoken from some very long and mythical sleep. The effect was transfixing. You could have heard a pin drop when the song ended. But then those six great beats kicked off "Dreaming" and Deborah came alive, taking the crowd with her. The last ten years suddenly became irrelevant—it could have been 1979 again. Harry tore off her sweater to reveal a minidress underneath.

The musical feast that followed included a string of Blondie favorites but never came off maudlin or nostalgic. Morever, the timelessness of the old material only exposed how innovative it actually was. Songs like "Rapture" and "The Tide Is High" fed the hungry crowd, which diversely reflected a mix of diehard Blondie fans and newcomers.

As soon as those first piano strains of the new single ("I Want That Man") were heard, another roar went up. The band was tight, and Deborah obviously enjoyed the switch to newer stuff. Already drenched in sweat, she would fling herself like an electrified rag doll about the stage, then suddenly freeze like a pillar of salt.

The old magic, the endearing klutziness was back. But the real magic was that element that no camera seems ever to capture—Debbie has an aura that can electrify a thousand people in a second. There's something mesmerizing, and alas, unrecordable, about the way she covers a stage, the way her expressions shift from one ironic extreme to another, her constant attachment/detachment from the crowd that makes one sometimes feel as if one is watching a hologram. Her presence can evoke the surreal in its most profound sense, or she can seem as broad as the stroke of a cartoon. She is otherworldly.

And sometimes surprisingly sinister. When the band broke into "Cautious Lip," an old Blondie sleeper from the *Plastic Letters* LP, a smoldering and motionless Debbie played it eerie, and every swaying body in the room froze to watch the possessed angel. And in the old Blondie raver "Detroit 442," she was a blur too fast to follow. The frenzy only mounted when she bit the head off a rose and spit the petals into the first three rows: "This bud's for you!" she deadpanned.

The roller coaster took another poignant dip during "Brite Side," an emotional and obviously personal number for Deborah, presumably written during dark days: of course, it's a love ode to Stein, who once penned one for her, about her penchant for falling asleep to the lullaby of late night TV in the song "Fade Away and Radiate." The moment was all the more touching for those who know the pair of fifteen years has romantically parted ways.

"Andy Warhol, this one's for you!" shouted Deborah into the darkness to kick off the new "Comic Books" which aptly describes the transformation of a cartoon buff into a larger than life fantasy figure. (Guess who?) Like everything else, it fit in perfectly. No gap between old and new. And the screaming crowd couldn't get enough. Debbie must have caught the wave, for two thrashers, "Forced to Live" and "Bike Boy" rose the room temperature sufficiently for Harry to rip off her dress and perform the encores in only a black bra and stockings.

The show surpassed expectations. Deborah was a hothead powerhouse. It was excitement of the variety one doesn't easily experience at rock shows anymore—an honest, unhyped high. As Norman Mailer said of Marilyn Monroe's performance in the movie "Gentlemen Prefer Blondes": "...in the end, it transcends entertainment and becomes a kind of affirmation...one is more attracted to the idea of life by the end of two hours" (Mailer, 1973).

Mandy Rohr
Germany
The Blondie Review, Art Issue II, Summer 2002, Copyright © 2002.

"Accidents Don't Just Happen:
An Interview With Richard Harry"

by Brian La Fountain
(adapted and edited by Allan Metz)

Deborah Harry's father talks about his very special daughter. This article was originally published in Barry L. Kramer's Fan Mail *fanzine, issue #12, April 1991. It also was later featured in edited form in* Harper's *magazine in 1991.—Ed.*

A most interesting event occurred this past week! I met a gentleman who is a musician, about 60 years old, very worldly and talks a lot. I met him at Sam Snead's Tavern where I work and he comes in now to have a few drinks after playing in this resort hotel here in town. He gave me a photo of himself next to the Sphinx after seeing my Egyptian tattoo (an eye) which is on my upper right shoulder. Anyway, no matter where I've been, he's been there. He seems to be full of shit most of the time, and he is bothersome. His name is Frank. Frank Bittles. And, one day, he's talking about musicians. He's going on and on about old writers and songs.

I thought I'd add one he'd know. Cole Porter. "Oh sure." Of course he did. I told him about current artists doing his songs. He knew about that too! I said my favorite artist was on the remake CD...I told him Debbie Harry...you probably wouldn't know her...Blondie. He says, "You know what? I do know her! You know how I know her? I know her parents from when I used to play up in Cooperstown. She's adopted."

Well, I just fell back and said "What! You mean to tell me you know Richard and Catherine?" He said, "I've known Dick and Catherine a long time!" I freaked out because he was serious! He used the name, "Dick" which only someone who knew him would call him. I then got hysterical about "how well do you know them?" Well, it turns out it is only Debbie's parents he knows, and has only met her once or twice around 1975 or maybe the late 70s. I set up an interview to be held at the bar the following night. Frank said he could give me their telephone number. It was too much.

The next day, Frank calls me at work and says, "I have their phone number if you want it. I got it out of the Cooperstown phone book. I also copied an article about the Cole Porter project from *Down Beat* magazine." This is so neat! He says he can't come down tonight—he'll see me Friday. He did. The transcript follows.

Brian: How long have you known the Harrys?

Frank: We met over 20 years ago. About 19 years.

Brian: Really?

Frank: Yeah, in Cooperstown where I used to work. I used to play there. It's a small town.

Brian: Where did you work?

Frank: At the Otesaga Hotel. It's on the lake up there and their shop is near there.

Brian: And you went shopping there, or what?

Frank: Yeah. I've been there dozens of times. They're nice people, the Harrys.

Brian: They must be around 60 years old, right?

Frank: Yeah, maybe 60. 60s.

Brian: Do you remember anything at all, anything about Debbie?

Frank: I only met her twice. Back in...let's see...1975, I guess. All I remember was she was a blonde. She was with Catherine and Dick at a restaurant there called the Red Sleigh which is on the lake. Yeah, I saw her a couple of times.

Brian: (testing) Was she popular? Did you know she was "Blondie" back then?

Frank: I knew she was popular, but not really "big" yet, but she was big.

Brian: Really!

Frank: I just sent them some articles when I was in Fort Lauderdale, Florida, from, you know, those weekend mags.

Brian: *Parade,* etc.?

Frank: Yeah, you know, and I sent them clippings about her "coming out of retirement" last year.

Brian: Really? Well, thanks a lot Frank!

Frank: Give them a call, I sent a postcard telling them you'd be calling them.

Brian: I am definitely gonna call. I'm really nervous. I don't want to seem weird.

Frank: Oh, no! They're nice people. They'd love for you to call. Give them a call. I told them Brian would be calling from Hot Springs.

Brian: Great! I'm sending this interview to be printed in the *Blondie Fanzine* and *Fan Mail* and I'll send you a copy. It goes around to a lot of places and this is a neat interview.

Frank: (leaving) Good. Give them a call.

Well, the testing moment has arrived. I'm poised and ready to call Debbie Harry's parents' house in Cooperstown. Frank says, "I believe now they live above the store." I've got my portable mini-cassette recorder on the phone upstairs.

It's to no avail. No answer. And the same routine follows for a few, four or five days. I know if they are there they would surely have received Frank's postcard. On the fifth day I decided to give it another shot. Frank says he's worried. "Maybe they're on vacation. When they hear Frank sent you, they'll roll out the red carpet for you!" I set my recorder on one phone and ran to the next. One ring. Someone answers!!! The following is taken directly from the recorded interview, which concluded on March 7, 1991 at approximately 1:45 pm EST.

(ring)..."Around The House."

Brian: Yes, my name is Brian La Fountain, uh, I need to speak with uh, possibly Richard or Catherine?

Richard: Speaking...Richard.

Brian: Yes, Richard, um I'm speaking on terms of a fr- of a gentleman named Frank Bittles. I'm calling from Hot Springs, Virginia...(pause, waiting to see a response)...He said he would know you? He ah, he told me that I should feel free to call you. The reason I am calling is um, I don't know if this sounds really impersonal...

Richard: (jumping in) Is he the redhead?

Brian: Yes, he is. (Actually, it's reddish-gray).

Richard: OK! He's ah, part of the orchestra from the Otesaga Hotel?

Brian: Exactly!!

Richard: OK! You know we got that card from him.

Brian: Yeah?!

Richard: And, ah, we couldn't quite...I didn't know his last name, I've known him for 18 years, but only as "Frank."

Brian: I didn't believe him at first. I thought you know this is, you know, "No you don't!" So he said he'd send a postcard.

Richard: Yeah, he did!

Brian: (laughing) I just...

Richard: Oh yeah! He's very thorough.

Brian: He was worried that I...I've been calling you for a few days and he was worried that I...

Richard: (jumping in)...We just got in.

Brian: I see, well I don't want to sound really impersonal, um, but the reason I'm calling is I'm a big fan of, of Debbie's.

Richard: Uh huh.

Brian: Incredible fan, um...I'm 21-, 23! What am I saying? I'm 23! And there's a group of us that are hardcore fans and we've been following her for a while, but we've started things like the Collector's Society...Debbie's Collector's Society and um, I thought it would be incredible, I had mentioned to everybody that I might be able to talk to you just to say hello because I thought that would be incredible...(Mr. Harry begins laughing and I continue): ...and I—it's just an honor to talk to you and I want to tell you, you did a wonderful job raising Debbie, ha ha ha!!!!

Richard: Ha ha ha ha! We think so, too!

Brian: She's just...

Richard: We're a little conceited that way, and we think we've raised Debbie pretty good ourselves!

Brian: She is just phenomenal! And I just—it's, it's an honor to talk to you, I mean, I don't want to seem really weird or crazy, but...

Richard: (in a very understanding tone) Well, no, I appreciate it.

Brian: You probably get these calls...

Richard: (jumping in) Her music's changing a little bit, I'm a little disappointed.

Brian: Changing? Too pop you mean?

Richard: Ah, well, I don't know, it's not like the "Heart Of Glass" or "Call Me." ("Call Me" is spoken in a very strong accent almost sounding like "Cool Me").

Brian: "Heart Of Glass," which is my anthem, my favorite song in the world...

Richard: That's what I mean, but her recent ah, album, ah, it doesn't sound like it, and yet they're the same group.

Brian: Right.

Richard: Not the same group, but the ah, Chris and she still write together.

Brian: Right! I got to meet them, by the way, last year in DC for the first time...

Richard: Oh yes! Yeah, when she was in Washington.

Brian: Right! And uh, she didn't really look at me or speak to me like I'd expected, so I was really worried whether she thought I was crazy or, you know, weird because...

Richard: (jumping in) Well no, uh, don't feel—take it personal...she gets so much uh, uh, how should I put it? She gets so much attention.

Brian: Yeah, I was hoping that was...

Richard: Yeah, and high as, uh, she's...well, she's just gotten through a show and she's...her mind's up, way up high also.

Brian: Yeah. I've got pictures; I've got several photos that, you know, a friend of mine took. She asked us not to take pictures, but, my friend did and um, I've got some of me and Chris and he was really great, you know, he was just, he was always accommodating and, and really appreciative of the fans, and I knew Debbie is, you know, she's had this kind of stuff for years so she's just probably, you know, worn out from the touring and things, so um...I don't know.

Richard: That last trip to Washington was part of a two-month tour.

Brian: Uh huh.

Richard: Previous to that was another two-month tour uh, between Europe and Australia.

Brian: Right, I followed her through that...

Richard: (jumping in) So, if you can figure that out (I laugh) ah, and still be in one sane mind.

Brian: Yeah!

Richard: I don't know, I don't see how she does it, myself.

Brian: She's, she's great. I—I don't understand why she's not what Madonna is today (referring only to her popularity and chart success)...We are all just...

Richard: (loudly and in disbelief of my question) Well, you know why.

Brian: No, I don't!

Richard: Sure you do!

Brian: Because she...

Richard: (defensively) She took care of Chris and—

Brian: Oh, no no no—of course!

Richard: That put her out of the market for over three years.

Brian: Sure, I understand that! But I'm saying once they put her face back on the cover of any magazine she's still as...

Richard: Well, sure they all recognize her.

Brian: Of course! She's, she's...

Richard: Well, Deb doesn't like to be compared with Madonna anyway, but, ah...ah...

Brian: She stole so much and then took it all...you know, it's just...

Richard: Yeah.

Brian: But Debbie will never admit that in an interview. All these interviews I have she never admits that. They always ask her and say, "Don't you feel cheated?"

Richard: No. No, she doesn't.

Brian: She's, that's what's great about her, I don't know, this is really weird...talking to her Dad! Ha ha!

(He also has a big laugh, and I go on). It's really weird! (He's still laughing). I'm glad you're, I hope you have time to talk...

Richard: Yeah, we just ah, we just got home and we got the...We're working on getting the gift shop open, we're, ah, getting ready to clean up things.

Brian: Ah ha. Well, Frank said he was gonna, he's going up there in like a week, two weeks? Maybe two weeks?

Richard: Sounds early.

Brian: He's going back to work, and ah he...

Richard: Not till May first. Oh, wait a minute. The hotel may open around the 21st of April.

Brian: He said he was leaving early.

Richard: Uh huh.

Brian: But, he said he was gonna pick me up ah, one of your business cards and buy me something from "Around The House." (We both laugh a lot!)

Richard: How 'bout if I send you a couple...How many are, in the club down there?

Brian: Well you see both *Fan Mail* and the *Blondie Fanzine* are in Pennsylvania, but I'm a distributor of information. I collect information and get in touch with the publishers of the fanzines. There is a group of us that is heavy duty. About 18 people that I estimate are heavy duty. Heavy duty. Every day we're into it. For the past ten...

Richard: Well I was gonna send you signed pictures...hang on...

Brian: Oh God!

Richard: (after a long pause) Yeah, I have some I can send you.

Brian: Signed Debbie photos?!!

Richard: Yeah! Yeah! They're signed!

Brian: I've nev—the only autograph I ever had was when she signed my t-shirt, while I...(an uproar of laughter!)...while I was wearing it! I was wearing a Blondie t-shirt and ah, I don't know. I can't even describe to you...let me tell you what. I have thousands of dollars worth of Debbie Harry merchandise, a virtual shrine!

Richard: My God!

Brian: I'd like to tell her that, but I always thought that she would think I was this freak, this weirdo! But actually I'm not! I can afford it and it's my hobby.

Richard: Uh huh.

Brian: But, um. I've always wanted to tell her that...you know how devoted and appreciative of her I am. Everyone that's in this circle has thousands of dollars in their collection. And uh, we want her to know how much we appreciate her...

Richard: (sincerely) I'll tell her!

Brian: We are major fans...Should I give you my address?

Richard: Please! (I give him my address.) OK.

Brian: Let me tell you really quick! I know this is the only time I'll ever get to speak to you and I...(another uproar of laughter!)...just want to take full advantage of it! (He's very amused, and still laughing. I can't help but laugh too). I'm just really excited because I didn't expect you to pick up the phone. I've been doing this for, um, days and I just was shocked when you picked the phone up...Um, Debbie's—You know about her new motion picture, probably...

Richard: Yep.

Brian: Have you seen any parts of it? Yet?

Richard: Nope! She doesn't even know the name of it yet!

Brian: Oh, it's, it's called "After Midnight," right? That's what we're all hearing. I called her manager's office and they said it was "After Midnight."

Richard: Well, no. I haven't. I haven't spoken to her...Personally, I mean I haven't spoken to her particularly about the movie in the last several weeks.

Brian: I see.

Richard: "After Midnight" is the name of it?

Brian: Uh huh!

Richard: That's good to know! Ah ha. I'll, I'll know that cause I'm gonna see her, I hope to see her this Saturday.

Brian: Right! Well, I really appreciate the time you've spent, it's really phenomenal and um, I hope you don't mind, I was gonna transfer some of the information to the fanzine, that I got to speak to you and the date and...

Richard: Okee doke!

Brian: OK! I really appreciate that and everybody else is gonna appreciate it, too. We're all behind her!

Richard: Very good, it's good to hear!

Brian: OK!

Richard: Thank you again!

Brian: Thank you! Bye bye.

Richard: Bye bye, now.

Mandy Rohr
Germany
The Blondie Review, Art Issue II, Summer 2002, Copyright © 2002.

"Jazz Passengers & Deborah Harry: Great American Music Hall/San Francisco"

by Dan Ouellette

Down Beat, *December 1994*

A balanced review of Deborah Harry's performance with the Jazz Passengers on September 27, 1994, still relatively early in her stint with the band.—Ed.

While a good portion of the crowd was drawn to this show to see ex-Blondie Deborah Harry (they cheered wildly when the new wave diva graced the stage and tossed her kisses and a bouquet of roses), there was a strong contingent in the sold-out house intent on making the best of a rare West Coast opportunity to catch the quirky, experimental Jazz Passengers. Fans kept calling for old tunes, but saxophonist Roy Nathanson responded that even he couldn't remember how they went.

Was this really true or just a strategy for keeping the focus on the love song material from the Jazz Passengers' satisfying new album, *In Love* (High Street), starring an eclectic crew of 10 vocalists? Whatever the case, refreshingly off-kilter excursions full of Nathanson's squealing sax lines, Bill Ware's shimmering vibes runs, and Curtis Fowlkes' bold trombone riffs supported Harry (who appears on just one album track), who got to sing her heart out, negotiating with varying degrees of success the twists and turns of the delightfully atypical, rhythmically complex love songs.

The show got off to a great vaudevillian start with Nathanson reading a schlocky script about the invention of long songs while being pelted from offstage by plastic cups and paper plates. The rest of the band gradually appeared and laid the musical pulse down for Harry's entrance. Just as on the album, the vocal-oriented portion began with the gorgeous ballad, "Imitation Of A Kiss," which Harry didn't even come close to interpreting in the deeply soulful way Jimmy Scott does on the disc. However, the next tune was her vocal contribution to the album, the delightfully buoyant "Dog in the Sand," which she completely owned live. She also soared on the tango-inflected melody "Handsome Man From Fiji" and later torched the house with a fiery romp/finale through "Kidnapped." This prompted an encore, which, as consolation for Harry's fans craving her old hits, included a playful but less-than-inspired stumble through "The Tide Is High."

"Debbie Does the Commodore"

Review by Stuart Derdeyn
(adapted and edited by Allan Metz)

Drop-D Magazine *(Vancouver, Canada). July 12, 1996*

Performance review offering a Canadian perspective.—Ed.

The Jazz Passengers with Deborah Harry
Vancouver International Jazz Festival
The Commodore Ballroom
Vancouver, BC
June 23, 1996
Photography by Rodney Gitzel

I love the Jazz Passengers, and my Blondie vinyl is as dear to me as my KISS *The Originals* set, so I was ready for this meeting of the minds at the Commodore. Last time through town, this unit played a disjointed practice show to a paying crowd. Delightful to see what a year can do to a performance.

Dame Debbie was in excellent form, sporting high camp fashion and singing her self silly on all the material from the last J.P.'s release. Obviously, she is supremely comfortable with the format, leaving off mid-phrase to let the improvising go, stepping in to rap/scat her way into the noise, doing a dippy doodly dance step that all the adoring fans stage front kept trying to copy, but missed. That's why the lady is a vamp.

On a perfect planet, the Jazz Passengers would be bigger than Mariah Carey, shipping gazillions of units of their demented free-pop sounds to hungry fans all over. Vibes player Bill Ware and the violinist (not Jim Nolet) just smoked all night long. The show belonged to drummer E.J. Rodriguez and bassist Brad Jones, whose impeccable meter drive just kept anything from getting looser than it should. 'Bone player Curtis Fowlkes didn't make the gig, but whoever the barefoot, dreadlocked replacement was, he knew his way around the horn.

J.P's front-median Roy Nathanson was in fine form, blowing his sax—or saxES—and heckling the crowd and Harry. He kept insisting on calling her Baroness Von Stongbach and telling her to "watch out for the sharks." Harry just kept up the punch by taunting Nathanson during a twisted version of Blondie's "One Way or Another," when a star-struck (and was that a roll of change or...) fan hugged Dame Debbie, with lines like "I got one Roy, like your sax?" and other such.

Nathanson told the crowd, "If you care to dance naked on top of the tables, that's strongly encouraged," before a beautiful version of the decidedly soft and waltzy "Imitation of a Kiss." A version of "The Tide is High" kept the (weak-willed) fans from losing interest after the band went into the stratosphere on an instrumental soca/tango number.

Maybe the only reason, actually the only reason, the show was a sell-out was Harry's presence on stage. That said, she is part of a band now, and a band that anyone with musical appreciation sense can realize are taking pop music into the cutting edge big-time. Catch them anywhere on tour you can. You will love it.

"The Censored *High Times* Interview With Debbie Harry"

by Victor Bockris

INTRODUCTION

In 1996 the music editor of *High Times*, Steve Bloom, asked me to interview Debbie Harry. I had sporadically kept in touch with Debbie over the years, but we had hardly ever sat down together or had any kind of sustained conversation. We met at the apartment of an important photographer and New Yorker, David Croland. We had an animated conversation, after which Debbie drove me home in her enormous beat up old boat of a car. As I was working on the interview it struck me that it might be interesting to look back into some of the old material and see how it would work in with the new stuff. In retrospect, it should not have come to me as a surprise that they matched perfectly, for Debbie has always had a lot of continuity in her character, it's part of her strength. Anyway I called her up and explained that I had come upon some material that had not been used in *Making Tracks* but that fit in with what we had been discussing in the recent interview, with an emphasis on the influence of drugs etc. We talked it over and decided that this was a good opportunity for Debbie to speak out honestly about her heroin addiction back in the late sixties, and how it had affected her. Heroin was continuing to be a big problem for a lot of young people who didn't know much. *High Times* appeared to be the perfect magazine to address the subject in.

I went to work on welding the two conversations together and came up with a text that I felt was one of the best things I had done in the interview format for some time, and, in my humble opinion, one of Debbie's best interviews. Bloom was ecstatic with the results. The next thing I knew I received a copy of the galleys in the mail. Reading the piece, though in the cold light of hard type, I was even more impressed.

That weekend, as I was musing happily upon the results, I received a phone call from *High Times* publisher and long time friend, John Holmstrom. Holmstrom always speaks in a very level voice, it is quiet but full of authority. In his way he proceeded to tell me that we were going to have to make some changes in the interview, that we needed to cut out and replace some of the material.

"What material?" I asked him.

"Everything about heroin," he replied.

Had it been anybody but Holmstrom on the phone I would have let out a wild banshee curse and screamed them off the phone. But I knew this was checkmate, and there was nothing to talk about. I had learned by then not to agonize over such situations. It seemed hypocritical, but then *High Times* had long had a policy of celebrating soft drugs and drawing a hard distinction between them and hard drugs. Personally it didn't make sense to me. I felt they had a responsibility to deal with hard drugs, but I had always respected Holmstrom and *High Times* founder, Tom Forcade, and if that's what they wanted I would give it to them. So I quietly acquiesced. Luckily there was enough material on tap to make a perfectly good piece.

I am then, very happy to have the opportunity to publish here, for the first time in Allan Metz's Blondie anthology, "The Censored *High Times* Interview With Debbie Harry." It is, so far as I am aware, the only interview in which she has ever laid down these tracks.

Victor Bockris, Summer 2001, New York.

VICTOR BOCKRIS: What is the most important thing that's happened to you in the last year?

DEBBIE HARRY: Just this past weekend I had to drive upstate to see my Mom and Dad. I sort of had the same feeling I had at the beginning of Blondie. Then, I had this really wonderful instinctive drive, this guiding momentum, this energy, and I just had to use it. I was so instinctive. Everything was just there, you know?

Then, for a long time I didn't want any kind of energy like that. But all of a sudden, driving upstate, I thought, Gee, I wonder if I could do that again? And I just had this little feeling in the pit of my stomach that went, Yeah, I could, and maybe I would want to. But who focuses all their drive on work at my age? I was thinking, I'm

159

already doing it. This technical jazz singing with the Jazz Passengers and getting a real acting part in "Heavy" was much more of a revelation to me.

BOCKRIS: What is your daily life like these days? When you're living in New York and you're not touring, do you have any practical schedule?

HARRY: Well, I swim every day. If I'm not working that night, performing or going to a club to see a band, I'll get up at about 7:30, eight o'clock. I take my dog for a walk and feed the cat. Then I get the newspaper and read it for an hour. I drink coffee and have a pastry. Then I just do phones or tour plans or clean up the apartment. Try to get jobs. Rearrange traffic. I'm trying to organize doing a book of my own again.

BOCKRIS: You want to do your autobiography?

HARRY: Yeah, but I'd like to have more of a sex life before I write it. I mean, the book should be banned somewhere!

BOCKRIS: What do you remember about your teenage years?

HARRY: At 16, I found out about pot, which was unbelievable because nobody did it. I lucked out. I had a girlfriend, Wendy, who was a year older than I was and she had an older sister who was a real beatnik painter who lived in New York in a loft on Grand Street on the Lower East Side. She had travelled in Mexico and taken magic mushrooms and smoked pot.

BOCKRIS: What was it like when you first smoked grass?

HARRY: I first smoked grass when I was eighteen. It was like an acid trip. I took about three hits off a joint and it lasted for hours and hours and it was great. My whole life just ran in front of me and I realized a lot of things in a flash. I could see a lot of things very clearly. It didn't answer everything, though. I still had some emotional problems and a lot of pain in my body.

BOCKRIS: Did you go out with a lot of different guys in high school?

HARRY: When I was a freshman, my town had these stifled sexual appetites. It was really awful. No matter who you were, if you went out with a lot of guys you would get talked about and people would say you were a whore. It was this big paradox. So I ended up going out with one guy for a couple of months and then another guy for a couple of months. In my junior and senior years, I pretty much had one boyfriend.

BOCKRIS: Were you attracted to a particular type?

HARRY: No. But I was really oversexed. Really charged, hot to trot. Later on, when I got my driver's license, I used to drive up to this sleazy town near Paterson [New Jersey], and would walk up and down this street there called Cunt Mile. I would get picked up and make out with different guys in back seats of cars to get my rocks off, because I was so horny and I couldn't make out with anybody in my town.

BOCKRIS: Did you always have this idea of going to New York and becoming a star?

HARRY: There was quite a big jazz scene in 1965 on the Lower East Side when I moved there. I was into music more and more even though I was painting then. After taking my first acid trip, I started painting sound and decided I wanted to be in music. I hung out with bands and didn't paint anymore. But I had to learn how to feel good about myself, because I didn't like myself. To break up these patterns, I had to become what I wanted to be and who I wanted to be, and it took a long time. I felt that I was another person inside and that I wanted to come out, that I was in pain and always depressed and feeling terrible.

In 1967 I went into the music business. I was so depressed and so upset. I knew that I would do it wrong and get so far in one direction that it would make people think of me in another way. This happens to many people, like Lou Reed. I knew I couldn't do it the way I wanted to, so at the end of the Sixties I stopped doing music and took a lot of junk [heroin] because I thought it would calm me down and it did.

I had come to a point that seemed like a tunnel. I'd come to the entrance of a tunnel and I could either go down into the tunnel and continue or I could take this little winding road off to the side.

That's what I did at the end of the Sixties: I took a winding road off to the side. That whole time that I worked at Max's Kansas City and as a Playboy bunny I was doing junk.

It turned out to be the thing that kept me going. I worked like a beaver when I was a junkie. I had full-time jobs. I made money. I traveled. It made it so that I wasn't in such terrible pain and gave me time to outgrow my problems. So from, '69 to '73, I took a sabbatical.

BOCKRIS: When you came back out in '73, what was the first thing that you did?

HARRY: That was the early glitter period when I used to hang around the [New York] Dolls. They were put down by the critics, but they were the pets of the New York scene. That period—T. Rex, Jonathan Richman, the Dolls—was when I jumped back in mentally. I had a little car and used to drive them around, but I was more on the fringes of everything. People noticed me but I couldn't speak. It was really awful. I would be standing in a public place with my mouth hanging open and someone would tell me to shut it. I would go into ladies' rooms and cry. A lot of times I would try to sing and I'd get all choked up and all I could do was cry.

BOCKRIS: Did you lose this fear when you started to perform?

HARRY: The pain went away when I started performing with The Stilettoes in 1973. My intuition was no one was dancing to rock'n'roll. And that was what The Stilettoes wanted—to bring back rock dancing. I had really gotten rid of most of the pain before Blondie. But I still wonder about that fear. It must come from some kind of infant thing.

There are certain things that are going to take that pain away, and if you can find out what they are sometimes you can find out what it's about. I was thinking the other day about this latest heroin epidemic that's hitting New York. Though I'm not interested in getting into it myself, I realized that I may walk around with a lot of physical anxiety in my body. But that's what keeps me doing things. It keeps me driven, really striving to do something. I don't want to just lie back and not do anything. I want to keep doing. But I do suppose that junk can be a very useful medicine. I know people who have killed themselves that mightn't have if they'd had a shot of it to cool themselves out.

To me, there are two or three physical types. Some are in correct physical balance where a stimulus is a stimulus and a depressant is a depressant. Then there are people like you who are affected the same way, but they have this pain and are satisfied with it because it makes them do things; whereas my pain made me not do things, and a depressant made it possible for me to have the ability. It seemed to have the opposite effect. Like some children are overstimulated naturally and they are given stimulants to calm them. That's how it worked for me. Nobody understands that.

BOCKRIS: How did you learn how to use heroin for yourself?

HARRY: God. I don't know. I just did it. I got very, very, very stoned on junk and did a lot of yoga exercises, which involved heavy breathing and physical endurance in a certain posture and I got a very strong physical sensation like a rush, a paralytic rush that felt like I almost died. This happened twice. I remember the first time getting really scared, crawling, dragging my body across the floor to the bed saying: Now go to sleep and you'll wake up in the morning. The second time I said, Well, this is a message. I don't know whether it came from me or whether it came from outside, but the message was that I could quit whenever I wanted and that I should and that I was on the right track. I liked myself from then on. It happened in one realization, one violent physical shock from the drug.

BOCKRIS: You never had a bad time with heroin?

HARRY: It got to the point where it outlived its usefulness and it became a real worry to get it. I found myself consorting with people I wouldn't normally ever talk to: extortionists and slime people. I wavered back and forth for a while. It took a year to finally be rid of it. When it started I was in such pain that it was good because it relieved— blessed relief, thank you. Thank you and because of this relief I was able to talk to myself and get an understanding of what was happening to me. Sometimes I'm uncomfortable within my body. Sometimes I don't like to feel at all.

That's why taking drugs had a very strong attraction for me, because it made me bodiless, which is very nice. But after awhile the burden of the junk became real. The problems of the system behind junk became my problems and I wasn't willing to have them. I was using it in my life, but I didn't want it to become my life.

BOCKRIS: But it did give you the time and the clarity of vision to understand your situation, and that's what I think it does for someone at its very best. In a sense, it did that for William Burroughs, but he had to deal with it over a much longer period of time. But that's exactly what it gave him. And I've seen people do that for shorter periods of time.

HARRY: It just got to be this terrific treadmill of a rat race I was on. I even went to a psychiatrist a couple of times, which turned out to be a big beat. That was the only time I ever went to a psychiatrist. I went about three times. I just said, What's wrong? Why am I caught in this trap? That's when I was crying every time I opened my mouth. I was taking junk and I was still crying. I had to make a lot of money to support my habit and pay my bills and it was like, How could I get out of it? I thought maybe I should go to a psychiatrist. Maybe there's some deep-rooted thing I can get rid of through hypnosis. So I went to a psychiatrist who specializes in hypnosis. I was hypnotized partially. I started to go under, but I just thought this guy was taking his time. He could have done it faster. It was just another fucking rat race I was going to get into and I thought, Oh shit, I don't need this. Plus, he was very expensive, my God!

BOCKRIS: How are you feeling nowadays?

HARRY: It's been a period of evolution for me. I couldn't for the life of me have picked a better situation than the Jazz Passengers to experiment and to sing in a different way and perform in a different way and to know exactly what I wanted to do. It's very nice for me. It's like a great period of creative discovery.

BOCKRIS: Are you addicted to your work?

HARRY: I guess I am, but I just think it's the best thing to be productive and to be creative. What else are you gonna do?

BOCKRIS: How do you reconcile carrying around the enormous shadow of the legend of Blondie in the present?

HARRY: That's funny, because to me it's grossly out of proportion. It's ridiculous and preposterous, yet it's totally accurate in relation to what is considered really vital and really valuable in the culture. But it just seems totally out of proportion that I should be considered anything other than another singer. The mythologizing of it is absurd. I was just being a driven, obsessed, star-crazed rock'n'roller, and doing my best to be part of all that, and wanting to say a few things that were relevant at the time, and now it's gone way out of proportion.

The concept of the youth culture has an awfully powerful effect, which is incredibly fucking misleading. It's so boring, so incredibly ridiculous, but it controls many people's lives. They think they better get it done now because when they get to be forty-five they're not going to have anything.

BOCKRIS: Where do you see rock heading?

HARRY: The only place left for rock to go is toward more girl stars. There's nothing left for men to do. The only people that can express anything that hasn't been expressed in rock'n'roll are fags and girls. There's bound to be more male stars, but they can't express anything new. What girls are saying is: 'Don't treat me like that, treat me like this.' Which Nancy Sinatra initially did with 'These Boots Were Made for Walking'! That's the sort of predominant attitude. It's not the same as 'Take another little piece of my heart now,' or 'Baby love, baby love'—all that kind of gush. It's giving girls a chance to develop, get to the stage where their style of living and thought is the same [as men's], not some clandestine activity.

The thing that's fucked up nowadays is that it's not hip to be good. It's hip to be hip. It's hip to be chic or smooth or witty or fast, and the rules of the game are: If you can screw somebody and get away with not paying for something and make somebody else pay the price, that's cool. It's a horrible, rotten status quo, and it's not going to get any better by itself. That's the really bad thing about the downfall of religion. People aren't concerned with being good; they're only concerned with survival.

"Private Lesson: Debbie Does Jazz"

by Robert L. Doerschuk

Musician, *July 1997*

Deborah Harry's adjustment from rock to jazz, including the difference between singing in these two musical genres.—Ed.

New York, as they say, is a small town, so perhaps it's not so strange that the Jazz Passengers would wind up working with Deborah Harry. After all, various Passengers have been hauling their horns around the city's club circuit since the early Eighties, when saxophonist Roy Nathanson and trombonist Curtis Fowlkes began working with the Lounge Lizards. And Harry, of course, was the queen of clubs from the moment she and her band Blondie first blew the roof off of CBGB's in 1974.

They worked the same streets, but Harry and her future collaborators were separated by something bigger than their neighborhood: The singer's slicked-up variation on punk could never fit easily into the smoother contours of avant-jazz. One slammed while the other—in an ironic way, at least—swung.

Or so it seemed in those pre-postmodern days. In the Nineties, anything is possible—which often means that any collision of styles, no matter how bloody, is valid. For all the cross-pollination going on between the rock, jazz, hip-hop, and classical communities, rare is the artist who jumps a stylistic hurdle and arrives on the other side with a real understanding of what the aesthetic there is all about.

Deborah Harry is one of the few who have made the leap. On her two projects with the Jazz Passengers, the High Street release *In Love* (1995) and this year's *Individually Twisted* on the 32 label, she sings the band's original repertoire and a handful of chestnuts with a confidence and nuance of phrasing that's pure, undiluted, one-hundred-percent jazz. Now and then a bit of the fist-balling snarl of her Blondie roots breaks through, but in this context it sounds more like a jazz singer dabbling in new wave than the reverse.

What's the secret? Ms. Harry shrugs. "I've always liked abstraction and dissonance, strange chord combinations and notes. Blondie didn't really do that, but I've always liked bands that did. So given the opportunity to put some of that to use, it seemed like a nice thing to do."

That opportunity came in the form of an invitation from producer Hal Willner to sing "Dog in Sand," which would eventually appear on *In Love*. For Roy Nathanson, her performance revealed her potential as a bona fide jazz singer. "First of all, she brought this tongue-in-cheek quality, this goofy, romantic, Dada thing to the lyrics. And she's really an actress, which was perfect because singing, whether it's jazz, pop, classical, or new music, really is acting. It's about serving the narrative. Not only that, she has really good pitch and a beautiful sound. Plus, even though she doesn't really know a bunch of jazz scales, her ears are good. We do this song, 'Kidnapped,' that's got 'Giant Steps' types of changes in the A section. It's a chromatic song, and it's hard to hear. I mean, we had Mavis Staples sing this one, and it was very hard for her. But Debbie heard the harmonic stuff right off the bat. Intervallic stuff is rarely a problem for her. She can go for the interesting parts of the chords on the basis of where her ears take her—and, most important, these harmonic colorings augment the narrative."

As Nathanson sees it, the only problems Harry faced in getting a grasp on jazz were technical. "Odd rhythms can be difficult for her," he observes. "She does so many things intuitively, but some of these time signatures literally can't be felt, or they can be felt only after you've analyzed them. You have to actually count them out to have some idea of what's going on. Her way of getting is to just do it a lot. Like, the end of 'Kidnapped' is a 7/4 horn line over a 4/4 rhythm section base. Clearly you could just sing rubato over that. Mavis dealt with it by just doing some R&B yelping. But Debbie, because she sings very logically, figured out what she could do. At one point—this was actually both her and my idea—she read part of Robert Louis Stevenson's *Kidnapped* and screamed a lot. And since then, she's figured out a way to sing over the groove. She found what she had to do, and she never does too much."

Although Harry had some experience doing cabaret work in the early Seventies, it was through the Jazz Passengers that she made the successful morph from rock to jazz. The key, for her, was to listen to other singers.

"That's the first step, listening especially for breath control in the different style. My first reaction to singing jazz is that it's a different type of aggression. Rock & roll is physically aggressive but not necessarily mentally aggressive. With jazz, the aggression is totally intellectual. You have to be very still and focused to do all this intricate stuff and make it look like it's nothing. At first all I wanted to do was to hit the notes right; I was very absorbed in doing that. A few times, though, I would find myself in the moment, like the acting thing, and feeling the emotion of the piece. *Then* some startling things would happen to me musically. I would do some harmonic line that I hadn't planned out, because it was emotionally inspired."

Harry admits that her theory chops are "still limited" but insists that a combination of hard work and being open to change can make up for that. "If I came in with a note that was totally wrong, that wasn't too critical to the guys as long as I completely knew the songs as written," she points out. "As time went on, it became acceptable to fool around with them. Jazz people are like this; that's how they approach music, so that they have some kind of personal involvement and these moments can exist. That's a new experience for me, not to have to do everything the same every time."

One important difference between jazz and rock, the treatment of the backbeat, also played into Harry's education with the Passengers. "You're pretty much on the beat in rock," she says. "In jazz, as long as you know where you're heading, anything goes."

Nathanson concurs. "In rock singing, singers push the beat. When Debbie first sang with us, she didn't have a sense of laying behind. Since then, although she tends to still be on the beat, she knows what it means to lay back. She also chooses really interesting voice-leading. She stands right in front of the vibes, and with the vibes, although you've only got four voices, you hear just as much harmony as you want to hear. You don't get this bombardment of ten notes like you get with [pianist] Fred Hersch. That helps her because pop singers don't work with that many notes, so they make the ones that they have work. If you listen to her pop records, everything is chosen carefully, and she didn't throw that quality to the winds while singing jazz. That's why she sounds good."

In the midst of all this jazz stuff, Harry is taking time to record tracks for a Blondie reunion album, [*at the time of this writing, thought to be*] produced by Nick Rhodes and Warren Cuccurullo. [*Craig Leon produced this album, entitled* No Exit—Ed.]. Has working with the Passengers changed her approach to belting it out with her old band? "It's given me better control," she smiles. "I actually sound better singing jazz; my instrument is better for that. I can sound kind of shrill in rock, especially live, because there's a lot of pressure to recreate that sound [on the records]. That's why I tended to sing so clipped and punchy, but I can do more now. The more you work, the better you get, no matter what field you're in. I mean, I could have been working as an auctioneer and the same thing would have happened. If I had thought about it like that. But realizing what this voice has to do in this band [the Passengers] has just made me a better singer overall."

Solo Photo Section

Umbria Jazz Festival, Perugia, Italy, July 27, 1997
credit: copyright © Andrea Farina

Umbria Jazz Festival, Perugia, Italy, July 27, 1997
credit: copyright © Andrea Farina

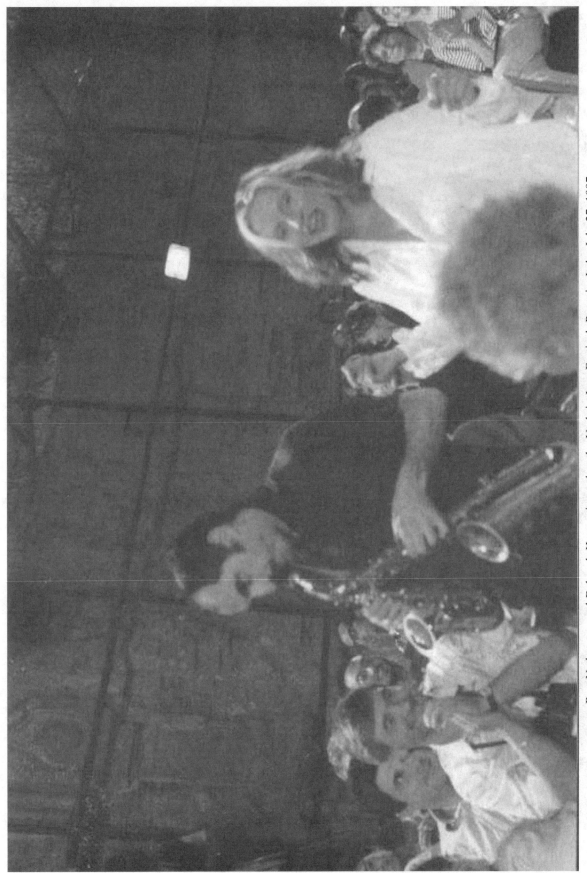

Roy Nathanson and Deborah Harry pictured at the Umbria Jazz Festival, Perugia, Italy, July 27, 1997
credit: copyright © Andrea Farina

Deborah Harry and Chris Stein arrive at Heathrow Airport, February 2, 1987
credit: copyright © Mirror Syndication International

Debravation tour, City Gardens, Trenton, New Jersey, May 22, 1994
credit: copyright © Joe Ryan

Seeing Deborah Harry in person the first time...left a clear impression on my mind. I felt immersed and taken by her natural beauty. She just has this spirituality about her. After all, she is one of the most attractive women to grace our times. Though I can't recall what song she was singing in this photo, it was definitely the pinnacle of the show. Deborah Harry and Chris Stein turned the place upside down!—*Joe Ryan*

Deborah Harry and Chris Stein, *Def, Dumb & Blonde* tour, Hornblower's Yacht, San Francisco Bay, October 17, 1989
credit: copyright © David Bartolini

Deborah Harry, The Country Club, Reseda, California,
October 23, 1989
credit: copyright © Luther Orrick-Guzman

I was merely a junior college student covering for my college paper one of the best concerts I'd seen to date back in 1989. I was lucky to get in, during that time she had tickets go on sale for The Roxy and a couple other clubs in Hollywood, but they sold out so fast that I was only able to get a ticket for The Country Club in Reseda, California. Although nervous, I managed to get some images of Deborah Harry I could be proud of. I'd never seen her perform live prior to that show other than on video. I remember *Def, Dumb and Blonde* being a new favorite album in my collection. The lights were dim and after an opening band had played, I was sure that the band members going on stage were Debbie's. The thump thump thump of "Dreaming" filled the venue with electricity as Miss Harry came on stage full of fire and beauty. The vision of an authentic Rock Goddess filled my camera frame as I snapped away at one of my childhood idols. She wore her trademark sunglasses, and a torn black T-shirt rolled up at the sleeves fastened by large safety pins.—*Luther Orrick-Guzman*

Debbie's short red form-fitting pants that came down slightly above her knees looked sexy. At her knees and below, Debbie displayed unique body paint designs. The red and black outfit was completed with a matching red belt, a red cap with short devil horns and tail in the back of the cap. Debbie at the time was in the best physical and vocal shape ever. The song set seemed short even though it really wasn't. She performed many popular Blondie songs, new solo songs, and obscure punk rock Blondie songs. My goal that night was to capture her in that red cap looking at me and then to capture her swaying her hair while she rocked out to "Comic Books." The stars were on my side that night. I am the proud photographer of some of my favorite color and black and white images of Deborah Harry. —*Luther Orrick-Guzman*

Luther Orrick-Guzman is the Entertainment Editor of a Latin men's magazine called *QV Magazine* and is its lead photographer on the West Coast. He also is a senior editor and photographer with *Latin Style*, an entertainment magazine, as well as a contributor to *Latin Vibes*, and other publications. Luther also does a lot of freelance (and freebies) to keep his name alive in the Latin magazine circuit.

Debbie did a solo concert at the Long Beach Convention Center as part of the Long Beach Gay Pride Festival in California. Debbie came out wearing what she described as a "cheap wig" that she ended up throwing out to the audience. Her entrance was breathtaking as she began to sing the best version of "French Kissin..." I ever heard. This was a much more playful and campy Debbie and I was more than thrilled to capture her on film after an audience member gave her a bouquet of roses and a sparkling tiara that she put on while performing "I Want That Man." Debbie playfully bit the rosebuds and spat out quantities of rose petals to the frantic Long Beach audience for another unforgettable show.—*Luther Orrick-Guzman*

Deborah Harry, Long Beach Convention Center,
Long Beach, California
copyright © Luther Orrick-Guzman

Deborah Harry, Lake Compounce Park,
Bristol, Connecticut, June 29, 1990
credit: copyright © John Atashian

Deborah Harry with the Jazz Passengers, Great American Music Hall, San Francisco, September 27, 1994
credit: copyright © Stuart Brinin

When I was assigned by *Down Beat* magazine to photograph Deborah Harry as guest vocalist with the Jazz Passengers, I didn't know what to expect. I mean, I was familiar with her as the lead singer of the punk rock band "Blondie," but this was jazz, after all.

What I witnessed was a woman who had matured as a singer and had added a lot of emotion to the music. Her sensual version of the song "Imitation of a Kiss," sung by Jimmy Scott on the Jazz Passengers' album *In Love*, was a prelude of more things to come. Her voice on some of the songs was haunting and mysterious. Ms. Harry seemed really captivated by the material, and her audience was swept up by it all—a great performance by a talented vocalist.—*Stuart Brinin*

Stuart Brinin has been documenting jazz and blues artists through his camera lens for over twenty years. While covering music festivals and concerts nationally and internationally, Stuart is also a regular contributor to *Down Beat*, *Pulse*, *Living Blues*, *Blues Access, Guitar Player*, etc. His work has also been published in the *New York Times*, the *Village Voice*, and *Rolling Stone* as well as a number of other major music publications. Mr. Brinin's photos have graced the covers of a number of CDs, including such legends as Charles Brown, Irma Thomas, Marian McPartland, Elvin Bishop, and Otis Rush. Stuart is also a staff photographer for SIPA Press, one of the largest photo agencies in the world. Please visit his web site at www.jazzwest.com/stu/index.htm from which this bio was adapted and reprinted with permission.

Deborah Harry with the Jazz Passengers, Great American Music Hall, San Francisco,
September 27, 1994
credit: copyright © Stuart Brinin

Deborah Harry and Chris Stein, Borderline Club, London, October 8, 1989
credit: Pete Still copyright © The Concert Photo Co.

Deborah Harry (with Chris Stein in background),
Town & Country Club, London,
November 30, 1989
Credit: Pete Still copyright © The Concert Photo Co.

Deborah Harry with the Jazz Passengers, Commodore Ballroom, Vancouver, British Columbia, Canada,
June 23, 1996
credit: copyright © Rodney Gitzel

Deborah Harry, October 6, 1989
credit: copyright © Mirror Syndication International

Deborah Harry, March 18, 1984
credit: copyright © Mirror Syndication
International

Deborah Harry, November 23, 1993
credit: copyright © Mirror Syndication International

Deborah Harry
credit: copyright © Mirror Syndication International

Deborah Harry arrives at Heathrow Airport,
February 2, 1987
credit: copyright © Mirror Syndication International

Deborah Harry, February 18, 1987
credit: copyright © Mirror Syndication International

Deborah Harry and Chris Stein arrive at Heathrow Airport, February 2, 1987
credit: copyright © Mirror Syndication International

Deborah Harry at BPI (British Phonographic Industry) Awards, February 9, 1987
credit: copyright © Mirror Syndication International

Four cultural icons: (l to r): Jean Michel Basquiat, Andy Warhol, Deborah Harry and Muhammad Ali
credit: copyright © Victor Bockris

Deborah Harry with the Jazz Passengers, Camden Jazz Café, London, England, July 1997
credit: copyright © Marc Millar

Deborah Harry in razor dress by Michael Schmidt
at "The Supper Club," New York City, March 13, 1993
credit: Bob Gruen / Star File

Deborah Harry and Joey Ramone, New York City, 1987
credit: Bob Gruen / Star File

Deborah Harry at the pre-screening party for Madonna's film, "Truth or Dare," at Laura Belle,
43rd Street, New York City, May 8, 1991
credit: Karl Feile / Archive Photos

Deborah Harry as Ezmeralda – The Psychic in "Red Lipstick" (1999) directed by Alexandra King
credit: copyright © Alexandra King

"On Acting" by Alexandra King

"Red Lipstick": "Two drag queens lose their jobs and go on a Bonnie & Clyde rampage around New York City...but neither one wants to be Clyde," was written with a part for Deborah Harry. I had gotten a message to Debbie that I was making a film and wanted her to play the role of Ezmerelda "The Psychic." She said, "Well, I am a psychic," and I said, "I've heard."

Debbie is great to work with. She brings so much depth to even the simplest of characters. When she walks on to a set, the whole vibe changes—you can feel the buzz, yet she is totally down-to-earth. The camera loves her and she never holds back. She gets right into it and isn't afraid to go past that place where most people draw the line. Her experience working with so many directors is evident. I've watched her bring a scene to life and get all the other actors around her to shine.

Alexandra King: Writer and Director

Alexandra wrote and directed her first feature film, "Red Lipstick," an imaginative, campy comedy. After turning down financing for "Red Lipstick" from Vista Street Entertainment, an LA-based distribution company, Alexandra decided to self-finance the entire project. This option allowed her to preserve artistic integrity, maintain creative control and gave her the chance to use innovative ideas and techniques to create a highly stylized film.

Alexandra delves into cutting-edge issues and presents them in a new light. After screening a rough cut of "Red Lipstick," she was hired by Pilgrims 5, a New York production company, to direct her second feature film, "Zoo." The film was shot in 35mm with a substantially larger budget. "Zoo" is a dark comedy set in the fictitious small town of Spraine, a seemingly upstanding community. A big city private detective is hired to track down an animal serial killer. The detective digs deeper as the killer draws him into a trap, reversing the roles of cat and mouse. The story unravels, revealing that nothing is as it seems.

While attending New York University Film School, Alexandra directed two short films, and numerous half-hour live and taped segments for CUNY TV, a Manhattan and Paragon cable access channel. Alexandra went on to direct promos for Comedy Central, fashion videos featuring designers such as Ralph Lauren and Bob Mackie, as well as a public service announcement for AIDS. She has also produced an extensive list of music videos as well as commercials and films.

Eight years of Meisner acting training, added another dimension to Alexandra's perspective, by improving her ability to understand and direct actors. It taught her that acting is revealing and enhanced her ability to incorporate imagination and life's unexpected changes from moment to moment into her work.

Alexandra's constant surge of new ideas always keeps her looking to the future. She is currently working on the script for her next film: an erotic thriller focusing on a love triangle trapped in sexual compulsion and obsession, with overtones of voyeurism and exhibitionism.

Alexandra King is a promising, new talent who is just starting to gain attention in the film industry. She possesses exceptional writing abilities, dynamic directing skills and an extraordinary style, along with unequivocal determination, unbounded creativity and a profound passion for film.—*Bio reprinted with permission from the* Red Lipstick *web site, www.red-lipstick.com*

Deborah Harry reciting lyrics she originally wrote for her former all-girl trio the Stillettoes in the show "101 Varieties" at the Pyramid Club, New York City, 1993
credit: © Jon Erkider / Retna Ltd

Designer/club impresario Michael Schmidt, Debbie Harry of Blondie and Joey Ramone of the Ramones
relax outside Squeezebox at Don Hill's at a birthday party for Debbie, July 1996
credit: © Jon Erkider / Retna Ltd

Squeezebox is the coolest place for rock shows on a Friday night. Not only did Debbie perform here but she would actually come to hang out! This was a night celebrating Debbie and Michael Schmidt's birthdays. The place was probably packed passed its legal capacity. It was so crowded around the stage during Debbie's performance that I couldn't lift my arms to take pictures. Afterwards, there was absolutely no air left in Don Hill's. I had to stand on a stool to take a breath of what little air was left among the carbon dioxide of the crowd. I bolted out the door and turned the corner only to find Debbie, Michael and Joey Ramone chatting and posing for pics. I got to give Debbie a birthday present (a set of Runes) and she actually grabbed me and gave me a great big kiss on the lips. It was unreal. I still remember how it felt and it's something that I still brag about.—*Jon Erkider*

Jon Erkider was born John E. Espinosa in San Antonio, Texas and moved to New York in 1992 to pursue his interests in the Arts and to be close to his heroes. He started taking pictures in 1987 and his photographs have been published in *Entertainment Weekly*, *Cosmopolitan*, *Penthouse* and the *Village Voice*. One of the highlights of his life was getting to announce Blondie on the Rosie O'Donnell show as "one of the four biggest Blondie fans."

"Photographing Debbie is always difficult. I still freak out when I see her. I still freeze up, get nervous, and even get too excited to concentrate on anything else. It's by far a hit-and-miss process when I'm looking through the camera because I never want to miss one beat of her in real time."—*Jon Erkider*

190

l to r: Deborah Harry, Joey Ramone, and Tina Weymouth (of the Tom Tom Club and, before that, the Talking Heads). This photo was taken at a Ramones show at the Greek Theatre in L.A. in August 1990 during a "Meet and Greet" backstage downstairs either before or after the show.—*Jeff Mayer*

credit: copyright © Jeff Mayer

The late Robert Jacks and Deborah Harry, New Orleans, New Year's Eve, 1997 – Courtesy of the late Robert Jacks

credit: photo by Wayne

Sonny Bono, Deborah Harry and John Waters on the set of the movie "Hairspray," 1987
credit: copyright © Scott Coblio

Deborah Harry, Maple Leaf Gardens, Toronto, Ontario, Canada, 1990
credit: copyright © Scott Coblio

Deborah Harry, The World, November 12, 1989
credit: copyright © Scott Coblio

Deborah Harry, The Marquis, New York City, 1990
credit: copyright © Scott Coblio

195

Deborah Harry, Squeezebox, New York City, Friday, July 15, 1994

The invite we received in the mail had a personal note from Michael Schmidt "Tina - Don't Miss This! you'll thank me later!" The night started early with an open bar at 10 pm that we missed; arriving right on time for the fabulous performances. We saw Michael and Deborah outside the packed club and slipped in through the side door with them. We made our way through the steamy crowd up to the front of the stage where Joey Ramone was master of ceremonies. Joey introduced the dazzling performers: Varla Jean Merman and Raven O. Then Sherry Vine, Mistress Formika, and Miss Guy all performed together in celebration of Deborah Harry and Michael Schmidt's birthdays. After the entire club sang Happy Birthday, Deborah went on stage to perform a slamming set of classic Blondie songs with the Squeezebox Band. That night, I photographed Deborah performing close up and also with her electrified audience. Afterwards, most of us spilled out on to the sidewalk to cool off and also cherish Michael, Deborah, and Joey.—*Tina Paul*

Deborah Harry, The World, New York City, Sunday, November 12, 1989
credit: copyright © Tina Paul 1989 All Rights Reserved

This was my first time photographing Deborah Harry in concert. There was a buzz around town all week before the two night sold-out shows which I didn't have tickets to. I went clubbing with friends on the second night and our first stop was The World, only we arrived just as the show had ended. My friends Robert and Tim Twin promoted shows at The World so they invited me back for the special third show added on the following night. While at The World, we heard that there was an after-party for Deborah at The Big Hunt Club so we went there. Bob Gruen was there with Matt Dillon but Deborah didn't show up. We later went to Florent for breakfast where we saw Keith Haring and Lysa Cooper dining also. Then even later we went to after hours at Lotto Club. Sunday was spent resting up for Deborah's concert. The friend I invited to go was late so when we arrived at The World, Deborah was already on stage. I first used my 200mm lens to get close up since it was hard to get through the crowd. Chris was also onstage, playing guitar with the band. It was so exciting for me to finally photograph Deborah in concert. At the time, I was photographing for *Details* magazine so I managed to go backstage after the awesome concert. There I saw Stephen Sprouse, Stephen Saban, and Robert and Tim Twin hanging out with Chris and Deborah.—*Tina Paul*

Joey Ramone and Deborah Harry, CBGB Gallery, New York City / Blank Generation Revisited
—Exhibition of Photographs from the Punk and New Wave Era / October 23, 1991 / 6-9 PM.
credit: copyright © Tina Paul 1991 All Rights Reserved

Of the many talented photographers represented in this exhibition, Bob Gruen was also celebrating his birthday at the opening party and hired me to photograph the occasion. Since this was a gallery show opening it was an early party. I arrived about 6:30 pm and had just missed Yoko Ono. Sean Lennon was there and gradually the Gallery became filled with friends and legends. For Bob's birthday, there were three round gourmet cakes and one large rectangle-shaped cake designed as a camera. All those in attendance sang Happy Birthday to Bob including Constance, Voltaire, Bebe Buell, Joey Ramone, Virginia Lohle, Cherry Vanilla, Deborah Harry, Miss Guy, Jo Jo Americo, Leee Black Childers, Jim Jaramush, and Phoebe Legere. Later on, there was a performance by Annie Golden. After some cake and more wine, some of the party moved outside to the sidewalk in front of the Gallery. This is where I photographed Joey and Deborah hanging out. Between the sightings on the walls and in the flesh, the night was a magical reunion of a creative community of friends. I was fortunate to experience this then, having not been there the first time around.—*Tina Paul*

198

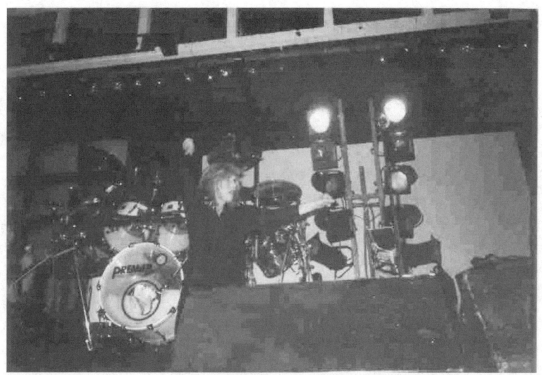

Def, Dumb & Blonde Tour, "Piper," Rome, Italy, 1989
credit: copyright © Sandro Monticelli

William Burroughs, Jean Michel Basquiat and Deborah Harry at Victor Bockris' apartment, New York City, Christmas 1986
credit: copyright © Victor Bockris

Deborah Harry and House Afire, Shine, New York City, February 14, 1998
Special guest Chris Stein...is welcomed to the stage for twisted versions of "Rapture" and "One Way"
while Lou Reed and friends held court in a corner booth!—*John Sibby*
credit: copyright © John Sibby

"workin it! debbie is the original avant CHANTEUSE rockin' out with Gretchen Langheld & her band, House Afire" by John Sibby

amidst the street hassle of broadway and canal an early evening crowd gather. a typical procedure among the hardcore. passing time with debbie folklore and sightings is common fare. a brief and barely audible sound check gets under way improvised and fragmented the stage is set. veiled from fans an open side door now reveals a translucent debbie harry flanked by mentor chris stein. gretchen langheld and some members of her band house afire sit illuminated by candlelight that permeates the inner sanctum of this club called shine...the guest list freak show will soon occupy these very same seats. as if the atmosphere inside isn't visually stimulating enough in itself, shortly before showtime debbie and friend lou reed casually stroll into the club together...slow motion surreal! debbie sans high camp fetish fashion in girl scout garb with white furry platform boots complete with signature wraparound shades, and lou with those eyes darting ultrafocused within the perimeters much to my amazement the two go unnoticed. Debbie continues to the back of the club while lou and new love laurie anderson meet with friends at one of the many reserved tables. the performance itself was much like these photos convey. several chaotic instrumentals begin this avant exorcism while debbie and chris wait on the sidelines eager to share in this uncompromising work. make no mistake when debbie harry takes this stage it seems all too obvious no other artist entrances nor indulges her fans like she is capable of doing. ms harry is indeed in people's DNA. the band's offerings stream together like visions of disenchanted reality vivid yet intangible debbie seems to channel this and create an atmosphere that knows no boundaries. if fans came to hear standard versions of the songs they know and love...they were to leave disappointed. familiarity did not preside over this evening's festivities. but when chris sat in on stage for two warped versions of blondie classics spewing off twisted modal tonalities everyone in attendance including the band was all smiles!...i think this show and many others like it were essential in setting the stage for the historic events that were yet to follow...the second coming. i can't imagine in this mundane current state of entertainment (for lack of a better word)...being without who we affectionately refer to as "debbie and chris"...

Texaco Jazz Festival, New York City, June 1-14, 1998
credit: copyright © Andrea Farina

Deborah Harry with the Jazz Passengers (including Roy Nathanson pictured at the right),
Luna Park, West Hollywood, California, September 30, 1994, the first show at 8 pm.
credit: copyright © Luther Orrick-Guzman

"Jingle Ball Benefit"

by Paul Parks
(adapted and edited by Allan Metz)

KFBM, Star 100.7 FM, San Diego, California
web site, www.histar.com

Blondie at Jingle Ball—Friday night December 7, 2001 was once again one of most looked forward to concert events of the year, the annual Jingle Ball Benefit Concert at the Cox Arena presented by Star 100.7 FM and sponsored by Viejas. Jingle Ball is a benefit concert to help raise funds for "Becky's House," a domestic violence shelter.

This year's Jingle Ball Concert turned out to be one of the biggest and the best yet. The lineup included the Barenaked Ladies, Sugar Ray, Alanis Morissette, Stevie Nicks, and Blondie.

Barenaked Ladies were the first to take the stage this year, having followed Bon Jovi in 2000. The Barenaked Ladies brought the packed house to their feet by pleasing their fans with songs such as "Brian Wilson," "Too Little Too Late" and the crowd sing-along "If I Had A Million Dollars." Next on the bill was Alanis Morissette. Alanis prowls the stage with her Joe Cocker-like spasms and hair that now rivals the length of Cousin It or at least Crystal Gayle's. She played some of her new stuff and her smash hit "You Oughta Know" from her acclaimed album *Jagged Little Pill*. Alanis may have been a hard pill to swallow for those youngest in attendance who came for Sugar Ray and for those a bit older who were there for Stevie Nicks and Blondie.

Next on the tamer side was Mark McGrath and the rest of the boys out of Newport Beach, Sugar Ray. The good-looking MTV hitmakers played all their favorites and had the teen boppers bopping in their seats. They played "Someday," "When its Over," and spreading love to San Diego in full Sugar Ray party style mode with "Fly." Next the revolving stage brought forward the matriarch of the night, Stevie Nicks. With the tightest and most talented musicians of the night behind her, Stevie and her band kicked into all her classics—"Stop Dragging My Heart Around," "Dreams," "Gold Dust Woman," "Sorcerer," "Stand Back," "Edge of Seventeen" and draped in her customary all-black flowing dress she played her signature song "Rhiannon." For her final song she came back out in a white sequined shawl and played her good friend Tom Petty's song "I Need To Know."

Last but not least, it was time for another veteran female rocker, Debbie Harry, fronting the famously known Blondie. Blondie did not disappoint either. Debbie came on singing the velvety "Dreaming" and throughout the performance the band played favorites like "One Way or Another" and the huge hit "The Tide is High."

Jingle Ball was truly a magical night of some of today's best artists. What started out as a benefit to raise money to open Becky's House has turned into one of San Diego's biggest annual concert events. Kudos and congratulations has to go out to Star 100.7 for their vision and making this all happen, to The House of Blues Concerts for booking the bands and their organization, and to Viejas and their fellow sponsors for helping make Jingle Ball a success and such a spectacular event.—*Paul Parks (adapted and edited by Allan Metz, with permission)*

Jingle Ball Benefit Concert, Cox Arena, San Diego State University, San Diego, California, December 7, 2001
credit: copyright © 2001 courtesy of KFBM, Star 100.7 FM, San Diego, California

Part III: Now

Deborah Harry and Chris Stein, Q101 Jamboree 99,
New World Music Theatre, Tinley Park, Illinois, May 22, 1999
They were the coolest in person.—*Theresa Heinz*
credit: copyright © Theresa Heinz

Interviews

"Don't Call It a Comeback: The Evolution of a Legend"

by Jeff Johnson

Original unedited version of article published in Fabula *magazine, 1998*

This article was written after Blondie's fall 1998 UK tour and before the release of the No Exit *album in February 1999. Among the topics covered are Blondie and Deborah Harry's influence and legacy, the reunion, the* Autoamerican *album, and speculation on future albums. Based on interviews with Deborah Harry, Clem Burke and Jimmy Destri.—Ed.*

I'm on the phone with Deborah Harry and I'm still getting over it. My dad's email message blinks across the backs of my eyelids every time they close: How do you interview a cartoon character? To Harry, I say, "So you've been quite active in your personal career since the last Blondie album 16 years ago." She coos her assent. "Does the reunion and new album nonetheless feel like a comeback?" Oops. "Well, it's definitely a reunion, [but] comeback is sort of a derogatory term somehow." As I scribble the word comeback on a page of my notes, then scratch it out of legibility, she continues: "We just wanted to make a good record and we managed to do that." Call it what you like, Blondie is back. At the time of this conversation, the band had just returned from an eight-week tour of the UK, their first in 16 years, to promote the upcoming release of their new album, *No Exit* (due from Beyond in February). Judging from fan response on the Internet, Blondie is ready to rock. I was able to talk with three of the four founding members of the band: drummer Clem Burke, keyboardist Jimmy Destri, and singer Deborah Harry (the fourth member is guitarist Chris Stein).

It's possibly more difficult to name a band fronted by a woman that is not influenced by Blondie than it is to name one who could not have existed without them. And though elements of Deborah Harry (then Debbie)—her look, her attitude, her delivery—appear everywhere in music and fashion today, as they have throughout most of the 80s and 90s, Blondie's sound has been just as influential as their style. As far as Harry is concerned, however, the issue seems to be one of origin. Is she a reflection of the world, or is the world a reflection in her mirrored glasses? After all, this is the band who got its name from the catcalls of men stripped to their stranded libidos by the passing of this future icon: Hey, Blondie! And that's the ageless beauty of Deborah Harry's Blondie character: She managed to stand out in a big way by submerging herself in the trappings of utter typicality. Granted, from that position she subverted those very trappings. Her blatant dye-job was black at the ends, a less than subtle inversion. Told early in her career that she should get out of the business (by no less than Patti Smith, purportedly), and that she was too pretty to rock, she proceeded to work it, to seduce and frustrate her crowd, to arouse and frighten every listener. Trashy? Yeah, sure. Sexy? Forget about it. Rockin? She's the fucking Rock Bird!

touched by your presence dear

So as word gets out that Blondie is reforming, people worry. Will they tarnish their platinum image? Prove they aren't as ageless as their music? Make us feel like suckers? High on the tide of critical acclaim for her work with the Jazz Passengers, Deborah Harry, for one, is not gonna make a fool of herself. After all the posing, all the identity play, she seems to know who she is, and she seems happy to be older and wiser. This is in fact the consensus of the band, and though it's a pretty typical sentiment for a mature band, the fact that none of the members of Blondie dismisses their early work makes it easier to swallow. One could even believe the intervening years have been a ripening silence for the band. It's a good sign they had been planning a much less ambitious project, and they decided they could do more. It's an even better sign that they made *No Exit*. According to Burke (who in recent photos looks spookishly identical to his image on early album covers), "First and foremost what we wanted to do was make a new record, because originally it had been put to us to get back together and do a compilation [with] one or two new songs, which I think would have been very transparent [and] superficial to our fans, and I think we would have done ourselves a disservice." Leery of lurching forward as another quick-cash reunion tour, the band took things slowly. "It's been going on for about three years, you know, the initial talks, and we only went public with it about six months ago." Meanwhile, various band members continued with their own projects (Harry has been singing with the Jazz Passengers, whose latest offering, 1998's *Live in Spain,* silences any doubts that her voice has retained its distinctiveness). Since they weren't rushing into things, they had time to attend to the finer points of musicianship: "We realized we needed to become a band again before we went any further with it," says Burke, "so we found a place to rehearse, figured out what kind of haircut to have and what kind of clothes to wear, and just tried to be a band and rekindle our friendships and our relationships with one another."

Yet another fortuitous sign is Harry's perspective on her latest incarnation (previous versions include being a member of the all-girl trash-vamp Stilettoes, H.R. Giger pin-cushion girl circa '81's solo debut *Koo Koo,* bomb-in-the-beehive mom in John Waters's *Hairspray,* virtual S&M queen of Cronenberg's *Videodrome,* ageing smalltown badmouthed waitress in *Heavy*). She seems to realize it's necessary to allow her persona to age as gracefully as she has. And where to begin? Where else? Her most effective hairstyle of late is a brilliant riff on the Blondie character of old: mostly black, with a fashionable 90s economy-bleach framing the hairline. And no accrual of decades could take away that captivating face. When asked to describe the further evolution of what she has in the past referred to as "the Blondie character" (see 1982's photo-packed *Making Tracks,* recently re-released by Da Capo Press, featuring text by Her Blondeness), she says: "I'm not so concerned with the facade of being a pop star or any kind of little sex object or idol. I did a lot of things from the third person and I think now it's much more immediate for me, much more personal and direct." Continuing in true diva form, she says, "I think at one time the Blondie chanteuse little kind of singer character really sort of outweighed the identity of the band as a group." When asked if their decision to work with Craig Leon, who produced Blondie's first record, signifies a return to some important aspect of the way the band works, her response is promising: "The mere fact that we actually did the record speaks for itself—I don't really care to be so analytical about it."

just another blondie album?

I wasn't sure what to make of *No Exit* when I first listened to it. The second time, I wasn't sure I liked it very much. I tried again. I took notes. On the third listen, I noticed that the album is sort of broken in half, and that "side two" was starting to grow on me. I worked my way backward, listening again and again. It got so the opening drumroll (yes, the album opens with a drumroll) drove my housemate from the room, her hair a pink flash disappearing behind her bedroom door. It was kind of like being a teenager, listening obsessively to a new album, waiting for it to catch on. Pretty soon my housemate got to hear me sing. As Burke puts it, "it feels like the next record, it just took 16 years to make." Or as Destri breaks it down, "It's just another Blondie record, you know?"

What did fans in 1980 think when they first heard *Autoamerican*? The album starts with a sci-fi string and horn arrangement, a score for the movie Blondie imagined they were making. Suddenly, we are caught in Debbie Harry's monotone tractor beam: "Based on the desire for total mobility, and the serious physical pursuit of religious freedom, the auto drove mankind further than the wheel and in remote areas even today it is forbidden as a device too suspect for human conveyance." By the end of her libretto, the auto is of course caught in "phase II gridlock" and "abandoned on the expressway." Cue the next song and start up the 80s ("so easy to Live It Up"). Before the side is over, Blondie has done a show tune ("hit it boys!") [*"Here's Looking At You"*—Ed.] and a reggae song ("The Tide Is High"). And before the needle lifts from side two, Blondie has unleashed the world's first number-one rap fusion song ("Rapture"). Oh, and like some ultramodern Babe Ruth, Harry calls the album's next shot to the upper decks when she sings, "I'm gonna be your number one" in the album's other chart topper.

"Do you think listeners have had a chance to sort of catch up to what Blondie's doing?" I asked Destri. "Maybe it's a more ready environment now, I mean maybe they expect the rap track and they expect the dance track from us now rather than being shocked by it the first time around, but at the same time rather than just try and be totally bizarre and push the limit, go like 10 years ahead again...I think we just remain what we are, and I think that works." Clearly, and thankfully, Blondie stretches themselves on this album, but not in a way that makes the listener wince. Says Burke, *No Exit* "feels like a soundtrack to me very much the same as *Autoamerican* did." What type of movie? "Probably a sort of film noir or something based on a French existentialist play, which is actually where the title comes from, a Jean-Paul Sartre play. [Blondie has] always kind of been part of our identities through the years even though we weren't working together, so there is kind of no exit to it and no escaping it in some ways." It must be noted that on the title track, guest rapper Coolio's posturing highlights Harry's talents. Her icy, distant "Who's gonna cry" siren song layered over and behind the music is far more effective, more sinister, stranger than anything foolio is capable of contributing to a Blondie song. Unlikely as it sounds, the band pulls off this homage to Sartre, replacing philosophy with attitude and keyboards straight out of Old Hollywood horror flicks. Who's gonna cry over you? Don't ask Blondie.

The album also harbors "Maria," a well-crafted pop rock song written by Destri and performed beautifully by Harry (look for it to be the first single); a steamy jazz number ("Boom Boom in the Zoom Zoom Room") with lyrics by Harry, which benefits greatly from her recent work with The Jazz Passengers; "Screaming Skin," a ska/dancehall reggae hybrid that glances back at the rare skin disease that inflicted Stein at the time of Blondie's breakup; the gorgeous, playful country ditty "The Dream's Lost On Me" (perhaps the gem of the album); the hip, Shangri-la singalong "Out on the Street" ("he don't hang around with the gang no more"); and the voodoo-jam "Dig up the Conjo" ("it's only a zombie, honey, hailing a cab"), which closes the album. It may sound schizoid, but it wouldn't be Blondie without the protean restlessness.

this is not an exit

If fan response is any indication, Blondie is not only limber, they're inspired. But is this the goodbye Blondie never gave us when 1982 saw them fade away and radiate? Burke opines, "I think we're definitely going to make another record. People have different ideas but I think for sure another record...but first we have to do this whole go-round." And Destri adds, "I think we'll probably do another record, and I'd like to take it sort of one step at a time and see how it goes. I'd like it to be a little more than a short run, I'd like it to be a few albums, and a few tours, and then I'd like to leave, but the main thing is to leave a legacy as strong as the one we left the first time around." Harry, unruffled, leaves me with, "I think we're just facing it as it comes. I think if you put a lot of pressure on yourself about future goals you know, it can become overburdensome."

Yeah, you know her.

Jones Beach, Long Island, New York, August 8, 1999
credit: copyright © Sylvia Diaz

"Lightning Strikes Twice"

by Paul Burston

The Guardian, *January 23, 1999*

Blondie on the road in England. Topics include Madonna, Blondie's musical influence and an overview of the band's history and Harry's solo career.—Ed.

After 16 years' absence, Blondie are back where they began—on the road and playing in small halls for slim pickings. The hate that made the band split is long forgotten, audiences are as ecstatic as ever, and Debbie Harry, icon of cool, is still the embodiment of blonde ambition. Life is good, they tell Paul Burston.

Debbie Harry is debating whether to buy a shirt she has seen in Joseph. "It's really beautiful," she sighs, running a gentle hand over her bleached-blond tresses and smiling happily. It's a smile so wide it looks almost painful, a smile so familiar it immediately brings back memories of school discos, skinny ties and Heart Of Glass. Then it's gone. She frowns, and fixes me with those sleepy, blue eyes. "But, y'know what?" she says. "It is very expensive. I'm not sure. What would you do?" I tell her that I would probably buy it now and worry about it later, and she snorts with laughter. 'He's a great believer in that,' she says, gesturing towards Chris Stein, who is sitting to her right. Stein has been at Harry's right-hand side, on and off, for the best part of 25 years—first as her live-in boyfriend and co-founder of Blondie, then as an occasional songwriting partner during her solo career. More recently, he has been the driving force behind the much-publicised Blondie reunion. Naturally, she takes a lot of notice of what he thinks.

'I think you should buy it,' says Chris in a voice that sounds like Woody Allen at full speed. 'You never know what could happen. You could die in a minute. A meteor could come through this ceiling and kill you right now.' 'That's so true!' Debbie says, becoming animated. 'Y'know, I gotta tell you. I was in Amsterdam, and the damned hotel was struck by lightning! While I was there! I was sitting there, in an atrium just like this, in the best hotel in Amsterdam, and it was hit by a lightning bolt. And I felt it! It sorta went wah! And then whoosh!'

'I was walking through Central Park once,' Chris announces. 'It was raining, and I had an umbrella, and a lightning bolt hit very near me. And that was exciting. The air crackled, and I felt like a kinda shock. It was really very exciting. People have their psychic abilities kicked up a lot when they're hit by lightning. I wouldn't mind doing it.'

But, by now, Debbie has lost interest. Without warning, the original silky-smooth, ambitious blonde pop goddess, now 53, brandishes her soup spoon and waves it in the air. 'No profiteroles for you!' she shouts in a strange German accent, stabbing away furiously. 'No profiteroles for yoooo!' On the opposite side of the table, Jimmy Destri, the keyboard player, pats his stomach guiltily and confesses that, yes, he is supposed to be on a diet.

It's Saturday afternoon at Conran's Bibendum restaurant on London's Fulham Road, and Blondie are in high spirits. Last night, the band were honoured for their lifetime contribution to the music industry at the Q Magazine Awards.

'It was wonderful,' says drummer Clem Burke.

'It was great,' Debbie agrees. 'Very straightforward. They were concentrating on the awards, not making it into a TV show. Unlike the US, where everything is a TV show and it just drags on and on. But this was very down to business. So there was some spontaneity to it.' 'And I do find Q to be a very credible magazine,' Clem chips in.

Chris looks confused. 'Really? I've never heard of it.'

Debbie slams her soup spoon down on the table and laughs. 'Q?' she says incredulously. 'You've never heard of Q?' Chris shrugs. 'I'm not in the loop, you know.'

For the awards ceremony, Debbie wore a skin-tight black dress covered with razor blades—because, she says, 'fashion should always be a little dangerous.' And she ought to know, better than anyone. This is the only woman who ever looked good in a Day-Glo yellow jumpsuit, the same woman who once sported a rather fetching dustbin liner and very little else for the video they made to promote the single Atomic. Today, she's opted for something slightly more demure—a blue check two-piece, complete with bum-bag and chunky boots.

'Still, it was nice what they said in the paper today,' Chris says.

'Really?' Debbie asks. 'What did they say?'

'Oh, you know. That we had been cruelly overlooked, and all this shit.'

Debbie catches my eye and giggles nervously. 'Really?' she says. 'Is that what they said? About us? Ha ha ha ha!'

It's hard to imagine that anyone could have overlooked Blondie in their heyday. Between 1978 and 1981, they clocked up five number-one singles in Britain (Heart Of Glass, Sunday Girl, Atomic, Call Me, The Tide Is High), plus a string of top-20 hits that guaranteed their place in pop history (Denis, Picture This, Hanging On The Telephone, Union City Blue). Their musical range was extraordinary, combining the sweet sounds of Sixties girl bands and surf music with the harsher elements of New York punk, disco, reggae and rap. Although nobody thanked them for it at the time, Blondie were the first to introduce rap music to a mainstream, white audience with their 1980 American chart-topper, Rapture. What's more, they pulled off a difficult balancing act, somehow managing to be both spectacularly popular and extremely hip at the same time. Posters of Debbie adorned bedroom walls everywhere. She was even guest of honour on the Muppet Show, which was about as big as anyone got in those days. On the other hand, Blondie were Andy Warhol's favourite group, and close cohorts of such well-known arbiters of cool as David Bowie, Iggy Pop and Patti Smith. You could say they were the original pop-art group.

The Blondie story began in 1974, when art student Chris Stein met former [Max's] Kansas City waitress and one-time Playboy bunny Debbie Harry. In 1975, they were joined by Clem Burke and Jimmy Destri, and started playing the New York downtown circuit centred on the legendary CBGBs club, where bands as diverse as the Ramones, Talking Heads, the New York Dolls and Television would draw small but loyal crowds. 'The initial CBGBs scene involved about a hundred people,' recalls Clem. 'There was a real sense of solidarity. Then, as time went on, it became a business. People started to feel a real animosity towards one another about who was going to make it.'

Nobody seriously expected Blondie to be the ones who made it big. When it started to look as if they might just be in with a chance, some people accused them of selling out. 'Which was ridiculous,' says Clem. 'Our whole aesthetic was about being successful. It was more analogous with Andy Warhol in a way, mixing art and commerce together. We wanted to reach as many people as possible. That's why Warhol made paintings of Brillo boxes and Campbell's soup cans, because everyone could relate to that. It was about finding a common denominator, which is also what Blondie has always been about in a way. Some people at CBGBs had more artistic pretensions, which we had, too, of course. But we were also very focused on the commercial aspect of it.'

And nobody more so than Debbie Harry. An adopted child who grew up in New Jersey dreaming that her real mother was none other than Marilyn Monroe, she was hungry for attention from the outset. She had previously been a member of an all-girl trio called The Stilettoes, and a large part of Blondie's commercial success was centred on her sexually upfront stage persona. So too was much of the criticism that followed. Long before Madonna started flaunting her underwear and offering to teach us about sex, Debbie was going on stage without any knickers, acting out the part of the sexually assertive, blonde bombshell, and being condemned for it.

'All the things that Debbie got rapped for are really commonplace now,' Clem says. 'To be a beautiful woman, and to play rock music, and to use her sexuality like that—people really came down hard on her. I remember there was one picture of Debbie with her tongue sticking out, licking a record. That caused so much trouble.' 'I did it all very consciously,' Debbie asserts.

'I wanted to inject some of that film-star glamour. And I didn't want to be portrayed as a victim. I felt that a lot of women in music sang songs about being victimised. I mean, I love Janis Joplin, and I love a lot of the old soul singers, but I really didn't want to do that. I'd had enough, y'know? So it just seemed, especially since I was in front of a rock band, and especially a rock band of all men, like the perfect opportunity to sing songs that were a little more playful about the situation. At the end of the day, it is all about the war between the sexes. But I wanted to be more playful about it. And also to sing in the third person, like with Sunday Girl. It was more like telling a story. My training, or my initiation into singing, came from this man I knew in New York who was a director and who taught Method acting. We worked together for a while, and he got me into this whole Method thing.

I really applied that to what I was doing on stage. It gave me an additional fuel, that I had all these points of view that I could play with. I think that distance is what gave it that extra aggression.'

Ultimately, it is also what led to Blondie's untimely demise. Slowly but surely, the distance between the real Debbie and the persona she adopted on stage created a distance between her and the rest of the band. People began to assume that Blondie was simply Debbie's alter-ego, that Debbie was Blondie, and that Chris, Clem and Jimmy (and, later, guitarist Frank Infante and bass player Nigel Harrison) were little more than backing musicians—despite the fact that they all shared the songwriting credits.

By the time Blondie released their fourth album, Eat To The Beat, in 1979, ardent fans had taken to wearing button badges proclaiming 'Blondie Is A Group.' But, by then, it was already too late. The band's 1980 offering, Autoamerican, was quickly followed by Debbie's first solo album, Koo Koo, sparking rumours that Blondie were about to split. In the event, they battled on for two more years, releasing their sixth and last album, The Hunter, in 1982 before internal tensions drove them apart.

By this time, Chris had fallen ill with a rare and often fatal genetic disease known as pemphigus. The story goes that Debbie spent the next few years putting her career on hold while she nursed Chris back to health—although later she would tell a journalist that rumours of her sainthood during this period had been 'greatly exaggerated.' Clem enjoyed a brief stint with the Eurythmics, while the rest of the band drifted into obscurity.

Debbie is the first to admit that the past 17 years haven't seen her reach quite the same heights she achieved with Blondie. Still, she didn't exactly sit around waiting for something to happen. She made a few inroads as an actress, most memorably as the deranged mother in John Waters' Fifties retro-kitsch film Hairspray. And she had some success as a solo recording artist with hits such as French Kissing In The USA and I Want That Man.

'But I was sort of on the B-list,' she says. 'I mean, French Kissing was a massive hit, but my relationship with Warners was really over by then. They were too busy pushing some other blonde. I felt overshadowed by their commitment to Madonna, and this feeling that I was being viewed as some sort of competitive thing that they couldn't devote much time or energy to. Those songs sort of happened on their own. They weren't really promoted.' She claims not to feel any real resentment towards Madonna, despite the fact that Madonna effectively stole her act. 'But she did it so well,' she says, without a trace of bitterness, or even a hint of sarcasm. 'She's a very smart woman, actually. I really respect her.'

By the mid-Nineties, Harry had more or less turned her back on pop, settling for the role of featured vocalist with contemporary free-jazz outfit the Jazz Passengers. 'I think I've been kind of lucky with that. I've had the chance to do a bit of experimentation, retreat from the spotlight of being a pop star, and just work as a singer and as an artist. Working with the Jazz Passengers is like what CGBGs offered to all of us in the beginning, sort of a workshop to experiment in. All artists need to hide behind closed doors sometimes.' Still, when people started turning up at Jazz Passengers gigs dressed in faded Blondie T-shirts, she couldn't resist the thrill of nostalgia. 'It was wonderful,' she says dreamily.

Somewhere along the way, she started calling herself Deborah ('I thought I was getting too old for Debbie'), and developed a reputation for being rather eccentric. In fact, reading some of the interviews she's given over the years, you could be forgiven for thinking that she was stark raving mad. She once spent an entire interview trying to slip the word 'masturbation' into the conversation as many times as possible. On another occasion, and for no obvious reason, she challenged the man interviewing her to a fist fight—over the telephone. 'But I say these things as jokes, y'know. Some of the people they send to interview you are so straight. I say these things to amuse myself, and then they start scribbling them down.' So it isn't true that she once planned to run away with Patti Smith and live in a lesbian commune?

'I do live in a lesbian commune,' she says, trying her best to sound convincing. 'Write that down. Debbie Harry lives in a lesbian commune.' Moments later, she starts howling like a dog, before announcing that she recently made a film about bestiality called Zoo. I'm not sure whether to believe her. 'You have a dog, don't you?' I say, nervously. 'Oh yeah,' she replies. 'I have a dog. A lovely dog called Chi Chi. She's a lap dog. She sits right on my crotch. Just like a big penis.'

She admits that some of the things written about her over the years have got to her. 'A few things have upset me, and that's when I've been at the end of my emotional tether. I mean, I get depressed about it all sometimes.' But surely, after all these years, she must be used to the pressures of being famous? 'Well, I've sort of been out of the game for a while,' she drawls. 'But I see stuff in the paper, and I have a good laugh. Stuff about

Geri and the Spice Girls. All the stuff about royalty in this country. And Clinton, of course. It's like, 'Oh my god!' But yeah, I suppose it's great to be back in the hot seat. It keeps your ass warm.'

Today, Debbie Harry's ass is warmer than it has been in a long time. The idea of a Blondie reunion was first suggested to her by Chris Stein three years ago. Debbie took some convincing at first, but now that things are up and running, she says she couldn't be happier. She's happy to be back in Britain, where Blondie enjoyed such widespread popularity the first time around and where she feels she has always been given a fair hearing. 'It's a good feeling,' she says brightly. 'Not bad. Doesn't hurt.' She's happy to be going back on the road with Chris, Clem and Jimmy. (Frank Infante and Nigel Harrison were excluded from the reunion plans, and are currently contesting the decision in court [*which ultimately ruled against them*—Ed.].)

Most of all, she's happy to talk about the new Blondie album, No Exit. It is, she thinks, a very good record, a fitting continuation of the Blondie story. If anything, No Exit sounds like the album Blondie should have made after Autoamerican, but didn't. And because Blondie's influence can be heard just about everywhere these days, especially in bands such as Garbage and Republica, the album sounds contemporary.

But doesn't it worry her that people are bound to measure it against former glories, that a band with Blondie's track record are destined to be forever haunted by their past? 'Not at all. What's really kind of interesting is that when we did those records, we created a formula that went on to be sort of a standard in the industry. But, at the time, when we handed in those records, often they were rejected. What I think we've done on this record is the best, the essence, or the most powerful versions of all the things we have stood for and done in the past. It's the ultimate Blondie record.' And the title? 'The title came from Clem,' she explains. 'Well, it came from Jean Paul Sartre. But Clem appropriated it.'

'Hell is other people', Chris says, quoting from the Sartre play No Exit. 'I think that really defines what it's like being in a rock and roll band.'

Of course, they are all willing to admit that there was a time when hell was other members of Blondie. 'I can't speak for everyone,' Debbie says, choosing her words carefully, 'but Chris and I were certainly estranged for a while.' In the past, she has been less tactful about the split, saying that 'hate had a lot to do with it'.

Still, all that is in the past now. 'I think everybody's enjoying it a lot more this time around,' says Chris. 'Coming back into it, I think we all know what's involved. The first time around, you don't know what a pain in the ass it can all be. Looking back, I think we really took it for granted. We thought we had all the answers. When you're a kid, you think you know everything.'

Only, they weren't exactly kids. Chris was 30 when Blondie notched up their first number-one single. And when Debbie sang Die Young, Stay Pretty, one of the classic cuts from the Eat To The Beat album, it wasn't without some sense of irony. She was 34 at the time. Ironically enough, this does the reunited Blondie no harm whatsoever. Unlike the recent Sex Pistols reunion tour, nobody is going along expecting Blondie to act like disaffected 20-year-olds. In an odd way, time is on their side. Besides, Debbie has little time for people who suggest that she is getting too old for this game. 'I just get better at it,' she says firmly. 'Right now, I am better than ever. Why shouldn't I be? It's the same thing I resisted before, about being considered a victim. It's all about traditional roles. But they are changing. Look around. It's a radically changing world.'

'No Exit is simply the next Blondie record,' says Clem. 'It just took 16 years to make, that's all. And we're very fortunate to have Debbie here to convey the whole thing.'

Hearing this, Debbie blushes slightly, rolls her eyes and lets out a little laugh. 'You're right about that!,' she says. 'You're damned right!'

Three weeks have gone by, and I'm waiting for Blondie to arrive at the studio where the photo-shoot is to take place. For Debbie and the others, it's been a hectic three weeks. They have performed in no fewer than nine different European countries. Reviews of the tour have been extremely encouraging. On the other hand, their schedule has been little short of punishing, involving long hauls through the night on the tour bus with very little sleep.

Two hours later, there is a slight commotion outside and Chris walks in, closely followed by Clem and Jimmy. They all disappear to a dressing room. Another five minutes pass before Debbie wanders in, dressed in a leather pirate coat and biker boots, with a scarf wrapped tightly around her head.

'How are you?' I ask.

'Beat,' she answers quickly. It turns out that two days ago, Blondie were on a plane from Dublin, destined for Glasgow. Halfway across the Irish sea, the plane developed a technical fault and was diverted back to Dublin, where they were told there would be a slight delay and offered the usual—food vouchers. This 'slight delay' turned into seven hours, by which time Debbie had fallen asleep in the airport departure lounge.

Later, with Chris again at her side, she re-enacts the scene, sprawling across the nearest chair, head hanging back, mouth open. 'I was probably drooling as well,' she giggles.

'The thing is, we're on a tight budget,' Debbie explains. 'Regardless of all the exposure and all the interest, it's been small halls and not a lot of money. We're doing this in a very traditional fashion.' The way she describes it, it sounds as though it's only the adrenaline from the shows that has kept them all going. 'It really has been extraordinarily good,' she says. 'I just can't believe it. And the audiences have been right there with us. In Scotland, they sang along to everything, except the new songs. And they even tried to sing along to them.' 'Last night, they all started singing Union City Blue before she opened her mouth,' says Chris.

'They sang over the guitar intro,' says Debbie. 'These guys usually frown at me when I do that, but they let the audience get away with it. But y'know, if we never do anything again after this, it'll be fine. We decided very early on to document it all ourselves, so we're filming everything as we go along. So, if we never do it again, we've always got that.' At this point, Clem and Jimmy reappear, dressed and ready for their close-up. (Debbie has insisted on doing her own hair and make-up, although she does consent to a little retouching). Jimmy is describing an episode that occurred five days ago at the Campione d'Italia, near Lugano. The band had won an Italian entertainment award, and were invited to perform in the middle of a casino, before an invited audience of film and music industry executives all dressed in dinner suits. 'It was like being in a Fellini film,' Jimmy says. 'We did a lip synch, which we're very loath to do as a rule.' He points at Clem. 'For some reason, this idiot decides to hop over the drums. So he hops over his drum kit, doing his middle-aged Keith Moon, and knocks down our bass player, who he picks up by the collar. By now he's in his 1977 'I'm a punk rocker' vibe. So he goes out into the audience, picks up a chair, and starts swinging it above his head. And there's this little Italian guy, who must have been a film producer or something, and he's screaming, 'No! no! no!'' 'He's exaggerating,' Clem says. 'I just freaked out a little, that's all.' 'The food was amazing,' Jimmy says. 'There was lobster, all these amazing sauces, profiteroles...' So Jimmy finally got his profiteroles? 'Oh yeah,' he says, grinning. 'I went through the whole thing just eating.' As soon as the photo-shoot is over, Debbie lights up a cigarette. As a rule, she allows herself only one cigarette a day when she's performing, but since today is her first day off in almost a week she has upped it to three. Still, she feels guilty—she has a show to do tomorrow.

Chris, Clem and Jimmy are discussing where to go for dinner. Clem suggests going to the Groucho Club afterwards. Debbie groans at the thought. She has some friends visiting from New York, and would really like to spend some time with them, but thinks she'll probably just go back to her hotel and have an early night.

'I'll just tuck myself,' she says. 'I'll tuck into some food, and then tuck myself up in bed.' She laughs. 'A double tuck! I'm gonna have a double tuck!' As she prepares to leave, I compliment her on her leather pirate coat. 'It's cool, isn't it?,' she says happily, hugging the coat against her body and swinging her hips from side to side. 'I bought it in Berlin. This shop has two branches—one in Berlin and one in Miami. Figure that out. But you know what? It just gets better the older it gets. It's a bit more chewed up, a bit more funky.' The following night, an older, funkier Debbie Harry struts out on to the stage at London's Lyceum Theatre, dressed in a sharp tailored jacket and slinky pencil skirt. She has the audience in the palm of her hand right from the opening bars of Dreaming, but she doesn't take anything for granted. She's been around long enough to know better than that. Behind her, supported by a second guitarist and a new bass player, the original pop art, New Wave punk rockers storm through their back catalogue like the seasoned professionals they are, whipping the mostly thirty-something crowd into a frenzy. And, sure enough, even the new songs are met with pockets of wild applause.

Afterwards, there's a small celebration back stage. I spot Jimmy first. He tells me he isn't at all happy with the show, that the sound was awful. 'We'll have to do a proper sound-check tomorrow,' he says. Clem and Chris arrive together, looking mournful. Evidently they're not very happy either.

Finally, Debbie walks in, dressed in the outfit she wore for yesterday's photo-shoot, and surrounded by a host of admirers. Saffron, the lead singer with Republica, is hovering close by, autograph book at the ready. Debbie stops and chats with her for a while, before turning to me. Her face is expressionless, almost glacial. 'So what did you think of the show?' she asks. I tell her it sounded great from where I was sitting.

'That's good,' she says, rolling her eyes and heaving a sigh of relief. 'I need to hear that.' Something tells me that she isn't entirely convinced, which seems rather a shame. Because, tonight, Blondie proved that they can still make it magnificent—even if only for a short while.

"Blondie: No Introduction Necessary"

by John Kappes

Alternative Press (AP) *magazine, March 1999*

Interview with Deborah Harry and Chris Stein. Topics include American new wave, dance music, the New York City scene, fame and its pitfalls, longevity in the music business, the commercialization of rock, and the continuing influence of Blondie's music.—Ed.

Blondie have always served as a needed reminder that you can catch more flies with honey than you can with vinegar. They were pop pranksters who made a marriage of image and content seem easy. From 1977 to 1982, Chris Stein and Debbie Harry were practically the poster kids for growing up in public, together going through boom and bust, sickness and health, in the glare of cheap flash bulbs. Sick of publicity, they nonetheless came back with their catchiest chorus, "Call me, call me anytime." Twenty years later, just as the reunited band are poised to step out with an all-new album titled No Exit, we did.

Blondie were always more into pure pop than a lot of the other American new-wave bands. Did you take a lot of abuse for that?
Harry: No, I actually think there was a kind of mutual appreciation going on, where we had respect for each other's forces. The thing we shared was attitude; antisocial attitude. There wasn't really a lot of warring about musical inspiration. There was some healthy competition going on, but it wasn't about the music itself.

Stein: Everybody was trying to outdo each other, to have the best idea.

Harry: But you'd always find a song that another band did that really turned you on. I think people were more interested in seeing the different personas, because everybody had this personality thing going on.

But things did seem to change by the early '80s, with hardcore punk, when you used to hear that this or that band wasn't "hard" enough. Blondie was one of the few bands then to cross over into dance music, at a time when the "disco sucks" attitude prevailed.
Harry: Well, that's a whole other, macho kind of thing. There's no way around that when you get into music that's about force rather than musicality. That's where you end up. I didn't really hang out in dance clubs or anything, but I always loved Chic. They were really smart and had good songs. I liked Kraftwerk too. With me, it's whether I like a song. After that. I don't give a fuck.

And that hardcore scene did seem to reach a dead end eventually. There's only so fast and so hard, and then what do you do?
Harry: Go deaf, go blind, I don't know. [Laughs.] Get off the stage. Go sterile.

One fascinating thing about the New York scene was that you had this group of people who knew each other, and somehow their music ended up winning over the country and then the world. Do you think it could happen again?
Harry: Of course it could happen again.

Stein: No way.

Care to elaborate?
Stein: When we were doing it, there weren't all these TV shows and periodicals everywhere. And it didn't happen that quickly; it took a long time. Look at the New York Dolls or the Velvet Underground. I mean, it was 1967 when their dark, leather album came out. They may be legendary now, but then they couldn't make a living. Even with four

No. 1 hits in America, Blondie was always a cult band. I don't think nowadays there could ever be a scene that could ferment like that. I don't think it would be allowed to ferment.

Harry: It was quite a concentration of people communicating in their different forms—press people, photographers, artists, musicians, actors—all doing this simultaneously in one little area. So it was really kind of an explosive mixture.

A recent VH-1 documentary on Blondie suggested that the attention Debbie Harry captured worked against the band's survival from the outside, through other people who helped disrupt the group. But surely fame also had some affect on you.
Harry: It's a real whiplash experience being in a successful band—all of a sudden you're sort of flung out there. Unless you have some kind of management that is able to take neophytes, people who have never been in the industry, and give them the information they need about what's going to hit them next, you're left to take lots of slaps in the face.

But I can't really say it's entirely management's fault. It's a difficult, weird little world to be in. All of a sudden you're just like the most tasty piece of candy on the shelf, and everybody wants to take a bite. Also, you're thrust into a position where anything you want, you can have—and you're usually just fresh out of school. Here you are, expected to be an artist, but you're thrown into a really tough business world. So you're really pulled in a lot of directions at the same time. To land on your feet is quite a feat.

Especially since one of your ideas was to send up the whole platinum-blonde obsession, it must have been hard to keep hearing, "It's you, it's you—Just dump these guys and you can do anything."
Harry: Well, the group didn't last. [*Pauses.*] It makes you appreciate somebody who does maintain a career for a very long time at a very high level. You can really appreciate the strength and fortitude and business acumen that comes along with it. I certainly didn't want to be in the hot seat that long. I consider myself coming more from an art-school or a performance-art background. I'm not really a showbiz person. Initially, anyway; I've certainly worked my way into it by now. So it was difficult to put my brain around these contrasting, fighting elements. To make people understand that what I was doing was, for me, a theatrical event, was impossible. They wanted to sell this product, and I was having an event. [*Laughs.*]

So how do you feel now about Blondie having become a product, a nostalgia item? What's it like when you walk by and see a Blondie keychain or a Blondie cupholder?
Stein: I think I've said before, I didn't just want to play the old songs, but I find I've been getting all sentimental about them. It's my own personal nostalgia. I can understand how they mean things to people, since they have that feeling for me, too. But with rock and roll everywhere now, on milk commercials, I don't know how attracted to it I'd be if I were a kid. It's definitely become one more product.

Harry: I can really hear our influence in retrospect, you know, when I listen to a Madonna or a No Doubt. So I'm really happy with the music. At our shows, we know what they're selling. We don't sell diddly crap. We keep it to t-shirts and posters, things people would want to have. There are no cupholders, darling.

Suggested Listening: Blondie

THE PLATINUM COLLECTION
Nearly the whole Blondie story is available on this two-CD compilation, including DJ remixes of "Atomic" and "Rapture." Beginners are advised to seek this out. **(Chrysalis/EMI, 1994)**

PARALLEL LINES ▲
With the megahit "Heart of Glass," this album adds the sheen, but something of its subversive charm is evident on the picture disc, where a bored-looking Debbie Harry can be seen licking a piece of vinyl. **(Chrysalis, 1978)**

PLASTIC LETTERS
At its best, rock is about albums as much as big tracks, and Blondie are best heard sequenced the way the band intended. Plastic Letters showcases pop that's tight but not smothered in a plastic sheen, that's alive with possibilities. **(Chrysalis, 1977)**

AUTOAMERICAN
Although this faced some tough criticism upon its initial release, in retrospect it stands out as one of the first multiculti rock records, mixing in Caribbean and dance rhythms at will. **(Chrysalis, 1980)**

"Entering No Exit"

by Cindy Rivers

Ink19.com *web site, April 1999*

Interview with Clem Burke. Topics discussed include Blondie's uniqueness, influence and legacy plus CBGBs and the reunion.—Ed.

Like it or not, fact is, before Madonna and Courtney Love, Deborah Harry was music's first bleached-blonde bombshell. Before the Beastie Boys there was "Rapture..." So even, back then, Harry, a former Playboy bunny and consummate diva, was "pretty fly for a white girl." And for all its quirkiness, no one can deny that Blondie crossed music boundaries, defied categorization, creating trends instead of following them.

"We were always kind of being ourselves," says drummer Clem Burke. "I think Blondie was a little ahead of the curve a little bit, which is why you're seeing so much interest in the band today. We weren't doing anything other than being ourselves. So we didn't really follow any trends. I think, if anything, we created trends. Not to be egotistical about it, but, certainly, when Deborah appeared for the first time with Blondie, there weren't too many women out there doing what she was doing." And, in 1999, that offer still stands.

For those lined up for more nostalgia, No Exit is a slick production, light on heavy subject matter, with a touch of whimsy and airbrushed sex appeal. The album's strongest track, "Screaming Skin," the quasi-reggae/punk tune, has as much finesse as a James Bond movie. From the new age feel of "Night Wind Sent" and the peculiar appearance of the Loretta Lynn-style country song "The Dream's Lost On Me," to the "faux jazz" song "Boom Boom in the Zoom Zoom Room," inspired by Debbie's stint with the Jazz Passengers, and which Burke wrote with Go-Go Kathy Valentine, Harry's cool arrogance, seductive demeanor, and apathetic expression are as timeless as ever.

"No Exit feels like the next Blondie record for us. For some reason, it took 16 years to make, [but] the audiences has been very accepting," Burke surmises. "When we decided to come back together, the first thing we decided is that, if we're going to put all this time, energy, and emotion into this, we wanted to create some new music. The first thing we did was we all began writing. We went into the studio, and created a new record, which is the reason we're all here today. And it gives us a feeling of credibility, the fact that we've reformed with new material."

Today, Burke is nursing a cold. He's sniffling, yet surprisingly, quite talkative despite the fact he and the band have been awake since the wee hours, conducting various interviews. In between hacking coughs, he's obviously still elated from last night's two-hour performance at Town Hall in Manhattan, also their first concert endeavor (filmed for VH-1) in New York City in sixteen years. That's a point not taken lightly, considering that if (Harry's former lover, and fellow band member) Chris Stein's illness—pemphigus, a rare skin disease that caused him to break out in blisters—hadn't contributed to Blondie's break-up in 1982, Harry's increasingly high-profile persona, which overshadowed the other band members' contributions, or the strain of the music business would have. "We made five albums in four and a half years," Burke points out. "That's a pretty tremendous work load, when you look at bands today taking maybe three years between albums. At the peak of our success, we were working really hard, and we basically got worn down. Maybe the band had run its course. The Beatles were only together for eight years. Why didn't the Beatles stay together forever? Most relationships end, and life goes on. Then, everyone felt as though Blondie had run its course, at that point."

Then, of course, there's that "historic" appearance at the American Music Awards earlier this year that marked yet another milestone, in which the band, collectively, decided to perform "No Exit," featuring rapper Coolio, despite the immediate success of the first single, "Maria," which recently debuted at #1 in the U.K. Also incorporating the Wu-Tang Clan and Mobb Deep (for the AMA appearance) along for the strange ride, "No Exit" goes from being Blondie's second foray into rap to a rap song tinged with punk and gothic metal, its remixed version nabbing a spot on the 200 Cigarettes soundtrack (a movie staring Ben Affleck, Christina Ricci, and Courtney Love).

In light of the album's current Top 5 status in the U.K., Blondie will return to the U.K., upgrading from mid-sized venues to stadiums, including London's Wembley Arena in May, to accommodate the overwhelming demand, in the follow-up to their successful six-week European tour, before embarking upon a U.S. tour in the late spring.

So what makes your reunion different from everybody else's?

I'm seeing a lot of reunions, but I'm not seeing a lot of new music. That's the whole difference with us. It was really important for us to make a new musical statement. It was most important for us to be able to interact musically, and make new music, not just go out there and rehash the old songs. What you're seeing a lot of with these reunions is, "oh, by the way, there's a new album." But, really, it's just a reissued album with one or two new songs. People can do whatever they want, but, to me, that really doesn't show me that the people really want to be together, and make music together. It seems like they want to just go out and play, and they think there's an audience there for it. I don't want to cast aspersions on anybody else, but I really think the main difference with all of these other reunions and ours is that we've made a great record. We're all really happy with the record. If there's any catharsis involved in any of this, everyone always asks, "What was it like when you guys [first] went in a room together to make music?" That felt natural. The only catharsis was when we completed the record, sat back, and said, "Yeah, this is a great record. We're all proud of this record. And now we're able to continue." I think had we not made a new record and been happy with it, we wouldn't have been able to go on tour. We wouldn't have been able to continue. It feels fresh for us because we have new music.

Would you ever consider performing at CBGB's again?

I would love to. I've been twisting everybody's arm to do that. It's such a viable place, still. And the owner, Hilly Kristal, is such a great guy. I would love to do it. Everyone seems to think it's a little too small. I mean, it would be chaotic, but I think rock and roll kind of thrives on chaos, so I think it would be a good thing.

When I was a kid, I used to think the band was from England. Now that I know you're American, do you care to clear up any other misconceptions?

We're all things to all people. We're very confusing. Some people think we're a disco band. Some people think we're a blonde girl. Some people think we're a rap band. Some people think we're a punk rock band, still.

So what are you?

I'd say we're, pretty much, a classic rock and roll band. If you look at the Beatles, and the Stones, for instance, they were all working in different mediums. They were a rock band. But then the Beatles would do something like ["Ob-La-Di, Ob-La-Da"], which was like a ska song. Or the Stones would do "Miss You," which was like a dance song. I think we were working in those terms, as well. The songs stand up as songs, but they way we perform them is dictated by how we feel that day. You can play the songs on an acoustic guitar, and they'll still stand up. And the band is really about songs.

How did the collaboration with Coolio come about?

Chris Stein has always been a fan of rap music. Coolio and Deborah had worked together, of all places, in Vienna. They were on the same bill when Deborah was doing her solo venture. And she had suggested that perhaps we should get Coolio to rap with us. It's interesting. There's a real energy I get from [rappers], and I think, conversely, they get [something] from us, because you realize most rappers are used to working in the studio with sampling, and all. When we all came together in Los Angeles to begin rehearsing for the AMAs, it was really an exciting time for everybody, because I would start a drum beat, or somebody would play a guitar lick, and those guys would pick up on it and start doing a rap. It was a more organic way of making music, which we were used to, but those guys were using technology more. Coolio went into some reggae thing we were jamming on. I've got a great tape of that. I'd like to work with those guys some more. I've been around a lot of different people, and I really get a strong vibe from Coolio. I rate him up there with Mick Jagger or Iggy Pop—or somebody like that.

Chris actually approached you guys three years ago about reuniting. What took so long to get back to together, and to make the record?

Once we decided to come back together, we realized we needed to become a band again, not just a business venture. So once it was decided that we'd be a band, we went away, and did just that: went to a rehearsal room, worked on new material, and forgot about the outside world. And let the music flow out of us. Everyone was working on other things over the years. (Burke spent the Eighties working with Eurythmics, while Harry tried her hand at acting in such films as John Waters' Hairspray). And the time just seemed right with the approach of the millennium. [Now] we have a new focus. One of the references to the title of the album, was there really was no escaping Blondie. There was really no exit from it. Certainly, Debbie and Blondie were synonymous. And, all of us, to a lesser or greater degree, were associated with it. Within the music business, that's how people looked at it: "This is Clem from Blondie..." Or, "This is Jimmy Destri from Blondie." So it was always part of our identity, and I think everyone was always hearing, "When's the band going to get back together?" We've put a couple of things into play now where we feel secure in our representation. And everyone feels confident enough to be able to do this now.

"No Exit in Sight: The Rebirth of Blondie"

by Dino Balzano

Frontiers Newsmagazine, *May 1999*

An interview with Deborah Harry focusing on the Blondie reunion and the No Exit *album. Subjects touched upon include Harry's role in the band, music critics, radio's categorization of music, touring, Harry as a "gay icon," Harry as a "diva," the enduring quality of Blondie's music, and speculation on whether Blondie would record another album.—Ed.*

"I always wanted to perform," says Deborah Harry, "although when I was little I thought I wanted to be a movie star because rock stars didn't exist then. But when rock started, well...that's when I went, 'OK, that's it! That'll be it!'"

And it was! A rock star she would become, and a pretty big one, too—thanks to her group, Blondie, and its succession of chart-topping and ground-breaking records released between 1976 and 1982. Of course, Harry—away from the band—also managed to satisfy her curiosity as to what it's like to be a "movie star," appearing in a variety of films over the years.

But on the day that SF Frontiers spoke with her she really didn't want to talk about anything to do with acting or 'Deborah Harry—the performer.' These days it's Blondie she wants to discuss—and, of course, the release of their new CD, No Exit.

No Exit professionally reunites Harry with former bandmembers Clem Burke, Jimmy Destri and (former lover) Chris Stein for the first time in 17 years—the last album the group put out was 1982's The Hunter, a critical and commercial flop. After its release, the group soon disbanded over well-publicized in-fighting and career exhaustion experienced by all. It was at this same time Stein was diagnosed with a rare blood disease, which nearly took his life and did take many, many years to recover from. Even if Blondie had wanted to continue, it would have been impossible.

But it was also Stein who came up with the idea to get the gang back together again. Of course, he had no problem with Harry, as they have been musically collaborating together on her four subsequent solo albums and have always been close—whether as lovers or not. But what about the others? Was it difficult to coax them into reuniting? "Well, I guess it was more complex and not so much difficult," notes Harry, in reference to Burke and Destri.

"What we did was work at it for a two-and-a-half-year period," she says. "We went through a lot of different levels of intensity. First we just got together and played. Then we talked about reuniting with [former producer] Mike Chapman. Then we went into the studio with Mike and we invited [former member] Nigel Harrison to come play with us. He said that he wasn't interested. Then we did some demos with Mike [and] some live shows with [former member and notorious wild-card] Gary Valentine, which was kind of interesting and fun. Then we went back into the studio with Nick Rhodes and Warren Cuccurullo from Duran Duran and we recorded two songs they had written. And all this time we were trying to interest EMI/Chrysalis in doing some work with us because they were going to do yet another 'Best of Blondie' album. We tried to get them to accept some new material instead, but that sort of fell apart...they weren't really interested in that. Finally we just made our own record."

And make a record they did—one that manages to maintain the distinct Blondie sound from yesteryear yet also discovers new musical elements to make that classic sound current and fresh. This was a trick few people, including many die-hard Blondie fans, thought they could do. But they did. And let's face it, not just any band can mix so many musical styles on one recording—ska (Screaming Skin), rap (the title track, No Exit), jazz (Boom Boom in the Zoom Zoom Room) and country (The Dream's Lost on Me)—and not only get away with it, but get away with it successfully. Though a few tracks may not quite make the mark (Double Take), No Exit not only shows great musical integrity, but, simply put, works.

Asked how she would compare No Exit to Blondie's six previous albums, Harry states: "The production is simpler, not so many layers. I think the compositions and the melodic lines are more upfront. We worked very hard in developing each song and we're better at it now, for some reason. We've all been working over the years regardless of whether we've had hits or not. None of us ever really stopped, we just haven't been working together as Blondie."

The work has paid off, too, as displayed in their live performances promoting No Exit. Time has allowed each, in their own individual capacities, to become better musicians. "I think that the band is really a good band now," says Harry. "It's a terrific experience to go out on stage as a singer with a band that you can really rely on. My job is somewhere between the audience and the band. I have to sort of float on top of what they do, so [the band] has to be something that I can rely on—and I can really rely on them now."

The reviews for No Exit range from ecstatic, as in Britain's Mojo magazine, to mediocre, as Rolling Stone seemed to feel. Does Harry get bothered by the more negative reviews? "It doesn't really affect me," she says. "[Reviews] are subject to so many variables. I've been sort of happy with the response. I was happy with the record, so after that, well...You know, writers have an agenda—they're not really clear what their criticisms are. If you took a panoramic look at all the stuff written [about No Exit] you'd find that anything that could possibly be said has been said. It sort of makes you think it has more to do with the writer than it does you."

The press and its reviews have not been the problem for the band so much as the world of radio. Luckily for the group, No Exit is able to maintain respectable record sales despite the lack of play it's receiving on the airwaves. Radio appears to want to peg the album as "adult contemporary," but that is not the listening audience who is buying the album at record stores or attending the live concerts. And "adult contemporary" is a tag that does not sit too well with a band that became famous for ground breaking and original music. "It's crazy, the world of radio," Harry says. "I really don't have a clue about the way things are worked these days. It seems overly complex to me and has a lot more to do with selling advertising time than it does with music. I'm sorry that they don't find the song (the first single, Maria) or the record airable."

Adult contemporary stations appear to find No Exit too progressive, while progressive stations find the album too tame. The urban contemporary stations—those with a heavy funk and rap rotation—have absolutely no idea at all what to make of it—especially the title track, a street-wise rap number featuring guest artist Coolio. Asked how this collaboration came about, Harry responds: "Well, I had worked with Coolio on a show in Belgium a couple of years ago. I liked him and we sort of hit it off. [Blondie] had been in the studio and we worked out the No Exit track, and I had done the rap entirely myself. I wasn't really convinced that this was really sort of an ethical or meaningful experience for anybody, so then I thought I wanted the character of the vampire [in the song] actually played by a rapper. I thought of Coolio and then we sent the track off to him and he completely took it in his own direction and put his social twist on it and wrote his own rap—which was just perfect and took this song to a whole new level."

As for other tracks on the album, Harry is especially fond of Boom Boom in the Zoom Zoom Room, an off-beat, bluesy, swing-beat track that is very reminiscent of her recent work with the band, The Jazz Passengers. "Kathy Valentine (of Go-Gos fame) cooked that one up," Harry says. "I think that Clem [Burke] sort of wanted to give me something that would be sort of like The Jazz Passengers. I found it very interesting that he would come up with that because he's such the 'pop-meister.' One of his favorite things is English pop bands, so I was very surprised when he actually worked on that one. I love the lyrics, too."

It's a song Harry enjoys playing on their current concert tour, which will put them in San Francisco at the Warfield on Sunday, May 30. The tour is not only displaying the improved-with-time talents of the band's musicians, but also a new-found confidence in the lead singer that was previously unseen at a Blondie concert. Sure, even at the height of Blondie's fame Harry was fascinating to watch with her passive, indifferent—yet tough—stance in front of the microphone. But these days, she also exhibits a comfort on stage as a performer—a comfort that can only come from loving what you're doing. Which is lucky for her, because Blondie is booked to play a lot of shows this year. "I think the touring that we're doing now will take us into the year 2000," Harry says. "I think that the world, the way it is today, and the amount of work that a group like Blondie can do on the road, is practically limitless. We really could work for quite a long time and I think that's what we'll probably do."

The subject of touring, though, and a nonstop work schedule, is a sensitive one for Harry, as it was a factor in the demise of the band in 1982. Plus, the stress from the demands of it all, Harry maintains, played a part in Stein's serious illness—a horrendous experience she will never forget. But the same mistakes will not be made a second time around. "I think we learned our lesson big time," she says. "I can't possibly explain the amount of stress we put ourselves through. It was just a stupid work schedule. It was a stupid fucking way of looking at having a career. We didn't really have a good idea of longevity and what it takes to have longevity. We were really pushed to the limit 99 percent of the time. We never took a vacation in eight years. I think we recorded four albums in three years, or something ridiculous like that. Our schedule was totally insane. I don't think that any of us would ever do anything like that again."

With this new, less-punishing tour, she has more time now to meet with her many fans. And in doing so she's been able to confirm something she's noticed for quite some time: Gay men and lesbians love Deborah Harry and Blondie. Gay men, in particular, simply eat her up. In fact, Harry has come to be considered a true gay icon—something she seems to be enjoying. "Well, I guess it's true," she confirms with a slight giggle. "I don't know, I just try to wear the highest heels that I possibly can!"

As for diva status, well, she's not so sure about that one. Asked if that term applies to her, she says, "Well, in some ways it might. I think it's easier to apply it to a solo artist like Cher, or someone like that. My identity is sort of this group, as well as a diva identity. I'm not strictly a diva; I really enjoy working in an ensemble tradition."

Well, Blondie is an ensemble—and Harry has no problems with the focus put on the band and not just herself—in fact, it's how she prefers it. Of course, at the same time, she allows herself to be the attention-grabber in order for the band to get more media attention. Hey, Deborah Harry is anything but stupid. And she's smart enough to recognize when something works and when something doesn't. Blondie—the 1999 version—works. "There's something about this 'Blondie' thing that catches on," she notes. "It seems to endure."

But is No Exit a one-time shot, or will the reincarnation of Blondie endure long enough to go back into the recording studio after this tour winds up? "You can ask Kreskin that one," she laughs, recognizing the fact that no one can predict the future—least of all the members of Blondie. The trick is to have fun along the way—a trick that Blondie has finally been able to achieve.

Jones Beach, Long Island, New York, August 8, 1999
credit: copyright © Sylvia Diaz

"A *Picture This* Interview With Clem Burke"

by Francois Wintein
(adapted and edited by Allan Metz)

Picture This, *July 1999*

Wide-ranging, extensive and substantive interview with Clem Burke by the editor of Picture This, *Europe's No. 1 Blondie fanzine.*—Ed.

Friday the 7th of May, time 18:20 and I'm lucky enough to be chatting away to Clem Burke in a hotel in London via telephone. We conversed for almost an hour and a half and thanks to an incredible feat of makeshift wiring and microphones, I am able to bring you the transcribed cut down version.

Fran: How's your schedule going?

Clem: Oh, it's going great. We've been doing promotion over here in Europe for three weeks or so. We started off in Germany, we did an AIDS benefit telethon in Germany and then we did something for Kosovo in Belgium. We've been running into all sorts of interesting people like the Italian guy Succaro who's the Bruce Springsteen of Italy, and the people from Roxette, all sorts of people. It's been good. Everybody's like looking forward to going home for a couple of days before we begin the US tour. We're doing P.J. Mortello benefit in the States on the 13th which is an AIDS and cancer research charity.

Fran: When do you leave the UK?

Clem: Actually tomorrow.

Fran: Busy schedule this time?

Clem: We did Top Of The Pops, pre-recorded, and we're doing SMTV tomorrow morning and we did the Pepsi Chart Show.

Fran: So it's all go!

Clem: Well yeah. It hasn't been quite as hectic as last time. Omnibus is going to do a programme on us. We met with them when we first arrived in London last weekend and they've been kinda following us around a little bit pointing cameras in our faces and things like that.

Fran: The first thing people want to know is what have you been doing prior to the Blondie reunion?

Clem: Well, right before the reunion I made a record with a band called The Plimsouls—a band in LA—and it just came out on a label, Fuel 2000, in the States which is through Universal and I think it's out on Music Disk over in France but I'm not sure what the release is here. Also right before the Blondie tour started, I did a session with David Bowie for the Rugrats movie but the song wasn't used in the end. It was called "Safe In The Skyline." It might turn up somewhere someday!

Fran: That's one for the bootleggers!

Clem: Yeah right! I did a record with Mark Owen not too long ago, actually, on his first solo album that Craig Leon produced. We were working on that right prior to the beginning of Blondie. We did that over at Abbey Road. It was when the initial plugs for Blondie coming back together were happening. I recorded a few records for Craig over the years so he was really excited and I'm glad he was able to come onboard and produce *No Exit* for us.

Fran: Were you surprised about the Blondie reunion or did you expect it?

Clem: Well, it was always in the back of my mind that we would do it. That's one of the reasons why the record is called *No Exit*. There really was no escaping Blondie. No, I wasn't really surprised. Maybe I was surprised at this point in time but I always thought it might occur at some point.

Fran: The fans would have demanded it!

Clem: Right, the fans have been great, you know.

Fran: How did working with the Eurythmics compare to working with Blondie? Were they more professional?

Clem: [laughs] What makes you say that?!

Fran: They appeared more cleancut, I dunno!

Clem: Well, you know, I met Annie and Dave in 1980 at the Embassy Club in the West End. She asked me to come over for Sunday lunch and we talked about music. I wound up going to Germany with them and making their first record while I was still in Blondie in 1980. That was a record called *In The Garden*.

Fran: Were you credited on that then?

Clem: Yeah, then they went away, kinda rethought things, did the *Sweet Dreams* record and then I did a tour with them. I think Dave has a little more business suss in a lot of ways. They actually wanted me to join The Eurythmics back then but I was still in Blondie at the time so I passed on that and shortly thereafter Blondie stopped working [laughs]. But I continued to work with them. I think they were a lot more organised.

Fran: I hear that they are going to reform, have you been approached?

Clem: I sort of have, yeah, but obviously we're doing the Blondie thing. This is really in my heart. I think they had gone through a lot of different things and by the time they did the Eurythmics, they had a little more business suss. They were happening just as we were stopping so maybe they learned something from us. Annie and Dave are similar to Debbie and Chris in a lot of ways; they are very creative, intelligent people. So there were a lot of similarities as well.

Fran: If you weren't a musician, what likely career would you have chosen?

Clem: Well, I was studying social sciences at college. I was always very interested in philosophy and sociology and I thought perhaps I may become a social worker, but I started my musical career so early on. I was very interested in why people do things which is kinda the science of humans, you know, like why are there so many Blues musicians in the southern delta regions of the U.S. So perhaps I would have done that. When I was a kid, I wanted to be a forest ranger.

Fran: Where are you living at the moment?

Clem: Well, mostly I'm living in LA. I moved there in the early eighties and I also have a home in the New York area.

Fran: Have you ever considered living in the UK?

Clem: Well, I did live in the UK. The longest I spent there was maybe seven or eight months at one time, which was sort of during the Blondie days. When I met Annie and Dave, I was living in the Mayfair area, actually, because we had some time off which is how I got involved with The Eurythmics, really, 'cos it was one of the times we stopped working.

Fran: Did you get homesick and just want to go back?

Clem: Well, somewhat, but I do like it over here. I did almost purchase a flat over here at one point—it turned out it had dry rot. I'm mostly based in LA now but of course with the Blondie reunion, I'm spending more time in my New York home.

Fran: Do you play any other instruments?

Clem: Yeah. I play a bit of guitar and bass and keyboards. I co-wrote a couple of songs on the new record [*at that time,* No Exit—Ed.]. I need to collaborate with other people but, you know, I fool around a little bit. I have a little home studio in my house in LA that I work on stuff.

Fran: Do you still use Premier drums?

Clem: Yeah, I do!

Fran: Do you get them free?

Clem: Yeah, I do but that's not really the reason why I use them. I've been dealing with the company for over twenty years and they've been very supportive of me, actually, in the other parts of my career. They've usually always helped out and I do like the drums and you know, the history of Keith Moon, etc.

Fran: Do you ever get nervous before a show?

Clem: I wouldn't say nervous, no. I like to feel anticipation and energy and I get excited about performing and look forward to it.

Fran: You never need a tipple before you go on?

Clem: Er! I've been known to have a drink before I go on, sure [laughs], but no I wouldn't say nervous; that's not how I would describe it. The day kinda revolves around the performance and I try to gear everything up and be in the right frame of mind for it so I do take all that into account.

Fran: When you play the drum solo in "Union City Blue," what goes through your head?

Clem: Hum! A lot of times I think about something like Keith Moon or something like that, you know.

Fran: Yeah...That's like your own part of the gig really, isn't it?

Clem: Yeah. I suppose. I mean, I always liked the drums on that song and I kinda get excited about that and what goes through my mind is if I'm going to toss the stick up in the air and if I'm going to catch it [laughs]. That's all that really matters, if I catch it or not, but it's fun when I do!

Fran: With all the great Blondie songs to choose from, how do you decide on the set list and who has the final say?

Clem: Well, I think we all worked on the set list together. A few people I know have an idea that the drummer has a good idea of how to sequence the list to keep a momentum going, but at the end of the day Debbie has to sing the songs. It's hit and miss a little bit. We don't put a lot of thought into it. We learned a lot more songs than the ones we played.

Fran: I thought the November tour had a great packed set list and what makes me laugh is that you see people in the press saying it was too long winded. You just can't seem to win!

Clem: Yeah and it seems like so much fun. It's over before we know it.

Fran: What's it like extensive touring again? Is it as stressful as, say, twenty years ago?

Clem: No, not really. I don't know if it was ever all that stressful for me. I mean, I enjoy it, but I guess when you're around a group of people for a long period of time, people can tend to get on each other's nerves. But I guess we are enjoying touring. We like performing more than we do going on TV shows and lip synching and things like that. Initially it was fun to do lots of interviews. I still enjoy it but...this is good 'cos I'm getting asked a lot of different questions. I'm enjoying touring. I kinda feel at home with airports and hotel rooms. I just feel like this is what I'm meant to do.

Fran: When you're not doing the performances, do you go round the shops or restaurants together or do you all go your own ways?

Clem: No, we all go out. Last night we went and had a meal together and we go out together quite a bit. A lot of it is spontaneous. I think a lot of people went to the London Tower and the London Dungeon today. No, we spend quite a bit of time together. I like to work out and go to the gym and sometimes Jimmy will go with me. I think when we're on the road we hang out quite frequently and we go out to meals quite frequently. Sometimes it's good to have some time to yourself.

Fran: What was your most memorable gig over the years?

Clem: Most memorable gig, hum...Well, it works on all levels. We did a gig before our first record [Blondie—Ed.] came out in Central Park on New Year's Eve. It was very cold [laughs]. I mean, I don't know why we were playing outdoors in January, er...December 31st, but that was quite a memorable gig. And the first one we played in Glasgow—I think it was '79, you know—the one that broadcast around the UK, that was very memorable for me. There's been quite a few gigs. Certainly a lot of the CBGB's and Max's are somewhat memorable. I remember we played at Max's Kansas City right before we went on tour with Iggy Pop and David Bowie in 1977 and we literally left Max's Kansas City at night and got into an RV that we had that had one bed in it, basically, and we made that one bed into...we all slept in the bed together and we drove up to Toronto to begin the tour. And the next thing we knew, we were on tour and we met David Bowie and Iggy Pop, so that was definitely a memorable occasion. So there's been a lot. Certainly a lot of these gigs that we just did now in the UK are going to be memorable for us.

Fran: The next question kind of ties in with the last one. Are there any plans for a millennium gig, December 31st this year?

Clem: Yeah, we do have a tradition of doing New Year gigs and hopefully we'll find a good one for this year. Debbie keeps saying she wants to play somewhere in South America so we'll see. I think there might be a chance we might just play in New York City on New Year's Eve. [Blondie ended up playing in Miami—Ed.]

Fran: What's the rider like nowadays?

Clem: Lots of fruit and vegetables, lots of water, a few bottles of good red wine...bottle of vodka.

Fran: No crates of beer?

Clem: There's beer. I think Leigh [Foxx] likes to drink beer. We try to stay away from mystery meat and things like that. It's basically vegetarian but we also like smoked salmon and turkey. It was really strange, we we're just in Spain and I don't think they do, like, turkey in Spain...very strange-looking turkey! But there is always a lot of vegetarian food available which is important for me and everyone tries to eat pretty healthily, actually, and that's really it, brown rice and things like that.

Fran: What's the most elaborate item you've ever had on a rider?

Clem: Most elaborate? Err, a drum kit set up in the dressing room!

Fran: Really!

Clem: Yeah [laughs].

Fran: Do you get a bigger buzz playing the stadiums or do you prefer to play the smaller intimate venues?

Clem: Well, we just did three shows with Bryan Adams and they were in these rather large bullrings and the response was really good, especially for "Maria" and some of the more well known songs. A big arena is fun if you see that the people are with you. It's really exciting. When we were started this up we were attempting to do a couple of smaller clubs but it just doesn't seem to work out soundwise and things like that. But I kinda like the sweaty clubs when the walls sweat and things like that.

Fran: I was rather disappointed on the November tour that most of the venues were seated and I think that always spoils the atmosphere slightly.

Clem: Yep.

Fran: I like to see people crush the stage!

Clem: Actually, when we did Barrowlands it was a very memorable gig for us. They did stand up. We were crossing the Channel and we decided to fly. It's like a twenty/thirty minute flight from Dublin to Glasgow and we were just about to arrive in Glasgow and the plane had to turn back because the landing mechanisms wouldn't work. They were frozen and the de-icer wouldn't work. I was supposed to meet my fiancée...her Gran for the first time because she lives up in Scotland. We were going to go out and have a meal and all that before the show and then it turned out that we got there a half hour late for the gig, said hello and then rushed on for the gig but it was actually one of the best gigs of the whole tour. I like Scottish people and we always have good experiences in Scotland. That trip actually showed me that the band was really strong because we just stormed in and did the gig with no soundchecks.

Fran: Who are the drummers you admired most?

Clem: Well, there are the obvious, Keith Moon and Ringo Starr, but there's a lot of other people. There's a guy called Earl Palmer, a drummer who plays a gig round the corner from my house in LA. He's in his mid-seventies now but he was Fats Domino's drummer and he is also one of the most recorded drummers in history. He was a big session drummer in the States in the Sixties. And there's people like Jay Kruper, Buddy Rich, Alvin Jones, and Tony Williams, who played with Miles Davis. Actually, Tommy Ramone from The Ramones and Jerry Nolan from The New York Dolls were both big influences on me. Al Jackson from Booker T and the MGs as well. You learn from everybody.

Fran: If you could have the choice of any band to play with in history, would you pick The Who?

Clem: Yeah...maybe them or The Beatles. I recorded with Pete Townsend on an album that he did called White City, which is one of the things I did after Blondie. It was a real honour to work with him. I also worked with Bob Dylan a little bit. I do a lot of different session stuff and I had a band right after Blondie called Chequered Past.

Fran: I've got the LP!

Clem: Yeah. Maybe The Who, but maybe The Ramones, too. I actually did play with The Ramones for a while. I just forgot about that...New York Dolls maybe, although they were never that successful.

Fran: They influenced a lot of punk bands in the UK.

Clem: Oh yeah, they were a tremendous influence.

Fran: If you had a time machine, which musical era would you most like to visit if you were in your teens?

Clem: I always say that I was born maybe ten or fifteen years too late, I would like to have been around in the sixties—me being a musician. The whole punk rock thing we went through for me was reminiscent of that revival of what happened in the sixties. It had that...like what was going on in CBGBs.

Fran: I was quite a young kid when the punk revolution came out so, for me, I would like to go back to the '76 era and live the experience.

Clem: Yeah, that was a good time, that was a good era. I was happy to be around that era as well. It was very vibrant, you know, very high energy time. Music was changing. I think you still hear those changes in music today.

Fran: What bands are you listening to at the moment?

Clem: Radiohead and I like the new Blur record a lot.

Fran: The love song one that they [Blur] brought out?

Clem: Yeah "Tender." The album, 13, is great. I'm listening to the new Tom Petty record [Echo] which is actually out now. I like the French band, Air, a lot. I listen to a lot of Miles Davis. I like Belle & Sebastian. I've listened to the John Barry compilation that just came out a while ago.

Fran: What about Oasis? What do you think of them because they say they are influenced by The Beatles? Can you see that?

Clem: Yeah, I like Oasis a lot. I'm looking forward to their next record. Interestingly enough, I've seen Oasis maybe ten times. We saw the first show they did at a place called Wetlands in New York City maybe five or six years ago. I saw that gig and then, it so happened, when they were on a couple of club tours. I would be in the same city so I saw them in Detroit. The last time I was in LA, I went to both shows. I'm friends with Martin [Arthurs], who's actually Bonehead's brother [*a reference to Paul "Bonehead" Arthurs*—Ed.]. He moved to LA.

Fran: They don't get too large an audience in America. I don't think they ever cracked it there, have they?

Clem: Well, they played two nights at the Universal Amphitheatre which is five thousand a night. Funnily enough, at the end of the err...Glen Matlock and I went to see them out at Jones Beach at the end of the Pistols tour. Glen's a friend of mine. He was in New York and we drove out to Long Island to see Oasis, with Manic Street Preachers opening. That was a good show, which was right before they quit—they just cancelled the tour. I did like Oasis a lot. I liked their influences. I think they are a better band with their new drummer Alan [White]. I saw a big change, but I have seen them about ten times and I do like them. I've seen Blur maybe twice.

Fran: Glen Matlock is playing really small low key pub venues at the moment!

Clem: He's playing now?

Fran: He's got a band, the name escapes me, but he's playing like one hundred capacity venues because he doesn't want to exploit the Pistols name.

Clem: Yeah, well, Glen's a musician. He enjoys playing. I'm like that myself.

Fran: I'd love to see Blondie play a hundred capacity venue.

Clem: Yeah, that would be great! Glen and I were going to have a band with Eric Faulkner from The Bay City Rollers at one point in the '70s. They were both really good song writers, but it just never came together.

Fran: You never wrote anything or played?

Clem: No, but they're big old friends of mine and we were actually trying to get Paul Weller to join as well, which would have been a kinda interesting band.

Fran: It would have been—probably successful too! How do UK fans compare to the USA fans? Are we more down to earth than the Americans?

Clem: Yeah. I think there is a better understanding of Blondie in the UK than there is in the U.S. I was speaking to this guy, Adam, who is the *Billboard* editor over here for the UK and he was just saying that how he felt we had laid down a lot of roots in the UK and it seems that obviously the UK fans have stayed with us and with the success of 'Maria,' it's just phenomenal to see that. When we got the *Q Magazine* award I was really happy about that because the UK has influenced my technique so much and it was great to have a magazine like that say that we influenced the music over here, so I think that is great. I don't think that everyone likes Blondie. I think a lot of people dislike Blondie [laughs], but I think that is a good thing, too.

Fran: I think the press like to make out they don't like Blondie, but I believe they actually do at the end of the day!

Clem: When we went away and now coming back, we received a lot of kudos and a lot of credibility for what we did, for all the things that Debbie did, and the band did back in the '70s. But British fans are great. The U.S. is a big place and I think the fans are somewhat different over there.

Fran: Do you feel disappointed, though, that you were never as big in the U.S. as you were in Europe?

Clem: Well, it's hard to gear that because we had four number one records in the U.S., but we do kinda still think of ourselves as an underground band in some ways. One of the things about us coming back together, I would like to go and play places where we never really spent that much time. Sorta like the South in the U.S. where I know we have a lot of fans, but we never really spent that much time down there and we never really did that much touring in the U.S. once we became successful. I think we probably spent more time over here. That's one of the pitfalls of being a band with a tradition of success...everyone wants you at the same time. I think we enjoy being in Europe. I think New York has more in common with Europe, although I love the Midwest. I really love America. There's a lot of really great places in America, too. It's a really big place. The type of success we had over there was different. We had a lot of commercial success, but maybe that didn't transcend into...there's so many different radio formats and things like that over there, but we were very successful in the States as well.

Fran: If there was one Blondie song in particular that you yourself think, "Wow, this was my best ever drumming, this is my masterpiece," which song would that actually be?

Clem: I actually like 'Rapture,' but a lot of people would say 'Dreaming' probably. You know, like fans of mine would say 'Dreaming.' People always tell me how much they like the drumming on 'Dreaming.' I kinda like 'Rapture.' I was trying to get that sorta funk groove going, that kind of thing. I was trying to be like Tony Thompson from Chic. So maybe 'Rapture.' I like the drumming on 'Maria' a lot.

Fran: I always thought your drumming on 'Atomic,' even though that's a basic song, was quite complicated with the cymbals and high hats.

Clem: Yeah, 'Atomic' is good!

Fran: Which is your favourite to play then? Would that be the same?

Clem: I like playing 'Rapture.' I think the whole band likes playing 'Rapture' a lot just 'cos it's kind of evolved quite a bit over the years.

Fran: And it's good to experiment and you've really arranged the songs so different!

Clem: I actually like playing 'Hanging On The Telephone' in concert a lot.

Fran: That's probably the Blondie song that is covered the most by pub bands!

Clem: Right, that's funny 'cos we didn't write that one! Coincidentally, the singer and songwriter Peter Case, who was in the band that I was in LA, The Plimsouls, also was in the band, The Nerves, which wrote and recorded 'Hanging On The Telephone' first.

Fran: Did it ever get anywhere?

Clem: The song?

Fran: Does it exist on vinyl?

Clem: Oh yeah. The Nerves were known. They were actually one of the first kinda punk, pop bands in the States. They were in San Francisco. And there's Jeffrey Pierce, who has a song ["Under the Gun"] dedicated to him on the new record [*No Exit*], who was the president of the Blondie fan club at the time. He sent us a tape of 'Hanging On The Telephone' by The Nerves when we were in Japan and that's when we heard it for the first time and thought, "Wow that would be a great song to cover."

Fran: And it certainly was! How does Top Of The Pops differ from twenty years ago?

Clem: Oh, I think top Of The Pops is much more relaxed now. Before, you would have to go and stay there the entire day and they wouldn't let you leave.

Fran: I heard they had subsidised beer back in those days!

Clem: They had subsidised beer?!

Fran: Yeah, free!

Clem: Oh yeah, they might of. I mean, there's always a bar there. I don't know if the bar was free back then. I don't recall. Certainly, I wasn't paying at the time. I remember Top Of The Pops would never let you use video. You had to be in the studio. They wouldn't let you prerecord it, for instance. Yesterday we prerecorded 'Nothing Is Real But The Girl' for it to be played once it is released and before that wasn't allowed. I remember one time we were on with The Jam and I was having this suit made at this shop behind Carnaby Street by this guy called Colin Wilde, who I don't think is around any more but he used to make all the clothes for Marc Bolan, for instance. And I had to go in for my final fitting to pick up the suit so I basically got into a taxi and left the BBC when Top Of The Pops was in Shepherd Bush. I rushed down to the shop and I really had to escape 'cos you weren't allowed to leave. So I go down there, I get the suit and I come back. I was wearing the suit and the first thing, Paul Weller looks at me and goes "It wasn't worth it!" [laughs]. Everybody was going crazy, like "Oh where is he?," and in fact, there also was talk that Rick Buckler was going to take my place in Blondie and then I would have switched and played with The Jam 'cos they were on later in the show. And so I came back in this red suit and everyone's like, "Oh my God!," but I liked it and I had a great time with Colin Wilde.

Fran: You recently wore that mod t-shirt again. Did you pick that up in Carnaby Street?

Clem: Not that one, no. They have those in New York as well. Keith [Moon] used to wear something similar. I think it's an RAF [*Royal Air Force*—Ed.] emblem!

Fran: It became associated with the mod movement in the UK.

Clem: Absolutely. I just kinda like the symmetry—the way it looks and it's kind of a mod icon.

Fran: And it's become your trademark as well!

Clem: Yeah. I try to stay true to my roots. It was great to see Debbie come back and look so fabulous and to have the blonde hair again. I was really excited about all that.

Fran: It wouldn't have been the same if she'd had brown hair!

Clem: No, people want to see certain things that they remember and I think it's kinda cool. She looks fabulous, you know.

Fran: Well, people don't like change at the end of the day!

Clem: Right, I kinda agree with you in some ways. People like what they like about a group or a singer and they want to try to keep that, but as an artist you need to evolve. I appreciate people trying to change because you know human beings do change as you get older and that has to be reflected in your music as well. So that's gotta be taken into account. I think that's a lot of bands and artists' downfall. You know, people don't like what they are doing anymore. But it is hard to stay at the same thing. We try to reach that happy medium. I mean, on the new album there are songs like 'Maria' and 'Nothing Is Real...' that are very reminiscent of the Blondie of the past and then we had to try some different things as well. I really like songs like 'Maria.' We'll see what the next record is going to be like.

Fran: Were you surprised when that went to number one? Or were you expecting it?

Clem: Yeah, I was surprised. I knew it was the single, but I was excited and surprised with the reception we received in the UK. I was very happy with it and I think that gave us a lot of encouragement to continue on. We made the record and we weren't really sure which way we were going to head with it. We were happy with the record, but things are going in stages. I think at this point we're going to be touring until the end of the year and we are going to make another record so we all kinda know that, but I think a lot had to do with the fans for showing so much encouragement.

Fran: For me, it was like...at the time I could never go to the gigs because I was at school or in my early teens and my parents wouldn't let me go to the gigs. So a lot of people, myself, and a whole generation of people had never seen Blondie.

Clem: Right exactly.

Fran: And I think that is what made it so exciting.

Clem: Yeah. I was with some people in Stockholm when we did the first gig. This airline steward and a couple of people said they were on their way to work on the train and they saw the ad. At first they just assumed that it was a Blondie tribute band so they just go so, like, excited 'cos they'd had something that they never thought that they'd see. So it's great to be able to do that again. So much time has passed. It's like a whole generation that's gone by, but we are picking up new fans as well.

Fran: Well, doing this fanzine, I am really surprised by the number of teenagers that actually write to me. But then again, the bands they listen to have influences taken from Blondie. They read these articles saying "Oh yeah we love that song, we love that *Parallel Lines* album," and I think they probably pick up on that.

Clem: Right. It's similar to when The Rolling Stones first came out and The Beatles. They were like playing Chuck Berry songs or like Muddy Waters and I got to know those artists via those bands, Beatles and Stones, not by first hand. So I think you're right there. So I think things would have picked up a little for the fanzine [*Picture This*—Ed.] too, am I right?

Fran: Certainly since I went touring with PT15 on last November tour, yeah, it's taken off.

Clem: That's good.

Fran: Did you personally mind being linked to the Punk and New Wave label?

Clem: Well...I didn't mind because I think if we had not been a part of the movement in music, I doubt we would have been as successful as we were in the early days. The press like to lump a lot of bands together to make some sort of a scene so there's something to write about and I can understand that. I didn't mind and in retrospect it's okay, but I don't think anyone really likes to be labelled, although we certainly came out of the New York Punk Rock scene.

Fran: What UK bands did you like at the time?

Clem: Back during Punk?

Fran: Yeah!

Clem: Well...The Jam, obviously. I don't think they were ever really a punk band. The Pistols, The Damned. We were quite friendly with The Damned and, actually, quite friendly with The Jam.

Fran: I used to work for The Damned!

Clem: Oh, you did?

Fran: Yeah. I used to drive the van and things like that. The thing with them is that they are still on the go, but they're not the original lineup.

Clem: Is Rat Scabies still playing with them?

Fran: No. It's basically the singer Dave Vanian and Captain Sensible, who used to be on bass but plays guitar now.

Clem: I saw a fantastic Damned gig at the Starwood in LA with Joan Jett the first time they came over and that was really great. And I saw The Jam at their first gig at The Whiskey in LA.

Fran: Hectic gigs, I bet?

Clem: Yeah, it was great. I liked a lot of New York bands back then. I liked Television, Talking Heads and The Ramones.

Fran: Did the spitting ever transcend the water?

Clem: No, not in the States. It never happened there, really.

Fran: I think Rat Scabies claims to have invented that!

Clem: Oh, Really?! Yeah...well, he used to do a fantastic thing—lighting his symbols on fire; that was really cool.

Fran: He IS a good drummer at the end of the day.

Clem: Oh yeah. He was at one of our shows in London!

Fran: Really? Which one, the Lyceum?

Clem: Yeah, he was.

Fran: I love many of the B-sides. Some of them have been singles in themselves. Do you think you could have had more number ones than you actually did?

Clem: I don't know. It's hard to say, really. We've had quite a few here.

Fran: A lot of people think 'Angels On The Balcony' should have been a number one. Do you agree with that?

Clem: I love Jimmy's songwriting and I like that song a lot. I'm not sure what we released off *Autoamerican* other than 'The Tide Is High' and 'Rapture.' I don't think we ever released another single. Yeah, I think 'Angels On The Balcony' could have been. It's a real great song. There's definitely other songs, 'English Boys,' I think, off the last record. Dave Stewart was staying around my place in New York at the time and I played him the album. That was the song he picked to be the single off *The Hunter*.

Fran: Do you ever get the say of which songs can be a single?

Clem: Well, you know, singles are really kinda determined by the record company. We've never really had any interference as far as making the albums, but I understand what the record company needs to do once they get the album. They play things to people and get the feedback. Nowadays everything is computerised, demographic this and that, researched. I'm not really that crazy about that, to get that in depth, but I do understand a record company going to a radio station for comments. I don't think there is any problem with having the record company choose the singles because we've already made the music and I think it's really rare nowadays when people just record a single. Like with The Beatles, The Who or The Stones, they would go in and purposely record a single. Sometimes the singles wouldn't even be on the albums!

Fran: And they wouldn't be too worried if there weren't any singles on the album!

Clem: Well, the sixties was a singles market and a single now is basically just a kinda advance on the album. It's kinda like an advertisement for the album.

Fran: And they could go and do a concept album and not get slagged off for it but, today I think it would be very hard for a band to do that.

Clem: Yeah, well, maybe we'll do that some day.

Fran: That would be great! Have you got a favourite Blondie album of all time?

Clem: Once again, I think I would have to say *Autoamerican*, although I really like the first record [*Blondie*] a lot. I think I like *No Exit* a lot. I like all the records. I mean, everyone says *Parallel Lines* is the classic record...

Fran: I always say *Eat To The Beat* is my favourite because...

Clem: *Eat To The Beat* was our most rock record. I like *Eat To The Beat* a lot.

Fran: I think for the fans, in particular, you stick to a point in your life in your teens and you pick that album of the era. That stuck with me when I remember seeing you on Top Of The Pops week after week and things like that.

Clem: Right, *Eat To The Beat*...The interesting thing was that it was our second album with Mike Chapman producing. When we made *Parallel Lines*, it was a very arduous process for us and he worked us extremely hard in the studio, which really made us better musicians. He was very meticulous in what he was doing and it was amazing because, you know, we kinda expected it be the exact same process the next time around. The whole thing was a lot looser and I think you can hear it in the music because I think we had already had the success that Mike wanted us to have with *Parallel Lines* and he let us go with the flow a little bit more on the second record with him.

Fran: Do you think you would ever have him produce another Blondie record?

Clem: Well, he produced some of the demos that we did very early on. We had a full start with Mike and I would like to work with him again. I think I would really like to work with Craig on this next record we're going to do because Craig is really like an extra member of Blondie at this point. He really did put a lot of time, energy and emotion into making this record [*No Exit*] happen for us. I would like to work with the people from ABBA or Phil Spector.

Fran: Have you been to see the musical play they're doing in London?

Clem: No, I haven't gone, but one of the greatest gigs I ever saw was ABBA in New York City at Radio City Music Hall. I was a big ABBA fan for their musicianship and their songwriting.

Fran: It's amazing how many artists from your era, they didn't admit to it at the time, but now say they were fans of them.

Clem: Yeah, well, I admitted it at the time. When we were in Sweden, we talked about that 'cos it was almost like the Blondie thing in some ways at the time. They were kinda so successful and just like in your face and on the radio all the time that people kind of took them for granted to a certain extent, sometimes. Now they're kinda like national heroes in Sweden, you know.

Fran: Going back to The Damned, Captain Sensible was always a big ABBA fan and he reckons that he wrote most of his songs by playing ABBA songs backwards and ripped them off basically!

Clem: [Laughs] They just had great production, great melodies, the music was really sophisticated for pop music, and the singing was great.

Fran: And again, like Blondie, they're timeless. You can play them today and they sound as good as they did twenty years ago.

Clem: Yeah, I mean, that's really the test of time.

Fran: I reckon the drummers in these numerous Blondie tribute bands have the hardest job of all. Have you heard any of these tribute bands and, secondly, do you approve of them?

Clem: Well, what's the saying? Imitation is the sincerest form of flattery, whatever that old saying is. Funny enough, there used to be a band called Platinum Blondie and Jimmy and I were over here before Blondie reformed. Jimmy was over here producing something and I came over to hang out with him. We looked in the paper and saw that this band was playing up in Fulham in a pub and it was a tribute band called Platinum Blondie. So we kinda just showed up. Obviously, they were fans and they recognised us immediately. This was before they began to play. They went into the dressing room and they came like in Blondie drag. I remember Jimmy was a bit disappointed because the keyboard player was a little overweight. And the drummer came out with the wig on 'cos he was a ginger headed guy. He came out with a black spiky wig. But we actually got up and played and it was really fun 'cos obviously Jimmy and I hadn't played any of those songs for a long time. I think we got up and played 'Rapture' and 'Dreaming.' We played a whole bunch of songs with them and that was really fun.

Fran: And this was in the UK?

Clem: Yeah, it was a pub up on Fulham Road that has a lot of tribute bands. There's one called T-Rextasy that plays there, have you heard of them?

Fran: There's loads of them on the go, so many in the UK.

Clem: They had a tribute concert in New York for three nights for the 50th birthday for Marc Bolan and the music director was Tony Visconti, who produced Marc Bolan's stuff and early Bowie stuff. I was in the house band along with Tony Shanahan (the bass player from Patti Smith), Richard Lloyd from Television, and we also had Tish and Snooky [Bellomo] who used to be in Blondie. They were the back-up singers doing all the high stuff and we had like a string quartet, a saxophone player and two keyboard players. All these people like Lloyd Cole, Joey Ramone and various people got up and did the songs, you know, and it was like a two hour show. Then, at the end, Tony Visconti, who's in touch with this guy from T-Rextasy, flew him over. At the end, this guy comes out, he's like a spitting image of Marc Bolan, and we did 'Bang a Gong' with him. It was really funny.

Fran: I like the ones that DO make an effort, but there's so many out there who aren't even fans. They'll just exploit the songs. You'll go up to them and want to ask them about the band, but they can't tell you anything about them and that annoys me.

Clem: Yeah, that's annoying. This guy who does T-Rextasy, I think his name is Daniel, is pretty interesting, but the Blondie tribute bands...I don't know if I would go out of my way to see any of them, but I think it's great. I like going to see Beatles cover bands. Over here, is the Bootleg Beatles. They're fun for me. There's a lot of them in the States.

Fran: There's a lot of money to be made in nostalgia!

Clem: I suppose, I mean, yeah, people want to be able to hear the music and it's great to hear it played live. I think that's the thing with the Blondie tribute bands.

Fran: You've already said there's going to be another album after *No Exit*. Have you actually started writing songs?

Clem: We've all started writing a little bit. I know Jimmy was working on something while he was here in London. Sometimes the road can be a very inspiring place to write because you have new experiences that you normally wouldn't have. You might meet somebody you wouldn't normally meet and that might help you inspire something. Debbie has continually said she'd go into the studio tomorrow. I think we all enjoy recording a lot and we enjoy performing live. I think everyone's come to the conclusion that the least enjoyable thing is just kinda going around promoting, talking about yourself.

Fran: Yeah, answering the same old questions must be tedious!

Clem: Yeah, I appreciate why that is. I also appreciate that it needs to be done and if you're in a different country then, of course, people are going to ask you the same questions because it is a different audience, but you can make it what you want to make it. You can always spin an interview a certain way and try to develop some sort of rapport with the person you're speaking to. My favourite interviews are kinda like this one because it kinda just popped up today. It's happened to me before. I've been in a bar somewhere after a gig or something and someone will just stick a tape recorder in front of me and it's "Would you mind having a word?" Those interviews always seem a lot more fun.

We did a massive press conference in Spain, which I thought was really fun. It was a big turnout, about two hundred people, in a screening room at Planet Hollywood, but obviously they are a bit more contrived and a bit more stressful in some ways. I like doing the fan-oriented type of stuff where people are really interested. I've never really minded talking to fans. Sometimes you get a journalist who doesn't really care—it's their job, they were assigned to it that day.

Fran: And what you do tell them, they always turn it around.

Clem: Sometimes. I am a fan of the music press and fanzines. I like all that sort of stuff. I really appreciate you doing the fanzine. It's great, it really is cool.

Fran: I read in an article that Chris Stein was married, is that true?

Clem: I think he's been married before, but he's not married now. [*This interview took place prior to Chris Stein's marriage to actress Barbara Sicuranza as, for example, reported on the* World Entertainment News Network *on 8 June 1999 and in the 14 June 1999 issue of* New York *magazine*–Ed.].

Fran: How about you? Any plans to tie the knot?

Clem: Hope so, yeah.

Fran: Millennium wedding?

Clem: The sooner the better, yeah. Just trying to sort out the Blondie thing.

Fran: I love "The Good, The Bad And The Ugly" bit in 'Atomic.' Whose idea was that?

Clem: I think it might have sorta been Jimmy's because I think 'Atomic' was sorta based on the "spaghetti western" type of theme and we just kinda elaborated on that. I think Chris carries it on as well, but I think it might of been Jimmy's idea initially. That's good. I like the way 'Atomic' is performed in concert. I think it is one of the high points.

Fran: Unfortunately, the radio stations don't seem to play 'Atomic' and I wondered if there was some sort of copyright problem.

Clem: What you mean from a live show?

Fran: Yeah, when they broadcast the Lyceum show on Radio 2, they missed out 'Atomic'!

Clem: Oh! I don't know about that, could be.

Fran: Okay, last question. Did the band have to rehearse much before the first reunion gig or did the songs come back naturally? Did you forget a lot of them?

Clem: We learned the songs and we did rehearse quite extensively before we went on tour. It was over a long period of time for a few hours a day. It wasn't like we did marathons of ten hours of rehearsal, but we did give ourselves a few months to get the band together, which was a very good thing for us to do because in the past, I think, we have been perhaps a little unrehearsed at times, Certainly, when we played in Washington a few years back, before we made the record, we were certainly under-rehearsed. We played a little loft party in a rehearsal studio the night before, like, for eighty people and the next day we went out and played to eighty thousand people in the daytime [*a reference to Blondie's first reunion show at the HFStival '97, RFK Stadium, Washington D.C., May 31, 1997*–Ed.]. There was a bit of a screw up there because we were supposed to go out much later in the day, but we were offered another gig that day, which management thought we were going to do. We were to play two festivals in one day, so they switched the Washington one to go on at, like, two in the afternoon, which I didn't really think was the best time slot for us. I prefer going on at nightfall and we were definitely under-rehearsed for that. We took a lot of time doing this before we went public with it, and I think we are reaping the rewards.

Fran: Yeah, it was a really tight set.

Clem: What we are trying to do is add some more new songs. There are so many songs I would like to play like 'Angels On The Balcony' or 'Man Overboard' from the first album. There are all kinds of songs that we could actually play, but it seems we don't want to make the show too long.

Fran: Hmmm...

Clem: Well, you don't mind. I certainly don't mind, but there are definitely a lot more songs in the Blondie catalogue that could be played than the obvious ones.

Fran: But if you get to the point where you're doing, say, three UK tours a year, you could rotate the set list.

Clem: Yeah, we could do...I mean, I really had to force everybody to play 'Denis Denis,' you know, which I really like. When we played in Stockholm the only criticism of the show...the headline read that we didn't play 'Denis Denis'!

Fran: And that was one of your first hits!

Clem: Yeah. I think that has a soft spot in people's hearts. There's lots of songs we could play that we don't.

As the interview draws to a conclusion, we say goodbye. I thank Clem for taking the time to talk to us and I wish the band a great success with the June dates. He and Jimmy, I think, were off to see a gig before they head off to the States.

"Bitz: Rock of Ages Puts No Limits on Blondie"

Sunday Mirror, *November 7, 1999*

Interview with Jimmy Destri, showing his personal side, including his thoughts on Blondie, the hit single "Maria," and pop music in general.—Ed.

In 1984 we thought it was all over. The best new wave band in the world called it a day and Blondie were no more.

Who could have banked on them coming back in 1999 with a new album that had pop poppets hiding under the tables.

Feisty and still ferociously good, Blondie stormed the charts with Maria, hitting the number one spot.

And the man responsible for penning that song, which marked the rebirth of Blondie, says he can't wait to get back to Ireland to play.

Keyboard player and songwriter Jimmy Destri has more Irish connections than you could shake a stick at.

"I've got about 25 Irish relations and any time I play there I end up staying out all night drinking. I can't go through Dublin without getting totally sick. I love it!

"My wife, Eileen, is from Kerry and her family still live there. So I feel a bit Irish even though my last name ends in an i."

Jimmy is delighted that Blondie have finally regrouped. When the band first split-up in-fighting was rife—and he confesses that he was out of control.

He says it was a difficult decision to reform.

"I always wanted to reform the group—we all did," Jimmy said. "But for a long time I thought: 'Maybe this won't work'.

"For me to invest emotionally in it and for it not to work would have been devastating.

"These days we've all matured a bit. Personally our relationships are a lot more mellow than they were.

"When Blondie split-up I was a little crazy. I was a nutter and I was a big problem in the band.

"But what happened to me was I married a tough Irish broad and she really straightened me out. She's of the Moriarty clan in Kerry.

"Even today I give her all my money when I get paid and she gives me back five dollars and says: ''That's yours'."

But what has Jimmy been up to since the band split?

"I was doing the usuals, writing a track here and there for an artist, but for a long time I wasn't 100 percent there.

"When Blondie split, I had had a lost weekend of three years.

"My wife helped me sort my head out, and after that I got out of music and didn't go back for a long time.

"I ran a contracting business which did very well. I didn't go back to music until I got bored with that."

These days Jimmy is much more centred, being a responsible father of two.

"I have a beautiful daughter who is also called Eileen—she's a good Irish stepdancer—and a son Jimmy.

"Eileen is 14 and Jimmy is two and, before you ask, I haven't got two different wives, just one Irish one who said 'Not tonight' for 12 years! We're very very happy together.

"I've become a typical older guy—I yell at kids to get off my lawn and all that."

Jimmy has written and co-written many of Blondie's hit tracks from Picture This to Atomic. And it was his pen alone that crafted Maria, the song that told the world Blondie still have what it takes.

So, Bitz asked, who is the legendary Maria?

"Maria's probably now an old Italian woman with a moustache," Jimmy laughed.

"No, Maria wasn't a real person—she was the culmination of all the beautiful girls a gangly, ugly and weird high school kid lusts after but can't have.

"But it's great what a guitar can do for a guy. Maria is the one that got away before my transformation.

"I just wrote Maria to be a pop song. I had no idea that it was going to be such a huge hit."

Blondie are enjoying themselves and their music much more these days and Jimmy feels the passing of time has a lot to do with it.

"Things are always crazy when you're younger. And when you speak to people who are older than you, they give you advice and you don't generally listen to it.

"But when you get older, you don't want things to be as crazy as they were. You stop and smell the flowers more.

"For Blondie, we had to check each other out and learn to be a band again but with No Exit we did exactly what we wanted to do.

"But I'm not preaching to anyone. We've all ignored good advice and we have to make our own mistakes as part of the learning curve. You have to take the rough with the smooth."

"We're going to do another album, this time one that's a little more scary and out there than No Exit," Jimmy said.

"And it's crazy that our ages should be brought up at all. Why should there be a time limit or a cut off point on rock'n'roll? "Who cares if the likes of Little Richard are 90, as long as they can still give people a good tune? I really don't. If an age limit was put on rock, you wouldn't have got some people's best works."

Jimmy is looking forward to the Blondie Irish dates and there's one song he can't wait to play live for his fans here.

"I really love to play Dreaming. Every song is like my child and I can't distinguish a favourite among them. But actually playing Dreaming live really does something for me."

At the minute, Jimmy's turntable rocks to everything from Blur and Radiohead to hip-hop from New York's Everlast.

"And I must say, I love REM, even if they are as old as us."

Jimmy Destri, El Rey, Los Angeles, February 10, 1999
credit: copyright © Sherry Gunderman

"Don't Call Me Debbie..."

by Euan Ferguson

The Observer, *February 20, 2000*

Article/interview with Deborah Harry. Among topics discussed are the music industry, Harry's looks, Marilyn Monroe, music as an art form, overpopulation, the current state of women and music, and Britney Spears.—Ed.

She looks a little tired, she thinks Britney is boring. Blondie's singer is all grown-up now—even if she still looks 31...

Top of the world, Ma. We are looking down, Deborah and I, on a helicopter. The helicopter is in turn looking down on the roofs of Manhattan's relative pygmies, skyscrapers of a mere 30 stories or so, steam from their air conditioning units racing white into the chill blue sky. The pygmies are looking down, way below, on flurried snow and dirty yellow taxis. All is silent.

'Hmm,' muses Ms. Harry. 'Integrity. Well, yeah. Of course you start out trying not to get involved with the money men. You have principles. But look at us! We're sitting here on the 44th floor of the Bertelsmann Building'—symbol of everything corporately megalithic about the music industry. 'I suppose I feel I've succumbed to the inevitable.'

It took a long time coming. Deborah Harry—she dropped the babyish Debbie years ago—refused to bow to the inevitable for ages. It wasn't until she was almost 40, she confides, 'that I realised I wasn't going to live forever. Until then I hadn't thought about it.'

Many things, it seems, have come along later for this woman. It's instructive to realise that, back in the early Eighties when Blondie first swept up the British charts, and every now-dad spent every waking moment lusting furiously after their gorgeous bottle-blonde lead singer, she was already in her early thirties: almost unthinkable now, when we're lucky if our chart-topping sex vixens are past puberty. So she's in her early fifties now, and touring again, gyrating madly in her red dresses on stages around the world, and finally coming to terms with the fact that she has to please the money-men, who are, after all, in the process of putting out a new Blondie album *(Livid)* for her.

Early fifties...I'd wondered whether she would look it up close. She certainly hadn't looked it at Glastonbury last year, but the stage was 50 feet away and the sun was making everyone look good. (She laughs as I remind her of some of the pieces written about her dancing: there was some bitchy press carping about Deborah's style, the implication being that she shouldn't really have been allowed to be there at that age. 'What the hell,' she smiles, dropping in a few other epithets—she swears blithely, fluently, sweetly—'I like a bit of verbal abuse now and then; I find it quite exciting.')

Up close, she looks it even less. Steady, calm, blue-green eyes, flawless skin, and those absurdly Slavic cheekbones...well, there's a certain tiredness to her, her face seems strangely larger than expected, and she happily bends forward to show me her very human, very brown roots: but fifties, no way. She's used to the compliment, but still takes it graciously. Had she ever minded her good looks, or worried that they got in the way? 'Not really. I suppose...when I was growing up, yeah, I got my fair share of perverts.'

She grew up in New Jersey with foster-parents, having been given up for adoption shortly after her birth in Florida. There were stories that she had fantasised for many years about being the daughter of Marilyn Monroe; she says she did idolise Marilyn, but not in that complex fashion, not in any seriousness. She has since, she says, taken some steps towards finding who her real parents were. 'There was certain information I needed to have for health reasons. But I never went beyond a certain point. Apart from anything else, I know too much about valuing my own privacy to want to intrude on someone else's.'

She still has no family of her own, but that doesn't cause her any particular worries—though she does admit she would have liked a child; it is 'one regret. But, then again, I haven't added to overpopulation. Because I've always objected to the fact that so many people just fuck and have children, that people are not planning children but just getting off sexually. It depresses me to think that most of the world's an accident.

'In terms of family, though, I feel that I am now content with who I am, and I have friends. I have, if you like, a family of choice.'

It's a very Sixties, Warhol phrase, and thus suitable. For people can forget, in the standard Deborah story—the years spent nursing her lover, Blondie guitarist Chris Stein, back to health after a serious illness; the split-up with Chris that followed; the silent years and acrimony and then, recently, the successful reunion and new generation of fans—that she was also a big friend of Warhol and player on the New York art scene.

The music—well, she loves it, she says, but it needn't have been music that made her name. Over the past decade she's also acted, written short stories—'they're OK, but I don't think I'm a great writer; for that you need a truly original voice'—and worked in art and photography; a true New York renaissance woman. 'Whether I had gone into rock'n'roll, or any other kind of performance, I think I would always have had been engaged in some kind of search,' she says, slightly annoyingly; there are too many fey Californian generalisations floating about for complete comfort. 'I'm always searching for understanding; for people to understand me, or for me to understand them. The beauty, the discrepancies, the horrors, the ugliness.'

But, in fact, it's OK when she talks like that: she backs her argument with quotes from William Gibson, and various Nigerian authors she's reading at the moment; and she is regarded in the art world as an intelligent critic. Also, she's refreshingly direct about the rest of her life—drugs ('well, yes,' she says, giving a smile. 'But not as much as before of course. I'm still a glutton for sensation. But there's not too much partying, really; I enjoy a glass of wine and a cigarette. But I can hardly keep up.') She smiles again when talking about men (she lives alone with her pet dog Chi-Chan). 'Yes I would like to meet the right guy, some day, of course. But, at the moment...well, I do, um, date now and again.'

Direct, too, on what's happening now in terms of women and music. 'Britney Spears and the rest...well, I think it's boring, quite frankly. Money seems to be the big motive, the only motive, behind everything. Which I suppose is understandable, but still...why did it happen that way? Well, I think it's misogyny, pretty much. The music-business world is not exactly heavily represented by women. And I'm not so much criticising the music, but—well, people used to try to say something, didn't they? People used to believe in things.'

She's an odd one, this rather cold, rather clever woman. Fifty-three years old, looking about 31, happily talking the language of pensioners.

"A Cheap Date Exclusive...Debbie Harry"

interviewed by Anita Pallenberg

Reprinted from Cheap Date, *No. 3, 2000*

Debbie and Anita discuss, among other things, Ted Bundy, American and British punk, Debbie's early days in NYC, Max's Kansas City, the Rolling Stones, the New York Dolls, girl groups, William Burroughs, Chris Stein, rap and hip hop, the beatnik scene, and, appropriately enough, Debbie as a "legend."—Ed.

Anita: So were you attacked by Ted Bundy?

Debbie: I had an accidental encounter with Ted. It was in the early 70's, and I was wearing very high platform shoes and I was staggering across Houston Street late at night, and I couldn't get a cab. So I was standing in the road...and he came around and asked me if I wanted a ride, he asked again and I said no. But he kept coming around because I was there. So finally I got in the car, and it was hot, it was so hot. And he smelled so bad. I looked at him, and he was a good-looking guy. But the smell...it was like poison. It was a smell that made me think, this guy has like this odd smell. So I looked over to open the window, and the window was open a tiny bit, and I looked at the inside of the door, there were absolutely no handles, like you couldn't get out of the car. So I started looking at the whole interior of the car without moving my hands, and I realized the entire inside of the car had been gutted, stripped; it was just a metal frame. The hair on the back of my neck just went weeeee. And I stuck my arm out, and I opened the car from the outside. I was sneaky. I just did it. I think he realized what I was doing, and he put his foot on the gas, and I was flung out into the street and picked up by a cab.

Anita: Fantastic. You got out.

Debbie: You know, at the time I didn't know anything about Ted Bundy, you know? I just thought "thank God I got away from that asshole" and I just carried on...and years later, after he was executed, I got on a flight and I picked up a *Newsweek*, and I'm reading this story, and it says Modus Operandi, and it describes how he looked, the inside of his cars, and the hair on the back of my neck once again went out, and I said 'Oh my God that was Ted Bundy.'

Anita: That's such an amazing story. Another question: are the English right in their criticism of American Punk, or are they just being snooty and English? They always put it down don't they?

Debbie: I don't know, you know? I always thought that they were somehow linked. The only difference I felt was that with the English punks it was more of a political movement, and in the States it was more of a musical counterculture that was against the powers that be. We couldn't get record deals, we couldn't get airplay. In the UK, up and coming music gets more favorably treated, it gets looked at with real sort of interest by the music community and by radio. The major difference was that over here it was not so much to do with a political statement. You know Ari [*Upp, aka Arri Up*—Ed.] was here the other night from the Slits and that was kind of exciting.

Anita: Is it New York that's fun, or is it the company that one keeps in New York that is fun?

Debbie: I think it's New York that can be fun. You know New York has a specific thing about it. There's always so much going on. For me now it's really my friends, I really treasure my friends. But I can always go to a club and see somebody I know, so I guess it's a combination of those things.

Anita: If I didn't have a flat in London, and somebody might as well live in it, I would probably live in New York, I've always loved New York. So what's wrong with the French? (hhhaaaa)

Debbie: They speak French. Hhhhaaaaa.

Anita: 'Cause they speak French. They move their mouths in a funny way. Uuh. Uuuhn. If you could be reincarnated as a piece of clothing, what would it be?

Debbie: I think I would want to be a cape.

Anita: Ahh. Very nice. What are your memories of working as a Playboy Bunny and as a waitress?

Debbie: Oh you know, the usual stuff. I think mostly I was proiferal [sic], kind of figuring it all out, seeing you know what the real people were doing. I came from a very provincial atmosphere. Suburbia, New Jersey. Grew up in a small town, in a family that was very "small-town," and I wanted the world you know. I really wanted to taste everything.

Anita: Did you have to pay the rent as well?

Debbie: Oh yeah! I couldn't really do it any other way. I was too stubborn to, you know, get some guy to pay my rent, I figured that was more work than for me just to get another job. So working at Max's Kansas City was great, I got to meet everybody, see all these fabulous people. Max's in the 60's was fantastic.

Anita: It was the best. I used to go to Max's all the time, but I used to spend most of the time in the bathroom, or upstairs.

Debbie: I used to spend a fair amount of time there myself. Oooopppppss! I'm sure I saw you in there. Hhhhaaaa.

Anita: People say 'Oh you were there, I passed you on the way to the bathroom!' Yeah! I have a great memory of Johnny Thunders because in those days I was still part of the Stones' kind of entourage, and I had a limousine waiting for me outside, and when I got out of the club the limousine had gone. Johnny had taken it and had gone on a ride around the lower east side; the red light district. I thought it was quite funny. That's about all I remember. It was a great place.

Debbie: It was the only place like that, ever. I didn't know that Mickey (owner) was a junkie at the time you know. My boss was a junkie, I was a junkie, everyone was a junkie.

Anita: I was a junkie! Running in and out of the limousine, up to the bathroom and that was it. I had one thing on my mind, I guess. One track mind. Although I know lots of things went on there. Andy Warhol...everybody was there.

Debbie: Hair the musical was written there, the whole thing. It was interesting. In the 60's it was an all arts place. Everyone went there. Hollywood went there, New York went there. All the artists used to go there and give them their work for free so that they could eat. Nobody's got the balls to do it now.

Anita: The Chelsea Hotel is a bit like that, where people used to pay in paintings. I've done my fair share of Chelsea Hotel. You?

Debbie: Oh yeah, I've sure done my Chelsea!

Anita: Which paid better? Being a Playboy Bunny or Max's?

Debbie: Probably in the long run, the bunny was more, but more labor extensive [sic] because you had to maintain a level of appearance. You'd have to go through the inspection line before you went to work. They felt they had some kind of ownership thing, that they could call you and expect you to drop everything and work. It was actually really quite offensive.

Anita: I lived at the Playboy club in London for about six months, the Stones did a lot of stuff there, and stayed there too.

Debbie: I think about the Stones, about the songs, the experiences that they had. Nobody can ever top that, nobody can come near that. That era and the scale have just gone. I mean it's staggering.

Anita: They are untouchable now which is good. Nobody can fuck with them, really.

Debbie: I always loved Brian (Jones) I always felt very bad about that. He was so talented.

Anita: Yeah he was, but he was not very well. It was very difficult with him. I think he also really didn't want to be part of the Stones anymore, by his own choice. He was really into the Blues. So you're singing on Ronnie Spector's records now? Which is your favorite Ronettes' song?

Debbie: You know what I really like about Ronnie? I always liked those songs, they were all so sexy. She was just so hot you know, so cute. Everything. Recently I introduced her to somewhere in Soho, a club, and she did some of her Christmas songs, and I thought that was so nice; for some reason I never wanted to go near Christmas songs, but it was so cool that she did that, and the way she did them—gave it that sound.

Anita: And other girl groups?

Debbie: How can I remember the names, my God, I don't know. There was this one song that I really liked called "Lower The Flame," it was a B side, and it was one of my favorite songs. I used to marvel at these songs, in the production there were outright glaring mistakes, they just pressed them up anyway—the B sides.

Anita: There is a lot I have forgotten from those days, I can remember bits.

Debbie: Why should you force your brain cells to remember a lot of stuff when the most important [sic] you can do is to come up with new stuff? For me you know, I'm busy writing now and trying to think of things that take the twist with all of the stuff [sic]. Why should I sit here and be chronological or like a machine with old information? It doesn't make sense to me.

Anita: It doesn't make sense to me, I can live without it, that's for sure. That year or another year, I can't remember. It's nice, you know? In my own head it feels good, I got these memories, sometimes I get a flash, it's like having your own buzzer there going on, which is good.

Debbie: What they are discovering about time and the universe, that is like the way we remember things, like the depths of perception. Something going back, receding.

Anita: I've certainly got a big black hole in my life which is the 70's.

Debbie: You know I always felt that that period, that all of those drugs that came around that wiped out a lot of us and obliterated a lot of stuff, was all politically sanctioned. I always felt that and Chris said that too: that a lot of people who really had something important to say or do were subdued.

Anita: Well, it is like the English colonial system, it's the best way to disempower [sic]. But for me the 60's was like ooooppps I'll take it, or oooppss wow there's that, I'll have that, I'll try that, I'll have another one of those! and by the end of the day, it was like a compulsion you know? Incredible.

Debbie: The new blend! HHHaaaaa.

Anita: Today it is more selective, people know more about it anyway. Back then it was like William Burroughs, I thought "well if he can do it!" He really was fantastic.

Debbie: He was tremendously strong, both physically and mentally, what a great mind. His last words as they loaded him into the ambulance were: "I'll be right back." Hhaaaaaa. They slammed the door up and took him away.

Anita: Yeah, I really miss those guys. What happened to Chris (Stein)?

Debbie: He's writing, he's married, he has six or seven cats and a big dog, and he's pretty much the same person you know. He's a real diehard liberal, he'll never change. Thank God.

Anita: It's amazing that you two stayed so long together.

Debbie: I'm very comfortable and happy with Chris, it's a good thing, something happens with our two minds, which automatically just fits together. Even now everything is sort of parallel. We don't even think about it, it just happens. I think we were lucky that we actually found each other. I never expected anything like that to happen, I never knew that anything like that even existed.

Anita: What is your favorite hotel in the world?

Debbie: The one that I had most fun at was the Gramercy Park Hotel, hhhhhaaa, I always had fun there, and the Chelsea was fun too, but it was kind of scary there—yep a little scarier! Hhhaaa.

Anita: Which New York Doll did you dig the most?

Debbie: I was crazy about David [Johansen]. I thought David was the hot stuff! But I was friends with them all, I liked the original drummer, Billy Murcia, but then I became friends with Jerry [Nolan], and Jerry used to play an early incarnation of Blondie.

Anita: What do you think of rap and hip hop evolution [sic]?

Debbie: Well, I always loved it, there was always something so exciting about it. Even when it was primitive I felt like it was folk music. Blues had an element of the speaking, the voice of the people, but rap became much more political in a bigger way, you know I thought that was really important. I thought this is really hot shit.

Anita: What I liked about it was that it really did express anger. What do you think of the clothes?

Debbie: They come up with great combinations of things. I guess that's all we're left with now is to make new combinations, right? There's no way you can actually do something that is original, it's all blending.

Anita: I love the jewelry, the nails, the hair, everything. Whenever I see those nails I get totally envious! Haaa.

Debbie: I don't have time to do that myself, I don't know how those girls get ready, it must have taken them days to get ready!

Anita: I'm glad the Afro is back in now. The only thing I've ever done is just bleach.

Debbie: Bleach!! Yeeeaaaahhh!

Anita: I started bleaching real early, and then I also managed to convince myself that I was a white blond baby. How would you have dealt with fame if you had been as young as other punk rockers?

Debbie: Gee, I don't know. I think I probably would have been a better star, I think I would have gone for it in a much more showbiz kind of way. Which probably would have been better in the long run, you know? You know what I really wanted to be was a beatnik, I really wanted to be an underground artist. That was really where my thrust was, being a pop star—I thought it was such bullshit you know? I knew it was bullshit, I didn't really give a rat's ass about any of it, I wanted to be famous, but I didn't really care about carrying it on, you know. In a sense it would have been better if I had approached it in a more legitimate showbiz kind of way.

Anita: I've got that beatnik thing as well, I've always done the kind of underground thing. I've tried the big time, and I didn't like a minute of it, I just don't like the way it works. I don't like the way it works still. There is that thing about being a legend, which you certainly are. I think there is a deeper thing than the showbiz kind of stuff.

Debbie: That was always what I felt was the beauty of Rock'n'Roll, it was entertainment and showbiz but yet it had the idea of the voice of the people, it had an essence to it which was socially motivated. Not that I want to change the world, you know? But it was sort of relevant to real life, it involved the real essence of poetry or the real essence of fine art. But it was also an entertainment. That was the real vitality.

"Telling Stories With Dream Logic"

by Jeff Miers

Article reprinted from Blue Dog Press *web site, March 30, 2001*

Jeff Miers waxes poetic on jazz, the Jazz Passengers, and, particularly, Deborah Harry.—Ed.

Music, born of a rebellious spirit of wanderlust and a desire to communicate on a transcendent level, is still often beleaguered by politics. A politics of separation; of apartheid, if you will. The art form has become territorial, and a desire for one to "stay with one's own," so to speak, has become the predominant ethic in musics as disparate and diverse as pop, classical and Jazz. Hence, Wynton Marsalis and his Lincoln Jazz Center Orchestra pay heed to tradition, which is fine, until it comes to exist in opposition to bold hybridizations which seek to move the music forward. And pop artists—Elvis Costello, for example—who strive to fuse a pop or rock approach to more complex, harmonically speaking, musical underpinnings, often do so at the expense of record sales. Not cool, but very real, nonetheless.

In the mid 90s, vocalist Deborah Harry, most famous as the peroxide-blonde punk chanteuse leading pop pioneers Blondie, joined forces with Avant jazz geniuses The Jazz Passengers, and the territorial moanings began in earnest. Led by saxophonist Roy Nathanson, The Passengers rose from the ashes of The Lounge Lizards, and by the time they met Deborah Harry, had garnered a serious reputation among those in the know as the leading light in the future of jazz, based on the strength of such albums as Implement Yourself, Plain Old Joe, and Jazz Passengers in Love. The Big Apple buzzed on the band's irreverent will to musical power; Nathanson knew the future of jazz lay in the composer and performer's ability to confidently blend styles, from Wagner to the West Coast Cool of the 60s. He set out to follow the mandate of the Jazz composer a artist.

So hardcore Jazz folk made a big deal about Harry entering their sacred ranks. The group's first full-length collaboration, Individually Twisted, offered a bold blend of surrealism and peerless Jazz chops; it garnered widespread critical acclaim, but sold poorly. Critics and open-minded listeners "got it," but label geeks missed the boat, either misunderstanding the forward-looking muse the band chose to follow, or claiming that it was simply too eclectic and esoteric to find an audience. Too pop to be considered Jazz, too Jazz to be considered pop, Individually Twisted—despite the star power wielded by Harry and guest Elvis Costello—disappeared far too quickly. Still, the band soldiered on, racking up rave reviews for their outstanding live shows, waylaid only by the Blondie reunion album and tour. Harry, who isn't a trained musician, proved herself to be a Jazz vocalist of the first order, finding her own melodic threads to follow in the dense chordal tapestry provided by the Passengers—Nathanson, trombonist Curtis Fowlkes, bassist Brad Jones, percussionist E.J. Rodriguez, vibe player Bill Ware, violinist Jim Nolet—and offering her own sense of dynamics and theatrics to the mix. The combined effect is simply stunning.

"I think everything is going fine," laughs Deborah Harry from her Manhattan home, referring to the Jazz Passengers' preparations for their first-ever collaboration with an orchestra. "We had a rehearsal yesterday, and we've been listening to all the tapes of our old arrangements, to try and re-learn them! So we've made it through our first run-through with all the orchestrations and stuff. At this stage, the Buffalo appearance is a one-off, but we'd like to bring this around to anywhere in the world that will have it! Roy and Bill Ware did all the arrangements for this show, and they really are quite special. So we're kind of hoping this grows into something bigger!"

The band seems to take perverse pleasure in combining elements that wouldn't fit together under normal circumstances. Avant Garde Jazz meets Cabaret meets surrealist comedy; not exactly a proven recipe for commercial windfall. Did Harry, coming from a proven, commercially successful entity like Blondie, have trouble fitting into this art for art's sake ethos?

"I think some of the band's ethic really applies and appeals to me," says Harry. "You know, I started playing with them sort of by accident. I was invited to sing on a track on the Jazz Passengers In Love album, by Hal Willner, the musical director and producer from Saturday Night Live, who was producing it. It all just kind of developed from there. So my approach to it was very much an approach of discovery. I wasn't really aware of all the things they had been up to, and the sort of approach that Roy has. He's a very...active, I guess is the word for the kind of person he is. (laughs) He's really into all different kinds of things. He has taken The Jazz Passengers through fantasy worlds, in a sense, doing all kinds of theatre productions, to standard Jazz gigs, to now this gig with the Buffalo Philharmonic. So it is kind of an odyssey, in a way. And yeah, I guess I fit into that straight away."

The music media may have made a big deal out of Harry's jumping horses in midstream, from the pop camp to the Jazz world, but it really shouldn't have come as much of a surprise to anyone who has followed her work closely over the years. Blondie, for example, never shied away from melody, to say the least. Sophistication was always part of the deal. One would be inclined to think that such naysaying concerning Harry's proclivity toward eclecticism would become rather annoying.

"I think what's happened to me over the centuries (laughs) is that I've gotten used to it. Everyone has an opinion. And everyone hears things their way. And so, inevitably, there is always something different said or felt or reacted to. And I guess that's sort of what makes it all worthwhile. Yes, sometimes it's hard to take. But sometimes it's like the most sumptuous feast!

"And, of course, there are two versions of me, in a sense. For the 'little me,' I just approached this whole thing from the point of view that it was a great musical experience. And then, when you get hit with the reality of the big world, the 'big me' sort of takes over and deals with it all. I think that, whenever you crossover, my experience has been that the people who are working very hard in their area really resent intrusion! They've worked so hard to achieve what they achieve, and they think that because you're trying to cross over, you're trying to usurp some of their power, some of their glory. And there is an adjustment to be made there, and I understand that. I sort of think that way too; I bridle at things myself. That someone's gonna' come along and try to do pop or rock who doesn't normally do it doesn't make me happy! It's perfectly natural. I guess you just sort of have to wait and see, and realize that people who are in the arts—especially the performing arts—often have multiple talents. They really have the ability to do many different things. So sometimes you just take off in a direction because it's working. And you stick with it, despite what certain people might have to say about it."

Shortly after beginning her collaboration with Roy Nathanson and cohorts, Harry reunited with Blondie. They recorded a strong album in No Exit, and hit the road before receptive audiences around the world. Though No Exit mined familiar Blondie terrain, one suspects that Harry brought some of the inspiration gleaned from her experience as a Passenger to the table when the band reunited.

"I think, if anything, it has just made me able to contribute more to the process," Harry says. "I'm more educated. I'm a better musician than I was. I've had a bigger experience. Not to say that I wouldn't have evolved just doing Blondie straight through; but this is the way it happened. So I really do feel that I was able to contribute more musical ideas, and really be a part of that statement than ever before. I think that No Exit was a way for us to say, 'Here we are; we're not dead yet!' We wanted to make a really high-quality Blondie statement. It's sort of funny, because I realize that, in some ways, it sounds really dated. Even to me. I sort of feel like, 'Wow! We're really funny! We're old!' You know? (laughs) But then, in other ways, the musical aspects of it are so beautiful that, as far as I'm concerned, they sort of transcend whatever the flavor of the month happens to be. I think that the guys in Blondie who write these wonderful, quite charming, beautiful melodies...they need to be heard. And I'm proud to be a part of that."

As proud as Harry is of Blondie, Roy Nathanson is of her; the saxophonist is thrilled to have Harry in his group, and he makes no bones about it.

"She's an absolute mofo!" he enthuses. "She is absolutely the baddest mother out there! I'm tellin' you, when I first got her in the band, I just knew that she would get it. There are a lot of people who might have more pipes than her that we could've gotten. But she actually has great pitch, totally amazing phrasing. She is a fucking genius! Totally happening! Just like all of the other fuck-ups in The Jazz Passengers! (laughs) The Jazz Passengers is made up of a bunch of talented fuck-ups! Really, this is an amazing group of people. That it isn't more famous than it is just completely baffles me. Completely!"

Nathanson is the principle composer in the group, but he's more than that; you need only speak with him for a moment to realize that this music is his life, that he invests each recording, each gig, with every particle of his being. The Buffalo Philharmonic collaboration, in many senses, represents a pinnacle of the man's artistic vision. These are, for the most part, his compositions. And frankly, there aren't many artists approaching music of such grand, cinematic scope. Having an orchestra embellish the Passengers' sound is a dream come true for Nathanson.

"These are predominantly songs that I wrote the music for, although Bill Ware wrote one, Curtis Fowlkes wrote one, and Brad Jones wrote one. Bill Ware did all the orchestrations for this stuff, for the most part, and it has really been a simply monumental task. Bill is such a brilliant guy, harmonically speaking. He's an absolutely fantastic arranger. So the band is sort of a semi-collective for this particular job, the Buffalo date. And we're hoping this will become the direction of the band from here on out.

"These songs are really like constructions. It's funny, because we've always gotten great reviews. Pretty much unanimously. But we've always been sort of in a quirky, weird place. Structurally, speaking, that is. Because, even though it's a really great Jazz band, and Debbie's really good, we do a lot of different things. "And I actually have always felt that orchestrating this stuff would bring it home to people in a way that it hasn't been before. Because the sort of cross-genre stuff we've always done has been built around the narrative. "And it's something that doesn't necessarily fit a jazz club, it doesn't necessarily fit this, it doesn't necessarily fit that. I think that that's great! I think that that's what people are supposed to do with art. They're supposed to make things that don't fit into strict categories, that are new! This is original music! I love Duke Ellington, but how many Duke Ellington covers do you need? So I think, in a weird way, we're hoping that this way of doing things, with Deborah, with the orchestra, will take this complex music and translate it into a better hearing of the songs. This stuff is not meant to be goofy, you know. It's meant to be dream-like! That's what we're trying to do. To have dream structures, and tell stories with dream logic. But that's what good composition was always supposed to be doing! It's not like we invented that! We're just a part of that tradition, and we're trying to bring our own thing to it."

Blondie performing on a television program, Stockholm, Sweden, October 1998
l to r: Jimmy Destri, Deborah Harry, Paul Carbonara, Leigh Foxx, Chris Stein. (Clem Burke is hidden from view).
credit: © Matthew Murphy—courtesy of Paul Carbonara

Profiles

"Blondie's Back..."

by Jim Farber

New York Daily News, *January 10, 1999*

Speculation on the reception Blondie would receive upon their return to the music scene, the No Exit *album, a brief history of the band, how it's different this time around, and Madonna.*—Ed.

The setting isn't terribly different from where it all began: a dank rehearsal studio in an ugly industrial nook of New York.

On this sooty winter morning, the original members of the quintessential Noo Yawk group Blondie have gathered in a studio not far from their '70s birthplace on the beat-up Bowery. They've come together again for some fine-tuning: They're about to embark on a quick Australian reunion tour following an appearance on tomorrow night's American Music Awards.

The TV gig will mark Blondie's first televised appearance in nearly 17 years. It also serves as a call to arms for the band's comeback campaign, highlighted by an album of all-new material, "No Exit," arriving Feb. 23.

"The main point of all this," says drummer Clem Burke, "was to get back together to make a record that's a new musical statement—not to just play our greatest hits."

Don't worry. The reconstituted Blondie plans to follow this album with a hit-filled national tour in the spring—the band's first road show since they scattered in the wake of ego squabbles, poor business deals, illness, exhaustion and bad faith in 1982.

In the four years before that, the punky band managed to wisecrack its way out of the arty CBGB Bowery scene to achieve national fame with four No. 1 U.S. hits. In their prime, Blondie mainstreamed punk, pioneered disco-rock, racked up the first rap hit on the pop charts, made the first long-form music video and changed forever the image of the female sex symbol in rock via frontwoman Deborah Harry, who presaged the multi-media juggernaut of Madonna.

Now 53, Harry still looks smashing. When she dashes into the studio for an interview, she looks like Lana Turner in her prime, eyes blackened by shades, head shielded in a scarf, the perfect mystery blond. Her attempts at anonymity succeed only in making her seem more like an icon.

The question is, will the world still think so?

"I'm sure I'll be a sex symbol to someone—probably some octogenarian," Harry says, settling into a couch. "It'll be Blondie with stretch marks."

But then she takes the question seriously. "Popular music has reached a certain maturity where I think people are willing to say that sexuality actually exists past the age of 30."

"Jagger still uses his sexuality and he's, what, 80?" cracks guitarist Chris Stein.

But what people will think about Harry's sexuality is just one question the band faces in its tricky relaunch. Can a big audience be found for both a tour and an album of untested songs? Stein has been a believer for three years. At the time, he noticed the band's original music was getting a lot more radio play. "When we stopped, there was a long period when we really weren't on the radio," he says. "All that started to change."

At the same time, Harry's solo career hit a dead end. She had put out three very good albums since the band's demise, but they went nowhere on this side of the Atlantic, gaining hit status only in the U.K. "I had such a difficult time getting those things promoted," says Harry. (Also in the '80s, she embarked on an acting career in films like David Cronenberg's "Videodrome" and the TV series "Wiseguy.")

'Glass' Reunion

Throughout her solo career, Harry kept collaborating with Stein; he wrote and produced songs on each of her works. Although they had ended their famed romance by the mid-'80s—and Stein went on to marry someone else—they rarely went more than a day without speaking.

But getting the other members back together took a bit more doing. Burke didn't like the first proposal for a reunion: a compilation record with just two new tracks. "That's such a transparent, superficial thing," he says. "Let's make a real record and come out as a real band again."

Stein then made his pitch to keyboardist Jimmy Destri. "I said, 'You would be kicking yourself if you didn't decide to do it,'" explains Stein. Eventually, Destri realized this was "like a second opportunity to buy Microsoft."

A new manager, Allen Kovac, helped fine-tune things. He had earlier coaxed comebacks for Meat Loaf and Duran Duran. Kovac signed Blondie to his own label, Beyond, distributed through BMG. But the group's four main members didn't ask the band's other two starters—guitarist Frank Infante (now an A & R man at Interscope) and bassist Nigel Harrison—to join them.

Infante and Harrison have filed a lawsuit, and the case is still pending. [*The ruling went against Infante and Harrison*—Ed.]. Harry says they can't comment on the case, but Stein insists the band's current lineup, rounded out by two hired hands, is Blondie's most musically adept to date, able to deliver a fuller live sound than in their commercial prime.

To prove it, the group kicked off their comeback in the fall with a celebrated six-week overseas tour that began in England, where they had their first breakout. According to Stein, the biggest difference between the initial run of the band and the most recent tour is that "before, you were always trying to convince someone of something. Now, everyone gets it."

The band felt misunderstood right from their earliest days on the Bowery. Harry's glamorous bombshell image came from the language of Hollywood, not rock—and that invited suspicion. Worse, her image often overshadowed the music—a zippy mix of '60s girl-group trash pop and punk rock.

"Debbie got so much criticism for being overtly sexual," says Burke. "Now, that's everywhere."

Despite the carping, Blondie started to get hits in England in '78, and broke stateside in '79 once they expanded their sound. They cooked up the first rock song to play in the then-pervasive discos, "Heart of Glass," which went No. 1. They went on to top the charts with another dance-rock song, "Call Me" (from the soundtrack to "American Gigolo"), "Rapture" (the first rap smash) and "The Tide Is High" (their nod to reggae).

They were a success, but Blondie was coming apart. The musicians resented all the attention going to cover girl Harry, who, in turn, felt she wasn't getting attention for the right thing: her music. It didn't help matters that, according to the band, bad business contracts left them with a small share of the now-huge profits.

By 1981, relations between the musicians were so rocky that some of the backing tracks were done by session players rather than actual members. In early '82, Infante sued the group, claiming they were trying to ruin his career by excluding him from meetings and recordings. While he remained in the fold, his dissension epitomized Blondie's problems. After their sixth album, "The Hunter," bombed, the group died.

Then, Stein almost died, too. In the early '80s, he suffered from a mysterious wasting disease thought by many to be AIDS. It turned out to be a rare genetic illness; Stein's health didn't stabilize until the late '80s.

In the meantime, something began to happen to the band's reputation. Slowly, they were becoming respected for all that had been controversial about them the first time around. According to Stein, a crucial element in the change was the use of the band's music in movies. "Films started using our music as defining moments of a time," he explains. "It showed that we had an impact on the culture of more than just rock'n'roll."

Harry also won a lot of respect from critics and audiences in the last few years for her nimble and wry guest appearances with the New York underground act the Jazz Passengers. On a cultural level, Harry's use of glossy imagery has come to be recognized as a key antecedent to Madonna. According to Harry, Madonna has never spoken with her, but she has come to her solo shows.

"Madonna has a genius for condensing, for taking the essence of what people do and making it extremely commercial," Harry says. "My thinking is much more subtle. I want to sneak into people's brains. She wants to smash people over the head. I find it a bit unnerving that someone would come and take this little needle that I try to get underneath the skin of people and make it into a baseball bat."

Even talking about Madonna makes Harry itchy. "She doesn't need the press. We do," she says.

True enough. The band acknowledges that, aside from Aerosmith's spectacular second career, most rock comebacks don't take hold for long. And a lot of time has gone by. When this New York band got going, it was back in the era of "Ford to City: Drop Dead."

As the interview comes to a close and the musicians get ready to play, Harry flatly states her priorities. "I just want to be happy with what I'm doing. As far as being analytical about the outcome, that doesn't interest me. I'm way more interested in what makes me cook musically.

"As far as the rest—well, we'll see, won't we?"

"Touched By Your Presence, Dear..."

by John Walsh

The Independent, *February 9, 1999*

Blondie and Deborah Harry's appeal, then and now.—Ed.

She had eyes like the Snow Queen, eyes that could look right into your heart and turn it to solid ice. There was no comfort in her gaze, no warmth, no interest. She sang with a kind of nervy blankness, as if the lyrics meant nothing to her, and, when she narrowed her eyes, you felt as if she must hate you. She was the most beautiful woman we had ever seen. We adored her. Her name was Debbie Harry, and she sang with Blondie, the most successful New Wave band in the restless period that immediately followed punk.

We were just out of university; we'd been through punk—the pins, the rage, the gobbing, the spiky hair and the radical typography—and, in 1978, we just wanted some intelligent rock'n'roll again. Blondie came sassing into the charts and dished it up: "Denis," "Heart of Glass," "(I'm Always Touched by Your) Presence Dear," "Sunday Girl." They were real songs, with real hooks, classy keyboard runs, torrential drumming. We danced to "Dreaming." We sang along to "One Way or Another" ("I'm gonna getcha, getcha, getcha...") like karaoke nerds. And whenever there was half a chance, we just gazed at Debbie Harry.

She looks out from the sleeve of the band's third album, Eat to the Beat, with the glazed hauteur of a supermodel, her eyes toxic with disdain, her lips set in a soaring pout, her eyebrows arched in the most minimal enquiry, her platinum hair swept in a couture wave down to her neck—around which is proprietorially twined the hairy arm of Chris Stein, her Svengali, co-writer, guitarist and boyfriend.

He was a sultry, Brooklyn-Jewish, brooding sort of chap, and we hated him because she seemed to belong to him. Debbie Harry, the icon of transatlantic independence, belonging to anyone. How did that work?

The band were full of contradictions, and they mostly resided in the gutter Aphrodite who fronted them. She was both baby-doll young and too old for punk; it was rumoured that she was over 30, although she dressed in plain white shifts and white boots; she reminded you of every blonde goddess you'd ever seen, from Monroe and Jean Harlow right up to Nico, but hers was a different blondeness, at once trashy and pristine. We knew she'd been a Playboy bunny, a waitress, a quondam junkie ("That's why her skin's so perfect," we explained, knowingly), but she was now a self-created goddess.

Things went wrong. When Blondie split up in 1982, her solo career wobbled uncertainly for 10 years. Debbie Harry shifted into shock mode. The sleeve artwork of her solo album Koo Koo was by HR Giger, the intestinally obsessed production designer of Alien, and featured Ms. Harry's cheeks punctured by long, rusty spikes. She appeared in John Waters' camp and rubbishy Hairspray movie, and in David Cronenberg's deeply unsettling Videodrome. The good times were over, for Ms. Harry and her fans.

A couple of years ago, I saw Debbie Harry again. She was singing with the Jazz Passengers at the Jazz Café in London's Camden Town, and I went along to check it out.

Can I bring myself to say what she was wearing? Can I say the word? Ms. Harry was wearing a jumper. A sensible, ordinary, pink wool jumper. Her head, which had always seemed a little disproportionately large for her slender frame, seemed to have broadened out, like a Hallowe'en pumpkin after a week in the window. Her hair was mousy-nondescript. Middle age had finally caught up with the goddess. She seemed nervous, diffident, a little reluctant to sing. And when she did sing, her voice was thinner than I recalled, etiolated, drained of energy, more pale than blonde. She did "One Way or Another" slowly, as a wistful plaint rather than a statement of gonna-getcha sexual intent. The whole evening felt like a sad experiment.

Now look what's happened. At the end of January, a song called "Maria" started winding around the airwaves, with a high chorus line sung as though by a nun in suspenders ("Mah-ree-ah/ Just gotta see her...") that sounded eerily familiar. The accompanying pop video was dark to the point of pointlessness, but through the murk you could make out the penetrating blue eyes, the trashy barnet, the sharp Giger cheekbones, all over again. "My

244

God, who's she?" breathed my 11-year-old daughter. We both gazed at Ms. Harry, now 53, radiating sexy hauteur, singing in front of the old line-up, Stein, Clem Burke and Jimmy Destri, apparently reborn.

What's odd is how pleased you feel about this comeback. It's by no means a typical reaction. The Nineties have been so filled with comebacks, retreads and recyclings that we sometimes seem to be in danger of entering a retro-universe, one that hits an evolutionary wall and then starts going backwards.

We may smile to see Lonnie Donegan putting out a new record, Muleskinner Blues, at the age of 70, or to find the Sixties crooner Englebert Humperdinck being dusted down, and the rebarbative Tony "Is This the Way to Amarillo?" Christie turning up on Top of the Pops. We may utter a sympathetic "Awww..." at the news that a job lot of effete Eighties poseurs (Culture Club, Human League and ABC) are sharing an evening of nostalgia, or when we find Duran Duran insisting that they're very much direct competition to Blur and Oasis these days. We may look in wonder at a playbill from Wembley Arena announcing a concert this May—"the All-American Solid Gold Rock and Roll Show"—starring Little Richard, Bobby Vee, Chris Montez, Little Eva and Brian Hyland.

Who's Brian Hyland? He sang "Itsy Bitsy Teeny Weeny Yellow Polka Dot Bikini" back in the days when Princess Margaret was going around on a motorbike.

But the fact is, there are some comebacks that are just not acceptable to the public and some that are. The Osmonds, no. The Bay City Rollers, no thanks. Hawkwind, nah. Bros, no way. But Roxy Music, ooh yes. The Clash, yes indeed. The Pogues, God yes. And Blondie are right there among the yeses. They were a group you never had to defend your interest in, or justify your liking for. Ms. Harry and her acolytes were geniuses at throwaway pop; that's what, paradoxically, made their songs so enduring. Ms. Harry's look was a construct, that drew attention to her black roots, her pancake make-up, her machine-tooled gleam of sex; that's why we took her to our hearts. We cared for her because she encouraged us not to. We loved her precisely because she turned out to have a heart of glass.

And we liked the band because their songs were incontrovertibly their own. Now, at the end of the Nineties, the hit parade is full of recycled songs, listless cover versions of hits from the Sixties and Seventies. Listen to 911's recent spotty warbling of Dr. Hook's "A Little Bit More," or Emmie's antiseptic disco version of Roxy's "More Than This," or Boyzone's overwrought mangling of the Bee Gee's "Words," and the forty-something parent smites his brow, stalks the living-room and tells his unimpressed children that they're listening to a series of pathetic simulacra, a plastic Echoland in which nothing is original except the singers' habit of wearing telephone-receptionist's headpieces while performing gymnastic dance routines that would have seemed dated to Pan's People, circa 1968.

We pick and choose authenticity in our lives. We choose these political beliefs, these clothes, this music, this shade of terracotta, this holiday destination, in the belief that, because they have a special reality for us, they are more intrinsically real than other beliefs, clothes, notes, colours, islands. We make them ours. We perform a series of passionate identifications with artifacts, selecting them from the cultural market garden, thinking they will combine in a harmonious, thousand-petalled display and that will be the picture of our soul. We may get it wrong all the time, but what we once chose was once part of our sense of who we were. That's what counts. And when a band such as Blondie comes back—driven by heaven knows what impulse of artistic or, more likely, financial need, but sounding true to themselves—you welcome them back, as you would regard with a wry smile a younger, handsomer photograph of yourself.

Why is this comeback so popular? Maybe the country is full of sentimental 35-to-45-year-olds who grew up with Ms. Harry's trash-goddess vocals forming the sound-track of their lives, and now—with the house, the garden, the mortgage, the children and the asparagus kettle—like to feel they're still grooving; that their heroine, their ice queen, is at No 1 in the charts, though of course they're far too mature to care about "charts." Perhaps the whole comeback culture is a saying-goodbye to the century by re-treading the boards we trod in youth. Somehow, you can't imagine a Culture Club Nostalgia Tour in the year 2001. It's that Big Nought, of course. The bands that used to make all the running have got just 10 months of final encores left before we hit Year Zero, and a whole new world of new acts, new music, new art forms, gets going.

I can't say. But I'll just go and put "Dreaming" on the record deck one more time. It's probably the best of the singles that conquered the world at the end of the Seventies, and it finds the goddess in reflective mode: "We don't stand on ceremony/ We just walk on by/ We just keep on dreaming". So do we, Deborah, so do we.

"Catching a New Wave..."

by Brett Milano

Boston Herald, *February 23, 1999*

Preview of No Exit *album, and the second time around is better for Blondie. Edited with the permission of the author.*—Ed.

What did it take to get the members of new-wave icon Blondie back together after a 15-year break?

"I guess it was the slivers under the fingernails that did it," said singer Deborah Harry.

But nobody really had to torture Harry to make her take the gig. "We talked about it and thought about it, and eventually I came around to the idea that it would be an enriching experience in my life," she said, shifting into mock-respectable voice. "It's good that some record company support and credibility is finally being heaped upon us."

In some ways, the group has never been away. Harry continued working with her longtime musical partner (and former romantic partner), guitarist Chris Stein, on a string of Blondie-sounding solo albums. And the string of Blondie reissues, greatest-hits and remix albums now outnumbers their original discs. It was the prospect of one more greatest-hits album that drove Stein and Harry to put the band back together for a new one instead, with keyboardist Jimmy Destri and drummer Clem Burke. The reunion effort, "No Exit," arrives in stores today. The band hopes to tour extensively this spring.

"Nobody felt good about another greatest-hits record," said Stein. "We've been back together for three years, but at first there was a series of lousy business deals. Our main idea for the record was to make it more minimal, less of a wall of sound—we did parts of it in my basement. Otherwise, the main difference is that we have better management. The old band was disastrous in that way. We got screwed around and that left us with too many bad feelings to continue. Now it's bizarre when I hear that we sold 50 million albums, because they only paid us for eight of them."

"No Exit" is one of Blondie's more diverse albums, ranging from old-fashioned pop to lounge ballads, hip-hop and even a country tune. But it's done with a sense of fun that was missing from the later group and solo albums. For Stein, the dark period included a bout with the near-fatal genetic illness pemphigus; and dealing with a longstanding substance-abuse problem.

"I just haven't had it together over the last 16 years," he said. "The band ended, the illness happened, and then I went through a long introspective period trying to figure out why I was getting so high for all those years. Everybody's feeling more positive now, and you can hear that on the album." Even the gangster rap on the title track is done with tongue in cheek.

"We had the title 'No Exit' before we made the album," said Harry. "It's not meant cynically—just that I have an identity with the public, and you can't get away from that."

Still, Harry's developed a deeper and more grownup singing voice, after recent tours fronting the Jazz Passengers. "In the past, Blondie's identity was a more girlish pop sound," she said. "Maybe I was getting a little tired of being in cutesy mode. Now I have more experience, like an actor does when they assume certain modes. You can develop characters better when you understand more about human nature."

"One Way or Another, Blondie Has Made It Back"

by David Bauder

Associated Press, *February 26, 1999*

On the Blondie reunion, the band's influence and legacy, including Deborah Harry's observation that she is "'very proud of Blondie, the things we did for music...'"—Ed.

Research, not sloth, led members of Blondie to kill a few hours in the afternoon watching MTV in a luxury hotel suite.

After 16 years away from the pop music world, these former chart-toppers needed to see what the competition was up to. Not much to hold Chris Stein's attention, it seemed.

"I don't really know any of this stuff," he muttered, "and I don't really have any interest in it, either."

Now it's time to wonder if the pop music world is interested in them.

With a reputation burnished by nostalgia, Blondie has re-formed and released its first album of new material since 1982. Rock reunions are often depressing jokes, but early signs here are encouraging. The first single, "Maria," entered the British charts at No. 1, and VH1 filmed Blondie's first New York concert appearance for a special that airs Sunday at 10 p.m. EST.

Hits like "Heart of Glass," "Rapture" and "The Tide Is High" made Blondie among the most commercially successful bands to emerge from the punk rock scene. The band was engagingly eclectic and frontwoman Deborah Harry was a tough girl with pinup looks who could sing, too.

Money tore them apart; when they weren't making much at the height of success, they turned on each other. Stein was also seriously ill for years with a rare genetic illness and Harry, then his wife [*Harry and Stein never married*—Ed.], effectively disappeared to help nurse him back to health.

With artists like Garbage successfully mining Blondie's territory, Stein thought the time was right for a second try. Blondie's not ashamed to admit it's trying to cash in.

"I thought that if I didn't do it, I would look back in 10 years and say I probably should have done it," he said.

Disillusioned with the music business, keyboard player Jimmy Destri had spent years working as a contractor. He had renewed his interest in music and, oddly enough, was in England producing a Blondie tribute album when Stein called to talk about a reunion. Drummer Clem Burke had stayed in music, working for Eurythmics and others, and was also willing.

Harry, soured by the band's final days, didn't immediately warm to Stein's suggestion.

"He needed to work on me for a while," she said. "I thought it was not a good idea at all. I just didn't want to delve in the past."

Stein's enthusiasm and her own pride won her over. She'd done some acting, released some poorly received solo albums and sung for the Jazz Passengers, but the work wasn't entirely satisfying.

"I'm very proud of Blondie, the things we did for music," she said. "I thought it was sort of a shame that I couldn't continue my career as Blondie."

Some bad blood lingers. Nigel Harrison and Frank Infante, who joined the original quartet after their first album, aren't involved this time and have sued their former colleagues because of it.

But the passage of time is great for changing perspectives.

"We would do photo sessions in the old days and the photographers would say, 'Debbie, come here and do some photos by yourself,'" Stein said. "Everybody would start complaining. Now everybody's happy because nobody wants to do the work anymore."

Harry is, after all, synonymous with Blondie for a lot of fans. Her inability to establish a solo career may have quietly proven the point that male band members would defensively make in the old days—that they were a group, not a bunch of backup players.

Time also puts Harry's influence in better perspective. She wasn't afraid to use her sexuality and in a male-dominated business, that was something new. Stein, 49, remembers an entire chapter of a book on Blondie devoted to a furious attack on Harry for showing a glimpse of her underwear.

In the wake of Madonna and other strong women in music, it seems a lot longer ago than 20 years.

"Somebody would have done it if not Debbie, but she happened to do it," Stein said. "It was something that was coming along with the rise of feminism in society. Debbie's statement was that she didn't want to be seen as a victim. It was a form of girl power."

Harry, 53, says she enjoys hearing women say she helped encourage them to follow a dream into music.

"I don't think her singing and her role as a musician was ever discussed in the first time around," Stein said. "Only her attitude was discussed and her stance, how she was acting. And as a singer, she was more than good."

It's the men in Blondie, oddly enough, who talk about Harry's influence on women when asked about the band's legacy. Harry instead mentions "Rapture," the 1980 hit that was the first exposure to rap music for many white music fans.

Blondie was always a stylistically restless band. Songs like "Denis" and "Dreaming" merged girl group sounds of the early 1960s with aggressive rock. "One Way or Another" was a rocker with attitude. "Heart of Glass" was bubbly disco. "The Tide Is High" was reggae.

So it's no surprise that the new album, "No Exit," is impossible to categorize—ska, lounge, even country music drifts by. Although "Maria" is a shimmering single, the album as a whole reveals Blondie as a band still trying to find its legs.

Harry calls it a first step, although the market place will ultimately determine whether there are any steps beyond it.

"I think if we had gotten together and tried to work it in a way that looked like we were trying to break the sound barrier or something, it wouldn't have been that much fun," she said. "I really think we needed to do a record that was fun for us and as good as we could make it without being too preposterous or overachieving."

Deborah Harry, G-A-Y club night, The Astoria, London, May 18, 2002
credit: copyright © 2002 Mandy Rohr.

Deborah Harry with the Jazz Passengers accompanied by violinists from the BBC Concert Orchestra, conducted by Robert Ziegler, as part of the Barbican Jazz 2002 series, Barbican, London, May 19, 2002
credit: copyright © 2002 Mandy Rohr.

"Blondie 2.0"

by Jim Greer

Gear magazine, March/April 1999

Observations on Blondie's European tour, Fall 1998, and more specifically, a memorable stop on that tour, the Barrowland Ballroom, Glasgow, Scotland, November 19, 1998; Blondie's pervasive musical influence.—Ed.

Debbie Harry is back, 16 years after Blondie self-destructed. Jim Greer joins the band on the road, and finds a legend reborn.

The tension gathers slowly, like the clouds of cigarette smoke spiraling towards the cavernous ceiling. Aging punks in 999 and Buzzcocks T-shirts, throwbacks to Britain's golden age of punk, mix with clumps of fresh-faced teenagers in pressed blue jeans, all clutching plastic pints of something called "lager" and talking excitedly. The 2,000-capacity ballroom in Glasgow, Scotland, is crammed to the gills, and the overstuffing and beer consumption have already prompted a couple of fistfights, quickly squelched by beefy security dudes in yellow jackets. I pity the poor rock band that has to come out and face these expectations, especially knowing that (for reasons which will be explained later) there's been no time for such niceties as a soundcheck.

House lights dim, prompting a full-throated roar from the throng. In near darkness, we can just see several shadowy figures take the stage to the accompaniment of swelling orchestral music over the PA. The music stops. The music starts. A low-pitched, mid-tempo, powerful guitar-and-bass chug. The crowd shows its approval by means of a ratchet increase in volume. The stage lights flower, the drums explode into my chest, and the keyboards take up the instantly-recognizable melody to "Dreaming." Debbie Harry, resplendent in red shirt and black skirt, haloed in spotlight, makes her way leisurely from the wings to arrive at the microphone just in time to sing the opening lyrics: "When I walked into the restaurant/You could tell I was no debutante." [*The opening line actually is "When I met you in the restaurant..."*—Ed.]. It's an inspired choice for an opener, both acknowledging the passage of time and, through sheer force of music, erasing with casual grace the 16 years separating this performance from the last. Blondie, despite earlier threats to "Die Young, Stay Pretty," is back.

Never mind the middle-aged paunches on the boys in the band. Never mind that Debbie has substituted a sophisticated, class-actressy stage presence for the raw sexual allure of her early days. By the end of the second song, "Hanging On the Telephone," I see people openly weeping, tears of glee streaming down their faces. The rest of the set is a revelation, a shiver-inducing hit parade that closes, before the encores, with a tribute to the band's mid-70s CBGB (legendary club) origins, the highlight of which is a track called "X Offender," from their eponymous debut album. The encores knock me down (but I get up again) as the band rips through "The Tide Is High" and "Rapture," then returns for a coruscating Plasmatics cover before closing, sweetly, with "Denis" from their second album, *Plastic Letters*. Less nostalgia trip than belated celebration of the concentrated power of the band's two-decade old catalogue, of the wisdom experience brings, and of 24-hour room service in nice European hotels, the Blondie reunion tour—which hits the US this spring—has what most of today's crop of one-hit-wonder alterna-losers can only dream of attaining: deep impact.

"It's been very heartwarming, doing the European tour," says Debbie Harry. We're sitting in an airport in Dublin, waiting four hours for a plane to replace the one that flew us halfway to Glasgow but had to turn back due to unspecified "mechanical trouble." (Hence the lack of soundcheck time.) "It's been a phenomenal experience, just this heart-rending, heart-melting, mind-boggling response. I didn't think this could ever happen again, truthfully. We got it together, and after all this time people are really happy and excited to see us. It's a wonderful reward after all the bad things that happened to us as a band."

Was the response in line with your expectations? I ask.

"1 didn't expect so much," responds Debbie. "I thought maybe half of the attention that we've gotten. I thought it would just be, you know, reunion, retro kind of thing. It's much more than that."

Everybody knows Blondie. An hour into our airport vigil, two old Irishmen with wrinkled red faces and white hair approach me and say, "Our curiosity's been piqued. Who's the pop group you're traveling with?"

"They're called Blondie," I reply.

"Blondie! Where's Debbie Harry?" they ask eagerly, and I point to a row of seats along which Harry is now stretched in unglamorous repose, trying to sleep, beret perched on her face. Clutched in her arm is Minkie, a stuffed monkey and tour talisman (his name is a tribute to Peter Sellers' immortal Inspector Clouseau). The band will not go onstage without Minkie in his accustomed perch alongside Jimmy Destri's keyboards. In London, when he's unaccountably left behind at the hotel, someone is dispatched to go fetch the recalcitrant rascal (that's Minkie, not Destri, of course).

The two old gents have the good sense not to disturb Harry's nap, but later, after Destri discovers an unattended airport microphone and begins issuing fake gate change announcements, a woman who I can only describe as possibly Blondie's biggest fan—she's huge—approaches Debbie for an autograph. "You don't see very many fat women over here," comments Harry matter-of-factly after the fan leaves. "Not like in the States."

"I've got a big head," interjects Destri, somewhat irrelevantly.

"Size 62. It's the biggest head in the band, except for Debbie. She's got an enormous head."

"I don't think I like the sound of that," comes the reply.

It would be hard to overestimate the influence of Blondie on the musical climate. From the band's gritty origins in the nascent CBGB "New Wave" scene in mid-70s New York City alongside the Ramones, Television, Patti Smith, and Talking Heads, to their metamorphosis into disco-fueled pop stars with the song "Heart of Glass," and on into multi-genre pop explorations like the reggae-fied "The Tide is High" and rap-homage "Rapture" (many suburban white kids' first exposure to rap), Blondie has forged a relentlessly inventive musical path that still resonates. Its influence can be felt on ska-pop bands like No Doubt, on the raft of female-led rock bands in the early to mid-90s (Elastica, Hole, Breeders), on electronic-oriented pop like Garbage, and on and on. The eclecticism of the Blondie approach has always been one of its greatest strengths.

Over and above the music, of course, was the sex-kitten-on-ice image fostered by Debbie Harry, an irony-laden pose willfully presented with great elan by Harry's bottle-blond savoir faire. So strong was the image she created, and so influential (see: Madonna), that it threatened at the time to overshadow the group's musical prowess, and indeed was one of the contributing forces to the dissension that eventually broke them up.

These days, at 53, Debbie can't project (nor wants to) the same dewy appeal she successfully mined in the band's heyday. Instead, she has impressive actorly skills to help convey the depth of her often complex lyrics. I wondered, though, to what extent she saw the image of "Blondie" as represented by Debbie Harry changing with the passage of time.

"I wasn't so sure about the Blondie thing for me at this stage in my life," considers Harry. "On my solo projects I was constantly confronted with 'Blondie! Blondie! What about Blondie?' People were always calling me that. And asking about a reunion.

"Obviously I can't be considered a pop tart at my age,' she says. "The whole idea would be ridiculous. The thing I've really learned is that as difficult as anyone's life is, the most important thing is to be as fragile as possible. And to really maintain that fragility and that sensitivity. That's a hard lesson to learn, because you don't want to do that, it's against nature. The natural thing is to protect yourself and put up your guard, and to get through. Alone."

What Debbie Harry did have to get through alone, in the wake of 1982's disappointing *The Hunter,* was a famously acrimonious split between the band members, some of whom were under the impression that their contributions were less than sufficiently appreciated. "We really didn't dislike one another so much as we were pulled apart by the people around us;' recalls Destri.

Stein also fell victim to a rare genetic disease, pemphigus, which attacks the immune system, from which it took him two years to recover. During this time he and longtime-lover Harry—the two have subsequently split, though they remain close friends—were subjected to all sorts of tabloid rumors (Chris has Aids, Debbie is an alien) regarding his convalescence.

Of course, the drugs didn't help either. "I was in a cab with Bob Dylan a few years ago," recalls Burke, who filled in the intervening years with low-profile band projects and high-profile session work with Dylan, the

Eurythmics, Mick Jagger, and others. "He said to me, 'Clem. Blondie: what happened? You were huge. 'Drugs,' I said. He just nodded. 'Ahh, drugs.'"

"We all got pretty fucked up," confirms Destri. "I was a walking chemical shake."

"We were all doing fucking drugs, and the stress...I just exploded," remembers Stein.

All of which begs the question: why go back? Even after 16 years, there's got to be a little fear involved with re-immersion in a situation that proved so traumatic.

"Well, I don't know if I had any fear, I just didn't want to do it" recalls Harry of her reaction when first approached by Stein. The reunion was set in motion three years ago by a strange chain of events beginning with Stein calling a listing in a New York newspaper to raise cash by selling some of his old gold records.

Turns out that the guy buying memorabilia was married to the sister of a girl who was the inspiration for the song "Denise" by Randy and the Rainbows, which Blondie retitled "Denis" and turned into its first hit record, at least in the UK. From that unlikely push, the reunion train gathered enough steam to produce not only a tour but a whole new album, *No Exit*.

"It was a gradual process." says Harry. "I wanted to give Chris the benefit of the doubt. I thought it might be good to do some recording, and that was the initial goal—do a couple of songs. I guess the combination of Chris being really inspired and the support of [our new management company] made me feel like, okay, I could actually do this."

While not entirely a return to form, *No Exit* is far from being the embarrassment it could have been. Rather than simply revisiting old territory, it's an apparent attempt to update the Blondie sound, while exploring newer interests like Harry's stint with the Jazz Passengers (see, especially, the new record's "Boom Boom in the Zoom Zoom Room"). The songs that work best, however, are the ones that hew closest to a recognizably Blondie line, like the first single, "Maria," a Destri-penned tune that's been going over gangbusters with audiences so far. Call *No Exit* a promise of things to come, rather than the fulfillment of a 16-year reverie, and you'll be closer to the truth. Because Blondie, having surmounted the peaks and valleys of a troubled career, give every indication of just getting started.

On the way out of Glasgow's Barrowlands, heading for the tour bus that will take us overnight to London, Stein and Destri poke through the wreckage of plastic cups, cigarette butts and discarded shoes, looking to see if anything of value has been left behind by the beer-sodden punters. "This is what it's all about," says Destri with evident emotion, surveying the mountain of litter in the deserted post-show ballroom. "I don't ever want to lose this."

"Hey! I found a lighter!" calls Stein, oblivious to his bandmate's epiphany. Somewhere between the two discoveries, between the trivial and profound, lies the secret heart of rock's uncanny ability to rejuvenate both itself and its true practitioners. For now, for Blondie, the promise of that rejuvenation is enough.

"The Blonde Leading the Blonde"

by Everett True

Melody Maker *(London), May 22, 1999*

Revised version of original interview (and sidebars) published in Melody Maker*, in which Nina Persson of the Cardigans and Deborah Harry compare notes—musical and otherwise—and whose careers and music seem to run along* Parallel Lines.*—Ed.*

What could be better than a decade-defining blonde pop icon? Erm, how about two of 'em? We introduce THE CARDIGANS' Nina Persson to her Seventies prototype, BLONDIE's Debbie Harry, to find out whether blondes really do have more fun.

ONE NIGHT in Seattle a few months back, loaded up on free beer and whisky and whatever, we wandered along to the King Cat Theatre to see those sweet, unassuming Swedish pop stars The Cardigans play. Nina's got a lovely disaffected, cooing voice, yes, but she's not exactly the most striking of rock presences onstage. Or so we thought!

Hours later, drunk beyond all reason, we are phoning England hurling abuse and general profanity down the phone at their PR (who we had also erroneously accused of ignoring our phone calls): "What the fuck do you mean, not putting us on the fucking guest list? Oh, not fucking important enough any more, are we? Scared we'll slag off your precious fucking wanker pop stars, are we? Well, her band's still shit, but you fucking never told us Nina has turned into Debbie Harry, did you?"

And so she had. The cool Sixties Mary Quant-style pop art dresses were a thing of the past. Ms. Persson had become a leather-clad rock vixen extraordinaire, neon light billowing through her hair, tight trousers fueling our fantasies.

What happened?

THE similarities between The Cardigans and Blondie are striking.

Both are guitar-led bands of four blokes, fronted by ice-cool blondes—teenage pinups both, neither adverse to wearing the odd garment of leather and rockin' out. Both groups' best-known singles were despised by their "real" fans, almost for the same reasons (Blondie's ubiquitous 1981 hit "Heart Of Glass"; The Cardigans' 1997 smash "Lovefool")—they both have a techno edge. Both bands are connected with films (Debbie Harry starred in several Eighties movies, including John Waters' "Hairspray" and the futuristic "Videodrome"; The Cardigans shot to worldwide fame after "Lovefool" was featured on the soundtrack to the DiCaprio movie "Romeo And Juliet"). Both acts have aspirations towards their marvelously light-of-touch pop music not being disposable, towards it being "art." And both acts went slightly off-the-boil after their third album.

Only one, however, has had a Number One hit in the Nineties. Which?

Step forward, Debbie Harry and Blondie.

THE scene down at the N1 photo studio is sheer pandemonium. Wasn't this meant to be a "Melody Maker introduces Seventies blonde pop icon Debbie Harry to Nineties blonde pop icon Nina Persson" scenario? So who are the other 30 or so people here? It's more like fucking King's Cross station than a King's Cross studio: all the assorted designers and assistant designers, personal managers, partners, PRs, hair stylists, make-up artists! To add to the general confusion and merriment, Debbie's band have shown up mob-handed ("Blondie is a band", as the old slogan went) and a tape player blasts out old punk '77 hits, including Blondie's seminal Sixties girl-group cover "Denis"—a song which still excites considerable controversy among the group themselves. Oops.

Nina seems remarkably unfazed by all the chaos. She sidles off to a tiny room, and starts doing her own make-up (very little required, actually). Debbie Harry is—scary. Her face looks identical to the way it did 20 years back when she was on our TV screens with her platinum blonde hair and blue disco dress, cruising her way through Number One after Number One after Number One ("Heart of Glass", the reggae-fied "The Tide is High", the peerless "Atomic," the ground breaking "Rapture" and "Call Me"). Her figure—well, let's be polite and say that neither white nor a bleedin' bum bag round the waist does much to flatter. Her little bobby-socks and schoolgirl shoes look rather incongruous, too.

Still. The singer of the first band to have UK Number Ones in the Seventies, Eighties and Nineties (This year's comeback single, the soaraway "Maria," could've been an outtake from their second album "Plastic Letters") looks damn fine for her age (53).

The photographer asks if I wouldn't mind taking the boys in the band down to the pub for a swift half to clear some space in the studio: so I do, and Clem and Jimmy and Chris leap at the chance to drop the "serious" interview stance and lie on cue when prompted (see below). The downside of such conviviality, however, is that I have far too much to drink for so early in the day and spend the majority of the time given over to the interview with the two blonde icons needing the toilet. Imagine! I'm sitting in the same damn room as Debbie Harry, my saviour of many a lonely teenage night, and all I can think about is that I'm dying for a piss. Maybe it's nerves. Yeah, that must be it!

Time to bring the two singers together for a chat.

IS there any difference between being a pop star in the late Nineties and in the late Seventies?

Debbie: "It's become so refined nowadays. There are so many more manufactured groups, like the Spice Girls, Boyzone, 'N Sync and All Saints."

Wasn't it the same in the Seventies, with disco?

Debbie: "It didn't seem quite the same."

Nina: They're not our colleagues. Their managers tell them exactly what to do. They don't work in the same way."

You have control over what you do?

Nina: "Yeah. I think so. The reasons why you do it are different. The boy bands are much more about entertainment, promotion—not music."

But you don't have too much control, right? I remember the first, highly controversial, Blondie marketing campaign—posters which read "Wouldn't you like to rip her to shreds?" underneath a picture of a scantily clad Debbie Harry. You must feel manipulated sometimes.

Debbie: "At times. Fortunately, we always had a voice in our material. It makes all the difference. There's nothing like writing songs for yourself. The bands in the old days were counter-culture. Now the music's been absorbed. Everything is a prime target for advertising."

Do you find the way film soundtracks appropriate songs, especially older songs which have attendant personal memories, distasteful? Once they're absorbed, the memories cease to be as personal, and thus another small part of life has been homogenised. "Lovefool" is a good example of what I'm talking about. And, of course, that bleedin' Ford Fiesta ad with that bleedin' riff from "My Favourite Game." Do you feel the way those songs were used altered their original meanings?

Nina: "No. It's just another excuse to make compilations. Sometimes, though, people will tell you of an awful movie that used your music, and you didn't know! That's bad."

Isn't that record company manipulation?

Debbie: "It's more a merchandising thing, using the catalogue to their advantage. It doesn't have much to do with artistic interpretation."

You both have the problem with people saying Blondie when they mean Debbie Harry, etc. Is that irritating?

Nina: "It was, until I realised there was no point fighting it. That's just the mentality of the business. We did spend our first three or four years fighting it. It did help us a lot, though. We gained from that, because people learnt to accept us as a band. Also, you get more comfortable with your role in the band."

Debbie: "It was kind of abusive years ago. It's hard from a personal point of view, because everyone feels they're being ignored and overlooked, and everyone gets anxious about their positions and careers. It's a scary thing. And I actually had a manager early on who tried to separate me from the band, telling me 'you don't need those guys', and he told them continually that they could be replaced. It wasn't true. To plant that seed into teenagers like Gary and Clem's minds was a totally life-threatening thing to do. It did create a lot of problems. Now, everyone's very assured of their identities. It's human nature to be insecure. This is a scary competitive business we're in, and you work so hard to put yourself into your work and to have someone just ignore you..."

'She doesn't need any tips on how to be a pop star from me...She's cool enough already'
—*Debbie on Nina*

IN conversation, neither lady is eager to give much away.

Debbie, of course, is an old pro at this—she seems much more eager to stress the business side of the music industry, having been burnt through bad contracts in the past. One of the reasons behind Blondie's reformation was clearly Debbie's tax debt. Nina, speaking in her second language, has always been naturally reserved: the antithesis of the atypical rock chick in many ways. (Why, then, the leather trousers?) It's time to try and steer the conversation towards the music.

There are certain surface similarities between your two bands. Do they run any deeper than that?

Nina: "Music-wise, both bands have a huge variety of moods. There's not one particular Blondie song. We have that, too."

Debbie: "That's because we're such an urban-influenced band."

Your backgrounds are very different. You come from a small village, Nina...

Nina: "Yeah, although it's a big town by Swedish standards. Everybody knew each other, so we had no choice but to form a band."

Debbie, you were very much part of...sorry, I was just about to put words in your mouth...

"OK."

...of a musical movement. Did you feel part of one?

Debbie: "We had a tremendous feeling for coming out of this small whole anti-social group in New York, and we weren't considered viable to the industry at the time. We were all signed with absolutely scoldingly disgusting record deals. They were meaningless in terms of making money, and for any of us to come out of that and sell millions of records is just a phenomenon. That's the truth of it."

Do you wish that maybe you'd come out of something like that, Nina?

Nina: "I feel very much I do, that I came out of the Swedish scene, all the bands we hung out with—the fact that Sweden is so big on exporting music, and, apart from ABBA and Ace Of Base and Roxette and all that, there's such a great scene, so much interest in music, completely comparable to both the American and English, in terms of how they adapt trends and make something which is not false. I totally feel part of that. On tour, of course, we've bought Soundtracks Of Our Lives and Kent along with us, among other Swedish bands. They totally make us feel like we're on an excursion."

It seems like with The Cardigans it would've been a process of discovery incorporating all the different styles of music, whereas with Blondie the influences were already present in their bohemian surroundings—even if they did start off by playing a very specific form of (guitar-led pop) music.

Debbie: "On those early records we tried to include different feels, like Latin influences, but we didn't pull it off very well. It came off sounding very crunchy, three instruments—but then when we transferred over to the keyboards and synthesizers, that locked it in better. It was also down to experience. At first Clem [Burke, drummer] didn't like reggae, and it would sound like shit."

That's one style The Cardigans definitely haven't tackled.

Nina: "No! That's an area we don't touch at all. That'd be hard, we don't have the strong rhythm section."

Debbie: "We did actually break some ground. We blended different elements that really up until then hadn't been considered as legitimate. We really did get a lot of criticism for 'Heart Of Glass'."

We didn't care in England.

"In the States we got really heavily mauled," replies Debbie. "It's a totally different world over here."

" 'Lovefool' was like our 'Heart Of Glass'," sympathises Nina. "To most people who watch MTV, we were instantly connected with that song, despite our previous three albums. Wasn't it the same with 'Heart Of Glass'?"

"Yeah, definitely," says Debbie. "And it was criticised because it had a techno underbelly, same as 'Lovefool'."

DEBBIE Harry's influence on other female singers is well documented.

At a time when females were definitely the exception in the music business, Debbie—with her sophisticated sexuality, her pout, her rock chick persona, the way she made it OK for girls to be smart blondes—was a revelation. She pioneered rap. She hung out with Andy Warhol and William S. Burroughs and all those seedy literary types back when it wasn't so acceptable to do so. She came from the NYC CBGB's art-punk scene—Ramones, Television, New York Dolls, et al. She was a punk in the pop context.

And that hair! *That* hair! Glistening, strawberry-blonde, always backlit with the light streaming through it, fluffed up and just a fraction mussed, always perfect. While Debbie Harry reigned, there weren't any fucking supermodels (an Eighties invention), there were no film stars to gawp over. She was the only star in the world.

She was the perfect positive Seventies female icon.

Is there an equivalent nowadays? Before we have a chance to discuss Blondie's Nineties contenders, talk turns to Blondie's old Seventies contemporaries, ABBA (also currently topping the charts).

During the photo shoot, the Blondie lads were discussing "Swedish sexuality" and debating whether the ABBA girls were sexy. From there, it was only a matter of time before they compared Nina to Agnetha [Faltskog] from ABBA, so Debbie brings up the subject.

Nina: "ABBA were like the bands we talked about before [Spice Girls, Boyzone, etc]. I met the guys, and they admitted it was very calculated. Björn [Ulvaeus] just couldn't understand why we wanted to tour. I tried to explain that was to help the music develop. ABBA was more about the hit-making, not the lifestyle."

Debbie: "Yeah, they were more of a showbiz entity. They had no position of street credibility."

Is that important?

Debbie: "It depends on the person. Nowadays, there seems to be a huge market for entertainment, glitzy stuff and also—What do they call it now—the alternative mentality. That mentality is essential for me. I appreciate good songs, but I must have emotional investment, too."

Let me run a few other names past you...

Nina: "We might not even know them."

Saffron from Republica.

Debbie looks blank.

Nina: "I don't really know."

Who's the new Debbie Harry, then?

Nina: "There's no one."

Debbie: "Yes, me! I'm the new one."

Is there anybody out there who's doing what you did 20 years ago?

Debbie: "Gee, I don't know. It's so hard to keep track of everything. I sometimes see vestiges of me. Everyone has a different slant on what they do. I see some of my funkiness in what Courtney [Love] does. I met her years ago, before she was Courtney. She's a rock kind of girl."

She doesn't exactly have your pop sensibility.

Debbie "No, it's totally different—but early Blondie was very rough, before we had Jimmy [Destri, keyboard player]. It was all guitar."

Nina: "It's a weird question. There's loads of great female artists in bands...maybe Catatonia? Cerys [Matthews] is amazing."

Oh yeah. She's a star.

Nina: "Yeah, a total sweetheart—and good for England, too (*Wales, actually*—Ed), because you've been stuck with all these pop/rock bands fronted by boring blokes. It's super-refreshing to see her."

Debbie: "I met her at the *Q* awards. Very dynamic."

Shirley Manson?

Nina: "Maybe not as much in-your-face, but definitely her too."

The Spice Girls?

Debbie: "The sales pitch around them is annoying. They have some strong opinions but it's not coming from within them. It's something that's applied. It's a veneer. Their material all leans on their merchandise persona. It's calculated. There's nothing that takes you by surprise."

Their live show is great—so was the film.

Debbie: "Yeah, it's a different entity. The film was very good."

Nina: "I loved the film. I love it when the Monkees and The Beatles play themselves."

255

Are you going to go into movies, Nina?

Nina: "I don't think so. There are too many people doing it better than I could."

Debbie: "I always did movies. I did movies before I did bands. When I was a little girl, I always said I wanted to be a movie star, but then I gravitated towards the East Village music scene which seemed much more available to me. I've been lucky that I've got some very interesting connections. Not commercial directors, very individual, stylised directors. I don't know if I fit into the film industry as an individual. At this stage of the game, I've become too much of a personality to go out and get parts. People perceive me in a certain way."

How?

Debbie: "It's hard to be that objective."

How does Nina perceive the Blondie icon?

"Shall I leave?" quips Debbie, in mock horror at what her youthful counterpart is about to say. "Yes, I'll leave!"

"What can I say?" smiles Nina. "All I know is what I've been reading and seen on TV. Obviously, Blondie was a very visually strong band. Good style has always been connected with Blondie and Debbie. Street cred aware, too. I'd like to be perceived as both things myself."

'She's an excellent singer and also an excellent example of a front figure for a band'
—*Nina on Debbie*

DID you feel that the sexual side of Blondie got pushed to the detriment of the music?

Debbie: "Er, obviously there was a lot of push on the cute aspect, the sex aspect, but I don't think audiences would have gone for that and that alone. We had things that were relevant to a lot of people, especially girls during that period probably. Marketing, it was a good flashpoint."

Do The Cardigans get pushed in that way?

Nina: "Not pushed. In the context of our band, we're five completely sexless people together. Also, it's just weird if you've never particularly considered yourself interesting or sexy at all. It's just a media thing. It's just fortunate to be part of that phenomenon."

Debbie: "There we go. It's the way of the world."

Nina: "Again, like the way women in bands get put in the front, that's a syndrome of the business—yeah, you're cute, and the world is still a little bit shocked even these days if you're a woman making music. Also, most of the bands we grew up with did not have a girl in the band, so it's a good gimmick to have, it separates us from the rest. It's just strange to see people reacting to it, because we feel so sexless."

Is there any advice you'd offer, in terms of the experience you've had, on what not to do as a pop star?

"She doesn't need any tips on how to be a pop star from me," says Debbie, protectively. "No one needs to tell her how to be cool. She's cool enough already. But if I had to say something, it'd be the obvious things: make sure your contracts are not full of surprises. Get good legal advice. Also, you should be educated about what management's supposed to do for you, and have a good rapport with your agent. Don't be pushed into anything, and retain control over your energy and your image, and your music."

Nina: "I was just shown these full figure cut-outs of only me, of course, and I had no idea about them. No, I wasn't asked, but it's always a good thing to ask after they've done it..."

Debbie: "Yeah. That happens all the time."

Nina: "And then it sounds like they were cautious about my opinion, but of course they weren't really."

Are you loaded?

Debbie: "Definitely not. I've actually been paying a huge tax debt which has grown and multiplied for 15 years. That's been my personal private nightmare."

Is that part of the reason Blondie are back again?

Debbie: "It is and it isn't. It is a business, and we're older and we know we can make some money from doing it—obviously that's a very attractive thing. Let's make some money, yeah! But we couldn't have done it if we had not come to some creative level of understanding. There was a lot of bad blood we had to flush out and take care of. It's a great idea!"

Nina: "Was it more fun last time you did it?"

Debbie: "Actually, no. The playing is much more fun this time. We had so many business problems back then. It was very frightening, and so problematic. Also, we were coming into the business and thinking we had some sort of obligation to act like a rock band, instead of behaving like musicians in the music business, which is our perspective now. We know how to be a band now. It's sort of like being with a bunch of brothers and sisters. Now, it's like being in a dyslexic, dysfunctional family. We don't have to think about it, it just happens."

One final question: can you see yourself following Debbie's blueprint to the extent where you're reforming The Cardigans in 2019?

Nina: "Because of how we work—the way we hang out together all the time and are each other's best friends—it could be super-cool, real fun. Just as long as we feel we could do it in a good way, because there's also many examples of bands who do things just because they have the name, so the option is there...and then the music they come out with is super-shitty. "11 of us come from academic families, so we still get asked, 'When are you getting a proper job?' by our parents. We still have to try to convince them that this is a proper job, that it's not all about shooting heroin and shagging rock stars..."

I'm sure I see Debbie wince at this point.

"...So if I don't submit to pressure and become a nurse, then yeah, we probably will."

NINA has one final thing to say to the journalist.
Nina: "We're betting the headline is 'Blonde On Blonde,' people have bet me a thousand pounds."
Debbie: "God, I hope not. It's been done so often already."

MY FAVORITE DAME: NINA ON DEBBIE'S INFLUENCE

WHAT DOES BLONDIE MEAN TO YOU?

Nina: It's a great band. That's one band I've been listening to for a big part of my life, even though when I was younger I was into their look more than their music. It was around 1980, when I was very young, so I remember the picture, the image more.

DID YOU EVER WANT TO BE DEBBIE HARRY?

Nina: I think she's an excellent singer and also an excellent example of a front figure for a band. It's like the exact same set-up as we're doing now, so I can relate to that, but I've never had that relation to music, that I wanted to take after someone else. They've been around forever—they never really quit, did they?

YEAH. IT HAPPENED ABOUT 1984, AFTER "THE HUNTER GETS CAPTURED BY THE GAME". THEY REFORMED IN THE LAST COUPLE OF YEARS.

Nina: So it is a reformation.

DID YOU EVER HAVE ANY PARTICULAR FAVOURITE SONGS?

Nina: Not really. I wasn't into it that much. I knew "Heart Of Glass," not very much more. It was more recently I started listening to their albums. *Parallel Lines*, that's a good one. She was older than me when Blondie started, wasn't she—in her late twenties?

YES. AND AT THE TIME IT SEEMED A LOT MORE IMPORTANT, BECAUSE OF PUNK.

Nina: It's not really that important, but in our case we've always been terribly young. Maybe we still are.

WHICH OF HER IMAGES DID YOU LIKE THE BEST?

Nina: When I first started seeing her records, it was during the "Hunter" period—a style which maybe wasn't her best, with the lion hair. But on those first few albums, Debbie looked stunning. Especially the *Eat To The Beat* cover. *Parallel Lines* is a great record as well.

DO YOU FEEL LIKE THE CARDIGANS ARE THE HEIRS TO THE BLONDIE THRONE?

Nina: No, not at all. We're two completely different things. Why, just because we're both blonde women? It's a different time and a different business...so who took after The Beatles then because they're boys?

OASIS, OBVIOUSLY.

BLONDIE AMBITION: BLONDIE ON BEING NUMBER ONE AGAIN

SO TELL ME HOW IT ALL STARTED: YOU CAN LIE IF YOU WANT.

CLEM BURKE (drums): We can lie? Well, all right!

JIMMY DESTRI (keyboards): For me, it all started when James Brown punched me in the chest. I was a little kid, fetching some tea and donuts from the corner store when James punches me. He goes, "Huh! I thought you were the kid who stole my wallet!" Uncle James! He soon put me to work cleaning his classic car collection. That's what gave me the bug—these old jazz guys doing rock'n'roll licks for the money at the Peppermint Lounge—that was my epiphany when I was 11, 12 years old. It happened to Clem [Burke, drums] the same time, when he was 10—Chris [Stein, guitar] and Debbie, too. Debbie once wrote a song called "English Boys," where she clearly stated that.

SO HOW DOES IT FEEL, RETURNING AFTER ALL THIS TIME?

CLEM: It feels like we've been in a cryogenic capsule, preserved, and it's happening all over again. We've just been playing some bullrings in Spain with Bryan Adams, and we've become allergic to bullshit. We almost did them on the fly—we were on the verge of lip-synching, and got thrust into it. We're Number One in Spain with "Maria" right now, so the crowds were crazy.

JIMMY: The real reason for [this] US tour is as a pre-tour to the main summer amphitheater tour. We're doing the Radio City tour right now, as "Maria" has just cracked Top 40. America is frustrating to artists who are used to success in Europe, because it just takes so long.

(JIMMY TALKS LIKE A MARKETING GUY FOR A WHILE.)

JD: Sorry to talk like a marketing guy, but it's been drilled into me.

CB: We've said this before, but we still think of ourselves as an underground band in the States, despite the fact we've had four Number One singles. America is our meat and gravy.

JD: Going to Mississippi and Alabama is more of a shock than going to fucking Thailand. That's a real foreign country. Clem likes it for some reason, I don't know—he's a masochist.

CB: I like the blues, the Delta, the romance and all that. Elvis's birthplace is in Tupelo.

JD: But they all want to kill you, man.

DID YOU EXPECT TO COME BACK WITH A NUMBER ONE IN THE UK?

JD: That's a loaded question. We didn't expect anything, so everything is pleasing.

CB: The roots were put down here in the UK in the Seventies are sustaining us right now. I like it when magazines give us Most Inspirational Awards, because the music scene here has influenced us so much.

AT ANY GIVEN TIME, THE MUSIC SCENE IS A BUNCH OF SHIT. DON'T YOU FEEL GUILTY ABOUT INFLUENCING A BUNCH OF SHIT?

CB: The music business is a load of shit, but there are a lot of kids out there with a lot of big dreams, and that's what fuels the music industry. The new XTC record is good. The new Blur record is good.

JD: There are redeeming qualities to any entertainment. It takes your mind away from fucking Bosnia. It's not supposed to be substantial. It's meant to be a diversion. That's the substance.

MORE BULLSHIT, PLEASE.

JD: ...So James adopted me for a while, took me into his home, set me onto washing his cars. Then I got a real job. Then I met these guys.

CHRIS STEIN (guitar): Then he stopped taking hallucinogenic drugs.

WHAT ARE THE DIFFERENCES BETWEEN NOW AND THEN, APART FROM THE FACT YOU'RE ALL 20 YEARS OLDER?

CHRIS: That's about it.

JD: It's basically the same shit. It takes you a little longer to get up in the morning. It takes you a little longer to fall asleep at night. You get up and you pee more.

CB: That whole credibility thing factor that exists now wouldn't have happened if we'd stuck together for 17 years and made fools of ourselves. We'd have been the Rolling Stones. There's a little curiosity about the whole thing. Our fans at concerts tell us it's like having their album covers come to life.

JD: Well-dressed raisins, that's the Stones. Debbie has taken what she used to do, focused it and taken it up a notch. Just using her eyes alone she can relate to the whole audience, and her movements are so much more broader and her voice is more subtle.

CB: It's an evolution.

JD: And the bathroom is closer to the stage, because we have to pee all the time.

ARE YOU ALL TAX EXILES?

JD: Victims, not exiles. No Swiss bank accounts.

WHY REFORM?

CS: To pay taxes. It's the Willie Nelson syndrome.

JD: Because we needed a little confusion in our lives, a little chaos, a little disorder—and to try and have some fun.

CB: And Chris has been quoted as saying he didn't want to feel this was something he could'a did, and in 10 years time regret not doing it.

CS: Now I know for a fact this is something I could've not done, easily.

CB: You think so? You hate doing this?

CS: It's getting to me. The worst thing is talking about yourself and analysing yourself constantly. Spending hours in self-analysis gets very annoying. The worst part is feeling like a salesman, feeling like you're in advertising when you want to feel like an artist.

CB: That's always existed in Blondie: art versus commerce. All Andy Warhol did was bring the two together and call it art while making money. A lot of things we did look calculated—"Rapture," "Heart Of Glass"—we were just trying to take a chance, do things that were the antithesis of us. But people now think we were being cynical because many of the chances we took then have become commonplace, whereas it was Chris' vision at the time. There's that paradox that exists in Blondie: art versus commerce. I just think of us as a bubblegum band.

THEY'VE JUST REISSUED ALL NINE ABBA ALBUMS IN THE US. WHY WAS IT THAT THEY WERE CRITICALLY REVILED WHILE BLONDIE WERE LOVED?

CS: ABBA wasn't involved in any kind of sexuality, or sexual stance.

CB: The girls were sexy.

JD: Not like Debbie.

CB: They wore tight pants and you could see their...

JD: No, they were so fucking wholesome.

CS: They were so fucking Doris Day.

CB: There's a Swedish sexuality to ABBA.

CS: You're crazy.

JD: They were sterile—not like Debbie, going on stage and pulling off a wedding dress to reveal slinky leather. That was a whole different thing. And the lyrics!

CB: One of the greatest concerts I ever saw was ABBA at Radio City Music Hall. It's all in the songs. The reason we're here today is because the songs have endured.

(ends)

"With Live Album and Plum New Year's Gig, Deborah Harry Embodies Blondie Once More"

by Deborah Wilker

Knight Ridder/Tribune News Service, *December 2, 1999*

Touring again and how it is different this time around, the difficulty of classifying Blondie musically, the Blondie Live *album, Kurt Cobain, Madonna, and survival in the music business.*—Ed.

There is no entourage when Deborah Harry enters a room.

She is fresh off the bus after an 11-hour travel day that began three time zones and two plane rides away. She has come in through the loading dock of the Jackie Gleason Theater, sneaking through an unlocked door, carrying her own bag, a water bottle and a stack of papers.

The other members of Blondie, who reunited last year after 17 years apart, trickle in just as unobtrusively, followed by a road manager and a handful of technicians. There are no makeup people, hairdressers or publicists by her side, no one in her orbit at all.

It's a world away from the days 20 years ago when Harry defined New York's fanciful New Wave scene; when she was muse to Warhol and seductress of all Manhattan; when the fortunes of the city's nightclubs rose and fell on a mere appearance by her.

Though she is once again the undisputed centerpiece of Blondie, Harry is less a celebrity and more a workaday musician than she has ever been—performing earnest concerts, introducing her new music to radio programmers, taking her vitamins and trying to get as much rest as her schedule allows. A current tour has taken her all over the world this year, including a recent stop on Miami's South Beach, where she'll perform again New Year's Eve as part of a wide-ranging international spectacle to air on ABC, the BBC and other networks.

Among her many charms is the elegant, almost serene manner in which she presents herself offstage—a complete turnabout from the nightly hell-raising she orchestrates in concert. In person she projects instant warmth, much as she does when she's acting in films and on television. Her long-running side career as a character actress has included memorable TV guest shots and, more notably, dozens of movies, spanning the art-house landscape from Woody Allen's "New York Stories" to the helmet-haired mother in John Waters' "Hairspray."

Just before sound check, she settles in backstage to talk about this busy past year, a time of critical success, personal reflection and solid commercial returns. She makes it clear right off that Blondie did not reunite for the fame and fortune, but doing well sure is fun.

In fact, there were more reasons to stay apart than to get back together, but eventually her former partner and bandmate Chris Stein wore her down.

"I thought it was a stupid idea, that he was mad, completely off his rocker; that he had just...slipped a few gears," she says, circling an index finger in search of some imaginary brainwaves. "But little by little, he just sort of convinced me."

Chief among her worries was that a reconstituted Blondie could turn out to be a lazy cash-grab, a walk down the greatest-hits aisle with nothing new to offer.

"You know, I think it's fine to sort of go out there and bang that old gong. I don't think it would be fair not to play that stuff," she says of classic Blondie cuts such as "Call Me," "Dreaming," "Heart of Glass" and "The Tide Is High." "It's fun and it is very rewarding to have the fans loving it. But to make it real, it has to be current."

So with the promise that they would indeed create something new, Harry acquiesced, going back to Blondie with Stein, keyboardist Jimmy Destri and drummer Clem Burke. The band's early guitarist, Frank Infante, and bassist Nigel Harrison were not asked to return. (Harry won't discuss the uninvited players, both of whom initiated legal action when they learned they would not be included.)

She emphasizes that there was never any dispute with Stein, once her romantic partner and still her closest friend. The story of how she sidelined her own career for years during the 1980s to nurse him through a rare, debilitating disorder called pemphigus is well known to her fans.

Yet by 1987, with Stein's health restored, the romance foundered. Still, the two remained close, collaborating on her solo albums and various side projects, and rarely going a day without speaking. The two have always worked in something of a secret shorthand, a vibe that frames their current stage shows as well.

"Chris and I both always had that urge to be groundbreakers. We both came from conceptual places...to want to do things that are startling."

There are now two albums to show for Blondie's rebirth: the well-received 1999 studio set "No Exit," and the brand new "Blondie Live," a chronicle of this year on the road. The live set inevitably includes lots of familiar hits, and for that Harry does not apologize.

"We are proud of what we've done. They're really good songs. In some cases we've reworked them and rearranged them and brought them into a different time period."

She knows it's a different time in her own life as well. At 54, she doesn't kid herself about the Top 40 or Hollywood and what it means when time marches on in show biz. When she stopped making music temporarily in the 1980s, her acting career soared, placing her among the most sought-after faces in independent films. But the calls don't come as frequently these days.

"It's running away from me, but I'm after it," she says with a laugh. "I'm always pursuing it."

Nor is it quite as easy to get a song on pop radio. Despite its effervescent hook, making a hit out of "Maria," the first single from "No Exit," took a lot of work in a market dominated by teens. And though she agrees there is always room for a handful of veteran voices on the air (comebacks by fiftysomethings Santana and Cher come to mind), she says her band has another problem in that it's tough to classify.

"We created our own dilemma," she says of Blondie's penchant for dabbling in everything from rap to disco, reggae to rock, punk to pop. "In an age of specialization, we were always taking things and mushing them together."

Still, it's been a rewarding year, with plans already under way for another studio album. Gone, she says, are the jealous battles and rampant mismanagement that tore the band apart at its height during the early 1980s.

"You know, the guys were teen-agers, some of them, when we started. We had a difficult situation. I was the lead singer, I was the pretty girl, I had the blond hair and I got all the focus."

The attention left her guilt-ridden, on edge and full of anxiety.

"Now we all sort of know who we are and who each other is. It's more relaxing. More fun. Our ambitions are in a better place. There's no insecurity about having a position in the band."

"I can understand the tragedy of Kurt Cobain," she says of the rock superstar who committed suicide in 1994. "I know it personally. I look back and think 'My God.' I really admire kids today that have such massive success and can hold on.

"I am completely in awe of Madonna. She's able to take that success and live with it and remain sane. I say that with a smile, you know."

These days Harry has no struggle with her own sanity, enjoying side gigs as a sometime jazz singer and a contentment in the pop spotlight that eluded her years ago.

"I'm proud of it now. I'm very proud to be Blondie. And you know, I know that I AM Blondie."

"Flirty Harry"

by Stuart Turnbull

www.sleazenation.com *web site and* Sleazenation *magazine, March 2001*

Earthy interview with Deborah Harry, focusing on her acting career.—Ed.

Although Blondie are back in the studio, these days Debbie Harry is more into acting. You'll soon be seeing her in the new gay porn flick The Fluffer. We share a sofa with New York's Downtown Queen.

Debbie Harry's presence permeates pop eternally, sublimely, segueing a well-rooted-in-the-underground stance with the commercial demands of the brash pop zeitgeist. US universities run major courses that deconstruct the Madonna phenomenon while out in the real world the best cheekbones and lips in pop continue to house a sage-like grin that knows exactly where it's been and where it's going—namely anywhere that Harry can tickle people's preconceptions.

However, Harry, we have a problem with using the name 'Deborah' here. Our rational aversion to the full pronunciation of the moniker is on account of an unfortunate exposure to the 1970 T-Rex hit Deborah (not written with Harry in mind), on which Marc Bolan falsettos the misguided couplet, "Ooh, Deborah / You look like a Zebra." This combined with the fact she always was 'Debbie' in our mind's eye ushered a certain confusion when the machinations of a solo career and the independence driven decision to reclaim the full length of her own name caused 'Debbie' to go 'Deborah.' Out of respect for the lady, however, we shall here introduce her as Deborah Harry, a woman we encounter mid-morning one Thursday in New York City, while, down Britain's alleyways scores of teenagers can still be found strolling in Blondie T-shirts. 1978 style.

But it's 2001?

"Hey. Well, wow, that's great. That's good to know. Yeah." enthuses the woman whose iconic visage continues to be screen-printed onto cloth. What's she up to now though?

"I'm doing great and feeling really good these days. Knock wood." she laughs, heartily. "How you doin'?...We're working on a new record," explains the Sunday Girl. "So it'll be interesting to see how that goes. It's always nice to make music."

Music, as we know, is not the only fruit she yields. Acting provides another favourite platform.

"I recently did a Sarah Kane play, Crave, at the Axis in Greenwich Village, I had a wonderful theatre experience and am desperate, actually, to continue acting and doing more work in that area."

British playwright, Sarah Kane, shook the London stage with her studies of violence before committing suicide in hospital, aged 28, in 1999.

"The play was sort of Sarah Kane's brain talking to itself," explains Harry. "It was very open and very serious. Sometimes people don't want to think about frightening things like that in their lives, because it's maudlin, I guess...It was a real test."

Another of her latest dramatic forays is in the new gay porn flick, The Fluffer, co-directed by Wash West and Richard Glatzer. West describes the film as "A dark tale of obsession." Set in the porno underworld, the plot focuses on a bizarre love triangle at the centre of which is hetty Johnny Rebel, a swarthy beefcake-cum-gay-porn star [*played by Scott Gurney*—Ed.]. Harry herself plays the lesbian club-owner, Marcella. We ask her how it went.

"Fluffer? Fluffer. Oh my gawd!" she howls. "Yeah. The name is the best part of it. Terrific. Erm, West was great and very sweet to work with. My part is a foil for the main character. I haven't seen it yet so I don't know how I'm coming off...Marcella is a typical, tough, businesswoman who deals with a girl with a few problems, an uptight teen."

The Fluffer ethos states, "Fluffer salutes all people who have ever worked in the adult industry." The film claims to reach the places Boogie Nights couldn't. West himself has experience of directing porn movies having garnered the Adult Video News award for 'best sexual performance' with his 1998 wrap, Naked Highway, while he was invited to screen The Fluffer at this year's Berlin Film Festival.

What's Debbie's own stance on porn, living as she does amidst the fuck-flick maelstrom of the 50 States?

"Porn? I think it's a good thing. But I wish it was more plot-driven instead of cock-driven. I would personally find it more 'titillating' if I were 'sucked' in by the story," she emphasises, conspiratorially. "But, it's fine the way it is. A lot of people get a lot of enjoyment out of it."

When asked what's her favourite 'erotic movie,' she demurs somewhat.

"I don't really have any. I see them...I'm not really a collector of porn. I have a few, I mean I could go look at the titles, but I'm not really into quoting titles." That bad, eh?

Some pop stars (you all know who. Think of a certain well known crim-hag) attempt acting but fall flat on their face.

"Yeah. Actually I think I'm a better actor than a singer." asserts Debbie. "The reason the singing thing happened was because it combined that with performance value as well. I think I've got an average kinda voice."

A strong one, though. Not easily ignored.

"Yes. Annoying," she laughs, self deprecatingly. "A funny kinda voice. An annoying voice. A good punk voice."

A punk rascal's beautiful howl. Like at CBGBs when you used to carry the drum kits and all.

"Yes, of course. Yeah, we all did. Oh yes." Harry hoots mockingly before delivering a deep and serious cadence. "I've had to carry things...It was awful. Oh my God." she adds, chuckling wildly.

Debbie never had to attempt to be one-of-the-boys, because she was always the leader of the gang, without all the prima-donna-isms. Moving on to what a typical Harry day involves these days, sighing in the face of an ever-pressing schedule, she lists the Big Apple hustle.

"...Trying to organise different projects, get the record moving. Helping Chris [Stein] put his studio together, making phone calls, talking to my agent, trying to get him to send me things, looking for jobs, looking for work. The usual."

The usual often being unusual roles in off-the-wall cinematic trawls. As Marcella in The Fluffer, for instance. Was the part actually written for you? we suggest, a touch cheekily.

"No." She pahs, dismissing our glib typecasting. But hang on, club-owner Marcella was a one-time Playboy favourite and, likewise, Debbie has been linked to Hefner's harem. Well, the evening drinking scene anyway. And strictly no centre-spreads she points out, assertively.

"I was a Playboy Bunny in the club, a cocktail waitress, but that was nothing to do with the magazine."

Her only experiments in the sphere of ass'n'titties exhibitionism have been of the art-film variety, and achingly charged performances at that in, for example, David Cronenberg's Videodrome...Videodrome...an escalating reverie permeates Sleazenation's psyche. Videodrome was a strange animal n'est pas?

"Videodrome...Yeah. That was a good one."

Harry appeared on teenage walls worldwide, cocksucker-pouting through a plethora of Blondie posters whilst simultaneously submerged in warped sci-fi sadomasochism.

"You're right. I was."

"Debbie Harry's in this really weird sex film. Debbie leads another life. But we can't get into the cinema to see it." squawked legions of disaffected young thrill seekers when Cronenberg's drooling, labyrinthine plot hit cinemas in the early 1980s. The film was splendidly extreme, as Deborah concurs.

"Yeah. Hey. I got lucky you know," she laughs, repeatedly. "I got lucky." Now chuckling with wicked relish, her joy betraying her status in the New York underground. A woman with a predilection for joints populated by the shades-at-night set, she discusses her dark side bent.

"Well, I'm not interested in things that are terribly predictable. I find that my whole life has been a complete surprise. When you look at the whole thing it looks kinda par for the course in terms of what a showbiz career would be. But I do lean towards things that are a little frightening to me..."

As her dog breaks into a series of jabbing yaps, laughing perhaps at diabolic suggestions coursing through her canine mind. The dog's owner continues.

"...I really appreciate things that frighten and challenge me. I don't like obvious humour, I like absurd humour, satire, and that leads to a darker sensibility. At first glance Blondie looks very clear-headed and poppy and safe, but it does have an underbelly." she adds, larking saucily.

'Okay Debbie, let's tickle that underbelly' comes our offer.

"Yeah, Okay." she agrees with a coquettish whisper.

She's looking sharp and street-tough here in Terry Richardson's shoot, but at the time of speaking hadn't seen the images. Did the shoot with the mustached one go well? we ask.

"You never know 'til you see the pictures. Erm...we had fun, it was not painful, so that's a plus," she trills optimistically despite adding, "I mean it could become painful when I see the pictures, but I hope not."

But foul contact sheets hardly ever sully Deborah Harry, surely? we goof before she tersely corrects our descent into sycophancy.

"Oh yes it does. That would be insane."

Okay mistress, we're all dog rough on occasion but beautiful on the inside, except that your beauty crushed many a sap.

Moving onwards, why spoil the fun by mentioning a serial killer? Something that we do in raising the spectre of the sadistic campus-creeper, Ted Bundy, from whose car Debbie fled following a mistaken but brief hitch-hike. Her tone lowers to an irritated scowl, instantly bored by our sensationalist hacking.

"Yeah...Yeah I did get in his car. A long time ago," She drags the words out in a laboured, weary drawl. "I've talked about it many, many times so I think we'll sort of..." Forget it?

Always 'there,' 'on it,' wrapped in an edgy glamour (her more recent, packed-into-leather appearances on Top Of The Pops were scoffed at by some fascist cynics, but they can fuck off) one wonders exactly what sort of clothes madame feels most comfortable in at the moment?

"Mmm." she ponders, patiently sifting her thoughts before answering. "It just depends on the occasion and the mood that I'm in. Sometimes I love getting really dressed up but during the day when I'm running around the studio I just throw something on..."

Nothing fancy, then. Debbie has developed an altogether more casual ensemble. "Lately I've been wearing double pants, two pairs of pants. I think it looks great, a higher waisted pair and a lower waisted pair." Practical, with that familiar kooky edge; a tad terrace-hard, even; eminently functional yet beguiling. She explains this new sartorial bent.

"It works for the cold, but I think it also looks great. It's funky." she trills, delighted, before ushering a polite silence. She's a listener, see, all the while tuning her ear to our dulcet English. 'When are you happiest?' we ask. "Uhu. Aha. Mmm. Yeah. When I'm being creative, or tapping into things...Like when you're working really hard and you feel the satisfaction of achieving something. I guess I'm really achievement oriented. I'm looking forward to turning out some good lyrics for the new record. That's always a lot of fun."

Always one to pen a great love song, an epic appeal to passion, Blondie's, and Deborah's, finest work has been used worldwide by sexual tacticions, your scribe for one, making compilation tapes to woo potential shags. Pretty Baby (aah), employed to usher in the romance before Atomic provides the climax. Along the way, Heart Of Glass to make known your vulnerable side. Pretty Baby always made for a classic opener, though.

"Yeah that was a good one. Thank you. Oh, I hope it worked."

It did. She was a communist nymphomaniac...Enough of people though, what about Debbie's dog? "Yeah, I've got a dog. A Japanese one. A tiny dog."

Cute, but is Debbie a dog fancier with a penchant for dressing her pet in couture?

"No. Actually she really hates clothing. She does however own a luxurious double-fur coat, real short fine fur like a duck-down underneath with a long, coarser fur over it, but believe me she does 'not' want to wear anything and she really does not do well in hot weather. She's a cold weather dog. She hates putting on clothes and runs away."

Harry's naked ambition is evident in a back catalogue of fine product, but at home, coseted in her apartment, to what extent do her ambitions turn to interiors. Is she bothered?

"I guess. It's sort of eclectic and cluttered at this point which I would like to change. My new point of view involves a desire to simplify things. I'd like to strip down." she purrs, hanging on to the phrase.

Time to get dressed. Does she feel she's been an important influence on fashion? "At the time in the early 80s when I was working with Steven Sprouse. Yes, that was quite a strong statement. It was Steve Sprouse coupled with a very few ideas of mine combined with the theme of the band. I think it worked really well."

They're all at it now of course, bright young metropoles sashaying forth in Deb's mould. When the reformed Blondie most recently hit the UK the cats lapped it up, Glastonbury providing a lasting testimonial to their appeal. Just what is it about Brit kids that makes 'em dig her so?

"They're loyal and wonderful and great and enthusiastic. There's nothing to compare it to. Just superdooper...It's pretty obvious that if people are there to see you at this stage of the game that they really love you."

Strolling the Naked City, we ask if she ever gets mobbed on the New York City streets these days?

"Well. I've learned that I can have a certain amount of anonymity. I choose the times and places to go, y'know, and it works that way for me. Going out on the weekends is not really comfortable for me...But I'm certainly not as famous as some of the really big megastars. Then I would get mobbed."

We recall a vision of her walking across a fog-layered Wandsworth Common in the very late 80s as some tabloid twats gathered to pick her apart. She'd put on weight so they were circling. Harry recalls South London.

"When I was staying over in England doing my solo records [in Wandsworth] I got to go to some of the early rave things where you'd drive out to the suburbs to some closed up factory building, and that was great. Those were really fun nights." These rekindled thoughts of partytime London evidently tickle her fancy. "You should tell me what clubs to go to now cuz when I get over there I'll need to know. What's going on? What clubs are great? Somebody told me about someone named Avis? Axis? Access? A DJ who records and does off-the-wall parties."

He DJs with sandpaper discs, licks windows, drives a tank and wears a bra. He's the Aphex Twin. "Yes, that's him. Is he still happening? And the sandpaper discs, did it work?" she pipes, marvelling at the Cornish noisenik's invention. It seems Debbie admires the prolific, creative stance, one, she points out, that is borne out of inspiration and not the Protestant work ethic. "The fact that so many people just get together and make music is very British. I've not seen it happen that intensely in any other part of the world."

Whereas America, for good and bad, has always been Film Central. What cinematic experience gave her the most joy?

"I think I had the most fun doing Hairspray with the dancing and music and everything. The cast was so off-the-wall and that was great. Everyone worked so bloody hard that off-set they were falling asleep."

Finding that most of her roles are a healthy challenge she ponders her method. "The most important thing for me in acting is concentration and focus, being really available to what's going on to feel totally 'where I'm supposed to be.' It sounds mystical what I'm saying, but it's actually very practical. To know what would be predictable, but then to really 'not' be predictable—I sort of like doing two parts at once, hearing a voice inside questioning everything that I'm doing, saying the lines at the same time...I dunno, almost like some kind of schizophrenia. I'm relatively inexperienced as an actor, but recently when I was doing the Sarah Kane play I made a lot of discoveries and am desperate to do more acting. So get me a fucking job!"

Reeling from this loud plea we ask her 'Away from the studio and audience, what nocturnal delights butter your muffin?'

"I really enjoyed a club called Mother at Jackie 60. That's closed now so they do parties once a month at Don Hill's. I go down there and I do enjoy that."

We've heard you like to take off in your car.

"Not really. Cuz I'm a workaholic and I'm really into what I do. I feel really lucky about being an artist. When I wanna get away I get away, but it's not like I'm always taking road trips."

A mischievous snigger issues forth before she explains her determination.

"I knew all along that I wanted to do exactly what I decided to do and fought real hard to get there. Anybody who struggles to do something in an industry that's based on an artform...it's bloodcurdling.

"But of course now that I'm not a teenager anymore, I really appreciate it. I see people who are my contemporaries who aren't happy with what they're doing whereas I'm very challenged by what I do."

We ask if she's considered writing a play or screenplay as Debbie's wit burns dry as a stick.

"I don't know if I'm that creative a writer. But I really am a great actress. I'm kinda amazing," Cracking up before retaining her composure, Harry gets back into deadpan. "I don't usually say this about myself but I know that. I'm a great actor. It's really funny but I am."

And in what other ways has Deborah Harry surprised herself?

"Only on a personal level of sometimes being stupidly blind in situations. It surprises me that I could be so insensitive at some points of my life. So, I'm surprised by my own insensitivity."

As are we all on occasion. That said, does she also see herself as a caring person, giving love and feeling love, like?

"Oh, I don't know. I don't go around thinking about that. It's not really my inclination."

You've spread a lot of love around though.

"Yeah...I went to a funeral yesterday of a great poet, a beat poet, Gregory Corso. And you know, great poets, real poets, practically 'don't exist,' anymore. They don't take a place in society that's terrifically important anymore. Here was this incredible wordsmith that died and he struggled all his life, to be a poet, and I'm just getting over that. I feel that...Oh..."

Debbie's voice tails off as she falls into a contemplative silence before continuing.

"He was a good friend. I didn't see him an awful lot. But we had a sort of [adopts a deep, sultry tone], 'a chemistry,'" Laughing fondly, breaking from a temporary melancholy, she giggles, "Yeah...we had a chemistry." before pondering a big question.

"But you were saying about love...There's this song that Patti Smith sang at the service, Nature Boy, and the last line of the song is 'The greatest gift, you'll ever...give or get, is love. And love in return." She then repeats the phrase, faster now. "'The greatest gift you'll ever give or get is love. And love in return.' You know, she said it, that really is all you need to know."

Perked up by this positive sentiment, we ask what her new day will bring?

"I'm doing something for this hearing thing. This woman, she has a music foundation called Hearing Aid, The Hearing Aid Music Foundation, it's about people who develop hearing problems from listening to loud music, and so I'm gonna do a little filming for that," Now speaking with a sweet, sharp timbre she continues, "Then I'm gonna go down and do a little work at the studio, then I'm gonna wait and see what happens for...tonight." Thoughts of 'tonight' bring a wicked laugh, full of energised mischief.

In the midst of all this gallivanting does she manage to make time for the mundane necessities of life. Does she fetch her own grocery or has she abdicated? Our question triggers a bawdy belly laugh.

"No I haven't abdicated my grocery shopping just yet. No."

Deborah, are you a fine cook?

"I don't usually cook for myself, but I do like to cook for my dad sometimes. And some of my friends I cook for, the brave ones."

Do you cook for your dog?

"My dog? Yeah, right. She cooks for herself. She does her own thing." Just like her owner.

Harry's position as a star is a good one. Not so transient; something very real that has lasted and endured the foibles of a trend-driven pop scene.

"Yeah, there's something very luxurious in that." she concludes before signing off.

"Thanks Sleazenation. It's been nice talking to you."

A new Blondie album will be out later this year.

For information about the film The Fluffer, including release dates, see www.fluffer.com.

"Debbie Deserves the T-Shirt"

by Grace Bradberry

The Times *(London), March 2, 2001*

Deborah Harry's fashion legacy.—Ed.

Debbie Harry has been there and done that as a pop icon, and now, thanks to D&G at this week's Milan shows, she has the T-shirt to prove her enduring allure.

Who says fashion doesn't dictate to us any more? Without the industry's totalitarian resolve never to invent anything new, how many of us would willingly return to the Eighties? Unlike the Sixties, which no one who was really there can remember anyway, when the Eighties returns it comes in horribly lucid flashbacks of batwing sweaters and legwarmers.

But this week at the Milan fashion shows, D&G played a blinder, reaching back to a place we *can* bear to go—Debbie Harry. Last season, Domenico Dolce and Stefano Gabbana paid homage to Madonna, with ra-ra skirts and "I love Madonna" T-shirts. One imagines they were enthusiastically bought by the singer's entourage, but who, apart from the makers of music videos, can get truly excited about Madonna as a style icon? From the first *Like a Virgin* video, in which she drifted through Venice in a gondola, one was dimly aware of being taken for a different kind of ride. In any case, true icons must fade from public view for a while, and Madonna never has.

D&G's first catwalk giveaway was a diamantéé-studded "French Kiss by Debbie" T-shirt, then there was the see-through, skin-tight black T-shirt with the legend, "Debbie Debbie Debbie." Then along came the "Call Me Debbie" number with a picture of a mobile phone.

Actually, Debbie Harry hasn't called herself that for years. Now in her mid-fifties, she's upgraded to Deborah. But this is good, because it means that "Debbie" has never had to grow up. She is frozen there, back in the early Eighties, when style began and ended with the cover of Blondie's *Parallel Lines* album (actually released in 1978), all pouty glares and black and white cool. (In those pre-rap days, the word "hip" denoted a part of the body, and nothing more.) There are so many reasons why Debbie Harry is the perfect rock'n'roll girl that it's hard to know where to begin. It is easy to trot out a biography, but at the age of 11 I was not the least aware that the woman wearing a swimsuit on *Top of the Pops* was a cohort of Andy Warhol and had hung out on the New York punk scene with the Ramones and Iggy Pop. Nor did I realise that Debbie was a former *Playboy* Bunny. I was also blissfully unaware that my pocket money was mostly going to her record company, not to her—Debbie Harry was one of the last of that foolhardy troupe of rock stars who apparently signed recording contracts without consulting lawyers.

You didn't need to know any of this to "get" Debbie Harry. And you still don't. Before you understood the resonances of the word "broad," it was clear that she was one. Her New Jersey twang came through even when singing *Pretty Baby*. Her bravery with a bottle of bleach was nothing short of inspirational. Her skirts were short, but her accessories, particularly her shoes (ref those white wooden-heeled mules on the cover of *Parallel Lines*), looked as if they might do damage.

She appealed as much to boys as to girls. What they liked was all too obvious—the legs, the Slavic cheekbones, the bee-stung lips that were all the more exciting in a pre-collagen era. Long before the Spice Girls took the phrase and degraded it, Harry represented girl power. She dominated her band of dark, broody men, including Chris Stein, who was also her boyfriend. Earlier blondes such as Marianne Faithfull, however talented, could never shake off the groupie tag. Other female stars were too forbidding—Chrissie Hynde had the glare without the pout. Debbie Harry, on the other hand, was anti-Establishment, but very, very pretty. The odd thing is that she was actually in her thirties when all this was happening—the age that her core fans are now. She had moulded herself, quite intentionally, into a sort of punk Marilyn Monroe. She had a knowingness about her and was well aware that she was giving teens something more dangerous than pop.

Afterwards came disillusionment for Harry, but that passed us by, because we had moved on to other things. The life-threatening illness of Chris Stein passed us by. We were unaware that while the band sold 25 million records, they were unable to buy mansions in Malibu (not that they would have wanted to). If we were lucky we missed the pictures of Harry during what she calls her "ice-cream years," when she ballooned and became the victim of cruel caption writers. But the great thing for us was that she disappeared, re-emerging a couple of years ago as a post-punk Lauren Hutton to thrill us over again with the album *No Exit* and the No 1 hit *Maria*. Occasionally Harry has sounded slightly bitter about the huge success of Madonna, but her status as the ultimate style icon may be on the point of vindication in T-shirt sales.

"Blondie Ambition"

by Will Stokes

Revised extended version of an article entitled "Attitude Icons:
Will Stokes Dives Once More Into the Bleach With Blondie Bombshell Debbie Harry"
from Attitude *magazine, June 2001*

Just what makes Deborah Harry an icon? Read on to find out!—Ed.

The spirit of Blondie is preserved in several characteristic images or states of mind: the sheen of a shining red convertible on a summer's afternoon; the thrill of the day before your birthday; the pouting lip-glossed strut of a 14 year-old at her first school disco. Faded happy childhood memories. Perfect cumulus speckling an azure sky. Your first flinching kiss. Or even that split-second camera flash where, just for a moment, you are in the spotlight. Tonight, *your* hair is beautiful!

If the term "Girl Power" had been masterminded in the late 70s it would surely have been applied to Debbie Harry, vocalist of Blondie. She was more than any female performer before her: she signed, sealed and delivered the whole Riot Grrrl/Girl Power aesthetic years before even Madonna (let alone Geri Halliwell) had started ragging her hair, and shared a similarly rebellious attitude. It was something that she instinctively understood. "I tried to avoid the hackneyed rock poses and movements," she says, "along with the usual use-me-abuse-me attitude of most girl singers."

Feminism meets force with handbag in tow.

Indeed, the general visibility of female performers at the time was roughly limited to two camps: furrow-browed singer-songwriters whose impact was fixed to how far they could drag a guitar-case and hip-flask (Joni Mitchell, Janis Ian) or flailing divas stranded at high-tide from a decade previous (Tina Turner, Cher). Crucially, while each of these women has both talent and far-reaching influence in their own right, the majority was masterminded by men, however arch their intentions. Music as a big bucks industry has essentially always been founded and forged through patriarchy.

But no record company mogul could have formulated Debbie's pouting attitude, fashion forging or trademark harmonies. Debbie wasn't born through a careful marketing dichotomy or built overnight from a kit. Neither did the band—as a performing and songwriting unit, they remained resolutely uncommercial for their first two albums at least. That was part of the attraction. Abba might have been the same hot property on international charts, but only Blondie fulfilled the "they can do it, so can I" ideal.

Equal parts mirth, melody and mayhem, Blondie virtually defined the emergence of a new musical direction at the convergence of the 70s and 80s. Their unholy alliance of disco, power-pop, reggae and the first stirrings of white hip-hop (with 1981's "Rapture") was motored more by the aggression of punk and nightspots like the legendary CBGBs than clever marketing or the whim of the Top Ten mentality of most singles acts. Blondie was never about sell, sell, sell. It was the genuine love of the groove that fired Harry's imagination. When dismantling the band after a disastrous and half-hearted tour planned for Japan in 1983, Debbie cited her view that Blondie "wasn't changing as a group enough for my tastes" as the prime motivation for the move. It was all of these small and contrasting details—looks, attitude, musical prowess—that contributed to Blondie's popularity as *the* band of the era and Debbie's status as one of the few women in music to kick ass on a truly global scale.

Debbie was the magnetic yet accessible spearhead/spokeswoman for a new generation, and blew all competition from the water like a peroxide atomic bouncing bomb. Her alluring combination of sex and sanity was just one eye-catching feature of Blondie: a bunch of thrashy and trashy pop-punks who'd first thrown down their MOD roots in a strop, strutted into the hit parade as Debbie pulled on her thigh boots and stamped curtly over anything that got in their way. Even the Disco Sucks! movement was mowed down in the face of Harry's irony, as Blondie unleashed "Heart of Glass" and later "Atomic" on an ebullient world. Those boots really *were* made for walking.

It was the blurring and polarisation of musical genres that would make Blondie a considerable worldwide force as the new decade beckoned. Each new hit showcased both a different musical direction and a new look for Miss Harry, with Debbie initiating some memorably tongue-in-cheek performances in the early history of pre-MTV videos and striking cover shots. As "Denis" became the band's first Top Ten UK hit in 1978, Debbie twirled in front of your family in a slashed swimsuit, her only accessories being stiletto heels. Photo-shoots for singles like "Picture This" (with its image of a starkly made-up Debs with blonde hair scraped back and suggestively licking the rim of a 12" single) gave her the appearance of a stern dominatrix while proving that Harry was more than capable of playing the classic pouting vixen when it suited her. At other times, as on the sleeve for "Dreaming," she simply commanded respect, looking perfectly able to keep the trains running on schedule. In a khaki-green PVC storm-trooper outfit, complete with wrap-around shades, cherry lips resolutely unsmiling, the message was clear: "Look if you like. But look out."

Debbie's early history is the stuff of fairytale: the Cinderella factor was obvious to her appeal. Born in Florida in 1945, and given up for adoption into a middle-class family in the homey suburbs of New Jersey, Debbie was never exposed to a starry stage-school upbringing. Experience of being a normal part of society was instrumental in her being able to cope with fame and fortune when she eventually found success and stardom. Living in the real world, as it were. But her attitude to being part of this society, even when only on the dysfunctional outskirts of it, was uneasy. As a young teenager, she had a typically rebellious attitude to her upbringing. "I used to wear black all the time and pretend to be tough," she laughs. Debbie's musical career, as part of rock band The Tri-Angels and later in the baroque-folk ensemble Wind In The Willows, began as an escape route to the banal routine of mediocrity and the painful state of loneliness and isolation. "I kept thinking about Janis Joplin and Billie Holiday and the blues. All the sadness and tragedy just kept going through my head." But despite the therapeutic qualities of blues and jazz, singing them wasn't her calling. The late 60s was a depressing time for Debbie, who said "I was upset most of the time," a problem compounded by a drug habit. "I had the weight of the world on my shoulders when I was younger, and I was very unsure, out of touch and half of what I should have been."

But coming to downtown New York gave her fragile confidence. She hung out with the hip Warhol glitterati at trendy venue Max's, and briefly worked as a Playboy Bunny. It was a veritable see-and-be-seen era. Debbie concocted a look "semi-exotic enough for an interesting evening," exuding confidence, intelligence and spontaneity. But behind the glossy exterior, Debbie was often unsure of herself. "I didn't know who I was, and often couldn't talk." But this insecurity led to her arming herself with an attractive array of armour. She instantly recognised the importance of sex as a weapon, and came up with the legend Blondie herself after being repeatedly asked by overweight truckers, "Come on blondie, give us a screw..."

But even then, Debbie knew that neither sound nor style could carry a band far without the other. "I wanted a combination of the aggressive Shangri-Las' rock and the round, solid vocals of an R&B girl group," she said, "and the overall idea was to be both entertaining and danceable." But The Stilettos, an early incarnation of Blondie, only began to receive press attention when Debbie motioned to turn the group into a thrift store on-stage explosion. And so Debbie later manipulated the contradictions of the bombshell/waif look and attitude as she formed Blondie with partner Chris Stein. "I had a black Morticia dress, a gold day-glo cross, gold lamé dresses, stupid wigs, a goldfish bowl with a goldfish in it called Mr. Jaws. I was developing the Blondie character. She wasn't quite there yet, but she was on her way." The humour that would manifest itself in her work was beginning to gel.

It was the dynamics of the Blondie persona in all its different traits—punkette, babe, little-girl-lost, trampy street urchin—that became the notable fuelling of their initial success, but Debbie was a pin-up who had the balls to match the boys. While millions of lusty schoolboys wanted to be with her (perhaps ironic in itself as Debbie was 33 even before Blondie scored their first hit) just as many girls simply wanted to *be* her, her inspiring mix of sex and sass proving irresistible. Her skin gleamed with the unmistakable neon glow of all the limelight absorbed, and though she was blonde, she was certainly not deaf nor dumb. Blondie, with Debbie as it's sharpened spearhead, steamrollered the late 70s chart detritus with self-penned pop missiles "Heart of Glass," "Atomic" and "Call Me," and cherry-picking from long-forgotten would-be classics like "Denis," "Hanging on the Telephone" and "The Tide Is High." It was the entertainment factor that Debbie was most concerned with. "Have a good time," was her motto, "and be happy." As Blondie shimmered on the collective global beat box, the world hummed back their happy confirmation.

Debbie was already the most famous blonde since Marilyn Monroe. Everyone knew who this cartoonish child-woman was—she landed like a hyper-cool New York space alien at an Our Price store in London in 1979, creating the kind of mass hysteria that was previously observed for The Beatles in the UK. Kate Bush aside, beautiful women who could do more than throw vacant glamour poses were few and far between. But Debbie had morphed into the comic yet sexy Blondie character so convincingly that on the eve of the release of their fourth album *Eat to the Beat*, pin badges were handed out with the slogan "Blondie Is A Group!" just to remind people that its vocalist was only one cog in a larger machine. But sparking this much attention, perhaps it's no wonder that Madonna, Debbie's successor to the title Miss America two decades ago, has borrowed heavily from both Debbie's relentless iconic posturing and trashy yet inspiring fashion ideal. In a recent spread in the US magazine *Style* dedicated to Harry, Mrs. Ritchie gleefully pushed the pleated skirts, skinny ties and straightened peroxide locks to the max, calling Debbie "a brilliant woman" and citing her as being among her biggest influence. "I never saw her perform live with Blondie," concluded Madonna in one interview. "I wish I did."

After Blondie inevitably imploded in 1982, like an atomic bomb set on an egg timer, Debbie outlined the reasons for the split, making clear that music was the answer to both her happiness and misery. "We got tired of the narrowness and limitations of what we were allowed to do, and what we couldn't do, imposed by expectations of past performances." It wasn't the money, or band bust-ups or drugs or suicide or sex. Just like the world expected, it was down to the grooves on those well-worn 45s.

Post-peroxide, Debbie continued to build upon the legacy of the previous decade. At times she played on the sex kitten image (hit single "French Kissing in the USA" sounds erotic even now) while at other times deliberately overplaying her playful siren reputation (the pouting "I Want That Man" and its tongue-in-cheek parent album *Def, Dumb and Blonde*) or eschewing the hackneyed iconic pose with disconcerting violence (debut solo shot, 1981's Chic-produced *Koo Koo*, featured a controversial sleeve by H.R Giger, where Debbie is pictured skewered by four metal pins through her head). Her iconic image remained crucial to her influence: it was no coincidence that she returned to being a platinum blonde shortly before regrouping Blondie. Meanwhile, she recently displayed true blonde ambition as she sang with the smoky Jazz Passengers ensemble and gave an impressive performance in "The Fluffer" (premiering at the 15th London Lesbian and Gay Film Festival) in which she played a lesbian strip-club owner.

The music remains as durable as elastic; everyone has their favourite Blondie rip-snorter. The bombastic "Rapture" (with its slouching, lazy beat, frankly sexy bass line and sky-high in the mix vocal) has been tweaked by all manner of R&B acts, from Foxy Brown to Glamma Kid). The classic "Atomic," meanwhile, with its Spaghetti Western guitar licks and inspirational credo ("Tonight, your hair is beautiful") has been regularly re-worked, most recently by Diddy and Tall Paul. The renewed interest in Blondie as band and Debbie Harry as cultural icon, twenty years after their heyday, is pretty impressive for a woman who initially rocked to Andy Warhol's beat—fifteen minutes and your time's up, indeed.

Debbie Harry is made of sterner stuff. Blondie received the coveted Lifetime Inspiration award at the *Q* Awards in London two years ago, with Debbie raising the ceremonial roof with "Heart of Glass." Her black lycra ensemble bejewelled with hundreds of genuine razor blades was an apt confection, perhaps, for a lady who has always been on the sharper edge of sex.

Or, as the song goes, "cool as ice-cream, but still as sweet." You live in dreams, Sunday Girl.

Album Reviews

"Blondie Makes a Grand Exit"

by Jim Farber

New York Daily News, *February 14, 1999*

Album review, Blondie, No Exit *(Beyond/BMG).*—Ed.

BLONDIE

"No Exit" (Beyond/BMG)

You can't fault Blondie for lack of ambition on their first album together in 17 years. The reunited group clearly hit the studio hungry to recapture every strong point of their original releases, and more. Over the course of 14 tracks, they race through an encyclopedia of musical genres, moving track by track from reggae to ska to dance-rock to girl-group pop to new wave to rap. They even add new sounds for them: jazz, psychedelic pop and country.

For a band that never wanted to be pigeonholed, "No Exit" dive-bombs any attempt. Unfortunately, it also makes for a bit of a mishmash. Even some multi-artist soundtracks hold together better.

You can't quibble much with the individual tracks. They're graced with melodies as sturdy as the band's classics. "Maria," an ideal melding of '60s girl-group pop and '70s punk, would feel right at home on a Blondie album like "Plastic Letters," while "Forgive and Forget" has the rich dance rhythms of a smash like "Call Me."

Singer Debbie Harry makes good use of her woozy persona, developed with The Jazz Passengers, in "Boom Boom in the Zoom Zoom Room," while "Out in the Streets" makes a fascinating production connection between the echoed yearning of an early Ronnie Spector single and the eeriness of modern trip-hop.

The nymph-like charm still evident in Harry's 53-year-old voice can make for odd listening in a song like "Under the Gun" (which recalls the new wave of songs like "Dreaming"). Harry seems more age-appropriate in "The Dream's Lost on Me," a ballad that mixes world-weary cabaret with weepy country music.

Then again, maybe age has something to do with why the band decided to run so relentlessly through the genres to begin with. At this point in their lives, it's more about commanding the craft to make all kinds of music rather than attempting to maintain a single youthful character. From the evidence here, modern Blondie can nail any style they like.

"Blondie With an Edge..."

by Joey Guerra

Houston Chronicle, *February 21, 1999*

Album review, Blondie, No Exit, *Beyond Records.*—Ed.

Celine, Mariah and Shania, watch your sequined backs. 1999 is shaping up to be a very good year for veteran divas.

Cher, at 52, has scored her first U.S. top-10 hit in a decade with the disco ditty Believe, which grooved ahead of songs by the younger likes of Whitney Houston, Brandy and Sarah McLachlan. Now, original new-wavers Blondie, fronted by the still-icy-hot, 53-year-old Deborah Harry, are returning after a 17-year absence. (Harry has kept herself busy with indie movie roles, solo work and a stint with the Jazz Passengers).

No Exit, due in stores Tuesday, has already made a splash overseas. The first single, Maria, entered the U.K. charts at No. 1, making Blondie the first group to top the charts in three consecutive decades. The song is impossibly catchy, a wind-blown mix of heavenly hooks and bell-ringing pop nostalgia.

Stateside, it's quite possible Blondie will strike a similar chord. During the band's heyday in the late '70s and early '80s, Blondie defied categorization. The mix of rock, rap, punk and ska resulted in a string of enduring hits (Call Me, Rapture, The Tide is High and Heart of Glass) and a legion of artists were (and still are) influenced by the band's sound and Harry's inimitable style.

In some ways, No Exit picks up where the band left off nearly two decades ago. A smattering of styles color the album; pop-powered choruses surge through a number of tracks; and Harry is still front and center, wooing and seducing as effectively and suggestively as ever.

But don't call this a comeback. Every song on the album is new—no Rapture '99 Remix, thank you very much. There's a real edge here, a growl in Harry's voice that's often as fierce and nervy as anything Courtney Love will ever do.

Transylvanian keyboard licks dominate Screaming Skin [*should be "No Exit"*—Ed.], which finds Harry sporting a bride of Dracula accent. The chaotic title track is an inspired rap duet between Harry and Coolio, filled with threatening guitar riffs and a doomsday chorus ("Who's gonna cry over you?").

Forgive and Forget is a bubbling electro-pop confection that finds Harry accessing the upper registers of her voice. Boom Boom in the Zoom Zoom Room rides a lazy-day lounge vibe, conjuring up images of coffeehouses and poetry readings. And Out In the Streets is a dead-on remake of the Shangri-Las' late '60s girl-group anthem.

The closing track, Dig up the Conjo, is the weakest offering on No Exit. The song is a mishmash of tribal chants and tepid instrumentation that fails to match the energy of the rest of the album.

For the most part, however, No Exit is a forceful return to form for one of pop music's most stylish innovators. The tide is high, and Blondie is indeed moving on.

3 stars

"Blondie: Behind the Music"

by Michelle Goldberg

Salon.com *web site, March 3, 1999*

A detailed analysis of the No Exit *album. Includes consideration of Blondie's influence and its place in music history, along with Madonna thrown in for good measure. Quotes extensively from three band members—Deborah Harry, Clem Burke, and Jimmy Destri.—Ed.*

The members of the reborn band discuss their past, their reunion and their first recording in 17 years, *No Exit*.

There's hardly a single major '90s pop music phenomenon that doesn't have its antecedent in the sugary, ironic, thrilling pastiche of Blondie. Madonna's obvious inspiration was Debbie Harry, not Marilyn Monroe ("Everybody admits that but Madonna," says Blondie keyboardist Jimmy Destri). The Spice Girls, too, are Harry's daughters. An ex-Playboy bunny, Harry perfected the marriage of airbrushed, blow-up doll glamor and tough, me-first attitude that every MTV nymphet strives for—the insistent, carnally aggressive chorus to "Call Me" prefigured do-me feminism by a decade. Even hip-hop, which everyone from *Vibe* to *Time* magazine acknowledges as the music of the '90s, has a few blond roots, for while Grandmaster Flash and Kool Herc invented it, Blondie brought it to the masses—"Rapture" was, after all, the first No. 1 rap song ever. The sweet and sour harmonies of critical darlings Sleater-Kinney follow straight from songs like "In the Flesh" and "X Offender," Blondie's punk takes on the girl-group sounds of the Shangri-Las and the Angels. The Beastie Boys are often credited for merging punk, funk, hip-hop and dance music, but again, Blondie did it first, pumping out disco hits and keeping their CBGB street cred at the height of the "disco sucks" backlash. This remarkable genre diplomacy was made possible by the band's sophisticated use of parody and winking exaggeration (especially the bitingly blase lyrics to "Heart of Glass") and by Debbie Harry's indomitable coolness—a glamour that, at 53, still seems to burn as intensely as it did two decades ago.

When Blondie announced that they were reuniting, 17 years after their less-than-mediocre final album, *The Hunter*, and subsequent rancorous breakup (two ex-members filed a lawsuit against the band), even loyal fans might have groaned a bit, picturing the pathetic recent Sex Pistols tour or the geriatric, increasingly self-parodic Rolling Stones. Once again, though, Blondie amazes, producing what may be the most triumphant comeback record ever. Unlike the desultory greatest-hits packages of Blondie's past-their-prime peers, *No Exit* has all the manic energy and confectionery gloss of classic albums like *Parallel Lines* and *Plastic Letters*.

"That's why we tried to work on all new music. We didn't want to do this retro trip. We felt it was really important that we do something fresh," says Harry. "I don't think we would have done it otherwise—we couldn't ever have pulled it off."

Says drummer Clem Burke: "I'm friends with Glen [Matlock, the Sex Pistols' bassist] and Steve [Jones, the Sex Pistols' guitarist], and they both seem to have regretted that they weren't able to make new music during their reunion. We didn't want to do this as a business venture, like 'Let's go out on tour and make a whole bunch of money.' If we were going to put all this time, energy and emotion into it, we had to become a band again. That's the difference between a Blondie reunion and a Sex Pistols reunion or a Kiss reunion. Those were more nostalgic, and they disappointed fans because they didn't make any new music. We all feel very credible now that we've made the new record."

The reception of the new album has been almost uniformly ecstatic. "Maria," the deliriously catchy, operatically passionate first single—a pop gem as perfectly crafted as any in their oeuvre—debuted at the top of the charts in Britain, making Blondie the first band ever to have a No. 1 U.K. single in the '70s, '80s and '90s. No one in the group ever expected to be so prominently back in the pop spotlight again, but at the same time they say there's no feeling of disorientation or déjà vu.

"It really does feel like just the next Blondie album. It could have come between Eat to the Beat and Autoamerican, or after The Hunter," says Destri. "My thing is that, even though I got married and started a really wonderful family and am happy being at home, the 16 years I was at home were the surreal years. Doing this feels right. There was no death after Blondie for me, but I felt incomplete, even with a family and everything. Now I feel very much at home, like ahhh yeah, where did we leave off?"

If anything, *No Exit* is the most ambitious Blondie record ever, tighter and more wildly eclectic than anything the band has done before. There's a whiskey-rough country tune on *No Exit*, "The Dream's Lost on Me," as well as a noirish ska song, "Screaming Skin," and the title track, a Gothic rap featuring a furious cameo by Coolio. It all works, probably because it's the kind of experimental fare Blondie have tackled from the beginning. And while *No Exit* is in no way a retrospective, there is a sense that Blondie are consolidating their influences, making a statement about their own inventive legacy. Hearing them pull off ska, rap, pop, country, jazz and old-fashioned torch songs on the same album gives a contemporary listener a new appreciation how visionary Blondie were in fusing hip-hop, punk and disco, three genres that appeared eons apart in the late '70s and early '80s.

"We've just done a remix of No Exit with Wu Tang Clan and Mobb Deep. They say the first time they heard rap was with 'Rapture'—it's funny, you'd think they'd cite NWA or Public Enemy," says Burke. "Had we not done 'Rapture' back then, I don't think it would have rang true to work with rap now. There is an acceptance of Blondie [in hip-hop], and people recognize Debbie as being, in a way, the first female rapper."

Coolio got involved with "No Exit" after Harry sent him a tape of the song—he responded by recording his own rap to go along with it: "His performance was extraordinary," says Harry. "We really didn't have any intimate collaboration working in the same room. He liked the song and he did his thing and sent it to us. The process was kind of existential, which sort of fits the title."

Maturity Born of Experience and Loss

There's also a strong jazz influence on *No Exit*, especially on Harry's vocals. The playfully snaky phrasing on the loungey "Boom Boom in the Zoom Zoom Room" and the funky "Happy Dog" seems gleaned from her work with the Jazz Passengers, a New York avant-garde jazz combo known for its theatricality and wild improvisations. Bittersweet ballads like "Double Take" and "Night Wind Sent" are ideal showcases for Harry in her chanteuse mode. Age agrees with Harry—her voice here is richer and sultrier, as sexy as ever but tempered with wisdom. "Double Take" especially aches with a world-weary compassion born of outrageous experience and resilience in the face of loss. After all, one of the most striking things about Blondie is that, despite their dizzying trip from the insanely nihilistic, drug-drenched New York punk scene to worldwide fame and then to relative individual obscurity, its founding members are all still alive.

"So many people have died in our lives, with the drug epidemic and AIDS epidemic," says Harry. "I was at a photo show about the punk scene at CBGBs a couple years back, and as I walked through the show and saw all the faces, I realized at least 50 percent of the people in the pictures were gone. I don't think that's normal for people in their 20s and 30s, except during wartime."

Adds Destri:

"We've gone though our own little hells. We consider ourselves lucky that we made it out the other end. We've lost so many friends to the plague, drugs, freak accidents. It's a rough game we're in, but my three closest friends all came through it unscathed." Seeing so many of their friends and contemporaries flame out or fade away may have lessened any bitterness the band feels about watching other artists get rich off Blondie's innovations.

"I was really proud when I heard our style go on and influence other people," says Destri. "But I also saw that people were having massively successful careers based on aspects of us, so there was a bit of jealousy there—but also a bit of gratification."

No Exit is such a fantastic album that it carries with it the melancholy question of how many other great records the band could have made if it had gotten back together sooner. "Clem and I were discussing this once. Clem sees a lot of glasses as half empty, whereas I see them as half full," says Destri. "Clem said, 'Man, we could have went on into the mid-'80s, gotten paid and walked away hugely successful.' I said to him that I believe if we had gone on, we would have made less and less inspired records and would have been left without such a great legacy. We would never have had the opportunity to come back as strong as we did."

Says Harry: "I'm lucky. I've had an interesting life, a lot of success and an equal amount of failure. No matter how famous any of us are, we all probably have the same ups and downs, some things that are good and some things that really suck. I think I'm happier now than I was when I was younger. I know more about myself. I've had a lot of really cool experiences. The worst part is thinking that someday it's going to be over."

She won't admit any resentment toward Madonna and her millions: "It's very funny, but everybody asks me about Madonna. Just in asking that question you have the answer. Some of the fundamental things she used image-wise were directly influenced by me, that's pretty obvious. In Madonna's defense, she has worked extremely hard in her career and she's done some incredible things. Some of her music is really great, and anyone who achieves that kind of success has of course worked her ass off for it."

Ironically, with her keen business sense and genius for appropriation, Madonna has made it easier to see the shrewdness behind Harry's persona and has illuminated Blondie's brilliance. When the band first made it big, after all, many critics saw guitarist and co-founder Chris Stein (then Harry's lover) as the brains behind the group. Harry's parody of the bitchy blond bimbo was lost on many, and her contribution to Blondie's music was written off. The women in rock who followed her, though, have made it impossible to condescend to Harry in the same way, and hopefully everyone who listens to *No Exit* will hear her influence.

"I think that people's eyes have been opened a lot," says Harry. "That sexist approach has changed, the industry has opened up a lot more, and it's now apparent what my real contribution was. I worked on the music. I put my ideas into melody. I wrote a lot of the lyrics. I created the style and attitude of the band. I was holding my own, honey."

Likewise, the rest of the band professes to have come to terms with the fact that for many people, Debbie Harry is Blondie—a misconception once so prevalent that the group adopted the blunt slogan "Blondie is a band."

"When I was younger, there was a point where I was like, damn, here she is and the photographers are pushing me out of the way again," says Destri. "But there are other things that I've always found worse than that—like digging ditches for a living, or having to do manual labor under a nasty boss. In the first incarnation of Blondie, I wrote a couple of great songs and I was very lucky to have this superstar sing them for me. Of course there's a lot of times when people don't recognize the members of Blondie for the creativity that they have, but at the same time it also hurt Debbie, because nobody looked past the image to her creativity."

In 1999, those conflicts seem fabulously far away, and Blondie have nailed their place in both the music history books and on the contemporary pop charts.

"If you asked me if I would do it all over again," says Destri, "I'd say give me a beautiful blond chick with a voice."

Concert Previews
and Reviews

"Still Hip, Still Gutsy, Still Clever and Still Blonde"

by Nicholas Barber

The Independent, *November 15, 1998*

Performance review, Newcastle City Hall, Newcastle, England, November 10, 1998. Edited with the permission of the author.—Ed.

Apart from rap reworkings of Bee Gees songs, pop music in the Nineties will be remembered primarily for the reunions. Every few months for the past decade, the members of a legendary band have patched up their differences, told lots of interviewers that they never felt the group had fulfilled its potential, then fallen out again. And as a music critic, my part in this process has been to grumble each time about how pitiful it is when icons travesty themselves.

Deep down, though, I don't see what's wrong with reunions. OK, so the musicians are after some easy money, but why do you think they got together in the first place? And OK, they're never going to have the same impact as they did the first time around, but how could they? Times change. If you go to a school reunion, you don't end up sitting through double French and sneaking behind the gym hall for a cigarette.

Purists may shudder, but I'm happy to have seen the Velvet Underground, Television and the Sex Pistols return from the grave. And, this week, I was happy to see Blondie barrel through their many hits at such a breathless pace that the crowd never stopped dancing, and Deborah Harry's joke about leaving the stage to put new batteries in her pacemaker had a worrying ring of plausibility.

Blondie scored nine Top Five hits in the UK, including five number ones, before they broke up in 1982. Now, the four main members—Harry, Chris Stein, Jimmy Destri and Clem Burke—have resumed trading, joined by a new bassist, a second guitarist, and, on some songs, an extra keyboard player. And they're sounding excellent, notwithstanding the lamentable cleaning up of their trashy guitar sound. It's the first law of rock reunions: if you're a band from the Sixties or Seventies who reform in the Nineties, your music's going to sound a bit Eighties.

There's no disguising the fact that Blondie aren't as young as they used to be. During the instrumental break in "Atomic," Jimmy Destri played the synth while kneeling on the stage with a cigarette in his mouth. Harry, whose face has been on more posters than Blu-Tack, is now 53, and a T-shirt and a tight, knee-length skirt are no longer the wisest outfit for her. More sensibly, the men in the band have realised that the way to hide their middle-aged spread is to stick to the black suits they always wore, except for a stern-looking Chris Stein, who has chosen grey to match his hair.

But age cannot wither Blondie. If they're not as young as they used to be, one of the keys to their success was that they never used to be very young in the first place. Harry was an unbelievable 33 before the group had any hits. So while a Sex Pistols reunion requires 40-year-olds to fake the furious alienation of their acne-ridden teenage selves, Blondie's oeuvre was always made up of mature, knowing art-rock with a generous dose of cabaret. The group started life by kidnapping the fresh-faced girl-group cooing of the Sixties and dragging it round the grimy streets of New York, and they ended up making some of the most bizarre and ambitious disco-punk-reggae-jazz ever to grace the charts. Don't forget that "Denis" has a verse in French for no apparent reason, and one of the earliest examples of rapping on a pop single consisted of Harry rambling on about a car-eating alien in "Rapture." Despite their reputation for ultra-cool urban pop, then, Blondie have always dealt in postmodern pastiche. So on Tuesday, the admittedly frightening sight of Harry hamming up her performance, tottering on her heels, and belting out the choruses with the brassy voice of a show-stopping vaudeville dame was somehow true to the Blondie spirit.

Clem Burke has aged best. On Blondie's album covers, Burke is the one who looks like Rodney Bewes from The Likely Lads. Now, sustained by fruit, tofu and treadmill work-outs, he is the most hyperactive yet disciplined drummer I've ever seen. He starts "Dreaming" with a fearsome drum roll, and then keeps it going for the rest of the song. And he still has enough energy to jump on top of the bass drum at the end, spinning one drum stick between his fingers and tossing the other in the air.

What's more astonishing is that Blondie's new songs, due for release on an album in February, are almost as clever and as deranged as the old ones. "Maria" in particular deserves its place on a "Best of Blondie" compilation. If only Harry would invest in a trouser suit and Stein and Destri would keep their jackets on, I'd have no reunion city blues at all...

"The Tide Is High Again
for Rejuvenated Blondie"

by Sarah Rodman

Boston Herald, *May 17, 1999*

Performance review, Orpheum Theatre, Boston, Massachusetts, May 15, 1999; opening of North American leg of the "No Exit" world tour.—Ed.

It was once more into the bleach as Blondie jubilantly launched its first North American tour in 16 years Saturday night at a sold-out Orpheum Theatre.

The band, enhanced by three touring musicians, played a taut, engaging 80-minute set that spanned the new wave popsters entire recorded career from 1976's self titled debut to its current critically and commercially successful "No Exit."

The only clue that time had passed was the humanizing bit of girth around the waists of the original quartet, guitarist Chris Stein, keyboardist Jimmy Destri, drummer Clem Burke and lead singer Debbie Harry.

Otherwise, it was nothing but net as the group dove into its rich musical history—a successful hybrid of punk, new wave, disco, pop and rock—to play not only familiar hits but a handful of fan favorites and a smattering of the best new tunes.

Emerging in a black leather skirt, sparkly gold top and shades, Harry hid her famous two-tone blonde mop under a hat during the insistent opener, "Dreaming," which, as all the songs ultimately did, featured the impressive drumming of Burke.

From there, the never dumb blonde discarded the hat and was left "Hanging on the Telephone," swinging and swiveling her hips to Destri's bopping keyboard sounds, bouncing along with the crowd to the ska rhythms of the new "Screaming Skin," and coolly cooing "make me tonight' to the bass grooves and Stein's understated guitar solo during "Atomic."

Harry, sounding as strong and icily seductive as before, swooped to her upper register for ancient album track "Union City Blue," crept down low for the jazzy "Boom Boom in the Zoom Zoom Room" and got her first spontaneous crowd sing along with '50s girl group-style hit "Sunday Girl."

The clangorous bell tones of current hit "Maria" rang out nicely against Harry's clarion vocals. "Call Me" featured hard-charging guitar riffs and keyboard swirls, while "The Tide is High" swung on a tropical vine. The primitively hip rhyming on an intense "Rapture" and a full-on punk rendering of the sinister "One Way or Another" capped the set. Closing with a crowd bolstered run through of "Heart of Glass," the band is off to a great new start.

"Blondie's Back..."

by Neva Chonin

San Francisco Chronicle, *June 1, 1999*

Performance review, The Warfield, San Francisco, California, May 30, 1999, including an excellent discussion of Blondie's significance and musical influence.—Ed.

They don't make sex symbols the way they used to. When Blondie vocalist Deborah Harry accepted a bouquet of yellow tulips from a fan midway through the band's concert in San Francisco on Sunday night, she showed her appreciation by biting off a mouthful of petals and spitting them back at the audience. Now that's a star. A punk. A fiftysomething woman. The crowd cheered itself hoarse.

For the first half of the '80s, Harry was the quintessential gutsy bleached blonde whose cool moves inspired Madonna, Courtney Love and No Doubt's Gwen Stefani. During their tenure as chart toppers, the band Blondie created a diva-and-band template still at work in groups ranging from Garbage to the Cranberries, and pioneered a pop-punk fusion that later became the signature sound of '90s indie rock. The difference is that they did it all with an impeccable, mega-platinum cool that no band or singer since has recaptured.

Sunday's sold-out reunion concert at the Warfield proved that after decades in retirement, Blondie has lost neither its cool nor its chops. In terms of attitude and delivery—if not technical execution, but more on that later—the show was a triumph that brought the audience to its feet with the first song and kept it there through the encore.

In a gray minidress, black tights and black stilettos, Harry looked as if she had stepped directly out of the stage's gray-and-black graffiti backdrop. She arrived onstage wearing sunglasses and kept them on until the fourth song, the suitably eye-opening "Atomic."

For those dying to know, she looked terrific: less gamine and sporting more curves, and all the more sultry for it.

As always, Blondie's male contingent—backed by three tour musicians on bass, guitar and organ—played calm second fiddle to their star. Isolated in a plastic cubicle at stage right, Clem Burke flailed at his drum kit as if he were still a kid burning calories at CBGB's. Guitarist Chris Stein, blond and looking impressively fit considering his grueling bouts with illness in the '80s, played it cool behind a pair of shades; and Jimmy Destri bobbed behind his keyboards with his usual ebullience.

Unfortunately, the night was marred by a miserable sound mix that buried vocals and guitars behind a monolithic wall of drums and bass. Whether the lopsided sound was a misguided attempt at creating a dance vibe or simply a case of engineers dozing over their control boards, it flattened songs such as "In the Flesh" and "Union City Blue," whose momentum relied on melody, not rhythm.

BEYOND THE AWFUL SOUND MIX

But the audience was too besotted with Debbie and the gang to care. Though the band's reunion album, "No Exit," released last month to mixed reviews, was represented by "Screaming Skin" and the radio hit "Maria," most of the 75-minute set was given over to old favorites.

There were play-by-numbers renditions of "Dreaming" and "Hanging on the Telephone" and extended dance jams of "Call Me," the pop-rap "Rapture" and, as an encore, the career-defining "Heart of Glass."

Honed through years on the road with the Jazz Passengers, Harry's voice had a huskier tone and more elastic range than when she was the growling chanteuse who made the "I'm gonna gitcha-gitcha-gitcha-gitcha" chorus of "One Way or Another" so much fun in 1979. This time around, the growl alternated between a sumptuous roar and a throaty purr.

NOSTALGIC EVENING

"Jimmy Destri has quite a history with San Francisco," Harry said after a bittersweet run through "Sunday Girl." "Those of you who have brain cells left will remember."

Most of the crowd probably didn't remember, but they pretended they did anyway. Nostalgia, done well, is a beautiful thing.

"In A Great Comeback, Blondie Has More Fun"

by Jim Farber

New York Daily News, *June 12, 1999*

Following their successful debut concert on February 23, 1999 at Town Hall in New York City, broadcast on VH1, Blondie makes a return engagement to New York for a concert at the Madison Square Garden Theater on June 10, 1999. Farber offers a review of that concert.—Ed.

Blondie did more than just take a skip through their back catalogue at their zippy reunion show at The Theater at Madison Square Garden Thursday. They surveyed the last 30 years of music history.

In one number alone, "Atomic," the group whipped together elements of ska, disco, new wave, surf-rock and spaghetti Western soundtracks. In other songs, they touched on '60s Brit-pop, girl group music, jazz, punk rock, reggae, rap—everything but zouk.

With such a reach, it became hard to see the group in nostalgic terms, though memory couldn't help but play a big part in the evening's thrill.

What a repertoire these guys boast! Ten faves from the band's golden era dominated the 90-minute show, from the opener, "Dreaming," to the inevitable capper, "Heart of Glass." In between, the band worked in four songs from "No Exit," their first LP in 18 years, and one that fully lives up to their legacy. Only one song from their earliest days turned up, "In the Flesh"—the ultimate slow dance song for a high school mixer, held circa 1964.

The look of singer Debbie Harry also indicated the past. Wearing a black leather skirt, shades and pink blouse, she tackled the look of a '50s girl gone bad. Yet given her zaftig figure and age (she turns 54 next month), Harry appeared most like Jayne Mansfield's mother.

Vocally, the years haven't diminished her. She nailed every role, from punk (in "One Way or Another") to coquette (in "Sunday Girl"). Ex-hubby Chris Stein [*Harry and Stein were never married*—Ed.] added colorful guitar parts while Clem Burke remains one of rock's powerhouse drummers. The group took on hired hands for the bass and second lead guitar parts (Leigh Foxx and Paul Carbonara, respectively). But they fit in with the rest like old friends. Their combined work made this reunion ideal, a mix of memory and fresh effort that rendered the separation between them seamless.

"Enduring Music Gives Blondie a Pop Legacy"

by Joey Guerra

Houston Chronicle, *August 26, 1999*

This concert preview covers the Blondie reunion, the No Exit *album, the song "Maria" plus Blondie's past history. Based on interviews with Deborah Harry and Jimmy Destri.*—Ed.

"Forgive and forget," Debbie Harry coos seductively on a burbling electro-pop track from "No Exit," the first album of fresh material from original new-wavers Blondie in almost two decades.

In some ways, that simple phrase seems a fitting mantra of sorts for the group, whose slew of enduring pop tunes, including No. 1 hits "Heart of Glass," "Call Me," "Rapture" and "The Tide is High," made Blondie an icon for generations to come.

The group found U.K. success with its 1976 self-titled debut album and its follow-up, "Plastic Letters," but it was Blondie's third effort, 1979's "Parallel Lines," that got U.S. audiences grooving to the mix of rock, rap, disco and reggae.

Harry released a solo album "Koo Koo," in 1982, which also marked the release of "The Hunter," Blondie's sixth album. Sluggish sales and building tensions, however, caused Blondie to lose some of its shimmer. Fist fights often broke out among the group's male members—including keyboardist Jimmy Destri, drummer Clem Burke and guitarist Chris Stein. (Bassist Nigel Harrison and lead guitarist Frank Infante joined the group in the late '70s, but are not part of the reunion.)

To make matters worse, Stein was diagnosed with pemphigus in 1981, a potentially fatal disease that caused him to break out in blisters all over his body. (It was the inspiration for "Screaming Skin," a track on "No Exit.") Harry, who was romantically involved with Stein at the time, spent the next two years nursing him back to health, but Blondie was no more—at least for a while.

Harry released a number of tepidly received solo albums in the late '80s and early '90s, and the other members busied themselves with families and side projects. Seventeen years later, however, Blondie is back.

"There's not as much acrimony as we once had. We all chose to do this now. We got this up and running," said Burke, 43, calling recently from a tour stop in Cleveland. The "No Exit" tour hits Aerial Theater Saturday. "We all put a lot of time, energy and emotion into doing this. We realize there's a lot of history amongst us, obviously. It almost kind of feels like a family—a dysfunctional one. I think we all respect one another, and we're having a good time with it."

"No Exit," Blondie's seventh album, marks a fine return to form for the group. It was released in February and brims with dark, edgy instrumentation and power-pop grooves and catchy choruses. Harry is as coolly seductive as ever, weaving effortlessly through rock, electronica and doo-wop.

"It's sort of hard to put your finger on (the album's sound)," said Harry, 54, calling a week earlier from her home in New York. "I guess that's just sort of intrinsic to our nature. The old Blondie records have some of that, too. I think primarily (I just wanted) to do a good record, the best record that we could do. After not having worked together for such a long time, just to sort of try to be cool and work with everybody and make the best of what we were and what we are today."

While "No Exit" is indeed awash in the sounds and styles of the '90s, it does seem a logical follow-up to the albums and singles that have made Blondie one of pop music's most enduring acts. Even during the band's 17-year absence, its music popped up everywhere—in movies, on dance floors, at parties—and consistently draws an enthusiastic response from fans of all ages.

"I guess they're good songs, you know? We were concerned with writing songs...not just sort of riffs," Harry said. "I think that the songs are complete thoughts in a way, and that sort of stays with you. I can't attribute it to anything more than a lot of good luck, really."

Burke offers a more concrete theory on the long-running success of the group's classic tracks, which he called Blondie's "legacy." He believes those past successes are enabling Blondie to re-emerge and continue to grow.

"Although we stopped performing, I really don't think the music went away," Burke said. "Especially in places like the U.K., we had a lot of success there in the late '70s. We laid a lot of roots down in places like that, as well as the States. We're sort of part of the musical fabric at this point."

That staying power ensured immediate radio play for "Maria," the first single off "No Exit." The wistful song about a mystery woman did receive considerable airplay and press in the United States, but it failed to make a significant impact on the charts. In the United Kingdom, however, Blondie remains as icy-hot as ever. The song entered the charts overseas at No. 1, making Blondie the first group to have No. 1 singles in the U.K. in each of the past three decades.

"I don't know if you can ever predict what's gonna happen with a record," Harry said of the song's disparate levels of success. "We did have a very good fan base over there and quite a reputation for pop singles. I think that song really fit into...their kind of market for singles. I don't know if "Maria" is exactly sort of an American-style song for right now, but we did get some airplay on it."

While Blondie has enjoyed widespread success with its new material, it would have been easy for the supergroup to package a greatest hits collection with a few new tracks and hit the reunion-tour circuit, a la Fleetwood Mac. Boom—instant success, without the pressure of a show full of new material that may or may not sit well with longtime fans.

"I think it's kind of obvious when a band is just kinda doing one or two new songs with a greatest hits type of thing. It doesn't really seem as though they wanna be a band, maybe. With us, we wanted to be a band again," Burke said, adding that the group hopes to record another album next year. "We wanted to be around each other again, and we wanted to create music with each other. God knows there have been enough Blondie greatest hits things as well. We wanted to see if the chemistry was still there."

"No Exit" also finds Harry trading rap licks with Coolio on the album's title track. It's a return to familiar ground for the singer, who introduced rap music to a whole new audience on Blondie's early '80s hit, "Rapture."

"I think what's always attracted me to rap is that it was a breakthrough event," Harry said. "What it did for young black artists, and for the black audience, was it gave them a voice that was kin to folk music. Rap just really had to happen,...and when it did happen it was so exciting and so obvious."

Harry and the other members of Blondie took the rap connection a step further this past January at the American Music Awards, where the band performed "No Exit" with Coolio, Wu-Tang Clan and Mobb Deep.

"I can't really say that I am the penultimate rap fan, that I follow doggedly at the heels of rappers, but...I've met Foxy Brown, and I like Lil' Kim and Missy Elliott," Harry said. "I think the stuff is fantastic. It's beautifully written, it's clever, it's rhythmically interesting. There's so much going on. It's good stuff."

In between her musical careers as both a solo artist and as a member of Blondie, Harry has built a varied and steady career as an actress. She was recently seen in the indie film "Six Ways to Sunday." Her most notable roles include Velma Von Tussle in John Waters' "Hairspray" and bitter waitress Delores (her strongest big-screen performance to date) in "Heavy."

"I find it very challenging to assume different characters and to work in the technical world of film," Harry said. "It's a real discipline, and I like that kind of work. That's what gets me off.

"To a certain degree, I think I've always approached Blondie as acting—sort of a discipline or event or challenge or whatever. Not to say that it's impersonal, but sort of the way that I develop the character. To work it onstage is sort of like acting in some ways. It's sort of weird. It's this sort of gray area, or crossover area, between some kind of performance art and becoming somebody else entirely."

When the band finally does hit the stage, expect the unexpected.

"First there's a dog act. Then we bring on the topless dancers, and then..." Harry pauses and lets out a laugh. "No, no. Just doing some of our old stuff and a lot of the new stuff. It sounds really good."

Given the group's enduring and ever-growing track record, it would be hard to argue with that statement.

"Blondie Respects Roots, Focuses on Present"

by Joey Guerra

Houston Chronicle, *August 30, 1999*

This concert review of Blondie at the Aerial Theater in Houston, Texas on August 28, 1999, includes references to Deborah Harry as a "precursor" to other female rock stars, like Madonna and Courtney Love, and to the band's "enduring" music.—Ed.

Don't blame Deborah Harry for being a star. The girl can't help it.

As the alluring center point of new-wave pop group Blondie, Harry got more than her fair share of attention in the late '70s and early '80s. Never mind the fact that Blondie was a group, as the band was forced to point out several times during its heyday. Without even trying, the platinum-haired goddess often stood solo in the spotlight, and tensions within the band developed. It inevitably contributed to Blondie's demise in 1982.

Fast-forward 17 years, and Harry is still the cool-as-ice ringleader of the reunited group, a precursor to stars such as Madonna and Courtney Love. During Blondie's fun and enthusiastic performance Saturday at the Aerial Theater, however, there were no pangs of jealousy to be found among band members. The music was most important.

At 54, Harry still retains much of her appeal, and she fully embraces a naughty sense of sexuality. Wearing a tight peach dress accessorized with sparkling jewelry, sunglasses and a pair of roses she held in her hand, Harry strutted and shimmied across the stage, often to campy effect. She adjusted her microphone's volume via a black pack wrapped around the outside of her dress.

The show was peppered with classic and obscure hits, kicking off with the nostalgic "Dreaming." As one would expect, the oldies incited the biggest reactions from the diverse audience, which included baby boomers, college kids and younger fans, all familiar with Blondie's enduring pop catalog.

Much of the band's set, however, consisted of material off "No Exit," the band's seventh studio album, which brims with a dark, urgent edge. Harry took a bite out of the flowers she was holding and tossed them into the crowd before launching into "Screaming Skin," a song inspired by guitarist Chris Stein's battle with pemphigus, a rare genetic disease that causes blisters to form on the skin.

Each of the key members—Stein, keyboardist Jimmy Destri and drummer Clem Burke—had a turn in the spotlight. (Two new members complete the lineup of the touring band.) For fans, however, this was clearly Harry's show. They screamed every time she came near the end of the stage or uttered a word.

Harry has always been a bit of an aloof performer, but that's part of her appeal. She always seems deliciously above it all, too cool for the room. She strained a bit to hit those coquettish high notes that became part of Blondie's trademark sound, but it was still exhilarating to see Harry cooing her way through an inspired rendition of "Rapture." She nailed the song's rap break, which clearly energized Harry and the crowd.

Many fans slipped into their seats when the band launched into a number of new songs off "No Exit," including "Nothing Is Real but the Girl," the heartbreaking lament "Night Wind Sent" and the lounge ditty "Boom Boom in the Zoom Zoom Room." The best of the bunch was "Forgive and Forget," a burbling electro-pop number that seems a natural progression from Blondie's past hits.

"The Tide Is High" brought the house back to its feet for an enthusiastic sing-along, and the energy stayed alive with a charged-up version of "Maria," the band's recent single.

From here, Blondie launched into an onslaught of riffs that would scare most of Lilith Fair's ladies off the stage and give Shirley Manson or Courtney Love a run for her money. Her hair soaking wet from perspiration, Harry plowed through the rock'n'roll catfight "Rip Her to Shreds," the anthemic "Call Me" and a punked-up version of "One Way or Another." The only thing missing was the mosh pit.

The thundering grooves returned for an encore that showcased Blondie at its best—then and now. The band weaved its way through a solid version of the disco-tinged "Heart of Glass," but it was during the Transylvanian licks of "No Exit" that Blondie proved its sound was as fresh as ever, with Harry effortlessly handling the raps live that were laid down on the album by Coolio. Don't call it a comeback: These guys are back for the long haul.

On Their Craft

"Blondie's Clem Burke"

by Adam Budofsky

Modern Drummer, *June 1999*

In-depth article on Clem Burke, "the best drummer New Wave had to offer." Includes discussion of Burke's career and craft as a "Premier" drummer.—Ed.

Blondie had it all in the late '70s: Perfect pop songs. New York street smarts. Hollywood glamour. Four Number-1 hits. And, in Clem Burke, the best drummer New Wave had to offer.

Of course, fame is often fleeting. By the early '80s Blondie was gone from view. Besides lead singer Debbie Harry, who released the occasional solo album and acted in some offbeat films, Burke kept a higher profile than any of his bandmates, recording and/or touring with Pete Townshend, Bob Dylan, The Eurythmics, Dramarama, Iggy Pop, Joan Jett, The Romantics, and The Plimsouls.

Technically speaking, though, Blondie never called it a day. An official breakup announcement hadn't been made, and their business affairs weren't officially dissolved. It was more like the band was put on ice for...like...sixteen years.

Now the four core members of Blondie—Burke, Harry, guitarist Chris Stein, and keyboardist Jimmy Destri—are back. The band's brand-new album, *No Exit*, features the exquisite hit single "Maria," which debuted at Number 1 on the British singles chart and almost as impressively at home. Primo late-night TV appearances and a scalding performance on this year's American Music Awards knocked out thirty-somethings with skinny ties in their closets and baggy-legged No Doubt kids alike. And Web simulcasts, VH-1's airing of their February 23 New York Town Hall concert, and tours through Europe and the States proved the once mighty band could still bring a cauldron of contagious live energy to boil.

In each forum, Clem Burke provides the sights and sounds that literally draw you in. This particular fan clearly remembers, as a teenager, being completely floored by Burke's Keith Moonish abandon on an *American Bandstand* performance of the gloriously tom-heavy hit "Dreaming." Twenty years later, Clem looks barely a day older perched behind his red sparkle Premier kit, trademark Beatle shag making a blur with each roundhouse16th-note fill. Like a poster boy for the drums, Burke visually and sonically represents the pure joy of hitting like *very* few other players do.

That Blondie has reunited at all is due in no small part to Burke's dedication and enthusiasm. At a Chelsea studio during a break between rehearsals for their current tour, Debbie Harry put it this way: "Ever since I've known him, Clem has been dedicated to rock'n'roll and being a pop star and musician. That's really all he ever wanted to be. It's his dream. He's worked for it, and now he's done it."

It's not just the trappings of fame that interested Burke in a reunion. Even more than working with legends like Dylan and Townshend, it's Blondie—the players, the music, the *idea*—that's closest to his heart, and the drummer says he and the others had no interest in simply re-treading past glories. "The whole impetus to get back together was to make a new record," Clem insists. "It wasn't to go out and play some kind of revival thing. We wanted to make a musical statement."

Though Clem says Blondie's record company initially wanted to release a best-of disc with a couple of new songs, "That was ludicrous in everyone's mind. There have been so many reissues of Blondie stuff, and I think it's unfair to people who are interested in the band to have to buy all the old songs again just for one or two new songs. I also think that our starting up again is somewhat of a media event, and it would have been a waste of time and energy to publicize the fact that we had another greatest hits album. So everyone agreed that if we were going to do this, we'd take our time and write new material."

According to Clem, Blondie's resurrection didn't come out of nowhere. "We always remained friends," he explains, "but we approached getting together to make music again slowly at first. We tried to become 'a band' again—finding a place to rehearse, figuring out what songs to do, what kind of haircut to have. *No Exit* has been three years in the making. We didn't want to just jump into this."

Tentative baby steps or not, after extensive rehearsing in Chris Stein's basement studio in downtown Manhattan, it became apparent to all that a Blondie for the '90s was indeed possible. "I don't think there was any one moment where we all went, Wow, this is great!" Burke clarifies. "It was more like, This *seems* like it could work; let's continue and see where it takes us." Where it took them was into a proper studio for six months with Craig Leon, who in 1976 produced the band's first, self-titled record. "We only spent six weeks of that time recording," Burke says, "but we did a lot of pre-production and writing. We all contributed to the album."

No Exit starts off with "Screaming Skin," an uptempo ska-rock number seemingly written with Clem's drum style in mind. "That sound at the beginning is a press roll from another take of the song that we processed," Clem explains. "I like that song a lot; it's one of the songs we do live now." Featuring a four-on-the-floor bass drum and a signature five-stroke roll orchestrated differently throughout the song and ending on a snare/crash accent on the upbeat, the tune is all energy, and reintroduces the band in a grand fashion.

"Forgive And Forget" sounds like it's programmed, but Clem corrects, "There *is* programming going on, but not drum programming. First I overdubbed the 16ths on hi-hat and the basic 2/4 on kick and snare over the keyboard sequence, and then I overdubbed the tom-tom pattern. That tight percussive sound is an empty water cooler that I played with my hands like a conga. That sounds very much like a sequencer, especially when you compress it. The whole percussion track was then mixed and processed. I've done that kind of thing before, like on 'War Child' from the last Blondie record. I learned that from Dave Stewart of the Eurythmics. There's a song on their *Sweet Dreams* record, which I didn't play on, but during the bridge there are milk bottles being played live over a sequencer. I like using organic sounds, like tables and chairs. In the old days they would use a guitar case a lot for percussion."

"Maria" proves that Blondie can still construct the perfect straight-ahead pop single. "I'm really happy we chose that song as the first single," Clem enthuses. "It's like a classic Blondie pop song, in the tradition of 'Sunday Girl' or 'Dreaming.' We were talking the other day, and out of the four Number-1s we've had, one aspect of Blondie that's *not* been a big hit is the 'Maria'-type sound. 'Heart Of Glass' is a disco song, 'The Tide Is High' is a reggae song, 'Rapture' is like rap/funk, and then 'Call Me,' which was co-written with Giorgio Moroder, was kind of based on a shuffle-boogie riff transposed into an electronic medium."

No Exit's title tune is a rap-rock piece featuring Coolio on vocals. Before you accuse Blondie of catering to the latest trends, though, remember that "Rapture," from 1980's *Autoamerican* album, successfully mixed rock and rap at a time when Rage Against The Machine were still starting food fights in grammar school. According to Clem, "For the drums on that song, I was basically trying to cop a Bonham feel. There have actually been a lot of Led Zeppelin samples that have turned into rap songs. In fact, Puff Daddy just did a thing with Jimmy Page with a similar vibe to it. 'No Exit' was a quick take for the drums, maybe the first take."

Burke states that *No Exit*'s title was his idea. "We were rehearsing on a particularly frustrating day," he recalls, "and I happened to look up and see a 'No Exit' sign. I studied some existential philosophy in college, and there's a play by Jean-Paul Sartre with the same title. It's basically about these people in a room who have died and are waiting to see if they are going to go to heaven or hell, and it transpires that they are already in hell, because they just keep getting on each other's nerves. That's sort of like the downside to being in a band. Nietzsche said that there is only madness in groups. If you are on your own, no one is going to think you're insane, but if you get out in society, that's when it's noticed. And there is a certain madness that arises out of being in a band situation. The third reason that the record was called *No Exit* is because Blondie has never really left me. People say, Oh, that's Clem from Blondie, or, That's Debbie from Blondie. It's always been with us in some way. You turn on the car radio and there might be a Blondie record on. We grew up with it. It's part of our lives."

Other cuts Burke points out are "Night Wind Sent," a quiet tune that he uses rods on, and the closing track, "Dig Up The Conjo," which was written around a drum groove inspired by Ringo's part on The Beatles' "Tomorrow Never Knows." Perhaps most unusual in the Blondie oeuvre is the half-time country waltz of "The Dream's Lost On Me." "I like playing in 3/4 and 6/8," says Clem. "But I was disappointed because there was supposed to be a tambourine overdub on that tune, which made it into a 6/8 feel, and for some reason the tambourine got lost. But I like country music a lot; I love Hank Williams, and I go to see Buck Owens play a lot. It's been said before, but I guess as you get older you realize there are only two kinds of music: good and bad.

"We've always played different styles," Clem relates, "and I think that's part of being a good musician—and certainly being a good drummer. The songwriter might come in with a song in a style you may not be used to playing, so it's good to be well-versed in different types of music, like understanding what a shuffle is and what a waltz is."

Clem suggests studying the masters to hear how different styles should be approached. "One problem I have is that a lot of rock drummers don't make it swing. If you listen to Chuck Berry or Little Richard or someone like D.J. Fontana on the Elvis records, they are doing a triplet swing beat. If somebody goes to play 'Johnny B. Goode' and starts banging out straight 8th notes on the hi-hat, that's wrong. Steve Jordan was so great in the Chuck Berry movie *Hail! Hail! Rock 'N Roll* because he really got that style down."

As Clem points out, Blondie has always betrayed varied influences. In fact, the drummer insists that the members' shared taste for The Ramones, The New York Dolls, The Velvet Underground, and girl groups like The Shangri-Las—whose "Out In The Streets" Blondie has finally committed to tape on *No Exit*—is what kept them together through their tough early days. "We had mutual musical ground that a lot of people didn't have at the time," he recalls.

Conversely, their individual obsessions also guaranteed that they not only mixed their common interests into one identifiable sound, but pushed each other into uncharted waters. "We all influence each other," says Clem. "Chris was always heavily into R&B; 'Rapture' was basically his song. I have a little more of a pop sensibility, but I also love Tony Williams and Miles and all that stuff. Over the last fifteen or twenty years I've been getting more into jazz—not that I'm a jazz player, but since Debbie was working with the Jazz Passengers, I decided to write this sort of fake jazz song, 'Boom Boom In The Zoom Zoom Room.' We all like soundtrack music, too, and if you are doing a film soundtrack you're not really writing one type of music. If you go back to the first Blondie record, we may not have executed all the styles we were attempting—maybe our thoughts were beyond our skills at the time—but we did have a lot of different styles on there."

As Debbie Harry suggests, Clem has always been driven to succeed in the rock'n'roll world, and his recollections of life as a young drummer in Bayonne, New Jersey bear this out. "Everybody around me seemed to think that becoming 'a rock star' was unobtainable, but I never felt that way. I felt that this was how I was going to be able to escape my working-class existence. I was on a quest to find the perfect lead singer. I always say that when I met Debbie I sort of found my Mick Jagger."

Burke says that as a kid his drum heroes were "the obvious people": Bonham, Ringo, Charlie Watts. "Early on I was always in one of the better local bands," Clem recalls. "We would do the whole Battle Of The Bands thing, and it wouldn't be unusual if we were the winners or in second place. My high school band entered this contest with deejay Bruce Morrow of WABC AM. You would record a song and send it in to the station—and they played ours on the radio. The finalists would get to go and play at a ballroom like the Hilton, but that year it was at Carnegie Hall."

Later Clem would hang out at a bar in New York called Club 82, where a band called The Stilettos, featuring Chris Stein and Debbie Harry, would open for The New York Dolls. "I was very influenced by that," Burke says. "There was a handful of bands that I liked that my friends didn't particularly like—Bowie, The Raspberries, The New York Dolls. I did have one friend in high school who was a couple of years older than me, and he was a big jazz freak. He actually toured with The Jazz Messengers at one point, and he influenced me in a lot of ways as far as stepping outside of AM radio. But when I saw David Bowie at Carnegie Hall in 1973, that was a big turning point for me. There was great musicianship going on, but it was also complemented by a great show and a great image. That's the direction I thought I should head in."

Around this time Chris and Debbie put an ad in the *Village Voice* that Clem saw. "I was probably about eighteen at the time, and I came over from New Jersey with my girlfriend on the bus to a little rehearsal loft on West 30th Street to meet them. It wasn't an 'audition' so much as a 'chat,' and we found we shared musical ideas and had common taste in bands like The Velvet Underground, The New York Dolls, Iggy Pop, and The Shangri-Las, and soundtrack composers like John Barry and Ennio Morricone.

"More than anything else, I think they liked what I was wearing," Clem laughs. "We were doing an interview with *People* the other day, and Chris was saying, 'I really liked the shoes that you had on.' I had seen a picture of Keith Moon with a sailor suit on, so I had a blue sailor shirt on. But I was immediately taken by Debbie's charisma."

Clem wasn't the only one. During a very early gig at a bar on 13th and 3rd called Monty Python's, during a time when "Platinum Blonde" was their unofficial theme song, an unusual incident hinted at things to come. "These people came in and wanted to hire us for a party in this townhouse downtown, for some equestrian show. All they said was, 'Just make sure the singer wears those boots.' Debbie had on these high-heel boots with some kind of fur around them, but the point is they were really taken by her. I'm sure we sounded pretty sloppy and horrible."

That amateurism wouldn't last too long, however, and as the band improved and scored more gigs on the seedy lower east side, they found themselves ensconced in a scene that would become the stuff of rock 'n' roll lore. With clubs like Max's Kansas City and an ex hillbilly joint called CBGB's as the focal points, New York's East Village became the breeding ground for the bands that would change the world. Rule-breakers like The Ramones, Talking Heads, Patti Smith, Richard Hell & The Voidoids, and Television found themselves crowned as kings and queens of the American punk revolution. Their individual styles might have been radically different, but their ideas pointed in bold new directions that would influence legions of bands for years to come. Blondie was right there in the thick of things, and would eventually become the most successful group of the whole lot. But—and this is well documented—it might not have ever happened for them if not for Burke's persistence.

"I think the first time I played at CBGB's was the night our original bassist, Fred Smith, quit. In between sets he told us he was leaving to join Television. Blondie briefly kind of dissolved because of that, but I kept pushing to continue, and I brought in a friend of mine, Gary Valentine. The two of us were living in a storefront on East 10th Street, and even through he wasn't really a bass player, he was very artistic. He didn't really audition for the band; he just read some poetry, then sat down at the piano and sang one of his songs. So then at least we had the nucleus of a band once again, and we continued from there. But when it looked like the band was going to stop, I decided there was no way I was going to let that happen. You know, perseverance is a big part of any endeavor."

After adding Jimmy Destri on keyboards, Blondie recorded their debut, which included the Australian hit "In The Flesh." Valentine left soon after, and the remaining four released *Plastic Letters* in 1977, which featured "Denis" and "(I'm Always Touched By Your) Presence, Dear," which catapulted the band to instant fame in Britain. Blondie-mania in America wasn't far behind. The follow-up album, *Parallel Lines*, featured an expanded lineup that included Frank Infante on guitar and Nigel Harrison on bass, but more importantly contained the hits "One Way Or Another," "Hanging On The Telephone," and the disco-crossover "Heart Of Glass." Blondie found themselves the focus of a media frenzy.

Nineteen seventy-nine saw the release of *Eat To The Beat*, which spawned two more hits: "Atomic," and the leadoff track, "Dreaming," a showpiece for Burke's crazed full-kit abandon. When it's suggested to Clem today that a lot of drummers would never be able to get away with playing with such "enthusiasm" on the follow-up to a hugely successful album, he replies dryly, "Honestly, even *I* was surprised that one got through like that. When we did *Eat To The Beat*, there was a real exuberance in the studio. On *Parallel Lines*, producer Mike Chapman was very much of a taskmaster; he'd be in the studio conducting us to keep the meter, almost like a Phil Spector type of thing. He worked really hard at making that record perfect, and it ended up being Chrysalis Records' biggest seller ever. We were on a roll, so he kind of gave us free rein on *Eat To The Beat*. So on 'Dreaming' we were like, Let's go for it! A lot of people say that they like the drums on that song."

Despite their huge success, the pressures of stardom began to wear on the band. Their next album, *Autoamerican*, though containing the hits "The Tide Is High" and "Rapture," received less enthusiastic praise, and egos, substance abuse, and a tireless schedule conspired to drag the band down. They managed to squeeze out one more album, *The Hunter*, before letting the whole thing fizzle out.

Initially Burke joined Nigel Harrison and Steve Jones from The Sex Pistols in the band Chequered Past, which toured and recorded one album. In 1985 the drummer worked with The Who's Pete Townshend on the album *White City*. "That was one of the high points for me," enthuses Burke, who can be heard on the cuts "Brilliant Blues" and "Secondhand Love." "Blondie was very popular in England, so Pete's management called mine—that's how I get most of my gigs, by word of mouth—and I went to Twickenham, where Pete had his studio, the Boathouse. Pete hadn't picked up a guitar in quite some time, and we hung out for about a month and jammed."

Clem was in heaven. An avowed Who fanatic, he relished the opportunity to occupy the seat his idol Keith Moon sat in for so many years. "Early on," Burke recalls, "all I cared about was Keith Moon and The Who. When I was about eleven or twelve, my favorite part of drum lessons was the last ten minutes, when I'd get to sit at the drumset and play along to my favorite record. I'd bring in 'My Generation.' At the end of the song the drums go nuts. 'My Generation' was a turning point for me because before that it was all the Charlie Watts and Ringo type of thing."

The experience clearly stuck. Rarely is one drummer's influence on another as clearly identifiable as Moon's is on Burke. So it's understandable that, when on September 7, 1978 Moon died of an overdose of anti-alcoholism pills, Burke was quite shaken. "I remember very distinctly where I was when I heard the news. We were on tour in Rotterdam, and we were ready to go to London to do three or four sold-out shows at the Hammersmith Odeon. The British tabloid press was full of headlines like "Who Drummer Dies" and "Keith Moon Dead At Thirty-One," and I was completely in shock. We played that night, and at the end I just kind of...actually, I wanted to get an ax and some gasoline, but no one would give them to me. So I wound up basically throwing all my drums into the audience as sort of a sacrifice to Keith. The roadies retrieved them, but I didn't want them back. I was really, really bummed."

Clem had in fact come close to The Who's inner circle earlier, in 1980 when he befriended Ringo Starr's son Zak. "Zak played drums on The Who's recent Quadrophenia tour," Clem explains. "He's such a great drummer. The first time I met him was at a club in London. I went to see a band, and this young kid came up to me and said, 'You're a drummer, right? My dad's a drummer.' And I go, 'Oh yeah? Has anybody ever heard of him?' He was such a sweet kid, really young.

"Zak invited me out to his house, where he had a set of Keith's drums—actually, the last set that he had, the white ones with brass fittings. The Premier people told me that Keith wanted them to be white with *gold* fittings, but gold is very fragile so they told him, 'You better rethink this, Keith, especially if you're going to be smashing them!' Plus, I'm sure Keith had a full endorsement, so..." Clem laughs at the thought, and continues, "Zak and I went out to where his dad was living and set up the drums and played them. That's something that I'll always remember. We've kept in touch; in fact Zak came to one of the shows that we just did in London.

"I was actually at the party for Kenney Jones when The Who asked him to join the band," Clem continues. "He was *very* happy. He's another one of my favorite drummers. I love The Small Faces, and I always listened to Kenney's drums; he was so great on all that stuff. That's why I like that band The Raspberries; I think they tried to copy The Small Faces quite a bit, though they had their own thing going on too."

In 1986 Clem recorded the Eurythmics' *Revenge* album, which contained the Grammy-winning single "Missionary Man." Though the album was stylistically less adventuresome than any Blondie release, Burke explains, "With the Eurythmics I became a lot more groove-oriented, but I always wanted to find a balance between Al Jackson of Booker T. & The MG's—who I listened to continuously—and Keith Moon. The *Revenge* record is a favorite of mine; I learned so much from working with Annie Lennox and Dave Stewart."

Clem had actually met Lennox several years earlier, when he was living in London. "After we made *Autoamerican*," he explains, "we took what turned out to be a two-year break. I was at a club one night...it seems I used to get a lot of work from hanging out in night clubs, doesn't it? I don't really hang out that much anymore, so it's lucky I'm back in Blondie! But anyway, ironically they had been playing *Autoamerican* in the club from start to finish. This very attractive woman came up to me and introduced herself. I was somewhat disappointed when she started talking to me about a band she had, but she said she wanted to maybe work with me. She told me she was a fan and that she had been in a band called The Tourists with her ex-boyfriend, and now they had this band The Eurythmics. They were going to Germany to make a record, and she asked if I would be interested in going."

Clem was, and went with Lennox and Stewart to a farmhouse outside of Cologne to work on *In The Garden*, beginning an on-again/off-again relationship that continues to this day. "I did some TV shows with them when the record was released, but I moved back to New York after that. We remained friends, though, and they would come and visit me at my apartment here. Later they regrouped and rethought things, and just the two of them made the *Sweet Dreams* record, with synthesizers and drum machines. They decided to put a band together to promote it, so just as the record was released, I went with them on a tour of the UK."

Burke was in the right place at the right time, because the album, which contained the hit title track, quickly became a smash. "England is such a small place," Burke explains. "You could release a record and six weeks later see it become this huge hit, and if you're on tour, the momentum really builds. So we went in a van and did a college tour of the UK, and at the end of that six weeks *Sweet Dreams* was Number 1. It was like something out of a movie. They asked me to join the band, but Blondie was still going at that time—even though right after that Blondie kind of ended."

Clem got a second chance with Stewart and Lennox when he joined up for the *Revenge* album and tour. Another huge hit, the record's success saw the band playing a three-year tour that included 70,000-seat stadium gigs in Europe, such as a Nelson Mandela benefit concert in Wembley Stadium. Dave Stewart turned the band's popularity into a lucrative producing role, including work for Bob Dylan, and he recommended Clem for the gig. "We spent a couple of weeks jamming," Clem recalled, "and I was convinced we were making the next *Blonde On Blonde*. I thought, 'This record is going to be *great*,' and then one track came out like two years later on the album *Knocked Out Loaded*." Clem good-naturedly laughs at the way things worked out—he's used to such things in the world of rock'n'roll, after all—and is just thankful for the opportunities presented to him by people like Stewart. "When Blondie was in London last, I had lunch with Dave, and there's talk of us doing some more stuff because they are thinking about doing another project. Dave has always helped me along with gigs. We have an interesting relationship, because I befriended him when I was more of a success than he was, and now he's obviously got more success than me!"

Of course, Clem's being modest in his self-assessment. In addition to his work with Blondie, The Eurythmics, Dylan, and Townshend, his drumming graced the splendid 1991 album *Hi-Fi Sci-Fi* by Dramarama, a band he was a member of for three years. He's also been a sometime member of The Romantics (of "What I Like About You" fame) and critics' darlings The Plimsouls, both of whom have new records out soon. He even worked with David Bowie on an unreleased cut intended for the recent *Rug Rats* film soundtrack.

Perhaps contrary to current drum wisdom, Clem says he gets calls not so much because he is some kind of musical chameleon, but rather because of his individual qualities. "I've been lucky," he insists. "People usually want to work with me because of what I do, so they do give me somewhat of a free rein—though of course I have to be aware of my situation and not go too overboard. With people like Dylan and Pete Townshend, a lot of the musical communication that goes on is not necessarily verbal anyway. Bob communicates through his guitar a lot, through his grooves. Pete is a little more eloquent about what he wants. But I think most musicians communicate through their music. I find that people who are so anal about what they want don't really have a clue in some ways; they don't let the musicians do their job, and they're not really setting the tone for good musical interaction."

A big part of what other musicians love about Clem Burke's drumming is simply the boundless energy he brings to the table. Go back to Blondie's "Dreaming," or the new album's opening track, "Screaming Skin," or Dramarama's "Hey Betty," and you'll hear an inherent liveliness that you don't necessarily get even from triple-scale LA studio cats. Perhaps that's because Clem treats playing in the studio just as he does playing live: "I just *go* for it when I play. In concert, I try to envision what I would like to see if I was in the audience. I am really inspired by people like Moon and Gene Krupa—such showmen. Buddy Rich too. I really like playing live, I like being in front of the audience. Blondie, The Romantics, The Plimsouls—they are all great rock bands in the traditional sense. Everyone rocks out."

Clem also understands that, well, you gotta *look* good while you're rockin' out, too. "One of the luxuries of being on tour now is that we have a wardrobe person. Tommy Hilfiger has been sponsoring us, and he made us all these great clothes, kind of like leather Rat Pack suits. It's kind of impractical, though. Even Charlie Watts, who is like a sartorial man of elegance and is always seen in a suit, doesn't wear one when he plays. The problem with wearing suits when you play a heavy rock gig is that the linings shrink."

When reminded of classic old photos of Gene Krupa, where you can often see proof of his vivacious performance in the huge patches of sweat on his suit, Clem can relate. "Yeah, that was part of his style. Krupa was amazing. And Jerry Nolan from The New York Dolls, he'd always wear the greatest clothes. I can understand why musicians, drummers especially, come out wearing shorts. But it's just not my style.

Lest we forget, it isn't *just* about being exciting and looking good with Clem. He's got the chops to back it up, in particular a strong bass drum foot, which he often uses in neat patterns with his hands. "Independence between your hands and feet is an important thing to develop," Clem insists. "I try to think of the foot as another hand. Practicing paradiddles between your hands and feet is one way to improve that. That gets your foot working on double strokes."

Though Burke's busy schedule has kept him from taking proper lessons, he says he'd like to find a way to work with some of the great drummers he's met since moving to LA fifteen years ago. "There's always room for improvement," he states. "There are a lot of good people in LA, like Ed Shaughnessy and Joe Porcaro, and they both give private lessons. I'd also like to take some lessons from Earl Palmer. I go and see him play quite a bit in LA. He plays every Tuesday night at this place near my home, and he's such an inspiration to me. He's got to be in his seventies, but he looks great, the chicks dig him, and he's such a gentleman. When Earl has his jams, all kinds of people turn up. Last time The Stones were in LA, Charlie Watts and Jim Keltner were there just studying his moves. Hanging there has really opened me up to a lot of interesting, great musicians.

"It's important not to get too complacent," Clem states firmly. "There are a lot of physical aspects to drumming, especially rock drumming, and as you get a bit older you really need to keep your muscles in tune. I'm an avid jogger and I lift some weights and things like that. I just really feel a need to be able to do that in order to help my playing. Plus, working with people like Dave Stewart and David Bowie is always a really good experience. That's how I *learn*."

"Back in Blondie:
Chris Stein's Quirky Riffs Revitalize Blondie"

by Michael Molenda

Guitar Player, *April 1999*

Following a brief review of Blondie's history, most of this feature article consists of an interview with Chris Stein on the finer points of guitars, studio work, and Stein's musicianship, including the various guitars he plays.—Ed.

In the late '70s, Deborah Harry's icy beauty and tough/tender voice so captivated audiences that many assumed her name was "Blondie" and that she was being backed by some very lucky—and very expendable- -musicians. It got so bad that a publicist distributed "Blondie is a Group!" buttons to remind journalists and fans alike that the group was indeed a group.

But one listen to No Exit [Beyond/BMG], the band's reunion CD, proves that the "boys" are, were, and always will be indispensable elements of the classic Blondie sound. In fact, the muted rhythm figures—typically with a hint of slap back—and moody single note lines of guitarist Chris Stein broadcast a Blondie song even before Harry enters the mix. As songwriter, guitarist, and Harry's former paramour, Stein is responsible for much of what glorified—or damned, depending on your perspective—Blondie as the most commercial act to bust out of the late-'70s new wave movement. Despite its punk roots and studied New York artiness, the band became one of the last old-time singles acts, releasing brilliant radio tracks such as "Rip Her to Shreds," "In the Flesh," "Denis," "Hanging on the Telephone," "Heart of Glass," "One Way or Another," "Rapture," "The Tide is High," "Call Me," and "Island of Lost Souls"—as well as many album tracks that sounded like singles.

Founded in 1974 by Stein and Harry, Blondie's first run in the spotlight ended in 1982, as band tensions, declining record sales, and a serious illness prompted the members to call it quits. (Stein suffered for two years with pemphigus, a genetic disease that covered his body in blisters, caused severe weight loss, and left him assaulted by rumors that he had AIDS. He is now fully recovered.)

No Exit—the band's seventh album, and its first new work since 1982's The Hunter—reunites Blondie's original permanent lineup, minus bassist Gary Valentine. Clem Burke is once again tossing energetic Keith Moon-isms into his drumming and Jimmy Destri is back on keyboards. On record and onstage, the quartet is aided by bassist Leigh Foxx and guitarist Paul Carbonara. (Coolio makes a guest appearance on the title track.)

Produced by Craig Leon, the album pays homage to Blondie's chart-topping past, filled with loud guitars, catchy melodies, and hybrid rock tunes infused with rap and reggae. (Not surprisingly, Mike Chapman, the man who produced the band's first big hit "Heart of Glass," worked with the musicians during the demo process). But unlike some reunion projects that smack of commerce and tired ideas, No Exit presents a band that has the chops, passion, and compositional smarts to remain relevant well into Y2K.

Stein, 49, started pushing the Blondie reunion three years ago, when he suggested releasing a greatest-hits CD with two new songs. Harry was not interested. But as he described making the new album with impassioned, concentrated explosions of dialogue, it became apparent not only how No Exit came to be, but how Blondie made its way to the top and how he overcame his crippling illness: Chris Stein's formidable will is not something that backs down easily.

Interview With Chris Stein

It has been 20 years since the band's last record, and yet the rhythm tracks on No Exit scream "Blondie"— even if you were to remove Deborah's vocals. Did you consciously develop a "band sound," or does something bizarre happen when you, Clem, and Jimmy step into a studio?

Chris Stein (CS): There must be a little bit of chemistry going on between us, but it's hard for me to be objective. Rhythmically, perhaps it's because I've adapted a certain way of playing to Clem's crappy timing! He's very creative with the rhythm, but that's because he plays organically. He brings a lot of emotion and enthusiasm to his playing and sometimes that's indicated by his speeding up and slowing down. I don't necessarily think that's bad, however. Drumming can get very rigid and boring. I guess it's all about feel. We play a certain way when we're together, and that thing becomes this familiar sound that people relate to as Blondie.

What do you feel is your stylistic contribution to the band sound?

CS: I don't know. I've always been a particularly weird player, actually. For one thing, I always play with a thumbpick and fingerpicks. I don't know many rock and roll guitarists who do. It's a pretty standard claw-hammer style. John Fahey was like a total god to me—a huge influence. I can play more fluidly with just my fingers, but I always go back to the fingerpicks to get the attack right. I'll do things like whack chords with my thumb and pluck two strings simultaneously rather than deal with the little delays you get when crosspicking.

Did you do a lot of pre-production to ensure that the recording sessions for No Exit went smoothly? After all, the band hadn't recorded together in quite a spell.

CS: No, not so much. We didn't work up a lot of stuff. We probably should have, because I'm now finding that the songs are evolving further as we play them live. A lot of the tracks on the record were first or second takes—and often they were the first, second, or third times that we had ever played the songs together. Craig wasn't into waiting for us to work up parts in the studio—he wanted to get the tracks down quickly.

So the sessions took on a 'first thought, best thought" kind of vibe?

CS: Yeah, yeah. But that makes for a lot of inspired moments. The guitar part on "No Exit," for example, was done really quickly. It wasn't worked out. I came up with it, played it, and that was it. When you can get that kind of immediacy into your playing, you don't mind if the producer takes bits of your performance and loops them or moves them around.

How did you typically record your parts?

CS: Well, I didn't use any amps. All of my guitar sounds were through the console and direct-to-tape, using a Boss GT-5 multi-effects processor. I just tweaked parameters until the guitar didn't sound like a straight, normal guitar. I'd add ring modulation and things like that. I'm into programming, so it was fun to mess around. It was way easier than dealing with amps and mike positions and all that stuff. Actually, the difference between having a big wall of amps in the studio and recording something direct is not that pronounced. With these digital boxes, I think you can make anything sound like anything if you fool around enough.

Do you arrange your guitar parts to leave room for Deborah's vocals, or do you just go for it and edit the performance later?

CS: I'm always conscious of conflicting with the vocals. In a concession to modernity, this record is very minimal—less "wall of sound"—and that helps the vocals cut through. But even when I'm playing lines while Debbie is singing—which is not something we did much in the past—you can hear her just fine. The minimalism makes that kind of counterpoint easier to pull off, and technology certainly helps the process. We recorded the album on an Otari Radar hard-disk system—our first digital recording—and that, along with all the digital signal-processing stuff, makes it easier to get a real precise performance down quickly. And it can be just one guitar, so it doesn't have to fill a lot of space. In the past, to get a good guitar sound, you'd often double or quadruple a part. The guitar would sound great, but the dense tone also took up a fair amount of space in the mix.

How much were the tracks digitally manipulated?

CS: The drums were fixed up, but we'd usually just correct a few things that went severely out of time. Some of the parts were looped, mistakes were fixed, arrangements were tweaked, you know, it was pretty much the way everyone makes records these days.

As your career spans the analog and digital eras, did you find yourself pining for the good old days of tape recording while making No Exit, or did you enjoy the process—and the sound—of the hard-disk system?

CS: I liked it a lot. For one thing, when we worked with [producer Mike] Chapman on Parallel Lines, I would kill myself trying to play a part exactly the same five times, and he'd never be satisfied unless each overdub was exactly the same. I mean, it took us two weeks to put "Heart of Glass" together because Chapman wanted every single beat right on the money. The stuff on that track is as precise as if it had been done with a MIDI sequencer. It took me hours and hours to play the song's repeating guitar part so that my performance and my Roland Space Echo were perfectly locked to the timing pulse. Now, you can do things like synchronize your delays to timecode by pressing a button. It's automatic! So for this album, I didn't bother knocking myself out. I'd get the part down once, and they'd move it around or repeat it as needed.

So from a performance standpoint, you feel it's much easier working in the digital domain?

CS: Well, I should say that I didn't dislike recording all those overdubs. It was an experience, actually. And there's definitely a sonic vibe and density that occurs when you overdub parts that is different from digitally manipulating them. I'd be at a loss today if I hadn't done that stuff—as difficult as it was. The idea of repetition is important in any kind of art form. And doing something 100 times and keeping it fresh is a challenge.

Do you still use your Steinberger guitar?

CS: On the album, I used the Steinberger and this other thing—it's called a Lindert and it looks something like a Danelectro. It's a very cool, very quirky guitar. Sonically, it's pretty jazzy—a dry, clean-sounding guitar. There's not much of an edge to it. I also have a custom Tom Lieber (see sidebar, "The Gigerstein" on p. 61 [*of the original article, and reprinted at the end of this selection*—Ed.]) that looks amazing. It's based on H.R. Giger's designs. Actually, I'm pretty casual about this stuff. To me, it's not so much what the guitar is, as what it sounds like.

But you've certainly remained loyal to the Steinberger.

CS: Well for one thing, it stays in tune. Plus the graphite construction gives the guitar a fluid, yet very hard attack. And, when I plug the Steinberger into a distortion box, the signal doesn't clip as it tends to do with single-coil pickups. I kind of gave up on Strats because they'd clip out with distortion boxes.

Do you change your setup for live gigs?

CS: It's pretty lean—the Steinberger, a Fender Hot Rod DeVille or Twin, a Boss Super Feedbacker, and Boss distortion, phaser, and delay pedals. I've discovered that the more decisions I have to make, the more frustrated I get. It's best for me to keep it simple.

In the band's heyday, Blondie was extremely adept at cross-pollinating white, new wave rock with rap, reggae, and what's now called world beat. Did you actively seek out and listen to music from other cultures?

CS: Actually, I've always been out of the loop in respect to listening to other music. All my references were—and are—internal. I listen to the stuff that's going on in my head, more than what's going on outside. I don't listen to bands. Most of my references for recorded music are from stuff I was listening to before I did the band thing. Maybe I'm afraid of change or something, but the first things I fell into--like the Stones, Hendrix, and all that '60s stuff—have stayed with me my whole life. I never even got into the second wave. I was never into Zeppelin, for instance. When Blondie started, I stopped being a music fan because I got so involved with doing it.

So how did these hybrids occur?

CS: For the most part, I don't recall them as being deliberate. Maybe I'd hear this stuff in taxi cabs or whatever. If something sticks in my head, that's it—it might appear somewhere else in some other form.

You've had the hit records and all the goodies and bummers that come with pop stardom—what are your goals today?

CS: In the past, the challenge was trying to make a hit record. It was an intense thing because you'd be trying to make something that worked on a million different levels. For example, a hit song has to work on a corporate level, a marketing level, a business level, and then on radio, where it hopefully becomes something that many people identify with. Now, the challenge is figuring out what the challenge is. It's sort of more Zen.

Did you ever experience a clairvoyant moment when listening to one of your songs, where you knew it would be a huge hit?

CS: That only happened with "The Tide is High." I knew the timing was right, that the song was catchy, and that we were in a position to get the track a lot of airplay. The fact that Debbie sang "number one" in the chorus didn't hurt. It was like an unconscious suggestion going on there.

THE GIGERSTEIN

The disappointing box office receipts of the last Alien flick may have put the torch to that series, but fans of H.R. Giger's designs for the film can get an "art fix" by attending a Blondie concert. Guitarist Chris Stein—a longtime friend of Giger's—recently commissioned New York luthier Tom Lieber to build an instrument based on the futuristic artist's work. The Lieber "Gigerstein" is the result of a three-way collaboration between the guitar builder, the artist, and the musician.

True to Giger's vision of melding organic and synthetic elements, the Gigerstein is constructed of wood, bronze, carbon graphite, and assorted "biological materials." The 25 1/2"-scale graphite neck and fingerboard are molded into a single, integral piece, and the guitar weighs 9 lbs. Electronics include four custom EMG pickups—each with its own volume and tone control. Lieber—who has built instruments for Paul McCartney, Jerry Garcia, Stanley Clarke, and others—values the one-of-a-kind Gigerstein at $57,000.—*Michael Molenda*

For more information on and pictures of the Gigerstein, please go to www.lieberguitars.com/gigerGtr.htm–Ed.

Chris Stein, El Rey, Los Angeles, February 10, 1999
credit: copyright © Sherry Gunderman

"Timeless Pop—On the Top—Again"

by Henrik Tuxen

Original unedited version of published article entitled "Blondie: No Exit," Total Guitar, *April 1999.*—Ed.

They were the scapegoat in the CBGB cradle of punk. Blondie, with the mysterious sexbomb Debbie Harry in front, and Chris Stein on guitar, repaid by conquering the world of pop. They were way ahead of their time and after 16 years in the dark, they're back again.

In the early seventies Deborah Harry starred as one of three female vocalists in the New York group the Stillettoes. One day the band recruited guitar player Chris Stein. As the story goes, Stein immediately fell madly in love with the five years older blonde, and pretty soon the affection was mutual. Debbie Harry and Chris Stein were the inseparable couple of the emerging punk/art New York scene, with a passion so intense, that their heated love even took place at the toilets of CBGB.

Besides music, Chris Stein was involved in everything from black magic, voodoo and photography in the early 70s, a multi-artist to be. A strange and mysterious man, the Jew who'd perform with Nazi symbols, and the occultist who created beautiful pop music.

Keyboard player Jimmy Destri has always contributed to Blondie's music, with his atmospheric keyboards and his fine ear for writing pop tunes. Drummer Clem Burke is the true pop star and entertainer of the group, who has played with the Eurythmics, among others, and been involved in producing. At one time Gary Valentine played bass and was replaced by Nigel Harrison in the heyday of Blondie's commercial success, which also featured guitarist Frank Infante. These people have all left their fingerprint on the unique Blondie sound, but the top of the hierarchy has never been doubted, not then nor today. The charismatic and seductive Debbie Harry in front, and the musical mastermind, Chris Stein, on guitar.

Total Guitar met the former couple before, during and after Blondie's Top of The Pops performance of their current hit single—the Jimmy Destri composition "Maria." A song which Chris Stein wasn't too convinced about in the beginning.

Chris Stein: I wasn't so sure about some of the songs this time. Like the "Maria" song, when I finally heard the finished song I realised how great it was, but I was still in doubt up until then.

"Maria" as well as the rest of the current album *No Exit*, actually sounds like a continuation of Blondie from the early 80s, ranging from the crystal clear hit singles to various experimenting mix of musical styles. Pretty logical to Debbie Harry: "What else could it possibly be than a Blondie record? We worked on this record very much from internal sources, from the inside out, we wanted to do a Blondie album."

You've named it No Exit. *Does that suggest that Blondie will stick around forever?*

Debbie Harry: "Probably. It means that Blondie seems to be an inescapable identity; there is no exit, there is no escape."

And talking about eternity, the longevity of Blondie's music has been quite astonishing. Years after the band's split, the album sales have been consistent and even rising in the 90s. What's the secret behind this apparently timeless success?

DH: "I could say the songs are good, they still hold up. We were adventurous in our combinations of styles, in using different electronic styles and combining different instruments. I guess it was just genius (laughing). I don't know, we just did it. It's hard to say about yourself that you're a genius, but the combinations of all the elements and Chris' ideas were very futuristic."

CS: "We just seemed to have hit that thing, its very intangible and hard to talk about, but it's something about archetypes. You hear something and it sounds familiar, as something you've heard before, like certain scales or melodies which are in your brain already. A little kid sings 'la la la la' and where does it come from? It's just in his head. Certain groups of people sort of tap into that. It sounds corny but sometimes I feel like I'm just filtering the music which is coming through me. It's like I'm a computer and I listen to things and then I clip them together just like that."

What inspires you to write music?

CS: "Inspiration is a hard thing to define, I could never force a song. If I sit down and try to write a song, it just doesn't work like that, and then sometimes it's just right there. Something which comes immediately, or very very quickly. Often I'll be in the middle of fucking nowhere, and something comes in my head and I know it's a good song, but...If I could write music it might be better, because a million songs just get lost because I don't remember them."

Let's Get Together Again

Jimmy Destri totally left music for some years and for many years Chris Stein suffered from a genetic skin disease. Besides this, the original members of Blondie have been engaged in all kinds of different musical activities and Chris Stein has been involved with a lot of Debbie Harry solo material, so why wasn't Blondie reformed earlier?

CS: "When we stopped playing in 1982, there was a period where we weren't really on the radio, and then from the middle and the end of 80s and all through the 90s, it's been building up. Plus, we kept being in touch with kids who were excessive fans who encouraged us to reform. It just felt like a good time to do it now."

DH: "It was basically Chris' idea. He felt that if we didn't grab the opportunity now, we'd might regret it later in life. It's pretty obvious that people are referring to Blondie as an inspiration for their music, and then there are a lot of females and lady singers in the business today, and I think that's very good."

Band reunions have become a pretty frequent phenomenon, especially when solo careers or new band constellations are running low, or not running at all. And very often these reunions only feature one or two of the original members. Nigel Harrison and Frank Infante unsuccessfully tried to prevent Blondie from using the band name through a lawsuit, since they were not asked to join the reunion. Neither was Gary Valentine, but besides this, the core of band in 1999 is the original band members. Was it either the original line-up or no reunion at all?

DH: (pragmatically) "Well, according to our agreement in the band, we can't call it Blondie unless the original members are in it, so that's the determining factor. But band reunions with hardly any original band members are not a good thing. It had to be the four of us."

What's been the greatest thing about the comeback?

CS: "I'd say the acceptance now, people are kind of understanding us now. When we started out people didn't know what the fuck we were doing."

DH: "The response from the audience coming to our live shows has been very very wonderful, all over Europe, UK and Australia. We all felt so good about it. I don't think that it could ever happen again, quite like that. Just coming out again after such a long period of time."

The Architect and the Blend of Styles

Listening to the old Blondie album is like a voyage through all the different musical styles which were present at the time—reggae, rock, punk, disco, Latin, and even rap—squeezed into well crafted pop songs. Was it an intentional desire to construct crossover music or merely coincidental creativity?

CS: "I just did what I liked to do. Almost nothing was planned out, just things we did automatically, because we felt like it. None of the stuff was studied, and we never had a plan; neither for this album. It's just that I like all this different stuff. As when I originally heard reggae music back in 1973, which became a movement and a style in the USA, I got really excited about it. Something also happened when I heard Dr. John's first album—stuff like that."

DH: "Chris was very influential in the sense that he wanted to include certain elements he admired. We really liked Chic, Kraftwerk and Kid Creole & the Coconuts and a lot of bands which were around, and also the *Saturday Night Fever* album was a big hit with us. But it's just as much about being from New York. There's all these ethnic groups around and they all sort of become a part of you—and then you start to synthesise everything together in your own way."

So what music has an impact on Blondie today?

CS: "I really don't listen to a lot of modern stuff. I really don't. I mean, Clem especially listens to everything but I'd never heard Oasis and the only reason that I heard R.E.M. was because Clem had the new CD on the bus. My fan days were sort of over when I started being in a band. I was a fan in the 60s hearing the Stones and Jefferson Airplane, which I was most enthusiastic about. Then there was the new wave stuff, like Ramones and the Sex Pistols album, but my fan time sort of went away. I always had something internal around my head, you know bits and pieces, and then I hear a lot of modern music driving around in taxis."

Jimmy Destri also writes a lot of songs, but you are known as the arranger or architect in Blondie. Is that so?

CS: "I sort of push everything, yeah. I try to be democratic, but in bands there's just no such thing as a democracy. Somebody has to make the final decision to get things going."

Would you say that Jimmy is the pop head and you're the experimentalist?

CS: "Maybe, on this record it's true. For instance, the "No Exit" song sounded really different in the beginning. I was the one who made it sound like a gothic, big sort of metal crash. People said it sounded like *Gangsters Paradise*, which I don't even know that well, but I'm exited now about working with all the rap kids. Coolio is on the record and lately we've done this song with some of the guys from Wu Tang Clan. Those guys are really cutting edge to me, they sort of take the place of the punk movement today, as white Rock'n'Roll is pretty safe now. In America there's the whole racial thing which takes it another step. In England it's nothing like the tension in America which is still there, and there's probably another 50 years before it goes away."

There's Only One Jimi

Although Debbie Harry always had a magnetic effect on the cameras as well as the world wide music press, Blondie was always a very guitar-oriented band, with great articulated guitar lines, designed by Chris Stein, for whom there was always one guitarist above everybody else.

CS: "Jimi Hendrix, there's never been anyone like him. Then I'd mention John Fogerty from Creedence Clearwater Revival. Then there's certain performances by guitar players like Junior Melvin, who did the solo on Bob Marley & the Wailers' *Concrete Jungle*."

Do you basically see yourself as a guitar player or rather an overall musician?

CS: "Not even a musician. I do photography and all this stuff. I don't even know what the fuck I do, some kind of media thing I suppose."

Here at "Top of the Pops" *you're playing a Stratocaster.*

CS: "That's just what I borrowed to play for this show. I've been thinking that when I go back to New York, I might get a deal with Fender to get some free guitars. I like the Stratocaster, but for a long time I used the Steinberger, like last night (*album launch party at the Sound Republic...*—Ed, Total Guitar). [*See "In the Box With Debbie" at the end of this article*—Ed.]. It's a weird black one, with the horns pointing upwards. I keep falling back on that one, but I'd like to try decent Stratocasters. All through the Blondie time I had a 1965 maple neck. It was great, I shouldn't have sold it probably, it's still right at heart."

If you should name some new great guitar players, who would you pick?

CS: "I don't listen to enough people, but I don't think that anyone has come close to the stuff that Hendrix was doing and I don't think that there's any of the new records which are as good as those records. The stuff from Beck is kind of original, but for the most part it sounds the same. I just saw these guys from Divine Comedy, I thought they were fantastic, I like them a lot. We saw them on another show, but I know that they're here today. Massive Attack is a different band that is really good. I see things that I really like, but I think that I saw too many MTV videos for a while and somehow the stuff that's on video is worse than what's on the radio."

Lots of stuff has been happening since Blondie called it a day back in 1982. Charts music today is primarily electronic and guitar music seems to go in and out of style and some people even claim that rock is dead.

CS: "For me the rock is dead thing comes from the fact that it has become so mainstream and safe, plus it's background music for everything in life. You wouldn't see a rock 'n' roll song for a milk or a car commercial 20 years ago, and now everything is fucking Rock 'n' Roll. And because it's everywhere, it becomes less mysterious and less dangerous in that respect. It's different with jazz, also the newer stuff. There are a few people who are very enthusiastic about it and they sort of study it. Jazz never was a really big movement, maybe it had its high point in the early sixties, but still it was never as big a thing as rock 'n' roll is, with the Beatles and the world-wide thing."

The Analogue Cut and Paste

Listening to songs like "Heart Of Glass," "The Tide Is High" and "Rapture" today, suggests that there's more to them than the obvious hit quality. Blondie sold 40 million albums and were known for their fashionable mod style, with the magnetic blonde fashion model in front. And the music was innovative and fresh, especially as Chris Stein really knew how to experiment in a recording studio. Craig Leon was originally in the A&R team which signed Blondie in '75 and later co-produced their debut album. On *No Exit* he's been the man behind the Blondie knobs again. *Total Guitar* spoke to him about the new sound.

Craig Leon: "Blondie were way ahead of their time, not only musically but also technologically. The technological level of today finally matches the way that the band always wanted to record. They used the principle of cut and paste way back in the '70s, which was very time consuming with the available analogue technology. In the '70s they defined the modern way of working, and the modern sound—but without the modern technology. As with Abba, it took a long time before people acknowledged how brilliant their music was because it was pop. I think that Blondie will get that recognition now musically, but also for their way of working in a studio."

Not surprisingly then, recording *No Exit* was an entirely different experience.

CS: "Yeah it's very exciting that the whole thing is digital now. We were able to capture a lot of inspiration, in the past we had to play something a 100 times just to get it and that would be the take for the whole song. It's really exciting what you can do with the digital stuff which you couldn't do on tape. 'Heart of Glass' is a song that you could do with midi, but it was all done manually, almost like the reverse process."

Debbie Harry similarly welcomes the technological revolution.

DH: "I used to hate making records. I've always liked the writing process and the creativity of it, but the grind and the repetition and the slow process of analogue recording was always very tedious and very uninteresting and boring. But this time it suited me very very well, I really enjoyed myself in the studio this time."

The technological aspect has flavoured the songwriting process as well.

CS: "I don't have a set way of writing songs. It's changing all the time and I've probably tried every possible way, but most of the time I do sequences and midi now and sometimes I go back and try to write on the guitar. I'll very often start with bass and drums. When I write songs, I always concentrate about playing and refining one piece. I never play through jams and then chop them up. Rather than making more from less, I'll make less from more."

The Feeling Is Gone

Blondie emerged in the heyday of the CBGB scene in New York. In a few scant years, artists like New York Dolls, Television, Talking Heads, Patti Smith and Ramones defined American punk, with new and powerful words and music, a strong and alternative cultural identity, and often colourful and provocative identity. At first, Blondie was the scapegoat on the scene. Regarded as a joke, Blondie were the support group during whose concerts something always went wrong. Patti Smith and Tom Verlaine of Television literally looked down on Blondie, something which still bugs Chris Stein. As Blondie took on the world, the other CBGB groups slowly vanished or became moderately successful, and over the years the special CBGB atmosphere has disappeared.

CS: "The CBGB feeling is gone."

DH: "CBGBs is very straight rock and roll nowadays. I have played there for old time sakes with the Jazz Passengers, we wouldn't do it with Blondie; it's too small. Then it's difficult to make it happen because of the sound on stage. It's OK for the audience but difficult for the bands."

When Blondie broke up it was partly because of bad business people, Chris Stein's illness and the generally explosive atmosphere between the band members.

Have things cooled down here at the end of the Millennium or is the same as it ever was?

DH: "Well, we know each other so well and the intensity increases when you're always close together. When you're on the road, you have no one else to go to. I've been in other bands, it's the same thing, you get sick and tired of other people's stupid habits, etc. But I think everybody now is a little more mature and then our management situation is better. Some things have improved—you live and you learn."

Is it odd for you to work with Chris just on a professional level?

DH: "It doesn't feel odd. We had a bit of a cooling off period when we separated. He married and since had a divorce [*and later remarried*—Ed.], but we have remained friends and he's my best friend. It's unusual since separation is often full of anger and even hate. But we have always stayed in touch, seeing each other at least once a week. We would have been best friends whether we'd lived together or not—if I've just met him and we'd never been together, we'd instantly become friends."

And hopefully that guarantees Blondie's future for a while yet.

In The Box With Debbie

"I'm in the phonebox [*i.e. phone booth in American usage*—Ed.] it's the one across the hall," the classic hookline from "Hanging On The Telephone," which makes "Ich bin ein Berliner" and "I did it my way" sound like washing powder adverts. It's Deborah Harry's opening line, January 20th 1999 in Sound Republic on Wardour Street, London. It's the official launch party for Blondie's impressive comeback album, *No Exit*.

As indicated, the party kicks of with the 2.17 minute powerpop anthem "Hanging on the Telephone," from Blondie's 1978 album, *Parallel Lines*, which to date has sold no less than 20 million copies around the globe. The sound is remarkably good and Debbie's voice is convincing, although she appears somewhat shaken and misses a couple of phone messages here and there. The BBC is on the spot and after a very strong eight song set, there are requests for the phonebox intro once again! Back in the old days, Debbie was known to skip a line here and there, and in many ways everything is just like it used to be. The words just won't come out in the correct order, and after a triple run on the "Telephone," the BBC allegedly gives up.

In many ways symptomatic for the evening. Blondie and boys have grown older, they look a bit tired and a little uneasy with being the centre of one of the biggest pop hypes at the moment. But, when on a roll, Blondie's very personal blend of disco, punk, reggae and pop, sounds as timeless and intoxicating, and Debbie Harry's voice as mysterious and seductive, as ever. Best expressed by her comment to the primarily young audience. "It's a strange new old world here in clubland tonight."

Now Photo Section

Deborah Harry, Argentine
recording artist Gizelle D'Cole
and members of the Gipsy Kings,
New Year's Eve, South Beach,
Miami, Florida,
December 31, 1999
credit: copyright © Mayra Cabrera

Sheffield City Hall, Sheffield,
England, November 13, 1998
credit: copyright © Kevin Munns

Sheffield Arena, Sheffield, England, November 25, 1999
Deborah Harry sat by the keyboards for the long intro to the song
"Nothing is Real But the Girl" (NIRBTG)—*Rachael and Kevin Munns*
credit: copyright © Rachael Munns

Tibetan Freedom Concert, Alpine Valley, East Troy, Wisconsin, June 13, 1999
credit: copyright © 1999, 2002 Barry Brecheisen. All Rights Reserved

New Year's Eve, South Beach, Miami, Florida,
December 31, 1999
credit: copyright © Teresa R. Hale

Teresa Hale has been a communications specialist in the corporate world for several years. In 1999, she began branching out as a freelance journalist and photographer in the music business, her real area of interest and expertise. She's currently writing and taking pictures for publications like *New York Waste, Picture This* Blondie fanzine and *The Blondie Review* with several other creative projects in the works. A native of Peoria, Illinois, she frequents New York City in search of creative opportunities and excuses to immerse herself in "the scene." Teresa attributes her inspiration to Deborah Harry and The Motels' Martha Davis.

E-mail Teresa at livewire@davesworld.net

l to r: Jimmy Destri, Deborah Harry, Leigh Foxx, Paul Carbonara, Chris Stein, Clem Burke
Apollo Theatre, Manchester, England, November 22, 1999
credit: copyright © Tommy Galloway and Jackie Williamson

Barrowland Ballroom, Glasgow, Scotland,
November 19, 1998
credit: copyright © Tommy Galloway and Jackie Williamson

Apollo Theatre, Manchester, England,
November 12, 1998
credit: copyright © Tommy Galloway and Jackie Williamson

Debbie Harry of Blondie performing with the Jazz Passengers (including Roy Nathanson pictured at the right)
The Knitting Factory, New York City, May 8, 2002
credit: © Jon Erkider / Retna Ltd

Both photos on this page: Barrowland Ballroom, Glasgow, Scotland, November 19, 1998
credit: copyright © Tommy Galloway and Jackie Williamson

Left: Deborah Harry with Robert Betts at Cathay Che's *Deborah Harry* book release party held at "Mother" nightclub in the "Slaughterhouse" district of New York City on May 31, 2000.
Credit: Stacy Betts

Below left: Deborah Harry (with Blondie) at Foxwoods resort/casino, Mashantucket, Connecticut at the "No Exit tour finale concert" September 10, 1999.
Credit: Robert Betts

Below: Robert Betts reaching to touch "a star." Foxwoods, September 10, 1999.
Credit: Holly Maikshilo

Deborah Harry and Argentine recording artist Gizelle D'Cole, New Year's Eve, South Beach, Miami, Florida, December 31, 1999

credit: copyright © Mayra Cabrera

Madison Square Garden Theater, New York City, June 10, 1999
credit: © Joe Ryan

What a night this was! I worked for 4 months to get the photo pass for this show. Thanks to a generous someone at Hiponline.com, the pass finally fell into my lap 2 weeks before the big show.

I felt it was extremely important to photograph this particular show. Blondie reunited playing a hometown show at MSG--nothing more need be said. It worked out better than I could possibly expect...this show was actually the premiere of a new set design and videos by multimedia artist, Rob Roth. The band against the backdrop simply just looked amazing through my camera!—*Joe Ryan*

"When 'the original Beat cLub undergrOuNd sex goDdess Icon frEaks'* reunite, you have no choice but to follow."

After having photographed the Grateful Dead for several years, covering Blondie seemed an unlikely choice. Though my loyalty had been tied to the Dead for many years, oddly enough Blondie was one of the first bands I remember listening to as a kid...so it was almost a natural thing to document these NYC shows. What was happening at the time of their reunion was just as important as it was in the 70's. These historic moments in music must be preserved for the future and I, for one, took it upon myself to cover this gig.

Photographically speaking, everything about the show was a refreshing challenge from what I was used to. Unfamiliar territory definitely keeps your guard up. Of course, Debbie is the focus and your aim is to capture that energy of hers on film in the allotted three songs you have to shoot. Not an easy task when you don't know what to expect. It's all adrenaline minutes before showtime waiting in the press pit!

And, of course, being behind the camera, you see the band from a unique point of view. You have better-than-front-row seats and you're practically face-to-face with the band. Debbie's on-stage persona is no doubt a photographer's delight—her expressions, emotions, and of course, those lovely poses! You just can't get it anywhere else. Hardly a second goes by that isn't worth photographing. This band just has that "something" most will never achieve...this has been very clear through my lens.

JOE RYAN
Photographer/New Jersey
www.gratefuljoe.com
*Quote from *No Exit* promotional material

Brighton Centre, Brighton, England, November 14, 1999
credit: copyright © Teresa R. Hale

Dockland Arena, London, November 13, 1999
credit: copyright © Teresa R. Hale

After concert party, Fox Theatre, Detroit, Michigan, May 23, 1999
credit: copyright © Ed Kary

Foxwoods, Mashantucket, Connecticut, September 10, 1999
credit: copyright © John Sibby

El Rey, Los Angeles, February 10, 1999
credit: copyright © Sherry Gunderman

Clem Burke and Deborah Harry at Blondie's meet and greet event for the *No Exit* album at Virgin Megastore, San Francisco, February 19, 1999
credit: copyright © David Bartolini

l to r: Jimmy Destri, Chris Stein, Deborah Harry, Clem Burke, Leigh Foxx, Gary Valentine
HFStival '97, RFK Stadium, Washington D.C., May 31, 1997
A rare photo of the whole reunited band at that time, including Gary Valentine.
credit: copyright © Brian La Fountain

No Exit tour, Massey Hall, Toronto, Canada, May 16, 1999
credit: copyright © Marcine Linder

No Exit tour, Massey Hall, Toronto, Canada, May 16, 1999
credit: copyright © Marcine Linder

"Photo Pass"

by Marcine Linder

Believe it or not, the life of a photojournalist is far from glamorous. Sure, we often get to photograph international stars, hang out at some of the coolest parties, and travel. But we are also herded around by the P.R. people like cattle, forced to crowd behind barricades in front of red carpets hoping the celebrity we were hired to shoot decides to stop by and pose for us. To the entertainment business, we are a necessary evil often treated with suspicion. My experience with the members of Blondie was a wonderful and rare exception.

I originally photographed the four re-united members at a press conference hosted by Canadian Music Week in March 1999. When they returned in May 1999 to play Toronto's legendary Massey Hall, I was fortunate enough to have been accredited to shoot their show.

I decided to try to get backstage access. I printed three custom 8 X 10's of my press conference image of the band. My plan was to try to bribe the security guard with one, give the second to the band to keep, and have the third autographed.

Fortunately, the security guard recognized me from prior shoots and had no problem bringing their tour manager out to meet me. He graciously invited me backstage where I was warmly greeted by the band. Chris Stein leafed through my portfolio books, and Clem and I compared luggage preferences. Debbie had a room to herself down the hall where she also kept her dog. I munched on the catering and sipped a beer while they autographed my print (which sadly, I have since misplaced, definitely a sore point!).

It never occurred to me to take my camera out of my bag, even for a snapshot. I was glad to meet the band and have a chance to hang out with them. I'll never forget the dressing down I got from a colleague after I left their dressing room aglow with excitement. He was shocked and even horrified that I hadn't attempted to take any shots. Those shots might have been worth a fortune, being so rare. He told me if I didn't change my ways, I'd never get anywhere in the business.

I didn't regret not trying to shoot any photos of them then and I don't now. I don't see myself as a member of the paparazzi or even a greedy, intrusive photo journalist. I like to think of myself as more of a documentary photographer. After firmly and angrily explaining this to my colleague, he backed down and decided that perhaps he could respect my point of view.

In the end, it appeared it all paid off. Normally, press photographers are allowed to shoot the first three songs of a concert and are then ushered out of the venue. We may only return if we have a ticket and have stowed away our gear off site. My shooting privileges were not extended, but I was allowed to stay for the entire show gear and all on the honour system. It was a fantastic show and have I gorgeous concert shots to remember it with.

Clyde Auditorium, Glasgow, Scotland, November 26, 1999
credit: copyright © Steve Castle

FROM L-R: CHRIS STEIN,   CLEM BURKE,   DEBORAH HARRY,   JIMMY DESTRI

BLONDIE   beyond

Photo Credit: Nitin Vadukul (courtesy of Beyond Music)

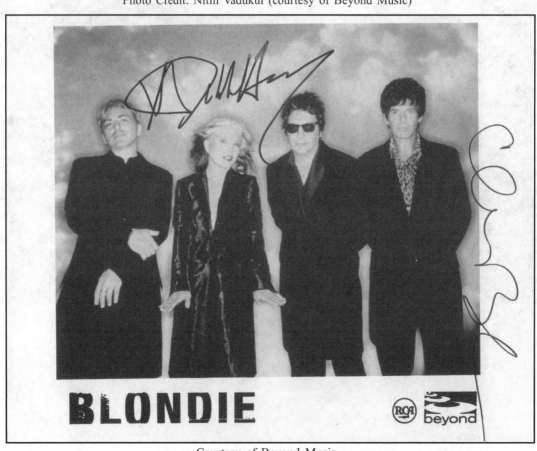

BLONDIE   RCA beyond

Courtesy of Beyond Music

Brighton Centre, Brighton, England, November 14, 1999
credit: copyright © Paul Renouf

Cathay Che book party, Mother, New York City, May 31, 2000
credit: copyright © Paul Renouf

Celebrity Theatre, Phoenix, Arizona, August 24, 1999
With confidence and determination, Deborah and her band mates take the stage...
My heart beats fast. I'm ready to go.—*Robert Tuozzo*
credit: copyright © Robert Tuozzo

Robert J. Tuozzo, having spent many years as a musician who toured the world, decided in 1992 to say goodbye to life on the road and founded Best Shot Entertainment. He played with many top musicians in bands such as Lou May and The Two Tones, 2103, and The Difference, to name a few.

Having gained notoriety and full knowledge of the music business, Robert still was not ready for the challenge of tour and business management. So he did the next best thing.

As a child, Robert always carried around a camera, so his love for photography also allowed him to relive his past; hence he began working as an entertainment photographer. With his love of music and his eye for detail, he soon became world renown, pointing the camera at hundreds of well-known musicians.

After seven full years of working with major corporations, Robert remembered how hard it was to get a break in the business as a musician, so he got involved with the local music scene in Phoenix, Arizona. Having all that stored knowledge of the workings of the music business, Robert was approached by several bands. He currently is responsible for major and indie labels, shopping his clients for record and distribution deals.

Robert also had throughout the years made several friends in the TV and film industry and appeared in full length films and TV. He is the staff photographer for *Loud Magazine* and has also business ties with KEDJ 106.3/100.3 FM—"The Edge" radio station in Phoenix, Capitol, and EMI, to name a few. He also has numerous credits for postings on the World Wide Web.

Robert has now thrown his hat into the management ring, signing such talent as Lock 44, Scarab, Scott Rowe, Mr. Nice Guy "A Tribute to Alice Cooper," and Mother Mercy, a band from Hollywood, California. Source—*"About" and "Bio" pages on Best Shot Entertainment's web site, www.bestshotentertainment.com. Adapted and reprinted with permission.*

John Waters and Deborah Harry at opening night
of the New York Film Festival, New York City, September 24, 1999
credit: WENN / Axel Bachelard

Deborah Harry of Blondie, Party in the Park, Hyde Park, London, July 4, 1999.
Deborah Harry performing to an audience of 100,000 in aid of the Prince's Trust and organized by Capitol Radio
credit: copyright © Mirror Syndication International

Cologne Palladium, Cologne, Germany, October 31, 1999
credit: copyright © Mandy Rohr, Witten, Germany

Haus Auensee, Leipzig, Germany, November 3, 1999
credit: copyright © Josephin Neumann, Leipzig, Germany

Euro '99 Tour, Exhibition Centre, Aberdeen, Scotland, November 17, 1999
credit: copyright © Marc Millar

FROM L-R: JIMMY DESTRI,   DEBORAH HARRY,   CLEM BURKE,   CHRIS STEIN

BLONDIE

Photo Credit: Rob Roth (courtesy of Beyond Music)

Blondie performing on the Today Show, New York City, June 4, 1999
credit: © Jon Erkider / Retna Ltd

In order to secure a front-and-center spot for Blondie's appearance, me and another die-hard fan named John Scott had to get to the NBC studios at 3:00 AM. It was worth it because we got to see Debbie and the band do the sound check at about 5:00. It was a high-energy performance and the coolest thing was that all the tourists from middle-America got so into it and knew all the words to the songs! John and I actually got 8 seconds of close-up airtime during "Maria."—*Jon Erkider*

Deborah Harry of Blondie taking a tour of the newly reopened Limelight, New York City, December 1998
credit: copyright © Jon Erkider / Retna Ltd / Retna Ltd, USA

Limelight was having yet another "re-opening" and was featuring some works by H.R. Giger. Everyone was in line waiting for the doors to open when Debbie and Chris walked out after taking a private tour of the opening. They told me they had just gotten back from Europe the day before and were so exhausted. I congratulated them on all the success they were having and told them how cool it was to hear a new Blondie single be played over and over on the radio again. Inside there were giant neon-blue *Koo Koo* light boxes on display over the right side of the main bar. I told Giger that his cover art of Debbie has yet to be matched even in the genre of goth and shock rock.—*Jon Erkider*

Joey Ramone's memorial show, CBGBs, New York City, April 30, 2001

331

"Life's A Gas: Joey Ramone's 50th Birthday Bash," Hammerstein Ballroom, New York City, May 19, 2001
credit: copyright © 2001 Sherry Globman. All rights reserved

House of Blues, Las Vegas, March 10, 1999
credit: copyright © Sherry Gunderman

Private concert, Orlando, Florida, October 8, 1999
credit: copyright © Jeremiah Jenner

Jimmy Destri, backstage, Parkpop
Festival, Zuiderpark, The Hague,
The Netherlands, June 27, 1999
credit: copyright © Inez Buijtenhek

Blondie concert in Campione d'Italia, Italy, 1998
credit: copyright © Sandro Monticelli

Q101 Jamboree, New World Music Theatre,
Tinley Park, Illinois, May 22, 1999
credit: copyright © 1999, 2002 Barry Brecheisen.
All Rights Reserved

Leigh Foxx, Sheffield Arena, Sheffield, England,
November 25, 1999
credit: copyright © Kevin Munns

l to r: Leigh Foxx, Deborah Harry,
Chris Stein, Paul Carbonara
Zazz Bash, Excalibur, Chicago, Illinois,
September 17, 1999
credit: copyright © 1999, 2002 Barry
Brecheisen. All Rights Reserved

Jimmy Destri
Clyde Auditorium, Glasgow, Scotland,
November 26, 1999
credit: copyright © Steve Castle

Sheffield City Hall, Sheffield, England,
November 13, 1998
credit: copyright © Kevin Munns

Plymouth Pavilions, Plymouth, England, November 29, 1998
credit: copyright © Frances Garrett

This photo was taken at Plymouth in November 1998, marking the last night of the Blondie Euro 1998 Fall tour. Accordingly, champagne had been brought onstage when Blondie went offstage and when they came back they all toasted and congratu-lated each other. I got this nice shot of the band with champagne glasses.—*Frances Garrett*

l to r: Chris Stein and Paul Carbonara
Dockland Arena, London, November 13, 1999
credit: copyright © Tommy Galloway and Jackie Williamson

Poole Arts Centre, Poole, England,
November 28, 1998
credit: copyright © Daniel Porter

Celebrity Theatre, Phoenix, Arizona,
August 24, 1999

As I peered through my viewfinder, I saw
Deborah's reflection in the Plexiglas that surrounded the drum kit. I grabbed this once-in-a-
lifetime shot.—*Robert Tuozzo*
 credit: copyright © Robert Tuozzo

Clem Burke with the Romantics, the club "Scream,"
Los Angeles, September 2000
credit: copyright © Greg Raspet.

Clem Burke with the Romantics, The Viper Room,
Hollywood, October 2000
credit: copyright © Greg Raspet

Both the Scream and Viper Room shows were fantastic.
After the last song at the Scream show, Clem jumped up
from behind the drums on to his kit and gave the crowd
a salute. The Viper Room show was the kind of show
where the Romantics shine.—*Greg Raspet*

Good sound and a good crowd. Clem really got into it
and you could really tell he was enjoying himself, inter-
acting with the other members of the band and really
giving a great show.—*Greg Raspet*

338

Deborah Harry at Click + Drag at FUN

by Sylvie Ball

Deborah Harry performs at Click + Drag's monthly happening at FUN, a Chinatown nightclub, NYC, March 8, 2001

Deborah Harry at Click + Drag at FUN

by Sylvie Ball
(adapted and edited by Robert Betts)

This original article was extracted and adapted from The Blondie Review.
Volume 1, Issue 3, June, 2001.—Ed.

Deborah Harry performed in a "hard-edged" cabaret act with the Nuclear Bomb Babies (Rob Roth and Garrett Domina) at Click + Drag's monthly happening at FUN in Chinatown (NYC) on March 8, 2001.

Click + Drag is a nightclub monthly extravaganza of kinky dressing referred to as "cyber-fetish" by event founder-producers, Rob Roth and Kitty Boots. For four years, Roth and Boots have been perfecting the high maintenance evening that was formerly held at "Mother" (which closed in June 2000) and "Jackie 60's" before relocating the party to FUN, a garage-style nightclub on a stretch of Madison Street in Chinatown known as "Mechanics Alley." Impresario Chi Chi Valenti (the third founder in chief of Click + Drag) is back this season to help evolve the club interface with her special brand of stream of consciousness MCing. Fun is located at 130 Madison Street and Click + Drag happens every second Thursday of the month. Visit their web site at www.clicknyc.com. British transplant Kitty Boots was at the door, enforcing a strict cyber-fetish dress code with imperious exactitude.

Inside, some bartenders and waitresses turned fashion on its head by wearing men's underwear as tank tops—turning the briefs upside down and cutting out a section of the crotch to create a "new neckline." Rubbernecking ran rampant while one creature after another wafted across the room dressed in one of the night's themes: women in floor length tulle chatted with men in apocalyptic neon wigs…young men in gas masks and pumps crossed paths with stately drag queens…men and women in "all black" rubber and vinyl added a sinister note to the mix. Platforms reached improbable heights. The gay and the straight intermingled with carefree aplomb. Male and female go-go dancers dressed in military-fetish flanked the stage. By midnight the place was starting to buzz.

At 1:20 AM, the crowd to the right of the stage parted and a very serious looking Chi Chi Valenti dressed in black military fetish with patent leather gloves came out to center stage and introduced Deborah Harry and the Nuclear Bomb Babies with a cordless mike. Following in Chi Chi's path, you could see Deborah's blonde hair emerging through the crowd. Deborah climbed onto the "very basic" stage with a lot of swagger and took the hammer from Chi Chi and said hello to everyone in the audience. She was radiating her hallmark combination of glamour and punk attitude and the audience was ecstatic.

Deborah was wearing her long hair loose and off her face. She was mostly platinum blonde in the front with some dark blonde spikes towards the back that fell about her shoulders. Her makeup was stunning. I would like to know who her makeup artist was that night because I would love to give him/her credit for the flawless expert application of "heavy, Hollywood" makeup that was both campy and gorgeous. Her skin was luminous. Her outfit was right out of her vintage Blondie character scrapbook. She was wearing a sleeveless swingy black minidress that moved well with her and naughty black satin thigh-high boots. Underneath, she was wearing a sheer flesh-colored body stocking with long sleeves that probably gave her some support and comfort on stage.

The Babies, Rob Roth and Garrett Domina, assumed their stance behind Deborah wearing matching pinstripe suits with red ties and pumps. Deborah's opening number was "Rip Her to Shreds." The energy in the room was intense. She paced back and forth across the stage with purpose as she delivered the song. Her facial expressions were a raucous mix of scowls, "in your face" stares, and plaintiff pouts. Her voice was full and rich and she sounded wonderful live. The Babies performed synchronized dance moves behind her and also acted as foils for her to react with and emote to…the way she might with band members…Harry's accompaniment was a taped instrumental track.

The second song performed was "Atomic" with the memorable lyric "Your hair is beautiful…whoa tonight!" This line makes a perfect caption for my photos of Deborah! [*See p. 339*—Ed.] By now, the boys are getting frisky…you know they're about to strip…

The final number of the evening was "One Way or Another" and the crowd joined in for the "Getcha getcha getcha's" and all screamed in unison for the lyric: "Some specials and RAT FOOD!" Deborah extended the microphone toward the audience to hear the words sung back to her. Meanwhile, the boys had been stripping for some time and had already busted out of their "breakaway" suits (now in crumpled piles on the stage) and were down to their black underwear ensembles complete with bras. The trio wrapped up the act and Deborah thanked everyone for coming, and the troupe quickly left the stage. The crowd gave Deborah and the Babies a nice round of applause. The whole act took about 15 minutes. The troupe performed the act again a week later (March 15) on the cruise ship "Atlantis." The Nuclear Bomb Babies were redubbed the Lunachicks for the cruise.

Part IV: In Retrospect

Early in Blondie reunion,
104fest, Riverside Park, Agawam, Massachusetts, June 1, 1997
credit: copyright © John Atashian

Overviews

"What Was Blondie's Cultural History, Legacy and Success?"

by John Hart
(adapted and edited by Allan Metz)

Sources used for research in this selection (which is written from a British perspective) include books by Simon Frith and Howard Horne, Cathay Che, Jon Savage, Clinton Heylin, Legs McNeil and Gillian McCain, Keith Negus, John Holmstrom, Lucy O'Brien, Simon Reynolds and Joy Press, Roy Shuker, Simon Frith, and Deborah Harry, Chris Stein and Victor Bockris. Television/video sources include "Alive and Kicking" (BBC), "Behind The Music-Blondie" (VH1), "Once More Into The Bleach" (BBC), "Punk and The Pistols" (BBC), and "The Trouble With The Seventies" (Thames Television). E-mail sources were from Gary Valentine and Sam Hill. Complete citations for these and other cited sources are listed in the "References/Bibliography" of this book.—Ed.

Introduction

In the world of rock'n'roll, there have been bands and groups that have captured the imagination of the contemporary youth of the day, so much so that many of these bands and groups are still household names today. The Beatles, the Rolling Stones and Jefferson Airplane are synonymous with the 1960s. Think of 70s bands such as T-Rex, Sweet and Slade and you conjure up images of huge platform shoes, males in makeup and the most colourful images to be seen in an otherwise drab grey decade. Yet the 1970s was a decade in which a new form of music and social movement made its mark. Punk and new wave gave birth to hundreds of bands, some of which had aspirations ranging from advocating social upheaval, the chance to play the guitar in front of an audience or the chance to be a worldwide success. This overview is going to look at one of the most successful innovative bands that came out of the 70s: Blondie

Fronted by Deborah Harry, Blondie would, in its eight-year career, travel from being a "sideshow" of the New York, underground punk scene to being idolised in Europe, the Far East and, eventually, the United States. This overview will look at what motivated Blondie, its effects on the fan, the historic breakthrough of a woman fronting a band and the experimentations and innovations of Blondie that brought about worldwide recognition. But, first of all, what was punk and how did it come about?

I. A New Era and a New Movement

From the fifties through to the present time, music has been a rallying cry for the contemporary youth of its day. From the early days of the youth movement when the likes of Buddy Holly and Eddie Cochran were denounced as "playing the devil's music," to Roger Daltrey singing how he would like to "die before he got old," Grace Slick of the Jefferson Airplane singing "feed your head," and Johnny Rotten exclaiming how he wants to "destroy the passerby," recording artists such as these have always captured the hearts and minds of the young. The only difference between the examples given was that the circumstances were varied. The new rock'n'roll of the fifties accompanied the prosperity of that decade. The Who exemplified the growing awareness of youth's newfound freedoms and Jefferson Airplane was the pinnacle of the hippie movement, which gave youth a new mystical angle to view life and society. Yet the punk music that arose from the middle to the late 1970s was born from an era of economic slump and rising unemployment, leading to a general bewilderment of modern society. The postwar political consensus, which had brought left and right together, was breaking down. The ideologies that governed the liberal democracies in the West were going their separate ways. The birth of the New Right on both sides of the Atlantic challenged the entrenched beliefs and policies of established political parties and governments. It wasn't only the world of politics and economics that was undergoing a challenge. The biggest upheaval that had happened to music since the advent of rock'n'roll was about to happen.

P u n k—'worthless person,' 'devotee of Punk Rock pop music' (Oxford English Dictionary 1994)

"We created it, let's take it over" Patti Smith 1976

Many people believe that punk was a British creation. That sadly is not true. The most famous and, indeed, outrageous punk bands were from Britain. The Sex Pistols insulting Bill Grundy on daytime television and the Stranglers hiring strippers to perform at an open-air concert are now the stuff of punk legend. Yet the first part of Patti Smith's words hold true. Punk was an American creation and Blondie was very much a part of that creation. How did it all begin?

New York's Soho and Greenwich Village always have been the "underground Mecca" for those seeking a Bohemian lifestyle. Bands such as the Velvet Underground exemplified this. Products of artist Andy Warhol, the Velvet Underground were a combination of art and rock all rolled into one. The Velvets achieved three features, which were to sow the seeds for punk to grow. First, they appealed to the art/rock student. Punk was to grow from the imagination of the art/rock student. Second, they became famous for their live performances. Playing live is essential to gain experience if a band is to establish itself within the music industry. Third, when playing live, a band is able to create a kinship with the audience and the community at large. Without realising, the Velvet Underground had laid the foundations for the next generation of young musicians from New York. As Jerry Harrison, formerly of the band Talking Heads, puts it: "It [punk] all started with the Velvet Underground and all the things identified with Andy Warhol." (Frith and Horne, 139)

This generation of young followers centred on the art colleges of New York. The Mercer Arts Centre was the most significant with its population of pop art-oriented students. One of these students was Chris Stein, the founding member of Blondie. The highlight of his student career was when his band, back in his high school days, had the opportunity to open a gig for the Velvet Underground. In the early to mid-1970s, playing live in the New York club circuit provided the necessary venues and experience to build a rapport with the audience, especially the young. In a television interview, Chris Millar, better known as Rat Scabies, drummer with the British punk band the Damned, explained why young people became supporters of this form of musical entertainment. Big bands of the time like Genesis, Emerson Lake and Palmer and Yes required high ticket prices to see them perform and maintained a rich lifestyle to which the average youth could not relate. In contrast, bands like Dr. Feelgood and Eddie and the Hotrods came on to the music scene and played in venues such as pubs and clubs that were much more accessible both in terms of price and the having the opportunity interact with the band after a show. (Thames Television, 1994)

Though viewed from a British perspective, this was happening on both sides of the Atlantic. Richard Nusser, music critic for New York's *Village Voice,* noted that, during the early seventies, the music from the late sixties had become an economic product. The youth of that time had watched the commercialisation of music that was supposed to be alternative and different. Rock music was now to be played on expensive stereos and at huge concerts where, if you were lucky, the lay of the land would enable you to view the band as a tiny dot on the horizon. Punk music was the opposite. "The new punk bands played within touching or throwing distance, and the music meant that it could be played on a cheap transistor radio and still sound good." (Frith, 159)

The new bands playing in the clubs and pubs showed the contemporary youth of the time that there was an alternative to the consumer driven "supergroups" of the early seventies. The most famous venues for this new "underground" movement was the 100 Club in London's Oxford Street and CBGB's OMFUG or, to give it its full title, Country Blue Grass and Blues and Other Music for Uplifting Gourmandizers. It would be wrong to argue that punk grew simultaneously in America and Britain. As already mentioned, punk's first roots were sown in New York in the early seventies, whereas Britain had to wait until 1975/1976 for punk to root itself. British punk appeared as a far more fierce aggressive form. It was far more of a social and political movement than its American counterpart. The Sex Pistols derided the adult world and the establishment, and the Clash even questioned the ethics of having to go out and work. Much of this culminated in the formation of the Rock Against Racism movement born out of the necessity to combat the growing influence of ultra-right racist groups in Britain. American punk had more to do with innovative styles and how far the musicians and artists could push out the boundaries of their own creativity. Artists such as Patti Smith would read poetry on stage while groups such as Television would turn up at gigs wearing outdated mod suits while all around people would still be wearing the style of the Glam-rock period. Punk rock in America was about how you could be different from what was happening at the time. No other band better exemplified this than Blondie.

II.

The first section has dealt with the how punk came to be born in America, what inspired it and how it differed from its more famous or infamous British cousin. Let us now turn to the band that is the object of this overview, Blondie.

344

"Blondie is a Group!"

Thus stated the badges that, at the height of Blondie's fame, its fans would wear on their lapels. You could be forgiven for believing that Blondie was Deborah Harry. From the early incarnation of Blondie, the music press and the media in general have played up that notion. The truth is that Blondie was and still is a group of people that played in a band under the name of Blondie. This section will, hopefully, dispel any myth that Blondie was the lead vocalist and not the band. It would be pointless, however, to write an overview or biography of Blondie and only mention Deborah Harry in passing. As this part of the overview is about the band members, Harry's role and the image that she portrayed will be dealt with in its entirety in section V.

Chris Stein: Guitarist/Songwriter

For me, the band members of Blondie were all equally important, so I apologise if they are listed in some order of preference or importance. But Chris Stein was the most obvious choice to start off with. Blondie would not have become a reality without him. Chris Stein's family background was you might say 'typical East Coast Liberal' in outlook. His mother and father had been trade union activists during the thirties and both his parents had an interest in the world of art. Growing up in Brooklyn, New York, his original intention was to be an Egyptologist. Instead, Stein later attended the Mercer Arts Centre in New York. It was here that Stein's "avant-garde" creativity began to grow. While acting as a roadie and occasional stand-in guitarist for Eric Emerson's Magic Tramps, Stein began to hang around the originators of punk bands such as the New York Dolls. While he was at the Mercer Art Centre, Stein heard about a "funky" group called the Stillettoes in which Deborah Harry was a member. Stein and Harry would become professional and personal partners. Stein has been accused of having a Svengali like relationship with Harry, plotting both her career with Blondie and subsequent solo career. Stein dismisses this as nonsense. "'It was very much a trade-off...So we filled each other out with what the other one was lacking...Plus the Svengali thing suggests that the whole thing was preconceived and it wasn't—we made it all up as we went along.'" (Che 1999, 138-139)

Clem Burke: "Premier" Drummer and Ardent Anglophile

Had it not been for an ad in the *Village Voice* asking for a "high energy freak drummer" to attend a rehearsal for a newly "re-formed" band, it is highly likely that Blondie may not have gotten off the ground. But the son of a New York society band drummer was the original music enthusiast.

When Burke joined Harry and Stein in late 1974, the whole idea of having any kind of band was very much undecided. The original bassist, Fred Smith, had left to join Richard Hell's band, Television. This had left Harry and Stein feeling very pessimistic about the future. Burke's enthusiasm and constant prodding helped keep Harry and Stein going. Deborah Harry writes: "Clem kept telling us [Harry and Stein] we were good, that we had something" (Harry, Stein and Bockris, 26). Harry explained that when she and Chris Stein visited Burke at home they were surprised at how many music magazines filled his room (BBC Television 1999). Clem Burke was a true pop star in waiting.

The reason why the word "Anglophile" is used here is because the sixties "invasion" of America by British bands had a deep impact on Burke. Ever since he was a young boy, Burke had always wanted to be a pop star. With a father who played the drums and the memory of Keith Moon's rolling drum roll on "I Can See For Miles" etched on his brain, Clem Burke was captivated. Posters of the Who and the Yardbirds, the epitome of sixties Britain, would adorn the walls of his room. When performing a gig or a concert, Burke would often wear a Union Jack shirt or a red, white and blue target set on a white T-shirt, a symbol that was synonymous with the British band the Who of the 1960s. In 1975, Clem Burke travelled to Britain for a six-week visit. While in Britain, he saw Dr. Feelgood perform at a packed Hammersmith Odeon. The fact that Dr. Feelgood had previously been part of the "pub circuit" playing in pubs and clubs all over London did not escape Clem Burke's notice. If a band such as Dr. Feelgood could accomplish this kind of success then so could other burgeoning bands. Dr. Feelgood added an extra drive into the ambitions of the playing at CBGBs.

Jimmy Destri—Keyboard Player "Deluxe"

It could so easily have been Dr. James Destri. Former pre-med student Jimmy Destri was the last member to join Blondie in its original lineup. Destri already had some band experience, playing the keyboards in Milk 'n' Cookies, another band which graced the New York club circuit. Destri was to be a good link between the art college-educated

Stein and the "pop" enthusiasm of Burke. Deborah Harry confides that the main reason Destri was selected to join the band was his wardrobe appealed to the band. (BBC Television 1999)

Last But Not Least

There were three other musicians who at one time or another performed with Blondie. Gary Valentine, Blondie's original bassist, and an old school friend of Clem Burke, performed and toured with Blondie up until their second album. He left the band due to conflicts of interest over what direction Blondie should take. Frank Infante, another old school friend of Clem Burke, replaced Gary Valentine, and Nigel Harrison, from the backwaters of Princes Risborough, England would perform with Blondie up until the band's break up in 1982. With the lineup of Blondie almost complete, this overview now turns its attention to Blondie's lead singer, Deborah Harry, and the part she played during Blondie's early years.

"I Wanna Be A Platinum Blonde" (Deborah Harry's first song written in 1974)

As you have read, Blondie is a band. Yet Blondie is a character as well. Blondie the character, played by Deborah Harry, would front the band from the very beginning. This part of the essay will look at how Blondie the band started out and at how Blondie the character evolved. Deborah Harry had experimented with hydrogen peroxide, that little bottle of chemical dye that could be found at the back of the bathroom cabinet, used by young and not so young girls to change their hair colour. Many healthy minded children and teenagers fantasise about living an alternative lifestyle or of following an exciting career. Deborah Harry was no different. She would often sneak down to her parent's cellar, open up the trunk of discarded clothes and dress herself up as one of the stars of the "silver screen." Harry had a particular fascination with perhaps the ultimate female icon of the time, Marilyn Monroe. It had been rumoured that Monroe had given up a child for adoption in the mid-1940s. With Harry herself adopted, this was a perfect reason to fantasise about Marilyn Monroe being her mother.

In 1965, after leaving school and graduating from college, Deborah Harry crossed the Hudson into New York with ambitions to be an artist. Like many ambitions, they often have to come second to what is known as life's realities. Needing a regular income, Harry took on various jobs, including being a Playboy bunny. Harry gained some experience in the music world, performing in a folk band called Wind in the Willows. With the release of their first and only album, which had only limited success, the band broke up. This did not deter Harry from further pursuing a career in music. Never the most self-confident person, though, Harry would often turn up at auditions for bands and not be able to utter a single word. With this in mind, Harry turned to drugs, to quell any insecurity. Obviously, this could not last long without ending in catastrophe. Thankfully, Harry weaned herself off of drugs and went back to New Jersey to live with her parents.

In 1972, Deborah Harry returned to New York. This time there would be no looking back. The year 1972 was the time of David Bowie's Ziggy Stardust, Sweet and T-Rex—the era of Glam-rock. New York had seen the transition from hippie/folk bands such as Wind in the Willows to the New York Dolls and the Magic Tramps. Much of the Glam-rock scene focused on the Mercer Arts Centre. Because Glam rock was the most visually stunning and exciting form of music there had ever been, the art students could roll their fascination and interest in music and visual images into one. In the same year, a small underground club opened that would provide an opportunity for the young "avant-garde" musician, CBGBs.

Skinny Ties and Broken Guitar Strings

One of the numerous groups that played at CBGBs was a singing group called the Stillettoes, a band that was more visual than musical. Performing cover versions by such groups from the previous decade as the Shangri-Las, the Stillettoes concentrated on image rather than sound. This approach made the band popular with the CBGBs audience by giving an air of humour and lightness to their performances. It was after a gig performed by the Stillettoes at a New York bar that Harry and Stein formed a private/professional partnership. Stein, not having any commitments, became a guitarist with the band. Due to resignations and the opportunity for bigger and better things, Harry and Stein found themselves in charge of the band. Harry and Stein were unhappy with the direction it was taking. Amusing the audiences with their lighthearted onstage performances were not going to get the band noticed by New York's music critics. Harry and Stein formed a Stillettoes Mk2. However, a Stillettoes Mk1 or Mk2 was not going to matter. Bands such as Television and the Ramones and art-rockers such as Patti Smith were drawing not only the crowds but also the attention of all-important music journalists and critics. One of the problems was that the

Stillettoes relied heavily on cover versions of previous hit tracks. Bands such as those mentioned played their own material, though all the bands would, during a gig, play covers. While the Stillettoes had original material, such as 'Platinum Blonde,' there was very little originality. Originality in music is important if a band wants use the creativity within its ranks to carve out an identity on a particular music scene such as CBGBs in the mid-70s. Cover versions can be very well done and exciting for the listener to hear an alternative version. It may even be commercially successful for a cover version to be released as a record. Yet if a band wants to be more creative, then too many covers will hold it back and not get it noticed.

Clem Burke's timely arrival and his enthusiasm for music largely helped to keep Harry and Stein interested in maintaining the band. After a brief stint as Angel and the Snake, the name Blondie was chosen, thanks to the catcalls of passing New York motorists concerning Deborah Harry's hair. The remaining Stilletto band members left to become students or musicians in other CBGB bands that appeared to have more of a future. By the end of 1975, Blondie's lineup would be complete with Gary Valentine on bass guitar and Jimmy Destri bringing a new sound to the group with his Farfisa organ. By the beginning of 1976, after months of rehearsal, Blondie came out of its "self-hibernation" and prepared itself for "fame" of a kind.

Blondie became famous playing at CBGBs as the band that wouldn't become famous and successful. Bands like Television and the Ramones and artists such as Patti Smith came to be recognised by the A&R (Agent & Repertoire) people as bands with the potential to produce great albums and to be commercially successful for the record companies—all the bands, that is, except Blondie. Blondie had experienced many problems in the previous months: performing badly onstage, amplifiers not working properly, guitar strings snapping halfway through a number, and other similar difficulties that many bands face when starting out. Rock journalist Alan Betrock summed up Blondie's live act. "Blondie were a real good recording band. I brought a couple of people to see 'em and I was really hurt and upset because they just couldn't play live, they'd stop in the middle of a song and start all over again, the amps would go out, the guitar would go out, strings would break and they wouldn't have extra ones." (Heylin, 163) These problems can be ironed out over time as playing technique improves and confidence grows. But what happens if a band's image is holding it back, as Heylin suggested? (Heylin, 163) One of the many definitions of punk was to do something within the music industry that was not normal practice such as a woman fronting a band. There had been female vocalists and songwriters before punk came along. With the exception of Janis Joplin, most women either had been solo artists or part of a band while very few had fronted a band. In the new punk movement, if people were brave enough to ascend the stage and sing then they had the right to do so. This notion included women. Again, with the exception of Janis Joplin, females on stage still had to have a visually exciting look to them. A good singing voice was not enough, especially if there was a large male audience, which in the music world there inevitably always is. No one was going to award the likes of Patti Smith or Poly Styrene from X-Ray Spex prizes for best looking singers but in the brave new egalitarian world of punk, this no longer mattered. Punk meant women on stage were the equals of men and that was all that mattered.

When Deborah Harry and Blondie took to the stage, it was as if CBGB's novelty act had arrived. Harry's good looks and Blondie's "fluffy" sixties style sound was contrary to what the other bands were performing and the image the other bands were portraying. When Deborah Harry performed on stage, with the glamour you'd expect from a devotee of Marilyn Monroe, it was as if she was putting the clock back to a time when women could only succeed due to their looks and not their ability. This was, however, unfair criticism from certain quarters within the CBGBs punk movement. As already stated, punk was about doing things differently. By wearing clothing such as a miniskirt and thigh high boots and by bringing a sexual dimension to the contemporary scene, Harry was playing the part of a punk. With the band dressing as mods, straight out of a scene of *Quadrophenia,* Blondie was not conforming to the ripped jeans, tattered denim, crinkled shirt style that the other punk bands were wearing. Blondie was carving out an image for itself that set it apart from the other bands. This did not make Blondie and Deborah Harry, in particular, very popular among certain quarters within the contemporary scene. Blondie's "light-hearted" approach was at odds with the more serious pretensions of certain CBGB acts.

Within the punk scene at CBGBs, there was a form of solidarity among the various bands. Friends would come to support various gigs and much of the audience would consist of other bands giving mutual support. The lure of fame and fortune, however, overrode any form of solidarity when the A&R people started to show up and scrutinise the various acts. Bands that had been cooperative with each other now became competitive as different acts vied with each other for the attention of the A&R people. Commercialism had entered into the CBGBs scene. The alternative world of punk music was starting to die just as it had begun to grow. With the careers of Television, The Ramones and the Patti Smith Group now taking off, Blondie was being left behind. Yet Blondie's alternative style of music would eventually pay off.

III. California and Britain

The fortunes of Blondie were about to take a turn for the better, but what drove them on? After all, the band had failed to make an impact as the Stilletoes as well as Angel and the Snake and the early performances of Blondie had courted very little positive attention. According to Blondie's former bassist, Gary Valentine: "As to our motivation during the CBGBs days, that's simple: success. Like everyone else, we wanted to get a record deal, make a great album, and make a million dollars." (Gary Valentine, e-mail message, 1999) This was the collective idea motivating Blondie. On a personal level, Gary Valentine explained his own individual reasons. "I always knew that I wanted to write good music, and that I believed in my creative ability and knew that I had to find an outlet for my self-expression. For me, this opportunity first came along with Blondie and then with my writing." (Gary Valentine, e-mail message, 1999) The self-belief described by Gary Valentine, of the band and the individual, was about to be re-warded.

In the spring of 1976, Blondie signed their first record deal, not with one of the huge record companies such as EMI, but with Instant Records, one of the many record companies that had been started in the 1970s. It grew in conjunction with punk and represented a form of commercial rebellion against the mighty and often abstract power of the long established record companies. Instant Records, under the stewardship of Marty Thau and Craig Leon, had been taking a keen interest in Blondie. Veteran record producer Richard Gottehrer, Marty Thau and Craig Leon asked Blondie, who at this time would have needed very little persuading, to record two songs for Instant Records that Blondie had been playing at CBGBs for some time: "X Offender" and "In The Sun." The two songs were taken to various record labels, but the established labels were still very wary of the new form of music growing on both sides of the Atlantic. These companies were not about to take risks with their investors' capital over a music phenomena which might prove to be ephemeral. Blondie was bypassed. Fortunately, a small record label called Private Stock took a risk and put up the money for Blondie's first ever album, *Blondie*. Recorded in the autumn of 1976, *Blondie* was released in January 1977, the year that came to known as the year of punk. The only other bands that had released punk albums were the Damned and Dr. Feelgood from England and the Ramones and Patti Smith from the United States. Blondie had become the fifth. When recording an album, a band—regardless of musical genre—has to tour to successfully promote it. The idea of touring is to make contact with the public who may or may not already be converted to your music, thereby promoting existing material and keeping in mind future song and album releases. An audience is a market and to keep hold of a market, it is necessary to keep the audience interested in your latest material—in this case, music. Blondie was no different. If anything, bands like Blondie and the wider punk movement needed to do this as punk was about keeping in close contact with the people, especially young people. Punk, like any version of rock'n'roll, was about youth. If Blondie was to have greater success than they already had, they would have to break out of New York and into the wider world.

With mass communication, such as radio, being able to infiltrate the homes and minds of potential fans and followers, bands are at an advantage, as their music will preceed them. Though, of course, this can prove to be a disadvantage; recall the reception the Sex Pistols encountered during their 1978 tour of America—anarchy and mayhem! Much depends on the individual DJs. If a DJ does not believe in the music or the album, it will be given little or no airtime and thus no publicity. Thankfully, there were DJs in the UK such as John Peel, who were willing to promote punk music through the airwaves. In America, however, there was no national broadcasting service such as Britain's Radio One. An enterprising DJ may well play punk on a radio station on America's east coast yet it does not mean the same will occur in the midwest or west coast of the States. Blondie's break radio-wise came in Los Angeles, where local DJ Rodney Bingenheimer played Blondie's album.

California was still living in the shadow of the hippie generation that, like modern day pilgrims, had moved there for an alternative lifestyle. Yet this had happened the previous decade and like many social movements, it had withered away. As such, the younger generation was looking for something new on the horizon. Teenagers would still be dressed in flared trousers and sporting shirts with patterns matching a botanical garden. Rodney Bingenhiemer was a DJ at KROQ radio, a small-time radio station in Los Angeles and one of many independent radio stations dotting the United States. Bingenheimer acted as a "human conductor rod" looking out for new forms of music to be played and connected to the radio station's listeners. After hearing Blondie's song "X Offender," Bingenhiemer played Blondie's album continuously over the radio. So much so, that the teenagers were anticipating the arrival of the album's creators. Blondie played gigs at legendary venues such as the Whiskey A Go-Go and each was a sell out. Blondie had filled a vacuum. It could, of course, be argued that any band bringing something new to the west coast would have been greeted with such enthusiasm. But in the eyes of the young Californians, Blondie were a different kind of band. The "art meets pop" world of New York had not reached Los Angeles and so the youngsters were interested in the music rather than what was behind it. Pleasant Gehman, a student who worked on a small punk fanzine summed up the attitude of the youngsters to Blondie. "'In New York, they had that whole arty faction that looked down on Blondie. We had that whole fuck art, let's dance type thing out here and Blondie was prefect for us.'" (Che, 1999, 46, and 44-46 for material up to this point in this section). Blondie also was setting trends. Besides the music having made an impact on the young fans, so did Blondie's fashion. Out went the sandals, flared jeans and flowery shirts; in came the white shirts, skinny ties and sharp suits. Imitation is a sincere form of flattery. Blondie had made their mark on both sides of the United States. Now it was time to make an impact on the other side of the Atlantic.

Globalisation is a word that has entered into the public domain in the last twenty or so years. It is usually associated with economics and international politics. Yet in the world of music and culture, globalisation has been in existence certainly since the fifties when rock'n'roll first appeared in our private homes and public places. From its origins in America's south to its extension to Britain and the western world, rock'n'roll has crossed national boundaries with total immunity, meeting very little opposition on the way. The 1960s had seen the "British Invasion"; a time when bands such as the Beatles, the Rolling Stones, the Dave Clark Five, the Animals, Herman's Hermits and the Who had crossed over the Atlantic and conquered America's youth. Since then Britain has been at the centre of music and youth culture. The Cavern, Glastonbury and the 100 Club are names synonymous with British music and are known around the world. In fact, it could be argued that music has been only one of a handful of successes that Britain has accomplished in the postwar world. The British are rightly proud that their music ranks alongside that of America's, which still dominates the global music industry. For Blondie to break into the UK and become a success would be a worthy achievement. British teenagers were not "starved" of modern music like their contemporaries in California. There was plenty of homegrown talent, ready to fill any musical vacuum if it ever occurred. British youth were not, unlike the young Californians, waiting in anticipation for a band to cross thousands of miles with their new album, but what the British youth did have was social anxiety.

The 1970s were a period of self-reflection for Britain. The economic situation was poor, unemployment was steadily rising and soon to reach the one and a half million mark, inflation was eroding the purchasing power of the housewife and the narrow gap between between left and right grew larger as the postwar consensus broke down. Industrial strife and workers' "sit-ins" led many people to wonder if Britain was becoming ungovernable. There were one or two bright spots on the horizon. Britain would soon be self-sufficient in oil. The "black gold" of the North Sea would solve the nation's energy problems and put the "Great" back into Britain. There was always, of course, the Queen's Silver Jubilee to look forward to; though the growing numbers of young people queuing at the job centres may have disagreed with the last point. If ever a nation was ready for musical upheaval, it was Britain. British punk bands like the Sex Pistols or the Clash could readily identify with the situation facing British youth: the Sex Pistol's rage against the "system" (Anarchy in the UK) to the Clash representing youth's frustration with songs such as "White Riot." Neither Blondie nor any of New York's finest could do this. The situation in Britain was unparalleled elsewhere. What is more, the teenagers involved were from a specific class. The hippie movement and the New Left/ student protests of the sixties were predominantly middle class in character. With such a bleak future, the working class kids from Britain really did have an "axe to grind." This view was not lost on Deborah Harry who writes, "The American protest movements of the sixties were inspired by comfortable middle-class college kids. The English kids of the seventies got jobs at seventeen if they could, and certainly most couldn't afford to go to a university." (Harry, Stein, Bockris, 79) With American punk bands and Blondie, in particular, coming from a different economic, political and social situation, would they be able to make an impact in Britain?

The impact of Blondie on the British fan was shown by the enthusiastic reception given by British fans to the band. During one of Blondie's many tours of Britain, the mass of fans managed to bring Oxford Street in London to a complete standstill as fans attempted to get a brief look at the band and Deborah Harry, in particular, during a record promotion. This type of mass reception had been reserved for groups such as the Beatles and "teenybopper" groups like the Bay City Rollers. Past welcomes were usually made up of young teenage girls, screaming hysterically like a scene from "A Hard Day's Night." Many of the people who made up the crowds for Blondie were teenage boys and young men. This was mainly due to the fact that a sexy good-looking blonde was fronting a band, but also because the music Blondie played was a compromise between the "rawness" of the Sex Pistols and the mainstream sound of a band such as ABBA. Punk did not afflict every British teenager. Youngsters may well have been disillusioned with the abstract aloofness and wealth of "supergroups" like Emerson, Lake & Palmer or Genesis. This did not mean that the average teenager would quite happily follow the antics of the British punk movement. Blondie offered them a "halfway house." For many youngsters, punk bands like the Clash and the Sex Pistols would bring a political and social meaning to their songs, to which the average 70s teenager may have found difficult to relate. Blondie did not do this. One such British fan who has admired Blondie throughout the years is Sam Hill, lead singer of Britain's only Blondie tribute band, Once More Into The Bleach. Hill, who plays the role of Deborah Harry, has expressed what she believed to be behind the success of Blondie with the British fan. "Listening to Blondie's lyrics, it's all very 'tongue in cheek'; have you ever heard a Blondie song with Deborah Harry singing about a lost love? Blondie was about escapism. Not everybody wanted to be reminded about how bad the world [was]. Much of the music was very 'heavy' around the time of punk; Patti Smith, Television, were all great bands/artists etc., but they were always 'moaning.' Blondie was passed off by this 'clique' as being 'frivolous' and having no sense of direction. Yet Blondie was able to keep up with current trends and in some respects predicted them. Other bands with their emphasis on creating 'serious music' became too narrow and could not move on. Blondie, not being attached to any form of music, allowed them to have the freedom to extend the limits of their creativity." (Sam Hill, 2000)

At this time, Britain had never experienced a band that was fronted by a woman and neither had the rest of the world. With the exception of the United States, no other country has ever shown much in the way of new innovations within music. This may sound rather prejudiced but until the 1980s, no other country has consistently introduced new forms of music or successful bands. Germany was famous for being the home of Kraftwerk and Sweden gave the world ABBA. These bands are a musical "one-off," whose country's music industries seem only to be able to produce a successful international band every ten years or so. Blondie was totally new even to the British youth; not just by having a female lead vocalist but an incredibly good-looking one, too. In this sense, Deborah Harry filled an adolescent vacuum. Britain's young men had been devoid of a female icon for sometime. Not since the likes of Sandi Shaw and Twiggy had there been a female icon.

IV. America: Blondie Comes Full Circle

By 1978, Blondie had released two albums, *Blondie* and *Plastic Letters*. During this time, bassist Gary Valentine had left the band due to differences of opinion and had been replaced by Frank Infante and Nigel Harrison. These two albums had given the band unparalleled success in Britain and around the world. "In the Flesh," a song from the *Blondie* album, gained Blondie recognition in Australia when released in conjunction with a video of the band. *Plastic Letters* had achieved two top ten hits in Britain with "Denis" and Gary Valentine's parting gift "(Always Touched by Your) Presence Dear." With tours of Western Europe, Australia and the Far East firmly cementing Blondie as an international band, the one country which Blondie yearned for successful recognition had ignored the band and the wider punk movement: the United States.

Though America was the birthplace of punk, punk seemed to be the "runt of the family," the musical child America did not want. There were only a few years separating the period of punk music from the upheavals of the 1960s, when America's youth arose to question the American way of life and the entire system under which Americans lived. The memories of Professor Timothy Leary studying the effect of "mind trips" along with the Merry Pranksters and the Grateful Dead handing out LSD to the youth of America still rumbled in the minds of America's adults and establishment. Punk may have been acceptable for underground music venues, but not to be played on radio and given any recognition. American society was not about to pulled apart again as it was in the sixties. Blondie, The Ramones, and Television had achieved breakthroughs in Britain without inciting inner-city riots. Blondie would have to rethink their position if they wanted to make inroads into the American music industry. One punk band that refused to rethink its position within America was the San Francisco-based band, the Dead Kennedys.

Without doubt the most politically motivated punk band within America, the Dead Kennedys were refused radio time and shunned by the mainstream record companies. This was due in part to lyrics containing political messages such as genocide in Cambodia, western business involvement in South Africa, American foreign policy and the ridicule of censorship in the United States. The Dead Kennedys formed their own record label, Alternative Tentacles, which provided the band with success in Europe but not in America. The lead singer, Jello Biafra, would go on to be a critic of censorship in America during the eighties. Blondie was not on any political or social crusade; their reason for existence was to be musically creative and commercially successful and if that meant adapting to mainstream America, then so be it. Blondie, however, was now fighting a "music war" on two fronts. The band was attempting to keep up its punk/new wave credentials with the British fan while attempting to break into the mainstream American music market and appeal to the American listener. Richard Gottehrer, who had produced Blondie's first two albums, found this very difficult. "'On that second record [*Plastic Letters*] it was hard for me to grasp the point they were trying to make. There were conflicts in general about just which songs to do....'" (Heylin, 309)

Parallel to the punk movement grew a new music phenomenon: disco. The film "Saturday Night Fever" had given disco the opportunity to explode on to the music scene. It was also a strand of music that America found acceptable and enjoyed. The conservative right would not particularly like the idea of a group such as the Village People apparently flaunting the idea of homosexuality on television, but there is no pleasing some people. The fact remained that disco was hugely popular and would open new opportunities for Blondie. Richard Gottehrer was replaced by Mike Chapman, who had produced the seventies Glam-rock band, Sweet. The result was Blondie's third album, *Parallel Lines*. The album was not so much a jettison of previous material Blondie had been working on and performing, but in fact an album which took the band back to its roots. The hit song "Heart of Glass," which finally broke through to the American market and made number one, was a reworking of "The Disco Song," a track which Chris Stein had written during the very early days of Blondie. It was one of the songs that critics within the CGBG scene had used to accuse Blondie of "fluffiness." Chapman, known to be something of a perfectionist along with the band, took hold of "The Disco Song," a "funky" electric guitar sound, and reworked it into the "disco-meets electro-pop" that we know today. Blondie's "fluffiness" had gone full circle but now with tremendous results—a number one single and an album which would sell over six million copies. "Blondiemania," for so long absent from America, had arrived. From here on, Blondie's innovative qualities would be in great demand. So far this essay has looked at Blondie's beginnings, the personalities involved, Blondie's British success and the band's reinvention that broke through to the American market. But there was one character within Blondie who took more acclaim and criticism than any other rock personality during this period: Deborah Harry.

V. Deborah Harry: Pioneer and Figurehead

No written piece of work on Blondie could be complete without an entire section devoted to the lead singer and front person of the band, Deborah Harry. It would be like writing about the Theory of Relativity without mentioning Albert Einstein. But Deborah Harry was not just the lead vocalist of a popular band, but was, in fact, a pioneer of women in rock, albeit in her own unique style. Women had entered the male-dominated realm of rock during the 1970s as conformists. Patti Smith, Suzi Quatro and Chrissie Hynde are example of women who came to front their respective bands by becoming one of the men or "one of the lads," a quaint English saying. Any kind of femininity about these artists was jettisoned as they put on their leathers and emulated the male rock musician's toughness. This was thought of as a necessity since it appeared to be the only way for women to be part of the rock scene. The "tomboy" look prevailed over the "girly" tendencies of the female rock "wannabees." This phenomenon is not exclusive to just the music industry. For women to succeed in traditionally male-dominated industries, it seems that they have to emulate men, even acting more masculine than the men themselves. Rock critic Lester Bangs once wrote, "She may be all high and mighty on TV, but everybody knows that underneath all that fashion plating she's just a piece of meat like the rest of them." (O'Brien, 139) Men and perhaps even women realise that whatever women attempted to do in music, it is all part of an act. Deborah Harry would show that there was another way of women breaking into that male-dominated world—one that did not require conformity or "self-purification" of femininity—but in fact played up her femininity to her audience.

As mentioned earlier, the heroines of Deborah Harry's childhood had been the stars of the silver screen. The Marilyn Monroes and Ava Gardners of this world have indulged their femininity and held their own against their male counterparts. But these women were, by and large, untouchable—the "aristocrats" of the American republic. It would not be right for Deborah Harry, in the "egalitarian" world of punk and new wave, where young fans were financially restricted, to be viewed as "untouchable" and an advertisement for the latest catwalk trend. Harry would combine glamour and a sense of egalitarianism. The clothes Deborah Harry wore were inexpensive glamour clothes and her dyed-blonde hair still showed the roots of its original colour. Teenage girls would watch her perform on stage and within a day would have dyed their hair blonde. She could play the part of Jekyll and Hyde—from the cute vulnerable girl singing "In the Flesh," a song that sounds like a schoolgirl having a crush on the leading male student [*Harry is thought to have written this song as a result of a crush she had on David Johansen of the New York Dolls—Ed.*], to the "viciousness" of "Rip Her To Shreds," lyrics that would not be out of place in a violent B movie of an all-female street gang. Beckoning the male audience to love her and the female audience to imitate, Deborah Harry would become centre stage for Blondie and the girls and women who wanted to make it into the world of music.

Two problems arose from the above. The publicity Deborah Harry enjoyed did cause some internal problems within the band. Blondie was not just Deborah Harry but five other males who all had their own qualities to give. However, glamour magazines and centrefolds were not interested in what Clem Burke the drummer was doing or how he was looking. A photo of Chris Stein or Jimmy Destri on the front page of *Tatler* was not going sell more copies. Deborah Harry's face would. This helped fuel the public's general perception of Deborah Harry being Blondie, much to the consternation of the other band members. The second problem is that every unit of people—be it a band, a business or even a state—needs to have a figurehead. The role of such a person can be passive, proactive, visual or someone who takes a back seat. In Deborah Harry's case, it was a combination of roles, which were visual and proactive: the presentation of the band like an ambassador (visual) and a songwriter and performer (proactive). When the performance of this unit, in this case a band, is going well, you will take the credit—i.e. demand for your photographs, imitation of your appearance. Blondie never had a period in their career when once they were successful, they then declined and then rose up again. But as Harry was the band's representative, she was the one who had to justify her position and the band's style to an inquisitive and potentially hostile press and media, which was also very much a male-dominated industry. Deborah Harry had entered a male-dominated sphere not by imitating males, but by using and indulging in her own femininity.

VI. Albums and Culture

The first perception of a band or a group is through its songs. Though we now live in a world where image is so important, no band/group has ever become successful through image alone. It does not matter how "photo friendly" people are; substance, in this case songs, cannot be substituted. This section will attempt to describe Blondie's albums—the varying aspects that they took and the innovation behind them. To gain a real feel for the albums, however, it is best to go out and buy them. This isn't a plug on behalf of Blondie, but as already mentioned, in the music world, there is no substitute for the ear!

Blondie—Blondie's Innovative Beginning

The first Blondie album paid homage to everything Middle America would find abhorrent. Put simply, the album is about aggression and the anxieties of contemporary youth. Within the eleven tracks are references to shootings, stabbing, underage sex and the smoking of cannabis. Everything, in fact, that young people growing up in a city such as New York could relate to. In terms of image, the photo on the album cover enforced the idea of Deborah Harry fronting an otherwise all-male Blondie, with Deborah Harry at the front of the band and the other members queuing up behind.

Plastic Letters—Punk Becomes New Wave

Plastic Letters was Blondie's second album and one that was to be the end of Blondie's period as a punk band. In fact, by 1978, the UK release of *Plastic Letters* had coincided with the transformation of punk into new wave. Out went the Sex Pistols and in came groups such as the Undertones with tracks dedicated to familiar themes such as youth and adolescence. Though the music tempo was often just as energetic as punk rock, the lyrics contained within new wave tracks differed. New wave lyrics dealt with the boy-girl relationship and the individual teenager as opposed to the social and political "rage" of punk rock. This is audible in *Plastic Letters*. Blondie's famous "foot tapping" song, "Denis," is a great example of this. In the autobiography *Making Tracks: The Rise Of Blondie,* Deborah Harry explains how *Plastic Letters* has a "dark quality about it." (Harry, Stein and Bockris, 79) This is true. There is a brooding sense of "something lurking round the corner." Harmonic songs like "Bermuda Triangle Blues" and "Poet's Problem" that lull you into a sense of warmth and security, suddenly give way to energetic tracks like "Detroit 442" and "Cautious Lip." These songs blow away any pretensions that *Plastic Letters* is anything but a rock album, one that was made to appeal to the (European) discontented youth of the late 1970s. The album is full of contradictions and surprises. Harmonies, punk tracks and even comedy scenarios like "Love At The Pier" all find their way into the album. Unlike most bands from the late 1970s, when you bought an album by the Clash or the Damned, you knew basically what you were buying: energetic rage from the Damned and political and social messages from the Clash. *Plastic Letters* was Blondie's "Pandora's box." You just did not know what you were about to let out of your speakers.

Parallel Lines—Blondie Conquers America

Blondie's third album, *Parallel Lines,* had but one purpose. It was not to show the world's audience that Blondie could deviate into the world of disco or electro-pop, but to break into the American music scene; not the underground music scene from where Blondie had originated, but the mainstream audience of the media and the record buyer. Blondie's music had so far been relatively ignored in the U.S. In an ideal world, the music fan and the music industry would come round to your style of music. Sure, Rodney Bingenheimer had played Blondie to an appreciative young Californian audience. But KROQ Radio and Rodney Bingenheimer were broadcasting to a relatively small audience and not across the United States. Blondie needed an album that would appeal to the mainstream audience and *Parallel Lines* was the result. The first thing that strikes you about *Parallel Lines* is the album cover itself, with the male band members standing in front of a black and white striped background and Deborah Harry standing out in front. There is no doubt about who is fronting the band. With the male band members dressed in black suits, black ties and white shirts and with Deborah Harry wearing a white slipover dress, the whole style is non-threatening—smart, respectable and mainstream, everything that would appeal to the American public. The only rebellious streak on the album cover is that some of the male band members are wearing sneakers. Not everything on or in this album, however, is black and white. Whereas Blondie's previous album covers had been set against a black background as on the cover of *Blondie,* or a street scene with a police car as the main feature on *Plastic Letters, Parallel Lines* is completely different. The album cover is a break from Blondie's recent past as are the songs inside. The cover is ambitious and diverse and represents a growing confidence within Blondie as they launched their third album.

The songs within *Parallel Lines* stretch from the mysterious sounding "Fade Away And Radiate" to the energetic "11:59," the sleazy "One Way Or Another" written with reference to an ex-boyfriend who had stalked Deborah Harry some years before, to what may be considered the ultimate disco anthem, "Heart Of Glass." Yes, the album is mainstream in sound, yet it "broke" in America and still managed to hold on to Blondie's existing new wave market. By 1978, the year of the album's release, punk had burnt itself out and had firmly become new wave. Previous punk bands also were changing their style of music and lyrical content. Bands like the Clash also were now entering into the world of reggae. With "Heart Of Glass" and "Sunday Girl" achieving chart success in America and Britain, respectively, Blondie's return to the style which they had made their own during the days of CBGBs, and for which they had been criticised, had paid off. With *Parallel Lines* selling over six million copies worldwide, Blondie was now one of the most famous bands in the world.

Eat to the Beat—Power Meets Pop

If *Parallel Lines* represented Blondie's breakthrough in America, *Eat to the Beat* was Blondie's most powerful sounding pop album. The album's first track treats you to drummer Clem Burke's "finest hour." The fast, powerful, rolling drumbeat of "Dreaming" contains the use of a drum kit that Keith Moon would be proud of. From here on, the listener is treated to such tracks as "Union City Blue," a song that symbolised Blondie's entry into the world of vibrant energetic music that still appealed to mainstream audiences. What is most significant about *Eat to the Beat* is that it was the first album released in conjunction with a music video.

Performers and fans alike have accused music videos of trivialising music. (Negus 1999) Certainly there is a big emphasis on image. But image has always been important in music. It depends on how far the sound of a band is substituted for the image and it is highly improbable to substitute sound altogether. As observed previously, people still rely on the sound of a band/group in deciding whether to purchase a record or album and not solely the image. The Spice Girls have relied heavily on image to summarize their idea of "Girl Power," but without producing music that appeals to the potential fan, the image would come to nothing. The image is a spin-off and the music video allowed this "spin-off" to be screened on television. *Eat to the Beat* could now be seen and heard at the same time.

Autoamerican—Pushing the Boundaries

Since cars have become an everyday part of our lives and are no longer seen as a luxury for a wealthy few, we have become infatuated with them. We are told we use our cars far too much and that Britain, America and the developed world will face gridlock, traffic jams and an even more polluted planet unless we stop using them as much. This may or may not be true, but the situation is that we love our cars. Many of us view cars not as a form of transportation, but as an extension of our individual freedom and indeed own living room. *Autoamerican* is an album born out of tribute to the fascination we have for our four-wheeled friends. Blondie always wanted to connect with what they were performing to the daily lives of the public. With *Autoamerican,* Blondie could relate to people's connection with the car.

At the beginning of this overview, it was noted that the appeal of punk was about connecting to your audience either by playing at a small gig or rejecting the wholesale commercialisation of music and remaining local, artistic and reflecting youth concerns. Blondie managed to relate to people and place a higher emphasis on the commercial aspect of their work. These two factors combined to allow Blondie to have a mainstream sound. From *Parallel Lines* onwards, there were to be no songs concerning violence or other such "shock material." It was the mainstream that appealed to America, which is why three of Blondie's albums (*Parallel Lines, Eat to the Beat* and *Autoamerican*) were so successful there. Combining art and commerce led to Blondie introducing ethnic and street music into its mainstream sound.

Rap was the underground music scene for New York's young black population. Mixed in with graffiti, rap had a very visual side. Yet it was a form of music confined to young blacks. Chris Stein and Deborah Harry, always looking for new forms of sound, adapted rap music in *Autoamerican*. The resulting song was "Rapture." With an accompanying video that incorporated much of New York's "avant-garde" set such as artist Jean Michel Basquiat, rap was introduced en masse to the mainstream audience. Rap music became one the most successful forms of music during the 1980s and this success continues to flourish to this day. Reggae, so long confined to the world of the Rastafarian, was another form of music which Chris Stein and Deborah Harry picked up on. Producer Mike Chapman had his doubts about adapting a reggae-tinged sound, predicting that it would not appeal to white America. ("VH1—Behind the Music—Blondie") Reggae was from a completely different culture, one that was not easily compatible with mainstream America. Blondie adapted reggae in the song "The Tide Is High." "Rapture" and "The Tide Is High" both were number one hits in the United States. Underground, ethnic music had made it into mainstream American and western music culture. *Autoamerican* had the most varied mix of sounds that Blondie had ever done: rap, reggae, jazz, show and even orchestral music with the opening track "Europa." Blondie was now experimenting with different sounds and *Autoamerican* was the product of this experimentation.

The Hunter—An Album Too Far?

The Hunter was Blondie's last album before the band was to break up in 1982. By the time this album was produced, Blondie was a band in name only. Between *Autoamerican* and *The Hunter,* the members of Blondie had gone their separate ways, trying out new ideas with different bands. Deborah Harry released her own album, *Koo Koo,* and Jimmy Destri did the same (*Heart on a Wall*). Clem Burke, the "pop specialist" wanting to broaden his horizons, fell in with an up-and-coming British band, the Eurythmics, whose lead singer, Annie Lennox, would become another female icon for her time. While Blondie had not formerly broken up, the close collaboration of Blondie as a unit was gone. *The Hunter* was an album lacking the enthusiasm and energy which had come to symbolise Blondie's work. The album sounds rather like Blondie had come to their end, putting out one more album for old time's sake (not to mention to keep previous contractual agreements). Though there are several songs that are as good as anything Blondie had done previously, the album fails to capture the listener's attention. The albums that had gone before were the kind that you would play all the way through. With *The Hunter,* this is not the case. Thanks to the advent of the compact disc (CD), you are able to pick and choose what tracks you want to hear. This would be a good description of *The Hunter,* a very "picky" album. The fans certainly thought so at the time. While *Parallel Lines* had sold over six million copies, *The Hunter* failed to sell more than twenty thousand when it was released in 1982.

The Hunter's lack of success is not necessarily due to the material within the album. From 1980 to 1982, Blondie ceased to be a touring band. Deborah Harry and Chris Stein became more interested in the production of music whereas Clem Burke and Jimmy Destri were insistent on the need for a band to tour. The problem of bands concentrating on production instead of touring, which had occurred in the early '70s, was happening to Blondie. Blondie was becoming a "music factory," producing music solely for consumption by the fan. Blondie's last tour, promoting *The Hunter* in 1982, showed that it could still attract the masses. The packed venues were full of fans wearing their Blondie t-shirts and greeting with enthusiasm the songs Blondie performed. Yet the enthusiasm was reserved for the work Blondie had previously done. Lester Bangs once wrote, "'If the main reason we listen to music in the first place is to hear passion expressed—as I've believed all my life—then what good is this music going to be?'" (Frith 1987, 14) Bangs wrote this before *The Hunter* was produced. At the time, I would have disagreed with the statement. Bangs appears to accuse Blondie of creating music "for its own sake." This was unfair criticism. While we as an audience were very much interested in the form and style of Blondie, especially Deborah Harry, we also were interested in the content. If style and image were the only keys to success, why did *Parallel Lines* sell over six million copies? Because of the album's content and lyrics. If fans were just interested in image, we would all have posters and badges of Blondie and Deborah Harry, but we would not have their albums. *The Hunter* was an album which represented producing "music for its own sake." It represents Blondie having "one more go," or "a final fling" with the fans. Unfortunately, Lester Bangs' statement, which at the time was wrong, was by 1982 quite correct.

VII. Reunion and Conclusion

"Nobody can say we didn't hold out for fifteen minutes"—*Attributed to philosopher, Jean-Paul Sartre*

The above quote, inside Blondie's new album, *No Exit,* could have been made for Blondie, in answer to their critics from the early days of CBGBs. In 1997, fifteen years after Blondie broke up, the original lineup, excluding Gary Valentine, got back together for a new album. The history of music is full of bands that have reformed, trying to relive the glory days of their long distant past. In 1996, the Sex Pistols reformed for a short period, but only managed to play the old songs. When the Sex Pistols played at Finsbury Park in 1996, many of the people there attended more out of curiosity rather than as followers of the band. The innovative Blondie not only wowed a new generation with previous songs, but actually produced a new album, *No Exit.* With this, Blondie has entered into the record books as the only band in Great Britain ever to have had seven number one hits, in three different decades, with "Maria" entering the number one slot in the UK in February 1999. If Blondie produced music "for music's own sake," surely the band would have been quite happy to play just the "old favourites." This would certainly be less risky, both financially and in terms of music credibility. Blondie has been playing to packed venues, in front of audiences with a mixture of the young and the not quite so young—the over thirties who can remember Blondie the first time around to teenagers who have only heard of Blondie when their parents play their old favourites on a Saturday morning.

Punk, new wave, and power pop are different forms of music that have graced our radios and stereos for over twenty-five years. Blondie brought all of them to us. Blondie has been an important part of bringing different kinds of music such as reggae and rap to mainstream society—music which we may not otherwise have listened to. The whole punk/new wave genre is a period of music full of the excitement and innovation that the young generation of the time created. It is a period that has yet to be surpassed by anyone or anything in the world of music. This overview is really only scratching the surface since so much can be written about Blondie and their background. Hopefully, this essay will motivate people to delve into the past, to a time when music was not the predictable monotonous form of art that, as some may argue, music has become today.

Clem Burke, El Rey, Los Angeles, February 10, 1999
credit: copyright © Sherry Gunderman

"Blondie: The Misfits"

by Barney Hoskyns

Provides an excellent in-depth overview of Blondie–both past and present—and is the original unedited version of the article published in Mojo *magazine, February 1999.*—Ed.

"And you don't stop/Do the punk rock..."

I'm bumping down Manhattan's Seventh Avenue in a taxi, staring through the window in amazement at a ginormous Levi's ad in the garment district. The thing consists simply of a vast image of the Sex Pistols, with a slogan running vertically alongside it. The slogan reads "Our models can beat up their models." A quarter century after the halcyon days of CBGBs, I decide that this slick slice of corporate co-opting provides a fitting millennial epitaph for punk rock.

An hour later, sitting in the cavernous Space photo studio down in Chelsea, I mention the billboard to Debbie Harry and Chris Stein and we all agree that it's, huh, mighty ironic. It probably isn't ironic at all, but it is eloquent testimony to American capitalism's ability to subsume and tame just about anything it wants to—an indication of how far we've come from the days when the entertainment industry wouldn't touch the Sex Pistols (or Blondie) with Brobdingnagian bargepoles.

Stein: "Everything is so tightly worked out now. It used to be like, Gee, let's just go on a TV show!"

Harry: "The industry's changed a lot. There really are no surprises. Everything is so carefully routed."

It may be that Blondie are more sensitive to the wholesale changes in the music business than most of their fellow CBGBs legends—those, at any rate, who are still alive. For unlike Patti Smith, who recently returned to recording after years of domestic hibernation, or Television's Tom Verlaine, who produced many of the tracks on Jeff Buckley's posthumous *Sketches* (*For My Sweetheart, The Drunk*), Blondie happened to have sold millions of records, helping to transform punk into the much more palatable "new wave" music of the late '70s and early '80s. Keyboard player Jimmy Destri could well be speaking for all four members of the reformed original Blondie when he confesses that there was "a certain amount of guilt involved" in the group's success.

"Blondie weren't *ever* geared up to be the stadium-rock type of band that they became," says the amiable Craig Leon, who co-produced the band's first album in 1976 and then returned twenty-two years later to pilot their new No Exit. "You've got to realise that they went from being The Band Least Likely To Succeed to signing to Chrysalis, probably the best record label of that era, and having big-time L.A. management. Anybody who said they knew Blondie were gonna be as big as they became would be full of crap. Blondie were not sitting around thinking, We're gonna have six No. 1 singles. If Clem got his picture in a magazine, he would have been the happiest guy in the world, and that was about it."

The same could almost be said of New Jersey boy Burke twenty years later. Of the four original band members, Blondie's drummer seems the least damaged by the saga of the band's rise and implosion. Slender as a rake and looking nary a day older than he did in 1977, Burke remains the enthusiastic heart of Blondie, a true fan. Craig Leon says that when the group recently dropped in on a session he was producing at Abbey Road, Burke—who'd worked at the studio with Leon on, of all things, a Mark Owen album—instantly became an unofficial tour guide, pointing out the piano John Lennon had played and showing them where Ringo's drums had been set up.

Just as Burke had much to do with urging the demoralised Blondie of late 1974 to keep going, so it was he who pressed for the reunited band of the late '90s to do this thing right. "The whole criterion was that it was important for us to become a band again before we tried to do any of this stuff," he says. "And that's what we've been doing over the past two years really. We didn't just decide to do this tour and then go and rehearse for a week and then go out. The management might have been in it for the quick kill, but as they got to know us they saw it would take a little time and energy on everyone's part in order for this to manifest itself."

Burke is seated on a sofa next to Jimmy Destri, the former hospital orderly and sometime Milk And Cookies tinkler whose Farfisa keyboard chords added the crucial musical touch that set Blondie on their trashy peroxide-pop course. The Italian pretty boy of 1977 has aged less well than Burke, but the endearing Brooklyn street charm hasn't deserted him. Occasionally, as the two men speak and interrupt each other, there are flashes of good-humoured friction that recall the volatility of the old days.

Destri: "You know, I think I'm part Chris Stein and part Clem Burke."
Burke: "Man, that sounds horrible. How d'you live with yourself?!"

With a fine regard for hierarchical etiquette, Destri and Burke have arrived at Space a half-hour before Harry and Stein. Dressed all in black, they're readjusting to the business of being pop stars, although one senses that both men are well aware of the risks the group is taking in bringing Blondie back to life. The good thing, they say, is that this time around they've been able to enjoy the various processes of writing, recording, and rehearsing.

Burke: "We keep using the analogy of us being a dysfunctional family, but I think it's still very apropos. It's like any relationship you go back to, be it an old friend or an old lover—you bring a lot of emotional baggage back with you. Sometimes that can work to your advantage. We've all been in therapy over the years, so that's a big help—"

Destri: "I think we look at each other in a lot funnier light now. We don't take each other as seriously."

Burke: "Plus we're more aware of the business aspects. I mean, we were always pretty much business-sussed, but as someone once said, it's the price of an education. It's just to get to the other end of it, is the thing. It's not unusual to get ripped off in the music business, and I don't know if we have more or less of that than other people, except now people are smarter—"

Destri: "We have a bigger background of getting reamed, so therefore we come with a little more cynicism. And that cynicism does breed a humour of like, 'Oh, don't tell me that!' It puts a sorta lump in your throat and paints you a little green with envy when an artist that sells half the records you do is living in a mansion in Highgate. But then some kids my age went to Vietnam and didn't come home, y'know?"

Later, after a respectful interlude, Clem Burke will sit in on my conversation with Debbie Harry and Chris Stein. It's almost as though he wants to monitor how well the interview is going.

"Someone asked me if we anticipated great success with this record," he interjects after Harry's told me how much she hates rehearsing. "And I said that, for me, success was that we'd made the record. I mean that sincerely. That we actually got back together and made the record. So we already are a success."

The quiet dignity with which he says this contrasts with Harry herself, who on this grey autumn afternoon seems strangely anxious and distant. Perhaps it's the unwelcome pressure of a photo session that will undoubtedly focus on her, triggering uneasy memories of her status as one of pop's major pinups. "She's not very relaxed when she's approaching photo sessions," says author Victor Bockris, the confidant whose 1982 collaboration with Harry and Stein, *Making Tracks: The Rise Of Blondie,* has just been reissued in the U.S. by Da Capo. "When they do these Blondie things, so much more is on her shoulders than anyone else's. Because she is Blondie, she is the person everyone really wants to talk to."

While Stein, droll and laconic, slouches droopily at his end of the sofa, Harry sits tensely at the other, her mind apparently elsewhere. She doesn't say much, and defers often to her ex-partner.

I ask the pair if the fame that suddenly swept Blondie away from their Lower East Side roots after the 1979 disco-pop No. 1 "Heart Of Glass" had in any way isolated them—from their friends, from their musical peers, from the rest of the band.

Harry: "I felt kind of cut off, yeah. And then of course the scene had changed so much, and it happened rather quickly. So I really had no place to go where I was just little me with my little friends. That had evaporated in the time that I had gone out."

Stein: "I'm more isolated now, I'll tell you, than I ever was in those days."

Harry: "Are you?"

Stein: "Yeah! What the fuck is there to do in fuckin' New York now?"

Harry: "Yeah, that is true. People really have gone their separate ways. I think what I really felt isolated about was that I had no anonymity, in that I couldn't just slink around the streets being my own usual cruddy self."

Stein: "But then you have to consider the inverse, which is not getting anywhere."

Harry: "I don't know if that's true. I think that you can adapt to anything, and if you aren't successful and you don't get big popularity, you can find happiness doing other things. I mean, this is not the only thing in life that's gonna make you or me or Joey Schmoe happy. You can hold on to your artistic integrity. Those things are kinda precious, and you compromise constantly when you're reaching out or you're getting bigger."

For a moment it's as if the idealistic hippie-chick who warbled away in '60s folk-rock troupe Wind In The Willows had suddenly blotted out any trace of the trashy street Venus who fronted Blondie and loudly proclaimed to the world that she was "no debutante." It also reminds me that—according to received wisdom—Harry sacrificed any real chance of solo stardom in order to nurse a dangerously ill Stein back to health in the mid-'80s. Debbie Harry is nothing if not diffident when it comes to the matter of her celebrity.

"She wasn't like one of these ambition people who kill to get to the top," says David Johansen, who became a close friend of Harry's after the demise of the New York Dolls. "I think she's an artist, essentially. One of the great things about her stage persona in Blondie was that you could see her nerves. That to me made the show more interesting, instead of saying, *I'm just this indomitable spirit.* She was like, I'm doing this, but it's not easy. And that was part of the charm for me. She's ultimately an intellectual. The whole Marilyn Monroe thing was just like a Jungian archetype. Sure, she turned herself into that archetype, but she did it as an art project."

"I think Debbie always had this great sense of irony," says writer and Blondie acolyte Glenn O'Brien. "I think she always was completely aware of the difference between your intentions and how you're perceived. She could play off of being the Marilyn Monroe figure, but actually she was kind of Arthur Miller and Marilyn Monroe wrapped up into one. She had a lot of life experience to draw on when she was writing lyrics and putting herself together. She'd been a Playboy bunny and a waitress at Max's Kansas City, she'd seen the Dolls and Andy Warhol. So she had a good education to work from."

Could the story of Blondie, then, be of an "art project" which parodied and ironised stardom but miraculously metastasized into bona fide megafame? Start with the dressing-up-box dreams of a pretty adopted girl in Hawthorne, New Jersey; add the morose attitude of a skinny Jewish black-magic-dabbler from Brooklyn; work in the whole background of Andy Warhol's glitzy decadence; and lo, what of all things you wind up with is a quintessential New York pop band whose sassy snap and '60s referencing legitimately catches fire on a global scale.

"Blondie were sort of the exception to the CBGBs rule in that they were actually a very good-looking group," says Marty Thau, who signed the band to his Instant Records production company in 1976. "They were young and they were happy and positive, and their songs were loaded with hooks. They were really the pop dream."

When Chris Stein first clapped eyes on the pert platinum blonde singing with a girl-trio-fronted band called The Stilettoes, the New York underground was moving to embrace the trash aesthetic at the heart of pop. Five years younger than Harry and a roadie for Eric Emerson's Magic Tramps, he swiftly finessed his way into The Stilettoes.

"Chris was always a weird guy," says the group's prime mover, Elda Gentile, who'd recruited Harry after running into her at Max's. "When you went into his apartment there was nothing but black magic memorabilia all over the place. When he saw Debbie, he had the hots for her, like, unbelievably. I was even a little surprised that she went for it. Let's just say that he was very, very smart the way he handled her. I knew he wanted her body, soul, and spirit, but he played it very cool to get her. He nurtured all her insecurities. See, everybody loved Debbie because she had this Marilyn-Monroe-in-the-gutter quality, but she was very insecure, and a little bit paranoid." (Harry's early '70s flirtation with drugs, including heroin, stemmed from this insecurity.)

The Stilettoes' Rock Follies-meets-Riot Grrrl pop took the form of camp covers (Labelle's "Lady Marmalade," the Shangri-Las' "Out In The Streets," the latter reprised on *No Exit*) and became briefly hip among those in the know: Bowie and Iggy checked them, and Keith Moon swung by a legendary lesbian dive called Club 82 to gawp. Harry was funky-but-chic, Stein a platform-stacked glitter boy. The couple fell so deeply in love that they were once discovered *in flagrante* in CBGBs' notoriously revolting bathroom. "That's true love, making it in the toilet at CBs," chuckles Joey Ramone, whose band was rooted in the same customized teen-pop tradition as Blondie.

When The Stilettoes broke up in August 1974, Harry and Stein took the remnants of the band with them, playing their first CBGBs shows as Angel & the Snake. Within a couple of months Blondie was born, evolving through a series of unstable lineups over the ensuing year. Even as she sung lines like "I wanna be a platinum blonde/ Just like all the sexy stars," Harry, alone in the spotlight for the first time, looked nervous and uncertain. "The weak part about them, as I recall, was that Debbie was not that confident," says Victor Bockris. "She would try to do things and then kind of look to the audience to see if it was right."

Tiny and incestuous though it was, the CBGBs scene scorned Blondie as lightweights. Next to Patti Smith's Rimbaud readings or Television's tense jamming, Blondie's ditsy True Confessions pop sounded lame. "Patti absolutely looked down on us," says Stein, a trace of hurt in his voice even after all this time. Concurs Harry, "she was very competitive."

"There were a lot of little cliques in those days, and probably still are," says Craig Leon. "These were all people running around thinking they were French Symbolists, and here comes Blondie, who are really like true punks and actually much more the mass-media future band than any of the others. In a way, some of those CBGBs bands might have been the dead end of progressive rock'n'roll. Not a lot of people really see that."

Pretty much everyone who saw the early Blondie at CBGBs or elsewhere agrees that they stunk live. Even the late Alan Betrock, who included the group in the first issue of his pioneering *New York Rocker* in January 1975 and financed a primitive Blondie demo, admitted the shows were completely chaotic. "They never had it together onstage," he told me not long before his death. "The guitar would break, and they'd have problems. That's why I thought their métier would be to record, and why we went and did this demo in Queens in some guy's basement." (Four songs were recorded: "Platinum Blonde," "Puerto Rico," "Thin Line," and "Out In The Streets," all done live with a couple of guitar overdubs. For "Out In The Streets," Debbie sang the three harmony parts herself. At the very end of the session, Chris suggested they cut what he called "The Disco Song," the prototype for "Heart Of Glass.")

One night in May 1975, Clement Burke made his debut on drums and bassist Fred Smith quit to join Television—a departure so devastating to Harry and Stein that they almost threw in the towel there and then. (Harry still blames Patti Smith, then Tom Verlaine's paramour, for Fred's defection.) Burke rallied them, and brought in an old school friend named Gary Valentine to play bass. Come the fall, James Destri and his trusty Farfisa were on board and Blondie were being re-evaluated by the CBGBs crowd. "I remember going to see Debbie at CBs at this time," says Elda Gentile. "I think she'd discovered that Blondie identity and was able to run with her."

When Craig Leon at Sire Records got wind of the nascent scene down on the Bowery, he convinced '60s pop veteran Richard Gottehrer (The Angels, The Strangeloves) to come down and check out the bands. During a series of recordings for a Live at CBGBs album, Debbie Harry charmed Gottehrer into producing a single by Blondie. "I remember going to a rehearsal and watching them play and grinning from ear to ear," says Gottehrer. "These were people that had great songs and were playing arrangements almost beyond their means. The execution wasn't perfect, but it had so much spirit. So that got me interested."

"Sex Offender," written by Harry and Valentine and based on the latter's traumatic experience of knocking up his underage girlfriend, was recorded at the comparatively plush midtown studio Plaza Sound and sounded killer. Retitled "X-Offender," it shocked many of Blondie's detractors into a begrudging respect. Perhaps most bizarrely of all, it was released on Private Stock, a label known principally for Frankie Valli's 1975 No. 1 hit "My Eyes Adored You."

"We ended up on Private Stock because everyone else passed on Blondie," says Marty Thau, who shopped the single around town. "There were a number of good-sized companies who came to see them, but even those in A&R circles who knew what was going on downtown were hesitant because they didn't believe in the so-called punk atmosphere."

According to Thau, most of the work on "X-Offender" and the first Blondie album was done by Craig Leon. "Richard Gottehrer was in the studio and thought he was in charge," he says, "but it was really Craig who was the backbone of the whole thing." Leon himself is self-effacing as to the accreditation; perhaps producing The Ramones and Richard Hell's seminal "Blank Generation" was enough for him. But he'll concede that he had more than a little to do with "shaping the sound that Blondie carried through all the way until they got really experimental with disco and rap."

"They were shambolic," he adds, "but through that you'd start hearing this great kind of recreation of the Shangri-Las mentality, mutated with all these other things. So I got to thinking, Well, I kinda know what they're going for: there's this little Herman's Hermits guitar thing here, and it's coming from all these different sources. Then it hit me why they had never come across on tape, because that really had to be channelled into, like, Let's take the best bits of all these ideas and make it so you can actually hear them one at a time!"

For Leon, Blondie, initially released on Private Stock in February 1977, bridged the group's very different camps: Stein and Harry's arty humour and Warholesque subversion, Burke's *Tiger Beat* anglophilia and Hal Blaine-meets-Keith Moon playing style, Destri's Rascals-nurtured New York pop smarts. In the delectable "In The Flesh"— inspired by a crush Harry had had on David Johansen and featuring Brill Building queen Ellie Greenwich on backing vocals—it also boasted Blondie's first hit (No. 2 in Australia).

"Clem's influence was the perfect counter-punch to Chris' artier side, and that was really a driving force," says Destri. "It was actually part of the thing that kept me there. Because I walked in with this vision of my own— you know, here are my songs, and this is what I want to do. And it was Clem who sorta took me aside. Otherwise Chris and I would have banged heads from day one."

"I always knew the songs were pretty well sussed," says Burke. "There was a nucleus of maybe fifteen, sixteen at the time, and there was also the taste we all had in cover songs. I didn't know too many people in my group of friends who really liked the Shangri-Las or the Velvet Underground. They were all in their bedrooms trying to be the next Jimmy Page. There was a specific vision we had that not many people had at the time."

As Blondie's sound crystallised, so the band's '60s thrift-store mod look came together. "The reason we got these clothes is because they were what we could afford at first," Debbie Harry recalled in 1979. "I was always raving in the early days about straight leg pants. Bell-bottoms used to really make me crazy because they'd swoosh and get in the way and I was always falling down in them." A key influence on the band's skinny-tie, narrow-collar image was that of designer Stephen Sprouse, who lived for a while in a Bowery loft with Harry and Stein and urged them to make bright colours and monochromatic simplicity a Blondie trademark.

From a British perspective, Blondie were a knowing power-pop antidote to the splenetic rage of punk—a retro dream for the Phil Spector fan in all of us. We loved the nod to West Side Story in "A Shark In Jet's Clothing," the surf-pop homage that was "In The Sun," the B-movie goofing of "Kung Fu Girls" and "Attack Of The Giant Ants." Not to mention the sheer gleeful trashiness of "Rip Her To Shreds." (An infamous early Chrysalis ad featured a pic of Debbie and read WOULDN'T YOU LIKE TO RIP HER TO SHREDS? Countless spotty young onanists wanted to do exactly that: in the delicate words of a boy interviewed for Fred and Judy Vermorel's marvellous *Starlust,* "I'd like to screw the heart off Blondie, and I said heart not arse"). In May 1977, we got to see the band when they came to England to support critics' darlings Television, and nine months later we made their gender-reversing adaptation of Randy & the Rainbows' 1963 hit "Denis(e)" a No. 2 smash.

Watching Blondie at the Hammersmith Odeon on that tour, did I honestly think they were better than Television, whose brilliant Marquee Moon had just come out? Of course not. But when I walked out of the gig, I realised Blondie had been a lot more fun than Verlaine's navel-gazing quartet. Amusing, then, to hear from Blondie twenty-one years later how miserable Television (and "Patti's clan") made life for their support act.

"We were pretty much at the bottom rung of the totem pole in the CBGBs scene." says Destri. "I think the only reason we went to England with Television was that we had a label and they were willing to put support on the tour. And we all knew each other. Miles Copeland, who promoted that tour, figured we wouldn't fight on the bus, that type of thing. So we went out, and the audience reaction was great for us. And that was the first indication that maybe somebody else gets this."

As good to Blondie as London, was Los Angeles, where—following February 1977 gigs at the Whisky-a-Go-Go—the band was quickly embraced by a burgeoning new wave scene and welcomed with open arms by scenesters like KROQ jock Rodney Bingenheimer. "L.A. was pretty inspirational for us," attests Burke. "We were able to get out of New York, and it was certainly a much less jaded type of audience, more open to the kind of trash aesthetic we were putting forward. It was a different sorta demographic."

Away from the CBGBs in-crowd, Blondie were starting to cross over. By the 1978 release of *Plastic Letters*—a darker collection of power-pop which nonetheless included "Denis" and its fine follow-up Brit hit "(I'm Always Touched By Your) Presence Dear"—Debbie Harry had become a star, a pop permutation of the luscious dumb blonde blueprinted by Monroe and filtered through the likes of Jayne Mansfield and Mamie Van Doren. With hindsight, what she really resembled was an Eastern bloc country's idea of Dumb Blonde sexiness. ("She looked like a corn-fed Polish girl," recalled Ritty Dodge, who'd worked alongside Harry as a Playboy bunny.) "I wanted to come across as a naughty, sexy, tarty woman who was really living," says the queen of the pop shiksas.

"Debbie and Chris come out of the beatnik tradition, and those people did not see themselves as entertainers," says Victor Bockris. "On the other hand, she once showed me how she would transform herself from Debbie Harry into Blondie: the different layers of makeup she used, and how she got dressed. And I must say, it was quite fascinating, because as she was doing it, by the time she was finished, I was very turned on. It was like, Now I'm Blondie, a sort of pouty cartoon character."

"Both Marty Thau and Richard Gottehrer said to me that the way I performed and sang and the way I wrote was so different from the person they knew socially," Harry says. "They just couldn't put those two personalities into one person. I guess they thought that I should be always completely raving and carrying on."

It should be said that Harry's elevation to sex-symbol status was always tempered by the knowledge that she and Chris Stein were lovers—a unit unto themselves within Blondie. Indeed, the band's manager Peter Leeds was so concerned about the detrimental effect of Harry somehow being sexually unavailable to the world that he suggested she and Stein split up.

Harry: "We always operated as a couple, and that's how it sort of went. Although I was very decisive or instigating a lot of stuff, Chris would have to sort of be the one to tell people—"

Stein: "Nobody now realises how much criticism Debbie got for being overtly sexual and doing the stuff that was commonplace among male performers."

Harry: "For the times I guess I was sort of shocking, but compared to today's standards it was nothing. There weren't very many girls around, and the ones that were were pretty strong-willed. Lydia Lunch was around a little bit later on. There was Tina Weymouth. Of course women's lib was in the press at that time, and all that stuff was going on. At that time I really did not want to do stuff that victimised women. That was clearly a motive."

Again and again in the Blondie story one comes back to a central conundrum: how a besotted bohemian couple came to front one of the biggest pop acts in the world, and how they did (or didn't) handle it. Plus, as an adjunct to that, how they were royally screwed by almost everyone along the path to success.

Perhaps the biggest turning point in that path was Blondie's signing to Chrysalis, whose English boss Terry Ellis was as smitten with La Harry as the callowest of schoolboys. "She'd be screaming and throwing things and screaming at everybody backstage," he remembered in a recent VH-1 *Behind The Music* special. "It was that kind of friction and energy that made them exciting and made them wonderful." Early pictures he saw of Harry, Ellis says, "shrieked stardom."

"After the Pistols, so many bands just got eaten up," says Elda Gentile. "The real good thing that happened for Blondie was that Chrysalis were very smart. They *developed* Blondie over three or four albums—they *worked* them, which is an unheard-of thing in this day and age. Debbie did have an opportunity to be groomed for the industry and do something really fantastic."

A catalyst for this fantastic something was Australian producer Mike Chapman, half of the great Chinnichap glam-rock team which had churned out early '70s hits for the Sweet, Mud and Suzi Quatro. (More recently, sans Chinn, Chapman had delivered hits for Exile and The Knack.) "Mike Chapman actually inherited a lot of the efforts of what we did way back then," says Craig Leon. "But I don't want to slight him, because in my opinion he is probably the greatest producer of the '70s pop era. And he really made Blondie into something commercial and worldwide when he got a hold of it."

Swanning into New York's Power Station studio in his aviator shades, a cigarette jammed into a naff white holder, Chapman announced that he was going to make a masterpiece. What he actually produced, in the summer of 1978, was a crossover album par excellence—what Lester Bangs in his book entitled *Blondie* called "New Wave for that great mythic Ozzie and Harriet audience out there in the heartland."

"*Parallel Lines* is good tight listening," Chapman later reflected. "That's what Blondie's all about...I didn't make a punk album or a new wave album with Blondie. I made a pop album. If the radio stations would only forget this evil word 'punk.' It's modern rock'n'roll."

"Modern rock'n'roll," in Chapman's definition, included the reworking of "The Disco Song" a.k.a. "Heart Of Glass," a *bête noire* for the band's hardcore fans but an American No. 1 hit in March 1979. How ironic that a song recorded almost as a novelty—a perverse New York nose-thumbing to the Disco Sucks crowd—should have been the one to propel Blondie into the big time. But propel them it—and *Parallel Lines*—did, in the process fostering an entire American wave of lame noowave skinny-tie bands.

Parallel Lines introduced a new Blondie lineup, with Gary Valentine replaced by ex-Silverhead Brit bassist Nigel Harrison and the guitar sound bolstered by a runty-looking guy called Frank "The Freak" Infante. (Harrison and Infante nearly managed to sabotage the Blondie reunion last year by refusing—as members of the financial partnership that is "Blondie"—to give it their blessing. In addition they sued Harry, Stein, Burke and Destri for $1 million, claiming their finances had been mismanaged and demanding a re-auditing of the Blondie books.)

In Britain, where they were bigger than ever, *Lines* spawned four hits, including two No. 1s in "Heart Of Glass" and "Sunday Girl." "Blondiemania" was no exaggeration for what the band experienced at events like in-store signings. Suddenly, says Debbie Harry, "everyone was at you, at you, at you..."

Back in Manhattan, a mixture of local pride in their success and resentful envy served to cocoon the band still further in a strange bubble of fame. "When we started getting attention, it was such a weird thing," says Chris Stein. "Everybody was just a bunch of fucked-up maniacs on the streets, and it seemed like a fluke, I think, all around. And that this attention was almost unreal and we'd better all jump on it. As a result, everybody got very competitive."

"Of course everyone was jealous," says Craig Leon. "None of the other bands had hits, apart from Patti with 'Because The Night.' Blondie were the only ones where you could actually point to a chart and say, 'Here is one of the CBGBs bands and they're up there with David Soul!' I'm sure it got a lot of people angry, because Blondie were so haphazard and lackadaisical about the way they played."

"One of the things people really forget is the fact that Debbie and Chris wrote most of these hits," says Alan Betrock. "I mean, Patti Smith's hit was written by Bruce Springsteen. Debbie and Chris were writing all these songs, and they were worldwide hits that sold millions of records. None of the other New York bands could match that. And I don't think people give that songwriting team enough credit. People don't realise how much work and dedication it took for them."

With manager Peter Leeds putting them on nonstop worldwide tours, the inevitable happened, only it was exacerbated by a uniquely New York surliness and recalcitrance. First the band weren't talking to each other, and soon they couldn't stand to be in the same room. Barrels of laughs all round. "Everybody would always disagree about everything," Stein says. "Debbie and I would disagree with each other, the band would disagree with us, the band would disagree among themselves. The whole thing was turmoil."

"They went through the same thing a lot of groups go through, where there's success and then everybody's ego gets inflated," says Glenn O'Brien. "In the old days of jazz you'd have a group and there would be a leader and there would be sidemen. But then the whole notion of the pop group came along, and even though Chris and Jimmy were the principal songwriters, and Chris in a way was the musical director, and Debbie the star, all of a sudden Frankie Infante thinks it's a democracy. And I think that democracy and successful bands is just something that's never been resolved."

Manager Peter Leeds failed to mollify the growing friction. Nor did the cash flow run smoothly. O'Brien: "People don't realise that Debbie and Chris would be calling up Chrysalis and saying, 'Where's the money?,' and Chrysalis would say, it's in the pipeline. There was a big lag between the time they got famous and when they actually earned anything. I think they were taken advantage of by a lot of people. I don't think Blondie were very lucky."

"Leeds gave birth to Blondie, in a sense," says Victor Bockris. "He put them on their first world tour, and he played a few tricks with them and got them a higher profile. But he also planted the negative seeds in the very basis of their career. Subsequently it wasn't smooth sailing, and Blondie has always been somewhat troubled by financial situations. Debbie and Chris were very straightforward about things, and expected to be treated straightforwardly. And they weren't."

With the release of 1979's *Eat To The Beat,* Blondie switched their management to L.A. bigshot Shep Gordon. But Gordon wasn't ideal for them either. "Shep was a real game-player, and he was operating on a lot of different levels," says Bockris. "I don't think Blondie was the most important thing in the world to him." This didn't stop *Eat To The Beat* continuing the group's meteoric rise, featuring as it did "Dreaming," "Union City Blue" and the glorious "Atomic," Blondie's third British No. 1. Much of the record, though, sounded cold and antiseptic, making an odd contrast to the sexuality ostensibly projected by Harry. (Lester Bangs—who *en passant* claimed that he "couldn't even work up a decent pornographic fantasy" about Debbie—argued that Blondie's music had become "a wall.")

When the touring stopped, Harry and Stein retreated to a townhouse they'd bought on East 72nd Street, hiding away from the glare of cameras. In his splendid "oral history of punk" *Please Kill Me!,* former punk figure-head Legs McNeil notes that at some point he actually began to feel sorry for Harry. The former fun-loving scenester, he said, "just seemed so lonely."

"The Debbie who really likes to have a good time tended to get less available, and in a sense less wanted," says Victor Bockris. "Because when she was Blondie, so many people wanted a bit of her that the only time she could get away from all that was when she and Chris would hole up in their apartment and not see anyone. And there were certain periods when Chris was very depressed because of the whole Peter Leeds situation, and I just think it wasn't easy for her. We think it's ridiculous for rock stars to complain when they're making so much money and they have all this crap that everyone wants, but the fact is that it is really painfully isolating in a way that very few people understand."

To an impartial observer, the onset of Blondie's demise must have been obvious. Asked about the band's unravelling, Chris Stein replies simply that "it was never ravelled...the band exploded and then I exploded." Clem Burke says that between 1980 and 1982 he saw no one in Blondie socially. Which only makes 1980's *Autoamerican* more remarkable for its stylistic range, not to mention the huge success of the pointedly un-Blondie-ish singles "The Tide Is High" and "Rapture," the first a cover of the Paragons' reggae classic, the second the first real example—five years before Run DMC's "Walk This Way"—of white pop interfacing with black hip hop.

Unfortunately, the same could not be said of 1982's *The Hunter,* the disastrous last album by Blondie Mk. 1. (For this fan, the writing was really on the wall when the band paired up with Giorgio Moroder for 1980's horrible electro-rock smash "Call Me"). In six years, Blondie had gone from being one of the most vibrant pop bands of the '70s to being mere MTV fodder. Stein, in any case, was becoming visibly ill, wasting away and becoming worryingly pale. I assumed he was a junkie; his friends thought he must have contracted a scary new virus then beginning to ravage America's gay communities.

"Nobody knew what was wrong," says Glenn O'Brien. "We thought maybe he had AIDS but how did he get AIDS because he didn't do any of the things you're supposed to do to get AIDS. You could see he was like a skeleton." Victor Bockris: "No one used to see them at all, they wouldn't even answer their phone. It was hellish for a while. Basically Debbie stood by Chris. There was a period for a few months where he might have died." Stein's disease was eventually diagnosed as the rare and potentially fatal skin condition pemphigus vulgaris.

With Harry and Stein all but disappearing from view, Blondie quietly dissolved, the band's other members scattering to find gainful employment. Clem Burke played with Eurythmics, and then with The Romantics and various other power-pop-rooted entities (most recently the reformed Plimsouls). Jimmy Destri released an unheralded 1982 solo album, *Heart On A Wall,* bounced around Europe, and eventually settled for life back in Brooklyn as a contractor. Nigel Harrison played with Burke and ex-Pistol Steve Jones in Chequered Past, then wound up working in A&R for Capitol and Interscope.

Harry and Stein finally re-emerged in the mid-'80s, with Stein apparently on the mend. "I can remember Chris coming over to my apartment to meet William Burroughs," says Victor Bockris. "It was amazing to see him because he was a completely different person—so turned on, and so funny, just talking and talking. That was in 1986, and it was definitely the moment at which I recognised he was back completely. It did take a few years, because it wasn't just a physical illness. The fallout at the end of Blondie also created enormous stress. To get out of the tangled web they were when he fell ill was very complicated and took a long time and was very boring and stressful."

Harry, whose solo career had started rockily with 1981's much-ridiculed, Chic-produced *Koo Koo,* returned to make *Rockbird* (1986) and hit with the bubbly, inane "French Kissing In The USA." She also continued the movie career she'd begun with *Union City* (1979) and David Cronenberg's *Videodrome* (1982), appearing as Sonny Bono's wife in the John Waters romp *Hairspray* (1988).

"Of course I was kind of lost after Blondie," she says, "but I kept on trying to figure it out. And then I wanted to make more records. I guess the best thing that I know now is what it really takes to be creative and to hold on to my artistic soul. And I guess I really didn't know that, I didn't know how to activate it. I think one of the reasons that I was so attracted to Chris is that he is so naturally adept at expressing that constantly. And it's taken a while just to become habitually in touch with that, and just to live my life like that."

"Many women going through what she went through might easily have fallen apart and become very dispirited or very bitter," says Victor Bockris. "Debbie maintained a pretty good attitude towards all this stuff. I never saw her go through periods of long depression: she might have had difficult times up and down, but she wasn't someone who fell into deep depressions. She's a person who basically got up and tried again."

Although they split up at the end of the '80s, Harry and Stein remained close friends and continued to work together—on *Def, Dumb And Blonde* (1989) and *Debravation* (1993), neither terribly captivating. "I Want That Man" was another overproduced piece of late '80s schlock, and another hit. Who really cared? Meanwhile Blondie's influence peeped through only in the underwhelming form of The Primitives, Transvision Vamp, and Kim Wilde. Of course, there was that Madonna broad...

More cred-boosting by far was Harry's work with The Jazz Passengers, a loose-knit New York bop ensemble who may have heard her initial (and very credible) stabs at jazz singing on *Autoamerican.* "It's much more about real singing, which is definitely what I'm more adept at," Harry says. "I really am good at that. So it was as much of a revelation to me. I work very hard to be a good singer and I study, and I've kept working. In my performance I consciously hold back from dancing too much because I know that it's going to affect my singing. I really work to be a musician, and I contribute to the arrangements as much as I'm capable of doing. And that's what I love. I get joy from that."

"I think the Jazz Passengers thing was really good for Debbie," says Glenn O'Brien. "It enabled her to make music and even improve her skills while taking the spotlight off her and just being one of the boys in the band. That was a situation she was never in before. And I think she's more one of the boys in Blondie now than she was in the beginning. She's not playing up the glamour part so much as just being a great entertainer and kind of a freak."

"In a weird way Debbie has become a lot better than she was," says Craig Leon. "All of them have grown up, but she has gone off into a completely different area and done very well creatively in it. She's become really good at it, to the point where it lights bulbs in my head as to doing a real Debbie Harry jazz album."

Leon says that trying to incorporate the new, jazz-oriented Harry into a reactivated Blondie sound was "probably the biggest challenge for her and for me and the band as well". While *No Exit* kicks off with a super-charged blast of vintage Blondie pop ("Maria") and returns to the band's Shadow Morton girl-group roots ("Out In The Streets"), it also takes in a slew of very different genres, each bringing out a new element in Harry's voice. There's the slinky hepcat jazz of "Boom Boom In The Zoom Zoom Room," the stomping ska-pop of "Screaming Skin," the Gothic hip hop of the title track (featuring Coolio), the hyper-sequenced, *tres* '80s "Forgive And Forget," and a lovely, sensuous reverie called "Night Wind Sent." If anything, *No Exit* is too eclectic for its own good.

"Getting herself comfortable with even singing in a pop style again was hard," says Leon. "I mean, she's having fun doing it, it's not like she doesn't enjoy it. It's just totally different to what she's been doing for the past few years, and it's probably musically a little less interesting than the avant-garde things she's recorded."

All of which begs the question of just how keen Harry is to re-enter the arena of Anglo-American pop culture as "Blondie." At 53, she may have a rough ride at the hands of ageist commentators. "I truly hope this Blondie thing is a wonderful success for her, because she really deserves it," says Elda Gentile. "People look at a person like Debbie and think, Oh, she lives such a glamorous life, but I don't think that's really true. I think she works hard to live up to the image of Blondie, and the pressure on her must be enormous right now—especially in this day and age where if you're not 16 years old you're not cool."

"She's probably old enough to be the mother of a lot of people in her audience, but she's still like a wild thing," says Glenn O'Brien. "And that's sort of a phenomenon. I've been saying, 'Look, you should come out there looking like June Cleaver.' She thinks she should look like Marilyn Manson, but what's more surprising than coming out looking like a Serial Mom?!"

The best news for the moment is that the group's reunion has been, for the most part, a happy experience. With the trusted Leon at the controls and the powerful Left Bank management team behind them, Blondie have found a renewed zest for life as a band. Even the arguing has been fun this time around. "There's always this melting pot of ideas on the same song," says Craig Leon. "It can still get pretty violent with everybody fighting for their ideas: Chris wanting it one way, Jimmy wanting something here, Clem wanting something there, and Debbie kind of serenely sitting back and saying, 'When you guys get it together, I'm going to give you the hit melody and vocal.' It's all just because they all have a fabulous sense of pop history."

"They always quarrel, but now they have more informed and amusing quarrels than they used to," says Glenn O'Brien. "During the recording sessions they were having a lot of fun kind of goofing on each other. I think there's a real appreciation that's even been enhanced because of the years where they didn't see each other. It's almost like they never broke up."

Sitting with Blondie at Space, on the eve of their first tour in over fifteen years, the band appear cheerful enough about their prospects.

"As it goes along week by week," says Chris Stein, "I think everybody's getting much more positive about the whole thing. The last tour Debbie and me did, what'd we do? Two of the fuckin' hit songs, maybe. And I can remember people leaving and going, 'Well yeah, but I had no idea what that was about.' Five years ago I wouldn't have wanted to do the old songs, but now I feel real positive and real emotional about doing them. And unless we get heavily bombarded by tomatoes and beer cans, I think it's going to be fine."

There are no tomatoes in evidence when, six weeks later, Blondie take the stage at Poole's Arts Centre for the penultimate gig of their European tour. Instead the Saturday night crowd gives the band the rapturous welcome that's become routine on the tour—a welcome born of equal parts nostalgia and curiosity. At the Arts Centre you can spot the punk vets who've hung up their safety pins and joined the mortgage set, but you can also see Debbie-ettes who were still in nappies when Blondiemania reigned.

For a few numbers the performance looks tired and uninspired. Harry, wearing a '40s hourglass suit that suggests a 1974 Roxy Music backing singer's outfit, seems tentative as she tackles the sequenced rock-pop of "Forgive And Forget." Meanwhile the others look like L.A. musos. Leigh Foxx, black jacket sleeves rolled up to his elbows, has the temerity to play a *bass solo* on "Atomic." From The Shangri-Las to...Spyro Gyra! Is it meant to be ironic?

But as the show goes on, Harry, her voice huskier and more Joni Mitchell-ish than it used to be, loosens up and starts to enjoy herself. When the Poole boomers bob as one to "Sunday Girl," clapping along on the bridges with Harry, the band goes with the flow. "Oh baaaybeh...my sweet baaaybeh," Harry coos, and for a second we're transported back to girl-group heaven—Brooklyn, summer '64. By the time the band reach "Rip Her To Shreds," via "In The Flesh" ("the song that got us away from New York City and into the big wide world"), everybody's happy.

"NO ONE CAN SAY WE DIDN'T HOLD OUT FOR 15 MINUTES," reads the back of the Blondie tour t-shirt, the quote daftly attributed to Sartre (author, lest we forget, of a play called *No Exit*). It's not as if the band don't realise how sad these reunions can be. (The coming week will bring to nearby Bournemouth not only Duran Duran but the hot-ticket triple bill that is Culture Club/ABC/Human League...ah, Paul Morley, what did you start all those years ago?) After obligatory encores of "Denis," "The Tide Is High," and "Heart Of Glass," Blondie shuffle off and leave us with our warm memories of picture discs and *Top Of The Pops*.

"And you don't stop..."

"Personally for me it's been very stress-free as a result of so much acceptance," says Chris Stein *après le gig*. "I think Debbie's the most worn-out, because I get to sort of phase out, whereas Debbie's level of focus is a lot higher."

Stein says the tour's first date in Stockholm was "dismal" but that almost every subsequent show has been a blast. The previous weekend's pair of dates at London's Lyceum had brought out everyone from gnarled war heroes like Rat Scabies to Blondie-inspired Britpop babies like Theaudience. "I'm more familiar with the faces from the old punk days," says Stein, "but Clem is up on the new breed."

Burke: "Speaking of old punks, take a look at my lucky Carnaby Street punk bracelet. Only three pounds, man."

Stein: "We went to fuckin' Hermes and they had them for three *hundred* pounds."

Burke: "So we were inspired to buy the ones for three pounds. Although I did get my girlfriend a punk necklace from Vivienne Westwood for seventy quid."

Stein: "A mere drop in the bucket."

Burke tells me it's "getting boring saying how good everything's been going." Only a hilarious incident in Lugano, Italy, where Blondie were being presented with a highfalutin' cultural award—previous recipients: Fellini, Callas, Nureyev—provided any hiccup along the way.

"It was this black-tie fuckin' situation," says Stein. "Polanski was there with some eleven-year-old dancer. I don't know if it was his date. And Clem got progressively drunker and drunker and tried to leap over his drums, and he fell on Paul [Carbonara] and Leigh [Foxx] in front of this whole crowd of bejewelled courtesans. It was a disaster, but at the same time it was a major existential moment."

"I had completely forgotten that I had drunk three bottles of champagne, and also that I had my Annello & Davide Cuban-heel Beatle boots on," says Burke. "So I go over the drums and next thing I know I'm on the floor on top of Leigh, and then the drums come crashing down in a chain reaction, and all you hear is five hundred people going, *Oh my God*...in Italian, of course."

Stein: "By the way, the award was a really beautiful thing with a marble base and silver shit and a fuckin' gold mask, whereas our fuckin' *Q* award must have cost all of four dollars—"

Clem: "But the *Q* award means a lot—"

Destri [piping up in the background]: "Fuck the meaning! It's cheap!"

Burke: "But let's face it, what are Fellini and Maria Callas compared to Weller and Massive Attack?"

I turn around and see that Debbie Harry has emerged from her dressing room to pose for pictures with a pair of peroxide-blonde girls, each wearing the "Vultures" t-shirt Harry used to model back in '77. Pop's sometime Marilyn Monroe looks glazed but happy.

"You girls were *relentless* tonight," she tells the Blondie girls, her arms spread round their shoulders.

"Vulture women together!!"   —   Thanks to Kate Simon, Howard Thompson and David Fricke.

Clem Burke of Blondie, 2002
credit: © Robert Matheu / Retna Ltd

"The Power of the Visual Image"

by Scott Coblio
(edited and adapted by Allan Metz)

The author notes "the power of the visual image" for Blondie, as reflected in the photography contained in this book.—Ed.

Simply speaking, Blondie was a visual band. At a time when many rockers were faceless (Alan Parsons, Foreigner, et al) Blondie grabbed hold of pop iconography, borrowing and stealing and pasting together what would become a brilliant abbreviation of American Pop history.

"...lighthearted as if from another time, yet not at all another dead slice of sixties nostalgia" raved Lester Bangs in his *Village Voice* review of the debut album. Indeed, Blondie's visual and aural attack seemed not so much to make time stand still as eliminate it altogether. In Blondie-time, it was as if all eras enjoyed simultaneous co-existence. Yesterday as tomorrow.

And thereby hangs what must be called Blondie's secret weapon—transcendence. Blondie's appeal lingers because they transcended their times. By going backward and sideways, they ended up forward. Viewing any videotape of their many television appearances in the late seventies, one is immediately struck by how futuristic the band looks in contrast to their audience. On a televised 1978 "Midnight Special" appearance (an all-disco show attempting to capitalize on the success of "Saturday Night Fever"), Debbie performs in a Stephen Sprouse single-strapped mod mini and thigh boots while women with Ogilvy perms and lycra hustle by with their earth shoe-and-bell-bottomed boyfriends. It looks more like the collision of two cultures than a merging of them. But then, that's precisely what it was.

Once the group started selling in the States (they had already been topping charts in Europe and Australia for a year or two with hits like "In the Flesh," "Denis" and "Presence Dear") they—and specifically Debbie—became a platform for visual artists of all types to interpret. "The Image" became a franchise: Blondie a la Annie Leibovitz. Debbie a la Scavullo, a la Avedon, a la Mapplethorpe, H.R. Giger, Andy Warhol, David Cronenberg, Blondie a la mode. It is fair to say that Debbie's extraordinary looks and personal style became part of global consciousness, or as *Creem* magazine put it, "the glittery gage by which we measure our own cool."

As Harry became a visual abbreviation for the group, one looked with anticipation to see how each new artist would interpret Blondie. Often the results created a kind of art all its own...in a sense, publicity as art. It was a concept that had already been introduced by Andy Warhol in the sixties. In the seventies, however, Debbie and the boys took a lot of flack for it, and whispers of "sell-out" were heard ringing all the way back to CBGBs' darkest corners. In fact, it seemed for a time that Blondie, by virtue of their very success, would become the ultimate scapegoats of the "new wave" they helped create.

But time has been kind to Blondie and their Warholian touch. The world's a hipper place, and the band's avowed purpose to "manipulate the media" no longer sends frightened townsfolk running to light the torches. The music has proven to endure (witness "Maria" hitting the number one spot in England, 1999) and their influence on music, style and fashion can be seen daily in the countless bands and female singers who travel a road that Debbie and the boys helped pave.

As Chris Stein once observed, Blondie was really a "'pop art band'" and not a "'pop band'" (Freydkin). For a moment in time, Deborah Harry became a mirror of popular culture, reflecting its many facets and trends without losing—as have many since—a hold on herself that connected and gave life to all the roles she would play before the photographer's lens. The bombshell, punky pin-up, child-woman, sophisticated lady or rock chanteuse, always paying a twisted homage to convention before ripping it to shreds.

And the band balanced the glamor with a gritty counterpoint, so that Debbie's stunning visuals could be all the more effective by contrast. And let's not forget that the songwriting talents of Chris and Jimmy, especially, are a huge part of the Blondie "voice" and "persona." By singing songs written from a male perspective, Debbie was able to be "bisexual or asexual," which no doubt accounts in part for the group's huge cult status with people from all walks of life.

For the window of time that they occupied center stage in the media's eye, Blondie, like all true stars, created a light that resonates in the eye and the imagination long after their proverbial 15 minutes were up.

If the music has its own legacy, then let these images tell their own story.

Here's to the light.

"state of the arts? (transparencies circa 2000)"

by John Sibby

i

out of context, it would seem justifiable to consider the trite meaningless
examples of the media saturated, current flavor, trendy ranks.
adored by most, abhorred by few.
what a pathetic fallacy.
catchy phrases like legend, icon, diva are blurted out with careless abandon
and are sadly rendered a shallow new meaning.
this interest is seemingly applicable to these contrived clichéd people who impose on our consciousness...
safe, hopelessly choreographed, state-of-the-art, prefab, poseur
parody...contribution? yeah right, check back in, say, twenty-five years? ten minutes?...
enter one debbie harry through ambient distortion mingles seductively among us
personifying burroughs' meanderings and serving as a superb counterbalance
by rejecting defunct mainstream ideology.
these angst-ridden narratives executed with point blank nyc swagger and grace
are veiled with anti-marilyn sentiment.
classics like x offender, rip her to shreds, sunday girl, union city, shayla explore
far beyond its girl group referencing and pent up mosaic sexuality.
they totter inadvertently in live show succession.
the dense contrast rests solely on the band's ability to translate the intangible
with multi-dimensional beauty.
origins hint of debbie's decades old dream state reality of
mathematical equations, articulating exuberant colliding passages.

ii

if opposites attract than debbie and chris would have simply overlooked one another...
ground zero...
this shared dialect would reinvent, restructure and redefine music while
interjecting urban streetscape visuals long before rap reestablished this genre.
initially shrugged off but forced to reconcile with this sound, so-called critics scurried to categorize it.
surface labeling zeroed in on a perceived tempest persona...how dull!
debbie had their attention alright and the joke was on them...time was ticking.
while america's heart skipped a beat, producer chapman hit em where it counted.
this masterpiece would both propel and disengage the band.
(being a romantic, one can only hope that fame was not the boys' main objective).
this landmark expression advocates the perverse dichotomy between mainstream and clandestine nuance.
two other offerings, eat to the beat and autoamerican, complete the trilogy
reestablishing america's demure fixation.
numerous chart successes fill the pockets of higher-up record execs...
everybody was happy...except the band.
the hardcore know it's the b-sides that really make us tick...
if these disks represent an all-encompassing view of what the band is about,
then the hunter, with its revaluating discord, represents its closure.

iii

time was no longer ticking; it was up...
the sons of the silent age get together to make a little noise...
global reverberation results.
hey what can i say...
america found safer, saner, more predictable bedfellows...
let 'em have 'em!
...till blondie pushes the envelope one more time!...

"Debtalk"

by Victor Bockris

INTRODUCTION

When I was looking through my Blondie files researching "Blondie's Punk Roots" for this book, I came across these random unpublished passages of Debbie talking about, among other subjects, aliens, fame, politics, love and illusion. They represent a sampler of Debbie's mind at work. Read them out loud. Find their rhythm. They are her voice portrait, tracking the rhythm of her speech, capturing the way her voice track sounds.

Reading these passages back today reminds me of how much I learned from talking with Debbie and, I have to add, Chris. One of the things I admired most about them was that they had succeeded at the complex task of collaborating on their lives and careers, making them one and the same thing, while being in love. Many of the things Debbie said could just as easily have been said by Chris, so shared was their thinking. Not that they agreed on everything. Rock 'n' roll is made out of tension and there was a lot of healthy tension between Debbie and Chris.

ON THE BOWERY WITH BURROUGHS

Because of their Beatnik roots, I was particularly happy to introduce Debbie and Chris to William Burroughs, at my apartment in N.Y.C. in 1980.

"DEBORAH HARRY: You live next door to where we used to live on The Bowery. We used to live in a haunted building.

WILLIAM BURROUGHS: What haunted it?

HARRY: On top of the liquor store, we lived in an old doll factory that had employed child labor.

CHRIS STEIN: When we moved into the place things went berserk. They were flying around all the time.

HARRY: Fires...

STEIN: It was three floors, a real big floor through.

BURROUGHS: Were you fixing it up?

STEIN: No it was totally destroyed, but I found these old things in there from the forties, old plaques.

HARRY: There were bullet holes in the windows from the Mafia when they had the place.

BURROUGHS: Well now what were these psychic phenomena that occurred? Tell me about it.

HARRY: There was an entrance that came up from street level, a narrow long staircase that was very dark, and at the top of the staircase there was a flat wall with a doorway in it and Chris decided to paint this wall black because he thought it would make it nice, and then there was loud knocking and he saw a little boy.

STEIN: Flashed on a little kid. It was more like a feeling than actually seeing. It was more a presence...

BURROUGHS: Did you have any impression of the child's age?

STEIN: Eight, nine.

BURROUGHS: Was there anyone in the vicinity of this whole operation that young?

STEIN: No, there were no little kids around.

BURROUGHS: 'Cos you probably know about poltergeists. They almost always manifest themselves through young people..."

ON ALIENS

Debbie was not an intellectual or bookish person, and made no attempt to pretend to be, but she was hip. She had read *Howl* and she had been around, and in those days New York was a wonderfully intelligent place.

The photographs at the end of *Making Tracks*, in which Debbie emerges as an H.R. Giger character, along with some of her lyrics, point towards Debbie's avowed interest in aliens. She is a firm believer and will be among the first to go. You know she'd be great in outer space.

"I think it's natural that somewhere in the universe, there would exist other forms of life, and I would naturally assume that these other forms of life have intelligence. I know a little bit about Wilhelm Reich and his business about some aliens being bad for us—I can understand that. I mean, I should think that we would have some kind of malignant confrontation with aliens, because we have that kind of confrontation right here with our *own* species.

But then again, I think that...now, I'm thinking more and more about other dimensions, that UFOs are like coexisting kinds of things that come and go through dimensions.

Einstein brought a lot of stuff that was fiction into the realm of scientific reality, and I really, I believe in that...Because of those things that happened to me when I was a child—having scientific knowledge about things that I suddenly knew about that I had no way of knowing about—I just believe that all this is possible, I believe that the human brain is limited by all these emotional traps, and like folklore. If we could get beyond this, I mean physical reality is a lot for us to conquer, and I don't know...it's like the bodiless mind or the mindless body, it's like which one? and where does it go? and how far does it go? I mean, we've come from the mindless body, and are we approaching the bodiless mind? We're a long way from *that*."

ON THE BAD

I first met Debbie in the apartment of a mutual friend on the night of the great New York Blackout in 1977. We sat talking in the living room in the pitch black dark. So, although I knew Debbie was sitting across the room from me, I could not see her. I remember her laughing.

At that time she had been on the New York scene for ten years. She and Chris were on a high. They had recently returned from their world tour and were still living in a hotel suite. One night we all went up there to see Godard's "Alphaville." Debbie was well grounded in the axis between the N.Y. nightlife and the New York underground. Consequently she was able to see things a lot more clearly than most of her peers.

These quotes give an accurate impression of Debbie the moralist who kept really remarkably well attuned, despite the truly enormous amount of shit she had to put up with. I don't think I know anybody else who has managed to remain essentially good, while being constantly ripped off, on a daily basis, by people she had spent time with. Perhaps it was because of her long apprenticeship in the music business. By the time she made it she was wiser than her contemporaries in the punk scene. She didn't come off as superior or anything like that, it was just that, over time, I began to see that there really was a lot more to Debbie Harry than met the eye.

Debbie worked very hard. Once she succeeded she had no choice, other than throwing the whole thing over, but I don't think that ever seriously entered her mind.

"The bad is overpowering the good. People don't talk about being good anymore, they don't care about what's good, they don't try to act good for the most part, they try to just get ahead, or they try to be successful, or they try to be powerful. See, when I grew up I always felt that nobody ever said exactly what they meant. They always talked in opposites. If they said one thing, what they really meant was the exact opposite. Nine times out of ten this turned out to be true. I think that it's true for everyone in the world today.

Being good is not the criteria. Success is the criteria. Power is the criteria. And this leads one to deal in opposites. If you're really going to be good, you don't sign a group to a record at an unfair percentage. You give them something real that they can live off, so they're proud to be doing what they're doing and will therefore create better material. But this isn't done. Artists are squeezed. They try to squeeze every little ounce out of them for the least amount of money, especially in the record business. And that's the way it is, that's the general rule of thumb throughout the world today.

I don't think I'm a goody-goody but I certainly don't think that I'm a baddy baddy. I have a very strong limit about how I will treat other people and what I will do to them, and what I will accept from them. But in turn I'm not treated like this, and that's what I know and that's what I've gotten out of this whole thing. If we are fucking on this planet and we

369

have to survive, and there is nothing here but us and the animals and sticks and stones, and we had to go out and find some rabbits to eat, you know fucking well you'd go out and do that. And that's when you know what is good.

I know so many people who don't work, and yet somehow they expect to get a lot of money for what they don't do. All they try to do is hustle their fucking buns. That's it. They don't really go out and like fucking work for six hours a day at some menial task just to have enough money to buy food or pay the rent. They try to avoid that at all costs, and that leads to the devaluation of what reality is."

ON POLITICS

Debbie learned a lot from her life, from the unusual opportunities her position gave her to meet people and see things from obtuse angles. And she used it all. So many people who pass through the great arc of fame are so dazzled by it that they never enjoy the moment. They're frozen by awe and the horrible thought that it might all go away tomorrow. All they do is worry.

In these passages, Debbie comes across as a hard-hitting moralist. She speaks with the experience of the sixties still bright in her memory, but the lessons of reality in place. She surprised me with how emphatic she could be. She also really had more of a worldview than most people I knew.

"I'm really upset about politics. I don't mind capitalism, I think that free enterprise is very stimulating. At the same time, you get these brash twenty-one year olds who come in and say 'I'm going to change the world,' without taking any practicalities into account. And it's bullshit. I approve of the fact that people want to try to change things, but phew! Why don't they just come in and say 'I'm going to learn about the world and then if I'm lucky I'm going to survive.' That's the hippest thing, but most revolutionaries or rebels can't possibly think like that.

I think the people in Communist countries suffer from a lack of free enterprise and initiative with all that red tape, but I think it's disappointing for young people to be brought up in this system. Let's face it, most people in this country are educated very well and taught to have respect and to be truthful and be on the positive side. I mean, education is leading towards that, but the government that exists is very contradictory and very hypocritical to that.

Everything should be more clearly defined. There should be more definition. What will happen is, in order for people to get more definition they're also going to get more ideology, whether they want it or not. Instead of really defining what's happening totally and then adding ritual to it, they will form an ideology and not really interpret anything."

ON PSYCHIC

One time Debbie, Chris and I were floating through London in the small living room in the back of a gigantic Damiler limousine. Chris was telling me about a wonderful psychic vision he had had on the Isle of Man off the British coast, where they had just been filming videos for *The Hunter*. Debbie was waving to people in the street and passing cars like the Queen. We were all equally interested and experienced in psychic phenomenon of every kind.

"The psychic thing is so important because it's one of the only areas left to go. Either that, or maybe it takes two steps backward to go one step forward. They might have to put the clamp on everything to get everybody to suddenly get to this point and recognize the present. They had to build a fucking wall around Berlin."

ON SCHOOL

Debbie was super aware of Blondie's audience. She and Chris were dedicated to trying to use whatever ways they could to reach out to the kids who were still in school and confused. I was always impressed by how much attention they paid to their young audience. They knew thousands of kids read their interviews and they often tried to really say something useful. Or at least reach out an understanding hand. They vividly recalled how difficult their own childhoods had been.

"I don't have any problems with any of the stuff that's taught in school. Personally I think that's fine, but I think they should make more things available and people should be able to pick and chose a bit more at an earlier age. There's no reason why some poor kid who's working in the metal shop and really not interested in anything else should have to take a lot of other stuff. It just causes him pain to have to try.

In the United States everybody is lumped together in their education. In the communist countries specialization is the most important thing. They just can't afford to teach everybody on an equal level, they have to specialize from an early age. You have to be worth an education to get it."

ON CARS

Debbie grew up in a series of dull, small towns in upstate New York and New Jersey. It was difficult being an alien. She passed through the years getting involved where she could.

Debbie was famous among the CB's crowd for her car. She was a generous liftgiver and often drove people home, or drove large groups of people around town, clubhopping. This reflection of interest in cars came when we were talking about what *Making Tracks* was going to be about. At one point, we thought it was going to be about cars.

"I guess I always knew secretly without admitting it that, because of the structure of society, men were always instructing women in the ways of the world, because women weren't involved with it as much. In high school, I learned a lot about cars from my boyfriends, because cars were the big thing and everybody had a car or liked cars. I really learned a lot about the mechanics of a car, although I never really took a car apart, I knew how to identify the various malfunctions just by the sound of the motor."

ON LOVE

Debbie was endlessly interested in figuring out the big questions for herself.

"Love is the biggest thing because there's nothing else. One of the strongest instincts of man is to perpetuate the species, and that's what it comes down to but companionship and the idealization of this basic biological function comes out in all these twisted ways. People are so confused about it. Maybe there's a lot of things missing that people really need to balance themselves out."

ON FAME

This is a realization people were having in the punk scene around 1975. Today most young people caught up in the excitement and glamour of fame wouldn't understand it at all. Nowadays everybody is still buying into the same old illusions they were buying into, when punk came along to stop all that. Fame, like size and speed, is among the top ten American illusions. Just because it's bigger doesn't mean it's better. Just because you're famous doesn't mean you're happier.

"I think people are coming to realize more and more that fame is a less and less attractive proposition. It used to be that everybody wanted to be famous, then people realized that being famous is not a particularly great deal at all. In fact, the major part of it is a pretty bad deal. It's a terrific invasion of privacy. It just changes your whole life and basically it just gives you money in exchange. It just gives you money, but it leaves you totally vulnerable to every fucking person who knows how to read."

TALKING WITH DEBBIE

On the roof deck of their penthouse on East 58th Street, in my apartment, in hotel rooms and cars in London, L.A. and New York, backstage, upstairs, peering out the window, at the Mudd Club, parked outside some dealer's place in the West Village, on the phone, I talked with Debbie. From 1977-1982 we had a good relationship, we made a good piece of work together with Chris, *Making Tracks: The Rise of Blondie* (Da Capo, New York 1998). We never had any problems. It was really great and it was fun. If anything I think I was a bit slow, a bit stupid in their world. They moved so much faster and did so much more than I did in any given week that they seemed to almost live in a different world. They were addressing the world every time they put something out—being released on the same day in thirty-two different countries. That makes you feel different.

I think the most outstanding thing about Debbie is that she managed to stay so grounded when she went so high. Maybe that's why she didn't die as a result of the precipitous fall Blondie took in 1982-1983. I never sensed any kind of fear in her. Most people I know you can see their fear, or they talk about it. There was one stage when it was hip to be scared, to be like the paranoid who is a person in possession of the facts. Anybody who isn't terrified all the time is out of their mind, William Burroughs opined.

One thing I did realize about Debbie early on was that she had grown up on the axis between the beatniks and the hippies, so that at the start of the eighties she would be interested in meeting William Burroughs. When Patti Smith had the opportunity to sit down and talk with Burroughs she talked endlessly about herself. Debbie, on the other hand, actually had a conversation with William. That's the difference between them. Patti was bullshitting, Debbie was really there. It's not that one is better than the other, it's just that they're different. Debbie Harry and Patti Smith were very different people. Wherever she emerged Debbie was by her nature a classic American pop icon. In 1969 she was a Lower East Side Slum Goddess in the East Village Other. In 1979 she was the queen of the punk scene. She should have played Boadicea, the British Queen who beat the occupying Roman army, almost throwing them out of England.

She was a very sensitive person so she felt every little nuance of the hard-boiled world in which she was making her living. One of the great things about her was that she never showed contempt for people, she never looked down. She could be angry, she might despise someone, but her sunny disposition, her "we'll-cross-that-bridge-when-we-come-to-it" attitude, kept her on a steady track.

Reading over this piece more than twenty years after it was recorded I feel how much she had earned the right to her opinions. Nobody knows how fucking hard Debbie Harry worked during the Rise of Blondie. I remember once sitting with her on the large comfortable gray couch in the living room on East 72nd Street. We were waiting for her manager to pick us up and take us to a meeting at Dell, the publisher distributing *Making Tracks*. I suddenly realized that sitting straight up, neatly togged out, washed and polished, Debbie was asleep.

"Deb...Deb, what...uh...are you alright?"

"Yeah...I'm Ok."

"Is anything wrong?" I asked.

"No," she replied, slightly annoyed. "I just wrote and recorded a fucking album in three weeks! I'm tired!" She sounded slightly exasperated, and I realized that even I, who had seen her every day she had been in town over the past year, didn't realize how much work went into doing that. This was *The Hunter*.

Chris used to spend eighteen hours a day in the studio, they rarely slept more than four hours a night if that, often staying up for a couple of days without sleep. The pace is fast. The stakes are high, your adrenalin is pumping and you do what you can. Writing and recording an album in three weeks, however you cut it up, is an enormous amount of work, especially when the weight of its success rests upon the success of the songs and your singing voice. I remember breaking into her office with Chris, shrieking about some problem with the book. Debbie was studiously typing up a sheaf of lyrics on a giant IBM machine, working hard. She was pissed off because we broke her concentration.

ON HEALTH

One of the things that divides the men from the boys in the entertainment world is the individual's strength. Brian Jones fell out of the Stones largely because he was asthmatic. His increasingly frequent breakdowns became a serious drag on his band. I don't ever remember Debbie being sick. She was often exhausted and lying on her bed watching TV because she worked so hard. But she was and is a strong person.

"I know a lot about my body because of intuition and sensitivity. I don't know anything about it in terms of heredity. I really don't know anything about my parents. Recently my mother told me that there was a tendency in my genes for diabetes, but I generally don't have any problems. My health is very good. I'm very sensitive to anything that changes. But I hardly ever catch cold."

ON ILLUSION

This is the sort of thing Debbie would come up with that would set me thinking, realizing how close I was still living at times to just such illusions...

"I know a groupie, a girl who started fucking around when she was twelve, and became a famous groupie and travelled around the world. By the time she was sixteen she was tired, embittered and feeling that she had met every body and fucked everybody, and done everything and didn't have much to live for. She started going downhill at that age and by the time she got to be twenty-three, she felt that she should drop off the face of the earth, and subsequently has. Girls like that have no career, no ambition, they think that they're old and used up. It's like—wow, what a tragedy! I mean like really, *what a tragedy*, and it's just the culture. It's really preposterous. *Oh God! I'm so glad that I got away from that.*"

Comprehensive Discography
Commentary

"Blondie: Once More (Into The Bleach)"

by Ralph Heibutzki

Discoveries, *September 1999*

Comprehensive overview of Blondie's discography from an American perspective. Following introductory material, a thorough chronological analysis is presented. Concludes with book and magazine references to Blondie.—Ed.

When Gary Valentine crowded into "true bohemian squalor" in New York's East Village in the summer of 1975, he wanted nothing less than to rewrite his story: "I'd left home, under a cloud of various troubles; basically, at 18, I said, 'I'm going to be a poet, a rock star, a writer, or [an] artist.' And that's you how do it—you have to live rough, try and make it, and go to a place where things are happening.

"You go from New Jersey, which couldn't be on the farther end of the galaxy, and suddenly, you're in the center of it [bohemian life], just over the [Hudson] river. If you're gonna have a straight job, you do one thing; if you wanna be an artist, that's what I did."

Time's incinerator has recast much of the East 10th Street that Valentine embraced nearly 25 years ago. Gentrification has overtaken the junkies and youth gangs, while the storefront he shared with a friend—where his fingers piddled around on a broken piano—is now a Tai Chi studio. Yet nothing quenches the fans' interest in the years 1975-77, when Valentine composed, played bass, and toured with the cartoon that conquered the world, Blondie.

Few bands have been so extensively documented, or gossiped about; everyone has a Blondie story up their sleeve, whether in *Please Kill Me: The Uncensored Oral History Of Punk* (Grove Press: 1996), or *MOJO's* recent "New York Naked City Special" issue. [*See pp. 66-74 and 356-365 of this book*—Ed.]. Teenage girls marked their mirror time to lead vocalist Deborah Harry's chiseled pout, and the warring tastes of drummer Clem Burke, keyboardist Jimmy Destri, bassist Nigel Harrison, guitarist Frank Infante, and her partner, founder/guitarist Chris Stein.

Almost twenty years have passed since Blondie ascended into platinum Valhalla, doing what more highly-touted peers never did: putting the "singalong" back into singles, and selling records by the gross.

Long before Madonna or Courtney Love parlayed their bowed mouths into icon status, Harry graced *Rolling Stone's* "Random Notes" column whenever she changed her hair color—from black, to blue, brunette, green and silver—yet never stopped presenting herself as smart, sexy and self-assured.

When Blondie clicked, the results were dazzling. Its 1979-81 hits ranged from icy disco ("Call Me," "Heart Of Glass"), slinky reggae ("The Tide Is High") and pop-hiphop collages ("Rapture"). At their peak, they were unstoppable, whether "Rapture" spun as backing music during an NBC-TV "Facts Of Life" episode, or an Alabama DJ used "The Tide Is High" to psyche up the Crimson Tide football team, earning a call from Harry, *Trouser Press* noted in 1981. A year later, Burke mentioned hearing "One Way Or Another" at baseball games.

It's hard to imagine a better example of mainstream acceptance, which Burke now admits never envisioning: "My whole thing was going to Woolworth's, and getting 89-cent records. I thought we had a limited audience."

Few bands have been more analyzed, or misunderstood, especially when Blondie spun out in 1982 following poor ticket sales, an ineffectual album *(The Hunter),* Stein's near-fatal bout with an obscure disease (pemphigus vulgaris) and Infante's mysterious ouster. That goes double for the plethora of compilations (1981's *Best Of Blondie;* 1991's redundantly titled, *The Complete Picture—The Very Best Of Deborah Harry & Blondie*), remixes (1988's *Once More Into The Bleach*), and cover versions.

Blondie's freewheeling aesthetics can accommodate whoever climbs aboard, such as UK bands like Sleeper covering "Atomic" on the *Trainspotting* soundtrack—or rapper Coolio on the swooning goth-pop of "No Exit," the title track of Blondie's first album in 16 years (Beyond Music/BMG). Yet the reunited quartet of Burke, Destri Harry and Stein remains harder than ever to pin down.

How Harry, 53, feels about revisiting the old neighborhood is unclear, as the *San Francisco Chronicle* found last February, when the questioning veered from her current solo project: "Listen, this is supposed to be about the Jazz Passengers and their show—I don't know if we should be talking about all this Blondie stuff so much."

Nor are Blondie's publicists more helpful, as their vague promises ("Interviews will be scheduled some time next week") dribble into sphinxlike nonchalance ("We don't know if any interviews will happen"). Besides, they plaintively plead, doesn't everyone know that Blondie is a group?

Resurrecting that 20-year-old slogan might elicit different answers from Burke and Infante, who find themselves on opposing fences. Where *No Exit* vaulted Burke past numerous Nineties sideman gigs (The Eurythmics, Plimsouls, and Romantics), Infante, with Harrison's support, sought to block the reunion. Since Blondie had been a partnership, they contended, the reunion could not occur without their blessing, or a share of the proceeds. (A separate $1 million suit against the reunited lineup for alleged financial mismanagement is pending. [*The ruling on the suit subsequently went against Infante and Harrison.*—Ed.].

The punches and counterpunches sounded familiar enough when the author asked Harrison for an interview in fall 1996, shortly after he'd been named to run Interscope's A & R (Artists & Repertoire) department.

Citing his responsibilities ("I'm burned out from being on the phone so much"), Harrison politely declined. "I'm still musically scarred from my experiences in Blondie, as far as talking about this stuff goes—that's what you're up against." He still couldn't resist a punch line: "It's really easy for us now; all we have to do is sell the records!"

Yet climbing the mountain once is tough enough; climbing it a second or third time is even sweeter, because all those frictions mean nothing when every car radio is playing your song, hour after hour—if only for a time. "When we stopped, it's like, you have the winning lottery ticket, and you didn't cash it in," said Infante. "I remember coming back from a tour, and 'Call Me' was #1 on the radio. I was in the limo with Clem, and that was it. It's what you're workin' for."

The Bleaching Years: 1974-77

Forget who did what to whom. To Burke, rock'n'roll means the clothes, gestures and songs that make a band great. "When I joined Blondie, my favorite band was the Bay City Rollers, because of the energy they had," he said. "When I met Chris and Debbie in '74, I was 18, and really into bubblegum, which was the early impetus for Blondie, 'cause it's all kind of connected."

In Deborah Harry (born in Miami, Florida, July 1, 1945) and Chris Stein (born in Brooklyn, New York, January 5, 1950), Burke found a couple who'd paid, repaid and possibly overpaid their dues. Stein's previous bands included First Crow To The Moon (1967), whose lone break had been supporting The Velvet Underground, and the folk-rock Morticians (1965-66), who did one gig ("a promotional thing for a local barber—opening his shop!" he marveled in 1978 for Pete Frame's "Smouldering In The Bowery" family tree).

More recently, he'd played bass for the Magic Tramps, fronted by another rock martyr in Eric Emerson, one of several inspirations for Lou Reed's "Street Hassle." Since gigs were scarce, Stein left to join the Stilettos (though he kept making tapes with Emerson).

Harry had an equally convoluted performing history. She'd begun singing in late 1966 with the abrasive free-jazz combo FNUC&B (First National Unaphrenic Church & Bank), whose saxophone and percussion assault got no gigs, except a weekly radio show. Harry then joined Wind In The Willows, whose self-titled album (Capitol SKAO 2956: 1968) made no impression, even amid prevailing Sixties folk-rock winds. Soured by her first bout with big time rock, Harry bounced around as a health spa instructor, Playboy bunny and waitress at Max's Kansas City, which is where photographer Leee Black Childers remembers spotting her in 1970.

"As I recall," said Childers, "she was working as a hairdresser in New Jersey, and at night, she would waitress in the back room of Max's Kansas City—you didn't make much in tips, because everybody was pretty broke, but at least you got to be in the back room! She was very pretty, and everybody was always hitting on her. She always had ambitions of performing."

Harry even survived a ride with notorious serial killer Ted Bundy on New York's East Side, as *Q* readers learned this spring: "—I wasn't going to get a cab so I got into the car—the windows were all closed except for a fraction. I looked down to open one and there were no handles." Alarmed by the man's "incredible odor," Harry wriggled an arm outside to open the door, and run away. Only after reading a *Newsweek* story of Bundy's escapades, for which Florida executed him in 1989, did Harry realize whose car she'd shared.

While the New York scene is always associated with CBGB's and Max's Kansas City, unsigned bands had no outlet until 1972, when the Mercer Arts Center, on Mercer Street, gave the New York Dolls' stack-heeled raunch a crack at its 350-capacity Oscar Wilde Room, which they quickly packed every night. The Dolls graduated to Max's, which had caught some of rock's most gripping scenes, such as Lou Reed's final gigs with the Velvet Underground. But Max's booked signed acts, so did clubs like My Father's Place, on Long Island, while The Coventry's unsigned bookings favored emerging metal acts, like Kiss, or Blue Oyster Cult. In such a climate, the Mercer remained ground zero for the new scene until the building literally collapsed in August 1973.

Fired up by the Dolls' initial triumphs, Harry joined the Stilettos with vocalists Rosie Ross and Elda Gentile in October 1973. Conceived as a ballsier, contemporary girl group, the seven-piece combo started gigging at "this dirty little bar on 24th Street called The Boburn Tavern," she told Pete Frame. "We were a lot of fun, but we weren't too musical."

"It was almost like the Andrews Sisters," said Childers. "It was an interesting way of putting a group together, because they really did have their own style. Rosie was [singing] Thirties and early Forties, Elda was Fifties—she did Alice Ghostley songs—and Debbie did bluesy-type stuff. Debbie had very short hair, which was brown at the time.

"They'd sing together, but would have their turn at the microphone—that's when I first met Chris, at one of those shows. I found him very bizarre-looking, because he was wearing almost more makeup than all three of them put together, sitting there with very heavy eyeliner, all alone at the table watching them."

The Stilettos briefly became hip; David Bowie and Iggy Pop checked them out, as did the late Who drummer, Keith Moon, who caught them at Club 82, an old drag club which filled the void for roughly a year after the Mercer's collapse. That's where Burke first saw Harry, as well as the Dolls, and Wayne (later Jayne) County. He considers Club 82 "the predecessor to CBGB'—it was run by these butch lesbian people, and they had a rock night. It was on East Fourth Street, around from where the Fillmore East used to be."

But then Club 82 stopped booking bands in summer and fall of 1974, while Max's—despite promising weekends for new bands who impressed on slow nights—closed for about a year in December, citing financial hassles. The resulting vacuum allowed a new club owner to establish an unlikely presence in one of New York City's grimiest areas—the Bowery.

When Hilly Kristal had opened CBGB's in December 1973, he was ready to book country acts and poetry readings—until guitarists Richard Lloyd and Tom Verlaine convinced him to book their band, Television, by reassuring him, "Yeah, we play that, and some originals, too." What Kristal had envisioned as country bluegrass & blues changed after March 31, 1974, when Television started a month-long Sunday residency, which drew 20 to 30 people; followed by the Stilettos in May and The Ramones' hyper-minimalist aggression came in August.

Club 82 lost relevance as glitter dried up, so its crowd "migrated to CBGB's, and cut their hair somewhere along the way," said Burke. "I remember tripping over [late New York Dolls guitarist] Johnny Thunders down the stairs! [Drummer] Tommy Ramone [of The Ramones] was the weirdest [figure]—he was this guy, in a sea of shag haircuts, wearing a velvet jacket and a pair of bellbottoms."

Chris Charlesworth's July 6, 1974 *Melody Maker* roundup showed Harry a glint of what might happen if the right person ever saw her potential, when he reckoned the Stilettos had some songs "well worth putting on vinyl." They, along with The Brats—led by ex-New York Dolls guitarist Rick Rivets—The Fast, Television and Teenage Lust showed explosive promise, if someone captured it properly, Charlesworth wrote, even if the scene seemed little more than "learning a few chords, applying lipstick and bingo!"

When the Stilettos crumbled in August 1974, Harry walked away with something greater—the start of a personal and creative partnership with Stein. If they hadn't known each other when Childers first saw them, "they certainly knew each other after that night," he adds. "I have to give both of 'em credit, especially Debbie; they were very devoted to each other. It was a very, very promiscuous time in those days; the phone booth at Max's Kansas City was for blow jobs. If you wanted to make a phone call, you had to go down the street."

Assisted by Stilettos bassist Fred Smith and drummer Billy O'Connor, Harry and Stein added two backup singers (known only as Jackie and Julie) to become Angel & The Snake. They played a near-empty CBGB's on August 16 with The Ramones, whose ten songs whizzed past in 15 minutes. Guitarist Ivan Kral joined that October, but after just three months, jumped ship to join Patti Smith—who'd carved out a strong local poetic reputation (and had even played Max's in December 1973). It wasn't a pretty picture for those not considered to be going places.

"There were these other bars, [like] Monty Python's, where people could play, but it wasn't a scene, except for people who were in bands," notes Valentine. "We would see The Miamis, this great, fun band—they wrote great pop tunes, sort of sarcastic, but with wit. Debbie used to cover one of them [their songs]. You'd go to their gigs, they'd go to your gigs. The audience was the other bands!"

The musicians' lives had more in common with punk's low-budget connotations than their diverging musical styles, Childers notes, since anybody could rent large lofts in the Bowery—as Harry and Stein soon did— for rock-bottom rates. The conditions were another matter, as Childers discovered when using the toilet: "There was a pipe that came out of the wall; out came a rat, and it ran right across the floor. There were stories based on those kind of places, that when you were sitting on the toilet, the rats would also swim up! If you choose the rock 'n' roll lifestyle, that's part of it."

Jackie and Julie lasted till January 1975, when Snookie and Tish replaced them on backing vocals, with Harry as lead singer. The original vocal trio's blonde hair may have inspired a name change to Blondie & The Banzai Babies, until someone finally suggested dropping the second half altogether. Valentine's not sure who deserves the credit, citing "the story of the tribe handed down to me." "Debbie got guys whistling and saying, 'Hey, Blondie!', and they became Blondie. There was always, inevitably, confusion over whether Blondie was Debbie [or the group]."

The next five months nearly tore Blondie apart. When O'Connor opted for law school, Smith suggested someone well-known as a skilled, dynamic drummer—Clement "Clem" Burke (born November 24, 1955), whose arrival coincided with the shorter name, and first demos. Burke's influences read like a British Invasion roll call— "all the obvious people," he notes, including the Beatles, the Kinks, and the Who, as well as Booker T & The MGs, and The Raspberries. "I was at a crossroads," said Burke. "I was playing with Lance Loud, [also] The Mumps, and I auditioned for Patti Smith, but it's good I didn't get that gig—I'm a major Patti Smith fan, but I wouldn't have owned a house!"

Burke saw what the art-rock crowd didn't: "Debbie had conceptual ideas from the beginning. When I met her, I definitely knew she had something special. I never doubted that."

By contrast, Stein's dark energy never quit. "He had this Alice Cooper fixation at the time," said Burke. "He was really creative on guitar, but he'd present an idea, and you'd have to work with him [as he presented it]."

Childers admits he initially found Blondie "a little poppy" for his liking: "I was living with Jayne County at that time. We were getting ready to see Blondie, and I said, 'There's not really much guts to 'em.' And Jayne knows her rock'n'roll; she really knows it, and she started quoting words and riffs: 'Are you crazy, this is the greatest band right now! Listen to it, don't look at it!' And I was taught my lesson that night in the bathroom, while we were putting on our mascara. I was making the same mistake a lot of people did—they were looking, and not listening, to her."

Burke's March 1975 debut marked Smith's last gig; his colleagues heard their old bassist was taking Richard Hell's slot in Television, between sets at CBGB's. Figuring the fun had ended, Snookie and Tish quit too (later singing for The Dropouts and The Sic F*cks, then opening the punk clothing store Manic Panic). To Harry, it smelled like the Kral affair, while Stein "half-heartedly" tried out for Thunders' implosive post-Dolls combo, the Heartbreakers. Undaunted, Burke suggested auditioning an old New Jersey acquaintance he'd known in high school, who'd just found his range (middle C) on the broken piano—Gary Valentine.

"He wasn't really a bass player at all. He was a poet; he played one of his songs on piano, and Chris and Debbie accepted him," said Burke.

For Valentine, joining Blondie let him express his Sixties-era British influences to their wildest extent: "We found all these great secondhand shops over in Hoboken [New Jersey]. You'd find peg-leg pants, [or] paisley and polka-dotted shirts in their wrappers, in the back of the shop, since they went out of style—they were practically giving them away." That was just as well, too, judging by Blondie's earliest group shots, where Burke and Stein sport longer hair well removed from their later neo-Mod styles, and Valentine sticks to his trademark shades, even as Harry already glows for the camera.

It's the same quality that attracted late multimedia artist Andy Warhol, "because he knew exactly where she was coming from," said Childers. "And she realized it didn't have to be perfect, she didn't have to look like [Sixties fashion model] Twiggy. We used to go to that loft in the Bowery and do photographs all the time, so she could experiment with how she looked."

Such tastes defined Blondie, along with the unsigned Marbles, and Ramones, as part of "a Sixties retro contingent", while Richard Hell, Patti Smith and Television "were all influenced by French Symbolist poetry, trying to combine the arty and the pop world," said Valentine. "Hey, it got me—I was [also originally] into it!"

That retro streak also found expression on Blondie's first recordings, made only a month after Valentine joined. Worried about the band's hit-or-miss live reputation, Alan Betrock—who'd later edit the *New York Rocker,* and write books on Sixties girl groups—supervised a demo session of the Shangri-Las' "Out In The Streets," "Platinum Blonde," and "The Disco Song," a jokey Stein funk-rock number.

"I was playing about a month when we did those," said Valentine. "He [Betrock] wanted to manage: 'Let's make a demo!' And so he brought us into a studio out on Long Island, someone's garage, basically. It wasn't anything fancy, but it was great; I hadn't done anything like that. But that was a different sound. 'Platinum Blonde' was Debbie's signature song, an old campy number." (The demos have reappeared on *The Platinum Collection,* while "Out In The Streets" has also resurfaced on *No Exit*.)

Much has been made of Blondie's lack of live consistency, before and after they became established, but Childers doesn't remember hearing about it, as most bands were doggedly unpolished. "If anybody was inconsistent, it was the Ramones," he said. "When [bassist] Dee Dee Ramone got onstage, you didn't know whether he was going to be in tune—it didn't matter if Blondie had an off day, or hit off notes. It wasn't like they had to be perfect; it was even better if they weren't!"

Infante also takes a generous view: "I wouldn't call it [the early sound] a racket. They were playing pop songs, but they weren't polished. I prefer a situation like that, instead of playing the same stuff over and over."

By summer of 1975, Max's reopened under Tommy Dean's management, leading to what many writers have termed a "club war" against CBGB's, with separate audiences and bands. But Childers dismisses the idea, as both clubs were barely seven blocks apart—CBGB's on Bleecker Street, Max's on 17th Street and Park Avenue South—and had no problem allowing the bands to jump between them. "Whoever you pulled, you got the whole door—the club didn't take any of it," he said. "So you played both clubs, because you had to eat!"

That didn't mean Dean and Kristal weren't above copying each other, as proven when Max's hosted its own unsigned bands festival and double live album after CBGB's broke that ground in June 1976. The largely teen audiences didn't care either way. "First of all," said Childers, "it was very inexpensive to go, if you were a kid from Long Island—it was walking distance, so you didn't have to take taxis, or subways. A lot of kids would go to both, just to see what was going on. It was a social scene, too."

While many fans think the bands got more competitive after A & R men began coming, the sensible ones already worked on their music, which eliminated those "just doing it for the glamour," like Teenage Lust, or the Harlots Of 42nd Street, said Childers. Even the Ramones, "who made it appear that they didn't care, were working really hard on their music," he adds. So was Blondie.

Childers learned how much Blondie cared after placing a full-page *Village Voice* ad announcing the return of the Heartbreakers, whom he was managing, to Max's after a long layoff. Richard Hell had quit, so Thunders suggested announcing the band's return with a photo of the new lineup brandishing guns, "which, of course, we couldn't afford," laughs Childers. "In those days, you could take the ads in, and pay later—and usually not pay later. So that's where my mind-set was. Blondie were opening on Friday, The Vest on Saturday.

"So, really, at the last minute, I thought, 'Whoops! I'd better put in the other bands.' It [the names] wasn't tiny, but it wasn't big—but Blondie, all of them, got very angry with me for that. I'm sure you know the history of the Heartbreakers—the catch line was, 'see 'em before they die.' It didn't occur to me I was going to offend Debbie, but she's right, and I'm wrong."

The band improved when Jimmy Destri (born April 13, 1954) joined in October. He came from the Anglopop-driven Knickers, which boasted future *Trouser Press* editor Ira Robbins' guitar (and, in the original band, singles reviewer Jim Green, on bass), but managed only two gigs during its year-long life. Destri's burbling keyboards cemented Blondie's march away from the garage to straight pop, though nobody knew his style would fit so well, said Burke: "We wanted a piano, he had a Farfisa [organ], and it was a mistake! People thought that we did it on purpose, but we didn't, really."

When Burke trotted off to Britain for six weeks that fall, the band stopped playing and embarked on some good old-fashioned woodshedding. "Chris, Debbie and I had moved into the loft that was a block and a half from CBGB's—there's lots of stories connected with that place," laughs Valentine. "We'd all written songs; we all hunkered down, and practiced without Clem. When Clem returned, we did a lot of practicing..."

The new quintet bowed February 14, 1976 at CBGB's, marking the first time that Blondie found its onstage identity, Harry has stated. Valentine agrees: "Jimmy had come to see us a few times at [a gay bar called] Mother's [on 23rd Street], and was hanging out; he was very eager to play."

With the A&R gold rush still well off, Blondie cut its May 1976 debut single, "X Offender"/"In The Sun" (Private Stock PVT 105). Valentine's A-side drew on the trauma of knocking up his underage girlfriend: "Told me that law, like wine, is ageless; the public defender/You had to admit you wanted the love of a sex offender." (The lyric also mandated a strategic title change to avoid misinterpretation.) "It was definitely a Sixties sound; not to blow my own horn, but Blondie was 'X Offender,'" said Valentine. "We closed [gigs] with that, it was sort of an anthem, and got us the record deal. It defined what Blondie was about; we were getting more and more poppish."

"X Offender" had actually been cut for Instant Records, a production company of ex-New York Dolls co-manager Marty Thau, Sire Records producer Craig Leon, and Richard Gottehrer, who'd written and produced for Sixties groups like The Strangeloves ("I Want Candy"). Instant had already convinced Blondie to sign a two-single deal before CBGB's showcased them at June's unsigned bands festival, beside Richard Hell (fresh out of the Heartbreakers), Talking Heads, and Television.

The resulting *Live At CBGB's* album (Atlantic SD 2-508: 1976) turned out to be something of a farce, since most of the major acts, including Blondie, refused to let their tracks be used. Despite that setback, Blondie won Gottehrer over with raw conviction, in Burke's mind: "Richard came to our rehearsal to audition us for the album. He was blown away that we had 20-30 songs, because nobody [else] could play."

The reviews bore him out; where buyers might reasonably have expected Talking Heads, or Television, Kristal stuffed the album with second- and third-tier acts like The Shirts and Tuff Darts. Thau convinced Private Stock, best known for Frankie Valli's #1 1975 hit, "My Eyes Adored You," to buy the "X Offender" single for $2,500, and option for an album. Private Stock signed them after a June 17, 1976 CBGB's gig.

"It was a definite, solid look," said Valentine. "We played in tune, we didn't flub, we had a stage presence, and it worked. We went from being a band that would open for anybody to packing CBGB's [for] three nights running."

The debut album, *Blondie* (Private Stock PS 2023: 1977) was cut at New York City's Plaza Sound, Radio City Music Hall, where the composer Stravinsky had once set up. A suitable beginning for a trash-camp album, essentially done live in the studio, that opposed the prevailing ethic of four long songs per side. "Attack Of The Giant Ants" and "A Shark In Jet's Clothing" nestled comfortably by the hissy cattiness of "Rip Her To Shreds." "X Offender" and "Man Overboard" deftly revamped the Sixties girl group sound, while "In The Sun" updated surf.

Now running *Trouser Press,* Robbins felt the songs took a backseat to their sonic trademarks of crisp handclaps, shouted choruses and snapping fingers. Destri's two songs aside, Blondie still packed rare charm and raw promise, he said: "What people are going to think outside of New York I won't profess to imagine, but it's going to get played around my house."

"There was still a lot of stuff left over from previous incarnations Chris and Debbie had had—some old glam stuff, and campy sort of things," said Valentine. "My influences were British Invasion, Velvet Underground, and later, Television. Jimmy's were similar, and Clem's a walking rock 'n' roll encyclopedia, so we decided to go in that direction, and that's when we became very identifiable." Meshing Harry's and Stein's leanings to Burke's and Destri's street-level tastes sounded like a nightmare, but it worked on vinyl, as Blondie had already learned to serve the song, not the writer's ego.

"The first record was very innovative, and 20 years ahead of its time," said Burke. "It was really experimental stuff, in a lot of ways." He cites "X Offender," which pushed Blondie into a newly creative level in the studio, rather than just reproducing its live sound, like so many bands did. "Gary played guitar, Chris played bass. That intro, he [Gottehrer] kind of took from 'My Boyfriend's Back.' When they put it on the jukebox at CB's, everybody flipped. It really made an impression on me; he really captured something special with that song. To this day, it's one of my favorites."

Blondie hit the road by January 1977, a month before their album appeared. They found themselves lionized in Los Angeles, where personalities like longtime KROQ DJ Rodney Bingenheimer wasted no time adopting them. Supporting Iggy Pop made the trip even sweeter, since his music figured "among the stack of albums that we listened to religiously," said Valentine.

"To me, that was an incredible thing—I hadn't flown before," he said. "I hadn't really been outside New York that much. The second time we played [in Los Angeles], people were wearing skinny ties, and mod suits.

We definitely had an influence. That was adolescent rock heaven. We were staying in Beverly Hills, running up incredible tabs, doing all the things you do when you're 20, and somebody says, 'OK, you're a rock star now.'"

The next critical moment came in May 1977, when Blondie toured Britain for the first time, having been handed a seemingly impossible task: supporting Television, whose *Marquee Moon* album had just appeared to unanimous critical hosannas. While Harry has cited that tour as a miserable affair, Valentine dove headfirst into a country that had fascinated him since childhood: "What I did, more than anything else, was running out to bookstores, because I was a nut for fantasy, weird fiction, occult, and magical stuff—we were all into that sort of thing."

Valentine doesn't exactly recall a rivalry, but two distinct camps that happened to be sharing a tour: "There was the 'art' camp, and we were just the lowly rock'n'rollers. I began to admire them [Television], and appreciate their music; seeing [guitarists] Tom Verlaine and Richard Lloyd play every night was great!" Yet neither guitarist talked much to each other, much less anyone else, which may explain how some people found them pretentious.

"There was one funny moment in some hotel, with Jimmy, Clem, myself and Verlaine in an elevator, and Verlaine's standing in front of the button; somebody said, 'Going down, Tom!'" said Valentine. "He had this atmosphere of being detached, the 'bemused poet.'"

Valentine's merriment evaporated when Blondie came home, and management called ("this was before the days of answering machines," he notes) on July 4, 1977, to say he'd been ousted. "I wanted my own band, I wanted to play guitar more, I wanted to sing," he said. "At the end of the show, I would [sometimes] switch off; I didn't want to take away from Chris playing guitar. I just thought, 'Why not? We can play different instruments, too.'"

Balancing five opinions may have proven too much if "Chris and Debbie had in mind: 'OK, a song from Gary, a song from Jimmy,'" said Valentine. "We were sort of the George Harrisons [of Blondie], in a way, and I kept writing more and more songs." He cites "Scenery," a first-album outtake featuring his 12-string guitar: "I felt that Debbie did a lax vocal, because she wasn't into it; maybe she didn't want two songs by me on the album. As long as I stayed where they thought I should be, it would be all right, but I wanted more [responsibility]." (The song is featured on *Blonde And Beyond*, where listeners can make up their own minds.)

What miffed Valentine most was knowing his proposal to record—and tour—for the second album had been roundly ignored: "I remember telling the manager that—as soon as I said that, I got a call saying I was out. It became, 'Well, if you apologize to Debbie...' I said, 'I don't really want to do that.' A month later, I packed my things, and went to L.A."

The Lipstick Years: 1977-79

With an album due, Burke nominated another New Jersey acquaintance to play bass. That was Infante, already something of a local legend in World War III, an MC5-type band that never played without hassles: "All these social misfits would come out, and the cops, too. We were loud, into 'the revolution,' but the songs were good. There'd be trouble whenever we played, because we were down on everything."

Right away, Infante sensed something different afoot: "They were just having fun. 'Blondie has more fun'—that was a slogan. It wasn't a serious 'muso' thing; the energy was there, and the songs were there. Before I joined, the bands I was in were trying to be more musical."

But Burke still seethed: "The second record was more of a transitional experience—I was pissed that he [Valentine] left. I brought Frank into the fold, but it wasn't really a unit [yet]. I remember doing the photo session, going, 'Somebody's missing.'"

Somewhat predictably, the drummer quit, but soon came to his senses, "The weird thing about Chris and Debbie was, they always needed a scapegoat—I spent a lot of time trying to keep people in the band. Somebody was always on the outs." A month later, Chrysalis bought out Blondie's Private Stock contract, followed by the band's decision to buy out its deal with Gottehrer, who still produced *Plastic Letters* ("Richard didn't know what was going on, but we did," said Burke). Chrysalis promptly reissued both albums in October 1977.

"It all got totally done behind closed doors," said Burke. "Production deals are pretty dubious. I can't say enough about Richard, because he really helped us, but he had us tied up, basically. And we were $500,000 in debt, instantly.

"We were up on this high-rise, twelve floors up, literally trapped in this room, and Jimmy said, 'Here's the phones! Let's call England, let's call France!' Contracts were flying back and forth. I think the sun came up when the deal was done—it was the most cathartic experience for us."

So was *Plastic Letters* (Chrysalis CHR 1166: 1978), which wound up darker than its predecessor, thanks to Destri's growing army of synthesizers, and songs like his "No Imagination," whose nightclub decadence borrowed from Lou Reed's "Lady Day." Clever lyric twists abounded, such as Stein's "I'm On E," which talks about inner emptiness, he told *Trouser Press* (note the driving references). Still, titles like "Bermuda Triangle Blues" or "Youth Nabbed As Sniper" ensured not everything turned out heavy and meaningful.

Gottehrer's offhand approach sometimes jarred with the band's yearning for more fleshed-out arrangements. "His idea of production was to put handclaps on it [a song]," said Burke. "He wasn't real precise; he was more into creating a mood."

"That was another trip," agrees Infante. "His approach was, 'You do four takes, and pick the one you like.'"

Yet the songs that stuck longest came from unexpected sources. Figuring that DJs needed a proper calling card, Harry suggested redoing Randy & The Rainbows' #10 U.S. 1963 hit "Denise," which became Blondie's first genuine hit in February 1978, peaking at #2 U.K. (Chrysalis CHS 2204), after a gender change to "Denis." It didn't trouble the U.S. Top 40.

In April, Valentine's parting shot, "(I'm Always Touched By Your) Presence, Dear" (Chrysalis/EMI CHS 2266)—which had remained on *Plastic Letters,* as a tribute to his departed energy—reached #10 U.K. "Blondiemania" had begun. "*Plastic Letters* has a lot of interesting songs, some of Jimmy's, particularly," said Burke. "Debbie had the brilliant idea to cover 'Denise'—I guess she knew it when she was a kid, and it became a big hit."

That led to a funny experience miming "Denis" for the U.K.'s "Top Of The Pops," whose guests were not allowed to play live. "You'd pretend to record your backing track, and they already had this multitrack recorder," said Burke. "I remember the English MU [Musicians' Union] guy [asking] in the control room: 'Can't you guys stomp in time a little more?'"

Plastic Letters peaked at #10 U.K. and #72 U.S. Emerging regional magazines like the *Illinois Entertainer* predicted stardom: "Coupled with her denim sexuality, Harry possesses all the ingredients needed for media personality status." (Not a bad call, since that March 1978 write up came a full year before 'Heart Of Glass' broke.)

Figuring it needed a fulltime bassist, Blondie hired its sole English member, Nigel Harrison, best known from the glam band Silverhead (of the immortal couplet: "16 and savaged/so young and so ravaged"!), and Nite City, keyboardist Ray Manzarek's last real band project (after The Doors). Harrison's November 1977 arrival permitted Infante to move back to guitar: "Sometimes, Jimmy used to do the bass, and we'd have two guitars; sometimes Chris would play bass. There was no rhythm and lead guitar approach, we just played parts. It wasn't like one guy played rhythm, and held it down."

To warm up for recording, the band revisited Los Angeles, where Infante met such larger-than-life characters as singer Tomata DuPlenty of The Screamers, who made videos, as they considered records a "dead medium": "That was their concept, because they were film guys. I remember when we played The Greek Theatre, and our manager hired a Sherman tank, and we drove through the streets with it! That was insane, but pretty fun.

"A lot of good things were happening—then it became, 'You're not allowed to do this, you're not allowed to do that.'" Blondie then returned for a short U.K. tour, whose ads now centered around Harry, captioned, "Wouldn't you like to rip her to shreds?" The taste and timing of such moves surely escaped the woman who'd survived Ted Bundy's raunchy interior, but if Harry has a grudge, her *Q* interview didn't say: "It's press, as they say in the business."

From there it was six lengthy months of touring, wherever Blondie could snatch a foothold—Australia, Japan, and Thailand, all sandwiched between forays back to Britain. When the band finally caught its breath in March 1978, the red ink had deepened—but so had the international fanbase so crucial to stardom. "It meant you were [now] in debt for $750,000, but I had a great time," said Burke.

Some truly surreal moments came in Australia, whose isolation (16 hours from America alone) means trends take longer to penetrate. "People were afraid of us, and everything was magnified," said Infante. "They thought we were this punk rock thing from outer space. It was good, because it was new to everyone."

Stranger still, "In The Flesh" (Chrysalis/EMI K-6973) became a #2 hit there, through no connivance of the band, said Burke: "This guy had a show, the 'Top Of The Pops' of Australia, 15 years before MTV. They had a video for 'X Offender,' but played the 'In The Flesh' video instead, which was to our benefit—because it was a more commercial song, and it featured Debbie a little more."

To crack the big time, Blondie needed someone who could translate their quirky diversity into mainstream success. They met that person in Mike Chapman, whom the band would find an exacting, sometimes exasperating taskmaster. Best known as the hand who guided glam acts like Mud, Suzi Quatro and The Sweet, Chapman's philosophy was simple: if the first take sounded fine, the second might sound better. If a song lacked the right hook, find one.

From his perspective, Blondie seemed like an exciting challenge. He caught them during a three-night stand at Los Angeles's Whiskey A Go Go, and became hooked. "Mike was a songwriter—I mean, he wrote [The Sweet's] 'Little Willy,' one of the most bubblegum songs of all time," said Burke. "He appreciated a lot of qualities that other people didn't really appreciate."

In contrast to Gottehrer's bare-bones style, Chapman drove Blondie to double or triple their parts, doing and redoing them multiple times as the occasion demanded. "He definitely drove us nuts at the beginning," said Infante, "because we weren't into stuff like that. He was really into getting the timing right, even the guitar parts. I'd do it over and over to get it pretty precise. The basic tracks were always me, Clem and Nigel."

As might be guessed, such exactitude often made Chapman unpopular. "I once threw my keyboard at the guy—a $50,000 synthesizer. I picked it up, threw it," Destri confessed to *Trouser Press* in September 1982, "and said, 'You play it.' But he could do the same thing to me. That's how we battle it out, and that's why it works."

The resulting album, *Parallel Lines* (Chrysalis CHR 1192), catapulted Blondie to the big time; Chapman's philosophy captured layered guitars, keyboards and vocals that practically stopped on a dime. In his hands, the unexpected served as punctuation, such as the multiple Harry vocals on "One Way Or Another"'s free-for-all ending ("where I can see it all/find out who ya call"), or former King Crimson guitarist Robert Fripp's glacial blast in Stein's "Fade Away And Radiate" ("I hear how you spend nitetime/wrapped like candy in the blue blue neon glow").

But *Parallel Lines* was Blondie's show, and sharpest tunes yet, including Destri's moonily dramatic "11:59" ("Lock up all your memories/get outta here, you know that we can run"), and Infante's cryptic "I Know But I Don't Know" ("I lose but I don't bet/I'm your dog but not your pet"): "I was in a room one night, and it just came out. It's a Zen thing."

Stein's songs exuded edginess, such as "Sunday Girl"'s love turned sour ("Live in dreams Sunday girl"), while Harry's emotional expressions were more direct ("Just Go Away," "Pretty Baby'). The group tore up Buddy Holly's "I'm Gonna Love You Too," and a moody pair of songs from Jack Lee, whose own band, The Nerves, had broken up. "Hanging On The Telephone" lamented long-distance romance ("I'd like to talk when I could show you my affection"), while "Will Anything Happen" waxed ambivalence about success ("I always said you could make it/Just don't forget that I said it").

"He [Lee] just came down to the studio in a taxi, and he had those two songs—I haven't heard anything since, but I don't think that he has any complaints," said Infante. (When Burke joined the reunited Plimsouls, "Hanging On The Telephone" still packed enough staying power to make their setlist, too.)

Without a doubt, though, *Parallel Lines's* centerpiece was Blondie's unlikeliest—"Heart Of Glass," a Harry-Stein collaboration which had been performed since 1975 as "The Disco Song". What had begun as a funk spoof yielded Blondie's first major hit, as Harry spat out her disappointment ("Once I had a love/and it was a gas/ soon turned out had a heart of glass") over a glistening, six-minute disco-pop sheen.

The group wanted a "Kraftwerk-meets-Bee-Gees" sound. "Jimmy had that Kraftwerk synthesizer; by that time, he had a cheap Roland synth," said Burke. "There's a weird 6/8 [time signature] skip in the middle—that was Mike's idea." Vocals came last when Harry made her lyrics official, leaving Chapman free to improvise guide vocals: "It was fun, because he'd sing, make in-jokes as he went along," said Burke. (The ever-prepared Chapman made sure to record an alternate lyric for "soon turned out/to be a pain in the ass," which certainly soothed many a skittish DJ.)

Chapman's work yielded lightning results in Britain. "Picture This"/"Fade Away And Radiate" (Chrysalis CHS 2275) shot to #12 in September 1978 (with a limited 12" "Blonde" vinyl sleeve), while "Hangin' On The Telephone"/"Will Anything Happen?" (Chrysalis CHS 2266) went to #5 in December, without trying hard. *Parallel Lines* did equally well, selling a million copies by February 1979, when it topped the U.K. charts for four weeks.

Back home the enthusiasm seemed cooler, Burke recalls: "When we handed in *Parallel Lines,* the A & R [Artists & Repertoire] people decided there was no single—and wound up issuing 'I'm Gonna Love You Too,' because of the Buddy Holly revival."

Gary Busey's epic performance as the late Fifties rocker in "The Buddy Holly Story" (1978) did not salvage "I'm Gonna Love You Too," which bombed. Chrysalis tried "Hanging On The Telephone" (Chrysalis CHS 22771), when that single flopped, "Heart Of Glass" (Chrysalis CHS 2295) finally turned the trick, soaring to #1 on the U.S. and U.K. charts. It also revived *Parallel Line's* sagging fortunes; where the album had taken an agonizing 35 weeks to break the U.S. Top Forty; it had peaked at #6 by March 1979.

Such was the song's mystique that the late conceptual artist Andy Warhol threw a party to celebrate its success at (where else?) New York's disco bastion, Studio 54. (The band were reportedly playing Milan, Italy, when they learned of their success.) For a week, "Heart Of Glass" bested other disco smashes like Peaches & Herb's "Reunited" (#2), Amii Stewart's overheated remake of "Knock On Wood" (#3), and Gloria Gaynor's classic, "I Will Survive" (#5). The irony of winning the pop lottery with an overhauled demo hardly needs any elaboration. "Heart Of Glass" was the final straw for those who'd cheered the New York Dolls, or Ramones. Here lay proof, if anybody still needed it, of Blondie's treasonous ambitions.

The criticism especially stung when every major band tried disco songs in 1978-79. The Rolling Stones took little flack for "Miss You" (1978), nor Lou Reed, who used "Disco Mystic" to showcase his touring band on *The Bells* (1979). Donna Summer, then considered the genre's reigning diva, returned the favor by using The Doobie Brothers' lead guitarist Jeff "Skunk" Baxter on her crossover smash, "Hot Stuff."

Whatever Blondie did would never please its old crowd, especially as labels shied away from the "p"-word (punk) and switched to "New Wave" (borrowed from the Fifties French cinema school) in marketing bands. As critics picked up the distinction, Blondie found itself treated less deferentially than artists mining pure rock tradition, such as The Clash.

If so, they weren't listening when Blondie started, Burke maintains, as early sets had included such well-known R&B gems as Labelle's "Lady Marmalade." "Chris was always trying to get it ['Heart Of Glass'] where it would be a disco song. He and Debbie listened to a lot of black music, in fact."

At the same time, "Heart Of Glass" shot Harry into the pole position. Where the roadies' T-shirts had declaimed, "Blondie Is A Group," fans and journalists took Harry to be Blondie, a conflict that has been blamed for its demise.

Although some publications—notably *Trouser Press,* a supporter from way back—still mentioned all band members on equal terms, the "Blondiemania" tornado had little trouble sucking Harry and Stein down its funnel, and leaving everyone else in the cold.

Harry blames Leeds for playing the band against each other, enough reason to fire him despite a well-earned reputation for efficiency. "He told the boys they could all be replaced. I was the only one that was important. From then on they were always a bit afraid of what might happen." (Alice Cooper's longtime manager Shep Gordon replaced Leeds.)

Burke has a different take. "It [Harry's media profile] was never really a nuisance. If you're a drummer, you have to accept a lot of things," he said. "The drummer's only as good as the people he's working with. I needed Debbie, and I accepted that. I was never going to be successful on my own."

"They [fans] heard the word 'Blondie,' and think she was Blondie," said Infante. "It didn't cause a problem with me; it might have caused a problem for someone else. But I said, 'If it's not broke, don't fix it.'"

Blondie singles experienced mixed fortunes as spring became summer 1979. In April, "Sunday Girl"/"I Know But I Don't Know" (Chrysalis CHS 2302) reached #1 U.K., but never made the U.S. charts (the U.K. 12" treated fans to a French-language "Sunday Girl.") But in August, "One Way Or Another" made #24 U.S. (Chrysalis CHS 2236), proving that when it comes to rock'n'roll formats, both countries are totally different planets. The band was probably too busy to ponder the difference, as Blondie kicked off a major tour in Scranton, Pennsylvania on July 4, 1979, supported by Rockpile (Nick Lowe and Dave Edmunds's loose aggregation), which ran much of the summer. The ride had begun; the challenge now lay in keeping the momentum going.

The Frantic Years: 1979-80

Blondie's next album benefited from some much-needed spontaneity, and ended up showcasing some of its most committed rock'n'roll; working in three top New York studios (Media Sound, Power Sound and Jimi Hendrix's creative playground, Electric Lady), Blondie banged out *Eat To The Beat* (Chrysalis CHR 1225) in three weeks. Where *Parallel Lines* had been a take-by-take affair, *Eat To The Beat* sidelined Chapman's infamous click-track, except for "Atomic"'s permafrost disco-funk. This time, Blondie worked up songs in the studio. This development pleased Infante, since "there was lots of guitar, and I was free to do what I wanted.

"For me, they're [the albums] so good, because they're all so different—'Victor' was a good song, because I wrote it. The musical idea came from Russia, somehow. The theme there was a Russian thing. 'The Hardest Part' was a good song, too. 'Die Young, Stay Pretty'—Debbie came up with the concept." Yet *Eat To The Beat* spun off no major hits while marching to platinum status at #17 U.S. "Dreaming" (Chrysalis CHS 2379) reached #27 U.S. in October 1979, while "The Hardest Part" flatlined at #84 U.S. in February 1980; an America knowing little about reggae could not, apparently, embrace it commercially.

Eat To The Beat topped the UK charts in September 1979, and sold healthily for nine months (300,000 initial copies, *NME* noted that fall)—no small factor in "Atomic"'s #1 (Chrysalis/EMI CHS 2410) in March 1980 (versus #39 US). "Dreaming" (Chrysalis/EMI CHS 2350) also topped #2 U.K. for a breath-taking eight-week run. "Blondiemania" continued unabated on NBC-TV's "Saturday Night Live", as a gallop through "Dreaming" saw Destri frug madly behind his keyboards and Burke—clad in a Mod-style T-shirt, with a target design—simply couldn't be contained. A subsequent stab at "Union City Blue" proved no less intense.

"They [NBC] lock you in a room for ten hours. I remember [comedian/host] Steve Martin coming and saying, 'Hi,'" said Burke. "There was a really good party afterward."

Eat To The Beat also yielded a full-length filmed version (Warner Home Video: 1980), which Blondie called its "video album," the first such project in rock. While The Kinks' live *One For The Road* reached consumers first, Blondie's effort had been ready months earlier, only to be stalled by union disputes. Burke doesn't know if the filming ("We spent a long weekend doing 12 songs") or the dispute ended up more tiring. "The weird thing was, we had this guy on harmonica, and invited him to be in the video. But there were no ground rules for that, so there was a big holdup."

Blondie adopted what many regarded as a curious strategy for such a visual band, alternating between rough concept videos, and dubbing album tracks over live takes for a handpicked studio crowd. *Trouser Press* suggested saving the $39.95 for Blondie tickets: "There should still be money left over for a good film, if you want visual entertainment."

Still, *Eat To The Beat's* video version came nearly 18 months before MTV made it mandatory for performers to exploit their visual side; the same might be said of Harry's film debut, "Union City." (The song "Union City Blue," which was not actually featured in the movie, peaked at #13 U.K. in December 1979.) It was a remarkable performance, considering the project had started as a home movie involving herself and Stein. Harry's role as a frustrated housewife broke no box office ground, but won major distribution after Blondie broke big. "Union City" marked the first in a string of film roles, and confirmed that Harry's appeal extended beyond Blondie. The following summer, she appeared beside Meatloaf in "Roadie," a quirky rock comedy whose soundtrack included Blondie covering Johnny Cash's standard "Ring Of Fire."

Blondie's multi-media profile also produced the theme song for "American Gigolo," which starred Richard Gere as a male prostitute; "Call Me" (Chrysalis/EMI CHS 2414) rocketed to #1 US and UK in spring 1980, with a different producer in Giorgio Moroder, known for his Eurodisco slant (and *Midnight Express* film soundtrack). "He [Moroder] had this basic synth track, Debbie had the vocal thing—I did the guitar part that goes 'duddle-a-dah, duddle-a-dah,'" said Infante. "All of a sudden, the song took on a whole new thing."

"Frankie played some great stuff on it," said Burke. "'Call Me' was something that we really needed; it got us to the next level, and another #1 [single]."

The band hoped "Call Me" would stretch Blondie beyond Chapman's orbit, but reports of a Moroder-produced album came to nothing, because his Continental tastes didn't match their own, said Burke: "Richard Gere came around, and it was a good time, but I don't think we could have done a whole album with Giorgio—he just didn't have any rock'n'roll roots." Blondie was in the catbird seat that summer; its million-selling albums and singles opened immediate entry into the celebrity fishbowl, with the usual mixed results.

The Cryptic Years: 1981-82

While *Eat To The Beat* had partially thrown off the old constituency, nothing had prepared them for *Autoamerican* (Chrysalis CHE 1290), whose overriding diversity made pundits wonder if Blondie had lost its collective marbles. Enlisting a 30-man orchestra on Stein's brooding baroque instrumental "Europa" threatened to make Blondie seem like guest stars on its material, along with illustrious alumni like saxophonist Tom Scott, percussionist Ollie Brown, and guitarist Wah-Wah Watson. Mutters of "pretentious" greeted the murky cover painting of Blondie standing on a roof, admiring Harry from afar—a perfect, if unintentionally ironic, visual report of the band's increasing disconnection from each other.

Other disquieting signals loomed beyond covers or credits. Touring had stopped after a sold-out U.K. swing in December 1979/January 1980, igniting suspicions the group felt it no longer needed the work. The never-ending internal friction was likely a more pressing reason (Burke has recalled not seeing anyone in Blondie from 1980 to 1982). Side projects were also frittering momentum. When *Trouser Press* profiled the band for its June 1981 cover ("Solo Albums, Outside Projects...But Blondie Is Still A Group!"), Harry and Stein were hunkered in New York City's Power Station—where Bruce Springsteen had camped for two years delivering *The River*—on a bold joint album with Chic's main men, the late Bernard Edwards, and his partner, Nile Rodgers. Burke was producing local bands (The Colors, The Speedies); Destri was making a solo album [*Heart on a Wall*—Ed.].

Valentine himself surfaced that fall as guitarist in Iggy Pop's touring band for the latter's *Party* album. Once again, old contacts just fell into place: "It's another of those strange links—[guitarist] Ivan Kral, who played in Blondie before me, jumped ship at the last minute, so they asked me, did I want to go? I learned the songs going up to Buffalo [New York], or something like that." (The band also included Burke, guitarist Rob Duprey, who'd been in The Mumps so long ago, and Carlos Alomar, David Bowie's guitarist/musical director.)

Not surprisingly, Blondie spent much of its time downplaying breakup rumors, as well as accusations that acceptance had stripped away its former urgency. Harry, herself weathering criticism for a three-year deal endorsing Murjani jeans on TV, alluded to dueling egos: " I don't feel any responsibility to go out and give a bad show right now. We'll work again, but we'll only tour where we want to."

To pretend the band had never thrived on conflict seemed ridiculous, when Burke recalled "a great fistfight" with Stein at a 1978 U.K. gig. Not quite, responded Stein, he'd really targeted Destri, "I pushed his Polymoog." If that was the price to pay for hits, the comments implied, so be it. Ever the company man, Burke acknowledged Blondie had no illusions about its new role as pop phenomenon: "The only place left for us to go where people think we are crazy is to hang out with Chuck Mangione." (Or, perhaps, Harry's duet with Kermit The Frog on "The Muppet Show," singing the puppet's theme song, "Rainbow Connection.")

Stein had bigger concerns, "We put out a whacko album with all kinds of crazy shit to open everyone's head up a little bit, and half the critics freak out." He probably meant *Rolling Stone,* which had accused him of "trying to destroy pop music." Seeing that arrow flung at the minds behind "The Attack Of The Giant Ants" was too much to tolerate. Yet, as Stein well knew, the gap between direction and expectations is pop-rock's oldest soap opera. For some fans, covering "Follow Me" from the Broadway musical "Camelot" confirmed the Blondie they loved barely existed. (Studio personnel must have thought so too, judging by this comment, clearly audible after the fadeout: "You're not going to put this on the album, are you?")

Reviewers were equally unforgiving. "Can't someone stop these people?" groused *Sounds,* whose one-star drubbing smarted from the Britain who'd embraced Blondie long before anyone else ("Rapture" is over six minutes long, I only survived four.") Yet *Autoamerican* deserved a fairer shake, especially for "T-Birds," a spirited Harry/Harrison stab at Sixties trash-pop; "Go Through It," and "Here's Looking At You," solid Harry/Stein pop confections, and Stein's funk-oriented "Live It Up." Destri contributed his own distinct songs, including "Do The Dark," which cast Satan as a disco dancer ("walk on glass with the master"), the sprightly "Angels On The Balcony," and "Walk Like Me," which revisited the scene's old jealousies.

Schizoid or not ("I think I'm the only musician that plays on every song."), Burke sticks by *Autoamerican*: "It's my favorite album. When it came out, I was in a club in London, and 'Europa' came on, and it really set the mood."

But Infante felt hamstrung dubbing parts he hadn't created, "Debbie and Chris were pulling away from the whole band situation. I guess Chris wanted to be the only guitar player, I don't know. There was a lot of friction at the time; I don't want to go into that."

Yet the carping meant little when "The Tide Is High," flipped with "Suzy And Jeffrey"'s (Chrysalis CHS 2465) camp car crash drama, shot to #1 in the U.S. and U.K. in October 1980. It held the top slot for one glorious week in January 1981—besting the murdered John Lennon's "Just Like Starting Over" (#2), and Kool & The Gang's "Celebration" (#3)—on the way to selling one million copies. Despite gloomy prognoses for a country still reeling from economic recessions, the public wasn't having any of the tastemakers' food for thought.

Where Blondie's own reggae attempt ("The Hardest Part") had bombed in the U.S. singles charts, its imaginative remake of The Paragons' 1966 Jamaican hit—floating atop glistening organ, mariachi horns, and burbling percussion—pulled fans towards the style like few other musicians had done. (The Paragons even reformed to capitalize, earning a *Rolling Stone* "Random Note" in the process.) "Michael [Chapman] took that whole demo and orchestrated it. That was the 'kitchen sink' song—I thought it was a good song," said Burke.

"Rapture" (Chrysalis CHS 2485) had the same impact on hiphop, exposing white listeners to the latest underground genre—three years before Eddie Van Halen's guitar solo on the Michael Jackson crossover smash, "Beat It." In six breathtaking minutes, Harry and company saluted their new friends, Fab Five Freddy (Fred Braithwaite), Grandmaster Flash (Joseph Saddler, DJ for The Furious Five)—and, near the fadeout, an otherworldly "man from Mars" whose diet happened to include cars and guitars.

Flash returned the compliment by including "Rapture" on his 1981 single, "The Adventures Of Grandmaster Flash On The Wheels Of Steel," which cut that song—and other popular DJ showcases, like Queen's "Another One Bites The Dust"—to create a devastating audio montage, firmly grounded by Flash's distinct scratch style. Harry and Stein dipped further into the crossover sweepstakes by providing theme music for Charlie Ahearn's groundbreaking hiphop film, "Wild Style" (1982). Harry herself played a trendy journalist trying to enter its graffiti artists' and rappers' world, only to be treated with cool B-boy disdain (appropriately introduced by snippets of "Rapture").

By March 1981, "Rapture"/"Walk Like Me" (Chrysalis CHS 2485) reached #1 U.S., beating competition like Styx's "The Best Of Times" (#2), and REO Speedwagon's "Keep On Loving You" (#3)—and #5 U.K. (flipped with "Live It Up"). It easily sold one million copies, the last time Blondie ever did so. "That was fun—I remember collaborating on that handclapping we were doing," said Burke. "That was so ahead of its time; Debbie and Chris were true innovators in the sense that Bowie was."

Even without a quorum on every track, or tour to push it, *Autoamerican* delivered the goods, peaking at #3 U.S., and #7 U.K. The Blondie brand name still packed a wallop; whether the proposed Chic summit could hit the same crossover grand slam remained an unknown question.

The answer to Harry's *Koo Koo* album (Chrysalis CHR 1347) boiled down to "no way" on its August 1981 release. To Harry's and Stein's utter disappointment, the chasm of black and white radio—which had also recently sunk "Protection," a proud rocker that Bruce Springsteen had written for Donna Summer—yawned as wide as ever.

Koo Koo seemed misbegotten from the start—not least for its H.R. Giger cover (of "Alien" fame) showing ten-foot spikes piercing Harry's immaculate complexion. London Underground Limited promptly deemed it "too upsetting" for subways, causing Harry to sigh: "People should be more sophisticated in their art."

When Harry attended a party for rapper Kurtis Blow ("The Breaks"), *Rolling Stone* reported, she wouldn't permit the resulting photos to be used, after hearing they'd appear in *New Musical Express,* whose attention the band no longer welcomed. *Koo Koo* got a warmer welcome in Britain, where audiences have enjoyed more exposure to black musical formats. It peaked there at #6, but struggled to reach #43 U.S.—where rock fans had never forgiven disco's dominance of the singles chart, and disco singles had frequently occupied half the Top Ten slots. The trailblazing hiphop singles Harry and Stein so admired rarely reached beyond the black audiences who bought them. (Remember: hiphop's premiere label, Sugar Hill Records, never got another Top 40 pop hit after The Sugarhill Gang's "Rapper's Delight" peaked there at #36 in autumn 1979).

Koo Koo landed firmly between two chairs. So did its singles, "Backfired" #43 U.S., #32 U.K.), and "The Jam Was Moving," which limped to #82 US in November 1981. *Trouser Press* pronounced the album "more snack than feast," with its featured artists too eager to tailor their styles to Chic's ("The shoe just doesn't fit").

"Things were really getting into decline at that point," said Burke. "I don't think that album was very good. I don't think that Nile Rodgers and Bernard Edwards were the best producers for her."

"Piss off. I love that record," Harry responded in *Q* to one reader's query. "The mix is bad, but the material is great." In truth, *Koo Koo* deserved a fairer shake than it got, and contains several killer tracks, including "Jump Jump," "Military Rap," and "Under Arrest," in which the foundations of Harry's solo style can clearly be seen. Like it or not, she was outgrowing the boundaries of her day job. No such ambivalence greeted *The Best Of Blondie* in October 1981 (Chrysalis CHR 1337), a repackaging to plug the gap between albums. Subtitled *The Singles-Only Album* by some wags for its hit-oriented focus—which did include three remixes, and the otherwise non-LP "Call Me"—the album still reached #4 U.K., and #30 U.S.

With future activity still a rumor, Destri's *Heart On A Wall* (Chrysalis) crept out to unanimous razzes in January 1982. Despite impressive support from Burke, guitarists Earl Slick and Carlos Alomar (David Bowie), and keyboardist Tommy Morrongiello (of Ian Hunter's band), Destri's wobbly warble does little to uplift beyond the doo wop-style title track, and the amusing stab at neo-metal of "King Of Steam." "It was a real horrible record, for a lot of reasons—because Jimmy can't sing, for starters," said Burke, "and I don't think the timing was right for any of that stuff."

Blondie returned to action in February 1982, with a recut "Rapture" featuring Fab Five Freddy and Harry trading lines on a free flexidisc (then a popular format, thanks to its novelty, and low production costs). Originally slated as a Christmas record, delay on delay pushed that idea into the new year. So ran Blondie's fortunes. Sessions for its new album started on New York turf, at the Hit Factory, with Chapman back at the controls, and idea tapes bouncing around, as always. To Infante, the unanimity smelled like a front when nobody invited him: "All I know is, the record was going down without me being involved in the basic tracks, and I got the lawyer involved."

An out-of-court settlement left Infante a member, and allowed him to overdub his parts—but only after everybody had gone home. Not surprisingly, he remembers little of recording *The Hunter:* "You could play me stuff, and I could say, 'What is that?' I don't even remember where I did it!"

The best moments—Harry's plaintive "English Boys", Destri's story-so-far of his band ("Danceway"), and "Orchid Club"'s bubbling Latin mannerisms—harnessed the old playfulness. So did an understated, lovely remake of Smokey Robinson's "The Hunter Gets Captured By The Game," to which Harrison told *Trouser Press:* "When I hear it I keep waiting for the whole drum kit to come in."

The Hunter had little else going for it. "Dragonfly"'s opaque, six-minute sci-fi wordplay might have fared better without such bloated fodder as "The Beast," which paled unfavorably to "Rapture," and "Island Of Lost Souls" (Chrysalis CHS 2063), a blatant "Tide Is High" knockoff. Issued as a single, it withered at #33 U.S. in June 1982, but still managed a #11 U.K. peak.

"That's when I was traveling separately," said Infante. "When we did the video—talk about island of lost souls, man, lemme tell you! When I was there, nobody would talk to anybody else; my lawyer said, 'Don't talk to anybody, [and] don't hit anybody.'" A month later, "War Child"/"Little Caesar" became Blondie's final chart entry, peaking at #39 U.K., and nowhere in America.

Only two years earlier, Blondie were consistently topping the singles charts; they now had to watch their album limp to #33 U.S., and #49 U.K., and earn a pounding from the British press ("Blondie could hardly sound any safer, stodgier and more senile"), or Mark Rowland of *Musician,* who blasted the lyrics ("which often seem to borrow their syntax from [U.S. Secretary of State] Alexander Haig," he wrote. "In the end, *The Hunter* is all hot sauce and no enchilada."

Burke doesn't think the band sold itself short: "It was the first time I'd ever felt confident; I really thought I was at the top of my game, playing well. We made a good record, in a lot of ways." He cites "English Boys" ("Debbie did a good job with the lyrics, there's a lot of imagery"), and "War Child" ("the Falklands War was going on [between Argentina and Britain], which didn't ring true for a lot of people") as the standouts.

Professional as always, Blondie pressed ahead, even after slow sales had scuttled the upcoming U.K. tour. Instead, they decided to retake America, sponsored by Pioneer Stereo (earning little of the flack that greeted the Rolling Stones' deal with Jovan cologne for their own fall 1982 outing; ironically, their hit, "Start Me Up," ended up on Blondie's fall tour setlist).

Infante watched sessioneer Eddie Martinez (of Run-DMC's "Rock Box" single) replace him: "It was, 'Frank, there's a problem,' and I said, 'Get somebody else, and pay me as if I was there.' The vibe wasn't the same. I didn't go to any shows, but that's what I heard from people who did." Gordon's pre-tour pep rally had little more success. "He said, 'You can go out and be millionaires, or sit at home on your ass, and sell a lot of records,'" said Burke. "And Chris said, 'Well, I'll just stay home, then.'"

Armed with a set that had long banished the older hits, Blondie's "Tracks Across America" slid through half-empty halls, to crumbling morale. "It was like a changing of the guard," said Burke. "Nigel and I got Duran Duran to open for us; by the end of the tour, they were the success, we were the failure." Stein himself was in no shape to remedy matters. When his rapid weight loss and emaciated condition became too frightening to overlook any longer, the tour folded, and so did Blondie, joining a distinguished roll call of bands closing up shop that year— The Jam, Squeeze and Theatre Of Hate. (Stein's illness was soon diagnosed as pemphigus vulgaris, a rare, near-fatal skin disease that is mainly caused, it seems, by stress.)

The final, prolonged tailspin marked a sad end to one of pop's smartest, most relentlessly melodic bands, though the outcome wasn't a shock, given Blondie's trouble with reconciling success and democracy—which bedevils bands in their sunniest periods. And while the Duran Durans were giving Blondie a run for its money, that wasn't the decisive factor. As Destri had so cannily predicted in 1981's *Trouser Press* feature, if Harry went solo, everyone would have to fend for themselves: "As a member of Blondie she's tied down; she deserves to be let loose."

"It's frightening to see how successful the band could have been," said Burke. "It was a great success, and a great experience, but a lot of things could have been done a lot better." He would wait almost 20 years to see that promise pan out.

Back To The Bleach

With Harry and Stein out of sight, Blondie quietly dissolved, and its members scattered to find gainful employment.

After the *Heart On A Wall* debacle, Destri bounced around Europe, taking the odd production job. Ironically, the one he desired most eluded him. "I met U2's manager [Paul McGuinness] one night and we sat around dropping hints to each other," Destri told *Trouser Press* in spring 1982. "If he reads this he'll know I'd really like to produce U2." It didn't happen, and Destri returned to Brooklyn, where he became a contractor before rejoining Blondie.

Iggy Pop's bands became something of a refuge for ex-Blondie members. Before his illness, Stein had formed Animal Records, an imprint label for artists not falling into the mainstream, such as avante-garde violinist Walter Steding. Stein accordingly produced *Zombie Birdhouse* (Animal CHR 1399), one of Pop's quirkiest, least-selling albums, to which Burke and Duprey also contributed. The touring band again featured Duprey, as well as Infante, who spent fall 1982 promoting the album. They followed up with yet more roadwork in spring and summer 1983, where Pop visited Australia and Japan for the first time.

"I didn't call him [Pop], he called me," said Infante. "He just let you do what you wanted, everything was real cool. He'd encourage you to get wild. He wasn't a maniac to where he made you feel intimidated, or bad about it. He was the boss, but he wasn't a tyrant about it." Infante reunited with Iggy Pop years later, blasting through the latter's "Five Foot One" with Hunt (drums) and Tony Sales (bass) on a "Tales From The Crypt" show that featured the late comic Sam Kinison as promoter Marty Slash, who gets his comeuppance after committing a murder at his club. "We did that in an afternoon, just one take; it was a good little thing," said Infante.

Since Blondie's demise, Infante has lent his guitar to a variety of one-off projects and sessions, most recently on Sylvain Sylvain's *Sleep Baby Doll* (Fishhead FCD 02142: 1997); he plays on the haunting "Your Society Makes Me Sad," the late Thunders' final song, and a frantic remake of the Dolls standard "Trash." Infante also supported ex-Dolls bassist Arthur Kane on 1994's *I Only Wrote This Song For You,* a Thunders tribute album, and has backed readings for the likes of ex-T. Rex publicist B.P. Fallon, and Mick Farren. He's also writing for himself, though only one thing holds him back: "I'm not as prolific with lyrics as I'd like to be, whereas with the guitar, I could sit down, and all kinds of parts come out."

Burke and Harrison collaborated once more, providing the rhythmic backbone for Chequered Past, a sort of punk supergroup featuring ex-Sex Pistols guitarist Steve Jones, and ex-Silverhead/Detective vocalist Michael Des Barres. "You have to owe somebody a million dollars to be in this band," Des Barres said at a New York gig (that also featured Infante) reviewed in *Trouser Press*. Having been together all of four days, Chequered Past's material ranged from a crunching rendition of the Go-Gos' "Vacation," Waylon Jennings' "Are You Sure Hank Done It This Way?," and highlights from each member's past resumes. "With a few more original tunes—and depending on how serious they are—they could go far," Jim Green nodded approvingly.

But Chequered Past's 1984 EMI *America* album turned out to be embarrassing poodle-metal fodder, proving that the best resumes are no guarantee against the worst excesses; Infante wasn't present for Cliché Hall of Fame titles like "Let Me Rock You" (as opposed to doing homework, perhaps?). When the album thudded into bargain bins, Burke joined the Eurythmics—the first among many bands to use his services—while Harrison went into management. In 1988, the *Illinois Entertainer* featured him touting Tami Show, a Chicago band whose time never came, "The fact that they had two great looking girls fronting the band was a bonus." Sounds familiar, doesn't it? Harrison soon moved into A&R for Capitol, then Interscope.

Thanks to a regimen of steroids, Stein recovered by the mid-Eighties, although a barrage of tasteless death rumors forced Harry to declare, "Stories of my sainthood have been much exaggerated." Harry kept acting, chalking up notable turns in David Cronenberg's "Videodrome" (1982), as the late Sonny Bono's wife in "Hairspray" (1988), and the odd TV gig, including the CBS-TV drama "Wiseguy" in March 1989, and July 1989's "Mother Goose Rock 'n' Rhymes," in which Harry played "The Old Woman Who Lived In A Shoe" on the Disney Channel. There have been numerous one-off projects, too, including her AIDS benefit duet with Iggy Pop, "Well Did You Evah!" on the *Red Hot + Blue* Cole Porter tribute album, and a romp through the Castaways' Sixties nugget "Liar Liar," which wound up on the soundtrack for Johnathan Demme's comedy, "Married To The Mob" (1988). (Others are better off forgotten, such as "Teaneck Tanzi," a play which cast her as a female wrestler beside the late comedian Andy Kaufman, and closed on April 20, 1983, after just one night).

Harry's post-Blondie outings have been a more mixed bag. After a low-key start with "Rush Rush" on the *Krush Groove* (1985) soundtrack, Harry returned to action with *Rockbird* in December 1986. Its results were inconclusive, despite crisp production from J. Geils Band keyboardist Seth Justman. "Secret Life" is typical in hinting of an impending revelation, then dropping the matter, while other lyrics ("got you on my mind and it's mind over manners") make little melodic impact. The most likeable song, "French Kissin' In The USA," got to #8 U.K., #57 U.S. in January 1987, but Harry didn't write it. (Other singles fared less well, such as "In Love With Love," which peaked at #70 U.S. in July 1987.)

Somewhere along the way, Harry's personal relationship with Stein ended, but they stayed friendly, and collaborated on *Def, Dumb And Blonde* (1989)—which yielded a #13 U.K. hit, "I Want That Man," while the album got to #12, leading her to tour Britain after a nine-year break. American fans stayed away, allowing the Mike Chapman/Tom Bailey (Thompson Twins)-produced affair to peak at #123. Stein also helped on 1993's *Debravation,* which made little discernable impact.

Part of the problem understandably lay in the Blondie remixes and compilations that flooded the market and forced Harry to compete against her old peroxide persona—such as December 1988's remix collection, *Once More Into The Bleach,* which peaked at #50 U.K. Its single, "Denis," peaked in the same spot, while a remix of "Call Me" got to #61 U.S. in February 1989. Such tactics almost predestined the current Blondie reunion before Harry and company reached the same conclusion.

The problem was Harry's competition, most notably Madonna, whose platinum blonde image was un-imaginable without the trails her predecessor had blazed. "I think she caused me a few problems at my American label, Warners, because they were so heavily involved in Madonna it affected the level of promotion I got from them," Harry told *Q* readers. Other threats came from Britain's Transvision Vamp and its singer Wendy James, The Primitives and Kim Wilde. In America, the closest equivalents remain Hole's Courtney Love, and Gwen Stefani, the centerpiece of No Doubt—a band whose internecine struggles eerily recall those of Blondie.

The biggest boost to Harry's cause came from The Jazz Passengers' *Individually Twisted* (32 Records: 1997), distinguished by a duet with Elvis Costello ("Doncha Go Away Mad"), and a funked-up remake of "The Tide Is High"; a live album is imminent [Live in Spain *(32 Records: 1998)*—Ed.]. The loose-knit, low-key ensemble approach allows Harry to concentrate on jazz singing, which fits her newly-husky range like the proverbial glove. She has surely earned that right, after remaining one of rock's most strongest, most distinctive presences.

After touring with Iggy Pop, Valentine hung up his guitar to pursue an academic and writing career. Now living in London, he'd just returned in October 1996 to find a message on his answering machine left by one of Stein's friends. Playing pop music was the last thing on his mind, as Valentine had just returned from covering an arts festival in Bosnia, and playing with gypsy bands in Istanbul, and Macedonia.

"She said, 'Chris is desperate to speak with you,'" said Valentine. "Now, I hadn't seen or spoken to Chris in ten years—I call him, and he's ecstatic: 'I want you to come to New York, because I wanna put the band back together.' I thought, 'what the hell, it's 20 years, let's just do it!'" Valentine flew to New York a month later, only to find "nothing happening—he [Stein] wasn't in the best [physical] shape, and there weren't any rehearsals," he said. "I literally was sticking around a couple months before we got anything done."

Then again, Blondie's best and worst work had happened under the gun. When rehearsals finally began, Valentine felt pleased his "Amor Fati" ("Love Of Fate"), a song The Know had done, was among three demos cut at the Hit Factory—where the reunited Blondie had already been working with members of Duran Duran. "The sweetener was, 'we'll do these songs [with Duran Duran], but we also get to work on songs of our own: mine, one of Jimmy's, and a song of Chris's,'" said Valentine. "I wound up playing guitar and bass, 'cause Chris never showed up to the studio, and it seemed great."

Valentine rejoined the reunited Blondie in spring 1997, for a showcase in New York City, followed by festivals in Washington, D.C., Dallas and Connecticut. "Those went well," he said, "everyone liked it, we were getting along fine, and the word was: 'OK, work on some songs, and we'll bring you back in a couple months."

Two months stretched to five. When Valentine returned to sort out immigration rules in New York, he again visited Stein: "He said, 'Well, we don't know if you're the right person for the live shows'—he wouldn't give me a straight answer why—'but we still want you on the album, and we still wanna do your song.' So I went back to London, and I never heard from him again."

The next Valentine knew, he'd been told flying him over would be too expensive, and *No Exit* had begun without him. "I called [producer Craig Leon]: 'Is my song on?' He said, 'No, it wasn't on the final mix,' he didn't know why. Clem said he fought for it: 'at least make it a B-side.'" Last fall's U.K. tour went ahead with another bassist. But Valentine, 43, remains undaunted, having recently fathered a son, Joshua, and formed Fire Escape with his partner, Ruth, who plays electric violin. The band is playing around London and hopes to make demos, while Valentine works on a book about occult influences on Sixties bands.

Where *No Exit* will stand among Blondie's work remains to be seen, with reviews being cautiously encouraging. As with most reunions, future activity depends greatly on circumstances, sales and temperaments. The agenda isn't so much a smokescreen, but a blank screen, which was half the fun of following Blondie in the first place. While Blondie often suffered for being ahead of its audience, Burke never forgets what first appealed to him about Harry's and Stein's original vision.

"Their aesthetic was, 'girl group-meets-Velvet-Underground-meets-New York Dolls.' I mean, the first album is probably the campiest," he said. "[The late critic] Lester Bangs loved the first album, and hated everything else. So did Julie Burchill and Tony Parsons [of *New Musical Express*]. I love those kinds of bands, where you hate 'em, or you love 'em. Extremes are the best."

Infante is of two minds about the issue. "That was one of the best things about the band," he said. "We could do anything we wanted. We could have done a heavy metal song. We had five people that could write, so it was a different thing. That might have been one of the problems that became too much to contain." To him, it's not surprising that *Parallel Lines* looms largest in people's memory banks: "All I know is, when the band was the band, that's when it was successful—because we had the producer, the hit songs, and the sound. That was the pure power of Blondie."

That power tasted especially sweet after "Heart Of Glass" ended those nights of chocolate milk and chicken salad sandwiches after a poor take. "There's so many bands now," said Infante, "so many good bands, too—whereas, when we did it, there were no blueprints, because the whole music business hadn't become what it is today." Looking back, the whole story seems like a casting director's fantasy, because its members could not have had less in common. In the end, the band tabbed "least likely to succeed" prevailed over its detractors through inspiration, and some good old-fashioned perspiration, too. "She [Harry] was really working hard, and it paid off," Childers believes. "I've been on tours with older, more professional bands, and after four weeks, they've wound down. The shows become sloppy, they begin to complain, they want to go home.

"She did a world tour that went on and on. Being on the road is hard work, much less in places with weird food, weird culture, and hotel rooms with scorpions in 'em—she never, ever complained. I always admired people who said they're going to do it [succeed], and they just do it, they don't pay attention to anything else. And she did that...Debbie dug her heels [in], and would not be forgotten—and she went to work."

Valentine, who still earns steady royalties from "(I'm Always Touched By Your) Presence, Dear," remains proud of his Blondie days, despite his recent experiences. "The early days were some of the best times of my life—I followed a dream, it came true, and that time made me confident about pursuing other dreams. What 18-year-old kid doesn't want to be a rock star?" he said. "I've done many different things, and Blondie is just one of them, but it's a good one."

Just how good became clear after Valentine got 100 e-mails from "people saying, 'oh, it's really great to see you're around; let me tell you, 'Presence, Dear' meant a lot to me, it's one of my favorite songs,'" he said. "People would say, 'When we met, that was the song that was on.' It's a small contribution to the culture, but to know that it did have an effect on people is very gratifying."

The author thanks Clem Burke, Leee Black Childers, Nigel Harrison, Frank Infante and Gary Valentine for sharing their insights. Additional thanks goes to Dave Bianco, Stacy Fox, Don Hargraves, Lisa D. Heibutzki, Barney Hoskyns and Anthony Salazar for technical/informational support.

BLONDIE: BOOK & MAGAZINE REFERENCES

Ironically, Lester Bangs, the man who hated everything after Blondie, bashed out the first major book—the imaginatively-titled *Blondie* (1980)—in mere days. The band fired back its authorized version, *Making Tracks: The Rise Of Blondie* (1982), credited to Harry (text) and Stein (photos), and cowritten with Victor Bockris—issued, ironically, after Blondiemania had long quieted down. (Da Capo has since reissued the book.)

Bangs, who also died that year, seems to have taken matters less seriously than the band did, judging by a comment from the posthumous *Psychotic Reactions And Carburetor Dung* (Vintage Books, 1987) collection: "One day I even wrote my obituary: 'He was promising...' Then it occurred to me: 'Shit, I can't even commit suicide...Look what I'd have for a tombstone: Blondie!'"

Blondie also get major attention in *Please Kill Me: The Uncensored Oral History Of Punk,* by Legs McNeil and Gillian McCain (Grove Press: 1996), and Clinton Heylin's overview, *From The Velvets To The Voidoids: A Pre-Punk History For A Post-Punk World* (Penguin Books: 1993), which are both still in print. Reference material can be found in George Gimarc's *Punk Diary: 1970-79,* and *Postpunk Diary: 1980-82* (St. Martin's Press: 1994 and 1997, respectively).

The reader is also directed to Pete Frame's *The Complete Rock Family Trees Volume 1 & 2* (UK: Omnibus Press, 1980, and since reissued); his "Smouldering In The Bowery...One" and "Out In The Streets" charts provide an excellent overview of the original New York punk scene (and far more pre-Blondie information than this writer had room to include).

Trouser Press (1974-84) covered Blondie in exemplary fashion; major articles include "Blondie: Parallel Construction" (Jim Green, October 1978), "Blondie: State Of The Union 1981" (Scott Isler, June 1981), and "Blondie: Pumping Vinyl" (Jim Green, September 1982), in which the band members commented on each album they'd done.

Finally: for information on Gary Valentine, or his new band Fire Escape, e-mail him at: "Email FireEscape" link at this url: www.cdbaby.com/cd/fireescape. For the official Blondie web site, see www.blondie.net.

Jones Beach, Long Island, New York, August 8, 1999
credit: copyright © Sylvia Diaz

"Nothing Is Real But the Girl"

by James R. Blandford

Record Collector, *September 1999*

Thorough overview of Blondie's discography from a British perspective. Following introductory material, an album-by-album analysis is presented.—Ed.

JAMES R. BLANDFORD REACHES INTO THE BLEACH TO LOOK AT TWENTY-TWO YEARS OF BLONDIE

Few bands have achieved a comeback as stylish as Blondie's. After a seventeen-year hiatus, the New York pop-punksters, one of the first bands to emerge from the Big Apple-based New Wave of groups such as the Ramones and Talking Heads, have waltzed effortlessly back to the top of the charts with a No. 1 album, "No Exit," and a No. 1 single, "Maria." Their iconic singer, the ultra-cool and impossibly sexy Debbie Harry, may be 53, but a recent sell-out tour—they're still on the road as I write—has proved that age means nothing when you're a living pop legend with a list of timeless hit singles to pick from. And, in addition to pleasing their original fans, Blondie have captured a new audience by tapping into current musical trends, including a track with Coolio and a dance update of the classic "[Out] In The Streets," both featured on the new LP.

THE BIRTH OF BLONDIE

Debbie Harry's musical career began in 1967 when she hooked up with folk-rockers Wind In The Willows. Founded by former civil rights activist Paul Klein, the seven-strong band featured the decidedly brunette Debbie on vocals. In the male-dominated music environment of the time, the Willows were bound to make some small impression and thanks to a manager named Peter Leeds—who would later go on to become Blondie's controversial manager—they landed a deal with Capitol, who released their eponymous debut LP in 1968. The LP sank without a trace, while a spin-off single, "Moments Spent," fared little better—although it remains little more than a curio for Blondie fans, "Wind In The Willows" has been reissued on CD in recent years.

The group split in 1969, disillusioned by the album's failure, and Debbie would spend the next few years battling with drug dependencies, occasionally returning to live with her parents and finding her place in the New York underground art scene. Short-lived jobs saw her working as a Playboy bunny and waitressing in the trendy Max's Kansas City, but performing live was Harry's prime motivation, and in 1972 she found herself joining female vocal trio the Stilettoes, singing high-camp numbers such as "Lady Marmalade" and the Shangri-Las' "Out In The Streets". The Stilettoes may not have been the most talented act of the day, but they were interesting enough in 1974 to be checked out by David Bowie and one Chris Stein, who was smitten with Debbie from the moment he saw her. Stein quickly joined the girls' backing band and formed a relationship with Debbie that was as creative as it was sexual, leading to Debbie's decision to leave the Stilettoes and work with Chris in a new and independent musical direction. At the same time, they took the Stilettoes' rhythm section with them, effectively consigning the group to oblivion.

The next year was spent working the club circuit under the moniker the Angel and the Snake, with a line-up consisting of Debbie on vocals, Chris on guitar, Fred Smith on bass and Bill O'Connor on drums. Their progress was somewhat undermined when Fred Smith left the band to join Tom Verlaine's Television, and the departure of O'Connor shortly afterwards threatened to destroy the band completely. However, they dropped the name the Angel and the Snake and enlisted keyboard player James Destri, bassist Gary Valentine and drummer Clem Burke, changed their name to Blondie and began gigging at legendary New York punk joint CBGB's, where they were soon to attract a cult following thanks to Debbie's outrageous on-stage antics and their refusal to fit the mould of the club's more dour acts such as Patti Smith, who famously frowned upon their initial efforts.

RECOGNITION

It was in 1976, during the recording of a "Live At CBGB's" LP that Blondie came to the attention of producer Richard Gottehrer. He watched the band rehearse and was immediately struck by their chaotic style and energy, something he felt could be better captured in a studio. He proposed that Blondie should do a single for the Instant Record label, so the band went into the studio and recorded "In The Sun" and "Sex Offender"—the latter penned by Gary Valentine and Harry and based on the former's traumatic experience of making an underage girl pregnant, for which he was arrested. The tapes were then played to Howard Rosen of Private Stock, a label best known for Frankie Valli's 1975 hit "My Eyes Adored You." Rosen was impressed enough to put the tracks out as a single, although "Sex Offender" was retitled "X Offender" for fear of controversy. So much for punk.

This first single also provided the band with their first major rarity. "X Offender" had appeared as an A-side in Europe, Australia and Japan, but not in the UK. However, prompted by US imports creeping into the UK in 1976, Private Stock's London office planned a commercial release, with "In The Sun" as the flipside. A catalogue number was assigned, PVT 90, but the disc never reached the shops, although 500 copies left the factory. The only known recipient of the single was the BBC Music Library, which received two stock copies on 9th March 1977. A handful of A-label promos was also prepared, the first known example surfacing at a UK record fair in April 1996. The disc itself has been valued at £750—the less affluent collector will settle for obtaining "X Offender" (albeit in a slightly remixed form) as the flipside of "In The Flesh," which sells for a more reasonable £20.

Blondie signed an album deal with Private Stock and in 1976 released their eponymously-titled debut, recorded with Richard Gottehrer. The LP didn't provoke much interest in the States, though it did engender a following in the UK. However, the band weren't happy with what they perceived to be a lack of success with Private Stock, prompting a move to British label Chrysalis, which re-released "Blondie" shortly afterwards.

Another single was plucked from the album, the attitude-driven "Rip Her To Shreds," while the romantic "In The Flesh" reached No. 1 in Australia. This was the album's only hit, although "Rip Her To Shreds" would later put in an apt appearance on the Nightmare On Elm Street 4 soundtrack.

PLASTIC LETTERS

The second Blondie album was recorded in 1977 after an exhausting Stateside tour with David Bowie and Iggy Pop. "Plastic Letters" saw the departure of bassist Gary Valentine, who was apparently unhappy with a management contract he felt forced to sign, and who was replaced by Nigel Harrison. The LP also saw the introduction of Frank Infante on guitar.

Released in February 1978, "Plastic Letters" was to be the band's breakthrough album in Europe, although like its predecessor it sold next to nothing in the States. Featuring a reworked cover of the 1963 Randy & the Rainbows hit "Denise"—Debbie's own choice—and the Gary Valentine-penned "(I'm Always Touched By Your) Presence Dear," the LP marked the band's departure from the rawer punk energies of their earlier work. Radio stations responded, as did the public, and the album peaked at No. 10 in the UK. Record Mirror noted that "Debbie Harry is neither of the things her accusers suggest, i.e. a glamour girl who eclipses Blondie as a band or a talentless visual gimmick sold like cornflakes. The band on this album are vital fun, no musical mekanoids, smart as suits and with a direction they never suggested on the first album."

"Denis" was the obvious first single, and took six weeks to reach its highest position of No. 2 in the UK, while "Presence Dear" hit No. 10 in May. The 12" of "Presence Dear" featured the Jimmy Destri-penned "Poet's Problem", which was unavailable anywhere else at the time (although it now appears on the remastered "Plastic Letters" CD, alongside an alternate working version of "Denis"). Other stand-out tracks on the album include "Detroit 442" and "Cautious Lip," both of which would play an important part in Debbie's solo live work throughout the 80s.

PARALLEL LINES

1979 was *the* year of Blondie-mania. "Parallel Lines," the band's third album, was recorded with Mike Chapman—one half of the famous Chinn-Chapman team and a hit producer twenty times over in the UK (Sweet, Mud, Suzi Quatro)—who had realised his ambition for American hits by relocating to Los Angeles, where he worked with power-pop bands like the Knack. Harry comments in *Making Tracks,* the band's official 'autobiography,' that "we weren't prepared for his level of expertise so we learned an enormous amount about how to record from him...Chapman helped us become more commercial, with tighter arrangements and perfect basic tracks."

The original inner sleeve for "Parallel Lines" featured the lyrics to a track called "Parallel Lines," which doesn't actually appear on the album. Some have explained it away as a 'poem,' but according to Debbie in *Making Tracks,* "the title is especially significant. It comes from a song we didn't have time to finish, but we used the name about communications, characterisation and the eventual meeting of different influences."

The cut that was to carry "Parallel Lines" to the top of the charts was the energetic disco-influenced "Heart Of Glass," a song that had been initially demo'd back in 1975 under the working title of "Disco Song." Based around a preset on a Roland Rhythm Machine, the backing track alone took ten hours to put down, but Blondie's efforts were rewarded when "Heart Of Glass" became the band's breakthrough as far as American success was concerned. While they had found fame and recognition throughout Europe and as far away as Australia, the States proved persistently tougher to conquer, and the Giorgio Moroder-inspired sound was exactly what was needed to sway an American audience. The single went platinum and pushed album sales over the one million mark—to date it has shifted in excess of 20 million! Blondie were well and truly established and Debbie Harry swiftly became one of the world's most photographed women.

EAT TO THE BEAT

"Eat To The Beat" was recorded at the Power Station in New York, with Mike Chapman taking control of the production for a second time. Debbie Harry notes in *Making Tracks* that they "were becoming more adventurous about songwriting and playing, having had three years professional experience. We were looser in the studio now, tailoring the material for recording."

In keeping with the filmic theme of the album, augmented by Debbie's acting debut in the 1950s-style thriller *Union City* as well as a cameo for the group in the movie *Roadie,* also featuring Meatloaf, the band released a film version of "Eat To The Beat." This was the first ever video-album and was intended to cash in on the burgeoning video market—and how with a retail price £29.95! Reviews were less than ecstatic however, with *Record Mirror* grumbling that "with a video anything is possible, yet this one was surprisingly tame. You've already seen two slices from it on previous editions of TOTP and the rest isn't much different, save for one song where Debbie is disguised in black wig, sunspecs and stockings. What about this 'Blondie is a group' campaign of old? You hardly caught a glimpse of the five other members."

The LP itself contained the band's first tentative foray into reggae with "Die Young, Stay Pretty," and produced another run of hit singles. "Dreaming" peaked at No. 2, while the follow-up, "Union City Blue"—confusingly not featured in the *Union City* movie—stalled at a disappointing No. 13. Nevertheless, three months later, the Harry / Destri collaboration, "Atomic," crashed straight into the British charts at No. 3, reaching No. 1 the following week. This was followed by the Giorgio Moroder-produced "Call Me," culled from the soundtrack of the movie *American Gigolo,* which provided the band with their third UK No. 1 (though "Eat To The Beat" failed to produce a single American No. 1).

AUTOAMERICAN

Blondie's fourth album was recorded in Hollywood with Mike Chapman at the helm once again. Debbie Harry has said that the band consciously wanted to rally against everything they had previously recorded. In an attempt to create a different Blondie sound, Debbie even tried inhaling helium, though, as the rest of the band disliked the result, the idea was dropped.

"Autoamerican" took more time to complete than anything else the band had recorded, with each track being discussed at length in order to "satisfy everyone." "Rapture" was attempted twice, one version being considerably slower than the released version; "T-Birds" was named after the LA girls' roller derby team; "The Tide Is High" included percussion consisting of eight tracks of drum-sticks being tapped on a piano bench, while "Do The Dark" was created late one night on a cassette machine. As a final flourish the band employed a thirty-piece string section for Chris Stein's "Europa" and a jazz combo to back Debbie on "Faces."

"Suzy And Jeffrey," the upside of "The Tide Is High," was inspired by a curious episode which took place as the band were in the studio. A young couple on their way to get the necessary blood tests for their marriage licence had an argument, prompting the boyfriend to drive their car into the studio wall. Nobody was hurt, but the crash led to a straightforward recounting of the incident complete with "Leader Of The Pack"-style revving noises and references to Perry Como and Orson Welles, who were also recording at the studios at the time.

"Autoamerican" was released in November 1980, and reached the Top 3 on both sides of the Atlantic. It yielded the usual crop of hit singles. "The Tide Is High" was a No. 1 hit in the UK while "Rapture," which reached the top spot in the States, stalled at No. 5 here. The single also has the distinction of being America's very first rap hit—pretty good for a white NY pop group. The "Rapture" 12" featured extended mixes of the title track and "Live It Up," both of which have since resurfaced on the CD issue of "Autoamerican."

THE HUNTER

In 1982 it became apparent that the runaway pace of Blondie's success was slowing down. The band was being pulled apart by growing internal tensions, due in part to the press concentration on their photogenic lead singer as opposed to their music. Furthermore, a British tour was cancelled due to apparent lack of interest. Harry had released a solo album, "Koo Koo," immediately after "Autoamerican," partly to make the point that Blondie was a group. However, the album's artwork, by renowned Alien designer H.R. Giger, proved too much for some—a gaunt-looking Debbie peered out of the cover with a slew of skewers piercing her cheek. The LP wasn't a commercial success, but the media saw it as evidence that Blondie had split up. Of course, they were wrong, although they weren't far from the truth—"The Hunter" would turn out to be the group's last album for sixteen years.

Recorded at the Power Station with Chapman taking on production duties yet again, "The Hunter" was released in May 1982. The LP featured the minor hits "Island Of Lost Souls" and "War Child," and reached the Top 10 in the UK and the Top 40 in the States. The title track was the group's cover version of Smokey Robinson's "The Hunter Gets Captured By The Game." "For Your Eyes Only" had originally been recorded for the James Bond film, though it was dropped at the last minute when Sheena Easton was recruited to record the movie's soundtrack. Other stand-out tracks on the album include "Danceway" and "English Boys," though critics and fans alike shunned it. In Cathay Che's biography of Debbie Harry, *Platinum Blonde,* Harry is quoted as saying that "we identified as both hunter and hunted, but obviously we were more of the hunted at that point. We were really marked for slaughter and decimated by a bunch of different people right around then as we had really bad business problems. The record company just didn't market it."

In February 1983, tensions within the band had come to a head and Blondie announced their break-up. Clem Burke went on to play with Eurythmics, while Debbie took a break to nurse Chris Stein when he was struck with the potentially fatal skin disease pemphigus vulgaris. Blondie's roller-coaster ride of success had ended. Or so it seemed.

BLONDE AND BEYOND

Throughout the years following the demise of Blondie, Chrysalis released a glut of Blondie compilations while Debbie Harry recorded a clutch of decidedly mediocre solo albums such as "Def Dumb And Blonde," "Rockbird" and "Debravation." The latter part of the 90s saw Debbie singing with the Jazz Passengers, taking in European and American tours as well as a '96 appearance at the Phoenix Festival. She also concentrated on her film career, consolidating earlier roles in films such as David Cronenberg's *Videodrome* with spots in John

Waters' *Hairspray* as well as an episode of *Tales From The Darkside* on US TV. The 90s also saw dance-mix reissues of some of Blondie's greatest hits as well as a number of remix albums such as the widely unappreciated "Beautiful—The Remix Album." The pick of the compilation albums has to be 1994's "Blonde And Beyond". Alongside a selection of B-sides and rare early tracks, this CD presents the previously unreleased demo of "Heart Of Glass"—here entitled "Once I Had A Love"—as well as rarities such as the Spanish language version of "Call Me" and the French version of "Sunday Girl." Effectively an official bootleg, the album also rounds up soundtrack appearances such as a live version of "Ring Of Fire" and a cover of Bowie's "Heroes." Definitely one for the fans and an excellent collection-filler.

NO EXIT

So, sixteen years on from the poorly-received "The Hunter," Blondie are back. Instigated by Chris Stein, now fully recovered from his illness, rumours of a reunion had been rife since 1996, but late '98 finally saw them become reality as Blondie took to the road on a sell-out tour. Including original members Debbie Harry, Chris Stein, Clem Burke and Jimmy Destri, the reunion met with a minor hitch when former members Nigel Harrison and Frank Infante were not asked to be involved. Inevitable litigation concerning the use of the band's name ensued, though this doesn't seem to have overly concerned Miss Harry and chums, as 'Blondie' had been arrived at long before Infante and Harrison appeared on the scene.

Blondie marked their reappearance on UK TV in January with a spot on the prime-time *National Lottery,* on which they showcased their comeback single, "Maria," which crashed into the charts at No. 1. The album, "No Exit," followed in February. Produced by Craig Leon—who also oversaw their eponymous debut back in 1976—the album features their usual range of styles, from the ska-flavoured "Screaming Skin," through the classical organ and rap blend of "No Exit"—featuring Coolio, no less—to the girl group dance meld of "[Out] In The Streets"—that old Stilletoes fave.

Blondie have certainly proved that they are not rooted in their past successes with this album, consequently attracting new fans as well as loyal oldsters. With a second single, the menacing disco-romp of "Nothing Is Real But The Girl," more UK concert dates lined up for the end of the year as well as talk of another LP, it looks as though Blondie are, as Take That [*'90s British teen pop group*—Ed.] might've put it, back for good.

Rolling Stone ranks *Parallel Lines* #6 among "The 50 Coolest Records" in its April 11, 2002 issue

Appreciations

"Icon of the Month: Deborah Harry"

by Aletha Milam

The Hipstress, e-zine, April 2001

At the close of the disco era, a new group set the music scene on fire and came to exemplify the new wave era in both sound and look. Blondie, fronted by magnetic lead singer Deborah Harry, changed music and fashion forever.

Debbie was unique. Her hair was an intentionally obvious bottle blonde. Her makeup was theatrical and dramatic. The band's sound was a hybrid of new wave, punk, and pop, with the occasional homage to disco or rap thrown in. Debbie's style was equally diverse and therefore, revolutionary. Think Madonna invented the platinum blonde with dark roots look? Nope. Debbie.

Think back to the "Heart Of Glass" video, the bands most "disco" song. Debbie swirls around in a dress made for Studio 54, with hair from CBGB's, and makeup from Vogue Magazine, uber lip gloss included.

Deb's influence is all over the place these days, from the riot grrls of Hole to the blonde ambition of Madonna. She made punk pretty and feminine without losing the essential edge of the style, providing some of the greatest music ever made in the process.

And this is why she is our icon of the month.

"'The Highest Compliment'"

by Everett True

I got into music late, at the age of 16. It wasn't until I heard Blondie covering "Denis" on my parent's radio that I finally understood the appeal of pop. I still think it one of the finest singles ever recorded—to rank alongside the Ramones, the Ronettes and New Age Steppers' "My Love"...

I once used a line from Blondie's "Atomic" to compliment my former friend Courtney Love: it was about the highest compliment I could think of, to quote a line from such a perfect pop song. Blondie were such perfection, it hurts to think of them even now.

"Deborah Harry: 'The Mark of a True Icon'"

by Cindy Rivers

In the early 80s, I remember listening to R&B radio mostly. And a song called "Rapture" had come on. And it was a girl rapping...

Actually, she was purring in comparison to the female rappers—Missy Elliott, Foxy Brown and Lil' Kim—today. But at that time, female rappers, albeit a sugarcoated one, were unheard of. But that voice would introduce the first blue-eyed rap song, giving way to the likes of the Beastie Boys, Anthrax and others...

Debbie Harry held her own in room full of testosterone, much like girl rappers today. But she was smoother around the edges than some of these "bitch hoes" now. Sure she was a sex kitten, too. But she had style. She was punk. She was pop. She was disco. She was Marilyn Monroe in wolf's clothing.

And she was certainly the first to have "blonde ambition" well before Madonna and Courtney Love were even on the scene. And well before Christina Aguilera and Britney Spears were even thought of. I'd consider "The Tide Is High" probably to be one of the first ska songs...

I imagine that it might be hard for someone who's not into music to see what a pioneering band Blondie was because the band was neither the most profound nor prolific.

But as for a less "academic" assessment, Blondie inspired me to listen to harder styles of rap. And Debbie herself (along with Lita Ford some years later) would inspire my dress in high school. At that age, I couldn't wear the stiletto heels. But I could certainly sport the flashy trash look.

She was cool well before people knew she was. And that's the mark of a true icon.

Amy Oravec
Philadelphia, Pennsylvania USA
The Blondie Review, Art Issue, Fall 2001, copyright © 2001

"Blondie: 'Some Love Never Dies'"

by Henrik Tuxen

Nov. 1978. First time in London, with my fellow 9th graders. The excitement is endless. Somebody turns on Top of The Pops in the hotel bar. A band named Blondie appears on the screen. The track is Picture This. Debbie Harry goes into the chorus, and every guy in the room falls instantly in love; no more no less. Luckily the same song is to be found at the hotel jukebox. Needless to say, Picture This rotates into constant repeat.

As the night progresses the atmosphere gets more and more intense; wildly exciting for everybody except our school teacher who threatens to send us home to Denmark on our own expense, if we don't behave.

Time for revenge: At 3 am, when all the hotel's approximately 1000 guests are firmly asleep, four 15-year-old guys sneak into a dark and deserted bar, searching for the jukebox. We silently manage to push the monster away from the wall, find the volume button on the back of the machine and turn it to max. We put in a coin, push number 34 for Picture This and hurry back to our room.

Seconds later the classic Chris Stein intro threatens to break down the hotel walls, and as Debbie Harry ensures us that 'all she wants' is this and that...teachers, guests and hotel staff are running around the hotel in sheer panic, trying to locate and stop the music. The loudest version of Picture This, ever, goes on for at least three minutes, before someone manages to pull the plug. The triumph is complete.

Pretending to be asleep, our beds are shaking from victory, fear, laughter and true love. For some reason we weren't caught, which would have resulted in an instant return ticket.

Shortly thereafter, four teenage boys fell asleep overwhelmed by London and dreaming of Debbie Harry. Some love never dies!

credit: copyright © Daniel Porter
Depiction of Debbie circa *Parallel Lines* period

"Blondie And Me"

by Ralph Heibutzki

While I always knew how tall Blondie stood among New York's original punk vanguard, I didn't truly discover them until my peers in rural southwest Michigan did. Our town's pair of primarily Top 40-oriented stores simply didn't carry the likes of *Blondie* (1976), or *Plastic Letters* (1978).

In my hometown, if you couldn't pack an arena, and play the muscular brand of hard rock that folks demanded back then, you didn't matter—so my epiphany arrived along with everybody else's schedule, after *Parallel Lines* (1979) and its smart, sassy leadoff single, "Heart of Glass."

Suddenly, my classmates glimpsed the immediacy of all this left-field stuff that I'd championed so relentlessly. Once your sensibilities had been filtered through Blondie's gritty camp-pop cocktail, with its knowing winks to Fifties and Sixties trash glamour, a steady diet of Foreigner, Journey and all their faceless corporate brethren would never again be as appetizing.

In my eyes, Blondie were the premier New Wave ambassadors, who were able to retain a unique identity, yet let everybody in on the secret when it actually sold records. My admiration for that ability only deepened with their "Saturday Night Live" TV appearance; seeing Clem Burke firing roll after roll of machine gun-style drumming during "Dreaming" has been forever burned into my memory.

Where the Clash and Sex Pistols captured your head, Blondie knew how to engage your feet, and your heart, as proven by their final smashes, "The Tide Is High," and "Rapture," which brought reggae and rap culture into Middle America's radios and living rooms.

Regardless of how their story finally played out, Blondie's impact has remained lasting, and enormous, if only for the group's readiness to mix up their competing musical personas, and inspiring others to do likewise—and for that alone, they deserve a thank-you.

Katy Burchell
Wales UK
The Blondie Review, Art Issue, Fall 2001, Copyright © 2001

"I Am Wearing Debbie Harry's Panties"

by Teresa R. Hale

New York Waste, *Summer 2000*

So here I sit, nearly naked, trying to write about how I became proud owner of panties once worn by punk's original femme fatale. One sentence and I avert my eyes from the computer screen to gaze blankly out the window at cornfields ad infinitum. Then heavily, like the supporting tendon at the base of my neck has been severed, my head falls toward my lap and the bikini briefs imprinted with "Do Not Deprave Yourself" that cling to my hips. Maybe there is a story in this.

Flashback to May 31, morning. I'm jet-bound from Chicago to NYC, beside a big guy with body odor who stares longingly at the pack of peanuts on my tray table. I push the headphones from my ears to the bridge of my nose, so the foam discs stifle the sweat stench. I reach into my duffel for a Baggie filled with safety pins and a slip adorned with a collage of ironed-on concert photos I recently shot of Debbie. Time to complete an original design that will grab the attention of Blondie's Golden Goddess.

Obviously I managed to do that. How else would I've arrived home with Debbie's famous, er, infamous panties tucked away in my American Tourister? Oh, the tales I could weave about how I came to possess the prized panties. But truth is, I'm owner of the undies because I was one of hundreds of fans who converged May 31 at NYC's club Mother for a party celebrating the release of *Deborah Harry,* a biography by Cathay Che, and an auction of Debbie/Blondie memorabilia to benefit the Humane Society of New York. *More later. Now back to the plane.*

Little time left in flight, and I've yet to put finishing touches on my party garb. Like all Mother parties, there's a dress code—this evening it's aesthetically innovative, Debbie/Blondie-oriented attire. I'm aiming for a cheap-chic, "Parallel Lines," Sprouse-inspired look (Stephen Sprouse designs many outfits for Debbie featuring his signature safety pins).

I form mounds of pins on my tray table, which during turbulence seems to rattle flight attendants. The big guy watches as I fasten the pins, one by one, until clusters cover the slip's ripped hemline and neckline, and form frames around the ironed-on images. "Are those pictures of that Blondie lady?" he asks. "Yeah." I fake a smile. "Would you like a few pins?" No answer. He returns to his laptop. I find a key and stab it into the nylon, making random slashes common to punk haute couture. The chaste slip I wore during adolescence to mask the silhouette of my shape from pimply-faced boys will soon make a public debut.

Fast forward a couple hours. Now in the Big rotten Apple, I get out of the cab a few blocks from my respite, the Chelsea Hotel, which provides enough walking time for pollutants to permeate the lining of my nostrils and replace the big guy's odor. It also gives me time to mentally prepare for the physical transformation that will soon occur.

In the hotel room, the metamorphosis of a Midwestern brunette into a replica of a platinum-topped pop star begins. First, makeup—lots of it—heavy on glittery blue eye shadow and Day-Glo lip gloss. Second, hair—lots of it, too. I cram my head into a bleach-blonde wig, pull chunks of my own hair through to mimic Debbie's trademark mane, tease and add a pair of black shades at the crown.

Finally, the outfit: Hot pink stockings, body-strangulating slip that reroutes midriff flab into titty territory, gold stilettos and the safety-pinned photo dress. Tada! Ready for a quality inspection. Up, down, turnaround, back to the mirror. Sadly, I haven't emerged from the depths of the cosmetics kit a Harry-ed clone; I look more like an extra in an '80s heavy metal video. Detecting my insecurity, my friend, sporting a "Blondie Boy" motif, reassures: "You're trashy and flashy. Deb will dig it!" With that vote of confidence, we head to Mother.

Upon entering her monumental gilded doors, nestled in the city's "Meat Market," clubgoers stuff cash into a donation jar for the Humane Society (in lieu of the usual cover charge), then scatter in various directions: The entryway, where a collection of photos documenting Debbie's career are hung and free copies of *Interview* magazine featuring a portrait of Debbie and her dog Chi Chan are stacked; the dancefloor, where a Harry-heavy playlist spun by notorious deejay Miss Guy puts fans in aural bliss; the bar, where vodka drinks are on the house until 10 p.m.; the stage, where Debbie-exclusive visuals produced by multimedia master Rob Roth are projected; and the basement, where fans are jam-packed in dark recesses hoping to catch a glimpse of "herself" upon arrival.

This is my first encounter with the legendary Mother, and the crowd is exactly as I'd envisioned: a conglomeration of her own Debbie-worshipping family members—nocturnal artistes, freaks, geeks, cross-dressers, free-thinkers, dream-seekers, fetishists and other khaki-condemning nonconformists who comprise the city's underground "ahts" [*New York pronunciation of "arts"*—Ed.] scene—and die-hard "Debheads" from all over the globe who've come to witness the illustrious icon in her element.

While anxiously awaiting Debbie's appearance, fans muddle through the mob to meet author Cathay Che and purchase hot-off-the-press, discounted editions of *Deborah Harry*. Copy in hand, I hover in a corner to absorb more of Mother's uninhibited creative culture—her inspirational vibe, bizarre brood and eclectic decor.

I start taking pictures: Two gals clad in fishnet stockings and animal prints propped against a zebra-striped wall, smoking cigarettes as dim light streaming from antique fixtures forms halos above their heads, *click*. A pair of trannies seated on a Victorian tapestry sofa: One with a Wendy O. Williams (rest her soul) do—silver, spiked ends with lavender roots—the other, wearing a feathered chapeaux and huge, dark, round sunglasses; both wrapped in short jackets, velour leopard and silver vinyl, respectively; smooth, pale legs crossed ladylike, *click, click*. Next my lens focuses on Empress-ario Chi Chi Valenti, who with husband Johnny Dynell, owns Mother.

With Debbie's entrance imminent, I squeeze through the crowd to chat with Chi Chi. I tell her that within Mother's embrace, I feel at home and unconditionally accepted for who I am, like a lost soul saved. I learn that I'm in good company. Mother has worked her maternal magic for nearly a decade, nurturing artists like renowned rock photographers Bob Gruen and Roberta Bayley, and other local celebs mingling amid the crowd.

"Debbie and Cathay are regulars; they're family. When the idea for the event came up, holding it here was a natural choice for them," says Chi Chi. "It wasn't as easy deciding which cause would receive the proceeds; there are so many worthwhile ones out there. We chose the Humane Society because all three of us own shelter dogs, and we're huge supporters of the organization's efforts."

I comment on the hordes of fans, and Chi Chi estimates that by now about 350 have packed the house. "Debbie draws quite a crowd!" she says, adding: "Debbie knew some fans would travel hundreds of miles to attend the party. She wants to show her appreciation for that, not hide out in some V.I.P. room. She truly wants this night to be memorable for fans."

Minutes later, Debbie is escorted into the party. Instantly, flocks of fans push toward her, trying to stay composed as tears of excitement stain their painted faces. I stand back from the billowing mass and observe.

Debbie's two-toned tresses—now more brunette than blonde—are pulled into a ponytail. Attire is unpretentious: Tuxedo-style black pants, simple sandals and a white tee-shirt imprinted with the word "holy" beneath a holey black mesh tank. Her breathtaking beauty remains: Flawless complexion, chiseled cheekbones, half-mast Marlene Dietrich eyes, and youthful, infectious smile.

Armed with Sharpies and cameras, fans graciously request autographs and photos. Some ask for kisses and float away with lipstick-stained insignias on their cheeks. Others get "flesh" autographs, like the woman who has Debbie sign her ankle so she can get the signature tattooed the next day. Throughout the mania Debbie is polite, conscientious and accommodating. When the madness subsides, she disappears to help Mother staff prepare for the auction.

Around 10:30 p.m., fans congregate on the dancefloor for an auction of unique Debbie/Blondie memorabilia. The Dueling Bankheads, a pair of raven-haired queens who perform side-splitting skits at Mother, take the stage as novice auctioneers but soon run the show like pros. The Bankheads and Chi Chi describe the gems up for bid while Rob Roth and Romy Ashby, Debbie's friend and contributing songwriter to Blondie, fetch and flaunt items for the audience. *Note:* Romy is especially gifted at teasing vulnerable bidders by dangling merchandise—like a pair of leggings Debbie wore on "The Hunter" tour—in our faces. Close enough that we want more but far enough that we can't touch.

Meanwhile, Debbie strolls on and off stage—winking, blowing kisses, spitting rose petals into the crowd, relating amusing and sentimental stories about various items—basically any action that might wear down will power and build up temptation so hands holding our bidding cards... *"Do I hear $800?"*... involuntarily rise... *"Sold for $800 to bidder #100!"*

I've withstood the urge to bid by focusing on the uncontrollable itching of my scalp...*friggin' wig*. But then Romy re-emerges, stands directly in front of me, suspends a pair of red lace silk panties from her index finger and sways the garment enticingly. *"Nope, not gonna work,"* I think to myself, wishing that billfolds came with alarms.

I try to tune out the sound of Chi Chi rambling on about how Debbie wore these particular panties in the "Kung Fu Girls" video...*blah, blah, blah*...Then right on cue, Debbie reappears with a plea: "Oh please don't let the city's pussy go hungry"...Suddenly my mind shifts to "Do Not Eat" warnings on silica gel packets, and I recall countless times I was tempted to taste it. Before I know it, my bidding card is high in the air. I just blew a wad of hard-earned cash on underpants.

At the close of the auction, 16 treasures have been sold including: a Chanel dog collar worn by Debbie's dog Chi Chan; a limited edition Debbie Harry doll; a Private Stock "X Offender" single signed by Debbie; a print of an H.R. Giger portrait of Debbie; a photo of Debbie taken by Blondie guitarist Chris Stein; original *Punk* comic books featuring "cartoon" Debbie; a framed *Interview* magazine cover of Debbie shot by Roberta Bayley; and a handful of custom-made clothes worn by Debbie.

Debbie hangs out after the auction to sign mementos for stragglers. She winks at me. I hoist myself onto the stage while safety pins pinch my flesh and ask for her autograph. Debbie bends down, pushes my slip to my hips, signs "X, Love, Debbie Harry" down the length of my thigh, then s-l-o-w-l-y underlines the signature. She stands and kisses me on the lips. Believe me: Debbie Harry could make the straightest of girls bend.

Still stupefied, I speak briefly with Cathay, who tells me that tonight's event raised more than $11,000 for the Humane Society of NY! She also mentions that some bidders questioned the authenticity of the panties that cost me next month's rent. She rids my doubt by adding that during the auction, Debbie stuffed the panties down her pants to give them "recent essence."

Ready to call it a night, I'm bidding farewell to fellow fans when I sense someone standing behind me. I turn to see Debbie. "Do you wanna get a couple pictures together?" she offers sweetly. *Flash, blink, flash, hug*...Then out the door she goes.

It's past 3 a.m. The crowd has become sparse. Martini toxins have settled in my forehead; my wig is lopsided, my feet are numb; and due to exhaustion, the euphoria of being in Debbie's presence has dropped in rank from an intense rubber cement high to a caffeine buzz. Still, the night has defied description, and saying goodbye to Mother is bittersweet.

Back at the hotel, I de-wig and undress, tossing remnants of a perfect evening into a pile at my feet. I lie on the bed and trace Debbie's autograph, which has left an imprint on my leg. I fall asleep to the sound of sirens and screeching tires on the streets below, and a continuous loop of Blondie tunes that plague my brain.

I wake to the same sounds, louder. Standing at the open window, I inhale carcinogens and witness a near miss between a pedestrian and a driver on 23rd Street: *"Hey, fuck you!"* *"No, fuck you...motherfucker."* I throw on some clothes and a Yankees cap, and head out to a diner. My friend and I sit outside, drinking espresso and reading personal ads in a swinger's rag, dismal with thoughts of leaving for our respective homelands. I eat a sausage link while a passerby scoops up the shit his dog took three feet from our table. I'm going to miss this city...*but I wish I'd ordered bacon instead.*

I'm jet-bound from NYC to Chicago, beside a big guy with body odor. I give him the pack of peanuts I saved from the previous flight, then watch out the window as the Statue of Liberty fades into the distance. As clouds replace her, my mind wanders to visions of people waiting in the airport of my hometown. I think about how they'll stare disapprovingly at the red snakeskin pants I'm wearing—the ones I bought in SoHo—and how they'll thank God I'm not *their* daughter. I think about returning to the corporate cesspool, where staying afloat means drowning. I think about packing the freak within me away with the platinum wig and once again donning a mask of Midwestern normalcy. Then I think that none of these thoughts really matter at all.

I am wearing Debbie Harry's panties.

"Deborah Harry: Diva!"

by Alan Foster

About.com web site, May 12, 1999

Remember Debbie Harry? If, like me, you were a gay teenager in the late seventies and early eighties, you're sure to remember her as the platinum-haired lead singer of Blondie, the darlings of New York's downtown scene who actually made disco cool.

In case you haven't heard, Debbie and the boys are back together, touring the world with their first album in 16 years, "No Exit."

Just what is the secret of Ms. Harry's appeal to gay men? In a recent interview in *HX Magazine*, she explains: "Gay audiences really like women who fall into the diva blonde thing. And I worked that for all it's worth."

As Blondie's lead singer, Debbie adopted a persona that parodied the blonde bombshell type. As a result, her often campy performances were not unlike those of a drag queen. Taking the drag diva thing one step further, she has frequently appeared at Wigstock, New York's annual drag festival. That, and her performance in John Waters' camp classic "Hairspray," have helped assure her place as a gay icon.

"Razor Deb"
Gothic-Impressionistic rendering in pastels
Stacy Betts
Shelton, Connecticut USA
The Blondie Review, Art Issue, Fall 2001, copyright © 1999

"Meeting a Goddess"

by Sherry Gunderman

Tonight was my last Blondie show of the millennium. I've followed this band for the past year as best I could. I saw them perform their first show in the states in 16 years at the El Rey in LA...then roadtripped to Vegas with some boy boys to see them at the House of Blues. Then there was the May show in LA...with shoddy nosebleed seating...and I had just about lost hope with ever meeting my idol. Tonight was mesmerizing. I've worked in a trendy LA bar for 5 years now. I've MET more "celebrities" than the common mortal...but this was the pinnacle of achievements. My friend David had won front row seats and backstage passes off a very cool DJ on a local radio station. He and his boyfriend took the front row seats...I got his purchased ticket for the first aisle behind the pit. A lesbian couple that David knew had come with us, as well as Lisa, a girl we met through the DHBIS (an Internet Blondie fan club). We were in scattered seating throughout the amphitheater, but no one cared. The lights dimmed and the show began.

I knew the routine by now. The boys came onstage first..."Dreaming" began to swell, and Debbie Harry made her way onto the stage in sunglasses and a sexy dress. The crowd went nuts. Since I didn't have to drive, I'd thrown back a few drinks before the show and that only added to it. Inhibitions went out the window and I danced like a crazy person. They played everything...old...new...I was shocked and disappointed that people around me weren't displaying their enthusiasm half as much as I was. Leigh Foxx locked eyes with me and winked. I waved maniacally and continued to dance. When the show wound down with "Heart of Glass," I turned to a sitting couple next to me...who sat through the WHOLE SHOW...and gestured for them to stand and said "I think you may know THIS one!"

The lights came up and people began to filter out.

David came bounding up, clutching our backstage passes. I was so close. My heart was in my throat. We told our friends that we would come out and rotate the passes so that everyone would get a chance to get backstage. When we went backstage, I asked people who were leaving for their passes, which most of them surrendered kindly. The bouncers wouldn't let us get back out to GIVE our friends the passes we had! We were in...and we were the only ones getting in.

I saw Clem Burke first. I sauntered over to him and let me tell you this: The man has found the Fountain of Youth. He's something like 15 years older than I am and looks better than I do! He was kind and sweet...signing my "Making Tracks" (Blondie autobio) and making an effort to spell my name correctly. All thoughts of mentioning a mutual friend to him dissolved in his presence. I was rather a blubbering idiot...in awe of these people...these people who create music that moves me and that I thrive on. I thanked him as best I could and drifted off in search of other band members, leaving Clem to other fans.

I found Jimmy Destri next. He was busy talking with two other guys...rather consumed with fans and friends...but I got an autograph and told him that I adored him before letting him go.

I turned around and right into Leigh Foxx, the bassist who has replaced Nigel Harrison on this time 'round with Blondie. Leigh was more human than any celebrity I've met in a long time. I thanked him for the music and the awesome show and he nearly blushed...said "Thank you so much! You know, people push me out of the way to get to Debbie...no one knows who I am!" I was shocked by this. I told him that the REAL fans, like ME, knew exactly who he was and his contribution to Blondie's sound. He kissed me on the cheek. I tried not to swoon.

I left him to other conversations and rounded a corner...hoping for the jackpot. I came close. Debbie had come out for a minute, was engulfed by fans, and went back to her room. Resignation in my eyes, I saw people swarming someone else like vultures. I literally pushed them out of my way. There was Chris Stein, Debbie's ex and my heartthrob. I crassly shoved my way in and handed him my book. Chris smiled as politely as a rock star who was tired and on the road could while dealing with rabid fans. He took the book, signed it, took time to draw a skull and crossbones...and then I said "One more thing" and held up my camera.

Chris sighed, annoyed, and I said jokingly, but with a truthful undercurrent, "C-mon, man! I know you're tired...but I've waited 15 years for this moment!" Chris complied with my meager request. I thrust my camera to some nearby girl and Chris lowered his sunglasses over his gorgeous eyes. We put our arms around each other and waited...and the camera was not going off. Chris was not hiding his annoyance. "What's the problem?"

I laughed and kissed him on the cheek. I said "No problem! She's just giving me more time to hang on to you!"

He honestly laughed at that one and was more friendly, tugging my pigtail and smiling big for the flash. I thanked him profusely and left him to other admirers.

I located David, who has met the band many times before and was not as starry eyed as I was. He was on a mission to see Debbie. I was beginning to think this wouldn't happen...as I had not seen hide nor hair of guitarist Paul Carbonara and figured that Debbie had escaped undetected.

We went and got some beers from the complimentary bar. I stood against a doorjam, sipping my beer and wondering if we should forfeit and leave. It was then that a diminutive blonde brushed past me with her head lowered and a stocky bouncer shielding her from looky-loos.

David and I locked eyes for what must have been a split-second. I set my beer down behind the door and followed her into a private parking area. She was booking it. I had to run. I called "Debbie!" a few times and realized that she was not deaf but ignoring me. I changed my tactic to "Ms. Harry! Ms. Harry!"

She turned to me when she reached her car. She looked truly annoyed with me. The bouncer threw his arms out at me. I huffed "The last thing I want to do is HURT her!"

The woman was staring at me...and what had seemed a hostile stare had dissolved into a stunning question on her beautiful face. I never realized how tiny she was. I never grasped how luminous she was. I asked as innocently as I could muster "Can I please take a photo with you?"

She smiled at me and motioned me closer. I turned to find David, my photographer, and nearly bumped noses with him. So with me a sweaty mess, and her makeup redone, wearing a leopard hat, I posed with the woman who reinforced my belief that we blondes can be tough, smart & beautiful at the same time.

I think I was blacking it out. I remember leaning my 5'8" self down to her. I remember the camera going off. I remember handing her my book to sign...and then I think I must have just been staring at her in awe...because she pinched my cheek and said "You are so CUTE!"

Like an underwater experience, I was shuffled to the back of a small throng of admirers. David got a kiss on the cheek and a brief hello, as he has met her many times and she remembered him well.

Debbie got into her waiting car, and fans waved. As she was backing up to leave and fans had left happy, she rolled down her window and waved directly at me...as I was standing there in a stupor on the sidelines. My brain functioned long enough for me to wave back and yell "We love you!"

She blew me a kiss and sped off into the Los Angeles night.

Now let me try to explain this a bit. I have really met a LOT of celebrities while living here in LA. Many of them I admire and was thrilled to meet. But this...THIS...this left me like a starstruck fool. Blondie the band is gregarious, kind, amazing. I've always been one of the fans whose mantra has been "Blondie is a group." I've never discounted the guys on any level. But Debbie Harry has this aura about her. She is an inspiration and a gift to music lovers everywhere. And now, my dear friends, I can die happy.

Rob Roth in limousine with Deborah Harry, who is holding a plush Chi Chi puppy given to her by Mandy Rohr after the performance at G-A-Y club night, The Astoria, London, May 18, 2002
credit: copyright © 2002 Mandy Rohr, Josephin Neumann.

"(Can I) Find the Right Words (to Say)"

by Jon Erkider

I recently ran into a schoolmate of mine from Texas in a New York City bar. After getting over the initial shock of meeting so many years later the first thing he said to me was daunting, "I still remember in 6th grade when the nuns made us learn that song you wrote about Saint Mary Mazzarello using the music to "The Tide is High!..." What?!

Yes, it was true. I was asked to come up with lyrics to be sung during a mass honoring the saint. Rebellious and insurgent from strict school doctrine, I chose the most unconventional song by my favorite band Blondie. "The Tide is High" was #1 and the perfect counterblast to what we were singing in class like "Time in a Bottle" and "Earthen Vessels." The lyrics were projected on to the walls of the church and the entire school sang over the Blondie single during mass! "...the first Salesian Sister of St. John Bosco was Saint Mary Mazzarello...daughter of Joseph and Madelyn Mazzarell o...oh-oh-oh..."

It wasn't the best interpretation of her life but enough to have the entire student body sing it to the Mother Provincial on her visit to our school. I guess everyone was a little nervous or maybe the volume was a little too loud, but you could definitely hear Debbie's voice over ours. As the Mother Provincial sat, so proud and beaming with delight, a line rang out so bold "...every girl wants you to be her man...but I'll wait my dear, til it's my turn..."

Ouch!

Let's just say I was never asked to contribute a song again.

It's amazing how so many people associate you with your idol even after 20 years later. I discovered Blondie in 1979 and if there's one thing that somebody knows about me is my love for Debbie Harry and Blondie. It is a defining, real characteristic that's part of your Identity. Your association is a synonym, a symbolic connection that is complimentary. It's always been that way and it hasn't changed and I know it never will. There is a certain group of people who live their lives in awe and in admiration for a favorite band or pop star. It is nothing puerile or silly or childish. It is an admiration based on true love. Love of Art, love of Music & Lyric and love of Person. It's an esoteric and eclectic group to be a part. And I find the only persons to understand how you might feel are others who love the exact same person or band that you do.

No one writes about these "die-hards," nobody cares to understand them, nobody takes them seriously. Since I was a kid my entire life has been completely influenced by Debbie and Blondie. The idea that an idol may have so much of a hold over someone may seem freakish and outlandish to the masses but it is not. My life has only become more rich and colorful and beautiful because of it. It's a fun thing and it's a good thing. And it's a real, legitimate, existing rock'n'roll manifestation.

I moved to New York from Texas to be close to my heroes—ok, to Debbie Harry. When I discovered Blondie, I discovered a whole new world. Because of them I read about the Ramones and Richard Hell and Johnny Thunders. Growing up I spent all my money on *Creem*, *Rock Scene* and *Hit Parader*. I engulfed anything that had to do with New York and punk, Andy Warhol, Stephen Sprouse, Lou Reed and the Velvet Underground. This obsession only made me yearn to come to the place that all my heroes created Art and called home.

It's very rare that a fan or devotee un-accepts his ardor from afar and makes attempts to come one step closer to the sidelines and fringes of an idol (dare I say friend or contemporary). It's always an unthinkable event, one that's only bemusing in fantasy or daydream. It's a fact that I fell in love, first, with imagery—the beautiful face of Deborah—but eventually fell in love with something that I genuinely find to be an entity that contains some of the best songwriters and musicians of Pop. And of course there is that voice.

Living in New York and being able to see Debbie and Blondie so many times and in so many ways has only made me more of an acolyte. They are no longer just pictures, or video images or voices on record but real, live people. It's a transition your mind eventually makes when you see them do real things, or speak to Debbie and see her smile or frown or twitch or pet her dog. It's magical and magnificent and fulfilling. How many times does a fan really get to come so close to their idols?

We are a small, misunderstood group who share such great love for one woman and one band. Our lives are made up of so much of her and them. Although I'm not trying to incorporate Blondie songs in schools, the influence of Debbie Harry and Blondie still affects me every single day. They are incorporated somehow in my daily life whether it's consciously or not. It may be hard for some to understand or grasp. It may even be unexplainable. Or it may just be that I can't find the right words to say...

"Blondie: 'A New Concept'"

by Scott Coblio
(adapted and edited by Allan Metz)

I was reading an issue of *16 Magazine* one day, and like any self-respecting fourteen year-old, trying to keep up on all the important world news. Most of it was about the Bay City Rollers, Leif Garrett and Andy Gibb, but in the very back in the letters section, a small black and white picture caught my eye. In it, a blonde woman of uncertain age stared blankly at the camera flanked by four men in suits with skinny ties. Somehow it was different from any picture I had ever seen. The woman looked hard and soft at the same time, like Marilyn Monroe if she'd been a gangster's moll and if someone had chiselled all her round features into angular points. The photo was like a puzzle I couldn't solve. Was she young or old? Were they friendly or nasty? Who were these guys? A woman fronting a group of men was still a new concept. Did she sing pretty falsetto folk songs? I didn't even know about punk rock yet. But there was a latent violence behind the placid expressions, and whether it was real or of the "Batman" variety I had yet to learn.

The letter said something to the effect of "...heard this great new group called Blondie, can you tell me more about them?" Hmmmm, Blondie. There was something soothing about the fact that the name conjured up images of comic strips. Maybe they weren't going to rob my parent's house after all. I made a mental note to look for a record as soon as I could save the $5.98.

Well, as the fact that I sit here writing this appreciation 23 years later will attest, I still find the Blondie puzzle to be an unsolvable intrigue. It seems Debbie and the boys are all of the things I wondered about, despite inherent contradictions. Debbie is tough yet tender, young and old, the band was nice and nasty, the music is both conventional and futuristic. Witness the debut album in 1976. Dare, if you will, to remember what Top 40 radio sounded like, then play "X Offender," "In the Sun," or "Rip Her To Shreds." Keep in mind that John Denver, K.C. and the Sunshine Band, the Eagles, etc. were dominating the charts. "Disco Duck" and "Convoy." For women, we had fluffy Olivia Newton-John and the countrified Linda Ronstadt. Sixties retro was so OUT. It hadn't happened yet. But here was Blondie, sounding like a party band that might have opened for the Doors or the Velvet Underground.

I got *Parallel Lines* for my birthday and literally felt my head expand to accommodate space for a little imaginary world where Blondie lived. When life sucked, when school was unbearable, when I wanted to be anything but a fourteen year old from a suburb, I went to Blondie-land. I even slept with headphones on, listening to the albums over and over until the headset would fall off in the wee hours of the morning.

When the band hosted "Midnight Special" in the fall of '79, I was there with my instamatic and tape recorder (in lieu of a VCR?). Debbie had short hair and was mod-looking in her blue Stephen Sprouse minidress and matching tights. At first I didn't like the way she looked. Bed-head for days, and tired! I was expecting something along the lines of the child-woman from the first album or the slick chanteuse from the *Parallel Lines* album cover. But it grew on me. There was something more interesting about a gorgeous woman who's messed up and hiding behind her hair; this was rock and roll! Had she looked as pristine as I'd hoped, she probably would have resembled a singing Playboy centerfold. Slowly I started to appreciate the irony and subtext of the band's imagery, and simultaneously became less of a bumpkin myself.

I followed Blondie religiously through to their demise in 1982 and then Debbie's solo career. Rush, Rush! Coincidentally, I was living in Allentown, PA in 1987 when "Hairspray" was shooting location scenes at the local amusement park. I auditioned to be an extra by singing "Polyester" and got a small part as a newsman. It was a thrill to see Debbie, Divine, Sonny Bono and John Waters all in one place at one time. I couldn't stop staring at Debbie. She looked unreal. I had a chance to talk to her briefly between takes and walked away shaking like a leaf. I was to meet her a handful of times over the years when, later on, I worked for numerous magazines and newspapers and got press passes to photograph Debbie's live shows for "Def Dumb and Blonde." She was always the epitome of grace and charm, even when she had a cold and the greeting lines were ever expanding.

I now work as a video editor in Hollywood, which has again made my path cross with Debbie's. A filmmaking acquaintance I know made his first feature film in 2000 called "The Fluffer" which featured guess who in a cameo role. He knew Debbie was my favorite and let me be an extra in her scene. Once more, we spoke and she was natural, amusing, thoughtful and sincere.

"In the Sun" will always be the quintessential Blondie song for me. It captures the feeling of youthful optimism and longing, with such a surge of energy and excitement that, by the time Debbie's longing for the "pineapple sky" and fading out singing "where is my wave?," I still get goose bumps and a lump in my throat.

"My Favorite Blonde"

by Scott Coblio

Scott also wrote a song about Debbie called "My Favorite Blonde."
Lyrics reprinted with permission.—Ed.

Debbie, all in blue
Debbie, I love you
In your culotte suit, oh-oh
And patent leather boots, oh-oh
You're my favorite blonde, oh I love you oh-oh
Blondie, I love you, oh-oh
Blondie I really do
I can tell what it's all about
I know you're all stressed out
But then you look at me, ah-oh
On black and white TV, ah-oh
I turn the lights out
So it's just you and me, ah-oh
It's just you and me, ah-oh
And you can sing to me
I turn my nightlight on
Then my whole room is gone
And then you look at me, oh-oh
And sing my favorite song, oh-oh
Debbie, Debbie
You can sing all night long, oh-oh
You can sing all night long, oh-oh
You can sing all night long.

"Deborah Harry: 'I'll Send You a Bill'"

by Brian La Fountain

I have had great luck in meeting people who know Debbie and have made arrangements to greet or speak to her at several events. Working with a friend of her father from New York, Frank Bittles, I was able to contact her dad after he was notified and asked that I might chat with him for the fanzines. [*See pp. 152-56—*Ed.].

I was involved in sharing information and updates with Barry L. Kramer and April Kincaid during the pre-www.blondie.net days. Days of fanzines like "Fan Mail" where Barry was the writer/publisher. Now, they work personally with the band and I keep in professional and friendly contact.

I have met Debbie and Blondie members five times and had the pleasure of sitting with Debbie after filming a set of two Jazz Passengers shows in D.C., (she allowed me personally beforehand to videotape two shows) and completing the lifelong ambition of explaining, in an unhurried situation, exactly what she and Blondie have meant to me.

When I explained that she was "The single most therapeutic element to my existence" and that she could never know how much she meant to the young people growing up trying to find themselves and that she gave us the "rules on cool"...she got up from her dressing room chair and put both hands on my shoulders, looked at me and said with a flat expression, then a tweaked smile, "Great, I'll send you a bill!" She then kissed my left cheek.

A gin and tonic and cigarette at the lounge downstairs beside her with her fuzzy-faux-fur (black of course) and shiny silver blouse, she turned around on her high perch at the bar and with the most gracious smile said "Thanks Brian, good night," as I walked out into the rainy night.

Mandy Rohr
Germany
The Blondie Review, Art Issue II, Summer 2002, Copyright © 2002.

411

"...The Greatest High"

by Steve Knight
(edited and adapted by Allan Metz)

Debbie Harry was the greatest influence of my life; even greater than Jesus because she never had to die for anyone's sins and I thought that was great. Debbie Harry is physically the most beautiful woman I have ever seen. I knew that at 14 years old. When she sang "Pretty Baby," I almost died.

I knew what it felt like to be a teenager in the 1960s.

I loved her more than my own mother.

It was all so sexual and it was all so exciting.

Her face was always the greatest high.

Blondie will go down in history as one of the greatest rock bands that ever were—for reasons that are not yet definable.

"An American Icon"

by Steve Knight
(edited and adapted by Allan Metz)

Adapted from e-mail message, Steve Knight to Allan Metz, May 26, 2001.—Ed.

I was skimming your Blondie book web site (www2.drury.edu/ametz/blonbook.htm) and I think it's about time somebody really wrote a book about the band. But as always (as in all the other articles or books) Madonna is a constant comparison to Debbie almost to the point of tedium. Debbie really doesn't need to be compared to her because she came before her and influenced all of us without Madonna. Although I admire Madonna's great confidence, I feel that it belittles Debbie to be compared to her, especially since Debbie is the queen of punk and her ideas and music are completely alien to Madonna's approach to art. The only thing they have in common is blonde hair. Another thing that I always find missing is any opinion or remark concerning the band from their peers such as Heart or Journey or Pat Benatar or their friends—i.e., Mick Jagger or other equally famous people such as Tina Turner or Debbie's idol Ronnie Spector who sat in on a Blondie recording session when Debbie was so nervous being in the same room with her that she couldn't sing. What about Diane Von Furstenburg or Liza Minnelli or Lorna Luft? These people generate a wider reading audience and bring a backbone and weight to the band that they deserve. And there are stories out there. Are they so hard to talk to? And wouldn't you want to interview them? Gwen Stefani and Garbage are nice but their opinions are as light as a feather—hero worship. How about some praise from Patti Smith? Now that would be important stuff if you could get it. How did the AIDS crisis affect Blondie and all the friends they must have lost? I really would like to know what David Bowie thinks of Blondie. Wouldn't you? People have to remember that aside from "Heart of Glass," *Parallel Lines* was a pretty awesome album and Debbie Harry rocked most teenage boys and girls at the height of disco in a way no woman had before. It was the end of the 70's and Blondie rang out the new era with a big resounding bell and everything changed after them. It was Debbie Harry's face singing that fucking great "Hanging on the Telephone." No more Fleetwood Mac, no more Led Zeppelin. After that it was Devo, Gary Numan, the Vapors, new wave. It wasn't David Bowie or the New York Dolls or Television (Blondie loves these people so much that they give them credit) but it was *Blondie* who broke into the mainstream. They changed music forever. *They put a big crack in the sidewalk and let out all the steam.* I remember. I was 13 years old. It saved my life. Their influence is astounding. Everyone has them to thank, even David Bowie for his comeback. He couldn't have done it without their influence. There's so much more to that band than the same old story. The history of that band is a made-for-TV movie, a great American novel, a heroic and epic love story. Debbie Harry is an American icon.

"Who I Admire"

by Dan Lideen

Dan is a very articulate high school student, who was a sophomore when he wrote this essay. As Dan explains it: "I had to write a 150 word literature essay about someone who I admire. So I picked...you guessed it, Debbie Harry. I wanted to share...my essay." What follows is the original essay with some additional material.—Ed.

"Dreaming...dreaming is free." This is a quote from a song by a band that I truly follow, called Blondie. But the person I admire most is the band's lead singer, Debbie Harry. Blondie may date back to the 70s, but they're still around today and Debbie Harry still carries a special charm that compels me to admire her.

I can't really describe what it is. If you calculated her age (55, going on 56 in July), you'd say she's old enough to be my grandma. But because of her hip attitude, glamorous image, and influential voice, you'd have no idea that this woman was a day over 30.

Perhaps it's her way of making songs. I have probably heard every Blondie song at least 100 times and I still can't get enough of her voice. Each song means something different. There's one in particular from her first solo album, *Koo Koo*, that I find very descriptive regarding her judgment of other individuals. In the song "Backfired," Debbie gives advice to others on how you should just ignore the ones that annoy you. "Who needs it?" (From the song "Nothing Is Real But the Girl" from the Blondie album *No Exit*).

It may be the way that she makes things look so simple. I have Blondie's first reunion concert in more than 16 years on the *Blondie Live* DVD. The way the band performs, you'd think you were in a time warp because of their youthful image that projects them to look as if they were in their 20s and 30s. There is one song in the concert, "Shayla," where Debbie simply stands there singing and makes it look so simple, you would believe that she was just talking to you. Her facial expressions made it appear that there's nothing to it and that life is worth living.

Maybe that's why I admire her. She makes a good impression. Converting herself into a pop icon was like building a character, so I've read in various sources. Ruined hair bleach jobs, and only bleaching the front and sides of her hair no less, would normally appear odd in society. But somehow, it worked beautifully, and it made a strong statement in the fashion industry. The impression she projects makes you want to be just as good as her–good-looking, fun, and musically talented. She makes you want to set a personal goal for yourself, and then go accomplish it. Don't wait around for something to happen.

Debbie Harry makes me feel so good about myself, and I'm sure she's touched many others also. I'm not quite sure what I'll do when she no longer is in the limelight, but she has definitely shown us that "dreaming is free." And that is so true.

Josephin Neumann
Germany
The Blondie Review, Art Issue II, Summer 2002, Copyright © 2002.

"blondie: 'nyc a-go-go...'"

by John Sibby

nyc a-go-go prime time circa 76-77
.

my first encounter with blondie's strikingly surreal lead singer debbie harry was at first glance much different than i had perceived her through vinyl and celluloid, once past the obvious sexual overtones.

debbie somehow reminds one of any number of women you 'could' have normally encountered
...but 'never' did.

this aura embodied within the band's music was the vehicle for her reality.

this privileged glimpse into this disproportional existence is virtually impossible to translate any other way
but up close...in person...

it is this very presence that has entranced me to pursue this euphoria producing reality
and peer into this realm time and time again...

life expectancy of pivotal bands is bleak and resurgence of one is usually null and void
...until now...

blondie's music encompasses my being...who I am...a fragmented passing glance through the corridors of time
provoking memories...creating new ones...—september 2000

Graphics designed by Robert Betts for *The Blondie Review,* issue #3, June, 2001 and Special Art Issue, Fall 2001.

Appendices

The Blondie Genealogy

Ancestor Bands of Blondie

researched and compiled by Robert Betts

This title originally appeared in The Blondie Review, *Issue 3, June 2001.*—Ed.

Wind In The Willows
Early 1962–Late 1968
Baroque folk-rock. Recorded a self-titled, one-hit wonder.
Debbie Harry, Paul Klein, Peter Britain, Steve DePhillips, Gil Fields, Ida Andrews, Wayne Kirby, Harris Wiener

Uni Trio
1966
A Saint Marks' jazz group. Debbie played with escaped convict Tox Strothhaw in this trio.

F.N.U.C. & B. (First National Unaphrenic Church & Bank)
Late 1966–Early 1967
Deborah and company played on Bob Fass' Show, WBAI (NYC) Experimental "Terry Riley" type freak jazz.

Morticians
1965–1966
Chris played for this Brooklyn band as did George Cameron who joined The Left Banke ("Walk Away Renee").

First Crow On The Moon (aka The Bootleggers)
1967
Chris joined this band and played local gigs at the Crazy Horse on Bleecker Street and opened for the Velvet Underground.

World War III
Early 1970
Frank Infante left them for Blondie #4

Luger
1972–Early 1974
Ivan Kral left them for Blondie #2.

Magic Tramps
1973
After being in art school, Chris joined this band for a short while before being drawn to the Stilettos.

Pure Garbage
Late 1972–Early 1973
Deb tried to join this band, but they broke up. She met Elda Gentile there.

Stillettoes (variously spelled as Stilettos, Stilettoes, Stillettos)
October 1973–August 1974
A significant period for Deb and Chris.
Other members included Elda Gentile, Amanda Jones, Rosie Ross, Billy O'Connor and Fred Smith

Total Environment
1973–1974
Clem played Carnegie Hall in a Cousin Brucie "Battle Of The Bands" gig called "Big Break."

Sweet Revenge
1974–1975
Clem left this group for Blondie #2.

Knickers
January 1975–December 1975
Jimmy Destri came from here to join Blondie #3.

Know
Feb 1978–?
Gary Valentine joined this band after leaving Blondie #3.

Farm, Smokey Rice Blues Band, Silverhead, Ray Manzarek (formerly of the Doors) with Hunt and Tony Sales—Nigel Harrison's resume until Blondie #5.

The Blondie Chronology

A Heritage of Six Generations in Four Decades

researched and compiled by Robert Betts

This title originally appeared in The Blondie Review, *Issue 3, June 2001 in an abbreviated form. Most of the other material based on and adapted from* rockonthenet.com *web site, 1999-2001, including additional material supplied by Allan Metz.*—Ed.

CURRENT MEMBERS: Deborah Harry, Chris Stein, Clem Burke, and Jimmy Destri

BIRTHDAYS: Deborah Harry (July 1, 1945)
Chris Stein (January 5, 1950)
Jimmy Destri (April 13, 1954)
Clement Burke (November 24, 1955)

RECORD LABEL: BMG / Beyond

BIGGEST SINGLE: "Call Me" (1980)

BIGGEST LP: *Parallel Lines* (1978)

FACTOID: Rock 'N' Roll Hall Of Fame's 500 Songs That Shaped Rock And Roll includes "Heart Of Glass."

QUOTE: "We're a pop art band. Not a pop band."—*Chris Stein, 1999 (Source: Freydkin)*

CAPSULE BIO

Blondie was one of the few "new wave" bands that grew out of the punk sound of the 70s and found pop and alternative success in the 80s. Blondie consisted of Deborah Harry (vocals), Chris Stein (on guitar), Frank Infante (on guitar), Clement Burke (on drums), Gary Valentine (on bass until replaced by Infante), Nigel Harrison (on bass), and James Destri (on keyboards). The band formed in New York in 1974 after Harry left a folk-rock group called Wind In The Willows (she had previously been in a band called The Stillettoes where she met Stein). The Blondie band name is said to have come from what truck drivers used to call Harry when she walked by.

SIX "GENERATIONS" OF BLONDIE

The more-than-casual fan with bookshelves full of DH/B reference material will recognize that the "dates" presented here vary slightly from one writer to another. Casual writing has no place in archival documentation. Consequently, we have chosen to go to more official sources. Since most of the band personnel changes didn't happened instantly, but rather over several weeks or more, depending on tours, gig dates and contractual arrangements, the "official" dates have been kept somewhat general. Therefore a good common area during the different transitions is generally believed to be suitable for appropriate dates; in this case, within one month. We believe the most accurate and best suitable dates can be taken from the work of Pete Frame with assistance from Kris Needs. Pete was enlisted to write in the official *Blondie Gift Book* of 1980. He presents a rather extensive and accurate Blondie chronology which he titled *The Blondie Family Tree*. Other reliable sources were referred to for comparison of accuracy and details.—Ed.

1st "Generation"—August 1974–October 1974
Debbie Harry, Chris Stein, Billy O'Connor. Fred Smith, Jackie, Julie

Debbie took half the Stillettoes to start this group. Their first two gigs at CBGB's was under the name of Angel and the Snake. Apparently a Chris and Debbie creation. Another early name was Blondie and the Banzai Babies. Thereafter and henceforth, the band was to be Blondie. Debbie, Julie and Jackie were all blondes until Jackie dyed her hair brown early on.

2nd "Generation"—October 1974–August 1975
Debbie Harry, Chris Stein, Clem Burke, Billy O'Connor, Fred Smith, Ivan Kral, Snooky and Tish Bellomo

Blondie cut their first demos in NYC with Alan Betrock. Ivan left the band in December and Fred left in May. Tish and Snooky went off to ultimately create a costume and cosmetics empire on St. Mark's Place in lower Manhattan—Manic Panic. Ivan never performed with the Bellomo sisters, Tish and Snooky, and stayed with the band for only three months. Clem's first gig was May 1975. Fred left the same month.

3rd "Generation"—August 1975–August 1977
Debbie Harry, Chris Stein, Clem Burke, Jimmy Destri, Gary Valentine

Gary joined in August, Jimmy in October. Richard Gottehrer secured a contract with Private Stock. Blondie was the third New York, New Wave, band to sign a recording contract. "X Offender" (single) and the album *Blondie* was produced at Plaza Sound. Album release: Private Stock, Feb. 77; Chrysalis, Nov, 77.

4th "Generation"—August 1977–November 1977
Debbie Harry, Chris Stein, Clem Burke, Jimmy Destri, Frank Infante

A very important 3 months. Chrysalis buys out Blondie's contract. *Plastic Letters* is recorded. The band goes on a Los Angeles tour. Fandom grows. New York Punk and New Wave from Blondie is immediately accepted on the West Coast. Tours are seriously discussed along with thoughts for future albums.

5th "Generation"—November 1977–early 1980s
Debbie Harry, Chris Stein, Clem Burke, Jimmy Destri, Frank Infante, Nigel Harrison

Major Australia and Japan tours. Chrysalis re-releases *Blondie. Parallel Lines* is released. *Eat To The Beat* is released. Nigel joins, takes bass position. No official breakup date was ever established. There was no official Blondie breakup, so there is no real breakup date. The last thing they did together was *The Hunter* tour, so one could say it happened at the end of that tour. It should be noted that Blondie Music, their publishing company, has never ceased to exist.

6th "Generation"—1995/1996+
Deborah Harry, Chris Stein, Clem Burke, Jimmy Destri, Leigh Foxx, Paul Carbonara

Leigh on bass, Paul on guitar for the reunion tours and TV shows. As with the breakup, there is no official reunion date. The reunion really happened in stages with the reorganization of the band members, management preparations, recording schedules, TV guest arrangements, tour plans, print and broadcast media promotions, etc.

The first discussions about the Blondie reunion took place in late 1995. Two demos, "Mine" by Jimmy Destri (still unreleased) and "Colorado" by Chris Stein (later released on *No Exit* as "Under the Gun"), were produced with Mike Chapman in mid-1996. The first Blondie reunion shows took place in 1997, starting with the HFStival '97 in Washington DC on May 31 and the 104fest, Riverside Park, Agawam, Massachusetts on June 1. These appearances were followed up in 1998 by additional shows and an international tour. See also "Time Line" on pp. 419–420.

TIME LINE

1976

Blondie released their first LP, *Blondie.*

1977

Blondie released *Plastic Letters* and had their Top U.K. hits with "Denis" and "(I'm Always Touched By Your) Presence, Dear." The same year, Blondie toured with Iggy Pop in the U.S.

1978

SEPTEMBER — It was Blondie's third LP, *Parallel Lines,* that got the band noticed in the U.S. and around the world. In the U.K., Blondie had more hits with the tracks "Picture This" and "Hanging On The Telephone" and, in the U.S., the alternative-disco hit "Heart Of Glass" went all the way to #1. Additional hits from the LP included "One Way Or Another" and "Sunday Girl." *Parallel Lines* was later ranked as the 52nd among the Greatest Albums of All-Time by *New Musical Express* (NME) and sold over 20 million copies worldwide.

1979

APRIL — Both *Parallel Lines* and the single "Heart Of Glass" were certified gold.

JUNE — *Parallel Lines* was certified platinum.
Eat To The Beat was released with the hits "Atomic," "Dreaming" and "Union City Blue." Blondie had their biggest pop success with the release of the single "Call Me" from the film, *American Gigolo.*

1980

FEBRUARY — *Eat To The Beat* was certified gold.
"Call Me" hit #1 and became the biggest single of 1980.

APRIL — The single "Call Me" was certified gold.

JULY — *Eat To The Beat* was certified platinum.
Blondie released *Autoamerican,* which gave them their third and fourth #1 songs in the U.S. with "The Tide Is High" and "Rapture."

1981

JANUARY — *Autoamerican* was certified platinum and the single "The Tide Is High" was certified gold.

MARCH — The single "Rapture" was certified gold.
By 1981 Blondie became more distracted as a group with work on individual projects and a lawsuit from band member Frank Infante (because "he had been left out of band discussions" regarding their future). Also during the year, Stein was diagnosed with the genetic disease, pemphigus, which is often fatal.

OCTOBER — *The Best Of Blondie* was released and Debbie's solo effort *Koo Koo* was certified gold.

1982

FEBRUARY — *The Best Of Blondie* was certified gold.
Blondie's success had faded with the release of *The Hunter.* Tracks such as "Island Of Lost Souls" and "War Child" were mild hits in the U.S. and the U.K. The band (un)officially called it quits when Stein had serious health problems. Debbie Harry continued to pursue a solo career while also caring for her companion, Stein.

1980s/1990s

Over the years since Blondie had broken up, several compilation LPs have been released including: *Once More Into The Bleach* (1988), *Blonde And Beyond* (1993) which contains unreleased, live, and remastered tracks, *The Platinum Collection* (1994), and *The Remix Project—Remixed Remade Remodeled* (1995). Debbie Harry has gone on to release 4 solo LPs: *Koo Koo* (1981), *Rockbird* (1986), *Def Dumb And Blonde* (1989), and *Debravation* (1993). In 1996, Stein began the process of regrouping Blondie for a comeback and contacted Destri, who was then producing, and Burke, who was working as a session musician. *Rolling Stone's* "The 100 Top Music Videos" includes "Rapture" at # 82.

1998

APRIL — It was announced that Debbie Harry and the gang of Blondie were back in the studio for a new LP. *Billboard* reported that only Harry, Stein, Burke, and Destri would regroup for the new LP, *No Exit.* Originally the intent was to get together to perform a few new tracks for a greatest hits collection. But instead, the makings of a brand new LP was in the works. Ed Thomas, Blondie's manager, said: "'They feel like greatest hits albums are made by bands that are trying to make a comeback...This is not a reunion, this is Blondie chapter three—or two depending on who you ask.'"— (source: *Anni Layne*, Rolling Stone, *posted on the "American On-Line" news service, April 29, 1998*)

1999

Blondie is #84 Singles Artist of the Year for "Maria."

FEBRUARY   Blondie's new LP, *No Exit,* was released and featured the first single "Maria" which already had topped the charts in England. When Blondie talked with MTV, the focus was on Harry's groundbreaking role as a woman fronting a rock band in the 70s: Destri commented: "She opened the floodgates kids" and Stein said "The male rock establishment, the male rock critical establishment was really sexist back in those days...and she got knocked very heavily for selling her sexuality..."

MARCH   Blondie returned to the Top 40 with "Maria." Stein told CNN: "It's a continuation. It feels like we were in the studio for 16 years. It was bottled up and this album was an outpouring." Burke added: "We have more acceptance and credibility from being away for so long. Our songs have have a life of their own. It's like having a career without having a career" (source: Freydkin). Harry told *Rolling Stone* that the title for their LP "...has to do with the fact that no matter where we go, we're Blondie. There was no exit for any of us not being identified with Blondie." *The Best Of Blondie* was certified platinum.

JUNE   Blondie performed at the Tibetan Freedom Concert.

JULY   Deborah Harry was ranked #12 on VH1's "The 100 Greatest Women of Rock 'N' Roll."
And in a parallel VH1 fan survey, Harry was ranked #6, even ahead of Madonna who came in at #7.

NOVEMBER   Blondie released a live LP, *Blondie Live*, featuring 19 tracks.
The Advocate named Harry as one of the "25 Coolest Women."

2000

In contrast to a busy 1999, the year 2000 represented down time for Blondie in terms of recording and touring, although some preliminary work had been done on the band's next album scheduled for release in 2002.

Deborah Harry was reportedly involved in a number of film projects such as "Firecracker," "Deuces Wild," "The Tulse Luper Suitcase" (also starring Madonna), "The Fluffer" and "Red Lipstick."

OCTOBER   VH1's "100 Greatest Dance Songs" included Blondie's "Heart Of Glass" at #79.

2001

Q magazine ranked Blondie's *Parallel Lines* at #16 among "The 100 Best Record Covers of All Time."
A *Maxim* magazine poll of the 1000 sexiest women ever included Deborah Harry at #178.

MAY   VH1's "100 Greatest Videos of All Time" included "Rapture" at #91.

JUNE   *Parallel Lines* is among "Shirley Manson's 10 Essential Women's Rock Albums" according to *Alternative Press (AP)* magazine.

SEPTEMBER   Rerelease of six remastered Blondie albums with bonus tracks: *Autoamerican, Blondie, Eat To The Beat, Parallel Lines, Plastic Letters, The Hunter.*

FALL   Deborah Harry selected as one of the "100 Essential Women in Music" in *Women Who Rock* magazine's Fall 2001 issue.
Feature article on Deborah Harry and Blondie's style and sense of fashion in *Detour* magazine's Fall Fashion 2001 issue.
Profile of Deborah Harry in "Notorious: The Legends Issue," *Nylon* magazine, September 2001 issue.
Chris Stein and Deborah Harry among the artists featured in "The Music Issue," *Vanity Fair,* November 2001.
Profile of Deborah Harry by Cathay Che in *The Advocate*'s December 4, 2001 issue.
Q magazine conducted a poll for the "Top 100 Women Who Rock Your World"— Deborah ranked #6.

2002

JANUARY   A photograph of Deborah Harry taken by Chris Stein (Vultures, baby dolls photo) is ranked fifth among *Q* magazine's 100 Greatest Rock 'n' Roll Photographs of all time.

Spin magazine ranks Blondie 37th among the 50 greatest bands of all time in its February 2002 issue. Go-Go's, Bangles, Garbage, No Doubt, and Pink cited as being influenced by Blondie. *Parallel Lines* named Blondie's "classic album."

FEBRUARY   *Parallel Lines* ranked #7 among the "Greatest American Albums of All Time" in *Blender* magazine's February-March issue.
Deborah Harry interview of NYC band, the Strokes, in *Interview* magazine's March issue.

MARCH   Deborah Harry and Chris Stein featured on the "Musicians" series, Bravo cable network, March 11.

Life magazine's countdown of "The Top 100 Rock & Rollers of All Time" included Blondie at #43 in its *Rock & Roll at 50* special issue, March 11, 2002.

Deborah Harry is among those featured in "Downtown Girls," a gallery-format article on the contemporary NYC music scene, in the March 17, 2002 issue of the *New York Times Magazine.* Also includes, among others, Laurie Anderson, Foxy Brown, Kim Gordon (of Sonic Youth), and Suzanne Vega.

For continuous Blondie news updates, see *The Blondie Review (TBR),* the DHBIS discussion list, Blondie.net, and *Picture This (PT).*

Selected Blondie Album Discography
(With Album Tracks)

Adapted from links on a former web page: The Blondie Home Page—Deborah Harry *and* Blondie: Discography —*maintained by Louis A Bustamante.*—Ed.

Blondie. 1976
1. X Offender
2. Little Girl Lies
3. In The Flesh
4. Look Good In Blue
5. In The Sun
6. A Shark In Jet's Clothing
7. Man Overboard
8. Rip Her To Shreds
9. Rifle Range
10. Kung Fu Girls
11. The Attack Of The Giant Ants

Plastic Letters. 1977
1. Fan Mail
2. Denis
3. Bermuda Triangle Blues (Flight 45)
4. Youth Nabbed As Sniper
5. Contact In Red Square
6. (I'm Always Touched By Your) Presence, Dear
7. I'm On E
8. I Didn't Have The Nerve To Say No
9. Love At The Pier
10. No Imagination
11. Kidnapper
12. Detroit 442
13. Cautious Lip

Parallel Lines. 1978
1. Hanging On The Telephone
2. One Way or Another
3. Picture This
4. Fade Away And Radiate
5. Pretty Baby
6. I Know But I Don't Know
7. 11:59
8. Will Anything Happen?
9. Sunday Girl
10. Heart of Glass
11. I'm Gonna Love You Too
12. Just Go Away

Eat to the Beat. 1979
1. Dreaming
2. The Hardest Part
3. Union City Blue
4. Shayla
5. Eat To The Beat
6. Accidents Never Happen
7. Die Young Stay Pretty
8. Slow Motion
9. Atomic
10. Sound-A-Sleep
11. Victor
12. Living In The Real World

Autoamerican. 1980
1. Europa
2. Live It Up
3. Here's Looking At You
4. The Tide Is High
5. Angels On The Balcony
6. Go Through It
7. Do The Dark
8. Rapture
9. Faces
10. T-Birds
11. Walk Like Me
12. Follow Me

Best of Blondie (compilation album). 1981
1. Heart Of Glass (Best Of Blondie Mix)
2. Dreaming
3. The Tide Is High
4. In The Flesh (Best Of Blondie Mix)
5. Sunday Girl (Best Of Blondie Mix)
6. Hanging On The Telephone
7. Rapture (Original Promo Single Version)
8. One Way Or Another
9. (I'm Always Touched By Your) Presence, Dear
10. Call Me (Theme From American Gigolo) (Single Version)
11. Atomic
12. Rip Her To Shreds

The Hunter. 1982
1. Orchid Club
2. Island Of Lost Souls
3. Dragonfly
4. For Your Eyes Only
5. The Beast
6. War Child
7. Little Caesar
8. Danceway
9. (Can I) Find The Right Words (To Say)
10. English Boys
11. The Hunter Gets Captured By The Game

Blondie: Blonde And Beyond (compilation album). 1993
1. Underground Girl
2. English Boys
3. Sunday Girl (French Version)
4. Susie And Jeffrey
5. Shayla
6. Denis
7. X Offender
8. Poet's Problem
9. Scenery
10. Picture This
11. Angels On The Balcony
12. Once I Had A Love (Blonde And Beyond Version)
13. I'm Gonna Love You Too
14. Island Of Lost Souls
15. Call Me (Spanish Version)
16. Heart Of Glass (Disco Version)
17. Ring Of Fire (Live)
18. Bang A Gong (Get It On) (Live)
19. Heroes (Live)

Blondie: The Platinum Collection (Disc 1). 1994
1. X Offender
2. In The Flesh
3. Man Overboard
4. Rip Her To Shreds
5. Denis
6. Contact In Red Square
7. Kung Fu Girls
8. I'm On E
9. (I'm Always Touched By Your) Presence, Dear
10. Poet's Problem
11. Detroit 442
12. Picture This
13. Fade Away And Radiate
14. I'm Gonna Love You Too
15. Just Go Away
16. Hanging On The Telephone
17. Will Anything Happen
18. Heart Of Glass (Original Single Version)
19. Rifle Range
20. 11:59
21. Sunday Girl
22. I Know But I Don't Know
23. One Way Or Another (Original Single Version)
24. Dreaming
25. Sound-A-Sleep
26. Living In The Real World

Blondie: The Platinum Collection (Disc 2). 1994
1. Union City Blue
2. The Hardest Part
3. Atomic (Original Single Version)
4. Die Young Stay Pretty
5. Slow Motion
6. Call Me (Theme From American Gigolo) (Original Single Version)
7. The Tide Is High (Original Single Version)
8. Susie And Jeffrey
9. Rapture (Original Promo Single Version)
10. Walk Like Me
11. Island Of Lost Souls (Original Single Version)
12. Dragonfly

13. War Child
14. Little Caesar
15. Out In The Streets
16. Platinum Blonde
17. The Thin Line
18. Puerto Rico
19. Once I Had A Love
20. Atomic (Diddy Remix)
21. Rapture (K-klass Remix)

Blondie: Picture This Live. 1997
1. Dreaming (Live in Dallas 1980)
2. In The Sun (Live in Dallas 1980)
3. Hanging On The Telephone (Live in Dallas 1980)
4. You Look Good In Blue (Live in Dallas 1980)
5. Slow Motion (Live in Dallas 1980)
6. Sunday Girl (Live in Dallas 1980)
7. X-Offender (Live in Philadelphia 1978)
8. Picture This (Live in Philadelphia 1978)
9. Denis (Live in Philadelphia 1978)
10. Fade Away And Radiate (Live in Philadelphia 1978)
11. A Shark In Jet's Clothing/I Know But I Don't Know (Live in Philadelphia 1978)
12. One Way Or Another (Live in Philadelphia 1978)
13. Heart Of Glass (Live in Dallas 1980)
14. 11:59 (Live in Dallas 1980)
15. Bang A Gong/Funtime (Live in Dallas 1980)

No Exit. 1999
1. Screaming Skin
2. Forgive And Forget
3. Maria
4. No Exit
5. Double Take
6. Nothing Is Real But The Girl
7. Boom Boom In The Zoom Zoom Room
8. Night Wind Sent
9. Under The Gun
10. Out In The Streets
11. Happy Dog (For Caggy)
12. The Dream's Lost On Me
13. Divine
14. Dig Up The Conjo

Blondie Live. 1999
1. Dreaming
2. Hanging on the Telephone
3. Screaming Skin
4. Atomic
5. Forgive And Forget
6. The Tide is High
7. Shayla
8. Sunday Girl
9. Maria
10. Call Me
11. Under The Gun
12. Rapture
13. Rip Her To Shreds
14. X Offender
15. No Exit
16. Heart of Glass

Bonus Track
17. One Way or Another ("Snoops" theme song)

"Louis A Bustamante: From Our LAB to Your Home: An Exclusive Interview"

by Robert Betts
(adapted by Allan Metz)

Reprint of an interview first published in The Blondie Review (TBR), *June 2001—*Ed.

He is seemingly tireless. If I didn't know better I'd swear that all he had to do was sit at his Mac and maintain four Deborah Harry/Blondie related e-mail reflector groups, his own multi-topic Tiki Lab list and web site, and along with Barry L. Kramer, the Official Blondie web site. I can't imagine how he finds the time, but Louis A Bustamante really does have a life. He is involved in several other projects, has other hobbies and— interests. But, it's for the DHBIS (and spin-off lists) that I, along with hundreds of others, are grateful. I know my life is indescribably richer for it. From there I get much of my current news and information, great pictures, new ideas and have made scores of new friends. Think about it—without that list, how would we possibly all know each other? How would we stay informed on the latest things the Blondies are doing? How would we ever get our daily fix of bleach? I question if there would be a TBR today if it weren't for "the list." Read about our little visit. You'll learn a lot about the guy who has brought so much to so many— my friend, Louis.

The Blondie Review: Louis, you are known to scores of online DH/B fans as the guy who keeps us all together, informed of the latest DH/B news and events, and encourages all the little fun things like interest polls as the moderator of the DHBIS mailing list (www.deborahharry.com). I'm sure you have another life. Tell us about your occupation and interests outside the world of DH/B.

Louis A Bustamante: I have a web design business that keeps me very busy. I also do photography and some graphic design, and I've created a whole range of characters with elaborate backgrounds that I would like to eventually spin off into cartoons, action figures, comics, etc. I am currently selling t-shirts of some of the characters online and you can currently see them hosting different pages on my web site. They are all members of a comic strip I used to do before I got involved with the DHBIS.

I also write and record my own music. I used to be in a band a long time ago called Chernobyl Cocktail, now I am working on a solo album titled "Car Cola Cola." I would like to concentrate more on music and collaborate with other musicians in the future.

As for outside interests, I guess the work I do is what's most interesting. I like typical stuff...going to see movies, hanging out with my friends, going out on the occasional date, that kind of thing. I like to travel. I'd like to see more of the world.

TBR: What other music groups you listen to?

LAB: I like a variety of music. My teenage years were from 1979 through 1985, so of course I like a lot of "80s bands"—a label which is not quite accurate because a lot of them have gone on to new things, which are just as good. And I have a ton of singles of all sorts. I'm a big pop fan. A typical stack of CDs on my stereo would include: Garbage, the Art Of Noise, the Toilet Boys, Nick Laird-Clowes (The Dream Academy, TrashMonk), a lot of disco, HI NRG, house music, Bananarama, gee, this is hard...My Bloody Valentine, a lot of film music, Nina Hagen, Boy George, Catherine Wheel, Ella Fitzgerald, the B-52's, Jayne County, Yma Sumac, Luscious Jackson, Pizzicatto Five, Dead or Alive, Iggy Pop, The Pretenders, Pet Shop Boys, Sonic Youth, Nick Heyward...the list goes on.

TBR: You are obviously a busy guy. I know that you maintain and moderate several e-mail reflector groups [information available at www.tikilab.com under "Mailing Lists,"—Ed.], your own web site and do a majority of the work for the Official Blondie site (www.blondie.net). Is that it, or is there something I'm missing?

LAB: Well, Barry and I split the work on blondie.net. I also design web sites for other people. I just got done doing a site for Teresa R. Hale (www.t-rae.net), which is all about her photography of Martha Davis and The Motels. And I just completed work on a movie called "Prude" for adhdfilms.com and I'm hoping to do more work with them.

TBR: When I joined the list, you were already in place. How long have you been doing this?

LAB: Gee, I can't remember! I've been a fan of Blondie since I was 12 years old, so I guess you could say I have been doing this in some capacity since 1978. I had the Deborah Harry Home Page web site up sometime in 1994-1995. I started it because I'd just discovered the World Wide Web and couldn't believe Debbie didn't already have a site up! I think it was that same year I took over the DHBIS, but I'd have to look through my backups to remember the exact date. I took over the list because the original owner had said to the members that it was too much work and he needed a replacement. I think it had been online about a year before that.

When I took over the list, it was literally a list of e-mail addresses, and I'd send out every post by hand to the entire list. If someone sent a post in, I'd copy the post to a new e-mail, copy the list of people to the "BCC" field, and mail it off. Obviously sometimes it was not an immediate send! I'd do it a few times a day or whenever I had a few minutes to spare. After that, I looked into getting an automatic mailing system with my ISP, and the "Majordomo Era" came into being. That was much, much easier and I just moderated the list. After I started the web page, I met Barry L. Kramer, who is an amazingly smart guy and knows EVERYTHING there is to know about Debbie Harry. Later, he and April Kincaid made it possible for me to start work on the Official Blondie web site. Eventually, I added some co-moderators and we changed over to a free list web site for the list, mostly due to the cost of the Majordomo list. I then upgraded to a cable modem for faster access to the list and the net in general. Ironically, I now pay more for my cable modem connection than I did for the list during the "Majordomo Era"!

TBR: Going to the very, very bottom line...what do you feel is the final purpose or result from the DHBIS and the other lists?

LAB: My original goal was to let other fans know that we were out there. When I first got on the net, there were no mailing lists or web pages on Deborah Harry. I had been talking to fans through the Prodigy system, using a friend's account. Debbie was solo at the time, so I started the Deborah Harry Home Page in order to get in touch with other fans. Later the DHBIS and DHHP became part of the same project, and I hooked up with Barry and his Debbie Harry Collector's Society (www.debbieharry.net). Blondie reformed, then came www.blondie.net, and that's how we got where we are today.

TBR: I think this is a silly question, but I have to do it: What do you get from all those efforts that cost money and personal hours to maintain?

LAB: I like to meet other fans and share our love and appreciation of a very talented individual and her very talented friends. I have met some truly unique and beautiful people through doing this, and I've gotten into some very interesting situations. Plus, I get to give something back to the members of Blondie, who I consider the most perfect rock band of all time. So it's worth it, I think.

TBR: Tell me who you admire, both professionally and by acquaintance, for their accomplishments, and why.

LAB: I admire my mother most of all. She's survived through a very difficult time. My father passed away suddenly five years ago, and they had been married for 30 years, so of course it was a huge blow to her. She grew up in the era when women were not encouraged to be independent, and she was pretty used to that role, but she is managing to continue on with her life, even though it's extremely difficult for her. So that's very inspiring.

Musically, I really admire the members of Blondie, of course! And composer/arranger Carl Stalling, from the Warner Brothers cartoons of the '30s through the '50s. He broke every rule concerning film

424

composition and was a real genius. No one's come close to him since.

TBR: What was your most memorable meeting with Deborah or any of the Blondies?

LAB: I'd have to say the second time I met Debbie. The first time was at a radio station and she were so rushed that she barely had time to sign an autograph for me (but she did).

The second time was at the Long Beach Gay Pride festival in 1996. Debbie had seen the web site by that time and she liked it so much, she pointed me out during the show as her "web Master" (an intentional naughty play on words), then soon after dramatically removed the blonde wig she'd been wearing while she sang and handed it to me (this was during her brunette *Debravation* phase). Unfortunately, the wig was stolen from me in the crowd. I fought like heck to hold onto it but it was way too crowded and I lost it. Debbie even stopped singing and was yelling at the guy through her microphone "Hey, give it back you jerk!". It must have been pretty funny to see.

Later, backstage we talked for a while and she posed for pictures and kissed me three different times! And when she asked me "They got the wig, huh?" and I pouted "Yes..." with very sad eyes, she pulled my head up and said "Don't worry, we'll get you another one." She was so sweet. However, I have to say, Debbie, I'm still waiting on that second wig!

TBR: I'm not decisive enough to do this, but would you tell me, either one or more, of your favorite Blondie albums? Solo albums? Singles? Remixes?

LAB: Well this changes every once in a while, but...

Blondie album—*Autoamerican*
Solo album—*Debravation*
Blondie single—"X Offender"
Solo single—"Sweet And Low"
Remix—"Atomic" (Diddy Mix), "Dreaming" (The Sub-Urban Mix) or "Union City Blue" (OPM Poppy Mix)

TBR: Same question, but movies.

LAB: My favorite Debbie movie is probably "Union City." I also liked her in "Intimate Stranger" but the actual movie is just OK. I think her best acting is probably in "Heavy."

TBR: What's in the future for "Listers"?

LAB: That depends on the "Listers"...I am open to suggestions!

TBR: Where does Louis Bustamante want to be a year from now in his endeavors?

LAB: I'd like to be doing something musical, continue with my artwork, and maybe live in a bigger city for a while, like New York or San Francisco.

TBR: For selfish reasons, I hope it's New York. Anyhow, and finally, is there anything you'd like to say to the readers?

LAB: Thanks for all the support I've received over the years and special thanks to Barry L. Kramer, Chris Stein, all the other moderators on the list, and of course, Debbie Harry. And for anyone not on the list, try it, you'll like it!

*   *   *

Editor's Note: If you are not a current subscriber to one of Louis' many e-mail reflector lists, but consider yourself a Blondie fan, you really owe it to yourself to go to his web site (www.tikilab.com) and see what you are missing. Besides the usual news, opinions and gems of information from Blondie's past at the DHBIS (information service), there are some really great pictures of Deborah and the boys to be downloaded at the DHBPL (picture list). If you think your lifestyle is too busy to read all those terrific posts every day, Louis has thoughtfully created the DHBNL (News List) which forwards only the news and event information posts from the parent DHBIS list. It's all free. More than half a thousand fans can't be wrong; try it, you'll be in good company.

Gerard Kuipers
Netherlands
The Blondie Review, Art Issue, Fall 2001, Copyright © 2001

"'Plastic Letters' Photo Exhibit Review: 'the downtown gotham blondie concert photos'"

by Eric Wiener
(Adapted and edited by Allan Metz)

East Village/About.com *web site, 2000*

Review of Joe Ryan's "Plastic Letters" photo exhibit, Starbucks, Astor Place, New York City, February 2000.—Ed.

"Plastic Letters" is a nineteen piece display focusing on both of Blondie's performances in New York City in 1999. Images from The Town Hall and Madison Square Garden concerts recount the band's triumphant return to their hometown. These framed photos are available for sale by the photographer. (See Joe Ryan's web site at www.gratefuljoe.com for more details).

If you need a good excuse to go grab a cup of coffee, run don't walk over to the Starbucks located at 13-25 Astor Place, New York City, before the current exhibit of Joe Ryan's photographs come down. Ryan is a good photographer and I am using the word "good" with the greatest respect. His shoots are clean and technically flawless, necessary for any rock photographer, but there also that quality that goes beyond good, and that comes from the energy of someone who loves what he is doing. It produces that something extra—the shoot, the expression and the moment that makes you just want to say, "Wow, that looked like an amazing show!" You might have missed the Town Hall show but don't miss the work of Joe Ryan.

The photographer described what it was like to photograph Blondie: "It took about 4 months of hustling to get that photo pass, so when I finally got to be in the press pit, it was all adrenaline! The band had so much energy, I almost exploded trying to capture all the amazing shots!"

Currently, Joe is working with many up-and-coming bands such as Joydrop, Grinder, Melissa Reaves, and Life in the Balance. His work will be featured in a book on the Grateful Dead and another on Blondie [*the latter referring to this book*–Ed.].

Pictured are some violinists from the BBC Concert Orchestra, Deborah Harry, and Roy Nathanson, Barbican Jazz 2002 series, Barbican, London, May 19, 2002
credit: copyright © 2002 Andrew Keating

427

"'Atomic' Photo Exhibit"

by Dawn N. Volkman
(adapted and edited by Allan Metz)

New Haven, CT/About.com *web site, March 12, 2000*

Review of Joe Ryan's "Atomic" photo exhibit, March 16, 2000–April 15, 2000, Starbucks, Chapel Street, New Haven, Connecticut.—Ed.

Joe Ryan has photographed everyone from the Grateful Dead to Rusted Root to Blondie and for the next month and a half, from March 11 to April 15, [2000], New Haven residents can catch his Blondie exhibit at the Starbucks Café at 1068 Chapel Street in downtown New Haven.

I met with Joe and John Sibby, the person who helped him get this particular gig, as they were about to set up the "Atomic" exhibit this weekend. I was very impressed both by Joe's love of the work and the skill he has with what he would call "capturing the moment."

He started out in the business photographing the Grateful Dead, which he says changed his life. Blondie seems, at least musically, very different from most of his other subjects, including Bruce Hornsby, the Black Crowes, James Taylor and Blues Traveler. When I asked Joe, "Why Blondie?," at first he said that he has always had an interest in them, listened to them and he just knew when they got back together he had to do it. Then, a sparkle came to his eyes as he described the "euphoria" he experiences while engaged in the work.

To paraphrase him, "three songs in the pit and then you're done and you have to capture that moment in those three songs—not get in the way—just get the feel." "It's such a rush for me," he says with wide-eyed enthusiasm. John adds, "Debbie [Harry] is in people's DNA." The photos, though, say more than can be relayed in our conversation. They capture the essence of "being there," the thrill of the concert, and of Debbie Harry's overwhelming stage presence with all its drama and emotion. By looking at them you get pulled in and you can almost hear the music. But, as Joe says, "I wish I could tell you in words, but I can't." You have to experience it yourself.

Joe has photographed quite a few different bands and says that you have to go through the process of "getting in" every time. Each time you have to work harder, you have to "show them" rather than simply relying on past credentials. Besides concerts, Ryan has also worked for Lockheed Martin and was the tour photographer for The Gourds in 1998. In the future, he plans to keep on doing concerts and says he would love more opportunities to travel with bands as they tour because it affords the opportunity to do a sort of still-life documentary of band life.

Deborah Harry with the Jazz Passengers, Barbican, London, May 19, 2002
credit: copyright © 2002 Andrew Keating

428

"Physiological Analysis of Clem Burke during Blondie's 1999 *'No Exit'* World Tour"

by Marcus Smith

University College Chichester, Research and Publications *web page, 2000*

Interesting and unique physiological study of Clem Burke while performing in concert. Bottom line: our favorite drummer is in good physical condition. Adapted and edited.—Ed.

Background:

I first became aware of the group Blondie in 1977 when a close friend bought me a 12 inch record, containing 3 tracks for 75 pence, from a local record shop ['Rip Her to Shreds,' 'In the Flesh' and 'X Offender']. I subsequently joined the Blondie Fan Club in 1979 and at the age of 15 years I witnessed Blondie play live for the first time at the England Birmingham Odeon (1980).

In 1998, to celebrate the completion of my PhD in Exercise Physiology, I went to see a re-formed Blondie play live at the Lyceum Theatre in London. It was during this performance that I had the idea of contacting Clem Burke to see if he would be interested in being involved in a research project aimed at increasing our understanding of the physiological demands associated with playing the drums during a live concert.

On Sunday 7th November 1999, prior to Blondie's performance at Wembley Arena (London, England), a meeting took place between Clem Burke, Dr. Tim Holder (Sports Psychologist, University College Chichester) and myself to finalise the research programme.

The results contained within this document are unique and may serve as the basis for future collaboration.

Schedule for data acquisition

Brighton International Conference Centre	(10th November, 1999)
Bournemouth International Conference Centre	(14th November, 1999)
Birmingham Indoor Arena	(23rd November, 1999)

Methods employed for data acquisition

(a) Heart rate analysis

Over the past 15-20 years, heart rate analysis has proven to be a useful technique in helping exercise physiologists understand the physiological demands encountered by athletes during training and competition.

A Polar Vantage NV (Kempele, Finland) heart rate monitor was used in each of the 3 live performances. The components of the telemetry system consisted of: (a) chest strap containing a heart rate transmitter and (b) digital wrist watch heart rate receiver. The receiver was programmed to record Clem's heart rate response at 5 second intervals throughout each 'Live' performance. The telemetry device was attached to Clem 60 minutes prior to the start of each performance. Following each concert the data was recalled using a Toshiba 100CS lap top computer and compatible software.

Results:

The data shown in Table 1 show the highest, lowest, highest average and lowest average heart rate response, in beats per minute (b/min), for each live performance.

Table 1:

Heart rate response of Clem Burke during 3 live performances during Blondie's 1999 No Exit *World Tour.*

Venue	Highest peak heart rate (b/min)	Lowest peak heart rate (b/min)	Highest average heart rate (b/min)	Lowest average heart rate (b/min)
10th Nov 1999	175 b/min Dreaming	112 b/min Forgive And Forget	166 b/min Dreaming	105 b/min Forgive And Forget
	175 b/min One Way Or Another	126 b/min Acoustic [The Dream's Lost On Me]	162 b/min Hanging On The Telephone	106 b/min Rapture
	172 b/min Hanging On The Telephone	130 b/min Rapture	160 b/min One Way Or Another	115 b/min Tide Is High
14th Nov 1999	161 b/min Dreaming	95 b/min Night Wind Sent	153 b/min Dreaming	102 b/min Night Wind Sent
	161 b/min Hanging On The Telephone	95 b/min Tide Is High	150 b/min Hanging On The Telephone	102 b/min Tide Is High
	158 b/min Call Me	97 b/min Acoustic [The Dream's Lost On Me]	138 b/min One Way Or Another	105 b/min Acoustic [The Dream's Lost On Me]
	158 b/min One Way Or Another		138 b/min Denis	
23rd Nov 1999	153 b/min Dreaming	84 b/min No Exit	142 b/min Dreaming	90 b/min Acoustic [The Dream's Lost On Me]
	153 b/min Hanging On The Telephone	85 b/min Acoustic [The Dream's Lost On Me]	142 b/min Hanging On The Telephone	99 b/min Tide Is High
	149 b/min One Way Or Another		130 b/min One Way Or Another	101 b/min Night Wind Sent

Observations:

The equation 220–age is often used to predict an individual's maximum heart rate. Therefore, according to this equation, Clem's maximum heart rate should be approximately 176 b/min (220–44 yrs = 176 b/min).

The single highest heart rate response was 175 b/min during the song 'Dreaming.' This suggests that at times Clem was playing close to his cardio-vascular capacity. Indeed, 'Dreaming' was shown to be the most physically demanding song off the playlist, followed closely by 'One Way Or Another' and 'Hanging On The Telephone.'

Of interest is the reduction in peak heart rate for the track 'Dreaming' from 175 b/min (10th Nov 1999) to 161 b/min (14th Nov 1999) to 153 b/min (23rd Nov 1999). There are several possible explanations for this reduction in peak heart rate:

(a)   through cumulative fatigue, as the tour progressed, Clem was unable to put the same degree of effort into each song

(b)   through cumulative fatigue, as the tour progressed, Clem was unable to improvise to the same extent around the basic framework of each song

(c)   a change in temperature between venues

(d)   suppressed sympathetic nervous activity

(e)   a lack of motivation

From observing Clem play, I believe that the most likely explanation is a combination of (a), (b) and (d). A follow-up study involving blood and urine analysis may help explain the observed reduction in peak heart rate response.

In relation to the highest average heart rate 'Dreaming,' 'One Way Or Another' and 'Hanging On The Telephone' once more proved to be the most stressful. It would have been very interesting to record Clem's heart rate response during an extended drum solo. In this respect it was unfortunate that the song 'Union City Blue' was not played during this set. If Blondie conduct a future World Tour I am convinced that Clem's maximum heart rate response would be higher if the following tracks were performed following each other: 'One Way Or Another,' 'Dreaming' and 'Union City Blue'.

The least stressful/physically demanding songs played during the world tour were: 'The Dream's Lost On Me'; 'Night Wind Sent'; 'Tide Is High' and 'Forgive And Forget.' There are many factors which contribute to the decisions behind formulating the playlist, such as demands placed on the vocalist, musicians and the audience.

Acknowledgements:

Clem Burke, Matt O'Connor, Deborah Harry, Chris Stein, Jimmy Destri, Leigh Foxx, Paul Carbonara, Matthew Murphy, Trisha Becker, Peter Danilowicz, Erica Lane, Annick Barbaria, Damien Wiles, Dr. Tim Holder and Paul Smernicki.

"Blondie in the Library"

adapted and edited by Allan Metz

The following two listings for the book Making Tracks: The Rise of Blondie *(1982 and 1998) were taken and adapted from OCLC's FirstSearch WorldCat database and are used with OCLC's permission. FirstSearch and WorldCat are registered trademarks of OCLC Online Computer Library Center, Incorporated. Thanks to Victor Bockris for suggesting the concept for this selection.—Ed.*

The following list identifies 120 libraries throughout the U.S. (and Canada) as of April 2002 that own the book Making Tracks: The Rise of Blondie *by Debbie Harry, Chris Stein and Victor Bockris (New York: Dell Publishing, 1982). Arranged alphabetically by state:*

Alaska
Fairbanks North Star Borough Public Libraries

California
California State University Northridge
Los Angeles Public Library
Oakland Public Library
Riverside Public Library
Salinas Public Library
San Francisco Public Library
San Francisco State University
San Jose Public Library
San Jose State University
Santa Ana Public Library
Solano County Library
Stanislaus County Free Library
Torrance Public Library
Ventura County Library

Connecticut
Bridgeport Public Library
Ferguson Library
Greenwich Library
Libraries Online, Inc.

District of Columbia
Library of Congress
Model Secondary School For the Deaf
U.S. Department of Veterans Affairs

Florida
Broward County, Library Division
Orange County Library System
Sarasota County Library System

Illinois
Alpha Park Public Library District
Broadview Public Library District
Chicago Public Library
DePaul University
Gail Borden Public Library District
Lincoln Library
Palentine Public Library District
Peoria Public Library
Robert T. Jones Public Library District
Schaumburg Township District Library
Schiller Park Public Library
University of Illinois at Urbana-Champaign

Indiana
Monroe County Community School Corporation
Saint Joseph County Public Library

Kansas
Kansas Public Library, Kansas City
Kansas State Library
Olathe Public Library

Kentucky
Boone County Public Library
Kenton County Public Library

Louisiana
Lafayette Public Library

Maryland
Enoch Pratt Free Library
Montgomery County Department of Public Libraries
University of Maryland, College Park

Massachusetts
Bunker Hill Community College
Cary Memorial Library
Framingham Public Library
Springfield City Library
Watertown Free Public Library
Western Massachusetts Regional Library System

Michigan
Bay de Noc Community College
Chippewa River District Library
Dansville High School Library
Genesee District Library
Kellogg Community College
Southwest Michigan Library Cooperative

Missouri
University of Missouri, Kansas City

Montana
Lewis & Clark Library

Nebraska
Bellevue Public Library
Omaha Public Library

New Hampshire
New Hampshire State Library Processing Center

New Jersey
Atlantic City Free Public Library
Camden County Library
Cape May County Library
Lakewood Free Public Library
Monmouth County Library
Rutherford Public Library

New Mexico
Santa Fe Public Library

New York
Buffalo & Erie County Public Library
Capital Regional BOCES
Clinton Essex Franklin Library System
New York Public Library, Brooklyn Branch Library
Nioga Library System
Onondaga Cortland Madison BOCES
Rochester Public Library
Southern Adirondack Library System
Upper Hudson Library System
Westchester Library System

North Dakota
Bismarck Public School District

Ohio
Cleveland Public Library
Cuyahoga County Public Library
Lima Public Library
Lorain Public Library
Northwest Bookmobile Center
Ohio State University
Public Library of Cincinnati/Hamilton County
State Library of Ohio

State Library of Ohio Catalog Center
Youngstown & Mahoning County Public Library

Oklahoma
Pioneer Multi-County Public Library
Southeastern Public Library System of Oklahoma

Pennsylvania
Bryn Mawr College
Bucks County Free Library
Citizen's Library
Oil Creek District Library Center

Rhode Island
Cranston Public Library
Providence Public Library
Warwick Public Library
Westerly Public Library

South Carolina
Spartanburg County Public Library

Tennessee
Center for Popular Music, Middle Tennessee State
University
Knoxville City School
Memphis & Shelby County Public Library
& Information Center
University of Tennessee

Texas
Houston Public Library
San Antonio Public Library
Waco-McLennan County Library

Vermont
Vermont Department of Libraries

Virginia
County of Henrico Public Library

Washington (State)
King County Library System
Washington State Library

West Virginia
Kanawha County Public Library

Wisconsin
Hedburg Public Library
Milwaukee County Federated Library System
Wisconsin Department of Public Instruction

Canada
University of Alberta
Vancouver Public Library

The following list identifies 51 libraries throughout the U.S. as of April 2002 that own the book Making Tracks: The Rise of Blondie *by Debbie Harry, Chris Stein and Victor Bockris (New York: Da Capo Press, 1998). Arranged alphabetically by state:*

California
Commerce Public Library
Cuesta College Library
Los Angeles Public Library
Sacramento Public Library
University of California, Davis, Shields Library

Colorado
Denver Public Library

District of Columbia
Library of Congress

Florida
University of North Florida, Carpenter Library

Georgia
University of Georgia

Hawaii
Hawaii State Library

Illinois
Chicago Public Library
Columbia College

Indiana
Indianapolis-Marion County Public Library

Maine
Bates College

Maryland
University of Maryland, Baltimore County

Massachusetts
Harvard University, Harvard College Library
    Technical Services

Michigan
Flint Public Library

Minnesota
Minneapolis Public Library & Information Center
Winona Public Library

Missouri
Washington University

New Jersey
Free Public Library of Newark, New Jersey
Princeton University

New Mexico
Farmington Public Library

New York
Columbia University
Cornell University
Ithaca College
New York Public Library, Research Library
New York University
Newsweek, Inc.
Queens Borough Public Library
School of Visual Art Library
Syracuse University

North Carolina
High Point Public Library

Ohio
Akron-Summit County Public Library
Bowling Green State University
Cleveland Public Library
Columbus Metropolitan Library
Cuyahoga County Pubic Library
Lakewood Public Library
Toledo-Lucas County Public Library

Pennsylvania
Carnegie Library of Pittsburgh

Rhode Island
Brown University

Tennessee
Nashville Public Library

Texas
Corpus Christi Public Library
McMurry University
Texas A&M
University of Texas at Austin

Virginia
University of Virginia

Washington (State)
Pierce County Library System
Seattle Public Library
Stafford Creek Corrections Center Library

Blondie, Deborah Harry and Related Web Links
(selected listing)

compiled by Allan Metz

Web links are subject to change. An online copy is at this book's companion web site, www2.drury.edu/ametz/blonbook.htm and will be kept current.—Ed.

Blondie, From Punk to the Present: A Pictorial History
(corresponding web site to this book) by Allan Metz
www2.drury.edu/ametz/blonbook.htm

Blondie: Legacy, Influence, Legend
(companion to this book) by Allan Metz
www2.drury.edu/ametz/blondie.htm

RollingStone.com—Blondie Main Page
(includes a link to book preview site!)
www.rollingstone.com/photos
(then search for blondie)

VH1: Blondie Web Sites
www.vh1.com/artists/az/blondie/websites.jhtml

MTV: Blondie Web Page
www.mtv.com/bands/az/blondie/artist.jhtml

Blondie Guide
www2.drury.edu/ametz/blonguid.htm

Blondie: The Reunion by Theresa Heinz
(includes info about this book)
www.members.tripod.com/theresaheinz/index.htm

The Blondie Review—TBR
(Robert Betts, editor;
Amy Oravec, associate editor)
www.geocities.com/theblondiereview
TheBlondieReview.html

The Debbie Harry Collector's Society
by Barry L. Kramer
www.debbieharry.net

The Deborah Harry Home Page
by Louis A Bustamante
www.deborahharry.com

Blondie—The Official Web Site by Barry L. Kramer,
Louis A Bustamante, and April Kincaid
www.blondie.net

Beyond Music
www.beyondmusic.com

"We Created It: Let's Take It Over!"
by Jessamin Swearingen
www.inch.com/~jessamin

The Blondie Archive by Fraser White
www.blondie.ausbone.net

In the Flesh...: The Deborah Harry Web Site by Ed Kary
www.community-2.webtv.net/espice/InTheFleshThe

Blondie Reunion—The Best of Blondie
by Theresa Heinz and Ed Kary
www.thrill.to/BlondieReunion

Blondie: The Complete Discography
www.geocities.com/recmod

Blondie—No Exit by Simon Skinner
www.theblondie.freeserve.co.uk

Picture This—PT (fanzine) by Francois Wintein;
cowriters: Amy Oravec and Sarah Burke
www.blondie2000.freeserve.co.uk

Union City: Tribute Site by Dawn Coates
www.unioncity.force9.co.uk

Deborah Harry Page by April Kincaid
www.members.aol.com/Dblswitch/DH.html

Forever Blondie by Al Hill
www.geocities.com/blondie2debbie/blondieindex.html

PHOTOGRAPHY LINKS

SLPStock Home Page (Kevin Kushel)
www.slpstock.com

Mick Rock Official Web site
www.mickrock.com

Ebet Roberts Web site
www.ebetroberts.com

Roberta Bayley Image Gallery on SLPStock link located
on Blondie From Punk to the Present...web site
www2.drury.edu/ametz/blonbook.htm

Stephanie Chernikowski Photography
www.angelfire.com/pop/artpix

Joe Ryan Photography
www.gratefuljoe.com

The John Sibby Gallery
**www.gratefuljoe.com/concerts/sibbygallery/
johnsibby.html**

Sherry Globman Rock Photography and Web Design
www.rocktographynyc.com

Best Shot Entertainment (Robert J. Tuozzo)
www.bestshotentertainment.com/main.html

Mirror Syndication International
www.mirrorpix.com

Concert Photo Company (Pete Still)
www.concertphoto.co.uk

Stuart Brinin Photography
www.jazzwest.com/stu/index.htm

Bob Gruen Homepage
www.rokkets.com/gruen

Fifi Studios (Tina Paul)
www.fifibear.com

Corbis
www.corbis.com

Retna
www.retna.com

Visages
www.visages.com

WENN—World Entertainment News Network
www.wenn.com

Concert Photos (John Atashian)
www.concertphotos.com

Marcine Linder
www.marcine.com

Michael Ochs Archives
www.michaelochs.com

Goth, Punk and Indie Photos:
The Mick Mercer Archive
www.mickmercer.com

Deborah's Magic (Mandy Rohr)
www.deborah.ixy.de

Teresa Hale's Gig Pix
www.t-rae.net

New Wave Photos (Philippe Carly)
www.users.skynet.be/phicarly

Sylviestock (Sylvie Ball)
www.sylviestock.com

"Kids Are People Too"

(adapted and edited by Allan Metz)

This was the height of Blondiemania and Debbie and Chris were in the mode that they could do *anything* art-wise. It was a new different time and they were anxious to do their art (music videos, art rock & pop, commercials, public access TV, rap, films...), and, at the same time, also edging into the mainstream (Q: Who do you listen to at home? A: Donna Summer). Debbie's confidence in this interview is astounding. She knew she was #1 and the "It" girl of 1980. At the time, there was no one else like her.—*Jon Erkider*

It was certainly a very different (younger) look for Debbie, who looks so cute in her blue outfit (I don't even know what it is called, but it was a very Debbie outfit to be sure) answering the kids' questions and chatting about her previous

jobs—as a secretary she did the typewriter hand gestures, etc...Some of the questions were: Is the group Blondie breaking up? and Are you and Chris going to get married?— *Ross MacDonald*

"What I most remember about Deborah Harry being on the show was that I was told she and the band were fans...that they often watched the show the next morning on the road after a concert. I was always amazed at how many adults enjoyed the concept." —*Emmy Award winning host Michael Young, 2001, www.AltonEnt.com*

Debbie Harry of Blondie (1980) arrives at the studio for a taping of the children's TV show "Kids Are People Too," New York City. credit: © Walter McBride / Retna Ltd

"Michael Young Interviews Deborah Harry on the Program 'Kids Are People Too'"

(c. late spring/early summer 1980 show)
Host: Michael Young
Guest: Debbie Harry (of Blondie)

Michael Young: Our next guest made her singing debut in a sixth grade play in Hawthorne, New Jersey. And her high school performing career included the annual variety show and baton twirling...<shots of Debbie's high school yearbook>. That's her right there, uh huh. Well, now when she performs it's a little different. As you can see from this...watch <a clip of the "Dreaming" video>. From Blondie, please welcome Deborah Harry! Hi! How'r you doin'?

Deborah Harry: Hi Michael.

MY: Come and sit down.

DH: OK.

MY: From baton twirling to this, huh.

DH: Yeah.

MY: Have a seat.

DH: I was always dropping the baton.

MY: Were you the one who dropped the baton?

DH: Yeah.

MY: Did it always embarrass you when you did that?

DH: Very much.

MY: There's a television commercial where somebody drops the baton and I always feel sorry for that girl whenever I see it.

DH: Ha! Ha!

MY: Did you know you were gonna be a performer when you were in high school?

DH: Umm, well, I wanted to be, but I didn't know if I would be.

MY: You mean you thought you wanted to be.

DH: Yeah.

MY: When you were doing those variety shows and stuff like that did you think 'from here I'm going to go to show business, this is my training' and that sort of thing? Did ya, ya know?

DH: Umm, no, not really.

MY: Well, then how did you do it when you got outta high school? How did you make that entrance into a show business career?

DH: I moved to New York and I just hung out with people who were musicians and artists. You know? Stuff like that. And I just sort of inched my way into it. I felt my way into it.

MY: Did you do the…umm…the obligatory years of starvation, waiting tables and all that sort of thing that performers have to go through?

DH: Yeah, everybody does that.

MY: How did you survive during those times?

DH: Uhhh…well…I dunno, I sorta ummm, ya know ya have to be obsessed, I think. You have to really want, want to do it, you know? And you have to really just sort of let all the other things out of your way…just be very dedicated.

MY: To do what you want.

DH: Yeah.

MY: You know, I think the perseverance aspect of it is about 80% of making it.

DH: Yeah.

MY: Ya know, 'cause I know for the longest time I had to convince myself that I could go on. Ya know, one day I would be on TV. But in the meantime, I had to do all sorts of jobs. Did you have all those jobs?

*DH: Yeah *chuckle*. I had every kind of job you can imagine. I was a short order cook at one time. I was a waitress.*

MY: The short order cook's the guy who says…"Deborah! Give us a hamburger..."

DH: Yeah.

MY: What else?

DH: I worked at a health spa teaching exercises. I was a salesgirl. I sold a lot of things. All different things.

MY: See, now I was a sales clerk also. I sold stationery.

DH: Oh, a secretary…

MY: I thought I was a good writer and they put me in stationery. And a secretary also.

DH: Yeah.

MY: Do you type and all that sort of stuff?

DH: Yeah.

MY: It's hard to imagine…Deborah Harry typing…

DH: <sly grin, air typing>

MY: What about those people now who knew you back when you were struggling? When you run into them, how do you feel? Does it remind you of those times?

DH: Uhhh, I don't know. I think uhhh I pretty much see the same people, ummm everybody that, you know, that was struggling then, has sort of gone on to, uhh not struggle. You know? So I still see them.

MY: So a lot of the people that were…uhh beginning a career with you have also reached a certain amount of success now?

DH: Yeah.

MY: Do they all sort of have the same kind of belief and positive attitude?

DH: I guess so. Hahaha.

MY: Did you communicate with your family during that time? Did they give you a lot of encouragement?

DH: Oh, yeah.

MY: Yeah.

MY: I know our audience had a lot of questions…'cause they were like, "When is Deborah coming out?" Haha. So, can we get some questions with ya?

DH: This is a very lively crowd.

MY: This is a verrry lively crowd. We got a good group today. Let's get a few questions...

Audience question: Are you still goin' out with Chris Stein?

DH: Yes.

Audience follow-up question: Are you gonna get married?

DH: Yes.

MY: Aha! You heard it here folks. Good question. He goes right for it!

MY: Okay, let's take a question here...

Audience question: I'd like to ask you if there is anybody in show business you idolize (from today)?

DH: Yeah, there's a lot of people. I mean the list is very long.

MY: Name us a singer that you would listen to when you go home.

DH: Ummm…Donna Summer.

MY: Okay, good question! Let's take another one...

Audience question: When you started your singing career, where were you found?

DH: Where was I found?

Audience follow-up question: Clubs?

DH: Oh yeah, clubs, private parties. Umm, in the sixties there were a lot of events they called happenings. And they were like in lofts downtown. Those were a lot of fun. Usually they were free. And people would just like try to do their number and get noticed.

MY: Okay. Almost like a showcase type situation where you performed for free in order for the record company to see you. Okay let's take a question right here...

Audience question: How did you get started?

DH: Ahh *chuckle*. Well…Ummm, through working with some of my friends. And we just got lucky I guess. Just kept at it.

MY: Okay, alright. Let's take one over here...

Audience question: I heard rumors that Blondie was going to break up. Is that rumor true?

DH: No, it's not true...I started that rumor! Haha.

MY: Haha...

Audience question: Umm, do your parents like your singing career?

DH: Yes, very much.

MY: Do they come to your concerts and stuff like that?

DH: Oh yeah.

MY: I can tell why, 'cause I'd go. Would you?

Audience follow-up comment: Yeah sure.

MY: Deborah Harry, thank you very much for being with us!

DH: Oh, thank you! <blows kiss>

Interview ends with "Call Me" playing in the background…

Transcription by Ross MacDonald, and reprinted with the permission of Ross MacDonald and Michael Young. Adapted and edited by Allan Metz.

"Wigstock 2001"
A Photo Essay

by Andrea Farina

Deborah Harry at Wigstock 2001, New York City, September 2, 2001.
credit: all photos this page, copyright © 2001, Andrea Farina

440

"Wigstock 2001"

by Andrea Farina

(adapted and edited by Robert Betts from *The Blondie Review,* vol. 2, issue 1, #5, December 2001)

Andrea Farina shares his photographs and writes about the 17th, and last, Wigstock celebration held on September 2nd at Pier 54 on the west end of 14th Street in New York City. It was an awesome and exciting celebration. Viva, the zipper dress, Debbie è così bello, abbastanza buon mangiare, è amore."—Robert Betts

The End of the Wigs

Wigstock began in 1984 as a free celebration of the East Village underground queer culture, held at Tompkins Square Park. By the '90s, it became an annual pilgrimage for fun-loving wig wearers and later moved west to Pier 54, with an admission price instituted to cover rising production costs. The festival has been the subject of a full-length feature film, "Wigstock: The Movie," directed by Barry Shils, produced by Klaus Volkenborn in 1995. Some of today's music industry's hippest stars including Deborah Harry, RuPaul, Deee-Lite, the B-52's, John Cameron Mitchell (director of the film, "Hedwig and the Angry Inch"), and Kiki and Herb, to name a few, have graced Wigstock's stages all over the years.

This year magazines and newspapers reported that with the 17th edition, the "Wig is Dead." The reasons seem to be that for two years in a row (1999 and 2000) torrential rains turned Wigstock into "Wetstock" with the resulting loss of attendance, which helped to amass a large debt. In "Wigstock: The Movie," Lady Bunny said, 'Mother Nature must be a drag queen, because look at this beautiful weather.' Last year instead she added, "Now she must have turned into a very bitter, old, and crabby drag queen."

This year portions of the proceeds benefit the Gay Men's Health Crisis.

"…I had to make good time to see you…"

Like many other performances of Deborah Harry in NYC, it wasn't hard to convince my friends to take a trip and attend what was to be the last Wigstock. For me, instead, it was the first Wigstock I've ever attended and only by the end of the day did I realize how much I'm going to miss this event.

About a year ago I had seen "Wigstock: the Movie" on videotape (which shows Debbie's picture on the cover but disappointingly doesn't include her performance) so I knew what to expect from the event. But being there was such a fabulous and different experience, a day that I will always remember.

The day before the show, we headed to New York City, from Washington, DC with great excitement. That Sunday, September 2nd, I arrived at Pier 54, an hour before the show, leaving my friends to explore Chelsea with the promise that we'll catch up later. I wanted to live the whole experience from the very beginning. The crowd was just beginning but several casts of "wigs" had already arrived strutting their stuff. I snapped a picture of one outlandish costume in which the wearer had breasts the size of a watermelons, and then an Edgar Allan Poe drag queen with a raven perched atop his head. I took these photos at first, just to test if the camera was working and also to capture the glamour and campiness of the moment. Unlike last year, when I attended the party at Mother for the release of Cathay Che's Deborah Harry biography and the batteries went out right at the beginning of the auction, I wanted to be ready in case Deborah Harry would show up unexpectedly. I had no clue as to when she was going to perform.

Arriving early I took a place in the front row, assuring a good view of Debbie when the time came. Trying to keep that place became a hard task with the ever-growing crowd as the show was approaching the final set around 8:00 PM. The audience was full of energy. The atmosphere moved to an ever-frenzied pace after each stage show. It was a gradual climax to the final anticipation—Debbie! The crowd, including a good amount of young and old in Debbie Harry and Blondie shirts, all seemed, as though they were there for her. This atmosphere afterall set the stage for the punk diva herself.

"In the sun, it's for everyone, in the sun we're gonna have some fun…"

Unlike the previous 2 years, the final installment of Wigstock was blessed with gorgeous weather; the sun was hot and shining over the Hudson River, which brought out hordes of wig wearers, and spectators alike. Wigstock's three sets saw a number of music legends and surprise guests as a tribute for a final time, usually accompanied by witty remarks by the hilarious Lady Bunny who wore the most outlandish outfits, and of course, wigs.

While Wigstock's first set highlighted a pair of unlikely Kate Bush tributes, the second set really kicked the event into gear with one of Bunny's beloved laugh-in tributes, during which a drag ensemble cracked bawdy, tasteless jokes like "What does Lady Bunny have between her tits that an 18-year-old doesn't? A bellybutton!" The jokes were fast and irresistible, and I just couldn't stop laughing. It was probably one of the most enjoyable moments of the whole show.

Among the performers were a lot of drag queens, so many that it's impossible to remember all of them, and some terrific people that are familiar names to me for being Deborah or Blondie associates. This troupe of wonderful characters who keep the spirit of Manhattan alive, like Chi Chi Valenti who founded legendary New York City nightspots like Mother and Jackie 60, The Dueling Bankheads, the ethereal vocalist Antony, the trans-sexual star Amanda Lepore, the voluptuous and "real" Bob, who are enthusiastic regulars in alternative happenings such as Click+Drag, where Deborah Harry often performs.

Being a rock fan, I just couldn't be more ecstatic being in the front row and seeing acts like The Toilet Boys, whose set included several great songs from their *Toilet Boys* CD and the legendary transsexual punk rocker Jayne County—performing her trademark "f**k off!" number.

One highlight was a special screening of the trailer for Mariah Carey's upcoming film, "Glitter," to which a flood of boos came from the audience. Lady Bunny countered, "Just paying off some bills!" Drag queen Lindsay followed as an utterly psychotic version of the recently troubled singer. An especially hilarious act featured performers Sheila Noxzema, Harmonica Sunbeam and Sugar Pie Coco doing a cover of the hit song "Survivor" by Destiny's Child. Other memorable acts included a performance by the hilarious Rene Taylor (the mother from "The Nanny"), dance artist Kevin Aviance, '80's sensation Book of Love, and The Dazzle Dancers, a dance troupe dressed in thin swaths of fabric and masks on the back of their heads. Although insult slinging and playfulness were the order of the day, all of the performers had some kind of unique talent.

My friends left in the afternoon to go get something to eat, and promised they would come back later to catch Deborah's performance. I was hungry, thirsty and couldn't even reach the restrooms, but it was worth it.

"… Sunset sliding, my time to rise and be dancing, dancing down the moon…"

By the time Wigstock's final hours and performers came around, warmth, affection and pride ruled. Now the sun had left its place in the sky, replaced by a beautiful full moon. Right after Bob and Amanda Lepore, Lady Bunny in a moment of personal reflection about her childhood introduced Deborah Harry. The magic moment had finally arrived. The music started, it was the remix of some old song but at first I couldn't quite figure out which one. Deborah Harry's accompanying dancers, The Fish Sticks (Rob Roth and Garrett Domina) entered the stage in synchronized dance, wearing pinstripe suits.

"Oh, your hair is beautiful…"

Yes! It's the Diddy remix of "Atomic" and there was Deborah Harry and she was not wearing a wig! She strided on stage confidently, formidably like a lion tamer. Maybe it's just me but the atmosphere of the event changed completely; she looked like a star that had just fallen to earth from space. She looked like she had just stepped out of the 1977 *Plastic Letters* album cover: Debbie in her most glamorous punk-rock days, with her hair long, straight, black in the back, bangs down her eyes, and red lipstick. She wore a mini zipper dress that was open almost all the way. And those boots—her trademark thigh high black boots. Only the techno beat of the Atomic remix reminded me that I was in 2001 and not in 1977, but also her stage presence. Her movements were graceful and entrancing (slightly reminiscent of the American Music Awards (AMA) performance in 1999); her singing confident, more than ever, strong and sensual.

I took pictures; I tried to listen, and to watch the other two male dancers who, by this time had already started to strip—too many thoughts were in my head. The performance was so short, too short, just the length of that song, and in retrospect, I can't understand how so many emotions and feelings I could experience in such a short time. Plus I was taking pictures, probably one every 20 seconds! It was exhilarating. The crowd went wild, everyone were all screaming. I was screaming. When the boys were down to just their bras and garter belts, the song was over. Lady Bunny came back on stage and tried to speak over the crowd's applause and screams. She asked Debbie what she does to keep herself so young and beautiful, Debbie replied "I eat fish sticks". Then after a couple more jokes, Lady Bunny admitting she always wanted to have sex with her over all the years they have known each other, Deborah Harry left the stage, with exactly the same attitude as when she walked in. What a great finale for the festival of wigs!

**"I even tried wearing a wig for a while, it was the right color but not the right style…
…gonna get some peroxide…"**

Soon after Debbie's performance, while Obie-winning actor-singer John Kelly was performing his traditional (and very moving) closing number, "Wigstock," (lifted from Joni Mitchell's "Woodstock"), I remembered the pictures that I saw of Debbie in a previous edition of this festival when she performed dressed like Eve wearing a blonde ankle-long wig. This year she thought that a wig was not the right style; she got that bottle of fresh peroxide once again because her hair was all "real" and more platinum blond than ever.

"Fade away and radiate"

What a night, it was past 10:00 PM now, and I had all I wanted. I reunited with my friends who never made it as close to the stage where I was. They told me that while they were leaving around 5:00 PM they saw Debbie coming to the pier, walking slowly with her "Fish Sticks." They commented on how blonde and beautiful she looks up close. One of my friends approached Debbie asking at what time she would perform. In her typical way she turned around, shrugged her shoulders and said (like she didn't care): "I don't know!" and continued to walk with her two guys.

I was happy for my friends, because it was the first time they met Debbie in person. I wish this wasn't the last Wigstock, because it was really great. That same night, I walked by the square where the first editions of Wigstock took place, where they say there would only be a few people, all in wigs and no commercial sponsors. Some say it was better back then, rather than when it became a bigger event. I just closed my eyes and thought that I had been lucky to be at least at the last Wigstock. There were a lot of cameras at this year's event, which means another movie will be released; this time, there's no doubt it will include Debbie.

About the Author and Photographer

Andrea Farina was born and raised in Rome, Italy. He lives in Washington, DC and works for the National Institutes of Health in Bethesda, MD. Andrea has a Ph.D. and works as a researcher in molecular biology. Rather than going back to Italy, Andrea would like to find work and live in New York City for awhile.

Andrea has been a Debbie and Blondie fan since 1979 when he first heard "Heart of Glass." In his own words, "The first time I met and talked with Deborah was in Italy at the Umbria Jazz Festival, July 1997 when she performed with the Jazz Passengers (see pp. 166-67). I saw her again several times in NYC with the JP's, at the *Fire at Keaton's Bar and Grill* show, at the Cathay Che book party at Mother, in "Crave" at the Axis Theatre, and during the *No Exit* tour in Washington, DC and San Francisco."

He continues, "I love so many songs that it's impossible to mention all of them here. I love her in "Six Ways to Sunday" and "Union City." I collect everything I can that's Blondie or Debbie Harry related—what else?" Andrea adds a note of appreciation, "I would like to thank David for helping me write the Wigstock article in proper English and Greg, Samer, and Pryia for putting up with me and my Blondie obsession."

"Mike Morton"

Mike Morton is best known for his photography work in the British press. He's been published in *Melody Maker*, *Smash Hits*, and *The Times*.

Mike began photographing musicians and performers at the age of 16, including The Eurythmics, Culture Club, Marc Almond, Divine, Siouxsie & The Banshees, Depeche Mode, Bauhaus, and The Cure. He moved to London at age 18 to pursue a professional career, working closely with Divine, Bronski Beat, Strawberry Switchblade, and Sigue Sigue Sputnik who first put Mike's photos on their record sleeves.

After working for *Melody Maker* and Sky TV, he photographed hundreds more artists, among them Debbie Harry, The Stone Roses, Nick Cave, Oasis, Erasure, Billy Idol, Alice Cooper, Rod Stewart, and Bryan Ferry.

Mike was brought up on the Isle of Wight and attended his first gig, the 1970 Isle of Wight Festival, at age 5. He first heard Blondie in 1977 on Radio Luxembourg and first saw them perform on his 13th birthday, September 10, 1978, at Portsmouth Guildhall.

More of Mike's work can be seen on *Dreamland,* a web site devoted to the life and work of filmmaker John Waters (www.dreamlandnews.com/morton/index.html).

Averneal Centre, Belfast, Northern Ireland, May 29, 1990

Miraldo Theatre, Milan, Italy, December 9, 1989　　　　**La Cigale, Paris, France, December 16, 1989**

"'A Very Jack the Ripper Christmas,'
The Slipper Room, December 22, 2001"

by Sylvie Ball

The Slipper Room on Manhattan's Lower East Side (167 Orchard Street at Stanton Street) was host this year for The Jackie Factory's 7th annual Christmas event, "A Very Jack the Ripper Christmas," conceived and directed by Chi Chi Valenti. The show combines two of her favorite obsessions—Jack the Ripper and the English music hall.

The setting is an imaginary English music hall in Whitechapel during the Ripper murders of 1888. The "Saucy Jack Revue" culminated with a special performance by Deborah Harry and The Fishsticks.

Deborah sang a song called "Goodnight Sweetheart."—*Sylvie Ball.*

Deborah flanked by The Fishsticks (Rob Roth and Garrett Domina)

credit: both photos on this page copyright © 2001 Sylvie Ball

445

"Deborah Harry, Gershwin Hotel, New York City, January 29, 2002"

by Jon Erkider
(adapted and edited by Allan Metz)

To think that I would ever hear Debbie Harry perform anything from *Koo Koo* or *The Hunter* these days would be absolutely unfathomable. But that is exactly what she did this night as part of Neke Carson's "Live From The Gershwin Living Room"—a series of Tuesday night performances at the Gershwin Hotel by some of New York's most talented and colorful artists.

A once-in-a-lifetime experience—it was a performance that was almost devoid of that famous singing voice. Debbie gave a poetry reading. Bespectacled in thick black frames, Debbie began the night by reading poems included in *Making Tracks: The Rise of Blondie* (written by Debbie Harry, Chris Stein, and Victor Bockris).

It was amazing to hear her read these little poems that I had read so many times over, and were written at that vulnerable period when Blondie was barely an idea and the attainment of fame was still years away. *Making Tracks* was the most personal Debbie ever got with her fans (aside from performing), and to hear her read from it in person was truly a special and emotional experience. I felt very privileged.

But the coolest thing was that Debbie read the lyrics to "Military Rap"—a song she penned for her first solo record, *Koo Koo*. It was such a rare treat considering that we never got to see her perform any of these songs live—and it seemed that the audience really got a kick of its content. The lyrics are fun. A befitting choice of Debbie's and, in its own right, a hilarious rap.

Another big surprise was Debbie's reading of the lyrics of "Dragonfly" (from *The Hunter*)—a cosmic commentary on the rules and consequences of an inter-galactic race! By far one of the oddest of Blondie songs, Debbie read lyric-by-lyric as it appeared in the record sleeve of the long-play album. It was so strange to hear her read all this outer-space jargon that I often wondered how she knew so much about it! Debbie sang some of the verses and eventually segued into reading like a martian or robot. The room was full of laughter by the end, and I realized again how way ahead of the times Debbie was in breaking ground and making songs that were unconventional, even unmarketable, and yet altogether ingenious.

Debbie Harry of Blondie, one-woman poetry reading as part of the series "Live From the Gershwin Living Room," Gershwin Hotel, New York City, January 29, 2002. Right: With Leee Black Childers.
credit: © Jon Erkider / Retna Ltd

Debbie got huge applause after reading the truly poetic and eloquent "End of the Run" from *Def, Dumb & Blonde*. True poetry, this composition more than hints at Debbie's reflections of the past and she read it with true feeling and delivered it with such fealty. It was my favorite part of the night. She read earlier and newer poems—one even as recent as October 2001, which was nuanced with thoughts and imagery arising from the aftermath of the September 11th World Trade Center tragedy. This is where she got her biggest applause. It was very personal and I feel very lucky to have experienced it. As a matter of fact, I can't forget it.

Afterwards, Debbie signed autographs and posed for pictures with fans for over an hour. The audience numbered over one hundred (the room only seated 60—most of whom had to watch the performance via a video monitor in the Red Room Beer Bar in the hotel lobby!).

Among Debbie's fans and friends who were present were Romy Ashby (*No Exit* co-songwriter and publisher of *Goodie Magazine*), photographer Rob Roth, Warhol superstar (and Gershwin Living Room performer) Penny Arcade, DJ Johnny Dynell, photographer/poet/performer Bobby Miller, performance artist Richard Move, Jackie 60/Mother family member Rose Royale, photographer and one-time Sid Vicious/Johnny Thunders manager Leee Black Childers, and Tommy Volume of Star Spangles.—*Jon Erkider*

Debbie Harry with Tommy Volume of Star Spangles
credit: © Jon Erkider / Retna Ltd

Afterword

by John Sibby
(adapted and edited by Allan Metz)

close examination of iconic bands is often times left better off distorted.
time provokes their due and finally a formal accounting of such fleeting moments is revealed.
there exists an underlying theme that so strongly insinuates the profound connection between
music and art; that, with a penchant for self-discovery, is at the nucleus of this delicate equation.

amidst a decadent new york city backdrop, a surreal and primitive art form developed.
perhaps out of desperation or simply by accident, its influence derailed and seeped into american
culture with such an uncompromising ferocity that the effects of this imagery have been mimicked
(rather unsuccessfully) throughout time.
you were either out or in and it was over before it began; so the story goes.
the mind's eye acknowledges no such departure; therefore, no exit "has" taken place.

indeed this is blondie personified.
enter the acute menacing prowess of singer debbie harry who, with eclectic urgency, inculcates
her hawthorne lineage through manic swept passages like some mesmerized modern-day
silent film ingenue in a chaotic trance;
concealing herself within mentor chris stein's glycerine-based static-charged phrases.
high drama indeed!

existing within this perimeter are flawlessly crafted three minute punk/pop/rock gems;
their delivery so precise and yet awkward and disproportional.
music does not create feelings; it validates them, and so the story goes.
existing within the canopy of specter-inspired offerings, seminal reconstruction takes place.
its lavish delivery conjures brilliant themes based on our own origins.
euphoric recall, retrospect, innuendo, future hope; all come into play
making this a unique personal experience.

history does not repeat itself, it disassembles in the stream of time.
just look and listen to clem and jimmy; its all about the music, isn't it?
the epitome of the dysfunctional family extend their fifteen minutes of fame.
just maybe we are their therapy...

mediocrity presents itself in various forms.
most are very compliant.
the books that are read, the tv that is watched, the music that is listened to.
their mere existence can shape our perceptions...

many thanks to blondie, then, for validating the other side...quite by accident indeed!...
the flaw, you see, is part of the attraction.
September 2001

About the Contributors

Dino Balzano writes for *Frontiers Newsmagazine*.

Nicholas Barber grew up in Scotland and lives in London. He has been the pop critic of the *Independent on Sunday* for six years and contributes to several other British magazines and newspapers.

David Bauder writes for the Associated Press.

Robert Betts is the editor of this book, publisher of *The Blondie Review* (a quarterly fan journal), and a Blondie archivist. He has published several books on various technical subjects. Robert is, by vocation, an audio design engineer of commercial, professional and home entertainment products. He has had extensive experience in broadcast and recording studio and public area/arena-stadium system design. Bob reports to be "...a drummer of (very) moderate talent and New York City punk wannabe from a lifetime ago." In his own words, "I am extremely proud of one of my greatest achievements: being the same age as Debbie Harry."

James Blandford is an Editorial Assistant for *Record Collector* magazine.

Victor Bockris was born in England, brought up in England and America, and has lived in New York City since 1973. He is the author of numerous books, including—*With William Burroughs, A Report from the Bunker*; *Up-tight: The Velvet Underground Story*; *Making Tracks: The Rise of Blondie*; *Warhol: The Biography*; *Keith Richards: The Biography*; *Transformer: The Lou Reed Story*; *Patti Smith: An Unauthorized Biography*; *Muhammad Ali: In Fighter's Heaven*; *Beat Punks*; and *What's Welsh for Zen: The Autobiography of John Cale*.

Grace Bradberry writes for *The Times, London*.

Adam Budofsky is Managing Editor of *Modern Drummer* magazine. He has played drums in various New York area bands over the years, and is currently with abstract psychedelicists Una Pong. He fell in love with Blondie after seeing them play "Dreaming" on "American Bandstand," which featured Clem Burke "lip synching" to his amazing drum performance from *Eat To The Beat*. When Adam found out Clem's drum hero was Keith Moon—the same as his—he decided Clem was even cooler than he originally thought. And like Clem, and Keith Moon before him, Adam plays Premier drums. He lives in New Jersey with his wife, Susanne.

Paul Burston writes for a number of newspapers including the *Sunday Times*, the *Guardian* and the *Independent,* and also is an author.

Neva Chonin writes about music, culture, technology and other topics for the *San Francisco Chronicle, Rolling Stone,* and other publications.

Scott Coblio was born in 1964 in New York and is a graduate of Long Island University. Scott wrote and sang the lead vocals in the Blondie-inspired band Koo Koo Boy from 1991 to 1996. The band released three seven-inch singles: "I'm A Monster"/"Vampire Girls" (1992), "Hate Me"/"Twist" (1993), and "Sixty Miles an Hour"/"Manhug" (1994), and three full-length cassette albums: *Every Freak For Himself* (1991), *We Are A Star* (1992), and *Sixty Miles an Hour* (1993). Also to his credit is a CD retrospective entitled *Welcome To Monster Island* (1998). He first met Debbie in 1987 in Allentown, Pennsylvania for the filming of the movie "Hairspray" in which he was an extra. Scott worked for various newspapers and magazines in central New York from 1987 to 1992. During that time, he photographed and reviewed several of Debbie's shows in New York and Toronto. Scott met Debbie a second time backstage at Toronto's Maple Leaf Gardens in 1990 and a third time in L.A. in 2000 for the filming of "The Fluffer," in which he was an extra again. Scott is currently working as a video editor in Hollywood, California.

Stuart Derdeyn is a reviewer for the online magazine, *Drop-D Magazine* (www.dropd.com).

Lisa Diedrich is a Human Resources liaison at the library of the University of Denver and has been a fan of Blondie since discovering Deborah Harry via the film "Videodrome" in 1991. Her interests include a fascination with the glamorous film stars of Hollywood's golden era. She maintains a Joan Crawford tribute web site called Joan Crawford Heaven: www.members.aol.com/HarlowGold/joancrawford.html. This page also includes links to these other web pages that Lisa maintains: Douglas Fairbanks Jr. Homepage, Kim Novak Lavender Blonde, Baby Doll Carroll Baker, and Glam Rock Tribute. She also has an equal fascination for the superstars of pop/rock music, particularly the stars of the 1970's and early 1980's. Lisa also has been a fan of Madonna since hearing "Holiday" on the radio in 1984 and has continued to follow her career since then.

Robert L. Doerschuk is a former editor of *Musician* magazine and two-time winner of the ASCAP Deems Taylor Award. He is currently senior editor of the keyboard channel at Music Player Network (www.musicplayer.com).

Jim Farber has served as Chief Pop Music Critic of *The New York Daily News* since 1990. His work also appears regularly in *Entertainment Weekly*. His essays have appeared in *The Rolling Stone Book of the '70s*, *The Rolling Stone Illustrated History of Rock 'N' Roll* and a dozen other books.

Euan Ferguson writes for the *Observer*.

Alan Foster is a freelance writer and Web developer with a background in psychology and public policy. Alan has been actively involved in gay issues for many years. His online experience began when he joined a gay BBS nearly a decade ago. He has since witnessed the growth of the online gay community from a localized phenomenon into a global resource. Alan lives in New York City with his partner, Esteban. Alan holds a bachelor's degree in psychology from the University of California, Irvine, and a master's degree in environmental psychology from the City University of New York. Alan writes that he's "a big Debbie/Blondie fan."

Michelle Goldberg is arts editor of *Metropolitan* magazine in San Francisco.

Jim Greer is West Coast Editor of *Gear* magazine.

Joey Guerra is a freelance music journalist in Houston, Texas whose work has appeared on amazon.com, music.com, todos.com and in the *KRBE Zone* magazine. He was formerly a music critic at the *Houston Chronicle* and has written for national dance-music magazines *FIXX*, *1,000 Words* and *Axcess*.

Sherry Gunderman grew up in Chicago. The first time she ever heard Blondie was at the roller rink in 1980 when "Call Me" was being played. Since that fateful day, she has had the chance to see Debbie perform during the "Escape From New York" tour and later on, after moving to Hollywood, the Blondie reunion in both LA and Las Vegas. Sherry is multi-tasking as a script supervisor on films and a writer whose first novel, "Blonde Phoenix," is in negotiations with publishers at this time. Her favorite Blondie song is "Sunday Girl," and she admits to having an unrequited crush on Chris Stein.

John Hart: "I was born in 1973, just early enough to retain the images and sounds produced by Blondie the first time around. After leaving school, I joined the British Army. From there on, I worked in various jobs ranging from office to factory work and even washing cars. Having always taken an interest in current affairs and social history, I joined Ruskin College in Oxford. It was at Ruskin where my fascination with the era of punk and new wave music was re-ignited when Blondie reformed. For my course, I decided to write an essay concerning Blondie and the social and musical background from whence they were born. In October of 2000, I will commence research on a new essay titled: Globalisation: Is It A New Threat To Democracy? My ambitions are work in adult education teaching politics and political economy and to see an end to all the boy/girl bands from around the world! To see Blondie in concert once also would be very nice!"

Ralph Heibutzki has written for a variety of publications since 1992, including record-collecting journals *DISCoveries* and *Goldmine*, as well as more technical-oriented publications, such as *Bass Player*, *Guitar Player* and *Vintage Guitar*. During that time, he has profiled some of blues, jazz and rock's most significant and dynamic performers, including Luther Allison, The Clash, Danny Gatton, Iggy Pop & The Stooges, Nirvana, Mick Ronson, and Sly & The Family Stone, among others. Heibutzki's endeavors have not been confined to the magazine world. In 1996, he contributed 28 profiles of hiphop performers to *Parents Don't Have To Like It*, a three-volume encyclopedia targeted to a Detroit middle school readership (Gale Research). He is currently working on a round of album reviews and biographies for the All Music Guide's Internet database (Ann Arbor, MI). His other projects have included writing liner notes for the UK compilation label Music Club International and Rhino Entertainment's five-CD Sugar Hill Records boxed set, to which he contributed one of three featured essays included in the accompanying booklet. Heibutzki lives with his wife, Lisa, in Hillsdale, Michigan, where he writes for the *Hillsdale Daily News*.

Barney Hoskyns is the author of *Across the Great Divide: The Band and America* (1993), *Waiting for the Sun: Strange Days, Weird Scenes and the Sound of Los Angeles* (1996) and other books. He has been U.S. Editor of *MOJO* magazine and is currently Editorial Director of *Rock's Backpages* (www.rocksbackpages.com). He saw Blondie support Television at the Hammersmith Odeon and enjoyed them more!

Jeff Johnson in the 80s was a kid who didn't mind hearing "Rapture" and "Heart of Glass" every day on the radio. While researching for his Blondie article, he came upon *Plastic Letters* and the self-titled first album and discovered an even better band than he'd known Blondie to be. He lives in Oakland with the Pink Avenger and writes for *Fabula* magazine (www.fabulamag.com). Send fan mail to jeff@fabulamag.com

John Kappes has written about music for *Alternative Press* magazine, where his interview with Deborah Harry and Chris Stein first appeared, Philadelphia's *Slant* and the Newhouse wire service. As J.K. Manlove, he carries on his own cult of personality with the band Ein Heit, which includes members of Seattle's Silkworm and released "The Lightning and the Sun" in 1997. He lives in Cleveland, where he is an editor for *The Plain Dealer*.

Steve Knight is an actor and published poet living in Los Angeles. He spent the last ten years in San Francisco where he worked with the internationally known performance art troupe SOON3, City College of San Francisco musical theater, LYRIC (Lavender Youth Recreation and Information Center) workshops, and spent every available minute at the famous SF bar Hole in the Wall—the closest thing to CBGB's and Max's Kansas City that he could find—great DJ's. His sister Traci Woolley is the lead singer of the popular San Diego band Tourette's Lautrec. He is an observer and imitator of life and greatly influenced by the face of Debbie Harry, the only woman to surpass Marilyn Monroe as the most beautiful woman of the 20th century in his mind.

Brian La Fountain is a naturalist at The Homestead Hotel Resort in Hot Springs, Virginia and has been an avid Blondie enthusiast for over 20 years.

Dan Lideen is a Minnesota native, born at the world-famous Mayo Clinic. He has always admired classic rock bands such as Blondie, and has been a fan since 1998. Dan has written many essays and poems for school assignments, and at 16 years of age, his first official publication is in this book. Aside from his writing talents, Dan also enjoys playing and learning music. Playing the alto saxophone in band since fifth grade, and figuring out how to play the piano for the last six years, he has developed a passion for music and how it is put together. Seeing Blondie as a role model and personal hero, Dan has been giving a lot of thought regarding his future. Whether it will be a career in the music business (which is very Blondie-influenced) or the film/TV business, Dan plans on being very successful in the entertainment world.

Allan Metz is a reference librarian at Drury University in Springfield, Missouri, who is a long-time fan of Blondie and has written about and researched female rock and pop singers in his endeavors as a music historian and bibliographer. He compiled this book and is co-editor (along with Carol Benson) of *The Madonna Companion: Two Decades of Commentary* (New York: Schirmer Books, 1999; Music Sales Corporation, 2000), which is part of the Companion Series. He also has compiled articles on popular music for the *Bulletin of Bibliography*: "Women in Rock and Roll: A Three-Part Bibliography" ("All Female New Wave Rock Bands of the 1980s—The Go-Go's, The Bangles, Bananarama; "'Tell It Like It T-I-Is': The B-52's"; "The Pretenders and Chrissie Hynde") 55, 4(December 1998): 265-300; "The Musical Legacy of Blondie: An Annotated Bibliography" 56, 4(December 1999): 189-217; "Two Rock/Pop Bibliographies: I. The Cardigans, II. Garbage" 57, 2(June 2000): 107-133; and "Blondie and Deborah Harry: A Comprehensive Bibliography" 58, 1(March 2001): 11-48. The author plans to continue working on other music-related projects such as being the webmaster of three Blondie sites—*Blondie: Legacy, Influence, Legend* (www2.drury.edu/ametz/blondie.htm), selected by VH1 as one of the five best web sites on Blondie; *Blondie, From Punk to the Present* (www2.drury.edu/ametz/blonbook.htm), which is both a companion to and a preview of this book; and *The Blondie Guide* (www2.drury.edu/ametz/blonguid.htm).

Jeff Miers is the Editor in Chief of Blue Dog Press, Buffalo, New York.

Aletha Milam is a freelance paralegal and aspiring fashion writer. Originally from El Dorado, Arkansas, she has traveled extensively for the past few years while working on location. She has enjoyed writing about female music icons and their influence on style as the editor of *The Hipstress E-Zine* (www.thehipstress.com). She currently resides with her Siamese cat and a large collection of retro dolls.

Brett Milano writes about and reviews music for a number of publications including *Stereo Review*, the *Boston Herald*, and the *Boston Phoenix.*

Michael Molenda is Editor-in-Chief of *Guitar Player* magazine, and Editorial Director of Music Player Media. He has been a music producer since the first wave of punk in 1976, and currently owns Tiki Town Studios in Mill Valley, California.

Dan Ouellette is a contributing writer to *Down Beat* magazine.

Anita Pallenberg has acted in such films as "Candy" (1968, as Nurse Bullock), "Barbarella" (1968, as the Black Queen), and "Performance" (1970, as Pherber). She also has been part of the rock music scene and an interview with Ms. Pallenberg appears in the book entitled *Star Culture* by Mark Sanders and Jefferson Hack (London: Phaisdon Press, 2000).

Daniel Porter lives in the UK. He has been a fan since the *Complete Picture* was released and is more of a solo than a Blondie fan. Dan maintains quite a large collection with a lot of rarities, which he has collected since around 1994. He got to see Blondie, met Debbie for the first time in 1998, has seen them seven times and met Debbie three times in that period. Dan also is a contributor to the *Blondie Archive* web site. At the time of this writing, he was working for Boots The Chemists in the Marketing Department and studying for a degree in Business. Dan has a wide range of musical tastes, mainly inspired by Debbie. The first song he remembers on the radio and actually liking was "French Kissin," which is probably why he is more of a Deborah Harry fan.

Cindy Rivers is a freelance writer/photographer who resides in the Chicago area and has written for numerous publications, including the *Chicago Sun-Times*, *Reader's Digest*, *Circus* and *Playgirl* magazines.

Charlotte Robinson is a Michigan native and graduate of the University of Michigan's English and Creative Writing programs. She contributes to PopMatters.com and the *Illinois Entertainer* and works as a proofreader at a Chicago law firm. Charlotte was previously the news writer for the All Music Guide and a frequent contributor to the All Music Zine. Although her musical tastes span several genres, she is particularly fond of 1970s British punk.

Sarah Rodman is music critic for the *Boston Herald*.

John Sibby: "i was born into a very complaisant all-is-relative surburbia in the late 1950s. my proof positive approach in validating my own existence came from exploring the neighboring urban counterculture of others. although not immediately evident, this would prove to be my salvation and my downfall...all in one. (subversive currents are an awakening in themselves). i was well on my way...compliance to the norm, socially acceptable reasoning or anything remotely resembling these trappings never came easy; in fact, never came at all. hence the quest for an alternative. the thought-provoking british offerings of the 60s set the foundation for our oblique predecessors. americana shaped itself in the midst of metro surrealistic tv parables, awkward and alienated, provoking an attitude in music which was indeed vast. subculture was not yet cliché and its participants from these arts were accessible...a far cry from arena rock's haughty presence. my incessant viewing of 70s rock publications (aka creem and circus) mirrored what i thought was the world around me. inevitably it was rock scene's photos that depicted an unsettling view of popular music's current state. the b&w undiluted still life behind the scene's imagery revealed no hidden agenda...you get what you see seemed in reality to 'be' the scene...gotta get there!...i did!"

Marcus Smith Ph.D. is Field Leader in Exercise Physiology at University College Chichester, England.

Chris Stein is guitarist and co-founder, with Deborah Harry, of Blondie.

Will Stokes was born in 1978 in Shropshire, England. He studied English Literature at the University of Liverpool and graduated in the summer of 2000. Will began writing on all aspects of popular culture for various publications, including *Attitude* magazine, for which his feature on Debbie Harry was originally commissioned. He has variously written on the popular appeal of playwright Joe Orton, 80s heroes Bananarama and the French art duo Pierre et Gilles, as well as writing an occasional column for *Attitude*. Will Stokes currently lives in London.

Jessamin Swearingen teaches in New York City and has had an abiding interest in Blondie and the New York punk music scene. This interest is reflected in her honors thesis, which has been adapted into a web site, offering many insights into Blondie and rock music generally. While you're at it, go to the "*We Created It; Let's Take It Over!' The Emergence Of Punk In America*" web site at: www.inch.com/~jessamin, from which many selections in this book have been adapted.

Everett True, as assistant editor of *Melody Maker*, was the first outside journalist to cover the Seattle music scene in early 1989, bringing Hole, Nirvana and Pavement and a host of other, sadly less known, bands to public attention. After a stint of writing about public transport in Melbourne, he now lives in Brighton, England with his fiancee Charlotte and his collection of Dexy's Midnight Runners records. He has a book out, *Live Through This* (London: Virgin, 2001), written about his experiences in the US in the early 90s—and it's a damn sight better than any "serious" biography because it's AUTHENTIC, ORIGINAL, ENTHUSIASTIC and FUN FUN FUN! A Ramones book is to follow.

Stuart Turnbull is Editorial Director of *Sleazenation* magazine.

Henrik Tuxen is a university graduate in Geography and Social Science. Bass player and semi-professional rock musician for 16 years. Full-time music writer in Danish and international magazines for the past five years. Born, raised and living in Copenhagen, Denmark where he lives with long time girlfriend, and three kids.

Gary Valentine was a bassist for Blondie from 1975 to 1977 and wrote the hit song "(I'm Always Touched By Your) Presence Dear" during that time. He has done freelance writing for a number of publications, including the *Times Literary Supplement*, *LA Weekly*, and the *San Francisco Chronicle*. He now lives in London and has a band called Fire Escape which has released one EP, "First Step," available via email at fe@musicbank.net and these urls: www.musicbank.net and www.cdbaby.com/cd/fireescape. Fire Escape performs frequently in London.

Dawn N. Volkman is a former editor of the New Haven, Connecticut web page on the About.com web site.

John Walsh writes for *The Independent* (London).

Russell White teaches cultural and media studies at King Alfred's College, Winchester, England and is a contributor to *Total Guitar* magazine. He is currently completing his PhD on Black Nationalism in hip-hop culture. "As well as being a top band, Blondie provided me with one of my first introductions to rap music (via 'Rapture' obviously)."

Eric Wiener is a computer consultant by day, a multimedia artist and musician by night, and an East Village resident 24 hours a day since 1993. During this time he's been intimately involved with the local art, journalism, dance, film making, theater and music scenes. On the "East Village" web page Eric edits for About.com: "I keep tabs on what's going on in the news and on the street. This is a place for East Villagers to express their ideas. This unique area of Manhattan is an incubator of creative energy, and open dialog benefits everyone."

Deborah Wilker writes for the Knight Ridder/Tribune News Service.

Francois Wintein is editor of the UK Blondie fanzine, *Picture This*.

Permissions

Anita Pallenburg. 2000. "A Cheap Date Exclusive...Debbie Harry." *Cheap Date* 3(2000): 12-17. Copyright © 2000. All rights reserved. Reprinted with permission of *Cheap Date* and the interviewer.

Jeff Miers. 2001. "Telling Stories With Dream Logic." *Blue Dog Press* web site. (30 March; Accessed 15 May 2001) <www.bluedogpress.com>. Copyright © 2001 Blue Dog Press. All rights reserved. Reprinted with permission of the author and Blue Dog Press.

Jim Farber. 1999. "Blondie's Back..." *New York Daily News* (10 January): "New York Now: Music" section, p. 19. 1999. (c) New York Daily News, L.P. reprinted with permission.

John Walsh. 1999. "Touched By Your Presence, Dear..." *Independent* (9 February): "Features" section, p. 1. Copyright © 1999. All rights reserved. Reprinted with permission of the *Independent*.

Brett Milano. 1999. "Catching a New Wave..." *Boston Herald* (23 February): "Arts and Life" section, p. 43. Copyright © 1999. All rights reserved. Reprinted with permission of the author.

David Bauder. 1999. "Rock Beat: One Way or Another, Blondie Has Made It Back." Associated Press (26 February): Friday, BC cycle. Reprinted with permission of The Associated Press.

Jim Greer. 1999. "Blondie 2.0." *Gear* (March-April): 84-86, 88. Copyright © 1999. All rights reserved. Reprinted with permission of *Gear*.

Everett True. 1999. "The Blonde Leading the Blonde." *Melody Maker* 76, 20(22 May): 24-25. Copyright © 1999. All rights reserved. Revised version of originally published article printed with permission of the author.

Deborah Wilker. 1999. "With Live Album and Plum New Year's Gig, Deborah Harry Embodies Blondie Once More." Knight Ridder/Tribune News Service (2 December). Reprinted with permission of Knight Ridder/Tribune Information Services.

Stuart Turnbull. 2001. "Flirty Harry." *Sleazenation* magazine and web site. (March; Accessed 14 March 2001) <www.sleazenation.com>. Stuart Turnbull, Editorial Director of Sleazenation magazine. All rights reserved Sleazenation magazine 2001.

Grace Bradbury. 2001. "Debbie Deserves the T-Shirt." *The Times, London* (2 March). © Times Newspapers Limited, 2001.

Will Stokes. 2001. "Blondie Ambition." Revised extended version of an article entitled "Attitude Icons: Will Stokes Dives Once More Into the Bleach With Blondie Bombshell Debbie Harry" from *Attitude* magazine 86(June 2001): 144-145. Copyright © 2001. All rights reserved. Printed with the permission of the author.

Jim Farber. 1999. "Blondie Makes a Grand Exit...*New York Daily News* (14 February): "Sunday Extra section, p. 19. (c) New York Daily News, L.P. reprinted with permission.

Joey Guerra. 1999. "Blondie With an Edge..." *Houston Chronicle* (21 February): "Zest" section, p. 6. Copyright © 1999. Houston Chronicle Publishing Company. Reprinted with permission. All rights reserved.

Michelle Goldberg. 1999. "Blondie: Behind the Music." *Salon.com* web site. (3 March; Accessed 23 April 2000). This article first appeared in Salon.com, at *www.Salon.com*. An online version remains in the Salon archives. Reprinted with permission.

Nicholas Barber. 1998. "Pop: Still Hip, Still Gutsy, Still Clever and Still Blondie. *Independent* (London) (15 November): "Features" section, p. 6. Copyright © 1998. All rights reserved. Reprinted with permission of the author.

Sarah Rodman. 1999. "The Tide is High Again for Rejuvenated Blondie." *Boston Herald* (17 May): "Arts and Literature" section, p. 37. Copyright © 1999. All rights reserved. Reprinted with permission of the author.

Neva Chonin. 1999. "Blondie's Back! Original Pop-Punk Diva Band Enraptures Sold-Out Warfield." *San Francisco*

Chronicle (1 June): C1. Copyright 1999. All rights reserved. Reprinted with permission of the *San Francisco Chronicle.*

Jim Farber. 1999. "In a Great Comeback, Blondie Has More Fun." *New York Daily News* (12 June): "New York Now: Music" section, p. 29. (c) New York Daily News, L. P. Reprinted with permission.

Joey Guerra. 1999. "Enduring Music Gives Blondie a Pop Legacy." *Houston Chronicle* (26 August): "Zest" section, 1. Copyright 1999. Houston Chronicle Publishing Company. Reprinted with permission. All rights reserved.

Joey Guerra. 1999. "Blondie Respects Roots, Focuses on Present." *Houston Chronicle* (30 August): "Zest" section, p. 1. Copyright 1999. Houston Chronicle Publishing Company. Reprinted with permission. All rights reserved.

Adam Budofsky. 1999. "Blondie's Clem Burke:...The Best Drummer New Wave Had to Offer." *Modern Drummer* 23, 6(June): 78-82, 84, 86, 88-90, 92, 94, 96. Copyright 1999. Reprinted permission of *Modern Drummer Magazine*, Cedar Grove, NJ USA.

Michael Molenda. 1999. "Back in Blonde: Chris Stein's Quirky Riffs Revitalize Blondie." *Guitar Player* 33, 4(April): 58-64. Copyright 1999. All rights reserved. Reprinted with permission of the author.

Henrik Tuxen. 1999. Original unedited version of the published article by the author entitled: "Blondie: No Exit." *Total Guitar* 55(April): 20-23, 25- 26. Copyright © 1999. All rights reserved. Reprinted with permission of the author.

John Hart. 2000. "What Was the Culture and Legacy Behind the Acclaimed Seventies Band: Blondie? College Project, Ruskin Adult College, Oxford, England. 2000. Copyright © 2000. All rights reserved. Reprinted and adapted with permission of the author.

Barney Hoskyns. 1999. Original unedited version of the published article by the author entitled: "The Misfits." *Mojo: The Music Magazine* 63(February): 64-76. Copyright © 1999. All rights reserved. Reprinted with permission of the author.

Scott Coblio. 2001. "'The Power of the Visual Image'" Copyright © 2001. Original essay. All rights reserved. Printed, adapted and edited with permission of the author.

John Sibby. 2000. "state of the arts? (transparencies 2000)." Original invited essay. Copyright © 2000. All rights reserved. Printed, adapted and edited with permission of the author.

Victor Bockris. 2001. "Debtalk." Previously unpublished quotations recorded and original commentary by Victor Bockris. Copyright © 2001. All rights reserved. Printed with permission of the author.

Ralph Heibutzki. 1999. "Blondie: Once More (Into the Bleach): Blondie Returns for Its Fifteenth Round." *Discoveries: For Record and CD Collectors.* 136(September): 41-51. Copyright 1999. All rights reserved. Reprinted with permission of the author and *Discoveries Magazine*, 700 E. State Street, Iola, WI 54990-0001.

James R. Blandford. 1999. "Nothing is Real But the Girl: James R. Blandford Reaches Into the Bleach to Look at Twenty-Two Years of Blondie." *Record Collector: CDs, Records & Pop Memorabilia* 241(September): 30-35. Copyright © 1999. All rights reserved. Reprinted with permission of *Record Collector.*

Aletha Milam. 2001. "Icon of the Month: Deborah Harry." *The Hipstress: The e-zine for hip chicks* web site. (April; Accessed 11 January 2002) <www.thehipstress.com>. Copyright © 2001. All rights reserved. Reprinted with permission of the author.

Everett True. 2001. "The Highest Compliment..." Original invited essay. Copyright © 2001. All rights reserved. Printed and adapted with permission of the author.

Cindy Rivers. 2000. "Deborah Harry: 'The Mark of an Icon.'" Original invited essay. Copyright © 2000. All rights reserved. Printed and adapted with permission of the author.

Henrik Tuxen. 2000. "Blondie: 'Some Love Never Dies.'" Original invited essay. Copyright © 2000. All rights reserved. Printed and adapted with permission of the author.

Ralph Heibutzki. 2000. "Foreword: 'Blondie and Me.'" Original invited essay. Copyright © 2000. All rights reserved. Printed and adapted with permission of the author.

Teresa Hale. 2000. "I Am Wearing Debbie Harry's Panties." *New York Waste* red hot summer issue (Summer 2000): 36-38. Copyright © 2000. All rights reserved. Edited by the author and reprinted with permission of the author.

Alan Foster. 1999. "Deborah Harry: Diva!" Reprint of article entitled "Divas! Part 3: Deborah Harry."*About.com* web site. (12 May; Accessed 28 October 2000). (c) 1999 by Alan Foster (http://gaylife.about.com), licensed to About, Inc. Used by permission of About, Inc. which can be found on the Web at www.About.com. All rights reserved.

Sherry Gunderman. 2001. "Meeting a Goddess." Original invited essay based on a manuscript entitled "Blonde Phoenix." Copyright © 2001. Printed and adapted with permission of the author.

Jon Erkider. 2001. "(Can I) Find the Right Words (to Say)." Original invited essay. Copyright © 2001. All rights reserved. Printed and adapted with permission of the author.

Scott Coblio. 2001. "Blondie: 'A New Concept.'" Original invited essay. Copyright © 2001. All rights reserved. Printed and adapted with permission of the author.

Brian La Fountain. 2000. "Deborah Harry: 'I'll Send You a Bill.'" Original invited essay. Copyright © 2000. All rights reserved. Printed and adapted with permission of the author.

Steve Knight. 2001. "'...The Greatest High'" Original invited essay and adapted e-mail message. Copyright © 2001. All rights reserved. Printed and adapted with permission of the author.

Dan Lideen. 2001. "Who I Admire." Original essay first posted on the DHBIS (Deborah Harry and Blondie Information Service listserv located on Yahoo! Groups, www.yahoogroups.com) and later supplemented by the author. Copyright © 2001. All rights reserved. Printed and adapted with permission of the author.

John Sibby. 2000. "blondie: 'nyc a-go-go...'" Original invited essay. Copyright © 2000. All rights reserved. Printed and adapted with permission of the author.

Robert Betts, Rock On The Net, and Allan Metz. 2000-2001. "The Blondie Geneology/The Blondie Chronology." Copyright © 2000-2001. All rights reserved. Adapted from *The Blondie Review*, Issue 3, June 2001 and *Rock On The Net* web site with the permission of *The Blondie Review* and the *Rock On The Net* web sites. (See below for more detail regarding *Rock On The Net*).

"Blondie." 2001. *Rock On The Net* web site. (Accessed 10 September) <www.rockonthenet.com>. Copyright © 2000-2001. All rights reserved. Adapted as part of "The Blondie Geneology/The Blondie Chronology" with the permission of *Rock On The Net*.

Robert Betts. 2001. "Louis A Bustamante: From Our LAB to Your Home: An Exclusive Interview." Reprinted from *The Blondie Review* (TBR), June 2001. Copyright © 2001. All rights reserved. Reprinted with permission of *The Blondie Review*.

Eric Wiener. 2000. "Plastic Letters." *About.com* web site. (Accessed 10 May 2000). (c) 1999 by Eric Wiener <http://eastvillage.about.com>, licensed to About, Inc. Used by permission of About, Inc. which can be found on the Web at www.About.com. All rights reserved.

Dawn N. Volkman. 2000. "Blondie Photo Exhibit." Formerly on *About.com* web site. (12 March; Accessed 10 May 2000) <http://newhaven.about.com>. Copyright © 2000. All rights reserved. Reprinted and adapted with permission of the author.

Marcus Smith. 2000. "Physiological Analysis of Clem Burke During Blondie's 1999 'No Exit' World Tour." *University College Chichester* web site. (Accessed 17 September 2000) <www.ucc.ac.uk>. Copyright © 2000. All rights reserved. Reprinted and adapted with permission of the author.

"Blondie in the Library." 2001. Copyright © 2001. All rights reserved. Adapted and edited with the permission of OCLC Online Computer Library Center, Inc.

"Michael Young Interviews Deborah Harry on the Program 'Kids Are People Too'" 2001. Original interview transcription. Copyright © 2001. All rights reserved. Printed, adapted and edited with permission of Ross MacDonald and Michael Young.

Andrea Farina. "Wigstock 2001: A Photo Essay." 2001. *The Blondie Review (TBR)* 2, 1(December): 7-12. Copyright © 2001. All rights reserved. Reprinted, adapted, and edited with permission of *TBR* and the author.

"Mike Morton," 2002. Revised bio adapted from *Blondie.net* web site. (Accessed 26 January 2002). <www.blondie.net>. Copyright © 2002. All rights reserved. Reprinted and adapted with permission of the author and Blondie.net.

Sylvie Ball, 2002. "A Very Jack the Ripper Christmas..." *Sylviestock* web site. (Accessed 5 February 2002). <www.sylviestock.com>. Copyright © 2002. All rights reserved. Reprinted and adapted with permission of the author.

Jon Erkider. 2002. "Deborah Harry, Gershwin Hotel, New York City..." Based on original message first posted on the DHBIS (Deborah Harry and Blondie Information Service listserv located on Yahoo! Groups, www.yahoogroups.com) and subsequently revised and edited. Copyright © 2002. All rights reserved. Reprinted, adapted, and edited with permission of the author.

John Sibby. 2000. "Afterword." Original invited essay. Copyright © 2000. All rights reserved. Printed and adapted with permission of the author.

Photo Essays

Mick Mercer. 2000. "Photographing Blondie." Original invited essay. Copyright © 2000. All rights reserved. Printed and adapted with permission of the author.

Marcia Resnick. 2001. "The Philadelphia Story: Blondie in 1979." Original invited essay. Copyright © 2001. All rights reserved. Printed and adapted with permission of the author.

Charlotte Robinson. 2000. "'I Just Took Pictures': Interview with Roberta Bayley." Reprint of article entitled "She Just Takes Pictures: Interview with Roberta Bayley." *PopMatters.com* web site. (30 August; Accessed 28 October 2000) <www.popmatters.com>. Reprinted and adapted with permission of PopMatters.com and the author.

Robert Betts. 2000. "You Know When to Take the Picture": Roberta Bayley In Conversation." Reprint of article entitled "Roberta Bayley In Conversation: An Exclusive *TBR* Interview." *The Blondie Review (TBR)* 1, 1(December, 2000) Copyright © 2000. All rights reserved. Reprinted and adapted with permission of *TBR* and the author.

Paul Parks. 2001. "Jingle Ball Benefit." *KFBM, Star 100.7)* web site. (Accessed 20 December) <www.histar.com>. Copyright © 2001. All rights reserved. Reprinted, adapted, and edited with permission of KFBM-FM, San Diego, California.

John Sibby. 2000. "workin' it..." *Joe Ryan Photography* web site. (Accessed 23 May 2000) <www.gratefuljoe.com>. Copyright © 2000. All rights reserved. Reprinted and adapted with permission of the author and Joe Ryan.

Alexandra King. 2000. "On Acting." Original invited essay. Copyright © 2000. All rights reserved. Printed and adapted with permission of the author.

Marcine Linder. 2000. "Photo Pass." Original invited essay. Copyright © 2000. All rights reserved. Printed and adapted with permission of the author.

Joe Ryan. 2000. "When 'The Original Beat Club Underground Sex Goddess Icon Freaks' reunite, you have no choice but to follow." Original invited essay. Copyright © 2000. All rights reserved. Printed and adapted with permission of the author.

Sylvie Ball. 2001. "Deborah Harry at Click + Drag at FUN." *The Blondie Review (TBR)* 1, 3(June): 27-30. Copyright © 2001. All rights reserved. Reprinted, adapted, and edited with permission of *TBR* and the author.

References/Bibliography

compiled by Allan Metz

A

Advanti, Reena. 2000. "Profile: South Asian Music Crossing Ethnic and Generational Lines" [transcript]. National Public Radio (1 June).

Advokat, Stephen. 1990. "Contemporary Musicians...Deborah Ann Harry." *CD-NOW* web site. (November; Accessed 22 February 1999 from former *Music Boulevard* web site which is now part of *CD-NOW*) <www.cdnow.com>.

Aizlewood, John, Andrew Collins, and Bill Prince, comps. 1996. *The Q Book of Punk Legends*. Enfield, Middlesex, United Kingdom: Guinness Publishing.

Albert, George. 1988. "A Blonde for the '80s." *Houston Chronicle* (11 December): 11.

"Alive and Kicking." 1999. BBC Television Broadcast (June).

Allan, Marc D. 1996. "Deborah Harry's Ambition to Revive Her Singing Career Means She's Ready to Put Blondie Together Again." *Indianapolis Star* (27 December): D1.

Allan, Vicky. 2000. "Roller Coaster of Love." *Scotland on Sunday* (16 April): S12.

Alter, Jonathan and Donna Foote. 1992. "The Cultural Elite." *Newsweek* 120, 14(5 October): 34.

"Alternative Action: March: Eve's Plum." 1994. *St. Louis Post-Dispatch* (3 March): 8.

Anderson, Ian. 2000. "The Wrap:...Bardot, Bardot (Warner Music)." *Waikato Times* (18 May): "Features" section, p. 9.

Anderson, Leigh. 1999. "No Escaping Blondie's Triumphant Return." *News Record* web site (University of Cincinnati). (3 February; Accessed 1 July 2000) <www.newsrecord.uc.edu>.

Anscombe, Isabelle and Dike Blair (text by). 1978. *Punk!* New York: Urizen Books.

"Any Questions: Deborah Harry: The Questionnaire with a Difference—You the Reader Get the Chance to Ask the Questions You've Always Wanted to Ask." 1993. *Guardian* (London) (28 November): O44.

Aquilante, Dan. 1998. ("Music Review"). "Version 2.0, Garbage, Almo Sounds." *New York Post* (12 May).

_____. 1999. "Blondie in Top Form." *New York Post* (25 February): "Living" section, p. 54.

_____. 1999. "'Exit' Poll: Yea and Nay. No Exit, Blondie, Beyond/BMG." *New York Post* (23 February): "Living" section, p. 54.

_____. 1999. "'Metasexual' Healing: Metasexual, Joydrop." *New York Post* (9 February), "Living" section, p. 52.

_____. 1999. "Rapture Recaptured." *New York Post* (12 February), "Living" section, p. 50.

Armstrong, Alistair. 1999. "Blondie, Chch [Christchurch, New Zealand] Musician Seal It With a Kiss." *The Press* (New Zealand) (27 August): 29.

Armstrong, Lisa. 2000. "The Midas Touch." *Times* (London) (5 June): "Features" section, p. 218.

Ashare, Matt. 1996. "Back Again: Lenny Kaye Returns With Patti Smith—But With a Difference." *Boston Phoenix* web site. (6 June: Accessed 19 July 2000) <www.bostonphoenix.com>.

_____. 1996. "The Goops, Lucky (Kinetic/Reprise)." *Boston Phoenix* web site. (29 February; Accessed 19 July 2000) <www.bostonphoenix.com>.

_____. 1997. "The Return of Ric Ocasek: Shakes It Up On *Troublizing*." *Boston Phoenix* web site. (4 September; Accessed 19 July 2000) <www.bostonphoenix.com>.

_____. 1998. "Shirley's Temple: Garbage Get Grrrl Power." *Boston Phoenix* web site. (7 May; Accessed 19 July 2000) <www.bostonphoenix.com>.

_____. 1999. "Action Figures: Bis and Vitamin C." *Boston Phoenix* web site. (26 August; Accessed 19 July 2000) <www.bostonphoenix.com>.

_____. 1999. "Live Wires: Eleven New Reports from the Concert Front." *Boston Phoenix* web site. (2 December; Accessed 19 July 2000) <www.bostonphoenix.com>.

Ashby, Romy. 2000. "Biking With Deb" [interview]. *Goodie Magazine* 5(2000): 4-18.

Augusto, Troy J. 1998. "The Cardigans." *Daily Variety* (11 November): 13.

Avery, Nicole Volta. 2000. "French Fashion Raises a Bona-Fide, Feminism Fuss." *Detroit News* (3 March): 3.

B

Balzano, Dino. 1999. "No Exit in Sight: The Rebirth of Blondie: An Interview with Deborah Harry." *Frontiers Newsmagazine* 18, 2.

Bangs, Lester. 1980. *Blondie*. New York: Simon and Schuster.

_____. 1987. *Psychotic Reactions and Carburetor Dung*. Greil Marcus, ed. New York: Alfred A. Knopf.

Bannister, Nicholas. 2000. "Object of Desire for Tycoons: Brand Values Gucci." *Guardian* (24 June).

Barajas, Victor. 2000. "Lead Singer Martinez Puts the Boss in Boss Hog." *Arizona Republic* (25 May): "The Rep" section, p. 12.

Baraka, Imamu Amiri. 1984. *The Autobiography of Leroi Jones/Amiri Baraka*. New York: Freundlich Books: Distributed to the trade by Scribner.

Barber, Lynden. 1990. "Generation Gap." *Sydney Morning Herald* (18 December): 12.

Barber, Nicholas. 1996. "Picture This: Next Month Deborah Harry is Singing at a Small London Club. To Celebrate, Nicholas Barber Gave the Original Blondie a Ring." *Independent* (London) (28 January): "Arts" section, p. 16.

_____. 1998. "Pop: Still Hip, Still Gutsy, Still Clever and Still Blondie." *Independent* (London) (15 November): "Features" section, p. 6.

Bardin, Brantley. 1999. "How To Go the Distance." *Mirabella* 95(March): 154.

Barker, Kim. 1996. "Rock On! Now Cleveland Has a Claim to Fame—"Rock 'N' Roll Museum." *Spokesman Review* (Spokane, Washington) (4 February): G4.

Barker, Kristy. 1999. "Maker Breakers: Venini." *Melody Maker* 76, 25(26 June): 11.

Barlowe, Neal. 1977. "Culture Hero: Blondie." *High Times* 22(June): 85-87.

Barnes, Ken. 2000. "Listen Up...: Nina Gordon, Tonight and the Rest of My Life." *US Today* (27 June): 6D.

Barry, Nicola. 1999. "Blonde on Blondie: Fans Will Flock Tonight to Aberdeen's Exhibition Centre to Hear Debbie Harry and Blondie—Iconic as Ever, Even After a 17-Year Absence. Nicola Barry Talked to the Pop Superstar." *Aberdeen Press and Journal* (Scotland) (27 November): "Showbiz: Music" section, p. 15.

Bartolini, David. 2000. "Okay...Let's Remind Everyone..." Online posting. *Blondie Bulletin Board, iMusic* web site. (2 July, 21:09:42 PDT; Accessed 6 July 2000) <www.imusic.com>.

_____. 2000. "...You Are a True Original..." Online posting [excerpt]. *Blondie Bulletin Board, iMusic* web site. (2 July, 21:13:16 PDT; Accessed 6 July 2000) <www.imusic.com>.

Bauder, David. 1999. "Blondie II: The Sequel: Harry and Company Are Giving It Another Try." *State Journal-Register* (Springfield, Illinois) (4 March): 25.

_____. 1999. "One Way or Another, Rock Band Blondie Has Made It Back." *Fort Worth Star-Telegram* (28 February): 3.

_____. 1999. "Rock Beat: One Way or Another, Blondie Has Made It Back." Associated Press (26 February): Friday, BC cycle.

Bayley, Roberta...[et al.]. 1996. *The Blank Generation Revisited: The Early Days of Punk* [mostly photography, including a number of Deborah Harry/Blondie photos]. New York: Schirmer Books.

_____, ...[et al.]. 1997. *Blank Generation Revisited: The Early Days of Punk Rock*. New York: Schirmer Books.

_____, ...[et al.]. 2000. *The Blank Generation Revisited: The Early Days of Punk*. New York: Music Sales Corporation.

Bayton, Mavis. 1998. *Frock Rock: Women Performing Popular Music*. Oxford, England: Oxford University Press.

Behrman, Lorne. 1996. "Alan Vega, Dujang Prang (2.13.61)." *Boston Phoenix* web site. (19 September; Accessed 19 July 2000) <www.bostonphoenix.com>.

Bell, Andy. 1991. "Blondie Had More Fun: Andy Bell of Erasure on the Nonsensical Appeal of 'Atomic' by Debbie Harry's Blondie." *Independent* (London) (10 October): "Arts Page: Riffs" section, p. 23.

_____. 1997. "Rebellious Jukebox: Andy Bell of Hurricane #1 Racks Up His Row of Number One Records: 1. Blondie, 'Heart of Glass' (From the Chrysalis LP 'Parallel Lines')." *Melody Maker* 74, 19(10 May): 19.

_____, Gaz Farmer, and Paul Mathur. 1999. "Chronic Jack." *Melody Maker* 76, 11(20 March): 39.

Benedict, David. 1999. "Definitely Debbie: Blondie, No Exit (Beyond/BMG)." *Melody Maker* 76, 6(13 February): 44.

Berenyi, Miki. 1992. "Rebellious Jukebox: Miki Berenyi of Lush Talks About the Records That Changed Her Life: 1. Blondie: 'In the Flesh' (from 'Blondie')." *Melody Maker* 68, 32(8 August): 34.

Berger, Arion. 2000. "RS Hall of Fame: Blondie, *Parallel Lines*, Chrysalis, 1978." *Rolling Stone* 842(8 June): 129.

Bernstein, Fred. 1981. "Blondie's New Wave Tide is High, But Now Debbie Harry Wants to Plunge into Films." *People Weekly* 15, 10(16 March): 88-89, 91-92.

"Best Pop Discs: Version 2.0, Garbage (Almo Sounds/Universal)." 1998. *Columbus Dispatch* (27 December): 7F.

"Beth Orton's Songs in the Key of Life." 1999. *NME* (New Musical Express) web site. (26 September; Accessed 2 July 2000) <www.nme.com>.

Betrock, Alan. 1977. "New Wave Hangs Ten." *New York Rocker* (July-August): 43, 46.

_____. 1982. *Girl Groups: The Story of a Sound*. New York: Delilah Books; distributed by The Putnam Publishing Group.

Bianculli, David. 2000. "TV Tonight." *Daily News* (New York) (10 May): "Television" section, p. 92.

_____. 2000. "TV Weekend." *Daily News* (New York) (26 February): "Television" section, p. 71.

"Billboard Charts: Blondie—*No Exit*." [1999?]. *Billboard* web site. (Accessed 20 July 2000) <www.billboard.com>.

"...Billie's Back—With Her Surname." 2000. *Evening Mail* (11 April): "Singles Review" section, p. 28.

"Bitz: Rock of Ages Puts No Limit on Blondie..." 1999. *Sunday Mirror* (7 November): "Features" section, p. 4.

"Black Box Recorder's Sarah Nixey on the Couch." 2000. *NME* (New Musical Express) web site. (14 May; Accessed 2 July 2000) <www.nme.com>.

Blackburn, Jimmy. 1999. Review of *Platinum Blonde*, by Cathay Che. *Melody Maker* 76, 22(5 June): 13.

Blackburne, Elaine. 1999. "The Singer May Have Aged But the Songs Are Still Timeless: Blondie, Telewest Arena, Newcastle." *The Journal* (Newcastle, England) (17 November): "Regional News" section, p. 5.

Blanchfield, Mike. 2000. "No Doubt Removes All Doubt: Return of Saturn, No Doubt (Interscope)." *Ottawa Citizen* (19 April): E5.

Blandford, James R. 1999. "Nothing is Real But the Girl: James R. Blandford Reaches Into the Bleach to Look at Twenty-Two Years of Blondie." *Record Collector: CDs, Records & Pop Memorabilia* 241(September): 30-35.

Blasco, Erin. 2000. "...Bif Naked, I Bificus (Atlantic)." *Sun-Sentinel* (Ft. Lauderdale, Florida) (28 April): "Showtime" section, p. 94.

Blondie. 1980. *The Best of Blondie*. New York: Chrysalis Records. Videocassette back cover container.

_____. 1983. *Blondie Live!* Universal City, California: MCA Home Video. Videocassette back cover container.

_____. 1989. *Eat to the Beat*. New York: Warner Home Video Inc. Videocassette back cover container.

_____. 1999. *Behind the Music: Blondie*. West Hollywood, California: Beyond Music; New York: BMG Distribution. Videocassette back cover container.

_____. 1999. *Blondie Live*. West Hollywood, California: Beyond Music; New York: BMG Distribution. Videocassette back cover container.

_____. 1999. *Blondie: The Best of MusicLaden Live*. Encore Music Entertainment America. Videocassette back cover container.

"Blondie." 1998. In *The Encyclopedia of Popular Music*. 3rd ed. Colin Larkin, ed. London; New York: New York: Muze; Exclusive distribution in the US by Grove's Dictionaries, Vol. I, p. 598.

"Blondie Ambition: Talking With...Deborah Harry." 1997. *People Weekly* 47, 6(17 February): 30.

"Blondie Announces First Leg 'No Exit' North American Tour—Their First in 16 Years." 1999. *Business Wire* (6 April).

"Blondie, Cardiff International Arena, Tuesday." 1999. *South Wales Evening Post* (11 November): "Showbiz: Music" section, p. 15.

"Blondie is Gone, Video Remembered." 1986. *San Diego Union-Tribune* (21 February): D15.

"Blondie Live: Philadelphia 1978/Dallas 1980, Blondie..." 1999. *Virgin.net* web site. (28 June; Accessed 4 July 2000) <www.virgin.net>.

"Blondie Makes a Comeback" [transcript # 99090200V02]. 1999. "Newsstand: CNN & Entertainment Weekly" (2 September).

"Blondie, No Exit, Producer: Craig Leon, Beyond 63985-78003." 1999. *Billboard* 111, 10(6 March): 25.

"Blondie Plans a Do at House of Blues." 1999. *Orlando Sentinel* (2 July): "Calendar" section, p. 6.

"Blondie, Recorded Live at HOB Las Vegas, Las Vegas, NV 3/10/1999." 1999. *House of Blues* web site. (Accessed 18 April 1999) <www.hob.com>.

"Blondie: The Life Story." 2000. *VH1* web site, "Fan Club" section. (Accessed 14 July 2000) <www.vh1.com>.

"Blondie Wow British." 1999. *The Press* (Christchurch, New Zealand) (2 July): "Features: Entertainment: In Brief, What's On" section, p. 24.

Blush, Steven. 1999. "No Regrets: Blondie Go Back to Their Roots." *Paper Magazine* (March): 62-63.

"Bobby Gillespie's Fan-ish Inquisition." 2000. *NME* (New Musical Express) web site. (5 February; Accessed 2 July 2000) <www.nme.com>.

Bockris, Victor. 1998. *NYC Babylon: Beat Punks*. London: Omnibus Press.

_____. 2000. *Beat Punks*. New York: Da Capo Press.

Bockris, Victor and Roberta Bayley. 1999. *Patti Smith: An Unauthorized Biography*. New York: Simon & Schuster.

Bogaev, Barbara. 1998. "Garbage Rock Critic Ken Tucker Reviews the New Album from Garbage, entitled 'Version 2.0' (Almo Sounds): Garbage's Debut Album, Released in 1995, Has Sold Over Four Million Copies" [transcript]. "Fresh Air" (16 June 1998).

Boot, Adrian and Chris Salewicz. 1997. *Punk: The Illustrated History of a Music Revolution*. New York: Penguin Studio.

Booth, Daniel. 1999. "Blondie: Wembley Arena, London." *Melody Maker* 76, 26(3 July): 38.

Booth, Philip. 1998. "Garbage Feasts on Past to Create Future." *Saratoga Herald-Tribune* (Saratoga, Florida) (16 October): 10

Boyd, Brian. 1999. "Born Again Blondie—Some 25 Years Ago They Came, Saw and Conquered. Now US New-Wave Group Blondie Are Doing It All Over Again With a New No. 1 Single and Album to Follow. Brian Boyd Glimpses Their Roots." *Irish Times* (13 February): 63.

Brazier, Chris. 1979. "Albums: 'Eat to the Beat' (Chrysalis...)." *Melody Maker* 54 (22 September): 30.

Bream, Jon. 1996. "Having Fun With Retro Sounds is No Problem for No Doubt." *Star-Tribune: Newspaper of the Twin Cities* (Minneapolis-St. Paul, Minnesota) (8 August): 5B.

_____. 1997. "Arena's Not the Place for No Doubt's Happy Pop." *Star-Tribune: Newspaper of the Twin Cities* (Minneapolis-St. Paul, Minnesota) (2 July): 4B.

_____. 1997. "Cardigans Offer Irresistible Retro-Pop Paradox." *Star-Tribune: Newspaper of the Twin Cities* (Minneapolis-St. Paul, Minnesota) (4 April): 1E.

_____. 2000. "Club Hopping in the City of Angels." *Star-Tribune: Newspaper of the Twin Cities* (Minneapolis-St. Paul, Minnesota) (14 May): 1G.

Bresnark, Robin. 1999. "Flatiron Maidens." *Melody Maker* 76, 26(3 July): 14.

Brinn, David. 1997. "No Doubt's Magic 'Kingdom.'" *Jerusalem Post* (11 February): 7.

_____. 1998. "Mad About Noel Coward." *Jerusalem Post* (12 May): 9.

_____. 2000. "The Apple of Her Eye." *Jerusalem Post* (22 February): "Arts" section, p. 10.

_____. 2000. "...No Doubt, Return of Saturn (Helicon)." *Jerusalem Post* (23 May): "Arts" section, p. 10.

Bronson, Fred. *Billboard's Hottest Hot 100 Hits*. New York, New York: Billboard Books, 1991.

Broomby, Beth. 2000. "Digital Dalkeith Could Kill Off CD." *Sunday Times* (9 April): "Features" section, p. 4.

Brown, G. 2000. "Creative Pressure: Second Time Around No Doubt Responds with 'Return of Saturn.'" *Denver Post* (14 July): E1.

_____. 2000. "No Time Like the Present for '80s Rockers." *Denver Post* (28 July): F1.

Brown, Glyn. 1998. "The Flying Scotswoman: Shirley Manson from Garbage is Rarely at Home. Glyn Brown Finds Out Why." *Independent* (London) (6 December): 2.

Brown, Mark. 1995. "A Stretch of Success: Profile: Elastica's Singer is Still Dazzled by the U.K. Band's Elevation to Overnight Sensation." *Orange County Register* (Santa Ana, California) (14 June): F4.

Browne, David. 2000. "Spaced Cadets: After Several Years of Delays, No Doubt Return, Presumably Older and Wiser. But Does Saturn Ring of Real Maturity?" *Entertainment Weekly* 535(14 April): 71.

Bruno, Mike. 1999. "Joydrop, Metasexual (Tommy Boy)." *Boston Phoenix* web site. (25 March; Accessed 19 July 2000) <www.bostonphoenix.com>.

Budofsky, Adam. 1999. "Blondie's Clem Burke:...The Best Drummer New Wave Had to Offer." *Modern Drummer* 23, 6(June): 78-82, 84, 86, 88-90, 92, 94, 96.

Budzak, Gary. 1998. "Garbage's Manson Offers Nods to Her Many Antecedents." *Columbus Dispatch* (4 June): 5.

Burchill, Julie and Tony Parsons. 1978. *"The Boy Looked At Johnny": The Obituary of Rock and Roll*. London: Pluto Press.

_____. 1987. *"The Boy Looked At Johnny": The Obituary of Rock and Roll*. 1st American ed. Boston: Faber and Faber.

Burnside, Anna. 2000. "Starlet Express." *Sunday Herald* (Australia) (9 July): 7.

Burroughs, William S. 1964. *Nova Express*. New York: Grove Press.

_____. 1978. *The Third Mind*. New York: Viking Press.

_____. 1981. *Cities of the Red Night*. New York: Holt, Rinehart, and Winston.

Burston, Paul. 1999. "Lightening Strikes Twice: After 16 Years' Absence, Blondie Are Back Where They Began—On the Road and Playing in Small Halls for Slim Pickings. The Hate That Made the Band Split is Long Forgotten, Audiences are as Ecstatic as Ever, and Debbie Harry, Icon of Cool, is Still the Embodiment of Blonde Ambition. Life is Good, They Tell Paul Burston." *Guardian* (London) (23 January): 8.

Bustamante, Louis A 1999. "Leigh Foxx Answers Your Questions." Online posting [excerpt]. *DHBIS* Mailing List. (24 September; Accessed 7 July 2000) <www.egroups.com>.

Buttars, Lori. 1999. "Blondie's New Turn—Touring." *Salt Lake Tribune* (Salt Lake City, Utah) (15 August): D3.

Buttolph, Angela. 2000. "An Eyeliner Can Win Friends and Influence People." *Sunday Times* (London) (23 April): "Features" section, p. 51.

C

Cameron, Keith. 1998. "Singles Archive, 16/5/98 *(Various)*." *NME* (New Musical Express) web site. (16 May; Accessed 2 July 2000) <www.nme.com>.

Campbell, Chuck. 1998. "Color Me Badd: More Like Colorless." *Knoxville News-Sentinel* (4 September): T12.

_____. 2000. "'N Sync Gets in Step with Backstreet Boys:...The Crow: Salvation, Various Artists (Koch)." *Knoxville News-Sentinel* (31 March): 18.

"Canadian Indie Band Database: Tuuli." 1994. *Jam!* web site. (Accessed 20 July 2000) <www.canoe.ca>.

Carrol, Jim. 1987. *Forced Entries: The Downtown Diaries, 1971-1973*. New York: Penguin.

Case, Sue-Ellen. 1989. "Toward a Butch-Femme Aesthetic." In *Making a Spectacle: Feminist Essays on Contemporary Women's Theatre*. Lynda Hart, ed. Ann Arbor: University of Michigan Press, 282-299.

Catlin, Roger. 1997. "Moby, Mighty Bosstones, Return of Blondie Highlight Riverside Fest." *Hartford Courant* (2 June): A4.

[Chaplin, Julia, comp.]. 1999. "Blondie Blasts Back." *Interview* 29, 1(January): 66-67.

Charlton, Katherine. 1998. *Rock Music Styles: A History*. 3rd ed. New York: McGraw Hill.

Che, Cathay. 1999. *Deborah Harry, Platinum Blondie: A Portrait by Cathay Che*. London: André Deutsch.

_____. 2000. *Deborah Harry*. New York: Fromm International.

Cheever, Susan. 1997. "Tori Amos." *Rolling Stone* 773(13 November): 104-105.

Chesterton, Ian. 1999. "Nightshift Live: Brassy: The Point." *Nightshift: Oxford's Music Online* web site. (November; Accessed 3 July 2000) <www.nightshift.oxfordmusic.net>.

Chick, Stevie. 1998. "Big Apple Tarts!" *Melody Maker* 75, 45(7 November): 25.

Chonin, Neva. 1999. "Blondie's Back! Original Pop-Punk Diva Band Enraptures Sold-Out Warfield." *San Francisco Chronicle* (1 June): C1.

Christensen, Thor. 1999. "'No Exit': Members of Blondie Say the Reunion is Permanent." *Dallas Morning News* (27 August): 63.

Christgau, Robert. 1996. "Consumer Guide: Sound Recordings." *Village Voice* 41, 41(8 October): 60.

Chung, Winnie. 2000. "New Doubts: The Californian Ska Band Are Back With a New Album and Attitude Says Winnie Chung." *South China Morning Post* (14 April): "Weekend Entertainment" section, p. 5.

Cigarettes, Johnny. 1998. "This Week's Singles, 24/10/98." *NME* (New Musical Express) web site. (20 October; Accessed 2 July 2000) <www.nme.com>

Clapp, Susannah. 1998. "The Best From the Arts in the Week Ahead...Critics' Choice." *Observer* (London) (27 September): 7.

Clark, Keith. 2000. "Evening of Destruction Review." *Bristol Evening Post* (United Kingdom) (16 March): 3.

Clark, Michael D. 2000. "A Good Time? It's No Doubt." *Houston Chronicle* (8 June): "Zest" section, p. 1.

_____. 2000. "Living Wisely: Rejuvenated Smith Returns 'Gung Ho.'" *Houston Chronicle* (2 April): "Zest" section, p. 6.

_____. 2000. "Santana Rescues Forgettable Year." *Houston Chronicle* (2 January): "Zest" section, p. 11.

Clifford, Mike, ed. 1992. *Harmony Illustrated Encyclopedia of Rock*. 7th ed. New York: Harmony Books.

Cocks, Jay. 1984. "The New Bad Boys of Fashion: Two Kindred Spirits Make Bright Clothes with Rock Brio." *Time* 124(29 October): 83.

Cohen, Debra Rae. 1979. "Blondie: A Dream Come True." *Rolling Stone* (29 November): 63-64, 66.

_____. 1980. "Punk's Dream." *Penthouse* 11, 6(February): 70-72, 74, 159-160, 162.

Cohen, Howard. 1999. "Blondie's Return Shows Group Still Can Soar in Concert." *Miami Herald* (2 September).

_____. 1999. "New Releases from Korn, Third Eye Blind, Savage Garden, Blondie: 'Live' (Beyond)." *Knight Ridder/Tribune News Service* (8 December).

Cohen, Jane and Bob Grossweiner. 1999. "A Rock And Roll Hall Of Fame Analysis." *CD-NOW* web site. (22 September; accessed 7 April 2000). <www.cdnow.com>.

Conner, Thomas. 1998. "Trash Talk: Garbage Goes to the Bin with 'Version 2.0,' A Meaner, Cleaner Version of Album One." *Tulsa World* (9 October 1998): 16.

_____. 1998. "Various Artists—Bespoke Songs, Lost Dogs, Detours and Rendezvous: Songs of Elvis Costello—Rhino." *Tulsa World* (22 May 1998): 14.

Conniff, Tamara. 1999. "Blondie Comeback Reaches AMA Show." *Plain Dealer* (Cleveland, Ohio) (11 January): 3E.

Connolly, Paul. 1999. "Singled Out." *Times* (London) (23 January): "Features" section, p. 12.

_____. 2000. "Singled Out." *Times* (London) (13 May): "Features" section, p. 12.

Considine, J.D. 1995. "Harry Isn't Blondie and Never Was." *Baltimore Sun* (19 May): 24.

_____. 1999. "Back Tracks: There's Still More Hendrix to be Experienced. Blondie's Roots are Showing, and TLC Tries to Stay Sexy, Cool and Crazy After All These Years." *Baltimore Sun* (23 February): 1E.

Courtney, Kevin. 2000. "Original Clubbers." *Irish Times* (29 July): "Weekend" section, p. 63.

Cowen, Andrew. 1998. "Blondie's Got a Heart of Class: Blondie, Wolverhampton Civic Hall." *Birmingham Post* (United Kingdom) (11 November): 15.

Craik, Laura. 2000. "Kudos Rules: Britons Show What Makes a Collection Sell." *Guardian* (London) (2 March).

Croft, Claudia. 2000. "Let It All Hang Out." *Evening Standard* (London) (23 March).

"Culture Club Celebrity Tips on What to Read, Spin and Surf." 2000. *InStyle Magazine* 7,6(June): 196.

Cunniff, Jill. 2000. "Deborah Harry: Unleashed: Pure Rock Fierceness." *Interview* (May): 64-65.

Curtis, Jim. 1987. *Rock Eras: Interpretations of Music and Society, 1954-1984*. Bowling Green, Ohio: Bowling Press Green State University Popular Press.

D

Dafoe, Chris. 1998. "New Recordings: Pop: Version 2.0, Garbage." *Globe and Mail* (Toronto, Canada) (28 May): C4.

Dalton, Stephen. 1997. "Kenickie, At the Club *(EMIDisc)*." *NME* (New Musical Express) web site. (3 May; Accessed 2 July 2000) <www.nme.com>.

_____. 1997. "Salad, Ice Cream *(Island)*." *NME* (New Musical Express) web site. (31 May; Accessed 2 July 2000) <www.nme.com>.

_____. 1998. "Garbage, Version 2.0 *(Mushroom)*." *NME* (New Musical Express) web site. (9 May; Accessed 2 July 2000) <www.nme.com>.

_____. 1999. "Blondie, No Exit *(RCA)*." *NME* (New Musical Express) web site. (5 February; Accessed 2 July 2000) <www.nme.com>.

Dancis, Bruce. 1999. "New Platinum Blondie?" *Sacramento Bee* (14 March): EN3.

Davidson, John. 2000. "Legging It Back to the Bad Old Days: John Davidson Hears Paris's Rebel Yell of Eighties Culture But, He Says, Go On, Make My Day, Punk." *Herald* (United Kingdom) (3 March): 26.

"Debbie Harry Not a Pioneer." 1987. Associated Press (6 July): AM cycle.

"Debbie Harry Sets the Record Straight: 'It's the Music That Sells Blondie, Not the Sex.'" 1980. *Rock Stars* 16(March): 42-44.

DeCurtis, Anthony and James Henke. 1992. *The Rolling Stone Illustrated History of Rock & Roll.* New York: Random House.

Dedrick, Jay. 1999. "Garbage Takes the Nomination and Runs." *Record*, Northern New Jersey (5 April): L7.

DeMarco, Laura. 2000. "Lilith Fair Is Fair Game for Blame: Has the Women's Music Festival Sapped the Boldness and Edge from Female Musicians?" *Star-Tribune: Newspaper of the Twin Cities* (Minneapolis-St. Paul, Minnesota) (7 May): 10F.

_____. 2000. "Lilith Fair May Be Handcuffing Women Musicians." *Times-Picayune* (New Orleans) (25 February): L17.

Dempster, Sarah. 1999. "Quinn: Glasgow King Tut's Wah Wah Hut." *NME* (New Musical Express) web site. (23 November; Accessed 2 July 2000) <www.nme.com>.

_____. 2000. "Angelica, The End Of A Beautiful Career *(Fantastic Plastic)*." *NME* (New Musical Express) web site. (25 April; Accessed 2 July 2000) <www.nme.com>.

_____. 2000. "Geneva, Edinburgh Venue." *NME* (New Musical Express) web site. (15 March; Accessed 2 July 2000) <www.nme.com>.

DeRogatis, Jim. 2000. "Catch Frisbie While You Can: All the Right Spins." *Chicago Sun-Times* (14 July): "Weekend Plus" section, p. 5.

_____. 2000. "No Doubt Strays From Roots." *Chicago Sun-Times* (26 March): "Real Life: Pop Music Review" section, p. 3.

Dickerson, James. 1998. *Women on Top: The Quiet Revolution That's Rocking the American Music Industry*. New York: Billboard Books.

Dickinson, Chris. 1997. "...And Real Ground-Breakers." *St. Louis Post-Dispatch* (7 September): 4C.

Didcock, Barry. 1999. "Parallel Lives." *Sunday Herald* (Australia) (6 June): 4.

Dingwall, John. 1998. "Blondie's Ambition Still Strong." *Scottish Daily Record* (27 November): "Features" section, p. 67.

_____. 1999. "Blur's Blondie Ambitions: A New Book Reveals Blur Like You Have Never Seen Them Before—Damon Albarn As Debbie Harry and as King Arthur, Before He Was Crowned the King of Britpop." *Scottish Daily Record* (9 July): 56.

_____. 1999. "Once More Into the Bleach: Back at No. 1, Debbie Harry Looks Back on Blondie's Lost Weekend." *Scottish Daily Record* (12 February): 49.

_____. 1999. "Tales of Bands in a Harry: Blondie and the Clash Made It Big on the Back of Punk. John Dingwall on Two New Rockumentaries." *Scottish Daily Record* (2 October): Saturday Magazine, "Features" section, p. 3/31.

Dingwall, John and Rick Fulton. 1998. "I'm Queen of the Uncool." *Scottish Daily Record* (10 July): 6.

Disco, John, Manda Rin, Sci-Fi Steve, and Daniel Booth. 1999. "Maria, Blondie (RCA)." *Melody Maker* 76, 5(6 February): 36.

"A Disposable Guide to Disposable Popsters." 2000. *Sunday Herald* (Australia) (25 June): 5.

Dix, John. 2000. "Punk Chicks Good To Go." *New Truth and TV Extra* (19 May): "Features" section, p. 15.

"Do You Have What It Takes? Guitarist Required, To Create and Replace." 2000. *The Pallantines* web site. (Accessed 5 July 2000) <www.palantines.com>.

Dodero, Camille. 1999. "Paperback Pick: An Interview With Elizabeth Wurtzel." *Boston Phoenix* web site. (8 July; Accessed 19 July 2000) <www.bostonphoenix.com>.

Doerschuk, Robert L. 1997. "Private Lesson: Debbie Does Jazz." *Musician* 224(July): 24-25.

Doherty, Harry. 1978. "Albums: 'Plastic Letters' (Chrysalis...): Mature Blondie." *Melody Maker* 53 (11 February 11): 20.

Dominic, Serene. 1997. "The Jazz Passengers Featuring Deborah Harry, *Individually Twisted* (32 Records)." *Phoenix New Times* web site. (27 February-5 March; Accessed 20 July 1997) <www.phoenixnewtimes.com>.

Donald, Ann. 1999. "They're All Still Wild About Harry." *Herald* (Glasgow, Scotland) (4 October): 18.

Doss, Yvette C. 1997. "The Second Wave: Rockinvasion '97 is the Most Ambitious U.S.-Spanish Rock Tour Ever." *Los Angeles Times* (15 June): 57.

Du Noyer, Paul. 1994. "Music, Maestress, Please!" *Q Magazine* (December).

_____, ed. 1995. *The Story of Rock 'N' Roll: The Year-By-Year Illustrated Chronicle.* New York : Schirmer Books.

Dunlevy, Tcha. 1999. "The New Ship Blondie: The Band Sails Back Into the Spotlight with Forays into Pop, Punk, Ska, Country and What Was Once Called New Wave." *Gazette* (Montreal) (4 March): D14.

Dunn, Jancee. 1993. "The 100 Top Music Videos: The Stars, The Scripts, The Stories, In Extreme Close Up: Rapture, Blondie, 1981." *Rolling Stone* 667(14 October): 98.

Duralde, Alonso. 2000. "Summer Reading Strand:...*Deborah Harry* by Cathay Che..." *Advocate* 814(20 June): 131+.

E

Eccleston, Danny. 1998. "It's Bin Done: Garbage (6/10). Version 2.0. (Mushroom)." *Times* (London) (9 May): 10.

Eck, Michael. 2000. "Rock Legend Lives On: 'Buddy...The Buddy Holly Story' Comes to Proctor's Friday." *Times Union* (Albany, New York) (3 August): "Preview" section, p. 34.

Eddy, Chuck. 1997. *The Accidental Evolution of Rock 'N' Roll: A Misguided Tour Through Popular Music.* New York: Da Capo Press.

Edwards, Mark. 2000. "Commercial Suicide." *Sunday Times* (London) (19 March): 37.

Elder, Bruce. 2000. "Pay TV Highlights:...Behind the Music: Blondie." *Sydney Morning Herald* (17 July): "The Guide" section, p. 12.

Ellen, Barbara. 1998. "Harry Ever After: Blondie, Wolverhampton Civic Hall." *Observer* (London) (15 November): 9.

_____. 2000. "Natural Blondie Highlights." *Times* (London) (4 February): 42.

Elliot, Paul. 1996. "No Doubt: Feelgood Rock Aims for UK Market." *Music Week* (6 July): 12.

Ellis, Robert. 1981. *The Pictorial Album of Rock.* New York: Crescent Books.

Ellison, Michael. 2000. "New York Stories: We Will Survive..." *Guardian* (19 June).

Ervolino, Bill. 1987. "Debbie: An Interview with Debbie Harry." *Long Island's Nightlife* 7, 2(February): 19, 32, 37, 113.

Evans, Gareth. 2000. "Tuesday Book: A Hard and Fast Elegy for Slough's Satellite Boys: Human Punk by John King (Jonathan Cape, Pounds 10)." *Independent* (London) (23 May): "Comment" section, p. 5.

Evans, Simon. 1999. "Pop With Wit and a Wink: Blondie NEC." *Birmingham Post* (United Kingdom) (23 June): 18.

"Everyone's Wild About Harry." 1978. *Rock On!* 6(October): 18.

"Excerpt from Interview with Blondie: From Search & Destroy #3, 1977." 1999. *RE/Search Publications* web site. (Accessed 20 July 2000) <www.vsearchmedia.com>.

F

"Fans' Notes: No Doubt." 2000. *Rolling Stone* 840(11 May): 42.

Farber, Jim. 1999. "Blondie's Back: The Tide Is High for Deborah Harry and Co, Who Have an Album of New Songs and a Concert Tour Ahead." *New York Daily News* (10 January): "New York Now: Music" section, p. 19.

_____. 1999. "In a Great Comeback, Blondie Has More Fun." *New York Daily News* (12 June): "New York Now: Music" section, p. 29.

_____. 1999. "Monsters of Melody: Powerman 5000 Surges Up the Charts With Its Hummable Ghoul-Rock." *New York Daily News* (10 August): "New York Now: Music" section, p. 38.

_____. 2000. "'Millionaire' Tries to Cash In With CD." *New York Daily News* (21 June): "New York Now" section, p. 38.

Farr, Sara. 2000. "Seen and Overheard:...Rock 'N' Roll Lives!!" *Dayton Daily News* (30 July): 5C.

Feber, Eric. 1999. "CD Reviews:...Blondie, 'No Exit' (Beyond/BMG Records)." *Virginia-Pilot and The Ledger-Star* (Norfolk, Virginia) (26 February): E12.

Finn, Timothy. 1998. "Software for Your Ears: Garbage and Massive Attack Release New, If Not Improved, CDS." *Kansas City Star* (21 May): F5.

_____. 2000. "No Doubt's Saturnalia Gwen Stefani and Band Run Circles Around '80s Roots Bands." *Kansas City Star* (15 July): E7.

_____. 2000. "On the Cusp of 'Saturn': Gwen Stefani Looks Ahead to a Life and Career in Orbit." *Kansas City Star* (12 July): F1.

"The 50 Most Essential Punk Records." 2001. *Spin* 17, 5(May): 108-110, 112.

Fitzpatrick, Kelly. 1999. "A Grayer Blondie Older and Wiser: New-Wavers Hit the Studio and the Road Again After Nearly 2 Decades." *Orlando Sentinel* (3 September): "Calendar" section, p. 8.

Fletcher, Tony. 1999. "Cardigans Less Comfy This Time." *Newsday* (8 February): B3.

_____. 2000. "...Patti Smith, 'Gung Ho' (Arista)." *Newsday* (14 April): D27.

Flynn, Andrew. 1999. "Blondie Not Just New Wave Relics." *Jam!* web site. (13 March; Accessed 20 July 2000) <www.canoe.ca>.

Foreman, Sue. 2000. "Live Reviews: Elastica, The Zodiac." *Nightshift: Oxford's Music Online* web site. (May; Accessed 3 July 2000) <www.nightshift.oxfordmusic.net>.

Fox, Barry and Kira L. Schlechter. 2000. "Only the Important Make This 'Best' List." *Sunday Patriot-News* (Harrisburg, Pennsylvania) (2 January): "Arts/Leisure" section, p. E1.

Frame, Pete. 1993, 1983. *The Complete Rock Family Trees*. London: Omnibus Press.

Freedberg, Michael. 1996. "Republica, Republica (Deconstruction/RCA)." *Boston Phoenix* web site. (23 May; Accessed 19 July 2000) <www.bostonphoenix.com>.

_____. 1998. "The World's Greatest Club Collection (Alpha Wave)." *Boston Phoenix* web site. (29 October; Accessed 19 July 2000) <www.bostonphoenix.com>.

Freydkin, Donna. 1999. "Reunited Blondie Rapturous Again." *CNN* web site. (2 March; Accessed 20 July 2000) <www.cnn.com>.

Fricke, David. 1995. "Smashing Pumpkins." *Rolling Stone* 721(16 November): 51-59.

_____. 1996-1997. "The Year in Recordings: Tragic Kingdom, No Doubt, Trauma/Interscope." *Rolling Stone* 750-751(26 December-9 January): 195.

_____. 2001. "The Father of Punk, Joey Ramone: 1951-2000." *Rolling Stone* 869(24 May): 45-46, 49.

Frith, Simon. 1981. *Sound Effects: Youth, Leisure, and the Politics of Rock 'N' Roll*. New York: Pantheon Books.

_____. 1988. *Music for Pleasure: Essays in the Sociology of Pop*. New York: Routledge.

_____. 1996. "Looking After Number One—Heart of Glass, A Single by Blondie." *Melody Maker* 73, 17(27 April): 55.

Frith, Simon and Howard Horne. 1987. *Art Into Pop: Pop Music Influence of Visual Arts, 1955-1985*. London, New York: Methuen and Co. Ltd.

"From Fashion to Fizzle: 26 of the Chosen Who Change the Way the World Dresses" [including Deborah Harry]. 1980. *People Weekly* 14, 13 (29 September): 26-27.

Frum, David. 2000. *How We Got Here: The 70's, The Decade That Brought You Modern Life*. New York: Basic Books.

Fugate, Katherine. "Childhood Dreams Can Come True." *Lesbian News* 21, 12(July 1996): 45.

G

Gaar, Gillian G. 1992. *She's a Rebel: The History of Women in Rock & Roll*. Seattle, Washington: Seal Press.

Gaines, Donna. 1997. "Let's Talk About Sex: Women Rockers Swagger Into the '90s with the Moves That Would Make Mick Jagger Blush." *Rolling Stone* 773(13 November): 91-92, 94-95.

Gale, William K. 1999. "Blondie Bringing Artistry and Attitude to Foxwoods." *Providence Sunday Journal* (29 August): E2.

Ganahl, Jane. 2000. "She's Young, Beautiful and No Doubt Conflicted: Stefani Better Make Up Her Musical Mind." *San Francisco Examiner* (17 April): D1.

Garcia, Chris. 1996. "Have No Doubt, They're Hot." *Press Democrat* (Santa Rosa, California) (19 January): D1.

Gardner, Elysa. 1998. "Blondie on Blondie: Deborah Harry and Co. Talk About What Isn't Your Usual Reunion Project." *Los Angeles Times* (18 October): 3.

_____. 1999. "Blondie Out to Disprove There's 'No Exit' From Its Past." *USA Today* (5 March): 9E.

Garelick, Jon. 1999. "Blondie: Little Symphonies." *Boston Phoenix* web site. (20 May; Accessed 19 July 2000) <www.bostonphoenix.com>.

_____. 1999. "Spice Girls: Alanis Morissette and Garbage." *Boston Phoenix* web site. (25 February; Accessed 19 July 2000) <www.bostonphoenix.com>.

Garner, Simon. 1999. "Review: For Blondie, Read Blandie, National Indoor Arena." *Birmingham Post* (Birmingham, England) (25 November): 14.

Garratt, Sheryl. 1996. "The New Rock Chic." *Sunday Times* (London) (4 August).

Geller, Dave. 1999. "Blondie, *'No Exit,'* Beyond Music." *Sound Waves Magazine* web site. (March; Accessed 19 March 1999) <www.swaves.com>.

George-Warren, Holly. 1997. "High Notes: Women Have Been Responsible for Some of Rock and Roll's Most Influential Recordings. Here's a Selective Discography." *Rolling Stone* 773(13 November): 179-181.

_____, ed. 1999. *The Rolling Stone Book of the Beats: The Beat Generation and American Culture*. New York: Hyperion.

"Get Out Your Dancing Shoes..." 2000. *Daily News* (New Zealand) (4 May): "Features" section, p. 23.

Gimarc, George. 1994. *Punk Diary: 1970-79*. New York: St. Martin's Press.

_____. 1997. *Postpunk Diary: 1980-82*. New York: St. Martin's Press.

Giltz, Michael. 1999. "Men's Best Friends: Wild, Willful, Or Both, These Are the Women Gay Men Find Wonderful—Whether They Want to Emulate Them Or Be Their Bosom Buddies." *Advocate* (23 November): 36-39.

Ginsberg, Allen. 1972. *The Fall of America: Poems of These States*. San Francisco: City Lights.

"The Goddess Still Rocks: No Exit, Blondie, Beyond Records." 1999. *Advocate* 780(2 March): 57.

Gould, Phil. 1999. "Tide's Still High." *Belfast News Letter* (9 November): "Features" section, p. 15.

_____. 1999. "Tide's Still High for Blondie." *Western Daily Press* (England) (10 November): "Features" section, p. 7.

Gowans, Scott. 2000. "'Coyote Ugly' Gives Unlikely Earnestness to Inspirational Tale." *Columbus Dispatch* (4 August): 8F.

Gracyk, Theodore. 1996. *Rhythm and Noise: An Aesthetics of Rock*. Durham, North Carolina.

Graff, Gary. 1999. "Blondie Ambitions." *Wall of Sound* web site. (Accessed 2 March 1999) <www.wallofsound.go.com>.

_____. 1999. "Blondie Members Find Reunion Source of Rapture." *Blondie Archive* web site. (27 February; accessed 9 July 2000) <www.blondie.ausbone.net>.

_____. 2000. "Song Choices of Silver and Gold: A Revelation Even to Neil Young." *Plain Dealer* (Cleveland, Ohio) (25 April): 6E.

Graham, David. 2000. "Split Personality Has Stranglehold on Fall 2000 Fashions." *Toronto Star* (9 March): FA2.

Grant, Steve. 1999. "Night of Nostalgia for the Eighties Sub Head: Blondie/Squeeze, New Coliseum, St. Austell, Thursday Night Only." *Evening Herald* (Plymouth, England) (13 November): 13.

Green, Jim. 1979. "Blondie: Progress Report from the Power Station." *Trouser Press* 42(September): 12-18.

_____. 1982. "Blondie: Pumping Vinyl." *Trouser Press* 77(September): 16-21.

Greer, Jim. 1999. "Blondie 2.0." *Gear: The Still New Magazine for Men* (March-April): 84-86, 88.

Gregory, Hugh. 1998. *A Century of Pop*. Chicago, Illinois: A Cappella.

Greig, Charlotte. 1989. *Will You Still Love Me Tomorrow?: Girl Groups from the 50s On*. London: Virago.

Gross, Terry. 2000. "Sarah Vowell Discusses Her New Collection of Essays" [transcript]. Fresh Air (20 April).

Guerra, Joey. 1999. "Blondie Respects Roots, Focuses on Present." *Houston Chronicle* (30 August): "Zest" section, p. 1.

_____. 1999. "Enduring Music Gives Blondie a Pop Legacy." *Houston Chronicle* (26 August): "Zest" section, 1.

_____. 2000. "Pop's Outsiders: Luscious Jackson Goes Upbeat, But Fights for Airplay." *Times Union* (Albany, New York): 14.

H

HairColor80. 2000. "I Am [a] No Doubt Fanatic Stopping By." Online posting. *Blondie Bulletin Board, iMusic* web site. (3 July; Accessed 6 July 2000) <www.imusic.com>.

Hanks, Robert. 2000. "Television Review." *Independent* (London) (14 June): "Features" section, p. 16.

Hanrahan, Jenifer. 2000. "Born to None: Neither Boomers Nor Gen Xers, They're a Generation Apart." *San Diego Union-Tribune* (4 July): E1.

Harden, Mark. 1999. "Reunited Blondie Back Up to Its Old Tricks: New CD Gives Group a Modern Sound." *Denver Post* (26 February): E1.

[Hardy], Loz. 1992. "Rebellious Jukebox: Loz of Kingmaker Talks About the Records That Changed His Life...5. Blondie: 'Picture This' (from 'Parallel Lines')." *Melody Maker* 68, 43(24 October): 37.

Hargreaves, Darron. 2000. "Show Focuses on Warhol's 'Real' Art." *Daily Yomiuri/Yomiuri Shimbun* (Japan) (13 April).

Harrington, Richard. 1998. "Garbage at 9:30, Curbing Nothing." *Washington Post* (29 May): B3.

_____. 2000. "No Doubt: They're Back—Seriously." *Washington Post* (7 April): C7.

Harrison, Andrew and Peter Saville. 2001. *Q: The 100 Best Record Covers of All Time*. Limited ed., collector's special. London: *Q* [magazine].

Harrison, Shane. 2000. "Trademark Sound on a Roll...: 'Return of Saturn,' No Doubt, Interscope..." *Atlanta Constitution* (13 April): D6.

"Harry, Debbie." 1982. In *Current Biography Yearbook, 1981*. Charles Moritz, ed. New York: H.W. Wilson Company, 191-195.

Harry, Debbie, Chris Stein, and Victor Bockris. 1982. *Making Tracks: The Rise of Blondie*. New York: Dell Publishing Company.

_____. 1998. *Making Tracks: The Rise of Blondie*. 1st Da Capo Press ed. New York: Da Capo Press.

Harry, Deborah. 1995. "Foreword." In Amy Raphael, *Never Mind the Bollocks: Women Rewrite Rock*. London: Virago.

_____. 1996. "Foreword." In Amy Raphael, *Grrrls: Viva Rock Divas*. 1st St. Martin's Griffin ed. New York: St. Martin's Griffin.

"Harry, Deborah." 1998. In *The Encyclopedia of Popular Music*. 3rd ed. Colin Larkin, ed. London; New York: New York: Muze; exclusive distribution in the USA by Grove's Dictionaries, vol. III, pp. 2418-2419.

Hassall, Carol. 2000. "Blond of Love for Sam and Her Idols." *Sunday Mercury* (19 March): 15.

"Hatlist...: Brassy, 'Good Times.'" 1999. *Nightshift: Oxford's Music Online* web site. (November; Accessed 3 July 2000) <www.nightshift.oxfordmusic.net>.

"Hatlist...: "Cha Cha Cohen, 'Cha Cha Cohen.'" 1999. *Nightshift: Oxford's Music Online* web site. (March; Accessed 3 July 2000) <www.nightshift.oxfordmusic.net>.

"Hatlist...: "Cha Cha Cohen, 'Cha Cha Cohen.'" 1999. *Nightshift: Oxford's Music Online* web site. (December; Accessed 3 July 2000) <www.nightshift.oxfordmusic.net>.

Hayt, Elizabeth. 2000. "Pulse: What I'm Wearing Now." *New York Times* (28 May): section 9, p. 3.

Heatley, Michael. 1993. *The Ultimate Encyclopedia of Rock: The World's Most Comprehensive Illustrated Rock Reference*. New York: HarperCollins.

Heibutzki, Ralph. 1999. "Blondie: Once More (Into the Bleach): Blondie Returns for Its Fifteenth Round." *Discoveries: For Record and CD Collectors* 136(September): 41-51.

Helligar, Jeremy and Helene Stapinski. 1999. "Bleach Bond: After 16 Years Apart, Blondie Takes to the Comeback Trail With a New Album and a U.S. Tour." *People Weekly* 51, 1(11 January): 123-127.

Henry, Tricia. 1989. *Break All Rules: Punk Rock, The Making of Style*. Ann Arbor, Michigan: UMI Research Press.

Herrmann, Brenda. 1992. "Rockin' Fashions Through the Years." *Chicago Tribune* (19 August): section 7, p. 9.

Hershkovits, David. 1989. "Wild About (Deborah) Harry: After Running Out of Hits, Deborah Harry Comes Back with a Monster New Album." *Paper Magazine* (October): 24-25.

Heylin, Clinton. 1993. *From the Velvets to the Voidoids: A Pre-Punk History for a Post-Punk World*. New York: Penguin Books.

Hilburn, Robert. 1985. "Sometimes It Was Harry Being Blondie." *Los Angeles Times* (1 December): 63.

_____. 1995. "Making Music Together: Remember the Old Days When All We Heard From Were the Boys in the Band? And When Women Were Left to Join Forces in All-Female Groups? Well, It's the '90s, So Forget All That. The Sound You Hear is Gender Bending." *Los Angeles Times* (19 March): 8.

_____. 1995. "Pop Music Strategy? That's a Stretch: British Sensation Elastica Worked Hard to Avoid the Hype That Goes with Comparisons to Icons Like the Pretenders and Blondie. But the More the Group Downplayed Things, the Bigger the Buzz Grew." *Los Angeles Times* (12 March): 5.

_____. 1999. "Aiming High and Wide: In Concerts That Display Both Artists' Desire to Push Their Boundaries, [Alanis] Morissette Tops [Sheryl] Crow for Complexity and Depth." *Los Angeles Times* (5 April): F1.

Hill, Edward. 1990. "Deborah Harry is Moving Forward But Using Her Past." *Plain Dealer* (Cleveland, Ohio) (12 February).

Hill, Sam. 2000. E-mail [to John Hart] (August).

Himes, Geoffrey. 1999. "Cardigans Not All Warm and Fuzzy." *Washington Post* (29 January): N17.

Hinckley, David. 1998. "Like You Just Don't Care: Rappers, 1981." *Daily News* (New York) (11 November): 55.

Hirshey, Gerri. 1997. "The Backstage History of Women Who Rocked the World: The Seventies: Sirens, Punks and Disco Queens" [profiles of women musicians, including Deborah Harry]. *Rolling Stone* 773(13 November): 70, 72.

_____. 2000. "Pink Cadillacs, Little Red Corvettes, Paradise by the Dashboard Light." *Rolling Stone* 840(11 May): 87-89, 91-92, 94-96, 98, 101, 104, 106-107, 109-112, 114.

_____. 2001. *We Gotta Get Out of This Place: The True, Tough Story of Women in Rock*. New York: Atlantic Monthly Press.

Histen, Michael. 2000. "After a Long Wait, No Doubt's New Work is Just OK: The 'Million Dollar Hotel' Soundtrack and Legendary Patti Smith Are Better Bets." *Portland Press Herald* (Portland, Maine) (23 April): 5E.

Holdship, Bill. 1999. "Nightstick: This Week (August 20-26): Blondie." *New Times Los Angeles* (19 August): "Music" section.

Holguin, Jaime. 1998. "B-52's Targeting the Future With Tour." *Jam!* web site. (22 June; Accessed 20 July 2000) <www.canoe.ca>.

Holmes, John Clellon, *Go*. Mamaroneck, New York: P. P. Appel, 1977, 1952.

Holmstrom, John. 1996. *Punk: The Original: A Collection Of Material*. 1st ed. New York: Trans-High Publishing Corps.

Holston, Noel and Jon Bream. 1995. "PBS Tackles History of Rock's Renegades, Punks and Princes." *Star-Tribune: Newspaper of the Twin Cities* (Minneapolis-St. Paul, Minnesota) (24 September): 1F.

Horowitz, Ben. 2000. "Youthful Chickclick Plays It Smart and Cool: RadioActivity." *Star-Ledger* (Newark, New Jersey) (23 July): "Spotlight" section, p. 3.

Hoskyns, Barney. 1996. *Waiting for the Sun: Strange Days, Weird Scenes, and the Sound of Los Angeles*. New York: St. Martin's Press.

_____. 1999. "The Misfits." *Mojo: The Music Magazine* 63(February): 64-76.

Howell, Peter. 1991. "The Lady is a Vamp, and Quite Proud of It." *Toronto Star* (30 August): D1.

Hudson, Heidi. 1999. "Music: Blondie, Atomic: The Very Best of Blondie, Polydor UK" [review]. *Lesbian News* 24, 7(February): 34.

Hughes, Mike. 1991. "TV or Not TV." Ganett News Service (13 November).

Hunter, James. 2000. "Boss Hog, *Whiteout*, In the Red: Itchy and Scratchy Grooves from Friction-Loving New York Fivesome." *Rolling Stone* 835(2 March): 96.

I

Idelson, Karen. 1992. "Curve Bends Descriptions of Pop Music." *Houston Chronicle* (11 June): 1.

"In Blue Track by Track." 2000. *Malay Mail* (Kuala Lumpur, Malaysia) (18 July): "Music" section, p. 4.

"In the Box With Debbie." 1999. *Total Guitar* (United Kingdom) 55(April): 26.

Infusino, Divina. 1988. "Tangerine Dream Eschews 'New Age.'" *San-Diego Union-Tribune* (21 September): C4.

_____. 1989. "Rock Role Model: Often-Imitated Blondie Star Sets Own Course." *San Diego Union-Tribune* (27 October): E1.

"Inside Track: The Roots of Rap." 1999. *Dallas Morning News* (26 August): 5C.

Irwin, Colin. 1986. "Delicate Cutters." *Melody Maker* 61 (15 November): 10-11.

_____. 1986. "Live! Throwing Muses, Kilburn National Ballroom, London." *Melody Maker* 61 (29 November): 19.

Isherwood, Christopher. 1945. *The Berlin Stories: The Last of Mr. Norris, Goodbye to Berlin*. New York: James Laughlin.

Isler, Scott. 1981. "Blondie: State of the Union 1981." *Trouser Press* 62(June): 19-23.

"It's No Doubt 'New' Will Climb Charts." 1999. *Florida Today* (2 April): 6G.

J

Jackson, Alan. 1999. "Cold Call." *Times* (London) (6 November): "Features" section.

James, Martin. 2000. "How to Milk Blondie for All They're Worth." *Independent* (London) (16 June): 14.

Jansen, Ara. 2000. "Boss Ska Party." *West Australian* (26 May): 10.

Jenkins, Mark. 1994. "Live's Vital Rock: Casual Chestnutt." *Washington Post* (10 June): N17.

_____. 1997. "The Cardigans' Swede Sounds." *Washington Post* (10 February): D7.

_____. 1999. "Blondie at Nation." *Washington Post* (21 May): C8.

John, Richard. 1999. "Blondie Announces Tour Dates; Tix on the Net." *Jam!* web site. (6 April; Accessed 20 July 2000) <www.canoe.ca>.

Johnson, Dean. 1999. "MixFest Reigns! Rain Doesn't Dampen the Enthusiasm at Foxboro Concert." *Boston Herald* (11 October): "Arts and Life" section, p. 35.

Johnson, Jeff. 1998. "Don't Call It a Comeback: The Evolution of a Legend." *Fabula: For the Female Mind* 3, 1(1998): 24-32.

Johnson, Kevin C. 1999. "Rap at 20." *St. Louis Post-Dispatch* (28 March): F1.

_____. 1999. "Recordings: 'No Exit,' Blondie/Beyond Records." *St. Louis Post-Dispatch* (19 February): E4.

Johnston, Emma. 1999. "Bellatrix, Camden Place, London." *Melody Maker* 76, 34(28 August): 38.

_____. 1999. "Blondie, Wembley Arena, London." *Melody Maker* 76, 44(17 November): 47.

_____. 1999. "Friday, We're in Love." *Melody Maker* 76, 26(3 July): 26-27.

Johnston, Katie. 1999. "Band's Fans Lap Up All Sassiness 'Blondie' Comeback Can Dish Out." *Gazette* (Colorado Springs, Colorado) (27 May): "Life" section, p. 6.

Johnston, Mary. 1999. "Mary Johnston's Column: Harry's a Hit." *The People* (28 November): "Features" section, p. 8.

Johnstone, Nick. 1999. *Melody Maker History of 20th Century Popular Music*. London: Bloomsbury.

Jones, Alan. 1999. "Chart Commentary." *Music Week* (27 February): 20.

Jones, Cliff, Charley Stone, and Nigel Hoyle. 1999. "Blondie: Nothing Is Real But The Girl (RCA)." *Melody Maker* 76, 19(15 May): 39.

Jones, Scott. 2000. "That's Entertainment." *Shoot* 41, 8(25 February): 32.

Jones, Stephen. 2000. "More Mature Sound for Billie Follow-Up." *Music Week* (18 March): 8.

K

Kappers, John. 1999. "Blondie: No Introduction Necessary." *AP* (Alternative Press) 128(March): 40-42.

Kassulke, Natasha. 2000. "Yahoo! Outloud Tour: From Noisy and Disappointing to Bouncy and Melodic." *Wisconsin State Journal* (22 February): 5D.

Kato, Yoshi. 2000. "What's New in Live Albums." *News and Observer* (Raleigh, North Carolina) (29 January): D6.

Keating, Matthew. 1999. "Rock & Pop: Blondie." *Guardian* (London) (21 June).

_____. 1999. "Rock, Pop & Jazz:...Blondie." *Guardian* (London) web site. (10 November; Accessed 14 July 2000) <www.guardianunlimited.co.uk>.

_____. 1999. "Rock, Pop & Jazz: Blondie." *Guardian* (London) web site. (19 November; Accessed 14 July 2000) <www.guardianunlimited.co.uk>.

_____. 1999. "Rock, Pop & Jazz: Skunk Anansie." *Guardian* (London) (13 October).

_____. 2000. "Rock, Pop & Jazz: Elastica." *Guardian* (London) (26 January).

Kielty, Tom. 2000. "Blondie, *Blondie Live*, Beyond." *Boston Globe* (6 January): "Calendar" section, p. 8.

King, Conrad. 2000. "Fibre Class: The Lotus Esprit May Be Light in Weight, But Its Nerdy Owners Know It Can Hold Its Own With Any Car on the Open Road." *Scottish Daily Record* (8 April): "Features/SATMAG" section, p. 17.

King, Courtney. 1998. "From Beasties to Luscious: Ex-Drummer Finds Satisfaction in Girl Group." *Patriot Ledger* (Quincy, Massachusetts) (8 August): 29.

Klein, Howie. 1979. "Blondie: They're A Group! Not A Girl." *Relix* 6, 3(June): 22-25.

Kletke, Mary Jane. 1996. "Blonde Ambition." *Jam!* web site. (12 June; Accessed 22 July 2000) <www.canoe.ca>.

Kot, Greg. 1995. "Garbage Contained: Band Cuts Loose As Its Metro Show Progresses." *Chicago Tribune* (8 November): 12.

_____. 1998. "Fickle Fans: Garbage's 2nd Disc is Dandy, But the Public's Not Buying It." *Chicago Tribune* (20 November): 60.

_____. 1998. "Garbage Day: A Smoother Shirley Manson Makes for a Ferocious Frontman." *Chicago Tribune* (27 November): "Tempo" section, p. 2.

_____. 1998. "Garbage: Version 2.0 (Almo)." *Chicago Tribune* (17 May): 9.

_____. 1998. "Playing It Safe: Some of the Year's Most Successful, 'Alternative' Rock Bands Seem Content to Just Cash In." *Chicago Tribune* (21 December): "Tempo" section, 1.

_____. 2000. "No Doubt Steppin' Out Tour Begins, Stefani Gets Down to Business by Working the Crowd." *Chicago Tribune* (26 March): "Metro Chicago: Arts Watch" section, p. 6.

_____. 2000. "Recordings: No Doubt, Return of Saturn (Interscope)." *Chicago Tribune* (16 April): "Arts and Entertainment" section, p. 10.

Kozak, Roman. 1988. *This Ain't No Disco: The Story of CBGB*. Boston: Faber & Faber.

Krebs, Gary M. 1997. *Rock and Roll Reader's Guide*. New York: Billboard Books.

L

La Grone, Paige. 1999. "Artist Spotlight: Blondie, *No Exit* (Beyond Music)." *Atomic Pop* web site. (Accessed 18 April) <www.atomicpop.com>.

Lacayo, Richard and Ginia Bellafante. 1994. "If Everyone is Hip..., Is Anyone Hip?" *Time* 144, 6(8 August): 48-55.

Laing, Dave. 1985. *One Chord Wonders: Power and Meaning in Punk Rock*. Philadelphia, Pennsylvania: Open University Press. Blondie: 32, 117, 137, 141; Deborah Harry: 102, 117.

Lamacq, Steve. 1991. "Carter The Unstoppable Sex Machine, 30 Something *(Rough Trade)*." *NME* (New Musical Express) web site. (16 February; Accessed 2 July 2000) <www.nme.com>.

Lanham, Tom. 1988. "Gun Club's Jeffrey Lee Pierce: Reckless Rocker Sobers Up." *San Francisco Chronicle* (10 April): 46.

Laurence, Charles. 1998. "Debbie Harry: Life After the Disco: Seventies Band Blondie and Their Pouting Pin-Up Singer Are Back—For Love or Money? Charles Laurence Reports." *Daily Telegraph* (London) (25 May): "Features" section, p. 13.

Lazell, Barry, ed. 1989. *Rock Movers & Shakers: An A to Z of the People Who Make Rock Happen*. New York: Billboard Publications Inc.

Lee, Craig. 1989. "An Unharried Harry." *Los Angeles Times* (21 October): F2.

Lee, Kate. 2000. "Elizabeth Reigns." *Us* (19 June): 16.

Lengel, Kerry. 1999. "Rising Tide: Lukewarm Waters Won't Stop Blondie." *Arizona Republic* (19 August): "The Rep" section, p. 34.

Lennon, John and Jann Wenner. 1971. *Lennon Remembers*. San Francisco: Straight Arrow Books.

"Let's Go: Friends in High Places: New Grass Revival Leader Reunited the Band for Garth." 1997. *Cincinnati Enquirer* (21 February): W35.

Levitan, Corey. 1999. "Allstar News: Blondie Triumphs in L.A. Show, One Way Or Another." *CD-NOW* web site. (11 February; Accessed 22 February 1999 from former *Rocktropolis* web site which is now part of *CD-NOW* <www.cdnow.com>; Accessed 9 July 2000 from *Blondie Archive* web site). <www.blondie.ausbone.net>.

_____. 1999. "Will Blondie Have More Fun?: Reunited '70s Hit Makers Aim for '90s Acclaim." *Rave! Daily Breeze* (Torrance, California) 6, 9(26 February-4 March): 25.

Lewis, Jason. 2000. "Born Before 1945? Well, You're Too Old to Listen to Radio 2." *Mail on Sunday* (14 May): 43.

Linden, Amy. 1999. "No Exit, Blondie (Beyond)." *People Weekly* 51, 7(22 February): 37.

Linkous, Mark. 1997. "My First Gig: This Week, Mark Linkous of Sparklehorse Recalls the Peroxide Pop Perfection of Blondie." *Melody Maker* 74, 36(15 November): 39.

"The List." 1999. *Globe and Mail* (Toronto, Ontario, Canada) (6 February): C23.

Loben, Carl. 1998. "Overproof, Rockers Hi-Fi (Different Drummer/WEA)." *Melody Maker* 75, 49(5 December): 44.

Loder, Kurt. 1990. "The Story of Blondie (1986)." In *Bat Chain Puller: Rock and Roll in the Age of Celebrity*. New York: St. Martin's Press, 180-198.

London, Herbert. 1984. *Closing the Circle: A Cultural History of the Rock Revolution*. Chicago, Illinois.

Long, April. 1998. "Blondie: Newscastle Civic Hall." *NME* (New Musical Express) web site. (24 November; Accessed 1 July 2000) <www.nme.com>.

_____. 1998. "Ronnie Spector, London Camden Dingwalls." *NME* (New Musical Express) web site. (16 December; Accessed 2 July 2000) <www.nme.com>.

_____. 1999. "This Week's Singles, August 14, 1999:...Brazen Hussies, Living In Fear Of Reprisals *(Year Zero)*." *NME* (New Musical Express) web site. (14 August; Accessed 2 July 2000) <www.nme.com>.

_____. 2000. "Thee Michelle Gun Elephant." *NME* (New Musical Express) web site. (25 April; Accessed 2 July 2000) <www.nme.com>.

"Losing Personal Contact in Rise of the Internet?" 2000. *Leicester Mercury* (29 March): 13.

"Love's Labour at Last: Hole Finish Album in London." 1998. *NME* (New Musical Express) web site. (1 April; Accessed 2 July 2000) <www.nme.com>.

Lustig, Jay. 1990. "Successful 'Brave' Rock Groups Offer Good Listening to Devotees of Anticommercial, Avant-Garde." *Star-Ledger* (Newark, New Jersey) (1 July).

M

Mabbott, Alastair. 1998. "Debbie Harry & Co. Back in the Beat." *Scotsman* (Edinburgh, Scotland) (20 November): 2.

Magnarini, Brian. 1996. "Garbage Belies Its Name at Bogart's." *Cincinnati Enquirer* (14 March): C5.

Mailer, Norman. 1959. *Advertisements for Myself*. New York: Putnam.

_____. 1973. *Marilyn: A Biography*. New York: Grossett & Dunlap.

_____. 1979. *The Executioner's Song*. Boston: Little Brown.

Malins, Steve. 1999. "Cash for Questions:...Debbie 'Deborah' Harry." *Q* 151(April 1999): 10-11, 13-14.

Marcus, Greil. 1993. "Ripped to Shreds." In *Ranters & Crowd Pleasers: Punk in Pop Music, 1977-92*. 1st ed. New York: Doubleday.

Marin, Rick. 2000. "Getting Over Gwyneth." *Harper's Bazaar* (February): 218-221, 280.

Mark, Lois Alter. 2000. "Music: Parent's Guide." *Entertainment Weekly* 536(21 April): 77.

Marsh, Dave. 1983. *New Rolling Stone Record Guide*. New York: Random House/Rolling Stone Press.

_____. 1989. *The Heart of Rock & Soul: The 1001 Great Singles Ever Made*. New York: Plume Books.

_____. 1999. *The Heart of Rock & Soul: The 1001 Great Singles Ever Made*. New York: Da Capo Press.

Martin, David. 1999. "The Tide Is In: Chris Stein Wades Through Blondie's Inevitable Return." *Phoenix New Times* (19 August): "Music" section.

Martin, Piers. 1999. "Bis, Social Dancing *(Wiiija)*." *NME* (New Musical Express) web site. (17 March; Accessed 2 July 2000) <www.nme.com>.

_____. 1999. "Venini, London Soho Wag Club." *NME* (New Musical Express) web site. (27 May; Accessed 2 July 2000) <www.nme.com>.

_____. 2000. "Scarlet Division, London W14 West One Four." *NME* (New Musical Express) web site. (21 March; Accessed 2 July 2000) <www.nme.com>.

Martinez, Gerald. 1999. "Blondie, No Exit." *New Straits Times* (28 February): 23.

Mason, Neil. 1998. "Crowd Pleasers." *Melody Maker* 75, 33(August 15): 37.

Masuo, Sandy. 1995. "No Doubt Puts On a Lively Show." *Los Angeles Times* (27 November): F6.

Matheson, Dan. 1999. "Popular Eighties Band Returns: Guest: Deborah Harry, 'Blondie'" [transcript]. Canada AM, CTV Television (26 July), 8:11:45-8:19:15 Eastern Time.

Mathieson, Jack. 1999. "Blondie's Rapturous Return." *Evening News* (Edinburgh, Scotland) (21 June): 28.

Mathur, Paul. 1993. "Platinum Brunette." *Melody Maker* 69, 28(10 July): 12-13.

_____. 1999. "Live—Philadelphia 1978/Dallas 1980." *Melody Maker* 76, 30(31 July): 34.

_____. 1999. "She Talks to Rainbows EP." *Melody Maker* 76, 3(23 January): 38.

Maunsell, Jerome Boyd. 2000. "Instrumental: St. Etienne's Sarah Cracknell Tells Metro About the Music That Made Her." *Times* (London) (10 June): "Features" section, p. 11.

Maurstad, Tom. 2000. "Metropolitan Museum of Art Exhibit Comes Up Short on 'Rock and Style.'" *Florida Times-Union* (9 January): D4.

McCormack, Heather. 1999. Review of *Patty Smith: A Biography*, by Victor Bockris and Roberta Bayley. *Library Journal* 124, 13(August): 91.

_____. 2000. Review of *Deborah Harry*, by Cathay Che. *Library Journal* 125, 6(1 April): 103-104.

McCormack, Ed. 1972. "New York City's Ultra-Living Dolls." *Rolling Stone* (26 October): 14, 16.

McCormick, Neil. 1998. "The New It Girl of Rock'N'Roll: First There Was Blondie's Debbie Harry. Then Louise Wener from Sleeper. Now Meet Cerys Matthews of Catatonia..." *Daily Telegraph* (London) (23 April): 23.

_____. 1999. "She's Back, and Better Than Ever: With Blondie at Number One This Week, Debbie Harry Talks About Splitting Up, Filling Out and Being With the Boys Again." *Daily Telegraph* (11 February): "Arts" section, p. 29.

McFarland, Melanie. 1999. "Blondie: This Concert Was All About Nostalgia and Bonding." *Seattle Times* (2 June): E1.

McGee, David and Anthony DeCurtis. 1997. "The Rolling Stone 200: The Essential Rock Collection: Blondie, Parallel Lines." *Rolling Stone* 760(15 May): 70.

McGill, Hannah. 2000. "Dancing in the Dark." *Sunday Herald* (Australia) (19 March): 6.

McHugh, Catherine. 1999. "Another 15 Minutes: LDs Nick Sholem and Peter Jennings Light Up Blondie's First Tour in 16 Years." *Lighting Dimensions: The Magazine for the Lighting Professional* 23, 10(October): 60-65, 102-105.

McInerny, Vivian. 2000. "The Look/Kooky Fashion..." *Oregonian* (16 July): L1.

McKenna, Kristine. 1986. "Fall Album Roundup: Debbie Harry: Candy-Box Pop: 'Rockbird.' Debbie Harry. Geffen." *Los Angeles Times* (23 November): 59.

McKown, Loni Smith. 1998. "Back to the Future: Native Hoosier Stephen Sprouse Uses '60s Pop Ethic, Andy Warhol Prints for His Modern Clothes." *Indianapolis Star/Indianapolis News* (29 January): 1.

McMullen, Marion. 1999. "TV: Tonight's Highlights." *Coventry Evening Telegraph* (England) (4 October): "Features" section, pp. 16, 29.

McNeil, Legs. 1989. "TopSpin." *Spin* (July): 6.

McNeil, Legs and Gillian McCain. 1996. 1st ed. *Please Kill Me: The Uncensored Oral History of Punk*. New York: Grove Press.

_____. 1997. *Please Kill Me: The Uncensored Oral History of Punk*. New York: Penguin Books.

Mehle, Michael. 1997. "14 Years After Breakup, Harry Still a Natural Blondie." *Rocky Mountain News* (Denver, Colorado) (2 March): 5D.

_____. 1999. "This Time Blondie's Having More Fun." *Rocky Mountain News* (Denver, Colorado) (21 February): 3D.

Menconi, David. 1999. "Where Were You in '82?" *News and Observer* (Raleigh, North Carolina) (7 March): G1.

Metz, Allan. 1998. "Women in Rock and Roll: A Three-Part Bibliography" ("All Female New Wave Rock Bands of the 1980s—The Go-Go's, The Bangles, Bananarama; "'Tell It Like It T-I-Is': The B-52's"; "The Pretenders and Chrissie Hynde") *Bulletin of Bibliography* 55, 4(December): 265-300).

_____. 1999. "The Musical Legacy of Blondie: An Annotated Bibliography." *Bulletin of Bibliography* 56, 4(December): 189-217.

_____. 2000. "Two Rock/Pop Bibliographies: I. The Cardigans, II. Garbage." *Bulletin of Bibliography* 57, 2(June): 107-133.

_____. 2001. "Blondie and Deborah Harry: A Comprehensive Bibliography." *Bulletin of Bibliography* 58, 1(March): 11-48.

Metz, Allan and Carol Benson, eds. 1999. *The Madonna Companion: Two Decades of Commentary*. New York: Schirmer Books, 141.

Mico, T. 1985. "The Immaculate Misconception." *Melody Maker* 60 (28 September): 28-30.

Mieses, Stanley. 1979. "B-52s: Bouffant Bop." *Melody Maker* 54 (13 January): 10-11.

Mikhail, Kate. 2000. "Rankin: Up Close and Personal..." *Independent* (London) (26 May): "Features" section, p. 9.

Milano, Brett. 1996. "Head Land: Doing It Without David Byrne." *Boston Phoenix* web site. (14 November; Accessed 19 July 2000) <www.bostonphoenix.com>.

_____. 2000. "Star Ghost Dog's Woman in Front Gets Over Her Stage Fright." *Boston Phoenix* web site. (Accessed 19 July 2000) <www.bostonphoenix.com>.

Mills, Nancy. 1996. "Flashes:...To Dye For." *Entertainment Weekly* 346(27 September): 14.

Milner, Greg. 2001. "Ramones Come Home." *Spin* 17, 5(May): 92-94, 96.

Miner, Cathy. 1997. "Ugly Beauty, Sweetness (Atlantic)." *Boston Phoenix* web site. (11 December; Accessed 19 July 2000) <www.bostonphoenix.com>.

Mirkin, Steven. 1999. "Music/The Week:...Blondie, No Exit (Beyond)." *Entertainment Weekly* 472-473(19-26 February): 140+.

"Misc. Info and References in Our Neo-Pre-Macro-Post-Modern Society." 2000. *The DEVO FAQ* web site (Accessed 15 July 2000) <www.akula.com/~drazz/devo>.

Moir, James. 2000. "Panning for New Gold." *Mail on Sunday* (28 May): 79.

Moir, Jan. 1993. "Public Lives: Back to Her Roots: In the Seventies, Debbie Harry Was Woman Seeking Fame and Fortune. She Got It. She Was Beautiful, She Was Big, She Was Blondie. And Now..." *Guardian* (London) (7 July): 8.

Molenda, Michael. 1999. "Back in Blonde: Chris Stein's Quirky Riffs Revitalize Blondie." *Guitar Player* 33, 4(April): 58-64.

Moon, Tom. 2000. "Welcome 2 the 80s: The Era of David Byrne, Blondie, and Bryan Ferry is Upon Us Again, in Music, Culture, and, Especially, Style." *Esquire* 133, 6(June): 123-137.

Moore, Lisa M. 1999. "Blondie: A Little Rapture, A Lot of Closure." *CD-NOW* web site. (17 May; Accessed 9 July 2000) <www.cdnow.com>.

Morris, Teri. 1977. "Going All the Way With...Blondie." *Bomp!* 17(November): 55-57.

Morse, Steve. 1992. "Concrete Blonde Stirs Some Soul in the Mix." *Boston Globe* (4 September): 88.

_____. 1997. "A Frothy Carnival with the Cardigans." *Boston Globe* (4 February): E3.

_____. 1999. "Starting the 'Party': Boston's Push Stars Ready to Shine with a Major Label Debut." *Boston Globe* (14 May): C15.

_____. 1999. "Women Reign at Grammys: Hill, Twain, Madonna, Dion, Crow Head Roster of Winners." *Boston Globe* (25 February): E1.

_____. 2000. "Kittie Spit." *Boston Globe* (25 May): "Calendar" section, p. 8.

_____. 2000. "Rockfords Reunites Old Pals." *Boston Globe* (11 February): C16.

Morton, Roger. 1998. "Earl Brutus, Tonight You Are The Special One *(Island)*." *NME* (New Musical Express) web site. (6 June; Accessed 2 July 2000) <www.nme.com>.

_____. 1999. "The Cranberries, London Shepherds Bush Empire." *NME* (New Musical Express) web site. (22 April; Accessed 2 July 2000) <www.nme.com>.

Mullaney, Andrea. 1999. "Bag Lady Leaves Us in Raptures." *Evening News* (Edinburgh, Scotland) (29 November): 32.

Mullen, Brendon and Marc Spitz. 2001. "Sit On My Face, Stevie Nicks! The Germs, Darby Crash, and the Birth of SoCal Punk." *Spin* 17, 5(May): 100-102, 104, 106.

Munro, Ronan. 1998. "Marine Research: Live Reviews 1998: NME Review of Oxford Point, 7 Nov 98." *Marine Research: Our World* home page. (Accessed 3 July 2000) <www.users.globalnet.co.uk/~queenb>.

Murthi, R.S. 1996. "Tracks:...No Doubt—Tragic Kingdom..." *New Straits Times* (28 June): 4.

Myers, Ben. 1999. "When Harry Met..." *Melody Maker* 76, 7(20 February): 23.

N

Nason, Peter Neil. 2000. "Florida's Pop Culture Knows No Peer." *Tampa Tribune* (30 April): "Commentary" section, p. 4.

"NBC, CBS Go Retro." 2000. *Washington Post* (30 April): Y3.

Needs, Kris. 1978. "Plastic Love: A Day With Blondie." *Zigzag* 81(February-March): 10-13.

Negus, Keith. 1996. *Popular Music in Theory: An Introduction*. Cambridge, England: Polity Press.

_____. 1997. *Popular Music in Theory: An Introduction*. 1st U.S. ed. Hanover, New Hampshire: University Press of New England.

Nicholls, Mark. 1999. "Blondie Proves as Popular as Ever." *Aberdeen Press and Journal* (29 November): "Showbiz: Music" section, p. 8.

Nichols, Natalie. 1999. "Blondie Returns With a Sophisticated 'Exit': Blondie, 'No Exit,' Beyond Music." *Los Angeles Times* (27 February): F10.

_____. 1999. "Blondie's Back With a Show That Rises Above Nostalgia." *Los Angeles Times* (31 May): F3.

Nicoletti, Christy. 1999. "Review:...Madison Square Garden Theater...New York City...June 10, 1999...Blondie." *Hip Online* web site. (Accessed 8 June 2000) <www.hiponline.com>.

"Nightshift, Gig Guide...: Sunday 7th, Idlewild + Brassy." 2000. *Nightshift: Oxford's Music Online* web site. (May; Accessed 3 July 2000) <www.nightshift.oxfordmusic.net>.

Nine, Jennifer. 1998. "His Name Is Alive." *Melody Maker* 75, 35(29 August): 37.

"1980: nme.com's Rock Years, 1963-1999." 1999. *NME* (New Musical Express) web site. (25 December; Accessed 2 July 2000) <www.nme.com>.

"1979: nme.com's Rock Years, 1963-1999." 1999. *NME* (New Musical Express) web site. (24 December; Accessed 2 July 2000) <www.nme.com>.

"No Exit, Blondie..." 1999. *Virgin.net* web site. (15 February; Accessed 4 July 2000) <www.virgin.net>.

Norman, Philip. 1982. *The Road Goes On Forever: Portraits From a Journey Through Contemporary Music*. New York: Fireside.

O

Obejas, Achy. 1995. "Democracy, Latin Rock Take Off in Tandem." *Chicago Tribune* (29 September): 2.

O'Brien, Glenn. 1986. "Debbie's Back: Debbie Harry and Chris Stein Talk About Blondie, Wrestling, Disease, Record Rating, Show Biz, Fear, and Fantasy." *Spin* 1, 9(January): 42-47, 49.

_____. 1999. "Blondie: A Biography." *iMusic* web site. (Accessed 5 May 1999) <www.imusic.com>.

_____. 1999. "Deborah Harry." *Playboy* 46, 6(June): 120-122, 167.

_____. 1999. "Platinum Blondie." *Out* 67(June): 78-83.

O'Brien, Lucy. 1996. *She Bop: The Definitive History of Women in Rock, Pop and Soul*. New York: Penguin Books.

_____. 1999. "The Woman Punk Made Me." In *Punk Rock: So What? The Cultural Legacy of Punk*. Roger Sabin, ed. London: Routledge.

O'Dair, Barbara. 1997. *The Rolling Stone Book of Women in Rock: Trouble Girls*. New York: Random House.

O'Hara, Craig. 1999. *The Philosophy of Punk: More Than Noise*. 2nd ed. Edinburgh: A K Press Distribution.

O'Hare, Kevin. 2000. "Audio Zone CD Reviews: Return of Saturn, No Doubt." *Portland Oregonian* (14 April): "Arts and Entertainment" section, p. 49.

O'Keeffe, Rory. 1998. "The Ultra Montanes, The Ultra Montanes *(Lakota)*." *NME* (New Musical Express) web site. (30 September; Accessed 2 July 2000) <www.nme.com>.

"Once More Into the Bleach." 1999. BBC Television Broadcast (October).

Oppegaard, Brett. 1999. "Back With Blondie: Rock Diva and Her Band Reunite and Hit the Road to Portland." *Columbian* (Vancouver, Washington) (27 May): F11.

Orr, Deborah. 2000. "A Few of My Role Models, After a Fashion." *Independent* (London) (21 June): "Comment" section, p. 5.

Osgerby, Bill. 1999. "'Chewing Out a Rhythm on My Bubblegum': The Teenage Aesthetic and Genealogies of American Punk." In *Punk Rock: So What? The Cultural Legacy of Punk*. Roger Sabin, ed. London: Routledge.

Ostroff, Joshua. 1999. "Blondie Ambition: Aging New Wave Band Fights to Remain Relevant with Youth." *Jam!* web site. (6 March; Accessed 20 July 2000) <www.canoe.ca>.

O'Toole, Lawrence. 1990. "The Debbie Harry Story: Beneath the Cool Exterior Lies a Truly Cool Individual." *New York Woman* 4, 9(June-July): 84-87.

P

Pagett, Karen. 2000. "Compilations:...Top of the Pops 2 (BBC)." *Birmingham Post* (27 May): p. 7.

"The Palantines WLTM Guitarist with GSOH and Telecaster." 2000. *Nightstand* message board. (24 May; Accessed 3 July) <www.nightshift.oxfordmusic.net>.

Pallenberg, Anita. 2000. "Debbie Harry" [interview]. *Cheap Date* 3(2000): 12-17.

Pantsios, Anastasia. 1999. "Harry and Crew Turn the Tide After Rocky Start." *Plain Dealer* (Cleveland, Ohio) (14 August): 5B.

_____. 2000. "No Doubt: Band Displays Reasons for Wide-Ranging Appeal." *Plain Dealer* (Cleveland, Ohio) (15 June): 9B.

Paoletta, Michael. 1999. "Blondie's Tide Rises Again As 'Exit' Tracks Aim For Dancefloors." *Billboard* 111, 10(6 March): 35.

Pappademas, Alex. 1998. "The Cardigans, Gran Turismo (Mercury)." *Boston Phoenix* web site. (29 October; Accessed 19 July 2000) <www.bostonphoenix.com>.

_____. 1999. "Basement Jaxx: The Fly Life." *Boston Phoenix* web site. (23 September; Accessed 19 July 2000) <www.bostonphoenix.com>.

Pareles, Jon. 1999. "No Debutante: Blondie Returns to Its Roots." *New York Times* (25 February): E5.

_____. 2000. "Gung Ho, Arista." *Rolling Stone* 837(30 March): 62.

Parnes, Francine. 1990. "Deborah Harry Sheds Inhibitions Plus." *Denver Post* (26 July): E7.

Passy, Charles. 1999. "Blondie's Bravado Was Better Before Harry Went Gray." *Palm Beach Post* (2 September): 3B.

_____. 2000. "The Rap Music Generation Gap." *Palm Beach Post* (30 July): 1J.

Patterson, Sylvia. 1998. "Nearly Dog! Tricky, London Kentish Town Forum." *NME* (New Musical Express) web site. (3 June; Accessed 2 July 2000) <www.nme.com>.

"Patti Smith: Gung Ho." 2000. *Independent* (London) (26 March): "Features" section, p. 26.

Paul, George. 1994. "Tracing the Roots of Blondie: Blondie, 'Blonde and Beyond,' Chrysalis/ERG." *Orange County Register* (Santa Ana, California) (7 January): P49.

Peraino, Judith A. 1992. "'Rip Her to Shreds': Women's Music According to a Butch-Femme Aesthetic." *Repercussions* 1, 1(Spring): 19-47.

Perrone, Pierre. 2000. "Obituary: Alan Betrock." *Independent* (London) (29 April): "Obituaries" section, p. 7.

_____. 2000. "Swoom Along With Stefani Live: No Doubt Hanover Grand London." *Independent* (London) (3 March): 13.

Perry, Claudia. 1999. "Blondie's Comeback—It's No Mere Flashback." *Star-Ledger* (Newark, New Jersey) (25 February): 51.

Perry, Tim. 1999. "Pop: The Five Best Gigs." *Independent* (London) (7 November): "Features" section, p. 40.

Persky, Marci. 1998. "Not a Bit Trashy: Garbage is Pure Rock Enjoyment." *Grand Rapids Press* (17 November): D4.

Petkovic, John. 1999. "Timeout: Harry Gets Into Role for Blondie Again." *Plain Dealer* (Cleveland, Ohio) (12 August): 1E.

Piccoli, Sean. 1999. "Blondie a Bit Spacey, A Bit Rusty: Dancer From the Crowd Finally Wakes Up Harry and Crew." *Sun-Sentinel* (Ft. Lauderdale, Florida) (2 September): 3E.

"Pick of the Week: This Week's Rock Pick." 1999. *Birmingham Post* (Birmingham, England) (20 November): "News" section, p. 3.

"Pop Notes." 1999. *Washington Post* (15 December): "Style" section, C5.

"Portrait of an Artist." 2000. *Herald* (Glasgow, Scotland) (24 July): "Arts" section, p. 16.

Potter, Alicia. 1999. "Rebel Forces: Tod Williams Defies Convention." *Boston Phoenix* web site. (2 September; Accessed 19 July 2000) <www.bostonphoenix.com>.

Powell, Betsy. 1998. "Arts:...Garbage, Version 2.0 (Universal)." *Toronto Star* (23 May): M8.

Powers, Ann. 1999. "Blondie Proves (Again) It's a Group, Not a Girl." *New York Times* (20 February): section 2, p. 41.

Prekop, Sam. 1999. "CD Spins: No Exit, Blondie (Beyond)." *Arizona Republic* (11 March): 27.

Q

Quill, Greg. 1986. "Harry's Still Blonde and Hip, But Icy Edge Has Thawed." *Toronto Star* (14 December): G1.

R

"Random Notes." 1997. *Rolling Stone* 766(7 August): 18.

Raphael, Amy. 1995. "Only Rock 'N' Role: One Year After the Suicide of Her Husband Kurt Cobain, Courtney Love is Leading a Sexual Revolution in Rock Music in Which the Girls Get to Play All the Best Riffs. The Question Is, Can the Misogynist Music Industry Follow Suit?" *Guardian* (London) (15 April): TT32.

Raub, Kevin. 1999. "Reel Big Fish's Blondie Fantasy Comes True." *CD-NOW* web site. (23 June; Accessed 9 July 2000) <www.cdnow.com>.

Raymaker, Derek. 1999. "Pop Review: Blondie, At Massey Hall, in Toronto, on Sunday." *Globe and Mail* (Toronto, Canada) (18 May): C2.

Rayner, Ben. 1998. "Savvy Pop Sensation Turns Out Slick, Sexy Product: Garbage's Day." *Ottawa Sun* (17 May): "Showcase" section, p. 8.

_____. 1999. "Blondie's Attracting New Generation of Fans: Reunited Band Finds Fresh Young Faces 'Inspiring.'" *Toronto Star* (9 March).

_____. 2000. "Hip Hop for the SUV." *Toronto Star* (8 April): "Entertainment" section, p. AR3.

_____. 2000. "Rock of Ageless." *Toronto Star* (2 March): "Entertainment" section, p. EN2.

"Reggae Facts and Fancies." 2000. *Malay Mail* (Kuala Lumpur, Malaysia) (12 May): "Entertainment" section, p. 4.

"Reissues Blondie Collection." 1995. *Guardian* (London) (16 September): 15.

Review of *Deborah Harry*, by Cathay Che. 2000. *Publishers Weekly* 247, 16(17 April): 62-63.

"Reviews—For Records Out On 13 July 1998:...Blondie: Atomic—The Very Best of Blondie..." 1998. *Music Week* (4 July): 10.

Reynolds, Simon and Joy Press. 1995. *The Sex Revolts: Gender, Rebellion and Rock 'N' Roll*. London: Serpents Tail.

_____. 1995. *The Sex Revolts: Gender, Rebellion and Rock 'N' Roll*. Cambridge, Massachusetts: Harvard University Press.

Riemenchneider, Chris. 2000. "Beyond Question: Gwen Stefani and No Doubt Hit Escape Velocity with 'Return to Saturn.'" *Austin American-Statesman* (13 April): "The Beat" section, p. 8.

Roberts, Chris. 1989. "Debbie Harry: The Blonde Leading the Blonde." *Melody Maker* 65, 38(23 September): 14-15.

_____. 1995. "Tonight, Your Hair is Beautiful." In *Idle Worship: How Pop Empowers the Weak, Rewards the Faithful and Succours the Needy*. Chris Roberts, ed. Boston: Faber and Faber: 96-127.

Robicheau, Paul. 1999. "Cardigans Lose Some Fluff and Wear Their Changes Well." *Boston Globe* (8 February): D8.

Robins, Jane. 2000. "Albert Hall Galaxy of Stars for Frail 'Empress' Elizabeth Taylor." *Independent* (27 May): "News" section, p. 11.

Robinson, Clare. 1999. "No Exit as Icon Blondie Returns: Blondie Just Refuse to Go Old and Grey. Clare Robinson Looks at the Band and the Inspirational Debbie Harry." *Evening Herald* (Plymouth, England) (5 November): "Supplement: What's On: Music," p. 35.

Robinson, Peter. 1999. "Love at Absolute Zero." *Melody Maker* 76, 33(21 August): 38.

_____. 1999. "Pacifica: New Electro-Pop Stars." *Melody Maker* 76, 28(17 July): 8.

Robson, Andy. 1999. "Blondie Gets Back to Her Roots." *Scotsman* (Edinburgh, Scotland) (9 February): 11.

Robson, Brit. 1999. "Blondie Turns Back Clock While Chiming in with New Tunes." *Star-Tribune: Newspaper of the Twin Cities* (Minneapolis-St. Paul) (Minneapolis, Minnesota) (17 August): 4B.

Rock, Mick. 1972. "Velvet Memories: Lou Reed Sees The Future, Darkly." *Rolling Stone* (26 October): 12-14.

_____. 2001. "It's Glamour Photography." *Q* 176(May 2001): 36-41.

"Rock On! Turning a Deaf Ear to the Notion of Retirement, These Musical Women Have Figured Out How to Keep Their Edge as They Age." 2000. *People Weekly* 54, 5(31 July): 84-87.

"Rock With a Conscience: A Short History." 2000. *Milwaukee Journal Sentinel* (14 April): 5E.

Rodman, Sarah. 1998. "Discs." *Boston Herald* (22 May): S23.

_____. 1999. "The Tide is High Again for Rejuvenated Blondie." *Boston Herald* (17 May): "Arts and Literature" section, p. 37.

Roland, Paul. 1999. *Teach Yourself Rock & Pop*. London: NTC Publishing Group.

_____. 2000. *Teach Yourself Rock & Pop*. New York: NTC/Contemporary Publishing Co.

Rose, Cynthia. 1985. "The Return of a Punk Pioneer: Deborah Harry Set Trends. Now Can She Follow Her Own Act?" *Dallas Morning News* (19 November): 1E.

Rose, Karen. 1976. "The Heartwarming Rise to Fame of Lenny Kaye." *Trouser Press* (June-July): 27-29, 31.

Rosen, Craig. 1994. "Modern Rock Opens Doors to Rap Tracks." *Billboard* 106, 26(25 June): 1, 120.

Rosen, Steven. 1995. "Name Change Worked Wonders for David Johansen." *Denver Post* (28 April): 29.

Ross, Curtis. 1999. "Second Chance: Blondie is Back and Hopes the Tide of Fan Support is as High as was 20 Years Ago." *Tampa Tribune* (31 August): "Baylife" section, p. 1.

_____. 1999. "Showing No Shades of Gray, Blondie Keeps Energy High." *Tampa Tribune* (3 September): 6.

_____. 2000. "Spin This:...Grant Hart, Good News for Modern Man." *Tampa Tribune* (23 June): "Friday Extra!" section, p. 15.

Ross, Mike. 1996. "Almost Blondie." *Jam!* web site. (1 July; Accessed 22 July 2000) <www.canoe.ca>.

_____. 2000. "Pump up the Volume." *Edmonton Sun* (2 May): "Entertainment" section, p. 25.

Rotondi, James. 1999. "The Katies (Spongebath/Elektra)." *Boston Phoenix* web site. (29 July; Accessed 19 July 2000) <www.bostonphoenix.com>.

"Roy Nathanson's Vision: Not Opera, Not Musical: This is Storytelling with Jazz." 2000. *CNN* web site. (9 June; Accessed 28 July 2000) <www.cnn.com>.

Ruggieri, Melissa. 1999. "Despite the Passage of 16 Years, Blondie Still as Blondie as Ever." *Richmond Times-Dispatch* (11 February): D13.

_____. 1999. "Longtime Artists Are Releasing Many of the Upcoming Albums:...Blondie, 'No Exit' (Beyond)." *Richmond Times-Dispatch* (4 February): D12.

_____. 2000. "Stefani Reigns On No Doubt's Saturn...: No Doubt, 'Return of Saturn' (Interscope)." *Richmond Times-Dispatch* (20 April): D13.

Ruggiero, Bob. 1999. "Convalescent Punk: Blondie Has New Record, Legs." *Houston Press* (26 August): "Music" section.

Russell, Deborah. 1994. "MTV: Monk Television? Savage's Good Taste." *Billboard* 106, 21(21 May): 37.

Russell, Mark. 1996. "Applause/Sounds:...No Doubt: Tragic Kingdom." *Evening Post* (2 May): 14.

S

Saban, Stephen. 1987. "Debbie Does Details." *Details* 6, 2(August): 99-103.

Sabin, Roger, ed. 1999. *Punk Rock: So What? The Cultural Legacy of Punk*. London: Routledge.

Sakamoto, John. [1995?]. "Elastica, *Elastica*..." *Jam!* web site. (Accessed 20 July 2000) <www.canoe.ca>.

_____. 1995. "Elastica." *Jam!* web site. (27 February; Accessed 20 July 2000) <www.canoe.ca>.

_____. 1997. "Anti-Hit List: John Sakamoto's Alternate Top 10..." *Jam!* web site. (27 May; Accessed 20 July 2000) <www.canoe.ca>.

_____. 1997. "Anti-Hit List: John Sakamoto's Alternate Top 10..." *Jam!* web site. (3 June; Accessed 20 July 2000) <www.canoe.ca>.

_____. 1999. "Anti-Hit List: John Sakamoto's Alternate Top 10..." *Jam!* web site. (12 January; Accessed 20 July 2000) <www.canoe.ca>.

_____. 1999. "Anti-Hit List: John Sakamoto's Alternate Top 10..." *Jam!* web site. (26 January; Accessed 20 July 2000) <www.canoe.ca>.

_____. 1999. "Anti-Hit List: John Sakamoto's Alternate Top 10..." *Jam!* web site. (9 February; Accessed 20 July 2000) <www.canoe.ca>.

_____. 2000. "Anti-Hit List." *Toronto Star* (10 May): "Entertainment" section, p. 51.

Sarig, Roni. 1998. *The Secret History of Rock: The Most Influential Bands You've Never Heard*. New York: Billboard Books.

Savage, John. 1991. *England's Dreaming: Anarchy, Sex Pistols, Punk Rock, and Beyond*. New York: St. Martin's Press.

Schappert, Jason. 1997. "120 Minute[s] Transcribed." Online posting [excerpt]. *DHBIS* Mailing List. (12 June; Accessed 12 June 1997) <dhbis@primenet.com>.

Scheck, Frank. 1997. "Random Notes Daily: Performance: The Jazz Passengers With Deborah Harry." *Rolling Stone* web site (17 February; Accessed 19 July 1997) <www.rollingstone.com>.

Scherman, Tony. 2000. "Music: The Week..." *Entertainment Weekly* 531(17 March 2000): 70+.

Schlechter, Kira L. 2000. "Poison's Wild Child Finds Antidote for Past: Sober DeVille Brings New Band to Hershey [Pennsylvania]." *Sunday Patriot-News* (Harrisburg, Pennsylvania) (11 June): E9.

Schruers, Fred. 1980. *Headliners Blondie*. New York: Tempo Books.

Schwartz, Andy. 2000. "Alan Betrock, 1950-2000." *Village Voice* 45, 16(25 April): 128.

Scott, Jody. 1998. "Blondie Award Highlights New Look at Old Talent." *Times* (London) (31 October): 13.

Searleman, Eric. 2000. "CD Spins: Platinum Girl: A Tribute to Blondie, Various Artists (Cleopatra)." *Arizona Republic* (8 June): "The Rep" section, p. 16.

Segal, Victoria. 1998. "In With the In Crowd, Theaudience, Manchester Apollo." *NME* (New Musical Express) web site. (27 April; Accessed 2 July 2000) <www.nme.com>.

Semon, Craig S. 1995. "Elastica Just May be the Next Big Thing: Elastica, Elastica (David Geffen Co.)." *Sunday Telegram* (Worcester, Massachusetts) (7 May): 10.

_____. 1998. "There Are Nasty Gems To Be Found in Garbage: 'Version 2.0,' Garbage (Almo Sound)." *Sunday Telegram* (Worcester, Massachusetts) (21 June): 9.

_____. 2000. "Ani DiFranco Sings with Passion and Intellect." *Sunday Telegram* (Worcester, Massachusetts) (13 February): "Datebook" section, p. 8.

Sexton, Paul. 2000. "Catatonia's 'Blessed' U.S. Venture: Hit Welsh Act Hopes for 'Equal' Success in States Via Atlantic." *Billboard* 112, 11(11 March): 11.

Shaw, Arnold. 1974. *The Rockin' Fifties: The Decade That Transformed the Pop Music Scene*. New York: Hawthorne Books.

Sheffield, Rob. 1995. "Blondie." In *Spin Alternative Record Guide*. Eric Weisbard, ed. New York: Random House.

_____. 1999. "The Sheffield Report." *Rolling Stone* 807(4 March): 31.

Sherr, Sara. 1999. "CMJ Turns Scary as Tropical Storm Floyd Rocks Like a Hurricane: CMJ Music Marathon, September 15 through 18." *Village Voice* 44, 38(28 September): 72.

_____. 1999. "Five Sticky-Sweet New York Honeys Jam On It and Let It Whip: Ladies Marmalade." *Village Voice* 44, 33(24 August): 113.

_____. 1999. "Sound of the City: Dreaming Out Loud." *Village Voice* 44, 9(9 March): 74.

Shook, Karen. 1994. "Belly Dancing: Echobelly's Debut Album Came Out Only Recently But, Live This Week, They Showed All the Assurance of a Band That Had Been Around for Years." *Guardian* (London) (15 September): 11.

Shore, Michael. 1985. *The History of American Bandstand*. New York: Ballantine Books.

"Show: Deco Drive" [transcript]. 1999. Video Monitoring Services of America (4 September).

Shuker, Roy. 1994. *Understanding Popular Music*. London, New York: Routledge.

Siegel, Jerrold. 1986. *Bohemian Paris: Culture, Politics, and the Boundaries of the Bourgeoisie Life, 1830-1930*. New York: Viking,

"Singles Archive, 29/11/97 *(Various)*." 1997. *NME* (New Musical Express) web site. (29 November; Accessed 2 July 2000) <www.nme.com>.

Smith, Andy. 1998. "Garbage's Manson Rules a Jam-Packed Lupo's." *Providence Journal* (3 November): F4.

Smith, Giles. 1999. "Blondie Roots Of." Review of *Platinum Blonde*, by Cathay Che. *Mail on Sunday* (London) (18 July): 66.

Smith, Liz. 1996. "Blondie Returns!" *Newsday* (12 September): A15.

_____. 2000. "The Jagged Side of Julia." *Newsday* (30 January): A13.

Smith, Patti. 1978. *Babel*. New York: Putnam.

Smith, Tierney. 1999. "No Exit." *Goldmine* 25, 6(12 March).

Snyder, Michael. 1994. "Q & A With Deborah Harry." *San Francisco Chronicle* (25 September): "Sunday Datebook" section, p. 44.

_____. 1995. "A Smart, Snappy Set From Britain's Elastica: Elastica: Elastica, DGC." *San Francisco Chronicle* (2 April): 40.

Solomon, Charles. 1997. "A Blondie for the '90s." *Jerusalem Post* (3 February): 5.

Somerville, Colin. 1999. "Punk's First Princess is Older and Wiser, But the Sneer's Still Here." *Scotsman* (Edinburgh, Scotland) (26 November): 16.

"Something Wicked This Way Comes..." 1999. *Nightshift: Oxford's Music Online* web site. (December; Accessed 2 July 2000) <www.nightshift.oxfordmusic.net>.

Spartos, Carla. 2000. "My Funny Valentine" [letter]. *Village Voice* 45, 8(29 February): 104.

Spitzer, Hanna. 1977. "Blondie." *Rock* 2, 5(September): 50-53, 93-95.

Steel, Gary. 1999. "Blondie Lose Heart of Class: Blondie, No Exit (Beyond/BMG)." *Sunday Star-Times* (New Zealand) (28 February): F4.

Steranko, James. 1983. "A Prevue Exclusive: Deborah Harry Talks Candidly About Movies, Music and Making the Bizarre Cinematic Thriller Videodrome." *Prevue* 2, 11(March-April): 22-27.

Sterdan, Darryl. 2000. "Sinergy Go to Hell and Back: To Hell and Back, Sinergy (Nuclear Blast)." *Jam!* web site. (15 July; Accessed 20 July 2000) <www.canoe.ca>.

Stevenson, Jane. 1997. "Devine Bovine Inspired Album a Winner: Cowboy Reviewed: Cowboy, Erasure (Mute/Maverick)." *Jam!* web site. (20 April; Accessed 20 July 2000) <www.canoe.ca>.

_____. 1998. "Blondie Joins in Revival Fun." *Jam!* web site. (7 August; Accessed 20 July 2000) <www.canoe.ca>.

_____. 1999. "Blondie True to Their Roots: Age Hasn't Dulled Frontwoman Debbie Harry's Famous Edge." *Toronto Sun* (17 May): "Entertainment" section, p. 52.

_____. 1999. "Cardigans Button Up." *Jam!* web site. (11 February; Accessed 20 July 2000) <www.canoe.ca>.

_____. 1999. "Deeper Shade of Blondie." *Toronto Sun* (28 March): S4.

_____. 1999. "An Intimate Evening With Elvis Well Spent." *Jam!* web site. (29 January; Accessed 20 July 2000) <www.canoe.ca>.

_____. 1999. "Lots of Discs But Only 10 Make My List." *London Free Press* (London, Ontario, Canada) (2 January): C3.

_____. 2000. "Going Psycho Over Soundtracks:...The Crow: Salvation (Koch)." *Ottawa Sun* (17 April): "Showbiz" section, p. 25.

_____. 2000. "Talk About Killer Tunes! What's On the Latest Movie Soundtracks." *Toronto Sun* (14 April): "Entertainment" section, p. 66.

Stevenson, N. 1999. *Vacant: A Diary of the Punk Years, 1976-79*. London: Thames and Hudson.

Steward, Sue and Sheryl Garratt. 1984. *Signed, Sealed, and Delivered: True Life Stories of Women in Pop*. Boston, Massachusetts: South End Press.

Stoute, Lenny. 2000. "Bad Girls Rock: A New Crop of Twentysomething Bands is Keen on Sexual Exploration." *Globe and Mail* (Toronto, Canada) (19 July): R4.

Stubbs, David. 1999. "This Week's Singles, November 6, 1999:...Blondie, No Exit." *NME* (New Musical Express) web site. (6 November; Accessed 2 July 2000) <www.nme.com>.

Sullivan, Caroline. 1997. "Republica Rule, OK? Caroline Sullivan on the Brixton Band That's Stealing the Limelight on Audioweb's UK Tour." *Guardian* (London) (17 February): T10.

_____. 1997. "Spite Girl: Watch It Saffron, Says Caroline Sullivan—The Debbie Harry of Brixton Could Get Quite Famous: Republica (Deconstruction)." *Guardian* (London) (28 February).

_____. 1999. "Heart of Class: Blondie's Comeback Has More to Live Up to Than Most. Caroline Sullivan on Their New Offering." *Guardian* (London) (12 February): "Guardian Friday Review Page," p. 12.

_____. 2000. "The Corrs, In Blue (Atlantic)." *Guardian* (London) (14 July).

Sullivan, Jim. 1988. "Primitives: A Bit Like Early Blondie." *Boston Globe* (6 December): 82.

_____. 1989. "Deborah Harry Hits the Medium Pleasure Level: Music Review: Deborah Harry, The Channel, [November 1, 1989]..." *Boston Globe* (3 November): 54.

_____. 1996. "No Doubt About It, Ska-Pop 'Just A Girl' Works for This Band." *Boston Globe* (5 April): 52.

_____. 1999. "Blondie: The Pop Needs Some Pacing." *Boston Globe* (12 August): E4.

_____. 1999. "A Strong Start to Blondie's Next Wave: Blondie at The Orpheum Theatre, Saturday Night." *Boston Globe* (17 May): C10.

Surowicz, Tom. 1994. "Now Hear This: Speedway/7th Street Entry." *Star-Tribune: Newspaper of the Twin Cities* (Minneapolis-St. Paul) (5 August): 17E.

Susman, Gary. 1999. "High Tide: Blondie are Back." *Boston Phoenix* web site. (25 February; Accessed 19 July 2000) <www.bostonphoenix.com>.

_____. 1999. "Luscious Jackson: Electric Honey (Grand Royal/Capitol)." *Boston Phoenix* web site. (24 June; Accessed 19 July 2000) <www.bostonphoenix.com>.

Sutherland, Mark. 1998. "The Audience." *Melody Maker* 75, 8(21 February 1998): 12.

_____. 1999. "Blondie, Sound Republic, London." *Melody Maker* 76, 5(6 February): 28.

T

Talotta, Vince. 1999. "Debbie Harry Still a Magnetic Performer." *Toronto Star* (17 May): "Entertainment" section.

Tariff, Jonathan. 2000. "New CDs...: 'Jackie Collins Presents Lethal Seduction.'" *Times Union* (Albany, New York) (29 June): P33.

Tarlach, Gemma. 1999. "Blondie Treats Diehards to a Rapturous Evening: Harry and Crew Rock Hard, Years After the Hits That Made Them Famous." *Milwaukee Journal Sentinel* (16 August): 6.

_____. 1999. "Familiar Problems Plague 'Fresh' Blondie." *Milwaukee Journal Sentinel* (15 August): "Cue" section, p. 12.

_____. 2000. "Stefani Proves She's More Than 'Just a Girl.'" *Milwaukee Journal Sentinel* (8 July): 6B.

Tarradell, Mario. 2000. "What's in the Changer? Blondie, Live (Beyond/BMG, 1999)." *Dallas Morning News* (13 January): 5C.

Tayler, Letta. 1999. "'Blondie' Returns to Its Roots in Comeback." *Newsday* (25 February): B9.

Taylor, Mark. 1999. "Platinum." *Bristol Evening Post* (4 November): "News" section, p. 4.

"10,000 Maniacs." 2000. *Portland Press Herald* (Portland, Maine) (11 May): 14D.

Teo, Kris. 2000. "No Doubt(s), Return of a Blockbuster Act." *Sunday Mail* (7 May): "Music" section, p. 19.

"This Day In Music For June 26, 2000." 2000. *BPI Entertainment News Wire* (19 June).

"This Week's Singles: 27 May 2000:...Quinn, The Next Time (*Lunardiscs*)." 2000. *NME* (New Musical Express) web site. (27 May; Accessed 22 June 2000) <www.nme.com>.

Thrills, Adrian. 1998. "Girls Are on Top, And We Love It." *Daily Mail* (London) (18 December): 48.

_____. 1999. "Blazing Return of Miss Cool: Blondie: No Exit (RCA)." *Daily Mail* (London) (12 February): 47.

Tianen, Dave. 1999. "Blondie Concert Moves to State Fair..." *Milwaukee Journal Sentinel* (15 July): 6.

Tiven, Jon. 1994. "Blondie Was a Group: An Appreciation" [liner notes booklet to CD, *The Platinum Collection* by Blondie]. New York: Chrysalis Records, Inc.

Tom, Sian. 1999. "Blondie." *First Cut* web site. (Accessed 4 November 1999) <www.firstcut.com>.

Trakin, Roy. 1981. "Debbie Harry." *International Musician and Recording World* 3, 9(September): 30-32, 35, 37.

Trebay, Guy. 2000. "What's Old is New Again: Check Your Closets, Music Fans. Vintage Heavy Metal Rock T-Shirts Are Back for a High Fashion Encore." *Orlando Sentinel* (27 July): E4.

Tribby, Mike. 2000. Review of *Deborah Harry*, by Cathay Che. *Booklist* 96, 16(15 April): 1512.

"Tributes" [to Joey Ramone]. 2001. *Rolling Stone* 869(24 May): 50.

"The Trouble With the Seventies." 1994. Thames Television Broadcast (May).

True, Everett. 1994. "From Hype To Eternity. *Melody Maker* 71, 39(8 October): 30-32.

_____. 1996. "Loose Cannons: You Like Sleazy, Grubby, Noo Yoik Rock? You Like NY Loose." *Melody Maker* 73, 35(31 August): 10.

_____. 1999. "The Blonde Leading the Blonde." *Melody Maker* 76, 20(22 May): 24-25.

Turner, Stephen. 2000. "Web Week." *Sydney Morning Herald* (22 April): "Computers" section, p. 3.

Tuxen, Henrik. 1999. "Blondie: No Exit." *Total Guitar* (United Kingdom) 55(April): 20-23, 25- 26.

U

Udovitch, Mim. 1999. "Blondie's Dark Roots: Deborah Harry Chats About Her Youth and Dreams of Being a Sex Worker." *Esquire* 131, 3(March): 56.

V

Vale, V., ed. 1996. *Search & Destroy #1-6: The Complete Reprint [1977-1979]: The Authoritative Guide to Punk Culture*. San Francisco: V/Search Publications. Blondie: 3, 9, 21, 39, 44, 54, 57, 69, 131, 135; Deborah Harry: 15, 54.

_____, ed. 1996. *Search & Destroy #7-11: The Complete Reprint [1977-1979]: The Authoritative Guide to Punk Culture*. San Francisco: V/Search Publications. Blondie: 20, 21, 49; Debbie Harry: 20, 21.

Vale, V. and Marian Wallace. 1998. *Swing!: The New Retro Renaissance*. San Francisco, California: V/Search.

Valentine, Gary. 1999. "'Must Be Into the Shangri-Las...'" *Mojo: The Music Magazine* (United Kingdom) 63(February): 76-83.

_____. 1999. E-mail [to John Hart] (May).

Valles, Marie-Noelle. 1999. "Blondie Makes Comeback to Top of Charts." Agence France-Presse (2 March).

Van Den Nieuwenhof, Liz. 1999. "The Lady is a Vamp." *Sunday Herald Sun* (Melbourne, Australia) (28 February): "Sunday Magazine," 6-9.

Van Matre, Lynn. 2000. "Leaders of the Pack, April 28, 1980." *Chicago Tribune* (20 February): "Arts and Entertainment" section, p. 4.

Varga, George. 1999. "Deborah Harry Returns as the Blond Leading the Blondie." *San Diego Union-Tribune* (27 May): "Night and Day" section, p. 9.

_____. 1999. "Dye Job: Blondie Reunion Shows a Bit Too Much Gray: No Exit, Blondie, Beyond: Suicide Blondie?" *San Diego Union-Tribune* (25 February): "Entertainment" section, p. 16.

Veitch, Dave. 1997. "New Release Too Ambitious: Cowboy Reviewed: Cowboy, Erasure (Mute/Maverick)." *Jam!* web site. (27 April; Accessed 20 July 2000) <www.canoe.ca>.

_____. 1999. "Benatar Goes Wandering: Synchronistic Wanderings, Pat Benatar (Chrysalis/EMI)." *Jam!* web site. (17 October; Accessed 20 July 2000) <www.canoe.ca>.

_____. 1999. "Luscious Jackson Keeping Their Head Up: Electric Honey, Luscious Jackson." *Jam!* web site. (27 June; Accessed 20 July 2000) <www.canoe.ca>.

Vejnoska, Jill. 1999. "'Cigarettes' Misses the Party, But Brings Hip Cast, Great Music." *Atlanta Journal-Constitution* (26 February): P8.

Velisek, Melanie, comp. 1996. "USA/World Newsmakers:...One Way Or Another, The IRS Is Gonna Getcha." *Florida Today* (12 April): 2A.

Verrico, Lisa. 1998. "Indisposable Pop: What Do You Get If You Cross Three Thirtysomething Americans and an Edinburgh Shop Girl? Garbage, Electric Rockers for the MTV Generation, Fronted by Tantrum Queen Shirley Manson. Lisa Verrico Braves the Storm." *Times* (London) (6 June): 6.

"VH1: What to Watch Coming Up on VH1, August 4-August 10." 2000. *PR Newswire* (3 August).

Vincent, Mal. 2000. "'Buddy' Recaptures the Innocence of an Era." *Virginia-Pilot and Ledger Star* (Norfolk, Virginia): E1.

Vivinetto, Gina.1999. "Audio Files: Blondie, Blondie Live (Beyond)." *St. Petersburg Times* (10 December): "Weekend" section, p. 18.

_____. 1999. "Audio Files: Blondie, No Exit (Beyond)." *St. Petersburg Times* (19 February): "Weekend" section, p. 16.

_____. 1999. "Blondie's Delivery New, But Music Close to Roots." *St. Petersburg Times* (South Pinellas Edition) (2 September): 2B.

"The Vulture Picks Over the Bones of Contemporary Culture." 1998. *Times* (London) (24 October): 46.

"The Vulture's 100 Best Albums of All Time: Part 2." 1993. *Times* (London) (4 December).

"The Vulture's Top 100 Cult Albums." 1999. *Times* (London) (16 October): "Features" section, p. 24.

W

Waddell, Daniel. 1999. "Blondie Back at No. 1 After 17 Years of Silence." *Daily Telegraph* (8 February 8): 5.

Walters, Barry. 1994. "A Harried Shot at Jazz: Ex-Blondie Star Seeks a Niche." *San Francisco Examiner* (28 September): C1.

_____. 1995. "Give Her a Gun." *Village Voice* 40, 9(28 February): 50.

_____. 1996. "Punk Rocked But the Lifestyle Was a Killer." *San Francisco Examiner* (21 July): B7.

_____. 1999. "[Electric] Honey Makes a Buzz at Lilith [Fair]: Kate Schellenbach of Luscious Jackson Muses on the Band's New Album and the Ladies' Fair." *Advocate* (20 July): 55-57.

Warburton, Richard. 2000. "Digit Ditties for Baffled Callers: Phone Code Shake-Up Brings Disdial Misery." *Birmingham Post* (22 April): "News" section, p. 5.

Warhol, Andy. 1975. *The Philosophy of Andy Warhol: From A to B and Back Again*. 1st ed. New York: Harcourt, Brace and Jovanovich.

_____ and Bob Colacello. 1979. *Andy Warhol's Exposures*. New York: Grosset & Dunlap.

Watson, Ian. 1999. "Sugar and Spice...It's Not All Nice." *Melody Maker* 76, 41(16 October): 17.

Weatherford, Mike. 1992. "Band Hopes to Revive Jamaican Dance Rhythm Night Beat." *Las Vegas Review-Journal* (27 March): 2C.

Webb, Jay. 1999. "Something Old, Something New from Blondie" [video reviews of "Blondie: The Best of MusikLaden" and "Blondie Live"]. *Dallas Morning News* (17 December): 11J.

_____. 1999. "Super Tuesday: After a Typically Slow First Month, The Record Industry Times Its First Salvo of New Releases to Coincide with Wednesday's Grammy Awards. These Albums Are Due in Stores Tuesday:...Blondie, No Exit, Beyond." *Dallas Morning News* (21 February): 6C.

Webb, Steve. 1999. "Blondie: Call Them, They're Alive..." *Sarasota Herald-Tribune* (27 August): 9.

"The Week." 2000. *Entertainment Weekly* 12, 539(12 May): 78+.

Weingarten, Marc. 1998. "Grammys '98: Insiders' Grammy Bets." *Los Angeles Times* (22 February): "Calendar" section, p. 7.

Weinstein, Marc. 2000. "Music: The Week...: Various Artists, The Crow: Salvation (Koch)." *Entertainment Weekly* 533(31 March): 70+.

Weisbard, Eric. 1995. *Spin Alternative Record Guide*. New York: Vintage Books.

_____. 2001. "25 Years of Punk." *Spin* 17, 5(May): 86-90.

Wells, Steven. 2000. "Blondie, Livid *(Beyond)*." *NME* (New Musical Express) web site. (1 February; Accessed 2 July 2000) <www.nme.com>.

Wener, Ben. 1998. "'80s Acts Try to Synthesize New Buzz: The B-52s Aren't the Only Ones on the Comeback Trail." *Orange County Register* (Santa Ana, California) (31 July): F8.

_____. 1999. "Back to Blondie: Sixteen Years After Its Breakup, The Reunited Group Has a New Album in Stores and a Tour on the Way—But Don't Call It a Cash-In." *Orange County Register* (Santa Ana, California) (23 February): F4.

_____. 1999. "Sound Check...: 'No Exit,' Beyond/BMG." *Orange County Register* (Santa Ana, California) (5 March): F46.

_____. 2000. "'High Fidelity' Leads Pack." *Orange County Register* (14 April): F57.

_____. 2000. "Inside Patti Smith Rock..." *Orange County Register* (11 April): F4.

_____. 2000. "She's the Genuine Article: Patti Smith Kicks Off an American Tour with Inspiring, Earthy and Rocking Sun Show." *Orange County Register* (14 April): F5.

_____. 2000. "Sleater-Kinney 'All Hands on the Bad One,' Kill Rock Stars." *Orange County Register* (28 April): F62.

_____. 2000. "Sound Check...: Patti Smith, 'Gung Ho,' Arista." *Orange County Register* (Santa Ana, California) (24 March): F52.

Wener, Louise. 1995. "Rebellious Jukebox: Louise Wener of Sleeper Talks About the Records That Made Her Want to Do It Till She's Sore...2. Blondie: '11:59.'" *Melody Maker* (London) 72, 8(25 February): 11.

"What's It All About? Telephones." 1998. *Melody Maker* 75, 46(14 November): 10.

Whelan, Alison and Stephanie King. 2000. "Summer and the City..." *Independent* (London) (2 July): "Features" section, pp. 8, 9.

White, Fraser. 2000. "Deborah Harry and Blondie's Place in Popular Culture." *Blondie Archive* web site. (27 April; Accessed 20 July 2000) <www.blondie.ausbone.net>.

White, Russell. 1999. "Going Blonde at CBGBs." *Total Guitar* (United Kingdom) 55(April): 28.

Whitelaw, Paul. 2000. "Changing the Tune." *Scotsman* (22 April): 19.

"Who's That Blonde?" 1999. *Hartford Courant* (9 September): "Calendar" section, p. 3.

"Why Are They Famous: Debbie Harry." 1998. *Independent* (London) (22 November): "Features" section, p. 3.

Wildman, David. 2000. "Bosnia's Balkan Tribes Finds Musical Voice in Boston." *Boston Globe* (7 May): "City Weekly" section, p. 15.

Wilker, Deborah. 1990. "Tide May Be Rising for Deborah Harry." *Houston Chronicle* (3 February): 3.

_____. 1999. "With Live Album and Plum New Year's Gig, Deborah Harry Embodies Blondie Once More." Knight Ridder/Tribune News Service (2 December).

Williams, Simon. 1999. "Catatonia, Derby Assembly Halls." *NME* (New Musical Express) web site. (22 March; Accessed 2 July 2000) <www.nme.com>.

Williams, Zoe. 2000. "Fab Five Freddy Wants to Give Some Love Back: Zoe Williams Talks to the Father of Hip Hop About His Big Plans for London." *Evening Standard* (London) (24 March).

Williamson, Nigel. 2000. "Poor Little Rich Girl." *Times* (London) (1 April): "Features" section, p. 14.

Wilson, Catherine. 1994. "Fade Away and Recreate: Picture This: Blondie is Back. Rescue Parallel Lines from the Depths of Your Record Collection, Reclaim Your Dark Roots and You're Ready to Go." *Guardian* (London) (24 February): T15.

Wilson, D.B. [1999?]. "Blondie." *Wilson & Alroy's Record Reviews* web site. (Accessed 20 July 2000) <www.warr.org>.

Wilton, Lisa. 1999. "Blondie: Back to Their Roots." *Jam!* web site. (6 March; Accessed 20 July 2000) <www.canoe.ca>.

_____. 1999. "Gotta Luv that Punk: Battershell Lives and Breathes It." *Jam!* web site. (29 November; Accessed 20 July 2000) <www.canoe.ca>.

Wirt, John. 1999. "Blondie Disc Should Please Old Fans, Win New Ones: Blondie, No Exit, Beyond." *Advocate* (Baton Rouge, Louisiana) (26 February): 9.

Wolk, Douglas. 2000. "Connections: Wire and Elastica Return." *Boston Phoenix* web site. (25 May; Accessed 19 July 2000) <www.bostonphoenix.com>.

Wright, Chris. "Robot Wars: How Soon Are We Going to See Thinking, Feeling Robots? The Answer May Lie Inside a Mechanical Head at MIT." *Boston Phoenix* web site. (23 December; Accessed 19 July 2000) <www.bostonphoenix.com>.

Y

"You Ask the Questions: Justine Frischmann." 2000. *Independent* (London) (14 June): "Features" section, p. 7.

Young, Charles M. 2001. "First Punk or Last Hippie?" [Joey Ramone]. *Rolling Stone* 869(24 May): 49.

Young, Cook. 1999. "Blondie Is a Really Good Looking 53-Year Old Chick." *NY Rock* web site. (March; Accessed 1 March) <www.nyrock.com>.

Young, Ron. 1994. "Deborah Harry to Mix Old, New." *San Antonio Express-News* (17 June).

Z

Zaslow, Jeff. 1999. "Designer Sweets: Harry on Lookout at Zazz Bash." *Chicago Sun-Times* (17 September): "WKP" section, p. 6.

Zuel, Bernard. 1998. "The Shirley Principle." *Syndey Morning Herald* (27 June): 7.

_____, ed. 2000. "Stay in Touch: End of the Line for Blond Bombshell." *Syndey Morning Herald* (12 June): "News and Features" section, p. 22.

Author Index

Subject Index

Clarification of terms is contained in parentheses. Magazine and book titles are in *italics*. Web sites are also in *italics* and are identified as such in parentheses. Authors' surnames are in parentheses following book titles. Page numbers in *italics* refer to subject terms contained in photo captions.

Name Index

Clarification of names is contained in parentheses (for example, aka—also known as). The four original members of Blondie—Deborah Harry, Chris Stein, Clem Burke, and Jimmy Destri—are not indexed due to the frequency of references made to them throughout the book. Page numbers in *italics* refer to names contained in photo captions.

McGovern, George, 23
McGrath, Mark, 202
McGuinness, Paul, 388
McKuen, Rod, 35, 41
McLachlan, Sarah, 273
McLaren, Malcolm, 32, 38, 39, 41, 43, 44, 50, 52, 55, 57, 74, 129, 131
McLauglin, John, *46*
McNeil, Legs, 46, 130, 134, 362, 391
McPartland, Marian, 172
Meatloaf (aka Marvin Lee Aday), 384, 394
Melvin, Junior, 298
Mercer, Mick, 95
Merchant, Natalie, 103
Merman, Varla Jean, 196
Metz, Allan, 13, 159
Miller, Arthur, 358
Miller, Bobby, 447
Miller, Henry, 68
Mingus, Charles, 81
Minkie (also variously spelled as Minky and Minkey) (Blondie tour mascot), 146, 250
Minnelli, Liza, 412
Minogue, Kylie, 146
Miss Guy, 196, 198, 403
Mistress Formika, 196
Mitchell, Joni, 268, 364, 443
Monk, Noel, 131
Monk, Thelonious, 81
Monroe, Marilyn, 24, 77, 80, 81, *111*, 138, 145, 146, 151, 209, 232, 244, 267, 269, 274, 346, 347, 351, 358, 360, 365, 367, 399, 409, 451
Montez, Chris, 245
Moon, Keith, 212, 221, 223, 225, 286, 288, 289, 290, 291, 292, 345, 353, 358, 359, 376, 449
Morissette, Alanis, 202
Morley, Paul, 364
Moroder, Giorgio, 67, 139, 287, 362, 384, 394
Morpheus (Greek mythology), 65
Morricone, Ennio, 67, 288
Morrison, Jim, 27, 45
Morrison, Van, 32, 45
Morrongiello, Tommy, 387
Morrow, Bruce (aka Cousin Brucie), 288. (See also Cousin Brucie)
Morton, Mike, 444
Morton, Shadow (aka George "Shadow" Morton), 363
Move, Richard, 447
Mrs. Ritchie, 270
Mueller, Cookie, 78
Murcia, Billy, 237. (See also Doll, Billy)
Murray, Charles Shaar, 52

Nathanson, Roy, 157, 158, 163, 164, *167, 201*, 238, 239, *305, 427*
Needs, Kris, 418
Nelson, Willie, 92, 259
Neuman, Barry, 132
Newton-John, Olivia, 409
Nicks, Stevie (aka Stephanie Lynn Nicks), 202
Nico (aka Christa Paffgen), 244
Nietzsche, Friedrich, 287
Nightingale, Annie, 147
Nixon, Richard, 21, 23, 56, 80
Nofsinger, David, 129

Nolan, Jerry, 44, 71, 74, 223, 237, 291
Nolet, Jim, 158, 238
Noxema, Sheila, 442
Nuclear Bomb Babies (Rob Roth and Garrett Domina), 340
Numan, Gary, 412
Nureyev, Rudolf, 92, 365
Nurse Bullock (film character), 473
Nusser, Richard, 36, 344

O'Brien, Glenn, 28, 78, 358, 362, 363, 364
O'Connor, Billy, 63, 66, 376, 377, 392, 416, 418
O'Connor, Des, 147
"Old Woman Who Lived in a Shoe, The" (TV character), 389
Olla, Carla, 147
Ono, Yoko, 12, 22, 198
Oravec, Amy, 13
Ork, Terry, 38, 49, 129
Orlovsky, Peter, 24
Orrick-Guzman, Luther, 170
Orton, Joe, 453
Owen, Mark, 220, 356
Owens, Buck (aka Alvis Edgar Owens), 287

Pacino, Al, 71, 145
Page, Jimmy, 287, 359
Palmer, Earl, 223, 291
Parker, Charlie, 80, 81
Parsons, Alan, 366
Parsons, Tony, 32, 390
Paul, Tina, 196, 197, 198
Peel, John, 348
Persky, Lisa, 74
Persson, Nina, 16, 252-57
Petty, Tom, 74, 202, 223
Pherber (film character), 473
Phillips, Anya, 26, 79
Piccarella, John, 49
Pickett, Wilson, 45
Pierce, Jeffrey Lee, 11, 225
Pierre et Gilles (French art duo), 453
Pink, 420
Pitney, Gene, 18
Plant, Robert, 103
Poe, Amos, 78, *89*
Poe, Edgar Allan, 80, 441
Polanski, Roman, 365
Pollock, Jackson, 48
Pop, Iggy (aka James Newell Osterberg), 33, 63, 74, *102*, 110, 130, 131, 134, 135, 147, 209, 216, 222, 267, 286, 288, 358, 376, 379, 385, 388, 389, 393, 418, 423. (See also Stooge, Iggy)
Porcaro, Joe, 291
Porter, Cole, 147, 152, 389
Postal, Jonathan, *113*
Presley, Elvis, 32, 56, 71, 92, 258, 287
Price, Diana (character), 147
Princess Margaret, 245
Puff Daddy (aka Sean "Puffy" Combs), 287

Quant, Mary, 252
Quatro, Suzi, 67, 351, 361, 382, 394
Quinones, Lee, 78

"Ramon" (Paul McCartney alias), 51

Ramone, Dee Dee (aka Douglas Colvin), 28, 53, 72, 378
Ramone, Joey (aka Jeffrey Hyman), 51-54, 130, 135, *187, 190*, 191, 196, *198*, 228, 358
Ramone, Johnny (aka John Cummings), 53
Ramone, Tommy (aka Tom Erdelyi), 51, 52, 53, 72, 223, 376
Raven O., 196
Reagan, Nancy, 29
Reagan, Ronald, 29, 53
Reaves, Melissa, 427
Rebel, Johnny (film character), 262
Reed, Lou, 21, 22, 23, 25, 26, 27, 28, 29, 37, 38, 39-41, 42, 43, *46*, 50, 57, 69, *102*, 130, 135, 146, 161, *200*, 375, 376, 381, 383, 408, 449
Reed, Sylvia, *102*
Reich, Wilhelm, 369
Resnick, Marcia, 26, 119
Rhodes, Nick, 164, 217
Ricci, Christina, 215
Rich, Buddy (aka Bernard Rich), 223, 291
Richards, Keith, 23, 24, 27, 81, 449
Richardson, Terry, 264
Richman, Jonathan, 161
Rigby, Amy, 92
Rigby, Will, 92
Riley, Terry, 416
Rimbaud, Arthur (aka Jean Nicholas Arthur Rimbaud), 31, 32, 41, 358
Rivets, Rick, 376
Riviera, Jake, 131, 132
Roberts, Ebet, 132
Robbins, Ira, 378, 379
Robinson, Smokey (aka William Robinson), 387, 395
Rock, Mick, 40, 110
Rodgers, Nile, 12, 144, 385, 386
Rodriguez, E.J., 158, 238
Roeg, Nicolas, 23
Rollins, Henry, 92
Ronson, Mick, 451
Ronstadt, Linda, 409
Rosen, Howard, 393
Ross, Diana, 76
Ross, Rosie, 63, 376, 416
Roth, Rob, 309, 340, 403, *407*, 442, *445*
Rotten, Johnny (aka John Lydon), 26, 32, 131, 343
Rowe, Scott, 323
Rowland, Mark, 387
Royale, Rose, 447
RuPaul, 441
Rush, Otis, 172
Ruskin, Mickey, 27, 29, 37, 235
Ruth, Babe (aka George Herman Ruth), 206
Ryan, Joe, 427, 428

Saban, Stephen, 197
Saddler, Joseph (aka Grandmaster Flash), 386. (See also Grandmaster Flash)
Saffron (aka Samantha Sprackling), 212, 255
Sales, Hunt, 388, 417
Sales, Tony, 388, 417
SAMO (character), 78
Sanders, Mark, 473
Sartre, Jean-Paul, 207, 211, 287, 355, 364

Band/Group Index

As in the Album/Song/Video index, although some bands include "The" at the beginning of their names, it has been omitted for purposes of uniformity. Blondie is not indexed due to the great frequency of references to the band throughout the book. Page numbers in *italics* refer to bands or groups cited in photo captions.

Album/Song/Video Index

Although some bands include "The" at the beginning of their names, it has been omitted for purposes of uniformity. Page numbers in *italics* refer to album or song titles contained in photo captions.

507

508

Photo Credit Index

Photo agencies and other clarifications are in parentheses, when applicable.

Illustrator Index

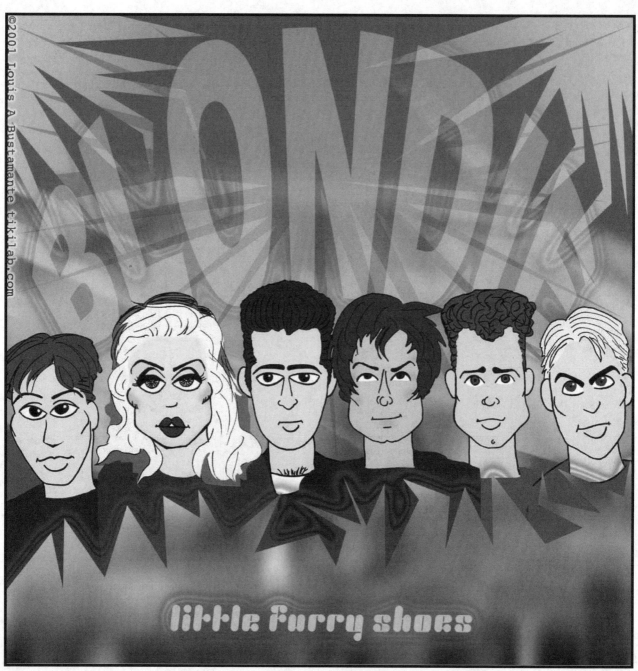

"Little Furry Shoes" by Louis A Bustamante, Phoenix, Arizona
Copyright © 2001
Owner/operator DHBIS (Deborah Harry/Blondie Internet Service) e-mail reflector group
www.deborahharry.com

Some Concluding Observations

Blondie is...
a band with one of the most successful reunions in rock history,
a band that has produced number one records in three decades,
a band with significant sales and chart statistics covering 26 years of rock and roll,
a band that has influenced the style of many modern artists and groups,
a band that has opened the doors for many modern artists,
a band that has been copied and covered...but never duplicated.

Adapted and edited from The Blondie Review, *issue 3, June 2001. copyright © 2001, Robert Betts.*